THE TWO SWORDS

Commentaries and Cases in Religion and Education

THE TWO SWORDS

Commentaries and Cases in Religion and Education

† †

We are told by the word of the gospel
that in this His fold there are two swords,
a spiritual, namely, and a temporal . . .
the one, indeed, to be wielded . . .
by the hand of the priest, the other by
the hand of kings and knights . . .

POPE BONIFACE VIII, *Unam Sanctam* (1302)

† †

By DONALD E. BOLES

The Iowa State University Press, AMES, IOWA, U.S.A.

DONALD E. BOLES is professor of government, Iowa State University, and a widely known political scientist whose field of special interest is public law. Besides this book, he is author of *The Bible, Religion, and the Public Schools,* Iowa State University Press; a body of articles in law, political science, and education journals; *An Evaluation of Iowa County Government;* and *Welfare and Highway Functions of Iowa Counties: A Quantitative Analysis.* In 1964 he served as a member of the Commission on Religion and the Schools of the American Association of School Administrators, which issued the report, *Religion and the Schools.*

© 1967 The Iowa State University Press
Ames, Iowa, U.S.A. All rights reserved.

Printed in the U.S.A.

Stock #1707

First edition, 1967

Library of Congress Catalog Card Number: 67–12132

PREFACE

THE PURPOSE and goal of this study are quite specific. It is directed toward school administrators and boards, theologians and lawyers, as well as teachers of school law and constitutional and civil rights law. Recognizing the topical quality of the subject, the book seeks to provide a comprehensive exegesis of the multi-faceted nature of the debate over religion in the schools. While the primary emphasis is upon the public schools, a variety of related problems have plagued private schools in different sections of the United States, and these, too, are explored.

This study attempts to demonstrate the complexity of the issues by illustrating the manner in which various courts (in most instances state supreme courts) have attempted to come to grips with the plethora of problems. Moreover, an attempt is made to broaden the breadth of understanding by illustrating the legal and philosophical reactions to the court decisions as found in legal, education, and religious journals as well as the mass media. As such, it should serve, among other things, as a handbook for educational policy formulators and decision makers who are increasingly faced with bitter disputes over the role of religion in the schools.

The need for a work of this nature was first called to my attention several years ago by the then-President of the national association of school law professors, Walter Hetzel. This need was reiterated by various leaders of the American Association of School Administrators during the period of time in which I served on that group's National Commission on Religion and the Schools. In addition, colleagues in both law schools and political science departments have noted the gap in comprehensive literature in this area.

A study of this sort cannot be completed without the cooperation and assistance of various governmental officials and librarians too numerous to mention. A special debt of thanks must go to Mr. Kermit Dunahoo, Mrs. Jean Downs, and Mr. William Turk who, at various times, aided me substantially in gathering and sorting the mountains of materials essential to a book of this nature. Needless to say, I alone am responsible for its shortcomings.

Ames, Iowa   DONALD E. BOLES

TABLE OF CONTENTS

INTRODUCTION

FEW DECISIONS of the United States Supreme Court have aroused as much public discussion and soul-searching as have the cases in which the Court declared a state-formulated prayer for the public schools of New York to be unconstitutional and shortly afterward declared Bible-reading exercises in the public schools to violate the Establishment of Religion clause of the First Amendment. The impact of these decisions on the public should not have been unexpected. After all, they dealt with two areas in which most Americans have a vital and personal interest—religion and public education.

This public awareness was reflected in many ways. An amendment—usually referred to as the Becker Amendment—was proposed in Congress to nullify the effects of the Supreme Court in these cases. Many veteran Congressmen admitted they had received more mail from their constituents on this subject than on any other matter in their tenure of office. The Republican candidate for the presidency in 1964 openly criticized the Court for its actions in these cases and many interest groups felt impelled to take a formal position on the subject of religion in the school.

The diverse nature of these groups is reflected in the hearings of the Judiciary Committee of the House of Representatives held in the spring of 1964. Such groups included not only most of the organized religious sects, and the National Council of Churches, but also organizations such as the American Farm Bureau, the American Legion, the John Birch Society, and the Liberty Lobby.

In essence, the current political debates on the subject merely transfer to the lay public a debate of long standing that has been carried on in scholarly and legal circles since the adoption of the First Amendment. In the minds of the framers the importance of the prohibition against an establishment of religion in the First Amendment is revealed by the fact that it is the first clause in the Bill of Rights. Nonetheless, from that day to this, there has been sharp disagreement as to which precise practices constitute a violation of this provision of the Constitution.

In modern times, a somewhat oversimplified exegesis of the opposing sides in the debate may be summarized in the following fashion. One school of thought, which includes many but not all Roman Catholics and most of the church hierarchy in addition to a few Protestants, maintains that the establishment clause merely prohibits the creation of a single state or national church. Under such an arrangement, if it were permitted, citizens' tax dollars would be used to support such a church regardless of whether the individual subscribed to its tenets or not. This school of thought argues, however, that the establishment clause does not preclude aid or assistance to all religious groups or incidental cooperation with religious denominations which might involve the expenditure of public funds.

The opposing school of thought which is composed of most Protestant groups, with the Presbyterians and Baptists following the most historically consistent position, plus most Jews, Unitarians, and Universalists, agrees that there is no doubt that the establishment clause prohibits a single state church. They argue, however, that the clause does much more than this. It creates, in Jefferson's words, a wall of separation between church and state. They point out that Madison, the author of the First Amendment, and Jefferson, his close friend, believed that this wall of separation prohibits all governmental aid of any sort to organized religion. This would include even indirect aids, and to bear out their contention they note Madison's and Jefferson's objections to public funds to pay chaplains, Madison's veto of a measure to incorporate the Episcopal Church in the District of Columbia, and a host of similar actions and statements by Madison—the man most responsible for the Bill of Rights.

The opinions of legal scholars run the gamut between the two extremes with emphasis on a variety of nuances far too numerous to even mention in passing. There are, for example, some writers such as Professor Philip B. Kurland, in his study *Religion and the Law,* who argue that the Establishment of Religion Clause and the Freedom of Religion Clause must be viewed as a single, combined entity. This is a point of view specifically rejected by the United States Supreme Court in the Engel case (1962) and in the Schempp case (1963).

The United States has avoided much of the strife that has plagued Europe and other parts of the world over the relationship between church and state in large measure because of the presence of the establishment clause of the First Amendment. Nonetheless, American legal history is replete with a host of cases covering a variety of subjects in which the controversy turns upon a definition of the Establishment and the Free Exercise of Religion clauses of the First Amendment.

Furthermore, the public schools have provided a key arena in which many of the most important battles have been waged. Thus while the legal status of these provisions of the First Amendment may prove a stimulating academic exercise for legal scholars and historians, it is a pressing, practical, and immediate problem for education policy formulators and school administrators.

No one can seriously challenge the principle that the Constitution is what the United States Supreme Court says it is. But while in recent years the Supreme Court has faced up squarely to a few of the problems involving religion and the schools, the fact remains that a host of other practices which some allege violate the religion clauses of the First Amendment have either never come to the Supreme Court or, if they have, the Court has declined to settle them on their merits.

State courts have been called upon to decide a far greater variety of practices which have been challenged as violating the provisions of the state and national constitutions dealing with religion. Therefore, this study includes an assortment of state supreme court decisions in some instances because they are indicative of a line of reasoning the Supreme Court has later followed, but in most instances because the state court has come to grips with issues on which the Supreme Court has not ruled.

This, of course, is not to imply that merely because a state court has ruled one way that the Supreme Court will automatically follow its lead. In some areas case cuttings are included of several state court decisions which take a diametrically opposed stand on the same practice. In those areas on which the Supreme Court has not spoken definitively, the state court decisions are included as illustrative of a line of reasoning which is, of course, controlling in that state, but which also may be assumed to be presented before the Supreme Court of the United States when and if that Court chooses to accept jurisdiction over a case involving similar issues.

Finally, it seems likely that the Supreme Court will be called upon to decide an increasingly greater number of cases challenging religiously oriented practices which affect the schools. This is in part traceable to the growing pluralism in our society magnified by the megalopolis, and metropolitan areas with their polyglot of religious sects. The days of the rural, religiously homogeneous community are numbered even in those states which are not overwhelmingly urban. The rural consolidated school drawing students from substantial distances increases the elements of pluralism, both religious and otherwise, in the nonmetropolitan areas.

The likelihood of litigation over questions involving religion and the school is heightened dramatically by the passage in 1965 of a federal aid to elementary and secondary education law which provides a potential for certain aids to parochial school students. The litigation possibilities inherent in this measure alone are immense as are its effects on traditional church-state relations in the United States.

TABLE OF CASES

*SMALL CAPITAL LETTERS indicate that case appears in text as case cutting; *italic numbers* indicate page of appearance.

THE TWO SWORDS

Commentaries and Cases in Religion and Education

CHAPTER ONE

Transportation

† †

THE GRADUAL DEMISE of the "little red schoolhouse" on the corner of the section line followed the industrial strides and similar developments in transportation and communication at the turn of the twentieth century. Furthermore, joint federal-state programs of highway construction and improvement of secondary roads followed the Supreme Court's implied approval of federal grants-in-aid in *Massachusetts* v. *Mellon,* 262 U.S. 447 (1923).

The ensuing consolidated school system, while multiplying the distance that pupils had to travel, also provided a partial solution to the problem of transporting students to schools farther from their homes. Centralization of available school funds in a larger school district thus made it possible to develop public transportation for such pupils. Legal problems quickly paralleled the expansion of the school transportation system, however. Various state courts found themselves faced with such questions as: *Must* school boards provide transportation facilities for the pupils in its district? Must they provide such transportation to *all* pupils regardless of the inaccessibility of isolated farm houses?

State courts repeatedly sanctioned mandatory pupil transportation only when it was required by statute. In absence of such applicable statutes, the school boards generally were allowed to exercise their own discretion. See Johnson and Yost, *Separation of Church and State* (1948) 153.

Religion was bound to creep eventually into the litigation over school transportation, thus creating a very thorny legal thicket. The rapid rise of private and parochial schools, which was to receive judicial acceptability by the Supreme Court in *Pierce* v. *Society of Sisters,* 268 U.S. 510 (1925), resulted in a determined campaign to secure public aid for the parochial schools. However, opposing efforts were more effective, as evidenced by the fact that in 1937 only Vermont lacked a provision in its state constitution prohibiting the expenditure of public funds for sectarian purposes.

The first controversy involving school bus transportation, *Oklahoma Railway* v. *St. Joseph's Parochial School,* 33 Okl. 755, 127 P. 1087 (1912), arose early in the twentieth century. There it was held that a regulation allowing public school children to receive reduced fares on public buses

3

to and from school should also be extended to pupils of St. Joseph's Parochial School. It was not until twenty-five years later that similar claims were upheld in another state. Then, in *Lewis* v. *Board of Education,* 275 N.Y. 480, 544, 11 N.E.2d 307, 743 (1937), an appeal was denied from a lower-court judgment which had upheld the policy of the board of education of New York City in allowing free transportation at public expense to all children attending free schools in the city of New York. In doing so, the state court of appeals agreed with the lower court's philosophy that "the Constitution no more forbids transportation to school children than it forbids supplying them with lunch."

Meanwhile, the supreme courts of Wisconsin and Delaware invalidated upon constitutional grounds policies of furnishing transportation to parochial schools. See *State* ex rel. *Van Straten* v. *Milquet,* 180 Wis. 190, 192 N.W. 392 (1923), and *State* ex rel. *Traub* v. *Brown,* 36 Del. 181, 172 A. 835 (1934).

However, a Maryland statute providing that children attending Baltimore county schools not receiving state aid should be entitled to transportation on school busses on the same terms as public school children was declared constitutional in *Board of Education* v. *Wheat,* 174 Md. 314, 199 A. 628 (1938). Such a function was considered to be in accordance with the state's compulsory education requirement. See also *Nichols* v. *Henry,* 301 Ky. 434, 191 S.W.2d 930 (1946). A similar conclusion was reached by the same court four years later in *Adams* v. *County Commissioners,* 180 Md. 550, 26 A.2d 377 (1942).

Contrastingly, *Hlebanja* v. *Brewe,* 58 S.D. 351, 236 N.W. 296 (1931), ruled that a parochial school is not part of the public school system, and thus its students would not be entitled to share in reimbursements for the transportation costs involved in traveling to another school in the district following the closing of the local public school. In this connection it is well to compare *Schiltz* v. *Picton,* 66 S.D. 301, 282 N.W. 519 (1938), which held that a bus owner who had contracted to transport school children was not required to transport pupils attending Roman Catholic schools in that city. That same year a state statute was struck down in *Judd* v. *Board of Education,* 278 N.Y. 200, 15 N.E.2d 576 (1938), that authorized the use of public funds for pupil transportation to institutions wholly or partly under the control or direction of any religious denomination. In commenting upon the New York state court's decision, a *Harvard Law Review* critic argued that a statute designed to reduce the transportation hazards for all school children is a valid exercise of police power, and any benefits that so accrue to parochial schools are incidental and immaterial.

The Oklahoma supreme court took the same position in *Gurney* v. *Ferguson,* 190 Okl. 254, 122 P.2d 1022 (1942). The Judd decision prohibiting such transportation, and rejecting the child benefit theory on the grounds that attendance at religious schools was fostered by transporting students to parochial schools by bus was reversed, however, by a subsequent constitutional amendment in New York.

The last transportation case decided by a state supreme court prior to the United States Supreme Court's ruling in the Everson case, which was *Bowker* v. *Baker*, 73 C. A.2d 653, 167 P.2d 256 (1946), sustained a decision by a California district court of appeals. The lower court had upheld permissive school transportation legislation against the contention that transportation to private or parochial schools violated the constitutional prohibition against the appropriation of public funds for the support of any religion or of any denominational school.

Of somewhat different nature was the issue involving state statutes *requiring* such transportation for parochial school children. Decisions of state courts striking down such practices as being contrary to state constitutional provisions may be seen in *Sherrard* v. *Jefferson County Board of Education*, 294 Ky. 469, 171 S.W.2d 963 (1943); *Mitchell* v. *Consolidated School*, 17 Wash.2d 61, 135 P.2d 79 (1943); and *Costigan* v. *Hall*, 249 Wis. 94, 23 N.W.2d 495 (1946).

Taking stock of the situation in the nation as of January 1, 1947, just prior to the Everson case, the Federal Council of Churches of Christ in America reported that there were 19 states and one territory which either constitutionally or by statute permitted the transportation of parochial school pupils at public expense. In addition, by the end of 1946 courts in seven states had disallowed such transportation whereas four states had supported such policies in their courts. These findings may be compared with those in Johnson and Yost, *Separation of Church and State* (1948) 164.

IMPACT OF THE EVERSON CASE

In 1947 the Supreme Court was faced with the problem of squaring public bus transportation to parochial schools with the Establishment of Religion Clause of the First Amendment. The case of *Everson* v. *Board of Education*, 330, U.S. 1 (1947), involved the validity of a New Jersey statute and school board regulation which authorized the payment of tax raised funds to Roman Catholic parochial school pupils in addition to public school pupils. The court declared for the first time that the establishment clause as well as the free exercise clause of the First Amendment were applicable to the state through the Due Process Clause of the Fourteenth Amendment.

Justice Black, speaking for a five to four majority, declared that such general welfare legislation did not "breach the wall of separation between church and state," and did not violate the Establishment of Religion Clause of the First Amendment.

A similar child benefit argument had been upheld in the textbook case of *Cochran* v. *Board of Education*, 281 U.S. 370 (1930). However, as

George W. Spicer pointed out in *The Supreme Court and Fundamental Freedoms* (1959), the Everson majority overlooked the fact that the recipients for these bus fare payments were selected by essentially religious tests. "Before making payments to reimburse parents for pupils' bus fares, the school authorities must ask whether the school attended is a Catholic school, and if it is not, the aid is not afforded."

The Everson dictates are similarly important for what they did not do as for what they did do. First, the Supreme Court held merely that there was no violation of the *federal* constitution. However, nothing was said about whether that particular statute, or similar statutes in other states, violated *state* constitutional provisions. This was considered to be a state matter to be settled in various state courts. Secondly, the Everson decision merely holds that states *may* permit public transportation for parochial school children. It does not say that such transportation is required.

† † EVERSON v. BOARD OF EDUCATION
330 U.S. 1, 67 S. CT. 504, 91 L. ED. 711 (1947).

Mr. Justice BLACK delivered the opinion of the Court, saying in part:

A New Jersey statute authorizes its local school districts to make rules and contracts for the transportation of children to and from schools. The appellee, a township board of education, acting pursuant to this statute authorized reimbursement to parents of money expended by them for the bus transportation of their children on regular busses operated by the public transportation system. Part of this money was for the payment of transportation of some children in the community to Catholic parochial schools. These church schools give their students, in addition to secular education, regular religious instruction conforming to the religious tenets and modes of worship of the Catholic Faith. The superintendent of these schools is a Catholic priest.

The appellant, in his capacity as a district taxpayer, filed suit in a state court challenging the right of the Board to reimburse parents of parochial school students. He contended that the statute and the resolution passed pursuant to it violated both the state and the Federal Constitutions. . . .

Since there has been no attack on the statute on the ground that a part of its language excludes children attending private schools operated for profit from enjoying state payment for their transportation, we need not consider this exclusionary language; it has no relevance to any constitutional question here presented. . . .

The only contention here is that the state statute and the resolution, insofar as they authorized reimbursement to parents of children attending parochial schools, violate the Federal Constitution in these two respects, which to some extent, overlap. *First*. They authorize the state to take by taxation the private property of some and bestow it upon others, to be used for their own private purposes. This, it is alleged, violates the due process clause of the Fourteenth Amendment. *Second*. The statute and the resolution forced inhabitants to pay taxes to help support and maintain schools which are dedicated to, and which regularly teach, the Catholic Faith. This is alleged to be a use of state power to support church schools contrary to the prohibition of the First Amendment which the Fourteenth Amendment made applicable to the states.

. . . It is much too late to argue that legislation intended to facilitate the opportunity of children to get a secular education serves no public purpose. . . . The same thing is no less true of legislation to reimburse needy parents, or all parents, for payment of the fares of their children so that they can ride in public busses to and from schools rather than run the risk of traffic and other hazards incident to walking or "hitchhiking." . . . Nor does it follow that a law has a private rather than a public purpose because it provides that tax-raised funds will be paid to reimburse individuals on account of money spent by them in a way which furthers a public program. . . . Subsidies and loans to individuals such as farmers and home owners, and to privately owned transportation systems, as well as many other kinds of businesses, have been commonplace practice in our state and national history.

. . . *Second*. The New Jersey statute is challenged as a "law respecting the establishment of religion." The First Amendment, as made applicable to the states by the Fourteenth, . . . commands that a state "shall make no law respecting an establishment of religion, or prohibiting the free exercise thereof. . . ." These words of the First Amendment reflected in the minds of early Americans a vivid mental picture of conditions and practices which they fervently wished to stamp out in order to preserve liberty for themselves and for their posterity. Doubtless their goal has not been entirely reached; but so far has the Nation moved toward it that the expression "law respecting the establishment of religion," probably does not so vividly remind present-day Americans of the evils, fears, and political problems that caused that expression to be written into our Bill of Rights. Whether this New Jersey law is one respecting the "establishment of religion" requires an understanding of the meaning of that language, particularly with respect to the imposition of taxes. Once again, therefore, it is not inappropriate briefly to review the background and environment of the period in which that constitutional language was fashioned and adopted.

A large proportion of the early settlers of this country came here from Europe to escape the bondage of laws which compelled them to support and attend government favored churches. The centuries immediately before and contemporaneous with the colonization of America had been filled with turmoil, civil strife, and persecutions, generated in large part by established sects determined to maintain their absolute political and religious supremacy. With the power of government supporting them, at various times and places, Catholics had persecuted Protestants, Protestants had persecuted Catholics, Protestant sects had persecuted other Protestant sects, Catholics of one shade of belief had persecuted Catholics of another shade of belief, and all of these had from time to time persecuted Jews. In efforts to force loyalty to whatever religious group happened to be on top and in league with the government of a particular time and place, men and women had been fined, cast in jail, cruelly tortured, and killed. Among the offenses for which these punishments had been inflicted were such things as speaking disrespectfully of the views of ministers of government-established churches, non-attendance at those churches, expressions of non-belief in their doctrine, and failure to pay taxes and tithes to support them.

These practices of the old world were transplanted to and began to thrive in the soil of the new America. The very charters granted by the English Crown to the individuals and companies designated to make the laws which would control the destinies of the colonials authorized these individuals and companies to erect religious establishments which all, whether believers or nonbelievers, would be required to support and attend. An exercise of this authority was accompanied by a repetition of many of the old-world practices and persecutions. Catholics found themselves hounded and proscribed because of their faith; Quakers who followed their consciences went to jail; Baptists were peculiarly obnoxious to certain dominant Protestant sects; men and women of varied faiths who happened to be in a minority in a particular locality were persecuted because they steadfastly persisted in worshipping God only as their own consciences dictated. And all of these dissenters were compelled to pay tithes and taxes to support government-sponsored churches whose ministers

preached inflammatory sermons designed to strengthen and consolidate the established faith by generating a burning hatred against dissenters.

These practices became so commonplace as to shock the freedom-loving colonials into a feeling of abhorrence. The imposition of taxes to pay ministers' salaries and to build and maintain churches and church property aroused their indignation. It was these feelings which found expression in the First Amendment. No one locality and no one group throughout the Colonies can rightly be given entire credit for having aroused the sentiment that culminated in adoption of the Bill of Rights' provisions embracing religious liberty. But Virginia, where the established church had achieved a dominant influence in political affairs and where many excesses attracted wide public attention, provided a great stimulus and able leadership for the movement. The people there, as elsewhere, reached the conviction that individual religious liberty could be achieved best under a government which was stripped of all power to tax, to support, or otherwise to assist any or all religions, or to interfere with the beliefs of any religious individual or group.

The movement toward this end reached its dramatic climax in Virginia in 1785–86 when the Virginia legislative body was about to renew Virginia's tax levy for the support of the established church. Thomas Jefferson and James Madison led the fight against this tax. Madison wrote his great memorial and Remonstrance against the law. In it, he eloquently argued that a true religion did not need the support of law; that no person, either believer or non-believer, should be taxed to support a religious institution of any kind; that the best interest of a society required that the minds of men always be wholly free; and that cruel persecutions were the inevitable result of government-established religions. Madison's Remonstrance received strong support throughout Virginia, and the Assembly postponed consideration of the proposed tax measure until its next session. When the proposal came up for consideration at that session, it not only died in committee, but the Assembly enacted the famous "Virginia Bill for Religious Liberty" originally written by Thomas Jefferson. The preamble to that Bill stated among other things that

Almighty God hath created the mind free; that all attempts to influence it by temporal punishments or burthens, or by civil incapacitations, tend only to beget habits of hypocrisy and meanness, and are a departure from the plan of the Holy author of our religion, who being Lord both of body and mind, yet chose not to propagate it be coercions on either . . .; that to compel a man to furnish contributions of money for the propagation of opinions which he disbelieves, is sinful and tyrannical; that even the forcing him to support this or that teacher of his own religious persuasion, is depriving him of the comfortable liberty of giving his contributions to the particular pastor, whose morals he would make his pattern. . . .

And the statute itself enacted

That no man shall be compelled to frequent or support any religious worship, place, or ministry whatsoever, nor shall be enforced, restrained, molested, or burthened in his body or goods, nor shall otherwise suffer on account of his religious opinions or belief. . . .

This Court has previously recognized that the provisions of the First Amendment, in the drafting and adoption of which Madison and Jefferson played such leading roles, had the same objective and were intended to provide the same protection against governmental intrusion on religious liberty as the Virginia statute. . . . Prior to the adoption of the Fourteenth Amendment, the First Amendment did not apply as a restraint against the states. Most of them did soon provide similar constitutional protections for religious liberty. But some states persisted for about half a century in imposing restraints upon the free exercise of religion and in discriminating against particular religious groups. In recent years, so far as the provision against the establishment of a religion is concerned, the question has most frequently arisen in connection with proposed state aid to church schools and efforts to carry on religious teachings in the public schools in accordance with the tenets of a particular sect. Some churches have either sought or accepted state financial support for their schools. Here again the efforts to obtain state aid or acceptance of it have not been limited to any one particular faith. The state courts, in the main, have remained faithful to the language of their own constitutional provisions designed to protect religious freedom and to separate religions and governments. Their decisions, however, show the difficulty in drawing the line between tax legislation which provides funds for the welfare of the general public and that which is designed to support institutions which teach religion.

The meaning and scope of the First Amendment, preventing establishment of religion or prohibiting the free exercise thereof, in the light of its history and the evils it was designed forever to suppress, have been several times elaborated by the decisions of this Court prior to the application of the First

Amendment to the states by the Fourteenth. The broad meaning given the Amendment by these earlier cases has been accepted by this Court in its decisions concerning an individual's religious freedom rendered since the Fourteenth Amendment was interpreted to make the prohibitions of the First applicable to state action abridging religious freedom. There is every reason to give the same application and broad interpretation to the "establishment of religion" clause. . . .

The "establishment of religion" clause of the First Amendment means at least this: Neither a state nor the Federal Government can set up a church. Neither can pass laws which aid one religion, aid all religions, or prefer one religion over another. Neither can force or influence a person to go to or to remain away from church against his will or force him to profess a belief or disbelief in any religion. No person can be punished for entertaining or professing religious beliefs or disbeliefs, for church attendance or non-attendance. No tax in any amount, large or small, can be levied to support any religious activities or institutions, whatever they may be called, or whatever form they may adopt to teach or practice religion. Neither a state nor the Federal Government can, openly or secretly, participate in the affairs of any religious organizations or groups and vice versa. In the words of Jefferson, the clause against establishment of religion by law was intended to erect "a wall of separation between Church and State." . . .

We must consider the New Jersey statute in accordance with the foregoing limitations imposed by the First Amendment. But we must not strike that state statute down if it is within the State's constitutional power even though it approaches the verge of that power. . . . New Jersey cannot consistently with the "establishment of religion" clause of the First Amendment contribute tax-raised funds to the support of an institution which teaches the tenets and faith of any church. On the other hand, other language of the amendment commands that New Jersey cannot hamper its citizens in the free exercise of their own religion. Consequently, it cannot exclude individual Catholics, Lutherans, Mohammedans, Baptists, Jews, Methodists, Non-believers, Presbyterians, or the member of any other faith, *because of their faith, or lack of it,* from receiving the benefits of public welfare legislation. While we do not mean to intimate that a state could not provide transportation only to children attending public schools, we must be careful, in protecting the citizens of New Jersey against state-established churches, to be sure that we do not inadvertently prohibit New Jersey from extending its general state law benefits to all its citizens without regard to their religious belief.

Measured by these standards, we cannot say that the First Amendment prohibits New Jersey from spending tax-raised funds to pay the bus fares of parochial school pupils as a part of a general program under which it pays the fares of pupils attending public and other schools. It is undoubtedly true that children are helped to get to church schools. There is even a possibility that some of the children might not be sent to the church schools if the parents were compelled to pay their children's bus fares out of their own pockets when transportation to a public school would have been paid for by the state. The same possibility exists where the state requires a local transit company to provide reduced fares to school children including those attending parochial schools, or where a municipally owned transportation system undertakes to carry all school children free of charge. Moreover, state-paid policemen, detailed to protect children going to and from church schools from the very real hazards of traffic, would serve much the same purpose and accomplish much the same result as state provisions intended to guarantee free transportation of a kind which the state deems to be best for the school children's welfare. And parents might refuse to risk their children to the serious danger of traffic accidents going to and from parochial schools, the approaches to which were not protected by policemen. Similarly, parents might be reluctant to permit their children to attend schools which the state had cut off from such general government services as ordinary police and fire protection, connections for sewage disposal, public highways and sidewalks. Of course, cutting off church schools from these services, so separate and so indisputably marked off from the religious function, would make it far more difficult for the schools to operate. But such is obviously not the purpose of the First Amendment. That Amendment requires the state to be a neutral in its relations with groups of religious believers and nonbelievers; it does not require the state to be their adversary. State power is no more to be used so as to handicap religions than it is to favor them.

This Court has said that parents may, in the discharge of their duty under state compulsory education laws, send their children to a religious rather than a public school if the school meets the secular educational requirements which the state has power to impose. . . . It appears that these parochial schools meet New Jersey's requirements. The state contributes no money to the schools. It does not support them. Its legislation, as applied, does no more than provide a general program to help parents get their children, regardless of their religion, safely and expeditiously to and from accredited schools.

The First Amendment has erected a wall between church and state. That wall must be kept high and impregnable. We could not approve the slightest breach. New Jersey has not breached it here.

Affirmed.

REACTIONS OF LEGAL PERIODICALS TO *EVERSON* v. *BOARD OF EDUCATION*

The Everson decision was greeted by overwhelming criticism in four of every five reviews that evidenced a definite stand. Scattered support in a few law reviews was either half-hearted or in some instances, vigorously favorable to the decision. Mere physical transportation to the doors of a parochial school was considered by Rev. Kenneth R. O'Brien and Daniel E. O'Brien in *The Jurist* (7:259) to be, without qualification, a temporal matter. A contrary argument was advanced in the *Oregon Law Review* (27:150) where it was suggested that children in other than public schools have no more right to public school bus transportation than do wayfarer travelers. An argument of expediency was made in the *St. John's Law Review* (21:176). There it noted that making attendance at private schools more difficult would result in channeling more students into the public school system, thus increasing taxpayers' costs.

Several reviewers plus the *New York Times* applauded the child benefit rationale as a sensible approach. On the other hand this position was characterized as "legal fiction" by Leo Pfeffer in the *Lawyers Guild Review* (8:387) and as clumsy and fictional in a note in the *University of Pennsylvania Law Review* (96:230). Correspondingly, a reviewer in the *Virginia Law Review* (33:349) concluded that both the school and the children were being aided. Just how far such aid, armed with the logic of the Everson opinion, would be allowed to expand into other areas was viewed with concern in several reviews. Professor Thomas Reed Powell asked in the *Harvard Educational Review* (17:73): "How can it be proper for the public to pay for transport to religious instruction and worship from Monday through Friday if it could not provide free rides to Sunday or Saturday worship?"

John C. Murray, writing in *Law and Contemporary Problems* (14:23), could find no historical, legal, or political support for Justice Black's concept of absolutism. Moreover, the *Marquette Law Review* (32:138) charged that the Everson decision amended the First Amendment by expanding its historically exclusive prohibition of governmental preference of one religion over others to now implant a Godless principle demanding complete separation. Other reviewers, however, supported the decision's accord with the purpose of the Founding Fathers in demanding an absolute separation of church and state.

Many observers objected to Black's historical interpretation of the Establishment of Religion Clause which held that no state aid was to be given to any religions. Others, agreeing with Black, declared that the Founding Fathers demanded that there be *no* state aid to religion. The whole question of aid to religious schools was dismissed as insignificant in the *Louisiana Law Review* (22:266) where an alternative test was prescribed in 1961 which would evaluate the extent to which the program "aids secular education which is objectionably colored by sectarian philosophy." As such, the Everson program merely relieved parents of expenses, and did nothing to impose religious precepts on the secular education of children, it was argued.

The public welfare argument was rejected in the *Michigan Law Review* (45:1001) as obscuring the underlying issues of indirect aid to religious institutions. Similarly, the fact that pupils attending schools run for profit were excluded from such public benefits was viewed with scorn in the *Cornell Law Quarterly* (33:122) where the validity of the safety-measure argument was severely assailed.

REACTIONS OF EDUCATION PERIODICALS TO
EVERSON v. *BOARD OF EDUCATION*

Of the education journals that took a definite stand on the Everson case, somewhat more than half viewed the decision with disfavor. Some, however, agreed completely with the Court's rationale. Others agreed with the philosophy of the child benefit doctrine, but would not apply it to public transportation for parochial schools. Still others objected to the Court's definition of the Establishment of Religion Clause of the First Amendment.

The child benefit theory was supported by J. L. Toner in *The American Teacher* (32:2, 1948). He included transportation in the same category as health services and school lunches.

L. R. Kuenzli in *The American Teacher* (32:2, 1948) saw transportation as benefiting the church rather than the child. While F. E. Johnson would have preferred to see this issue worked out on the local level, he speculated in *Religious Education* (43:201, 1948) that apparently a majority of the public condemned the Court's opinion that public transportation of parochial school children did not violate the concept of separation of church and state. He further contemplated that the Supreme Court would reverse the Everson decision if a similar transportation case came before it, as adjudged by the tone of the then-recent McCollum decision (which is discussed in another part of this book). In this same vein, the *National Educational Association Research Bulletin* (24:1, 1946) found that a majority of the state courts had not followed the child benefit doctrine in transportation cases. E. Fuller in *The Education Digest* (14:3, 1949) viewed the child benefit doctrine, however, as one which could, in fact, ultimately nullify the constitutional concept of separation of church and state. Concurring with this idea, B. H. Jarman in *School and Society* (67:44, 1948) was apprehensive that *any* practice of allotting public funds for parochial schools would open the floodgate to more extensive public financing of such schools.

W. W. Brickman in *School and Society* (67:245, 1948) took a completely opposite stand. He contended that the state should share in the upkeep of parochial schools since they help to reduce the load on public schools. Brickman saw no difference between public transporting of parochial school children and public financing of a chaplain in the United States Senate.

Both E. H. Dana in *Education* (69:124, 1948) and W. A. Wetzel in the *National Association of Secondary-School Principals' Bulletin* (33:66, 1949) did not agree with the Supreme Court's definition of the Establishment of Religion Clause in the Everson case. Dana argued that the church and the state have never been, and should not be, totally divorced. Wetzel, agreed in part, but suggested that the line of demarcation be drawn not between the state and religion but rather between the state and *ecclesiastical* religion. Some might speculate on the meaningful differences between religion and ecclesiastical religion.

EVENTS FOLLOWING THE EVERSON RULING

The supreme courts of Pennsylvania and Iowa were considering similar transportation programs at the time of the Everson decision. Their subsequent decisions demonstrated that state courts accepted without reservation the Everson dictate that public transportation to parochial schools was a state matter, so long as no other federal questions were raised. Consequently, the statute authorizing free transportation for any pupil to and from public schools was interpreted in *Connell* v. *Board of School Directors,* 356 Pa. 585, 52 A.2d 645 (1947), as authorizing free transportation for the public school pupils only, thus excluding parochial school pupils. A similar conclusion was reached in *Silver Lake Consolidated School District* v. *Parker,* 238 Ia. 984, 29 N.W. 2d 214 (1947). No mention of the Everson case was made in either.

Shortly after this the high court of Ohio was faced with a different but closely related problem. In *State* ex rel. *Church of Nazarene* v. *Fogo,* 150 Ohio St. 45, 79 N.E.2d 546 (1948), the Ohio court held that Sunday school and Bible school busses were not exempted from the annual state license tax. "Sunday school" and "Bible school" are terms which ordinarily mean a place for religious instruction operated in conjunction with a church, the court explained. Such terms, the court concluded, were not synonymous with the term "school" in the Ohio statute which exempted "school busses" from an annual license tax.

Bus transportation programs based upon permissive legislation in the absence of state legislation on the subject presented somewhat different problems after the Everson case. See *Connell* v. *Board of School Directors* and *Silver Lake Consolidated School District* v. *Parker,* discussed above.

The Missouri high court in *McVey* v. *Hawkins,* 364 Mo. 44, 258 S.W.2d 927 (1953), ruled that amending the 1949 statute, which authorized state aid or reimbursement for costs of transportation of school pupils, in order to specifically include transportation to private schools not operated for profit violated the constitutional protections of the public school fund and the maintenance of free public schools. Accordingly, the actions of a local board of education in furnishing such transportation were considered unauthorized, even though the record showed that the public school bus incurred no additional expense while transporting parochial school children for a portion of their way along the regular bus route without special stops to the parochial schools in the district.

Sharp criticism in the *St. Louis University Law Journal* (3:273) argued that the decision subordinated the practical importance of the health and safety of children to a strained philosophy that any practical law is unconstitutional if even an indirect benefit to religion is derived.

A statute empowering any town, city, borough, or school district upon majority approval of the electors to provide transportation services for children attending private schools therein, not conducted for profit, was declared in *Snyder* v. *Town of Newtown*, 147 Conn. 374, 161 A.2d 770 (1960), not to violate federal or state constitutional provisions respecting the establishment of religion. Recognizing that the furnishing of transportation for parochial students added additional expense to the town, the Connecticut court maintained that a statute serving a public purpose, as here, was not unconstitutional "merely because it incidentally benefited a limited number of persons." The court went on, however, to nullify the law because it would make available for private purposes the moneys derived from the school fund, in contravention of the state's constitutional provision stipulating that the "school fund" shall be "inviolably appropriated to the support and encouragement of the public, or common schools throughout the state, and for the equal benefit of all the people thereof."

Another related issue to plague some state courts concerned actions taken by individual school boards, without any permissive legislation or judicial sanction, to provide transportation to parochial schools within the specified district.

In *Board of Education* v. *Antone*, Okl., 384 P.2d 911 (1963) the Oklahoma supreme court held invalid the action of a school board on the grounds that the provision of the Oklahoma constitution forbidding use of public money or property for sectarian purposes prohibited the use of school busses operated at the public expense from transporting pupils to parochial schools. The court rejected the contention that such practices were justified on the grounds of public welfare.

Similarly, a Kentucky school board was denied the authority to use public school tax money for the transportation of children to parochial or private schools in *Rawlings* v. *Butler*, Ky., 290 S.W.2d 801 (1956). There the Kentucky high court adhering to its former decisions in *Sherrard* v. *Jefferson County Board of Education* and *Nichols* v. *Henry*, 91 S.W.2d 930 (1946), declared that the Nichols opinion did make it clear, however, that local governmental units could contribute tax money to supplement bus transportation for *all* primary-grade children living beyond a reasonable walking distance of their school, in compliance with the legislative act in 1944.

Of a similar nature, the Maine court in *Squires* v. *Inhabitants*, 155 Me. 151, 153 A.2d 80 (1959), ruled that the city council of Augusta in the absence of specific legislative authorization had no authority under its police power to provide for transportation of pupils to or from private schools, which were controlled and operated by the Roman Catholic Church. The court went on to say that a properly worded enabling act authorizing the expenditure of public funds for bus transportation to private schools, not operated for profit, would not violate state constitutional provisions concerning separation of church and state, and the expenditure of public funds for public purposes.

An injunction was issued by the Kentucky court in *Wooley* v. *Spalding,* Ky., 293 S.W.2d 563 (1956), to restrain the practice by the local board of education of stopping the operation of public school busses on religious holidays not legalized as state or national holidays. There it appeared that Protestant children in the area were being denied transportation to public schools on Roman Catholic holidays. The court's opinion covering many religious practices in the school district held that all practices of sectarianism should be abolished in those schools receiving public funds.

In the same year the Pennsylvania court issued a declaratory judgment in *School District* v. *Houghton,* 387 Pa. 236, 128 A.2d 58 (1956), which held that the board of directors of a school district could not upon its own discretion provide public transportation for pupils of an other than public school to the site of the public school. The court declared that it would entertain a proper judicial proceeding to determine the constitutional validity of such transportation *after* the legislature had authorized the practice.

MANDATORY TRANSPORTATION TO PAROCHIAL SCHOOLS

The Everson case had dealt with a state statute which permitted but did not require public school boards to transport students to parochial schools. Prior to this action by the United States Supreme Court, several state supreme courts had struck down state laws making it mandatory to transport students to parochial schools. The history of state supreme court attitudes toward state statutes and regulations making mandatory the transportation of students to parochial schools following the Everson decision suggests a more permissive view to such regulations, although there is by no means a unanimity of judicial decisions on the subject.

Quinn v. *School Committee,* 332 Mass. 410, 125 N.E.2d 410 (1955), held that the Massachusetts statute requiring transportation for pupils attending elementary school must be extended to include private elementary schools conducted by religious denominations as well as the pupils attending the public elementary schools. Similarly, the New Jersey court in *Board of Education* v. *State Board of Education,* 27 N.J. 76, 141 A.2d 542 (1958), overruled the state board of education's affirmation of the arbitrary discontinuance by the commissioners of education of the policy of transporting parochial school children, who were below the prescribed grade level (grades seven through twelve) for which the district public schools had been established, along the regular routes of the public schools.

The orders of the New York commissioner of public education *requiring* expenditure of public funds for transportation of pupils to parochial schools was upheld by the supreme court of Albany County, New York, in *Board of Education* v. *Allen,* 17 M.2d 1080, 192 N.Y.S.2d 186 (1959), below. Declaring that an amendment to the New York constitution permitted the state legislature to provide for expenditure of public funds for transportation of children to and from any school, the court found that the resultant expenditure of public funds for transportation to nonpublic schools was a constitutional expenditure, and thus did not violate religion clauses of either the state constitution or the First and Fourteenth Amendments of the United States Constitution.

† † BOARD OF EDUCATION v. ALLEN

17 MISC.2D 1080, 192 N.Y.S.2D 186 (1959).

Judge ELSWORTH delivered the opinion of the court, saying in part:

These are article 78 proceedings which raise issues as to the legality and constitutionality of orders of the Commissioner of Education requiring the expenditure of public funds for the transportation of pupils to parochial schools.

At the annual meeting of the Central District held on May 6, 1958, motions to provide such transportation were defeated. Appeals were taken to the Commissioner and sustained.

. . . .

Petitioner's most serious ground of attack is that the orders violate the state and federal constitutions. It is conceded that such question of a constitutional nature is here reviewable, and the Commissioner decided that such question should be left to the courts.

Undue emphasis is placed by petitioner on *Judd* v. *Board of Education,* 278 N.Y. 200, 15 N.E.2d 576, which held unconstitutional the use of public funds for transportation to nonpublic schools. Subsequent to that decision the 1938 constitutional convention proposed an amendment to what is now article 11, section 4 of the State Constitution to permit the state legislature to provide for the expenditure of public funds for the transportation of children to and from any school. Such amendment was approved by the voters at the general election of 1938 and became effective January 1, 1939. Therefore, the people of the State of New York have determined that the use of public funds for transportation to nonpublic schools is a constitutional expenditure.

The argument that the orders here in question violate the federal constitution also falls. *Everson* v. *Board of Education,* 330 U.S. 1, determined that a state may provide for the expenditure of public funds for the transportation of pupils to a nonpublic school without violating the First and Fourteenth amendments to the federal constitution. Petitioner seeks to distinguish the New Jersey statute from the New York statute and also on the facts. The distinctions made are not valid and material and the Everson case is deemed decisive.

Accordingly, the petitions are dismissed without cost.

OPPOSING VIEWS

In *Matthews* v. *Quinton*, Alas., 362 P.2d 932 (1961), a law authorizing the Alaska board of education to require school districts to furnish free transportation for pupils, insofar as it applied to pupils attending non-public schools, was declared violative of the Organic Act prohibition against appropriating public money for the support of nonpublic schools. The court discounted both the child benefit theory and the argument that such a statute was a valid exercise of the state's police power.

The *New York Law Forum* (8:424) contained a note sharply critical of this decision and argued that such transportation was necessary to avoid the dangers to parochial school students who now will be forced to walk to school. The danger factor was especially important in the case of Alaska, this reviewer felt, because of the great distances involved, the unusual weather and geographic hazards, and the wilderness conditions prevailing in many areas of the state.

An approach similar to the Alaska decision was reflected by the Wisconsin supreme court when interpreting a 1961 statute requiring public transportation for *all* pupils living the requisite mileage from the nearest public school. That court declared in *State* ex rel. *Reynolds* v. *Nusbaum*, 17 Wis.2d 148, 115 N.W.2d 761 (1962), that such a law violated the Wisconsin constitutional prohibition against the use of public funds to aid religious societies and in the process presented a rather complete summary of recent decisions in other states on the subject.

After declaring that 60 per cent of the state's approximate 500 parochial schools, all of which give religious instruction, lie within the prescribed area of authorized transportation, the court declared that such parochial schools stood a very good chance to benefit financially if the new act were put into operation. The Wisconsin court thus followed the Judd philosophy, which discounted the practicality of arguing the child-benefit theory. The Wisconsin court agreed with, and cited the ruling and rationale of a similar case, *Visser* v. *Noonsack Valley School District*, 33 Wash.2d 699, 207 P.2d 198 (1949), which accorded fully with Justice Rutledge's dissent in *Everson* v. *Board of Education*, 330 U.S. 1.

† † STATE ex rel. *REYNOLDS* v. *NUSBAUM*

17 WIS.2D 148, 115 N.W.2D 761 (1962).

Judge CURRIE delivered the opinion of the court:

Prior to the amendment of sec. 40.53 (1), Stats., by ch. 648, Laws of 1961, this statute required that school boards operating public elementary or high schools provide transportation to and from school for all pupils residing in the district two or more miles from the nearest public school they might attend, subject to the exception contained in sec. 40.55, Stats. Sec. 40.55, Stats. provides that secs. 40.53, 40.54, and 40.56 shall not apply to pupils who reside in cities, except that, if a city determines to furnish transportation on an optional basis, the same state aid shall be allowed as is provided by sec. 40.56. Because of the adoption of ch. 648, certain pupils attending approximately 500 non-public schools will be entitled to free transportation to and from the nearest public school they are entitled to attend.

. . . [W]e construe the statutory phrase "on regular routes approved for the public school bus" as not requiring actual residence on the routes themselves of either the public or non-public school pupils who are to be entitled to free transportation under the amended statute. This interpretation also obviates the necessity of passing upon a denial of equal protection of the laws argument advanced by respondent.

In addition to the denial of equal protection of the laws contention thus resolved, respondent advances further reasons why ch. 648, should be held invalid as violating various provisions of the United States and Wisconsin constitutions. However, we find it unnecessary to consider any of these except that which asserts that this enactment violates that clause of sec. 18, art. I, Wisconsin constitution, which provides: ". . . nor shall any money be drawn from the treasury for the benefit of religious societies, or religious or theological seminaries."

We construe "religious societies" to be synonymous with religious organizations, and, under the stipulated facts, practically all of the non-public schools, whose pupils are to be transported under the attacked act, are operated by religious organizations. Furthermore, at the time of the adoption of our constitution in 1848, the word "seminaries" was synonymous with the academies or schools. . . . Other courts have held that the term "seminary" includes primary and secondary schools. . . . Therefore, inasmuch as some religious instruction is given in all of the approximate 500 non-public schools operated by religious organizations or sectarian groups, certain of whose pupils are to be transported under the act, these parochial schools constitute "religious seminaries" within the meaning of sec. 18, art. I, Wisconsin constitution.

Because 60 per cent of these approximate 500 parochial schools located without the boundaries of cities are situated within distances which do not exceed one-half mile from public schools, it is fair to assume that a considerable number of pupils attending these schools will be afforded transportation under the new act if its validity is upheld. Those parochial schools, which now pay part or all of the cost of transportation of their pupils out of their school funds, stand to benefit financially by the operation of the new act. Others stand to gain through increased enrollment. Such an increase of enrollment is a benefit to these parochial schools. *Judd* v. *Board of Education* (1938), 278 N.Y. 200, 212, 15 N.E. 2d 576, 118 A.L.R. 789. . . . We quote with approval this statement of the New York Court of Appeals in the Judd case. . . :

Free transportation of pupils induces attendance at the school. The purpose of the transportation is to promote the interests of the private school or religious or sectarian institution that controls and directs it. 'It helps build up, strengthen and make successful the schools as organizations.' . . . Without pupils there could be no school. It is illogical to say that the furnishing of transportation is not an aid to the institution while the employment of teachers and furnishing of books, accommodations and other facilities are such an aid.

Therefore, the crucial question is whether the benefits which parochial schools would receive under the act are of a category to constitute a violation of sec. 18, art. I, Wisconsin constitution.

It must be conceded that there are benefits to religious organizations and parochial schools resulting from the expenditures of public funds which are not a violation of this constitutional prohibition. Examples are the providing of police and fire protection, the supplying of water and sewerage services on a basis whereby all the cost of the system or service is not charged to the users, and the building or improving of public sidewalks and streets. However, all of these public services and facilities are provided to the public, or to property, generally on a basis whereby no classification is made as to religious organizations or schools. It is this which distinguishes these benefits from those sought to be conferred by the instant act. Mr. Justice Jackson pointed out this line of demarcation in his penetrating dissenting opinion in *Everson* v. *Board of Education* (1947), 330 U.S. 1, 25, in these words:

A policeman protects a Catholic, of course—but not because he is a Catholic; it is because he is a man and a member of our society. The fireman protects the Church school—but not because it is a Church school; it is because it is property, part of the assets of our society. Neither the fireman nor the policeman has to ask before he renders aid 'Is this man or building identified with the Catholic Church?'

Professor Philip B. Kurland in his article, "Of Church and State and the Supreme Court," 29 *University of Chicago/Law Review* 1 (1961), draws this same line of demarcation, as did Mr. Justice Jackson, in considering the freedom of religion and establishment of religion clauses of the First amendment to the United States constitution. Kurland states his conclusion thus (at p. 96):

The freedom and separation clauses should be read as stating a single precept: that government cannot utilize religion as a standard for action or inaction because these clauses, read together as they should be, prohibit classification in terms of religion either to confer a benefit or to impose a burden.

It is apparent from the stipulated facts that while ch. 648 is so worded as to provide transportation to private schools generally, the private schools which stand to benefit from the act are the parochial schools. This is because of the 10 private schools in the state furnishing grade and high school education, five are located in cities in which the providing of public transportation is optional and the other five have most of their pupils in residence at their schools. Thus, the benefit conferred is in reality one confined to those religious groups which operate parochial schools.

There are, however, other valid statutes which benefit religious organizations, rather than the public generally. Perhaps the most prominent example is the exemption from taxation of religious organization or parochial school property in sec. 70.11(4), Stats. While the constitutionality of this and analogous provisions, under sec. 18, art. I, Wisconsin constitution, is not before us, we deem it important to point out the distinction from the instant situation. This distinction is that the exemption afforded by sec. 70.11(4) is not expressly or effectually restricted to religious organizations, as many other nonprofit organizations benefit from it. Thus, this tax exemption does not transcend the religious classification prohibition.

We have also given consideration to whether the benefits, conferred by ch. 648 upon parochial schools, differ in kind from the situation where parochial school pupils are permitted to attend certain specialized courses in the public schools. For example, it has been brought to our attention that pupils of certain parochial schools attend manual training and domestic science classes in the public schools. These parochial schools benefit in that they are saved the expense of providing the specialized equipment required for such courses, and of securing teachers trained to teach the same. However, let us assume but not decide that permitting children, who satisfy the age and residence requirements, to secure part of their education in the public schools, even though at the same time they may be in attendance at parochial schools, does not violate sec. 18, art. I, Wisconsin constitution. On this hypothesis it might be argued that permitting parochial school children to take advantage of transportation by public school bus, is a use of public school facilities equivalent to attendance at manual training and domestic science classes in the public schools. However, the essential difference, from a constitutional standpoint, is that riding school buses is not an educational objective of the state in itself, but merely an instrumentality to bring the pupils to the public schools where they will secure a public education. Under ch. 648, parochial school children are not to be transported to the public schools for the purpose of receiving any public instruction; rather, such transportation is merely a convenience to assist them in attending a parochial school.

One further argument needs mentioning on the issue of whether ch. 648 would benefit parochial schools in a manner prohibited by sec. 18, art. I, of the Wisconsin constitution. This is that the providing of transportation to parochial school pupils entails no more expenditure of public funds than would be required if these pupils were to attend public schools. However, this same argument would sustain the use of public funds to pay salaries of parochial school teachers or other direct operating expenses of such schools. Considering the objective sought by the framers of our state constitution in including the provisions of sec. 18, art. I, we are certain that the determination of whether religious schools receive a prohibited benefit from public funds is not dependent on whether the overall cost to the public treasury would be less or greater by reason of the operation of such schools than would be the case if all the pupils thereof were to attend public schools.

The legislature, in enacting ch. 648 entitled it, "An Act to amend 40.53(1) and 40.56(3) of the statutes, relating to the safety and welfare of all school pupils in the state." The attorney general argues that this act is sustainable on the basis that the transportation of parochial school pupils would promote their health and welfare. It could also be argued with equal plausibility that a direct grant in aid of public funds to parochial schools promotes the general welfare of the pupils of such schools because it aids in their education. In passing on the constitutionality of legislation as to whether it violates the particular prohibition of sec. 18, art. I, Wisconsin constitution, courts are not foreclosed by a legislative declaration that the act is in futherance of some facet of the promotion of the public welfare valid in itself, if the effect of the questioned act would in fact violate such prohibition had there been no legislative declaration of its purpose included in the title or body of the act. We are cognizant that a California intermediate appellate court, in *Bowker* v. *Baker* (1946), 73 Cal.App.2d 653, 167 P.2d 256, upheld the validity of an act, which provided transportation at public expense to parochial school pupils, on the ground that it promoted the welfare of the children. This was held in spite of a prohibition in the California constitution similar to the one contained in sec. 18, art. I, of our own constitution. Nevertheless, we do not find this California decision persuasive, or one which this court should follow.

A number of state courts have considered the validity, under state constitutional provisions, of statutes providing for the transportation of parochial school students at public expense. Six states have voided such acts on the ground that public expenditures to support any religious institution are invalid. . . . One of these states, New York, subsequently amended its constitution to authorize such transportation. . . .

Only one reported state opinion . . . has held such a statute to be for the benefit of the non-public school pupils and not in violation of state constitutional prohibitions similar to those contained in sec. 18, art. I, of the Wisconsin constitution. Four states have upheld the constitutionality of non-

public school pupil transportation acts, but did not consider constitutional prohibitions analogous to sec. 18, art. I, or statutes analogous to ch. 648. . . . Three states have invalidated such transportation systems on other than constitutional grounds. . . .

The most recent case passing on the constitutionality of a state statute providing for the transportation of parochial school pupils by public school buses is that of the Alaska supreme court in *Matthews* v. *Quinton* [Alaska, 362 P.2d 932 (1961)], decided in 1961. The statute before the court had been enacted while Alaska was still a territory, and the applicable provision of the constitution of the territory provided:

. . . nor shall any public money be appropriated by the Territory or any municipal corporation therein for the support or benefit of any sectarian, denominational, or private school, or any school not under the exclusive control of the government; . . . and all laws passed, or attempted to be passed, by such legislature in said Territory inconsistent with the provisions of this section . . . shall be null and void.

We deem this constitutional prohibition to be no more stringent in its prohibition than the last clause of sec. 18, art. I, of our own state constitution.

In an exhaustive opinion, the Alaska court reviewed the other decisions which have dealt with the constitutionality of statutes providing for transportation of parochial school pupils. It conceded that there was a division of authority, but, in spite of a strong dissent, concluded that the cases invalidating such statutes, because of state constitutional prohibitions, were the more persuasive. This view coincides with our own conclusion after carefully reading both lines of cases.

Most of the statutes ruled upon, in

the opinions of other courts, provided for the transportation of parochial school pupils directly to the schools attended by them. Ch. 648 does not do this, but only provides for their transportation to the nearest public school which they would be entitled to attend. We do not deem that this difference in any way affects the constitutional issue.

On this aspect of the case, the decision of the Washington court in *Visser* v. *Noonsack Valley School District,* [33 Wash.2d 699, 207 P.2d 198 (1949)], is pertinent. Washington first passed a law for the transportation of private school pupils which was interpreted in *Mitchell* v. *Consolidated School District* (1943), 17 Wash.2d 61, 135 P.2d 79, as authorizing such transportation to and from sectarian schools, and was held to be invalid under a prohibition in the Washington constitution similar to that of sec. 18, art. I, Wisconsin constitution. After this decision, the Washington legislature passed a new statute which provided:

All children attending school in accordance with the laws relating to compulsory attendance in the State of Washington shall be entitled to use the transportation facilities provided by the school district in which they reside. (Laws 1945, c. 141, § 13.)

Plaintiffs in the Visser case, parents of children attending a private religious school, instituted an action for mandamus to compel defendant school district and its board of school directors to permit plaintiffs' children to use the district's transportation facilities, which transported pupils to the public school. The complaint alleged that plaintiffs' children rendered themselves available for transportation along the route regularly established by the district for transportation of pupils and that the district had ample transporta-

tion facilities available for transporting plaintiffs' children. The court held, in spite of the fact that the transportation to be provided under the statute represented at least in part a legislative concern for the safety of children, that the Mitchell case was controlling and that the law violated the prohibition of the state constitution (art. I, § 11) that "no public money or property shall be appropriated for or applied to any religious worship, exercise, or instruction, or the support of any religious establishment." The opinion further pointed out, in answer to the argument that the law was an exercise of the police power for the benefit of the children to be transported to private religious schools, that the police power may not be exercised in contravention of plain and unambiguous inhibitions of a constitution.

In the instant case, the attorney general urges that this court should adopt the construction of sec. 18, art. I, of our constitution which the United States supreme court, by a five to four decision in *Everson* v. *Board of Education,* . . . placed upon the provisions relating to religion contained in the First amendment to the United States constitution. A sufficient answer to this argument is found in this statement appearing in the Washington court's opinion in the Visser case. . .

Although the decisions of the United States supreme court are entitled to the highest consideration as they bear on related questions before this court, we must, in light of the clear provisions of our state constitution and our decisions thereunder, respectfully disagree with those portions of the Everson majority opinion which might be construed, in the abstract, as stating that transportation, furnished at public expense, to children attending religious schools, is not *in support* of such schools. While the degree of support necessary to constitute an establishment of religion under the First Amendment to the Federal constitution is foreclosed from consideration by reason of the decision in the Everson case, supra, we are constrained to hold that the Washington constitution, although based upon the same precepts, is a clear denial of the rights herein asserted by appellants.

A prior opinion of this court, on the effect of sec. 18, art. I, of our constitution, is in strict agreement with this conclusion of the Visser case. In *State ex rel. Weiss,* . . . this court stated (at p. 207, 44 N.W. at p. 977):

Wisconsin, as one of the later states admitted to the Union, having before it the experience of others, and probably in view of its heterogeneous population . . . has, in her organic law, probably furnished a more complete bar to any preference for, or discrimination against, any religious sect, organization, or society than any other state in the Union.

Thus, we deem that the First amendment provision, which prohibits laws "respecting an establishment of religion," lends itself to more flexibility of interpretation than the provision contained in the last clause of sec. 18, art. I, of the Wisconsin constitution. Furthermore, as pointed out in Comment, A Constitutional Analysis of the Wisconsin School Bus Law, 1962 Wisconsin Law Review 500, the weight of authority since the Everson case is clearly against the constitutionality of providing publicly financed transportation and related aids to non-public school children.

For reasons previously stated herein, we conclude that ch. 648, Laws of 1961, is in direct violation of that portion of sec. 18, art. I, which prohibits the expenditure of any public funds "for the benefit of religious societies, or religious or theological seminaries."

Petition dismissed.

EVERSON IN RETROSPECT

Many of the cases discussed above were appealed to the United States Supreme Court. However, the Supreme Court denied the appeals in every instance, except in *Everson* v. *Board of Education.* An important declaration was made, however, by Justice William Douglas, a member of the five-man Everson case majority, in his concurring opinion in the School Prayer Case [*Engel* v. *Vitale,* 370 U.S. 421 (1962)], discussed in another chapter. He declared:

My problem today would be uncomplicated but for *Everson* v. *Board of Education,* 330 U.S. 1, 17, which allowed taxpayers' money to be used to pay "the bus fares of parochial school pupils as a part of a general program under which" the fares of pupils attending public and other schools were also paid. The *Everson* case seems in restrospect to be out of line with the First Amendment. Its result is appealing, as it allows aid to be given to needy children. Yet by the same token, public funds could be used to satisfy other needs of children in parochial schools–lunches, books, and tuition being obvious examples.

The impact of Justice Douglas' switch in thinking can not yet be assessed. No school bus transportation cases have been appealed to the

Supreme Court since his declaration in June 1962. The only holdovers on the present Court from the judicial personnel at the time of the Everson decision are Justice Douglas and Justice Hugo Black, the author of the majority opinion in the Everson case, and Justice Black wrote the majority opinion in *Engel* v. *Vitale*. At this juncture one can only speculate whether a disagreement between the two justices concerning the constitutional status of public support for transportation to parochial schools impelled Justice Douglas to write his concurring opinion in *Engel* v. *Vitale*.

SUMMARY

One of the most persistent and emotionally charged issues confronting courts and governmental policy makers has been the question of whether providing public funds to support the transportation of parochial school students violates constitutional or statutory prohibitions against an establishment of religion or the use of public funds for sectarian purposes. There is every reason to believe that this controversy will continue for years to come. For example, individuals supporting the use of public funds to pay for the transportation of parochial school students have organized themselves into militant pressure groups such as the "Citizens for Educational Freedom" pledged to oppose candidates for political office who oppose such programs or federal aid to parochial schools. Moreover, Justice Douglas' dramatic reversal in 1962 of his position supporting the constitutionality of such programs has suggested to some that the Supreme Court may be prone to take a second look at its decision in the Everson case of 1947 in which by the narrow margin of 5 to 4 the Court upheld the rights of the states to permit this practice if a state's constitution and statutes authorized it.

This chapter illustrates that the first litigation involving public aid for transportation to parochial school students occurred in 1912 where the constitutionality of the practice was upheld. From that date to the Supreme Court's ruling in the Everson case, however, the courts of other states in which the practice was challenged were sharply divided in their views concerning its constitutionality. In states where statutes permitted rather than required such public support, the courts of six states upheld the statutes while the courts of six states struck down such laws as unconstitutional. On the other hand, however, in the three instances where state statutes *required* public funds for practices of this nature, the courts in every instance declared such laws unconstitutional.

In three states the law was silent on the subject of whether a state was or was not authorized to provide public assistance for parochial school bus transportation. In every instance the state courts held that in the absence of specific legislation a school board or a city council was not authorized to use public funds for such a purpose. In Kentucky, however, the court authorized a local governmental unit to contribute tax funds for the transportation of *all* primary school students who lived beyond a reasonable walking distance from their school, but this was authorized by a general statute to this effect. Moreover, the Maine court held that a city council might provide transportation to private schools if a properly worded enabling act was adopted by the legislature.

An area as complex as this inherently has a variety of nuances. In one state the practice of halting public school transportation on Roman Catholic religious holidays was injoined. Tax exemptions for Sunday school or Bible school busses was prohibited in another instance.

Just prior to the Supreme Court's decision in the Everson case, the Federal Council of Churches of Christ in America conducted a survey of actual practices of this nature in the United States. That organization concluded that nineteen states and one territory permitted the use of public funds for the transportation of parochial school students either by statute or by constitutional provision. It found also, however, that by 1946, seven state supreme courts had declared such practices unconstitutional, while four state courts had found it constitutionally acceptable.

In 1947, the Supreme Court of the United States finally ruled on the substance of the question and concluded that the use of public funds to transport parochial students did not violate the First Amendment of the United States Constitution. The ruling in essence returned the issue to the states to determine if this practice was permitted by the state constitution and statutes. The Everson ruling raised almost as many questions as it purported to answer both because of the sharp split (5 to 4) on the Court and by the logic of the majority rationale, which Justice Jackson in his dissent said reminded him of Donna Julia who crying she would ne'er consent—consented.

The logical problems inherent in the rationale are dramatized by the reactions in legal periodicals. Four out of the five articles appearing in such journals analyzing the case were critical of the decision for a variety of reasons. While the adverse reaction was not as pronounced in educational journals, over half of the articles evaluating the Everson case were critical of the Court.

It would appear, moreover, that the Everson decision had no significant effect in clearing the constitutional waters for state courts. For example, where before the Court's action state courts had invariably struck down laws compelling transportation of parochial school students, following the decision, three courts upheld state policies requiring the transportation of parochial school students. Still another court held that transportation must be provided for parochial students in elementary schools. On the other hand, the supreme courts of seven states found, subsequent to the Everson decision, that providing public funds for transportation of students to parochial schools violated state constitutional provisions.

This seems clearly to be a live subject for litigation. The volatility of this issue is further revealed by a survey of the nation compiled by the Commission on Law and Social Action of the American Jewish Congress. This study, dated January 17, 1966 and titled, "Litigation Docket of Pending Cases Affecting Freedom of Religion and Separation of Church and State," reveals that as of that time six cases were pending before the courts of four states challenging the constitutionality of publicly supported programs of transportation of parochial school students.

On January 17, 1967 the Pennsylvania supreme court in a 5 to 2 decision upheld the constitutionality of that state's two year old bus transportation law which allowed the free bussing of both public and nonprofit private school children along established public school bus routes. Reversing its earlier position, the court in *Rhoades* v. *School District of Abington*, 226 A.2d 53 (1967), found that it would be illogical to exclude private nonprofit school children from public transportation when these pupils were not differentiated in other areas such as grades, promotion, and graduation. "Not only do law and reason refute any such differentiation [on the matter of transportation], but economics in good government dispels the concept."

The court cited *Everson v. Board of Education,* 330 U.S. 1 (1947) in finding that the Pennsylvania law did not violate the First Amendment of the United States Constitution. As to the charge that the law violated the religion clauses of the Pennsylvania constitution, the state court found "[t]hese assertions are so feeble of merit that they must fall in the slightest breeze of analysis." (See Appendix for the case cutting.)

CHAPTER TWO

Released and Dismissed Time

† †

AMERICAN EDUCATORS, while generally mindful that public schools them-selves should not impart religious education, nonetheless, historically have willingly opened the doors of the schools during school time to formalized sectarian exercises conducted by religious groups. Such cooperation by the public schools dates back to the educational reforms of 1882 in France, and was pioneered successfully in this country by Dr. William Wirt, Superintendent of Schools in Gary, Indiana, in 1914.

The Gary Plan, which served as a model for other "released time" programs, involved conducting of religious exercises *within* public school buildings by representatives of the various denominations. Participating students were released from their regular classes, while others not wishing to attend such services went to a separate room to study.

Other schools in adopting "dismissed time" programs altered the basic design of the Gary Plan by providing that the religious exercises were to be conducted *outside* the public school building.

State courts were wrestling with the constitutionality of such programs over twenty years before the United States Supreme Court finally came to grips with the issue. One of the more noteworthy developments to emerge from the state courts' decisions prior to action by the Supreme Court was the widely divergent conclusions reached by the different courts.

One of the earliest cases involving dismissed time programs in the public schools was *Stein* v. *Brown,* 125 M. 692, 211 N.Y.S. 822 (1925). There the supreme court of Westchester County, New York, held that the action of a local board of education in dismissing public school students to enable them to attend denominational services in the churches of their choice constituted an extra-curricular activity, in violation of a state law requiring the attendance of pupils during the entire time of the school session. Another statute prohibited denominational services in the public schools. Furthermore, the practice of students using printing presses owned by the city to print attendance cards for such programs was declared by the court to violate the constitutional prohibition against the use of public property to aid any religious instruction.

Two years later, the court of appeals of New York in *People* ex rel. *Lewis* v. *Graves,* 245 N.Y. 195, 156 N.E. 663 (1927), overruled the prohibition in *Stein* v. *Brown* of weekly programs of religious instruction in local churches. Emphasizing that neither public funds nor public property —the printing of the cards was done here by outside agencies—were being utilized, the court declared that the New York constitution and statutes merely intend putting religion in its appropriate realm rather than discriminating against it. Because the children who participated in the dismissed-time program missed no class recitations at the school, there was no violation of the compulsory attendance law, the court concluded.

In Illinois a writ of mandamus to compel a board of education to revoke its action authorizing a dismissed-time program was denied in *People* ex rel. *Latimer* v. *Board of Education*, 394 Ill. 228, 68N.E.2d 305 (1946). In finding no violation of state constitutional and code prohibitions, the Illinois court stressed that the plaintiffs had not charged that the board's action favored any particular denomination; nor did they include a clear statement of the exact amount of public time or money that was used in such a project.

In similar action, the district court of appeals of California in *Gordon* v. *Board of Education*, 78 C.A.2d 464, 178 P.2d 488 (1947), below, decided that the California program of dismissed time did not violate state constitutional provisions guaranteeing free exercise and enjoyment of religious worship nor the federal constitutional provision prohibiting an establishment of religion. The California court suggested that the most logical advance to be made in the science of sociology should be the unification of religious leaders in a coordinated effort to teach children faith and morality.

† † GORDON v. BOARD OF EDUCATION

78 CAL. APP.2D 464, 178 P.2D 488 (1947).

Judge BURNELL delivered the opinion of the court:

Section 8286 of the Education Code was added to our laws by legislative enactment in 1943. This section provides that pupils, with the written consent of their parents, may be excused from schools to participate in religious exercises or to receive moral and religious instruction. Upon complying with the provisions of the statute such absences are not counted in computing average daily attendance. However, allocations of state and county school funds are based upon average daily attendance.

The Board of Education of the City of Los Angeles adopted regulations setting up a plan of compliance with the statute, as follows: An Interfaith Committee composed of representatives of various religious denominations was to act as coordinating agent for the denominations participating in the plan. There were a number of such denominations so represented, including Catholics, those of the various Protestant faiths, and Jews.

At the request of the Interfaith Committee the Board of Education caused to be sent to parents of pupils in the Los Angeles schools literature describing the plan, and cards for the parents to return to the Board. These cards contained a form for the parents to sign consenting that the children take part in the plan, and designating the faith they were to be taught. The expense of preparation, printing or mimeographing and mailing of the literature and cards was paid by the school system. Teachers and superintendents of schools were directed to keep attendance records and to oversee the working of the plan.

As the plan operates, children are segregated according to the preferences expressed by their parents regarding religious instruction, transported from the school grounds to places arranged for by the Interfaith Committee, and there taught the doctrine of the church to which they have been assigned. Expenses of transportation are not paid by the school system, nor are the officers of the schools in charge of the children during their absence from school. Children not participating in the program remain in school and such teaching as they receive is optional with their teachers. . . .

Petitioner is a tax payer, and applied to the Superior Court for a writ of mandate to compel the Board of Education to discontinue the released-time plan. The petition alleged that the statute is void because it is in contravention of the Constitution of California, and that the released-time plan as carried on in Los Angeles violates not only the Constitution and laws of the state but also the Constitution of the United States. The trial court found against petitioner, denied the petition, and the case is now before this court on appeal.

The primary question for decision here is whether the operation of the released-time plan in Los Angeles under Section 8286 of the Education Code is unconstitutional.

Section 4 of Article I of the Constitution of California provides that:

the free exercise and enjoyment of religious profession and worship, without discrimination or preference, shall forever be guaranteed in this State; . . .

Section 8 of Article IX prohibits the appropriation of any public money for the support of any sectarian or denominational school,

nor shall any sectarian or denominational doctrine be taught, or instruction thereon be permitted, directly or indirectly, in any of the common schools of this State.

Section 30 of Article IV prohibits appropriations or the granting of anything "in aid of any religious sect, church, creed, or sectarian purpose."

The First Amendment to the Federal Constitution, applicable to all the states by the fourteenth amendment, provides that: "Congress shall make no law respecting an establishment of religion, or prohibiting the free exercise thereof."

These sections of our California constitution have been considered and applied in several cases in this state involving school affairs.

In *Evans* v. *Selma Union High School Dist. of Fresno County*, 1924, 193 Cal. 54, 222 P. 801, 802, 31 A.L.R. 1121, the Supreme Court of California held that the purchase of a King James version of the Bible by a school board for library and reference purposes is not prohibited by our law. In that case the Supreme Court observed that there is nothing objectionable in the use of religious books in our schools. To be objectionable such books must be "sectarian, partisan, or denominational in character." And the words "sectarian" and "denominational" are defined:

'Sect,' strictly defined, means 'a body of persons distinguished by peculiarities of faith and practice from other bodies adhering to the same general system' (Standard Dict.), and 'denominational' is given much the same definition. But the term 'sect' has frequently a broader signification, the activities of the followers of one faith being regarded as sectarian as related to those of the adherents of another.

. . . .

In *Bowker* v. *Baker,* 1946, 73 Cal. App.2d 653, 167 P.2d 256, 258, the District Court of Appeal of California held that section 16257 of the Education Code does not infringe constitutional prohibitions against appropriation of public funds in aid of religious sects or in support of denominational schools. This section authorizes the governing board of any school district to transport pupils attending private schools in school busses.

. . . .

In *Bowker* v. *Baker,* supra, a number of cases relative to furnishing of transportation by public school authorities to pupils of sectarian schools are cited; and some of them are analyzed. And the reasoning underlying the cases holding this practice to be lawful is summed up as follows . . .

The general line of reasoning running through those cases which uphold the right of the school district to provide free transportation for school children finds its starting point in the undoubted police power of the State to promote the public welfare by aiding in practical ways the education of the young. It is generally held that the direct benefit conferred is to the children with only an incidental and immaterial benefit to the private schools; that this indirect benefit is not an appropriation of public moneys for private purposes and does not violate any constitutional provisions against giving State aid to denominational schools.

And also in *Bowder* v. *Baker,* supra, the court finds support for its decision in a number of California cases holding that the Veterans Educational Act, Stats. 1921, Chap. 579, p. 967, is constitutional. This act authorizes the State to pay for the education of qualified veterans of the first world war in private schools when suitable facilities are not available in public or semi-public institutions, and also to pay for transportation of said veterans to such private schools.

. . . .

Research by counsel and the court fails to find any California case in which the released-time plan has been considered. There are two cases involving the operation of the released-time plan in New York. And New York's constitutional provisions and statutes forbidding state aid to sectarian institutions are similar to ours.

In *Stein* v. *Brown,* 1925, 125 Misc. 692, 211 N.Y.S. 822, the trial court of Westchester County, New York, held that the furnishing of cards for a released-time plan of religious education by the Board of Education violated constitutional provisions prohibiting the use of public funds or property to aid denominational schools.

But, in *People* ex rel. *Lewis* v. *Graves,* 1927, 245 N.Y. 195, 156 N.E. 663, a contrary conclusion was reached by the Court of Appeals upon substantially the same facts. In commenting upon these decisions in 141 A.L.R. 1151, it is said:

So far as appears, the only difference between the facts in the two cases is that whereas in the later case the cards upon which the parents of the pupils were to give their consent to the outside religious instruction of their children were furnished by agencies other than the school authorities, in the earlier case such cards were printed by the pupils as an exercise on materials furnished at the expense of an outside agency.

. . . In finally deciding the case . . . the Court of Appeals, which is the court of last resort of the State of New York, states:

Neither the Constitution nor the law discriminates against religion. Denominational religion is merely put in its proper place outside of public aid or support. . . .

The separation of the public school system from religious denominational instruction is thus complete. Jealous sectaries may view with alarm the introduction in the schools of religious teaching which to the unobservant eye is but faintly tinted with denominationalism. Eternal vigilance is the price of constitutional rights. But it is impossible to say, as matter of law, that the slightest infringement of constitutional right or abuse of statutory requirement has been shown in this case.

Thus it is to be observed that the trial court, the appellate division, and the court of appeals, the highest court of the State of New York (of which one of its members was the late Mr. Justice Benjamin N. Cardozo), were unanimous in upholding the constitutionality of a statute similar to ours of California and its application to a released-time plan of religious education in the New York school system.

Similar cases have involved the attention of the Illinois Courts.

In Chicago, Illinois, for the past sixteen years pupils have been excused by the school board for one hour a week to attend classes in religious instruction. What was done is described in *People* ex rel. *Latimer* v. *Board of Education of City of Chicago*, 1946, 394 Ill. 228, 68 N.E.2d 305, 309. . . . In commenting upon this application of the released time plan, the Illinois court says:

The school authorities in Illinois and in every jurisdiction in the United States have always been vested with discretionary power to determine what constitutes a sufficient excuse for absence from school, and the courts should not interfere or attempt to control the exercise of such power, unless it has been substantially abused. The regulation complained of does not do violence to the compulsory attendance law and in our judgment is a reasonable rule for the practical administration of the public schools.

. . . [We] do not find any constitutional or statutory violation by the board of education in this case.

In the latest Illinois case, *People* ex rel. *McCollum* v. *Board of Education*, 396 Ill. 14, 71 N.E.2d 161, decided by the Supreme Court of Illinois, January 22, 1947, classes were held in the public schools once each week. Teachers were supplied by religious denominations. Cards were used as in the California released-time plan. Separate rooms were provided for Catholics, Jews and Protestants, and for those pupils who did not desire to take part in the plan. Objections to this plan were presented by petition for mandate, upon the same legal grounds urged in the pending case, with the additional one that the classes were held in public school buildings. The Illinois Supreme Court followed its prior decision in *People ex rel. Latimer* v. *Board of Education of City of Chicago,* supra. In discussing the use of public funds in aid of the plan as applied in this case, the Court observes [396 Ill. 14, 71 N.E.2d 166]:

In the case of *Nichols* v. *School Directors,* 93 Ill. 61, 34 Am. Rep. 160, this court held that permission to hold stated meetings for religious purposes in the schoolhouse did not compel a taxpaper to aid in supporting a house of worship in violation of the above constitutional restraints. As the court there aptly said, 'It seems to us a very strained interpretation to attempt to bring the present case within the reach of either one of the above constitutional provisions.' The court there further said, 'Religion and religious worship are not so placed under the ban of the constitution that they may not be allowed to become the recipient of any incidental benefit whatsoever from the public bodies or authorities of the State.' This decision has been cited and followed by this court in a number of cases. It is our judgment the incidental expenses that might occur here are not in violation of the constitutional restraints insisted upon.

Whether the plan conflicts with Federal and State guaranties of religious freedom is also commented upon as follows:

. . . Certainly, such classes do not violate the freedom of conscience of any individual or group so long as the classes are conducted upon a purely voluntary basis. Freedom of religion as intended by those who wrote the State and Federal constitutions means the right of an individual to entertain any desired religious belief without interference from the State. Our government very wisely refuses to recognize a specific religion, but this cannot mean that the government does not recognize or subscribe to religious ideals. We find such recognition in the very preamble of our State constitution. The government does not recognize a particular faith but this does not mean that it is indifferent to religious faith. To deny the existence of religious motivation is to deny the inspiration and authority of the constitution itself.

This then brings us to a consideration of the California constitutional provisions and their application to the case at bar. Reference to the debates of the constitutional convention which presented the Constitution of 1879 to the people of California demonstrates that there was no thought whatsoever in the minds of the framers of that document in opposition to or of hostility to religion as such. They proposed to insure separation of church and state, and to provide that the power and the authority of the state should never be devoted to the advancement of any particular sect or denomination. Our pioneer forefathers did not have the remotest idea that they were laying the foundations of the great Commonwealth of California that was to be as a jejune, godless state; they believed one of the great pillars of our national strength to be the general acceptance of religion by our people.

. . . .

No one who keeps pace with the trends of modern society can deny that instruction of the youth of the state in faith and morality is of utmost necessity and importance. All too regretfully it must be said that in present-day American life the family as a unit has not done its part in this vital field of education of our boys and girls. Else juvenile courts would not be groaning under an avalanche of cases of derelictions of children. What more logical advance could be made in the science of sociology than the unification of religious leaders in a coordinated effort to teach children faith and morality—and for that purpose to excuse them from schools for one hour a week to go to the church or tabernacle or synagogue of their parents' choice?

Description of the released-time plan demonstrates it to be nonsectarian and not in violation of Sec. 4 of Article I of our constitution, nor of the Constitution of the United States.

. . . .

Again, research by counsel and the court fails to find any case in the United States Supreme Court directly in point. But there are two cases in that court which are helpful in determining the constitutional questions here involved. In *Cochran* v. *Louisiana State Board of Education,* 1929, 281 U.S. 370, 50 S.Ct. 335, 74 L.Ed. 913, it is held that the furnishing by a Louisiana School Board of secular text books without charge to private religious sectarian and other schools does not constitute aid to religion in violation of the Fourteenth Amendment to the Federal Constitution. "Its interest is education, broadly; its method, com-

prehensive. Individual interests are aided only as the common interest is safeguarded . . . ."

. . . .

Measured by the standards set forth in the foregoing authorities, in the operation of the released-time plan in Los Angeles, there is no appropriation of public money in support of any sect or denomination and no teaching of sectarianism in the school system of Los Angeles County in violation of section 8 of Article IX of the California Constitution.

And neither the California law nor the Los Angeles released-time plan is prohibited by section 30 of Article IV.

In addition to the constitutional questions appellant complains of rulings by the trial court excluding evidence of sectarian antagonism and ill feeling resulting from the conduct of the plan, and appellant presents several specifications of error of the trial court in finding or failing to find certain facts from the evidence. Whatever may have been the result of the application of the released-time plan is a matter of discretion of the Board of Education with which, in this case at least, the courts have nothing to do. From the findings as a whole, no error is apparent.

The judgment is affirmed.

THE UNITED STATES SUPREME COURT AND RELEASED TIME

Then the issue of *released*-time programs came before the courts for the first time. In *People* ex rel. *McCollum* v. *Board of Education,* 396 Ill. 14, 71 N.E.2d 161 (1947), the Illinois supreme court refused to grant a writ of mandamus against the Champaign public school board of education. In following the Latimer ruling concerning dismissed time, above, the court ruled in effect that the released-time program in Champaign schools did not constitute a use of public funds for sectarian purposes contrary to the constitution of Illinois and the state's school code.

Upon appeal to the United States Supreme Court, the lower court ruling in the McCollum case was reversed by an 8-to-1 vote in *Illinois* ex rel. *McCollum* v. *Board of Education*, 333 U.S. 203 (1948). Justice Black, writing the majority opinion, held that such a program constituted the "use of tax supported property for religious instruction and the close cooperation of the school authorities and the religious council in promoting religious instruction." Consequently, Justice Black held that the particular released-time program at hand violated the establishment clause of the First Amendment of the United States Constitution, and applicable to the states by the Due Process Clause of the Fourteenth Amendment.

† † *ILLINOIS* ex rel. *McCOLLUM* v. *BOARD OF EDUCATION*
333 U.S. 203, 68 S. CT. 461, 92 L. ED. 649 (1948).

Mr. Justice BLACK delivered the opinion of the Court, saying in part:

This case relates to the power of a state to utilize its tax-supported public school system in aid of religious instruction insofar as that power may be restricted by the First and Fourteenth Amendments to the Federal Constitution.

The appellant, Vashti McCollum, began this action for mandamus against the Champaign Board of Education in the Circuit Court of Champaign County, Illinois. Her asserted interest was that of a resident and taxpayer of Champaign and of a parent whose child was then enrolled in the Champaign public schools. Illinois has a compulsory education law which, with exceptions, requires parents to send their children, aged seven to sixteen, to its tax-supported public schools where the children are to remain in attendance during the hours when the schools are regularly in session. Parents who violate this law commit a misdemeanor punishable by fine unless the children attend private or parochial schools which meet educational standards fixed by the State. District boards of education are given general supervisory powers over the use of

the public school buildings within the school districts. . . .

Appellant's petition for mandamus alleged that religious teachers, employed by private religious groups, were permitted to come weekly into the school buildings during the regular hours set apart for secular teaching, and then and there for a period of thirty minutes substitute their religious teaching for the secular education provided under the compulsory education law. The petitioner charged that this joint public-school religious-group program violated the First and Fourteenth Amendments to the United States Constitution. The prayer of her petition was that the Board of Education be ordered to "adopt and enforce rules and regulations prohibiting all instruction in and teaching of religious education in all public schools in Champaign School District Number 71. . . . and in all public school houses and buildings in said district when occupied by public schools."

. . . Although there are disputes between the parties as to various inferences that may or may not properly be drawn from the evidence concerning the religious program, the following facts are shown by the record without dispute. In 1940 interested members of the Jewish, Roman Catholic, and a few of the Protestant faiths formed a voluntary association called the Champaign Council on Religious Education. They obtained permission from the Board of Education to offer classes in religious instruction to public school pupils in grades four to nine inclusive. Classes were made up of pupils whose parents signed printed cards requesting that their children be permitted to attend; they were held weekly, thirty minutes for the lower grades, forty-five minutes for the higher. The council employed the religious teachers at no expense to the school authorities, but the instructors were subject to the approval and supervision of the superintendent of schools. The classes were taught in three separate religious groups by Protestant teachers, Catholic priests, and a Jewish rabbi, although for the past several years there have apparently been no classes instructed in the Jewish religion. Classes were conducted in the regular classrooms of the school building. Students who did not choose to take the religious instruction were not released from public school duties; they were required to leave their classrooms and go to some other place in the school building for pursuit of their secular studies. On the other hand, students who were released from secular study for the religious instructions were required to be present at the religious classes. Reports of their presence or absence were to be made to their secular teachers.

The foregoing facts without reference to others that appear in the record, show the use of tax-supported property for religious instruction and the close cooperation between the school authorities and the religious council in promoting religious education. The operation of the State's compulsory education system thus assists and is integrated with the program of religious instruction carried on by separate religious sects. Pupils compelled by law to go to school for secular education are released in part from their legal duty upon the condition that they attend the religious classes. This is beyond all question a utilization of the tax-established and tax-supported public school system to aid religious groups to spread their faith. And it falls squarely under the ban of the First Amendment (made applicable to the States by the Fourteenth) as we interpreted it in *Everson* v. *Board of Education,* 330 U.S. 1. There we said:

Neither a state nor the Federal Government can set up a church. Neither can pass laws which aid one religion, aid all religions, or prefer one religion over another. Neither can force or influence a person to go to or to remain away from church against his will or force him to profess a belief or disbelief in any religion. No person can be punished for entertaining or professing religious beliefs or disbeliefs, for church attendance or nonattendance. No tax in any amount, large or small, can be levied to support any religious activities or institutions, whatever they may be called, or whatever form they may adopt to teach or practice religion. Neither a state nor the Federal Government can, openly or secretly, participate in the affairs of any religious organizations or groups and *vice versa*. In the words of Jefferson, the clause against establishment of religion by law was intended to erect 'a wall of separation between church and state.'

The majority in the *Everson* case, and the minority . . . agreed that the First

Amendment's language, properly interpreted, had erected a wall of separation between Church and State. They disagreed as to the facts shown by the record and as to the proper application of the First Amendment's language to those facts.

Recognizing that the Illinois program is barred by the First and Fourteenth Amendments if we adhere to the views expressed both by the majority and the minority in the *Everson* case, counsel for the respondents challenge those views as dicta and urge that we reconsider and repudiate them. They argue that historically the First Amendment was intended to forbid only government preference of one religion over another, not an impartial governmental assistance of all religions. In addition they ask that we distinguish or overrule our holding in the *Everson* case that the Fourteenth Amendment made the "establishment of religion" clause of the First Amendment applicable as a prohibition against the States. After giving full consideration to the arguments presented we are unable to accept either of these contentions.

To hold that a state cannot consistently with the First and Fourteenth Amendments utilize its public school system to aid any or all religious faiths or sects in the dissemination of their doctrines and ideals does not, as counsel urge, manifest a governmental hostility to religion or religious teachings. A manifestation of such hostility would be at war with our national tradition as embodied in the First Amendment's guaranty of the free exercise of religion. For the First Amendment rests upon the premise that both religion and government can best work to achieve their lofty aims if each is left free from the other within its respective sphere. Or, as we said in the *Everson* case, the First Amendment has erected a wall between Church and State which must be kept high and impregnable.

Here not only are the State's tax-supported public school buildings used for the dissemination of religious doctrines. The State also affords sectarian groups an invaluable aid in that it helps to provide pupils for their religious classes through use of the State's compulsory public school machinery. This is not separation of Church and State.

Reversed. . . .

Mr. Justice FRANKFURTER delivered the following opinion, in which Mr. Justice JACKSON, Mr. Justice RUTLEDGE, and Mr. Justice BURTON join:

We dissented in *Everson* v. *Board of Education*, 330 U.S. 1, because in our view the Constitutional principle requiring separation of Church and State compelled invalidation of the ordinance sustained by the majority. Illinois has here authorized the commingling of sectarian with secular instruction in the public schools. The Constitution of the United States forbids this.

This case, in the light of the *Everson* decision, demonstrates anew that the mere formulation of a relevant Constitutional principle is the beginning of the solution of a problem, not its answer. This is so because the meaning of a spacious conception like that of the separation of Church from State is unfolded as appeal is made to the principle from case to case. We are all agreed that the First and the Fourteenth Amendments have a secular reach far more penetrating in the conduct of Government than merely to forbid an "established church." But agreement, in the abstract, that the First Amendment was designed to erect a "wall of separation between church and State," does not preclude a clash of views as to what the wall separates. . . .

. . . .

Of course, "released time" as a generalized conception, undefined by differentiating particularities, is not an issue for Constitutional adjudication. Local programs differ from each other in many and crucial respects. Some "released time" classes are under separate denominational auspices, others are conducted jointly by several denominations, often embracing all the religious affiliations of a community. . . . It is only when challenge is made to the share that the public schools have in the execution of a particular "released time" program that close judicial scrutiny is demanded of the exact relation between the religious instruction and the public educational system in the specific situation before the Court.

The substantial differences among arrangements lumped together as "released time" emphasize the importance of detailed analysis of the facts to which the Constitutional test of Separation is to be applied. How does "released time" operate in Champaign? Public school teachers distribute to their pupils cards supplied by church groups, so that th eparents may indicate whether they desire religious instruction for their children. For those desiring it, religious classes are conducted in the regular classrooms of the public schools by teachers of religion paid by the churches and appointed by them, but as the State court found,

"subject to the approval and supervision of the superintendent." The courses do not profess to give secular instruction in subjects concerning religion. Their candid purpose is sectarian teaching. While a child can go to any of the religious classes offered, a particular sect wishing a teacher for its devotees requires the permission of the school superintendent "who in turn will determine whether or not it is practical for said group to teach in said school system." If no provision is made for religious instruction in the particular faith of a child, or if for other reasons the child is not enrolled in any of the offered classes, he is required to attend a regular school class, or a study period during which he is often left to his own devices. Reports of attendance in the religious classes are submitted by the religious instructor to the school authorities, and the child who fails to attend is presumably deemed a truant.

. . . The Champaign arrangement thus presents powerful elements of inherent pressure by the school system in the interest of religious sects. The fact that this power has not been used to discriminate is beside the point. Separation is a requirement to abstain from fusing functions of Government and of religious sects, not merely to treat them all equally. That a child is offered an alternative may reduce the constraint; it does not eliminate the operation of influence by the school in matters sacred to conscience and outside the school's domain. The law of imitation operates, and nonconformity is not an outstanding characteristic of children. The result is an obvious pressure upon children to attend. . . . [N]ot . . . all the practicing sects in Champaign are willing or able to provide religious instruction. The children belonging to these non-participating sects will thus have inculated in them a feeling of separatism when the school should be the training ground for habits of community, or they will have religious instruction in a faith which is not that of their parents. As a result, the public school system of Champaign actively furthers inculcation in the religious tenets of some faiths, and in the process sharpens the consciousness of religious differences at least among some of the children committed to its care. These are consequences not amenable to statistics. But they are precisely the consequences against which the Constitution was directed when it prohibited the Government common to all from becoming embroiled, however innocently, in the destructive religious conflicts of which the history of even this country records some dark pages.

Mention should not be omitted that the integration of religious instruction within the school system as practiced in Champaign is supported by arguments drawn from educational theories as diverse as those derived from Catholic conceptions and from the writings of John Dewey. Movements like "released time" are seldom single in origin or aim. Nor can the intrusion of religious instruction into the public school system of Champaign be minimized by saying that it absorbs less than an hour a week; in fact, that affords evidence of a design constitutionally objectionable. If it were merely a question of enabling a child to obtain religious instruction with a receptive mind, the thirty or forty-five minutes could readily be found on Saturday or Sunday. If that were all, Champaign might have drawn upon the French system, known in its American manifestation as "dismissed time," whereby one

school day is shortened to allow all children to go where they please, leaving those who so desire to go to a religious school. The momentum of the whole school atmosphere and school planning is presumably put behind religious instruction, as given in Champaign, precisely in order to secure for the religious instruction such momentum and planning. To speak of "released time" as being only half or three quarters of an hour is to draw a thread from a fabric.

We do not consider, as indeed we could not, school programs not before us which, though colloquially characterized as "released time," present situations differing in aspects that may well be constitutionally crucial. Different forms which "released time" has taken during more than thirty years of growth include programs which, like that before us, could not withstand the test of the Constitution; others may be found unexceptionable. We do not now attempt to weigh in the Constitutional scale every separate detail or various combination of factors which may establish a valid "released time" program. We find that the basic Constitutional principle of absolute Separation was violated when the State of Illinois, speaking through its Supreme Court, sustained the school authorities of Champaign in sponsoring and effectively furthering religious beliefs by its educational arrangement.

Separation means separation, not something less. Jefferson's metaphor in describing the relation between Church and State speaks of a "wall of separation," not a fine line easily overstepped. The public school is at once the symbol of our democracy and the most pervasive means for promoting our common destiny. In no activity of the State is it more vital to keep out divisive forces than in its schools, to avoid confusing, not to say fusing, what the Constitution sought to keep strictly apart. "The great American principle of eternal separation"—Elihu Root's phrase bears repetition—is one of the vital reliances of our Constitutional system for assuring unities among our people stronger than our diversities. It is the Court's duty to enforce this principle in its full integrity.

We renew our conviction that "we have staked the very existence of our country on the faith that complete separation between the state and religion is best for the state and best for religion." *Everson* v. *Board of Education*. If nowhere else, in the relation between Church and State, "good fences make good neighbors."

Mr. Justice JACKSON, concurring:

I join the opinion of Mr. Justice Frankfurter, and concur in the result reached by the Court, but with these reservations: I think it is doubtful whether the facts of this case establish jurisdiction in this Court, but in any event that we should place some bounds on the demands for interference with local schools that we are empowered or willing to entertain. I make these reservations a matter of record in view of the number of litigations likely to be started as a result of this decision. . . .

. . . If, however, jurisdiction is found to exist, it is important that we circumscribe our decision with some care. What is asked is not a defensive use of judicial power to set aside a tax levy or reverse a conviction, or to enjoin threats of prosecution or taxation. The relief demanded in this case is the extraordinary writ of mandamus to tell the local Board of Education what it must do. The prayer for relief is that a writ issue against the Board of Education "ordering it to immediately adopt and enforce rules and regulations prohibiting all instruction in and teaching of religious education in all public schools . . . and in all public school houses and buildings in said district when occupied by public schools." The plaintiff, as she has every right to be, is an avowed atheist. What she has asked of the courts is that they not only end the "released time" plan but also ban every form of teaching which suggests or recognizes that there is a God. She would ban all teaching of the Scriptures. She especially mentions as an example of invasion of her rights "having pupils learn and recite such statements as, 'The Lord is my Shepherd, I shall not want.'" And she objects to teaching that the King James Version of the Bible "is called the Christian's Guide Book, the Holy Writ and the Word of God," and many other similar matters. This Court is directing the Illinois courts generally to sustain plaintiff's complaint without exception of any of these grounds of complaint, without discriminating between them and without laying down any standards to define the limits of the effect of our decision.

To me, the sweep and detail of these complaints is a danger signal which warns of the kind of local controversy we will be required to arbitrate if we do not place appropriate limitation on our decision and exact strict compliance with jurisdictional requirements. Authorities list 256 separate and substantial religious bodies to exist in the continental United States. Each of them, through the suit of some discontented but unpenalized and untaxed representative, has as good a right as this plaintiff to demand that the courts compel the schools to sift out of their teaching everything inconsistent with its doctrines. If we are to eliminate everything that is objectionable to any of these warring sects or inconsistent with any of their doctrines, we will leave public education in shreds. Nothing but educational confusion and a discrediting of the public school system can result from subjecting it to constant law suits.

While we may and should end such formal and explicit instruction as the Champaign plan and can at all times prohibit teaching of creed and catechism and ceremonial and can forbid forthright proselyting in the schools, I think it remains to be demonstrated whether it is possible, even if desirable, to comply with such demands as plaintiff's completely to isolate and cast out of secular education all that some people may reasonably regard as religious instruction. Perhaps subjects such as mathematics, physics or chemistry are, or can be, completely secularized. But it would not seem practical to teach either practice or appreciation of the arts if we are to forbid exposure of youth to any religious influences. Music without sacred music, architecture minus the cathedral, or painting without the scriptural themes would be eccentric and incomplete, even from a secular point of view. Yet the inspirational appeal of religion in these guises is often stronger than in forthright sermon. Even such a "science" as bi-

ology raises the issue between evolution and creation as an explanation of our presence on this planet. Certainly a course in English literature that omitted the Bible and other powerful uses of our mother tongue for religious ends would be pretty barren. And I should suppose it is a proper, if not an indispensable, part of preparation for a worldly life to know the roles that religion and religions have played in the tragic story of mankind. The fact is that, for good or for ill, nearly everything which gives meaning to life, is saturated with religious influences, derived from paganism, Judaism, Christianity—both Catholic and Protestant—and other faiths accepted by a large part of the world's peoples. One can hardly respect a system of education that would leave the student wholly ignorant of the currents of religious thought that move the world society for a part in which he is being prepared.

But how one can teach, with satisfaction or even with justice to all faiths, such subjects as the story of the Reformation, the Inquisition, or even the New England effort to found "a Church without a Bishop and a State without a King," is more than I know. It is too much to expect that mortals will teach subjects about which their contemporaries have passionate controversies with the detachment they may summon to teaching about remote subjects such as Confucius or Mohammed. When instruction turns to proselyting and imparting knowledge becomes evangelism is, except in the crudest cases, a subtle inquiry.

. . . We must leave some flexibility to meet local conditions, some chance to progress by trial and error. While I agree that the religious classes involved here go beyond permissible limits, I also think the complainant demands more than plaintiff is entitled to have granted. . . .

The task of separating the secular from the religious in education is one of magnitude, intricacy and delicacy. To lay down a sweeping constitutional doctrine as demanded by complainant . . . is to decree a uniform, rigid and, . . . unchanging standard for countless school boards representing and serving highly localized groups. . . . It seems to me that to do so is to allow zeal for our own ideas of what is good in public instruction to induce us to accept the role of a super board of education for every school district in the nation.

It is idle to pretend that this task is one for which we can find in the Constitution one word to help us as judges to decide where the secular ends and the sectarian begins in education. Nor can we find guidance in any other legal source. It is a matter on which we can find no law but our own prepossessions. If with no surer legal guidance we are to take up and decide every variation of this controversy, raised by persons not subject to penalty or tax but who are dissatisfied with the way schools are dealing with the problem, we are likely to have much business of the sort. And, more importantly, we are likely to make the legal "wall of separation between church and state" as winding as the famous serpentine wall designed by Mr. Jefferson for the University he founded.

Mr. Justice REED, dissenting:

. . . I find it difficult to extract from the opinions any conclusion as to what it is in the Champaign plan that is unconstitutional. Is it the use of school buildings for religious instruction; the release of pupils by the schools for religious instruction during school hours; the so-called assistance by teachers in handing out the request cards to pupils, in keeping lists of them for release and records of their attendance; or the action of the principals in arranging an opportunity for the classes and the appearance of the Council's instructors? None of the reversing opinions say whether the purpose of the Champaign plan for religious instruction during school hours is unconstitutional or whether it is some ingredient used in or omitted from the formula that makes the plan unconstitutional.

From the tenor of the opinions I conclude that their teachings are that any use of a pupil's school time whether that use is on or off the school grounds, with the necessary school regulations to facilitate attendance, falls under the ban. . . . From the holding and the language of the opinions, I can only deduce that religious instruction of public school children during school hours is prohibited. The history of American education is against such an interpretation of the First Amendment

. . . .

This Court summarized the amendment's accepted reach into the religious field, as I understand its scope, in *Everson* v. *Board of Education*. . . . I agree, as there stated, that none of our governmental entities can "set up a church." I agree that they cannot "aid" all or any religions or prefer one "over another." But "aid" must be understood as a purposeful assistance directly to the church itself or to some religious group or organization doing religious work of such a character that it may fairly be said to be performing ecclesiastical functions. "Prefer" must give an advantage to one "over another." I agree that pupils cannot "be released in part from their legal duty" of school attendance upon condition that they attend religious classes. But as Illinois has held that it is within the discretion of the School Board to permit absence from school for religious instruction no legal duty of school attendance is violated. . . . If the sentence in the Court's opinion, concerning the pupils' release from legal duty, is intended to mean that the Constitution forbids a school to excuse a pupil from secular control during school hours to attend voluntarily a class in religious education, whether in or out of school buildings, I disagree. Of course, no tax can be levied to support organizations intended "to teach or practice religion." I agree too that the state cannot influence one toward religion against his will or punish him for his beliefs. Champaign's religious education course does none of these things.

It seems clear to me that the "aid" referred to by the Court in the *Everson* case could not have been those incidental advantages that religious bodies, with other groups similarly situated, obtain as a by-product of organized society. This explains the well-known fact that all churches receive "aid" from government in the form of freedom from taxation. The *Everson* decision itself justified the transportation of children to church schools by New Jersey for safety reasons.

. . . .

The practices of the federal government offer many examples of this kind of "aid" by the state to religion. The Congress of the United States has a chaplain for each House who daily invokes divine blessings and guidance for the proceedings. The armed forces have commissioned chaplains from early days. They conduct the public services in accordance with the liturgical requirements of their respective faiths, ashore and afloat, employing for the purpose property belonging to the United States and dedicated to the services of religion. Under the Servicemen's Readjustment Act of 1944, eligible veterans may receive training at government expense for the ministry in denominational schools. . . .

In the United States Naval Academy and the United States Military Academy, schools wholly supported and completely controlled by the federal government, there are a number of religious activities. Chaplains are attached to both schools. Attendance at church services on Sunday is compulsory at both the Military and Naval Academies. At West Point the Protestant services are held in the Cadet Chapel, the Catholic in the Catholic Chapel, and the Jewish in the Old Cadet Chapel; at Annapolis only Protestant services are held on the reservation, midshipmen of other religious persuasions attend the churches of the city of Annapolis. These facts indicate that both schools since their earliest beginnings have maintained and enforced a pattern of participation in formal worship.

With the general statements in the opinions concerning the constitutional requirement that the nation and the states, by virtue of the First and Fourteenth Amendments, may "make no law respecting an establishment of religion," I am in agreement. But, in the light of the meaning given to those words by the precedents, customs, and practices which I have detailed above, I cannot agree with the Court's conclusion that when pupils compelled by law to go to school for secular education are released from school so as to attend the religious classes, churches are unconstitutionally aided. . . . The prohibition of enactments respecting the establishment of religion do not bar every friendly gesture between church and state. It is not an absolute prohibition against every conceivable situation where the two may work together, any more than the other provisions of the First Amendment—free speech, free press—are absolutes. . . . This Court cannot be too cautious in upsetting practices embedded in our society by many years of experience. . . . The Constitution should not be stretched to forbid national customs in the way courts act to reach arrangements to avoid federal taxation. Devotion to the great principle of religious liberty should not lead us into a rigid interpretation of the constitutional guarantee that conflicts with accepted habits of our people. . . . The judgment should be affirmed.

REACTIONS OF LEGAL PERIODICALS TO *McCOLLUM* v. *BOARD OF EDUCATION*

The McCollum case stirred a variety of response in some three dozen law reviews. Clear disagreement with the decision was evidenced in about two-thirds of the reviews that took a definitive stand. A most resounding denunciation appeared in the *Marquette Law Review* (32:138, 145); "Take away the 'Everson [*Everson* v. *United States,* 330 U.S. 1 (1947)] Amendment,' reinstate the First Amendment, and the *McCollum* decision is clearly wrong." The most common argument of the dissenting reviewer evolved around the principle that our Founding Fathers "believed in freedom *of* religion, and not freedom *from* religion."

Criticisms of a more moderate nature frequently emphasized the Court's interference with a so-called "state function," the Court's assumption of a role as the National School Board, and the charge that the Court misconstrued the purposes of the First Amendment. The fact that government' reinstate the First Amendment, and the *McCollum* decision i religion was urged in some reviews. A note in the *Southern California Law Review* (22:423) contained references to other types of general support of religion which the Court had allowed. The fear that religion would be destroyed if it were not rooted in the hearts of young people was expressed in the *Fordham Law Review* (17:173).

A symposium on "Religion and the State" in *Law and Contemporary Problems* (14:1) contained the views of three noted scholars who disagreed sharply with the Court. First, Edwin Corwin supported aid to religion in general, and would incorporate "establishment of religion" into the Fourteenth Amendment solely when such an application involved invasion of somebody's freedom of religion, (14:1). Next, John Courtney Murray argued that absolute separation damages freedom of religion and parental rights, and is "unsupported, and unsupportable, by valid evidence and reasoning—historical, political, or legal—or on any sound theory of values, religious or social" (14:23, 40). Alexander Meiklejohn climaxed his criticism with the charge that the "sterile negativism" of such a separation doctrine "can express itself in the phrase, 'A state without religion and a church without politics' " (14:61, 71-2).

On the other hand, Milton R. Konvitz, writing in the same journal at the same time, argued persuasively that the Supreme Court had interpreted the First Amendment in the same manner as did Madison and Jefferson. He quoted with favor Justice Frankfurter's position that "Separation means separation, not something else." "Jefferson's metaphor," Frankfurter concluded, "in describing the relationship between church and state speaks of a 'wall of separation' not of a fine line easily over-stepped."

The decision also was hailed in several favorable reviews as upholding the historical tradition, the purpose of the First Amendment, and the American doctrine of religious freedom. The term "aid" was the focal point of such articles. A most impressive argument was made in the *Lawyers Guild Review* (8:387) and the *Rutgers University Law Review* (3:115) that the state was utilizing its school attendance laws to recruit pupils for religious programs held in public school buildings. An alternative test for determining such matters was suggested in the *Louisiana Law Review* (22:226). The proposed guideline was that a program should be evaluated according to the extent of aiding "secular education which is objectionably colored by sectarian philosophy." As such, the McCollum program of religious instruction within the public school buildings during school hours appeared unconstitutional, in the judgment of this review.

In addition, a half dozen other reviews either suggested a case-by-case approach or alternative programs which supposedly would be constitutional. A few reviewers correctly forecasted the Zorach decision of four years later. However, it was a common statement that McCollum had to be modified before any such desirable forms of "dismissed time" programs could be acceptable.

The 1964 report of the American Association of School Administrators, *Religion in the Public Schools*, summarized religious groups' reactions to the case.

The McCollum decision received a highly mixed reaction from religious groups in the nation. Roman Catholics were especially disturbed over it. Protestant Evangelicals were disappointed. The decision was praised, however, by the *Christian Century*, by Unitarians, Baptists, and most Jewish groups.

REACTIONS OF EDUCATION PERIODICALS TO *McCOLLUM* v. *BOARD OF EDUCATION*

Shortly before the McCollum decision, W. D. Cocking, in the *School Executive* (67:5, 1948) maintained that public schools should teach about religion, but not teach or interpret religion or religious beliefs. Such teaching or interpreting should be and must be left to the individual churches and religious groups and this must be done outside of school time and away from school premises, he argued.

The McCollum decision was generally viewed with disfavor in education journals. Many thought there was a definite place for religion in public schools. C. L. Hunt in the *Journal of Educational Sociology* (22:304, 1948) maintained that the public school system seemed to be the system most logically suited for imparting religious instruction. W. A. Wetzel, in the *National Association of Secondary-School Principals' Bulletin* (33:72, 1949), said that the Constitution, given the circumstances of the McCollum case, cannot be interpreted as forbidding all forms of religious education in public schools.

Other articles in the *National Association of Secondary-School Principals' Bulletin* pursued this same line by insisting public schools were not meant to be given an anti-religious slant by ignoring religion. Rather, it was urged that religion should be included in the schools to provide students with a sound preparation for life and to enlarge their knowledge and to insure cultural growth. In *Education* (71:353, 1951) F. E. Johnson also deplored the anti-religious ring in the McCollum decision. He found the doctrine ensuing from this case a challenge to organized religion, and thus totally inconsistent with the American tradition.

Other problems were seen by some as arising from the McCollum decision. W. A. Wetzel, in *National Association of Secondary-School Principals' Bulletin* (33:66, 1949), saw as a possible outcome that public school education would be left in shreds. In this respect, it was suggested in *Religious Education* (43:193, 1948) that the decision would make it possible for dissenting individuals or sects to oppose any teaching they dislike. The possibility that Protestants would be encouraged to set up their own elementary and secondary schools was seen as another possible problem for public schools in *Religious Education* (43:201, 1948).

A very different view was advanced by E. Fuller in *The Education Digest* (14:3, 1949) who agreed with the Supreme Court that separation of church and state did not mean an antireligious position should be taken by the public schools. Rather, good will between the two realms was desirable during that time when the actual meaning of separation of church and state was being legally defined. Fuller also supported the Supreme Court's decision on the grounds that our best interests are met by not having religious instruction in the public schools.

Two writers looked at the McCollum decision in terms of Bible reading and recitation of the Lord's Prayer, two practices common in many public schools at that time. M. K. Remmlein, in *Religious Education* (43:211, 1948), concluded that neither practice was implicity forbidden by the McCollum case. Furthermore, he thought, concerning programs such as Bible reading, that nothing should be implied, even as dictum, since the implications were so indirect. On the other hand, the possibility that Mr. Justice Jackson's concurring opinion formulated a theory whereby Bible reading and recitation of the Lord's Prayer would be declared unconstitutional was seen in *The Education Digest* (13:4, 1948).

Shortly before the McCollum decision, W. D. Cocking, in the *School Executive* (67:5, 1948) maintained that public schools should teach about religion, but not teach or interpret religion or religious beliefs. Such teaching or interpreting should be and must be left up to the individual churches and religious groups. But this must not be done during regular school time and must be held off the premises of the public school.

THE SUPREME COURT AND DISMISSED TIME

Since the McCollum decision left little doubt that "released-time" programs are clearly unconstitutional, the next step seemed the adjudication of dismissed time. In an unreported decision, the circuit court of St. Louis enjoined the continuance of the St. Louis system of dismissed time whereby religious instruction was held outside the school buildings, with no school supervision and no attendance records kept by the school teachers.

Just prior to the *Zorach* v. *Clauson* decision, a decision was handed down by the supreme court of Albany County, New York, in *Lewis* v. *Spaulding*, 193 M. 66, 85 N.Y.S.2d 865 (1951), in which the court found that the New York plan of dismissed-time, in which there was no expenditure of public funds, no credit given for such instruction, and no solicitation or supervision by the school officials in the religious programs was free from the objectionable features which motivated the United States Supreme Court to declare the Champaign plan of released-time unconstitutional in the McCollum case. In the Lewis case, the New York court felt that such programs could be challenged only if there was a finding that there was present an aid to religion. Since there was not, the program was upheld. Nor did the court find violations of the guarantees of religious liberty and separation of church and state as commanded by the United States Constitution.

Then in *Zorach* v. *Clauson,* 343 U.S. 306 (1952), the whole issue of dismissed time reached the United States Supreme Court for the first time. Therein, the New York Education Law provision which the New York city school board utilized to permit its public schools to release students during school hours for religious instruction outside of the school buildings, and without the expenditure of public funds, was upheld against the contention that such a program violated the First Amendment made applicable to the states by the Fourteenth Amendment.

The court in finding that New York had neither prohibited the free exercise of religion nor made a law respecting an establishment of religion within the meaning of the First Amendment, declared that there was no evidence in this particular case that such a system involved the use of coercion to get such students to enroll in such religious instruction. Declaring, "We are a religious people whose institutions presuppose a supreme being," Justice Douglas, speaking for a 6-to-3 majority, held that while the First Amendment prohibits governmental financing of religion or undertaking of religious instruction, it does not require governmental hostility to religion.

† † *ZORACH* v. *CLAUSON*
343 U.S. 306, 72 S. CT. 679, 96 L. ED. 954 (1952).

Mr. Justice DOUGLAS delivered the opinion of the Court:

New York City has a program which permits its public schools to release students during the school day so that they may leave the school buildings and school grounds and go to religious centers for religious instruction or devotional exercises. A student is released on written request of his parents. Those not released stay in the classrooms. The churches make weekly reports to the schools, sending a list of children who have been released from public school but who have not reported for religious instruction.

This "released time" program involves neither religious instruction in public school classrooms nor the expenditure of public funds. All costs, including the application blanks, are paid by the religious organizations. The case is therefore unlike *McCollum* v *Board of Education,* 333 U.S. 203 which involved a "released time" program from Illinois. In that case the classrooms were turned over to religious instructors. We accordingly held that the program violated the First Amendment which (by reason of the Four teenth Amendment) prohibits the states from establishing religion or prohibiting its free exercise.

Appellants, who are taxpayers and residents of New York City and whose children attend its public schools, challenge the present law, contending it is in essence not different from the one involved in the *McCollum* case. Their argument, stated elaborately in various ways, reduces itself to this: the weight and influence of the school is put behind a program for religious instruction; public school teachers police it, keeping tab on students who are released; the classroom activities come to a halt while the students who are released for religious instruction are on leave; the school is a crutch on which the churches are leaning for support in their religious training; without the cooperation of the schools this "released time" program, like the one in the *McCollum* case, would be futile and ineffective. The New York Court of Appeals sustained the law against this claim of unconstitutionality. . . . The case is here on appeal. . . .

The briefs and arguments are replete with data bearing on the merits of this type of "released time" program. Views *pro* and *con* are expressed, based on practical experience with these programs and with their implications. We do not stop to summarize these materials nor to burden the opinion with an analysis of them. For they involve considerations not germane to the narrow constitutional issue presented. They largely concern the wisdom of the system, its efficiency from an educational point of view, and the political considerations which have motivated its adoption or rejection in some communities. Those matters are of no concern here, since our problem reduces itself to whether New York by this system has

either prohibited the "free exercise" of religion or has made a law "respecting an establishment of religion" within the meaning of the First Amendment.

It takes obtuse reasoning to inject any issue of the "free exercise" of religion into the present case. No one is forced to go to the religious classroom and no religious exercise or instruction is brought to the classrooms of the public schools. A student need not take religious instruction. He is left to his own desires as to the manner or time of his religious devotions, if any.

There is a suggestion that the system involves the use of coercion to get public school students into religious classrooms. There is no evidence in the record before us that supports that conclusion. The present record indeed tells us that the school authorities are neutral in this regard and do no more than release students whose parents so request. If in fact coercion were used, if it were established that any one or more teachers were using their office to persuade or force students to take the religious instruction, a wholly different case would be presented. Hence we put aside that claim of coercion both as respects the "free exercise" of religion and "an establishment of religion" within the meaning of the First Amendment.

Moreover, apart from the claim of coercion, we do not see how New York by this type of "released time" program has made a law respecting an establishment of religion within the meaning of the First Amendment. There is much talk of the separation of Church and State in the history of the Bill of Rights and in the decisions clustering around the First Amendment. . . . There cannot be the slightest doubt that the First Amendment reflects the philosophy that Church and State should be separated. And so far as interference with the "free exercise" of religion and an "establishment" of religion are concerned, the separation must be complete and unequivocal. The First Amendment within the scope of its coverage permits no exception; the prohibition is absolute. The First Amendment, however, does not say that in every and all respects there shall be a separation of Church and State. Rather, it studiously defines the manner, the specific ways, in which there shall be no concert or union or dependency one on the other. That is the common sense of the matter. Otherwise the state and religion would be aliens to each other—hostile, suspicious, and even unfriendly. Churches could not be required to pay even property taxes. Municipalities would not be permitted to render police or fire protection to religious groups. Policemen who helped parishioners into their places of worship would violate the Constitution. Prayers in our legislative halls; the appeals to the Almighty in the messages of the Chief Executive; the proclamations making Thanksgiving Day a holiday; "so help me God" in our courtroom oaths—these and all other references to the Almighty that run through our laws, our public rituals, our ceremonies would be flouting the First Amendment. A fastidious atheist or agnostic could even object to the supplication with which the Court opens each session: "God save the United States and this Honorable Court."

We would have to press the concept of separation of Church and State to these extremes to condemn the present law on constitutional grounds. The nullification of this law would have wide and profound effects. A Catholic student applies to his teacher for permission to leave the school during hours on a Holy Day of Obligation to attend a mass. A Jewish student asks his teacher for permission to be excused for Yom Kippur. A Protestant wants the afternoon off for a family baptismal ceremony. In each case the teacher requires parental consent in writing. In each case the teacher, in order to make sure the student is not a truant, goes further and requires a report from the priest, the rabbi, or the minister. The teacher in other words cooperates in a religious program to the extent of making it possible for her students to participate in it. Whether she does it occasionally for a few students, regularly for one, or pursuant to a systematized program designed to further the religious needs of all the students does not alter the character of the act.

We are a religious people whose institutions presuppose a Supreme Being. We guarantee the freedom to worship as one chooses. We make room for as wide a variety of beliefs and creeds as the spiritual needs of man deem necessary. We sponsor an attitude on the part of government that shows no partiality to any one group and that lets each flourish according to the zeal of its adherents and the appeal of its dogma. When the state encourages religious instruction or cooperates with religious authorities by adjusting the schedule of public events to sectarian needs, it follows the best of our traditions. For it then respects the religious nature of our people and accommodates the public service to their spiritual needs. To hold that it may not would be to find in the Constitution a requirement that the government show a callous indifference to religious groups. That would be preferring those who believe in no religion over those who do believe. Government may not finance religious groups nor undertake religious instruction nor blend secular and sectarian education nor use secular institutions to force one or some religion on any person. But we find no constitutional requirement which makes it necessary for government to be hostile to religion and to throw its weight against efforts to widen the effective scope of religious influence. The government must be neutral when it comes to competition between sects. It may not thrust any sect on any person. It may not make a religious observance compulsory. It may not coerce anyone to attend church, to observe a religious holiday, or to take religious instruction. But it can close its doors or suspend its operations as to those who want to repair to their religious sanctuary for worship or instruction. No more than that is undertaken here.

This program may be unwise and improvident from an educational or a community viewpoint. That appeal is made to us on a theory, previously advanced, that each case must be decided on the basis of "our own prepossessions." . . . Our individual preferences, however, are not the constitutional standard. The constitutional standard is the separation of Church and State. The problem, like many problems in constitutional law, is one of degree. . . .

In the *McCollum* case the classrooms were used for religious instruction and the force of the public school was used to promote that instruction. Here, as we have said, the public schools do no more than accommodate their schedules to a program of outside religious instruction. We follow the *McCollum* case. But we cannot expand it to cover the present released time program unless separation of Church and State means that public institutions can make no adjustments of their schedules to accommodate the religious needs of the people. We cannot read into the Bill of Rights such a philosophy of hostility to religion.

Affirmed.

Mr. Justice BLACK dissented, saying in part:

. . . I see no significant difference between the invalid Illinois system and that of New York here sustained. Except for the use of the school buildings in Illinois, there is no difference between the systems which I consider even worthy of mention. In the New York program, as in that of Illinois, the school authorities release some of the children on the condition that they attend the religious classes, get reports on whether they attend, and hold the other children in the school building until the religious hour is over. As we attempted to make categorically clear, the *McCollum* decision would have been the same if the religious classes had not been held in the school buildings. We said:

Here *not only* are the State's tax-supported public school buildings used for the dissemination of religious doctrines. The State *also* affords sectarian groups an invaluable aid in that it helps to provide pupils for their religious classes through use of the State's compulsory public school machinery. *This* is not separation of Church and State. (Emphasis supplied.) . . .

McCollum thus held that Illinois could not constitutionally manipulate the compelled classroom hours of its compulsory school machinery so as to channel children into sectarian classes. Yet that is exactly what the Court holds New York can do.

I am aware that our *McCollum* decision on separation of Church and State has been subjected to a most searching examination throughout the country. Probably few opinions from this Court in recent years have attracted more attention or stirred wider debate. Our insistence on "a wall between Church and State which must be kept high and impregnable" has seemed to some a correct exposition of the philosophy and a true interpretation of the language of the First Amendment to which we should strictly adhere. With equal conviction and sincerity, others have thought the *McCollum* decision fundamentally wrong and have pledged continuous warfare against it. . . . In dissenting today, I mean to do more than give routine approval to our *McCollum* decision. I mean also to reaffirm my faith in the fundamental philosophy expressed in *McCollum* and *Everson* v. *Board of Education.* . . .

Here the sole question is whether New York can use its compulsory education laws to help religious sects get attendants presumably too unenthusiastic to go unless moved to do so by the pressure of this state machinery. That this is the plan, purpose, design and consequence of the New York program cannot be denied. The state thus makes religious sects beneficiaries of its power to compel children to attend secular schools. Any use of such coercive power by the state to help or hinder some religious sects or to prefer all religious sects over nonbelievers or vice versa is just what I think the First Amendment forbids. In considering whether a state has entered this forbidden field the question is not whether it has entered too far but whether it has entered at all. New York is manipulating its compulsory education laws to help religious sects get pupils. This is not separation but combination of Church and State.

The Court's validation of the New York system rests in part on its statement that Americans are a "religious people whose institutions presuppose a Supreme Being." This was at least as true when the First Amendment was adopted; and it was just as true when eight Justices of this Court invalidated the released time system in *McCollum* on the premise that a state can no more "aid all religions" than it can aid one. It was precisely because eighteenth century Americans were a religious people divided into many fighting sects that we were given the constitutional mandate to keep Church and State completely separate. Colonial history had already shown that, here as elsewhere, zealous sectarians entrusted with governmental power to further their causes would sometimes torture, maim and kill those they branded "heretics," "atheists" or "agnostics." The First Amendment was therefore to insure that no one powerful sect or combination of sects could use political or governmental power to punish dissenters whom they could not convert to their faith. Now as then, it is only by wholly isolating the state from the religious sphere and compelling it to be completely neutral, that the freedom of each and every denomination and of all nonbelievers can be maintained. It is this neutrality the Court abandons today when it treats New York's coercive system as a program which *merely* "encourages religious instruction or cooperates with religious authorities." The abandonment is all the more dangerous to liberty because of the Court's legal exaltation of the orthodox and its derogation of unbelievers.

Under our system of religious freedom, people have gone to their religious sanctuaries not because they feared the law but because they loved their God. The choice of all has been as free as the choice of those who answered the call to worship moved only by the music of the old Sunday morning church bells. The spiritual mind of man has thus been free to believe, disbelieve, or doubt, without repression, great or small, by the heavy hand of

government. Statutes authorizing such repression have been stricken. Before today, our judicial opinions have refrained from drawing invidious distinctions between those who believe in no religion and those who do believe. The First Amendment has lost much if the religious follower and the atheist are no longer to be judicially regarded as entitled to equal justice under law.

State help to religion injects political and party prejudices into a holy field. It too often substitutes force for prayer, hate for love, and persecution for persuasion. Government should not be allowed, under cover of the soft euphemism of "co-operation," to steal into the sacred area of religious choice.

Mr. Justice FRANKFURTER dissented, saying in part:

. . . The Court tells us that in the maintenance of its public schools, "[The State government] can close its doors or suspend its operations" so that its citizens may be free for religious devotions or instruction. If that were the issue, it would not rise to the dignity of a constitutional controversy. Of course, a State may provide that the classes in its schools shall be dismissed, for any reason, or no reason, on fixed days, or for special occasions. The essence of this case is that the school system did not "close its doors" and did not "suspend its operations." There is all the difference in the world between letting the children out of school and letting some of them out of school into religious classes. If every one is free to make what use he will of time wholly unconnected from schooling required by law—those who wish sectarian instruction devoting it to that purpose, those who have ethical instruction at home, to that, those who study music,

to that—then of course there is no conflict with the Fourteenth Amendment.

The pith of the case is that formalized religious instruction is substituted for other school activity which those who do not participate in the released-time program are compelled to attend. The school system is very much in operation during this kind of released time. If its doors are closed, they are closed upon those students who do not attend the religious instruction, in order to keep them within the school. That is the very thing which raises the constitutional issue. It is not met by disregarding it. Failure to discuss this issue does not take it out of the case.

Again, the Court relies upon the absence from the record of evidence of coercion in the operation of the system. "If in fact coercion were used," according to the Court, "if it were established that any one or more teachers were using their office to persuade or force students to take the religious instruction, a wholly different case would be presented." Thus, "coercion" in the abstract is acknowledged to be fatal. But the Court disregards the fact that as the case comes to us, there could be no proof of coercion, for the appellants were not allowed to make proof of it. Appellants alleged that "The operation of the released time program has resulted and inevitably results in the exercise of pressure and coercion upon parents and children to secure attendance by the children for religious instruction." This allegation —that coercion was in fact present and is inherent in the system, no matter what disavowals might be made in the operating regulations—was denied by appellees. Thus were drawn issues of the fact which cannot be determined, on any conceivable view of judicial notice, by judges out of their own knowledge or experience. Appellants sought an opportunity to adduce evidence in support of these allegations at an appropriate trial. And though the courts below cited the concurring opinion in *McCollum* v. *Board of Education* . . . to "emphasize the importance of detailed analysis of the facts to which the Constitutional test of Separation is to be applied," they denied that opportunity on the ground that such proof was irrelevant to the issue of constitutionality. . . .

. . . The result in the *McCollum* case . . . was based on principles that received unanimous acceptance by this Court, barring only a single vote. I agree with Mr. Justice Black that those principles are disregarded in reaching the result in this case. Happily they are not disavowed by the Court. From this I draw the hope that in future variations of the problem which are bound to come here, these principles may again be honored in the observance.

The deeply divisive controversy aroused by the attempts to secure public school pupils for sectarian instruction would promptly end if the advocates of such instruction were content to have the school "close its doors or suspend its operations"—that is, dismiss classes in their entirety, without discrimination—instead of seeking to use the public schools as the instrument for securing attendance at denominational classes. The unwillingness of the promoters of this movement to dispense with such use of the public schools betrays a surprising want of confidence in the inherent power of the various faiths to draw children to outside sectarian classes—an attitude that hardly reflects the faith of the greatest religious spirits.

Mr. Justice JACKSON, dissenting:

This released time program is founded upon a use of the State's power of coercion, which, for me, determines its unconstitutionality. Stripped to its essentials, the plan has two stages: first, that the State compel each student to yield a large part of his time for public secular education; and second, that some of it be "released" to him on condition that he devote it to sectarian religious purposes.

No one suggests that the Constitution would permit the State directly to require this "released" time to be spent "under the control of a duly constituted religious body." This program accomplishes that forbidden result by indirection. If public education were taking so much of the pupils' time as to injure the public or the students' welfare by encroaching upon their religious opportunity, simply shortening everyone's school day would facilitate voluntary and optional attendance at Church classes. But that suggestion is rejected upon the ground that if they are made free many students will not go to the Church. Hence, they must be deprived of freedom for this period, with Church attendance put to them as one of the two permissible ways of using it.

The greater effectiveness of this system over voluntary attendance after school hours is due to the truant officer who, if the youngster fails to go to the Church school, dogs him back to the public schoolroom. Here schooling is more or less suspended during the "released time" so the nonreligious attendants will not forge ahead of the church-going absentees. But it serves as a temporary jail for a pupil who will not go to Church. It takes more subtlety of mind than I possess to deny that this is governmental constraint in support of religion. It is as unconstitutional, in my view, when exerted by indirection as when exercised forthrightly.

As one whose children, as a matter of free choice, have been sent to privately supported Church schools, I may challenge the Court's suggestion that opposition to this plan can only be antireligious, atheistic, or agnostic. My evangelistic brethren confuse an objection to compulsion with an objection to religion. It is possible to hold a faith with enough confidence to believe that what should be rendered to God does not need to be decided and collected by Caesar.

The day that this country ceases to be free for irreligion it will cease to be free for religion—except for the sect that can win political power. The same epithetical jurisprudence used by the Court today to beat down those who oppose pressuring children into some religion can devise as good epithets tomorrow against those who object to pressuring them into a favored religion. And, after all, if we concede to the State power and wisdom to single out "duly constituted religious" bodies as exclusive alternatives for compulsory secular instruction, it would be logical to also uphold the power and wisdom to choose the true faith among those "duly constituted." We start down a rough road when we begin to mix compulsory public education with compulsory godliness.

A number of Justices just short of a majority that promulgates today's passionate dialectics joined in answering them in *Illinois* ex rel. *McCollum* v. *Education*, 333 U.S. 203. The distinction attempted between that case and this is trivial, almost to the point of cynicism, magnifying its nonessential details and disparaging compulsion which was the underlying reason for invalidity. A reading of the Court's opinion in that case along with its opinion in the case will show such difference of overtones and undertones as to make clear that the *McCollum* case has passed like a storm in a teacup. The wall which the Court was professing to erect between Church and State has become even more warped and twisted than I expected. Today's judgment will be more interesting to students of psychology and of the judicial processes than to students of constitutional law.

REACTION OF LEGAL PERIODICALS TO *ZORACH* v. *CLAUSON*

The Zorach case upholding the constitutionality of a dismissed time program was regarded by some legal scholars as an instance of the Court's backing-off from its much criticized position in the McCollum case.

Considerably fewer law review analyses followed the Zorach decision than its predecessor. The fact that the dozen or so reviewers were evenly divided over the merits of the decision lends support to a common impression that the Supreme Court was unable in the Zorach case to solve the multi-faced problem of squaring the whole idea of released time with the constitutional prohibition against an establishment of religion.

The opinion that the Zorach program involved coercion, as did the McCollum, was the main point found in the majority of the reviews which disagreed with the Court's stand. The charge was made in the *Southern California Law Review* (26:186) that no released-time program could avoid aspects of coercion and aid. On the other hand it was argued in the *Texas Law Review* (31:327) that a "dismissed program" involving unqualified release from the schoolhouse of all students at a given time would be constitutionally proper. A note in the *Rocky Mountain Law Review* (25:104) expressed concern because Jefferson's high "wall of separation" was being abandoned, while the *Southern California Law Review* (26:186) felt that a "desired social result was railroaded through." Just how the Zorach decision logically could be equated with McCollum rule was questioned in the *Georgia Bar Journal* (15:363).

Support for the Zorach decision in legal journals evolved mainly around the parental rights argument, as sanctioned in *Pierce* v. *Society of Sisters*, 268 U.S. 510 (1925). Reviewers reasoned that because a state must allow a child to meet his entire educational requirements in a parochial school, then it followed that parents may also direct the temper of the child's public-school education, and that the state can release a child for one hour a week to fulfill a similar religious purpose, as in the Pierce case.

The cooperation philosophy of the Zorach decision was described in the *Notre Dame Lawyer* (27:529, 539–41) as the "natural norm of the church-state relationship in a nation which has a religious orientation." Otherwise, a note in the *Louisiana Law Review* (22:266–Dec. 1961) presented the argument that since pupils went elsewhere for their religious instruction, the secular education would not be objectionably colored by sectarian philosophy, thus making constitutional, any such "aid" to religion.

An argument was made in *Columbia Law Review* (49:836) that the Zorach philosophy was constitutionally proper, but that the program in practice involved unconstitutional aspects of compulsion by public school officials.

REACTIONS OF EDUCATION PERIODICALS TO *ZORACH* v. *CLAUSON*

The Zorach decision was viewed favorably in a majority of the education journals which discussed the case. Some thought the decision departed from the trend of absolutism which had been started in the Everson case and followed in the McCollum, while others took a completely opposite view of the implications of the Supreme Court's rationale.

E. L. Shaver in *Religious Education* (48:38, 1953), wholeheartedly agreed with what he saw as a departure from Justice Black's principle of absolute separation of church and state. He felt the Court was correct in its interpretation that the government was not required to be hostile to religion and that the church and state are not to be completely and totally separate in all respects. Shaver applauded the Court's statement, "We are a religious people whose institutions presuppose a Supreme Being." L. A. Weigle, in another article in *Religious Education* (49:73–78, 1954) also viewed the Zorach decision in terms of a relaxing of the Court's doctrine of absolute separation of church and state.

However, F. E. Johnson in *Religious Education* (48:422, 1953) thought this decision did *not* modify the position of the Court in the Everson and McCollum decisions on aid to any or all religions. L. O. Garber in *Nation's Schools* (50:67, 1952) drew the same conclusions. He felt the Zorach decision could not be considered a reversal of the McCollum because the majority opinion in the Zorach viewed the two decisions as being consistent. Garber, in several other articles, also saw the possibility that the Zorach decision had not completely answered the question of released or dismissed time religious educational programs because of the strong dissenting opinions and the similarity of the Zorach case to the McCollum. Therefore, he concluded there might well be more litigation to settle the constitutional issue in plans differing from either released or dismissed time.

The American Jewish Committee came out strongly opposed to the dismissed time plan of the Zorach decision in *Religious Education* (50:232, 1955). The Committee insisted that the state was actually aiding religion by using part of the compulsory school day for religious purposes; that a divisive quality was present in the plan; that children who did not participate in the religious classes were denied the instruction disrupted or suspended during the hour of dismissal; and that records show that the program contributes to truancy because not all excused children attend the classes.

R. B. Tapp in the *National Educational Association Journal* (47:573, 1958), also opposed the dismissed time plan even though the Supreme Court considered it constitutional. He felt the plan was harmful to the public schools because the school day, which was already too short, was shortened even more. He also argued that the system had not effectively cut down on juvenile delinquency. Tapp considered dismissed time bad for democracy since the concept of separation of church and state was not being followed. By separating the children into denominational groups, Tapp thought the diversity in the nation was increased to the detriment of all.

J. E. Lookstein in *Religious Education* (49:95, 1954) found similar objectionable qualities in the unconstitutional released time plan declared unconstitutional in the McCollum decision, but apparently not in the dismissed time plan of the Zorach case. He even proposed this plan be extended to five days a week instead of just one to maximize the religious instruction.

J. Larson in the *National Educational Association Journal* (47:572, 1958) supported the Supreme Court's decision on the grounds that the dismissed time program was definitely beneficial to the children as a source of good training. The author could find no divisive quality in the plan. Rather, he concluded, it encouraged cooperation and was quite consistent with our tradition of separation of church and state. M. Howlett in *Education* (71:370, 373, 1951) also agreed with the Supreme Court. He considered the objection of taking advantage of compulsory school attendance for dismissed time silenced by *Pierce* v. *Society of Sisters.* "If the parents have the right to send their children to private or parochial school for full time, they certainly have the right to send them for one hour a week," he contended.

L. R. Ward in *Religious Education* (51:250, 1966), while not hostile to the dismissed time plan, felt that supplementing the public schools with religious instruction was not the answer because it accomplished too little. In a similar vein, an article in *Nation's Schools* (66:74, 1960) suggested that the schools teach *about* religion.

A variety of other articles discussed the Zorach case but took no position regarding the Supreme Court's decision. For examples see: A. E. Sutherland, *The Harvard Educational Review* (24:71, 1954); I. Starr, *Social Education* (16:361, 1952); and *National Educational Association Research Bulletin* (34:169, 1956).

JUDICIAL REACTIONS FOLLOWING THE ZORACH DECISION

The practice whereby the school officials of the state of Washington distributed the cards and made the announcements of the various programs in their classrooms was held to be an unconstitutional practice similar to that present in the McCollum case, but was absent in the Zorach case. Thus, the court was impressed with the effect of official influence upon the pupils while assembled as a "captive audience." In summation, the state of Washington court held that there were no constitutional limitations being contravened, since the school district may permit a dismissed-time school program as long as such program is practiced within the constitutional limitations.

Shortly after the Perry case the Oregon supreme court was confronted with a related problem in *Dilger* v. *School District*, 222 Ore. 108, 352 P.2d 564 (1960). The Oregon court held that the dismissed-time statute in question was not unconstitutional merely because of a failure to designate the particular official or board in the school system to whom application by the parents was to be made for such released-time programs, which were to be held inside the school system. The court went on to say that whereas the released-time statute made it mandatory that such religious instruction be given upon a proper application by a parent or a guardian, the Oregon statute did make it discretionary that the school administrator could adjust the time schedule for such instruction.

The Supreme Court ruling in the Zorach case, however, by no means solved the problems faced by state educational policy makers and courts in this area. In 1959 the *Perry* v. *School District No. 81*, 54 Wash.2d 886, 344 P.2d 1036 (1959) (discussed below) held that a dismissed-time program insofar as it involved distribution in the public schools of cards on which the parents gave their permission for their children to attend such instruction, and insofar as it involved the making of announcements or explanations by representatives of religious groups or instructors in the schools for the purpose of obtaining consent of the parents for participation of their children in the program, violated the state constitutional provision that no public money or property shall be used to aid religion, or religious instruction. In doing so, the court held that dismissed time itself has never been held to violate any state or federal constitutional provision; rather it is the manner in which such a program has been practiced that has constituted the violation. In other words, the state of Washington court concluded that each case must be determined by its own facts.

The court then quoted extensively from the Zorach case and held that the reasoning there was sound and that it reflected the reasoning of most state courts. The court, however, went on to find a significant difference in the facts of the Zorach case and the case with which it was confronted.

† † *PERRY* v. *SCHOOL DISTRICT NO. 81*
54 WASH.2D 886, 344 P.2D 1036 (1959).

Judge HUNTER delivered the opinion of the court:

This appeal involves the constitutionality of the released-time program carried on in Spokane in school district No. 81. . . . The findings of fact show that, on September 28, 1938, the school board by resolution authorized the release of public school children for one hour per week for religious education upon the written request of their parents. Since that date a released-time program has been in effect within school district No. 81, and since its inception the program has been primarily administered by the Spokane council of churches. . . . There is nothing in the board's resolution limiting the program to any particular church or religious faith. In recent years one parish of the Catholic church has participated in the program. The expense of the program is borne by the religious groups involved. No money out of the common school fund or tax funds is contributed to or received directly or indirectly by those instructing the religious classes. . . . The classrooms used for the religious instruction are located off the school grounds, usually in a nearby church. The procedural aspect of the released-time program is carried out in the following manner.

Early in the year, a representative from the religious group calls upon the principal of each individual school and provides a supply of cards upon which parents may indicate their desire to have their children attend the religious instruction. Depending upon the preference of the principal involved, the cards are distributed to the students either by the representative of the religious group or by the individual classroom instructors. In the distribution of these cards, the children are informed of the availability of the religious instruction and are requested to take the cards home to their parents. The Catholic parish involved distributes the request forms from the church, but there is no finding that they do not also distribute the cards in the public schools.

At the appointed hour for the religious instruction, those children whose parents have requested that their children receive the instruction, by signing and returning the request cards, are released from their regular classroom activities. They are met at the school by an escort provided by the religious group and are taken to the religious instruction classroom. At the end of the religious instruction, the children are returned to their public school classroom by the escort from the religious group.

The religious instruction period corresponds to a school period. In most instances this is from forty-five minutes to one hour, but not in excess of one hour. These religious instruction classes are held once a week, in some instances during all of the school term and in others during only a portion of the term. The children whose parents have not requested their release remain in the classroom where their public school activities continue. In most instances, where there are but few children remaining, the regular group instruction ceases, but the remaining children are kept occupied with special projects, additional individual help, or some other school activity, depending upon the discretion of the classroom teacher. The program is being carried out only in the elementary grades; all students are free to participate or not as their parents desire or request.

The school district, its directors, employees, and agents exercise no control or supervision over the instructors or the material used in any of the religious instruction classes, nor over the scope of the instruction. No report is made by any instructor of the released-time program to the teacher or employee of the district with respect to whether or not a child who was released to participate in the program had actually attended the class. No record is kept by the district or its employees as to actual attendance at the religious instruction classes. The responsibility for attendance at such classes is left with the person who escorts the children for the particular religious group. The children receive no school credit for participation in the released-time program. The function of the defendant school district is to facilitate the distribution of the request cards and thereafter note which children are to be released.

. . . Both parties consented that the constitutionality of the released-time program should be determined. . . . The trial court thereupon entered summary judgment holding that the released time program was constitutional. The plaintiffs have appealed.

. . . [T]he appellants contend the released-time program maintained by the respondent school district is in contravention of the following provisions of the United States constitution, our state constitution, and certain statutory provisions of the state of Washington:

United States constitution, amendment I: ". . . Congress shall make no law respecting an establishment of religion, or prohibiting the free exercise thereof: . . ."

United States constitution, amendment XIV, § 1: ". . . No State shall make or enforce any law which shall abridge the privileges or immunities of citizens of the United States; nor shall any State deprive any person of life, liberty, or property, without due process of law; nor deny to any person within its jurisdiction the equal protection of the laws."

Washington constitution, Art. I, § 11 (as amended by amendment 4): "Religious Freedom. Absolute freedom of conscience in all matters of religious sentiment, belief, and worship, shall be guaranteed to every individual, and no one shall be molested or disturbed in person, or property, on account of religion, ... *No public money or property shall be appropriated for, or applied to any religious worship, exercise or instruction, or the support of any religious establishment. . . .*" (Italics ours.)

Washington constitution, Art IX, § 4: "Sectarian Control Or Influence Prohibited. All schools maintained or supported wholly or in part by the public funds shall be forever free from sectarian control or influence."

RCW 28.02.040: ". . . . All schools maintained or supported wholly or in part by the public funds shall be forever free from sectarian control or influence."

RCW 28.27.010: "All parents, . . . shall cause such child to attend the public school of the district in which the child resides for the full time when the school is in session or to attend a private school for the same time.

The superintendent of the schools of the district in which the child resides, or the county superintendent if there is no district superintendent, may excuse a child from such attendance if the child is physically or mentally unable to attend school, . . . or for any other sufficient reason. . . ."

The released-time program in public schools is not a new question in other jurisdictions, but it is a question that has not been passed upon in this state. This court, however, has consistently strictly construed our state's constitutional prohibition against the use of public funds for any religious purpose, and has likewise so construed the constitutional mandate that our schools supported by public funds shall be free from sectarian control or influence. . . .

. . . .

It is safe to say that the released-time program in itself has never been held to be in contravention of the doctrine of separation of church and state, nor of any state or Federal constitutional provisions; it is only the manner in which it has been practiced that has constituted a violation. Each case is determined by its own facts.

In the McCollum case . . . the local board of education in Champaign, Illinois, participated in a released-time program wherein (1) religious training took place in school buildings and on school property; (2) the place for instruction was designated by school authorities; (3) pupils taking religious instruction were segregated by school authorities according to faiths; (4) school officials supervised and approved the religious teachers; (5) pupils were solicited in school buildings for religious instruction; (6) registration cards were distributed by the school and in one case printed by the school.

In the released-time program as practiced in New York state (*Zorach* v. *Clauson* . . .), none of the above factors was present: (1) there was no supervision or approval of religious teachers and no solicitation of pupils or distribution of cards; (2) the religious instruction was required to be held outside the school buildings and grounds; (3) no announcement of any kind was permitted in the public schools relative to the program, neither was any comment allowed by any principal or teacher on the attendance or non-attendance of any pupil released for religious instruction. All that the school did besides excusing the pupil was to keep a record, which was not available for any other purpose, in order to see that the excuses were not taken advantage of and that the school was not deceived, being the same procedure the school would follow in re-

spect to absence for any other reason. . . .

. . . .

The reasoning of the Zorach case . . . is sound and reflects the reasoning of the state courts which have passed upon the same question, except that of the state of Illinois to a limited degree in the McCollum case . . . It answers the contentions of the appellants in the instant case as to the violation of the United States constitutional provisions by the released-time program practiced in Spokane, as authorized by the respondent in so far as the facts of the Zorach case are here applicable.

The significant difference in the facts of the Zorach case and the instant case can be at once observed and that is the practice permitted by the respondent of the distribution of the cards and the making of announcements by the representatives of religious groups or school instructors relative to the program in the classrooms or on school premises. This practice was among those present in the McCollum case, and was absent in the Zorach case. Moreover, this *is a use* of school facilities supported by public funds for the promotion of a religious program, which contravenes Art. I, §11 of our state constitution. . . .

This practice has the further *effect* of *influencing* the pupils, while assembled in the classrooms, as a "captive audience" to participate in a religious program, contrary to the express provisions of Art. IX, §4 of our state constitution:

. . . All schools maintained or supported wholly or in part by the public funds shall be forever free from sectarian control or *influence*. (Italics ours.)

The appellants contend that the released-time program permitted by the respondent disrupts the instruction of the children remaining in the classrooms, to their detriment, and is a violation of the equal protection clause of the state constitution and the United States constitution. This contention is not supported by the record. To the contrary, the children remaining in school are assigned to special projects and receive the advantage of individual instruction during the released-time periods.

. . . .

Our state constitution like that of the United States and every state in the Union . . . indicates the framers were men of deep religious beliefs and convictions, recognizing a profound reverence for religion and its influence in all human affairs essential to the well-being of the community. . . . Our Preamble reads as follows:

We, the people of the State of Washington, *grateful to the Supreme Ruler of the*

Universe for our liberties, do ordain their constitution. (Italics ours.)

It was never the intention that our constitution should be construed in any manner indicating any hostility toward religion. Instead, the safeguards and limitations were for the preservation of those rights. No limitations of the constitution are contravened by the respondent school district permitting a released-time program in its schools, if practiced in a manner not inconsistent with the constitutional limitations as outlined in this opinion.

We hold the following practice in the released-time program, permitted by the respondent, to be in contravention of Art. I, §11 (as amended) and Art. IX, §4 of the state constitution, i.e., the distribution of cards in public schools, or the making of announcements or explanations for the purpose of obtaining the parents' consent for their children's participation in the released-time program, by representatives of religious groups or instructors in the schools.

The judgment of the trial court is affirmed. . . .

SUMMARY

Some of the most common practices in the public school carrying religious overtones, especially since 1914 and until the United States Supreme Court's action in the McCollum and Zorach cases, have been those exercises variously labeled as released and dismissed time. Released time has been defined in this volume to consist of programs whereby representatives of the various faiths, conducted on public school premises during the regular school day, for a certain period of time, instruction in the tenets of the particular sect. In the great bulk of such cases, student attendance in such programs was voluntary, however, if a student did not attend he was re-

quired to remain in the school (usually in the study-hall) and it was presumed he would study his secular subjects.

Dismissed time is defined in this work to consist of programs whereby
public school students were dismissed from the school during regular
school hours to attend programs of religious instruction off the premises of
the public schools. Again in the overwhelming percentage of cases of this
nature to be litigated, the religious instruction program was voluntary,
however, if a student did not elect to attend the religious exercise he was
required to remain in the public school. At this juncture it might be well
to note that some authorities use a slightly different definition of dismissed
time. The crucial difference seems to be that while the programs are conducted during the regular school day, all students are dismissed from school,
whether or not they attend the program of religious instruction.

From their inception, programs of this nature raised sharp and, at
times, bitter controversies in those states or communities which adopted
them. State courts, for example, were faced with cases requiring them to
judge the constitutionality of these programs for over twenty years before
the United States Supreme Court in the McCollum case in 1948 moved to
clarify the constitutional waters concerning released time programs. There,
the Court held that such state supported programs violated the establishment clause of the First Amendment since school facilities were used.

Time was soon to demonstrate that the term facility had a dramatically
different meaning to the various justices. Some saw it merely as including
the use of public school grounds and physical plant. Others were vehement-
ly insistent that the term meant not only that but included the official
school day or week which is normally formalized through statutes or administrative rules, and where sanctions exist to insure compliance with the
compulsory school laws.

The McCollum decision was sharply criticized in a variety of circles.
For example, over two-thirds of the law journal articles which discussed the
case were critical of the Court. While the reactions of education journals
were not as extreme, they generally disapproved of the Court's stance.
Moreover, the attitudes of general or popular periodicals also tended to be
critical.

The effect of adverse public opinion on future judicial behavior has
been the source of much speculation in recent years by both political
scientists and lawyers. Regardless of the school of thought one aligns himself with, there is more than a germ of evidence to suggest that the Supreme
Court follows not only the election returns, as Mr. Dooley observed years
ago, but also that the Court is influenced by law reviews and other scholarly journals analyzing judicial decision making. Thus there are some who
believe that public reaction to the McCollum decision explains the court's
action four years later in the Zorach case.

In the Zorach case of 1952, the Court upheld dismissed time programs primarily on the grounds that such exercises were held outside public school property and thus there was no state aid to religion. This was done over several vigorous dissents which noted that in the McCollum case, the term public school facilities was broadly construed so as to include not only the use of school property but also to include the use of hours in the state established public school day.

Nonetheless the law on released and dismissed time programs today appears to be that if the program is conducted on school property during the regular school day, the practice violates the establishment clause of the First Amendment. On the other hand, if such a program is conducted during regular school hours, but is held off the public school premises, and if no coercion is exerted by the public school authorities upon the student to participate in these exercises, the program does not violate constitutional prohibitions. This is contingent, of course, on the fact that such programs are authorized by the state's constitution or laws.

There was considerably less time devoted to an analysis of the Zorach case in legal periodicals than occurred over the McCollum decision. Those law journals taking a position on the Zorach decision were evenly divided between those who supported and those who opposed the Court. On the other hand, a majority of education journals supported the Court's stand. Moreover, a review of the popular press suggests there was less notice and emotion aroused by the Zorach decision.

Since the Zorach case, only two cases involving dismissed time have reached state high courts. The Washington supreme court in 1959 found such programs violated the state constitutional provision prohibiting the use of public property to aid religion. On the other hand, one year later, in 1960, the Oregon supreme court upheld the constitutionality of dismissed time programs against the contention they violated the Oregon constitution. There is little reason to doubt that this sharply divided attitude of state courts concerning dismissed time will continue.

One point seems clear, however, and that is that there has been a sharp decline in litigation on the subject of released and dismissed time since the McCollum and Zorach decisions. For example, a January 17, 1966, study by the Commission on Law and Social Action of the American Jewish Congress reveals that not one of the 18 cases involving church-state relations docketed in the various state courts involves the question of released or dismissed time.

A related subject which does seem slated to cause substantial litigation in the future involves so-called shared time programs which are referred to in the federal Elementary and Secondary Education Act of 1965, and which have been present in some states for a number of years. Such programs normally permit parochial school students to use the public school facilities for instruction on a part time basis.

At the time of this writing, the only litigation on the subject appears to be the case of *Morton* v. *The Chicago Board of Education*, alleging that such a program violates the United States and Illinois Constitutions. The trial court dismissed the complaint and an appeal is pending, on statutory grounds only, before the Illinois appellate court.

Because of the potentially large sums of money, both federal and state, involved in shared time programs it seems likely to be one of the most litigated areas in the field of church-state relations in the near future.

CHAPTER THREE

Prayer

† †

THE ISSUE of public-school-sanctioned prayer programs was not argued in the federal courts until the landmark case of *Engel* v. *Vitale,* 370 U.S. 421 (1962). Until that time, various forms of prayer exercises generally had been upheld in several state courts. Judicial sanction was given in one series of state cases that combined the Lord's Prayer with Bible-reading exercises. See *Moore* v. *Monroe,* 64 Iowa 367, 20 N.W. 479 (1884); *Billard* v. *Board of Education,* 69 Kan. 53, 76 P. 422 (1904); *Church* v. *Bullock,* 104 Tex. 1, 109 S.W. 115 (1908); *Knowlton* v. *Baumhover,* 182 Iowa 691, 166 N.W. 202 (1918); *State* ex rel. *Finger* v. *Weedman,* 55 S.D. 343, 226 N.W. 348 (1929); *Doremus* v. *Board of Education,* 5 N.J. 435, 75 A.2d 880 (1950); and *Murray* v. *Curlett,* 228 Md. 239, 179 A.2d 698 (1962). The United States Supreme Court, however, specifically overruled the latter decision of the Maryland court in *School District of Abington* v. *Schempp* and *Murray* v. *Curlett,* 83 S.Ct. 1560 (1963).

Nonetheless, in similar situations other state courts specifically held such exercises unconstitutional as in *People* ex rel. *Ring* v. *Board of Education,* 245 Ill. 335, 92 N.E. 251 (1910) and *Herold* v. *Parish Board of Education,* 136 La. 1034, 68 So. 116 (1915).

In a relatively recent case, Bible reading and Lord's Prayer exercises were upheld by the Florida supreme court, in the Chamberlin case, 143 So.2d 21 (1962). While the case was on appeal to the United States Supreme Court, definitive rulings were made in *Engel* v. *Vitale,* 82 S.Ct. 1261 (1962) and *School District of Abington* v. *Schempp,* 83 S.Ct. 1560 (1963). Thereupon, the United States Supreme Court, 83 S.Ct. 1864, vacated the lower opinion and remanded the case in light of the Engel and Schempp rulings. The Florida supreme court, Fla., 160 So.2d 97 (1964), refused to follow the federal court's dictates, and distinguished the Florida programs as being founded on nonsectarian considerations. Upon appeal, the United States Supreme Court summarily reversed the Florida court's determination as to the Bible-reading and Lord's Prayer issues. (For a more complete discussion, see the chapter on Bible reading.)

Following the Engel decision, three cases in addition to the Chamberlin case disallowed the religious programs of Bible-reading and recitation of the Lord's Prayer, all upon the authority of the Schempp decision. See *Sills* v. *Board of Education,* 84 N.J. Super. 63, 200 A.2d 817 (1963), *Johns* v. *Allen,* 231 F. Supp. 852 (1964), and *Attorney General* v. *School Committee,* Mass., 199 N.E.2d 553 (1964), all of which are discussed further in the chapter on Bible reading.

In *North* v. *Board of Trustees of the University of Illinois,* 137 Ill. 296, 27 N.E. 54 (1891), discussed in chapter on Curriculum, a rule of the trustees of the University of Illinois that required students to attend nonsectarian religious exercises in the university chapel, was declared nonviolative of the Illinois constitutional provision that no person should be required to attend or support any ministry or place of worship against his consent. *Commonwealth* v. *Renfrew,* 332 Mass. 492, 126 N.E.2d 109 (1955), held that religious objections to mere reading of the Bible and the recital of the Lord's Prayer in the public schools did not justify a violation of the state's compulsory attendance law. (See, for example, the chapter on compulsory education.) No violations of either state or federal constitutional provisions respecting religion were found in *Carden* v. *Bland,* 199 Tenn. 665, 288 S.W.2d 718 (1956). (See chapter on Bible reading.)

Another series of cases combined formal prayers and Bible-reading exercises. An order of the town school committee commanding such exercises was upheld in *Spiller* v. *Woburn,* 12 Allen (Mass.) 127 (1866), even though objectors were excused. *Hackett* v. *Brooksville Graded School District,* 120 Ky. 608, 87 S.W. 792 (1905), ruled that "A prayer offered by the opening of a public school, imploring the aid and presence of the heavenly father during the day's work, asking for wisdom, patience, mutual love and respect, looking forward to a heavenly reunion after death, and concluding in Christ's name, is not Sectarian, and does not make the school 'a sectarian school,' within the constitutional provision prohibiting the appropriation of educational funds and aid of sectarian schools."

A similar finding was made in *Wilkerson* v. *City of Rome,* 152 Ga. 763, 110 S.E. 895 (1921), in that an ordinance requiring prayer and Bible reading in the schools was neither an unconstitutional conflict with freedom of conscience nor the use of public money in support of sectarian institutions. However, a contrary result was reached in *State* ex rel. *Freeman* v. *Scheve,* 65 Neb. 853, 91 N.W. 846 (1902), where the action of a local school board without statutory authority in permitting a teacher to conduct, in her own words, "religious exercises" was declared violative of the constitutional provision prohibiting the use of public school funds for other than public school purposes.

A third set of cases tested programs involving prayers only. In *Dunn* v. *Addison Manual Training School For Boys,* 281 Ill. 352, 117 N.E. 993 (1917), the mere practice of offering a prayer in the Addison Manual Training School, which was under the direction of the Lutheran Synod, 'was considered not to constitute religious education, since there was no chapel and no minister assigned to the training school by the church. Therefore, the Illinois court concluded that the county could pay for the support of the children in the institution and not violate the state's constitutional prohibition against aiding sectarian schools.

In 1962 for the first time, the prayer issue went to the United States Supreme Court. In *Engel* v. *Vitale,* 370 U.S. 421, a six to one majority, Justice Black speaking, held that an official state prayer composed by the New York Board of Regents and made mandatory upon the public schools at the beginning of each school day violated the Establishment of Religion Clause of the First Amendment made applicable to the states by the Due Process Clause of the Fourteenth Amendment.

† † *ENGEL* v. *VITALE*
370 U.S. 421, 82 S. CT. 1261, 8 L. ED.2D 601 (1962).

Mr. Justice BLACK deliverd the opinion of the Court:

The respondent Board of Education of Union Free School District No. 9, New Hyde Park, New York, acting in its official capacity under state law, directed the School District's principal to cause the following prayer to be said aloud by each class in the presence of a teacher at the beginning of each school day:

Almighty God, we acknowledge our dependence upon Thee, and we beg Thy blessings upon us, our parents, our teachers and our country.

This daily procedure was adopted on the recommendation of the State Board of Regents, a governmental agency created by the State Constitution to which the New York Legislature has granted broad supervisory, executive, and legislative powers over the State's public school system. These state officials composed the prayer which they recommended and published as a part of their "Statement on Moral and Spiritual Training in the Schools," saying: "We believe that this Statement will be subscribed to by all men and women of good will, and we call upon all of them to aid in giving life to our program."

Shortly after the practice of reciting the Regents' prayer was adopted by the School District, the parents of ten pupils brought this action in a New York State Court insisting that use of this official prayer in the public schools was contrary to the beliefs, religions, or religious practices of both themselves and their children. Among other things, these parents challenged the constitutionality of both the state law authorizing the School District to direct the use of prayer in public schools and the School District's regulation ordering the recitation of this particular prayer on the ground that these actions of official governmental agencies violate that part of the First Amendment of the Federal Constitution which commands that "Congress shall make no law respecting an establishment of religion"—a command which was "made applicable to the State of New York by the Fourteenth Amendment of the said Constitution." The New York Court of Appeals, over the dissents of Judges Dye and Fuld, sustained an order of the lower state courts which had upheld the power of New York to use the Regents' prayer as a part of the daily procedures of its public schools so long as the schools did not compel any pupil to join in the prayer over his or his parents' objection. We granted certiorari to review this important decision involving rights protected by the First and Fourteenth Amendments.

We think that by using its public school system to encourage recitation of the Regents' prayer, the State of New York has adopted a practice wholly inconsistent with the Establishment Clause. There can, of course, be no doubt that New York's program of daily classroom invocation of God's blessings as prescribed in the Regents' prayer is a religious activity. It is a solemn avowal of divine faith and supplication for the blessings of the Almighty. The nature of such a prayer has always been religious, none of the respondents has denied this and the trial court expressly so found:

The religious nature of prayer was recognized by Jefferson and has been concurred in by theological writers, the United States Supreme Court and state courts and administrative officials, including New York's Commissioner of Education. A committee of New York Legislature has agreed.

The Board of Regents as *amicus curiae,* the respondents and intervenors all concede the religious nature of prayer, but

seek to distinguish this prayer because it is based on our spiritual heritage. . . .

The petitioners contend among other things that the state laws requiring or permitting use of the Regents' prayer must be struck down as a violation of the Establishment Clause because that prayer was composed by governmental officials as a part of a governmental program to further religious beliefs. For this reason, petitioners argue, the State's use of the Regents' prayer in its public school system breaches the constitutional wall of separation between Church and State. We agree with the contention since we think that the constitutional prohibition against laws respecting an establishment of religion must at least mean that in this country it is no part of the business of government to compose official prayers for any group of the American people to recite as a part of a religious program carried on by government.

It is a matter of history that this very practice of establishing governmentally composed prayers for religious services was one of the reasons which caused many of our early colonists to leave England and seek religious freedom in America. The Book of Common Prayer, which was created under governmental direction and which was approved by Acts of Parliament in 1548 and 1549, set out in minute detail the accepted form and content of prayer and other religious ceremonies to be used in the established, tax supported church of England. The controversies over the Book and what should be its content repeatedly threatened to disrupt the peace of that country as the accepted forms of prayer in the established church changed with the views of the particular ruler that happened to be in control at the time. Powerful groups representing some of the varying religious views of the people struggled among themselves to impress their particular views upon the Government and obtain amendments of the Book more suitable to their respective notions of how religious services should be conducted in order that the official religious establishment would advance their particular religious beliefs. Other groups, lacking the necessary political power to influence the Government on the matter, decided to leave England and its established church and seek freedom in America from England's governmentally ordained and supported religion.

It is an unfortunate fact of history that when some of the very groups which had most strenuously opposed the established Church of England found themselves sufficiently in control of colonial governments in this country to write their own prayers into law, they passed laws making their own religion the official religion of their respective colonies. Indeed, as late as the time of the Revolutionary War, there were established churches in at least eight of the thirteen former colonies and established religions in at least four of the other five. But the successful Revolution against English political domination was shortly followed by intense opposition to the practice of establishing religion by law. This opposition crystallized rapidly into an effective political force in Virginia where the minority religious groups such as Presbyterians, Lutherans, Quakers and Baptists had gained such strength that the adherents to the established Episcopal Church were actually a minority themselves. In 1785–1786, those opposed to the established Church, led by James Madison and Thomas Jefferson, who, though themselves not mem-

bers of any of these dissenting religious groups, opposed all religious establishments by law on grounds of principle, obtained the enactment of the famous "Virginia Bill for Religious Liberty" by which all religious groups were placed on an equal footing so far as the State was concerned. Similar though less far-reaching legislation was being considered and passed in other states.

By the time of the adoption of the Constitution, our history shows that there was a widespread awareness among many Americans of the dangers of a union of Church and State. These people knew, some of them from bitter personal experience, that one of the greatest dangers to the freedom of the individual to worship in his own way lay in the Government's placing its official stamp of approval upon one particular kind of prayer or one particular form of religious services. They knew the anguish, hardship and bitter strife that could come when zealous religious groups struggled with one another to obtain the Government's stamp of approval from each King, Queen, or Protector that came to temporary power. The Constitution was intended to avert a part of this danger by leaving the government of this country in the hands of the people rather than in the hands of any monarch. But this safeguard was not enough. Our Founders were no more willing to let the content of their prayers and their privilege of praying whenever they pleased be influenced by the ballot box than they were to let these vital matters of personal conscience depend upon the succession of monarchs. The First Amendment was added to the Constitution to stand as a guarantee that neither the power nor the prestige of the Federal Government would be used to control, support or influence the kinds of prayer the American people can say—that the people's religions must not be subjected to the pressures of government for change each time a new political administration is elected to office. Under that Amendment's prohibition against governmental establishment of religion, as reinforced by the provisions of the Fourteenth Amendment, government in this country, be it state or federal, is without power to prescribe by law any particular form of prayer which is to be used as an official prayer in carrying on any program of governmentally sponsored religious activity.

There can be no doubt that New York's state prayer program officially establishes the religious beliefs embodied in the Regents' prayer. The respondents' argument to the contrary, which is largely based upon the contention that the Regents' prayer is "non-denominational" and the fact that the program, as modified and approved by state courts, does not require all pupils to recite the prayer but permits those who wish to do so to remain silent or be excused from the room, ignores the essential nature of the program's constitutional defects. Neither the fact that the prayer may be denominationally neutral, nor the fact that its observance on the part of the students in voluntary can serve to free it from the limitations of the Establishment Clause, as it might from the Free Exercise Clause, of the First Amendment, both of which are operative against the States by virtue of the Fourteenth Amendment. Although these two clauses may in certain instances overlap, they forbid two quite different kinds of governmental encroachment upon religious freedom. The Establishment Clause, unlike the Free Exercise Clause, does not depend upon any showing of direct governmental compulsion and is violated by the enact-ment of laws which establish an official religion whether those laws operate directly to coerce nonobserving individuals or not. This is not to say, of course, that laws officially prescribing a particular form of religious worship do not involve coercion of such individuals. When the power, prestige and financial support of government is placed behind a particular religious belief, the indirect coercive pressure upon religious minorities to conform to the prevailing officially approved religion is plain. But the purposes underlying the Establishment Clause go much further than that. Its first and most immediate purpose rested on the belief that a union of government and religion tends to destroy government and to degrade religion. The history of governmentally established religion, both in England and in this country, showed that whenever government had allied itself with one particular form of religion, the inevitable result had been that it had incurred the hatred, disrespect and even contempt of those who held contrary beliefs. That same history showed that many people had lost their respect for any religion that had relied upon the support of government to spread its faith. The Establishment Clause thus stands as an expression of principle on the part of the Founders of our Constitution that religion is too personal, too sacred, too holy, to permit its "unhallowed perversion" by a civil magistrate. Another purpose of the Establishment Clause rested upon an awareness of the historical fact that Governmentally established religions and religious persecutions go hand in hand. The Founders knew that only a few years after the Book of Common Prayer became the only accepted form of religious services in the established Church of England, an Act of Uniformity was passed to compel all Englishmen to attend those services and to make it a criminal offense to conduct or attend religious gatherings of any other kind—a law which was consistently flouted by dissenting religious groups in England and which contributed to widespread persecutions of people like John Bunyan who persisted in holding "unlawful [religious] meetings . . . to the great disturbance and distraction of good subjects of this kingdom. . . ." And they knew that similar persecutions had received the sanction of law in several of the colonies in this country soon after the establishment of official religions in those colonies. It was in large part to get completely away from this sort of systematic religious persecution that the Founders brought into being our Nation, our Constitution, and our Bill of Rights with its prohibition against any governmental establishment of religion. The New York laws officially prescribing the Regents' prayer are inconsistent with both the purposes of the Establishment Clause and the Establishment Clause itself.

It has been argued that to apply the Constitution in such a way as to prohibit state laws respecting an establishment of religious services in public schools is to indicate a hostility toward religion or toward prayer. Nothing, of course, could be more wrong. The history of man is inseparable from the history of religion. And perhaps it is not too much to say that since the beginning of that history many people have devoutly believed that "More things are wrought by prayer than this world dreams of." It was doubtless largely due to men who believed this that there grew up a sentiment that caused men to leave the cross-currents of officially established state religions and deligious persecution in Europe and come to this country filled with the hope that they could find a place in which they could pray when they pleased to the God of their faith in the language they chose. And there were men of this same faith in the power of prayer who led the fight for adoption of our Constitution and also for our Bill of Rights with the very guarantees of religious freedom that forbid the sort of governmental activity which New York has attempted here. These men knew that the First Amendment, which tried to put an end to governmental control of religion and of prayer, was not written to destroy either. They knew rather that it was written to quiet well-justified fears which nearly all of them felt arising out of an awareness that governments of the past had shackled men's tongues to make them speak only the religious thoughts that government wanted them to speak and to pray only to the God that government wanted them to pray to. It is neither sacrilegious nor antireligious to say that each separate government in this country should stay out of the business of writing or sanctioning official prayers and leave that purely religious function to the people themselves and to those the people chose to look to for religious guidance.*

It is true that New York's establish-

---

* There is of course nothing in the decision reached here that is inconsistent with the fact that school children and others are officially encouraged to express love for our country by reciting historical documents such as the Declaration of Independence which contain references to the Deity or by singing officially espoused anthems which include the composer's professions of faith in a Supreme Being, or with the fact that there are many manifestations in our public life of belief in God. Such patriotic or ceremonial occasions bear no true resemblance to the unquestioned religious exercise that the State of New York has sponsored in this instance.

ment of its Regents' prayer as an officially approved religious doctrine of that State does not amount to a total establishment of one particular religious sect to the exclusion of all others—that, indeed, the governmental endorsement of that prayer seems relatively insignificant when compared to the governmental encroachments upon religion which were commonplace 200 years ago. To those who may subscribe to the view that because the Regents' official prayer is so brief and general there can be no danger to religious freedom in its governmental establishment, however, it may be appropriate to say in the words of James Madison, the author of the First Amendment:

It is proper to take alarm at the first experiment on our liberties. . . . Who does not see that the same authority which can establish Christianity, in exclusion of all other Religions, may establish with the same ease any particular sect of Christians, in exclusion of all other Sects? That the same authority which can force a citizen to contribute three pence only of his property for the support of any one establishment, may force him to conform to any other establishment in all cases whatsoever?

The judgment of the Court of Appeals of New York is reversed and the cause remanded for further proceedings not inconsistent with this opinion.

REACTIONS OF LEGAL PERIODICALS TO *ENGEL* v. *VITALE*

The Engel case which held that a state-composed prayer be recited in public schools was an unconstitutional establishment of religion, as prohibited in the First Amendment of the federal Constitution drew sharply divided public reaction.

Mr. William J. Butler, attorney for the Engel case, gave the following account in the *American Bar Association Journal* (49:444) of the initial impact of the decision:

> Within twenty-four hours, the decision came under severe attack from many religious leaders and public officials, and some educators. Thousands of critical letters and telegrams were sent to the Supreme Court and to Congressmen. Two ex-Presidents, Herbert Hoover and Dwight D. Eisenhower, opposed the decision. President Hoover went so far as to proclaim the end of the public school system in this country. Some support for the decision, however, came from President Kennedy, who, after noting that a decision of the Supreme Court is the law of the land and must be obeyed, suggested that Americans might do well to pray more at home and in church.
>
> The Roman Catholic hierarchy generally opposed the decision. The Jewish community almost unanimously supported it. Protestant groups were divided, but the powerful periodicals *Christianity Today* and *Christian Century* approved the result, as did such influential publications as the *New York Times*, the *New York Herald Tribune*, the *Washington Post*, the *St. Louis Post-Dispatch*, and *Time*.
>
> Within a week, a multitude of bills providing for a constitutional amendment to overcome the legal effect of the decision were introduced in Congress. One amendment soon had the endorsement of forty-nine state governors with only Nelson A. Rockefeller, of New York, abstaining.

A similar finding that some of the immediate public reaction to the case was favorable was made by Paul G. Kauper in the *Michigan Law Review* (61:1031). There he concluded that the decision was hailed by secularists and strict separationists as strengthening the wall of separation. He reported further support from "a substantial part of the press and a number of religious leaders and groups."

The decision was evaluated in over two dozen law review articles, with the slight majority of them being critical of the Court. Recurring charges were made that the prayer fell within the permissible confines of the Zorach decision's rationale permitting the accommodation of religion. It was also argued that First Amendment was designed exclusively to preclude official establishment of a church, and that programs of prayer had long been a customary component of the secular school's duty to provide moral and spiritual training to the young.

Arthur E. Sutherland, Jr., writing in the *Harvard Law Review* (76:25), declared that such religious controversies should be solved by other governmental agencies or by the people. Furthermore, the Court's application of its historical test in determining what the Framers meant to prohibit was attacked in the *Vanderbilt Law Review* (16:205, 212) for failing "to take proper account of modern changes in social institutions."

Charles E. Rice charged in the *American Bar Association* (50:1057) that the Court's inaccurate constructions have "tended to institutionalize agnosticism as the official public religion." The argument that the protection of a minority's rights should not involve discrimination against those of the majority was stated in *Missouri Law Review* (28:109).

Some of the main support for the Court's decision came unsurprisingly enough from the counsel for Engel, William J. Butler. Writing in the *American Bar Association Journal* (49:444), he claimed that much of the opposition to the Engel case was based upon ignorance of Madison's broad purpose embodied in the establishment clause of the First Amendment. He declared that the freedom being protected was from "state support or sponsorship of religion," and not "from religion" as charged by many critics. He also explained that state establishment must be restricted now "before a national or state church or religion is developed." His position that there is no such thing as a "little" or "non-sectarian" prayer was concurred with by several other reviewers, including Edmond Cahn, writing in the *New York University Law Review* (37:981).

However, David K. Udall declared in the *Arizona Law Review* (4:272) that permissive prayers should be allowed, but not state-prescribed prayers. In this connection, Leo Pfeffer noted in the *Rutgers Law Review* (16:735, 752): "State-sanctioned prayer has a long and ignoble history." Paul G. Kauper points out in the *Michigan Law Review* (61:1031), that the Engel rule protects both the believer and the nonbeliever from state compulsion and interference thus maintaining the dignity and religious significance of prayer. Correspondingly, the manner in which an American orders his relationship with God was declared in the *Tulane Law Review* (37:124) to have been insulated by the First Amendment from the political processes.

A warning was issued in the *Loyola Law Review* (11:358) that both church and state will suffer if the balance of power fails. This article further warned that "religious zeal should not misdirect governmental power" (11:358).

In passing, it was observed in the *Georgetown Law Journal* (51:179, 183) that the Court's wise avoidance of the literal-historical approach should be hailed as "perhaps the beginning of a fresh, and cautious, approach to the problem of church and state."

A half dozen reviews of the lower court decision divided evenly in their support of the court. Some of those critical of the New York court's allowance of the prayer found objectionable the psychological coercion, state supervision and influence involved in an unconstitutional practice of prescribing and official prayer. The decision was lauded, on the other hand, by some reviewers who claimed that such a prayer is an effective means of fostering good citizenship, and involves less subtle pressures than were approved under the "accommodation of religion" theory of the Zorach decision. An interesting policy was suggested in the *Syracuse Law Review* (11:285) that although dissenters cannot be forced to participate in such exercises, they also cannot use the First Amendment to prevent others from so doing.

REACTIONS OF EDUCATION PERIODICALS TO *ENGEL* v. *VITALE*

The reaction of articles in education journals to the Engel decision was varied and vociferous. It ran from endorsement to condemnation. The decision was regarded by some as a step toward defining and limiting the part religion should play in the public schools; others applauded the decision as a major step toward the rightful removal of religion from the public schools. A number of articles opposed the Engel decision on the grounds it was against the will of the majority of the people and deplored the onslaught of secularism. Several articles also deplored the emotionalism of the reactions to the decision.

A. B. Shaw in *Religious Education* (59:451, 1964), saw the Engel and the subsequent Schempp cases as helping to define and limit the role of religion in public education. He considered this important because public school curricula should include an acknowledgment of the influence of religion on man and culture.

The American Jewish Committee in *Religious Education* (50:232, 1953) supported the Supreme Court's decision. Organized prayer in public schools, it argued, is a form of worship and therefore cannot be sanctioned by the state without violating the establishment clause of the Constitution. S. Duker agreed that the Court barred all government sanctioned sectarian prayers in *Educational Forum* (27:71, 1962). However, he felt that nonsectarian prayers would probably not be effected by the Engel decision. He made no attempt to predict what the courts might say in the future concerning this intricate distinction. On the other hand, L. O. Garber in *Nation's Schools* (70:54, 1962) considered the implications of the Engel ruling to mean an end to Bible reading, repeating the Lord's Prayer, baccalaureate exercises, and Christmas programs in public schools.

In *Nation's Schools* (70:101, 1962), a poll based on a 4 per cent proportional sampling of 16,000 public school administrators, in which 42 per cent responded, showed 51 per cent were personally against the Engel decision. Forty-six per cent agreed with it and 3 per cent expressed no opinion. On the question of introducing an amendment to the Constitution permitting recitation of prayer in public schools, 46 per cent approved, 48 per cent disapproved, and 6 per cent were of no opinion.

Several other articles discussed the Engel case but the authors took no sides concerning the decision. See: I. Starr, *Social Education* (26:439, 1962); *National Educational Association Journal* (51:38, 1962); and *Overview* (3:60, 1962).

AN UNSETTLED ISSUE

That the Engel decision did not completely settle the question of prayers in the public schools became apparent in *Stein* v. *Oshinsky*, 348 F.2d 999 (1965). There a United States district court in New York declared that under the free speech and freedom of religion clauses of the First Amendment, school children are entitled to prayer. The prayer in this instance was distinguished from the unconstitutional Engel decision prayer which was prepared and prescribed by an agency of the state. The court pointed out that the latter programs involved a voluntary prayer which was offered by the children; no compulsion was involved, and the prayers were not prescribed by law.

The trial court's ruling, below, was reversed by the U.S. court of appeals on the grounds that the constitutional rights to the free exercise of religion do not require a state to permit "student initiated" prayers in the public schools. Moreover, the court of appeals concluded that the rights of freedom of religion and freedom of speech do not require a state to permit persons to engage in state-owned facilities whereever and whenever they desire. When this ruling was appealed to the United States Supreme Court, that body late in 1965 refused to accept jurisdiction by denying a petition for a writ of certiorari. Thus, the decision of the Court of Appeals stands.

On the other hand in *Reed* v. *Van Hoven,* 237 F. Supp. 48 (1965), a federal district court in Michigan ruled that public school students who wish to say prayers or read scriptures according to their choice in the morning before the school day begins or after the school day ends, should be permitted to do so, provided that they met in a room other than the regular home room, and completed their exercises at least five minutes before the regularly scheduled class day or did not commence them until five minutes after the completion of the regular school class day. Furthermore, the court insisted that a bell should signify the start of prayer exercises, and if a prayer was to be said during the lunch period, it should be a silent prayer engaged in during the moments of silence set aside for private meditation at the start of that period.

† † *STEIN* v. *OSHINSKY*
348 F.2D 999 (1965).

Judge FRIENDLY delivered the opinion of the court:

The decision in *Engel* v. *Vitale,* 370 U.S. 421 . . . condemning the "Regents' prayer" as violating the Establishment Clause of the First Amendment, held to be applicable to the states by the Fourteenth, was rendered on June 25, 1962, too late to affect the 1961–62 school year. The case now before us reflects a response to that decision by parents who think their children ought to have some form of religious observance while in public school.

The amended complaint . . . made the following allegations: The fifteen plaintiffs, of varying religious faiths, are parents of twenty-one children, ranging from five to eleven years in age. The children attend Public School 184, at Whitestone, N.Y., in grades ranging from kindergarten to the sixth. The defendants are Elihu Oshinsky, principal of the school; the members of the Board of Education of New York City; and the Board of Regents of the University of the State of New York. On October 5, 1962, Mr. Oshinsky "ordered his teachers who were instructing the kindergarten classes to stop the infant children from reciting the simple and ancient prayer:

'God is Great, God is Good and We Thank Him for our Food, Amen!'

before they ate their cookies and milk in the morning session," and "ordered his teachers who were instructing the kindergarten classes for the afternoon session to stop the infant children from reciting the simple and ancient prayer:

'Thank You for the World so Sweet,
Thank You for the Food We Eat,
Thank You for the Birds that Sing—
Thank You, God, for Everything.' "

He also "ordered his teachers to stop the saying of any prayer in any classroom in P.S. 184, Whitestone, New York." The Board of Education and the Board of Regents have instituted a policy banning prayers in the public schools even when the opportunity to pray is sought by the students themselves, and by so doing have "condoned and/or directed" Mr. Oshinsky's actions. The plaintiffs had joined in a written demand to the defendants "that our children be given an opportunity to acknowledge their dependence and love to Almighty God through a prayer each day in their respective classrooms"; defendants had ignored this. . . .

. . . We . . . cannot sustain defendants' contention that the complaint did not sufficiently raise a claim of denial of constitutional rights to the free exercise of religion and to freedom of speech "to warrant exercise of federal jurisdiction for purposes of adjudicating it". . . . But we think the court erred in its ruling on the merits.

Plaintiffs say that *Engel* v. *Vitale,* supra, and the later decisions in *Abington Tp. School District* v. *Schempp* and *Murray* v. *Curlett,* both at 374 U.S. 203 . . . (1963), held only that under the Establishment Clause of the First Amendment a state may not *direct* the use of public school teachers and facilities for the recitation of a prayer, whether composed by a state official as in Engel or not so composed but having a religious content as in Abington and Curlett; they argue that these decisions did not hold that a state could not *permit* students in public schools to engage in oral prayer on their own initiative. This may be true enough; if the defendants could prevail only by showing that permitting the prayers was prohibited by the Establishment Clause, the question would be whether the use of public property as a situs for the prayers, the consumption of some teacher time in preserving order for their duration, and the possible implication of state approval therefrom would attract the condemnation of *People of State of Illinois* ex rel. *McCollum* v. *Board of Education,* 333 U.S. 203 . . . (1948), or the benediction of *Zorach* v. *Clauson,* 343 U.S. 306 . . . (1952), and *Sherbert* v. *Verner,* 374 U.S. 398, 409 . . . (1963). Although we note in this connection defendants' serious contention that in the context of closely organized schooling of young children, "student-initiated" prayers are an illusion and any effective routine requires the active participation of the teachers, we shall assume, *arguendo,* in plaintiffs' favor that the Establishment Clause would not prohibit New York from permitting in its public schools prayers such as those here at issue. Nevertheless New York is not bound to allow them unless the Free Exercise Clause or the guarantee of freedom of speech of the First Amendment compels.

Neither provision requires a state to permit persons to engage in public prayer in state-owned facilities wherever and whenever they desire. *Poulos* v. *State of New Hampshire,* 345 U.S. 395, 405 . . . (1953). It would scarcely be argued that a court had to suffer a trial or an argument to be interrupted any time that spectators—or even witnesses or jurymen—desired to indulge in collective oral prayer. The case of the school children differs from that of spectators—although not from that of witnesses or jurymen—in that, so long as they choose to attend a public school, attendance on their part is compulsory. . . . But "[t]he student's compelled presence in school for five days a week in no way renders the regular religious facilities of the community less accessi-

ble to him than they are to others."
Abington Tp. School District v.
Schempp, supra, 374 U.S. at 299 . . .
(concurring opinion of Mr. Justice
Brennan). We are not here required to
consider such cases as that of a Moslem,
obliged to prostrate himself five times
daily in the direction of Mecca, or of a
child whose beliefs forbade his partak-
ing of milk and cookies without saying
the blessings of his faith. Cf. *Sherbert*
v. *Verner,* supra, 374 U.S. at 399 n. 1.
. . . So far as appears, the school authorities might well permit students to
withdraw momentarily for such necessary observances—or to forego the milk
and cookies, just as they excuse children on holidays important to their
religions.

Determination of what is to go on in
public schools is primarily for the
school authorities. Against the desire
of these parents that their children "be
given an opportunity to acknowledge
their dependence and love to Almighty
God through a prayer each day in their
respective classrooms," the authorities
were entitled to weigh the likely desire
of other parents not to have their children present at such prayers, either because the prayers were too religious or
not religious enough; and the wisdom
of having public educational institutions stick to education and keep out
of religion, with all the bickering that
intrusion into the latter is likely to
produce. The authorities acted well
within their powers in concluding that
plaintiffs must content themselves with
having their children say these prayers
before nine or after three; their action
presented no such inexorable conflict
with deeply held religious belief as in
Sherbert v. *Verner* supra. After all that
the states have been told about keeping
the "wall between church and state
. . . high and impregnable," *Everson*
v. *Board of Education,* 330 U.S. 1, 18
. . . (1947), it would be rather bitter
irony to chastise New York for having
built the wall too tall and too strong.

It was thus error to grant summary
judgment to the plaintiffs. We think
also that the case calls on us to direct
judgment dismissing the complaint.
. . .

. . . The Judgment is reversed, with
directions to dismiss the complaint.

SUMMARY

One of the hallmark cases handed down by the Supreme Court of the
United States in modern history was *Engel* v. *Vitale* where the Court held
a state sponsored prayer in the public school to violate the establishment
clause of the First Amendment. The importance of the case rests in the
fact that it voided practices common in many public schools since colonial
times. But more important, from a legal and practical standpoint, the
Court undertook a systematic and sophisticated analysis not only of the
establishment clause and the free exercise clause but also suggested that
they must be considered as two separate entities and further delineated
what criteria must be present for a violation of each of the religious
clauses to be demonstrated.

Speaking for the majority, in the six-to-one vote striking down state
sponsored prayer exercises, Justice Black, noted that while the estab-

lishment clause and the free exercise clause might overlap in some instances, they forbid two quite different encroachments upon religious freedom. "The Establishment Clause," Justice Black explained, "unlike the Free Exercise Clause, does not depend upon any showing of governmental compulsion and is violated by the enactment of laws which establish an official religion whether these laws operate directly to coerce nonobserving individuals or not. Inherent in this approach it would seem is the possibility the two clauses on religion might conflict with each other in a given situation, just as may the Freedom of Speech Clause and the Freedom of Religion Clause in other situations, for example."

Many of the critics of the Engel decision accused the Court of completely removing God from the classroom. The charge in itself reveals some interesting aspects concerning such critics' views of the celestial power structure. But the Court made it clear, however, that nothing in its decision should be construed as discouraging school children and others from reciting historical documents such as the Declaration of Independence, containing references to the Deity or singing "officially espoused anthems" which contain the composer's profession of faith in a Supreme Being.

Prior to the Engel ruling there had been a plethora of state court decisions on the subject dating from an 1884 decision of the Iowa supreme court in *Moore* v. *Monroe*. Frequently such litigation in the states was meshed with the issue of whether Bible-reading exercises in the public schools violated the First Amendment. The only generalization that might safely be made concerning state court attitudes toward such programs is that the states in which such litigation arose were almost equally divided concerning their constitutional validity.

Public reaction to the Engel ruling was widespread and intense. Editorial comment by newspapers, including such influential periodicals as the *New York Times* and the *New York Herald Tribune,* tended to favor the Court's position. Religious leaders divided sharply concerning the decision. Noted clergymen, including Cardinal Spellman, Cardinal McIntyre, and the Right Reverend James A. Pike, Bishop of the Episcopal Diocese of California, criticized the Court's position. On the other hand, Dr. David McLean Greeley, President of the Unitarian-Universalist Association, and the New York Board of Rabbis representing the Orthodox, Conservative, and Reform rabbinate of Greater New York vigorously supported the Engel ruling.

Despite the Supreme Court's ruling in the Engel case, the issue of prayer in the public schools can hardly be regarded as settled from a practical standpoint. For example, as one school administrator noted, while the official school policy prohibited such practices, he could not guarantee that individual teachers did not "smuggle" prayers into their classrooms. Also, practices of this nature may take an almost infinite variety of forms, thus the potential for litigation is increased. In this connection, at least one federal district court ruled in 1965 that prayer exercises which were voluntarily conducted either before or after the official school day, and which were not heralded by the official school bell, were not prohibited by the Engel ruling even though these programs were conducted in public school rooms.

CHAPTER FOUR

Bible Reading

† †

LITIGATION INVOLVING the constitutionality of Bible-reading exercises has concerned itself generally with answering three basic questions. The first and most important question is: Is the Bible a sectarian book? The second question need be discussed in detail only if the first question is answered in the negative. It is: May the Bible without note or comment be used as a textbook in public schools? The third question is: May the boards of education and teachers require compulsory attendance during the period set aside for Bible reading?

It seems clear that the states desire to keep inviolable the public school fund and to deny public aid to any sectarian instruction. However, the ambiguous provisions of the constitutions and codes of the various states have fostered widely varying judicial interpretations by the courts as to what particular practices are constitutionally allowable.

The classic case declaring Bible reading to be illegal was *State* ex rel. *Weiss* v. *District Board,* 76 Wis. 177, 44 N.W. 967 (1890). There it was determined that the practice whereby the teachers selected portions of the King James Version to be read in the common schools was contrary to the rights of conscience, and constituted sectarian instruction in violation of the Wisconsin constitutional provision declaring that "no man shall be compelled . . . to erect or support any place of worship." The court saw the issue before it as follows: "Is the reading of the Bible in the schools—not merely selected passages therefrom, but the whole of it—sectarian instruction of the pupils?"

The Wisconsin high court characterized Bible reading, even without comment, as "religious instruction." The fact that attendance was not compulsory did not affect the decision either, as the court pointed out that the departure of objecting students tended to destroy the equality of pupils and "puts a portion of them to serious disadvantages in many ways with respect to the others." The court did concede, however, that much of the Bible is not sectarian, and such parts may, therefore, be used in the secular education of the pupils if used in another publication other than the Bible.

The court concluded, however:

Hence, to teach the existence of a supreme being, of infinite wisdom, power, and goodness, and that it is the highest duty of all men to adore, obey, and love Him, is not sectarian, because all religious sects so believe and teach. The instruction becomes sectarian when it goes further, and inculcates doctrine or dogma, concerning which the religious sects are in conflict. This we understand to be the meaning of the constitutional prohibition.

The direct use of the Bible as a specific textbook was declared by the Wisconsin court to violate the constitutional provisions against sectarianism or interference with religious liberty. Thus, the Weiss ruling was utilized by the state of Washington supreme court in *State* ex rel. *Dearle* v. *Frazier,* 102 Wash. 369, 173 P. 35 (1918), in its disallowance of a Washington school's requirement of an examination of high school pupils on "the historical, biographical, narrative, and literary features" of the Bible, pursuant to the receiving of high school credit for such religious instruction.

However, the Wisconsin court went on to say that the use of textbooks founded on extracts from the Bible was not prohibited by the Wisconsin constitution even if sectarian doctrine could conceivably be inferred from such passages. This part of the rationale was adopted by the Michigan supreme court in *Pfeiffer* v. *Board of Education,* 118 Mich. 560, 77 N.W. 25 (1898), where the use of a book entitled *Readings from the Bible,* and consisting principally of moral precepts tied to the Ten Commandments, was allowed by the court as a text to inculcate good morals.

Prior to the Weiss case, Bible-reading exercises without comment had been upheld as constitutional in *Spiller* v. *Woburn,* 12 Allen (Mass.) 127 (1866); *McCormick* v. *Burt,* 95 Ill. 263 (1880); *Moore* v. *Monroe,* 64 Iowa 367, 20 N.W. 475 (1884); and *Hart* v. *Sharpsville Borough School District,* 2 Lanc. L. Rev. (Pa.) 346 (1885).

The same conclusion in accepting the constitutional validity of Bible-reading exercises was reached in the following cases subsequent to the Weiss decision: *North* v. *Board of Trustees* (discussed further in chapter on prayer), 137 Ill. 296, 27 N.E. 54 (1891); *Curran* v. *White,* 22 Pa. Co. Rep. 201 (1898); *Stevenson* v. *Hanyon,* 7 Pa. Dist. Rep. 585 (1898); *State* ex rel. *Freeman* v. *Scheve,* 65 Neb. 853, 91 N.W. 846 (1902); *Hackett* v. *Brooksville Graded School District,* 120 Ky. 608, 87 S.W. 792 (1905); *Church* v. *Bullock,* 104 Tex. 1, 109 S.W. 115 (1908); *Knowlton* v. *Baumhover* (see chapter on combining public and parochial school building facilities), 182 Iowa 691, 166 N.W. 202 (1918); *Wilkerson* v. *Rome,* 152 Ga. 763, 110 S.E. 895 (1922); *Kaplan* v. *Independent School District,* 171 Minn. 142, 214 N.W. 18 (1927); and *People* ex rel. *Vollmar* v. *Stanley,* 81 Colo. 276, 255 P. 610 (1927).

The Kaplan case, cited above, evidenced an opposite result from that in the Weiss case, yet it utilized a portion of the rationale of the Wisconsin court. The Minnesota court noted that the conclusions of the Weiss case were specifically stated as not to "banish from the district schools such textbooks as are founded upon the fundamental teachings of the Bible or which contain extracts therefrom. . . . Such textbooks are in the schools for secular instruction, and rightly so."

The majority in the Kaplan case then asked, "If textbooks may be used containing extracts from the Bible without violating the constitutional provisions, why may not selections therefrom be made by school authorities?" Consequently, the practice adopted by a local school board whereby the superintendent selected certain passages of the Old Testament from the King James Version of the Bible to be read, without note or comment, during Bible-reading exercises from which objecting students were excused was declared not to constitute sectarian instruction nor to convert the school or building into a place of worship within the constitutional prohibitions.

The supreme courts of a number of other states agreed with the Weiss ruling. In *People* ex rel. *Ring* v. *Board of Education,* 245 Ill. 334, 92 N.E. 251 (1910), the Illinois supreme court held that reading the Bible, singing hymns, and repeating the Lord's Prayer in public schools violated the state constitutional guarantee of the "free exercise and enjoyment of religious profession and worship without discrimination." The court held further that such religious practices in the public schools constituted sectarianism within the constitutional prohibition against appropriating any public fund to aid any sectarian purpose.

Of a similar nature, the supreme court of Louisiana in *Herold* v. *Parish Board,* 136 La. 1034, 68 So. 116 (1915), enjoined the board of school directors of Caddo Parish from activating the board's resolution requesting its teachers to open the school day by reading from the Bible, without note or comment, and by offering the Lord's Prayer. Noting that it is impossible to read the Bible without conjuring up religious and sectarian overtones, the court observed:

> To read the Bible for the purpose stated requires that it be read reverently and worshipfully. As God is the author of the Book, He is necessarily worshipped in the reading of it. And the reading of it forms part of all religious services in the Christian and Jewish churches, which use the Word. It is as much a part of the religious worship of the churches of the land as is the offering of prayer to God.

The key state case upholding Bible-reading exercises was *People* ex rel. *Vollmar* v. *Stanley,* cited above. There, the supreme court of Colorado ruled in 1927 that reading of the King James Version without comment in the public schools did not abridge the constitutional guarantees of religious freedom and enjoyment of religious worship without discrimination. Nor did such instruction constitute the expenditure of public funds to sustain a school controlled by a sectarian denomination, the court found.

That ruling became the almost classic rationale of those who supported Bible-reading exercises in the public schools prior to their prohibition by the United States Supreme Court. Disapproval of the use of a "sectarian" book, the Bible, for teaching "good government principles" was voiced in *Lawyer and Banker* (21:164). There, Frank Swancara pointed out that many schools were imparting such "mental food" without the use of the Bible.

Nevertheless, the issue of sectarianism was reserved by the Colorado court for another day:

> When comment or the reading of a given part is claimed to be teaching sectarian doctrines or tenet, the courts will consider that point, but it cannot be said that the whole Bible is so.

However, in its only reference to the Weiss case, the Colorado court pointed out that "Even in *Weiss* v. *District Board* . . . it is said that parts of the Bible are not sectarian. 'There can be no valid objection to the use of such matter in the secular instruction of the pupils.' Religious and sectarian are not synonymous."

The court went on to declare, however, that attendance at such exercises must be voluntary, the reasoning being that instruction not essential to the development of good citizenship cannot be forced upon objecting children in the public schools. Such a view was in opposition to that in the Weiss case, where voluntary Bible-reading exercises were enjoined.

Little attention was given generally in the other cases to the issue of compusory attendance. However, *Hackett* v. *Brooksville Graded School District* and *Spiller* v. *Woburn,* both cited above, recognized specifically that compelling students to participate in religious observances contrary to their own convictions would violate the constitutional guaranty of religious liberty and freedom of conscience. Of a similar nature see the Ring case, discussed above. For a contrary finding, see *Church* v. *Bullock,* cited earlier, in which the Texas supreme court refused to enjoin public-school exercises consisting of Bible reading, Lord's Prayer recitation, and singing of patriotic songs even though attendance was required.

One case, *State* ex rel. *Finger* v. *Weedman,* 55 S.D. 343, 226 N.W. 348 (1929), was concerned solely with the issue of compulsory attendance. However, the *obiter dictum* in the decision against it was so critical of Bible reading in general, that the statute permitting it was deleted from the South Dakota Code.

NONINTERFERENCE BY SOME COURTS

That some courts considered the question of religious practices in the public schools solely an educational matter was evidenced in several cases. In *Board of Education* v. *Minor,* 23 Ohio St. 211 (1872), below, the Ohio supreme court held that the courts have no rightful authority to interfere with the policies of boards of education in prescribing what instruction shall be given and from what books it shall be given. Noting in dictum that reading the King James Version of the Bible violated the rights of conscience of Roman Catholic and Jewish children, the court nevertheless ruled that the state's constitution neither enjoined nor required religious instruction and religious books in the public schools, and consequently denied the application for an injunction to enjoin enforcement of a resolution discontinuing the Bible-reading exercises. See also in this connection: *State* ex rel. *Dearle* v. *Frazier,* 102 Wash. 369, 173 P. 35 (1918), and *State* ex rel. *Clithero* v. *Showalter,* 159 Wash. 519, 293 P. 1000 (1930).

A similar result of judicial noninterference was reached by a county court in *Board of Education* v. *Paul,* 7 Ohio N.P. 58, 10 Ohio Dec. N.P. 17 (1900). There, a resolution by a board of education, in accordance with authority conferred by law, which prohibited religious instructions in the school, was declared final and therefore nonreviewable by the courts.

For the opposite point of view, see *Lewis* v. *Board of Education,* 157 Misc. 520, 285 N.Y.S. 164 (1935). There, the supreme court of New York County took the initiative but upheld the validity of a 1901 Greater New York Charter provision which prohibited the board of education from excluding "the Holy Scriptures, without note or comment, or any selections therefrom, from any of the schools provided for by this chapter." The fact that the provision further stated, "provided that nothing herein contained shall be so construed as to violate the rights of conscience, as secured by the constitution of this State and of the United States," was the determining factor in the court's judgment. (See the chapter on religious use of school buildings for a further discussion of the other issues involved in the case.)

GIDEON BIBLES AND THE PUBLIC SCHOOLS

A slightly different issue was involved in *Tudor* v. *Board of Education,* 14 N.J. 31, 100 A.2d 857 (1953), below. There the New Jersey supreme court determined that the policy of permitting the distribution of the Gideon Bible (conforming to the King James Version of the Bible) in the public schools constituted an establishment of religion in violation of the federal Constitution and the preference of one religion to the exclusion of others in violation of the New Jersey constitution.

That ruling evidenced a remarkable turnabout in judicial attitude from the same court's position concerning Bible reading in *Doremus* v. *Board of Education*, 5 N.J. 435, 75 A.2d 880 (1950), discussed below. By accepting the arguments used against Bible reading as permitted in the Doremus case, the court in the Tudor case left little doubt that it accepted a different concept of sectarianism. Henceforth the New Jersey court would consider as controlling importance in its interpretation of sectarianism those things of doctrinal significance which are unacceptable to specific religious groups.

† † *TUDOR* v. *BOARD OF EDUCATION OF RUTHERFORD*
14 N.J. 31, 100 A.2D 857 (1953)

Mr. Chief Justice VANDERBILT delivered the opinion of the court, saying in part:

The Gideons International is a non-profit corporation organized under the laws of the State of Illinois, whose object is "to win men and women for the Lord Jesus Christ, through . . . (c) placing the Bible—God's Holy Words—or portions thereof in hotels, hospitals, schools, institutions, and also through the distribution of same for personal use." In recent years it began a campaign to make available to pupils in the public schools of this country the so-called "Gideon Bible," which was characterized by the International in its pleadings as

a book containing all of the New Testament, all of the Book of Psalms from the Old Testament, all of the Book of Proverbs from the Old Testament; all without note or comment, conformable to the edition of 1611, commonly known as the Authorized, or King James version of the Holy Bible.

In furtherance of this campaign it applied by letter to the Board of Educa-tion of the Borough of Rutherford for permission to distribute its Bible to the public schools of that municipality.

. . . .

The proposal was considered at a meeting of the board of education on November 5, 1951, at which time there was voiced some opposition to the proposal by a Catholic priest and a Jewish rabbi on the grounds that the Gideons' New Testament was sectarian and forbidden to Catholic and Jewish children under the laws of their respective religions. The proposal, however, was passed by the board with one dissenting vote, the resolution adopted providing that "the Gideons International be allowed to furnish copies of the New Testament, Psalms, and Proverbs to those pupils who request them." . . .

. . . .

. . . At a principal's meeting on February 6, 1952 the following instructions were issued:

(a) Only names of pupils whose parents had previously signed for the Bibles should be used in any announcement.

(b) Pupils whose parents had signed for Bibles are to report to the home room at the close of the session and no other pupils are to be in the room when the Bibles are distributed.

(c) Any announcement of names for the purpose of reporting after school should not include a reference as to the purpose of reporting.

. . . .

The plaintiff Bernard Tudor is an adherent of the Jewish religion, while plaintiff Ralph Lecoque is a member of the Catholic faith, each being a New Jersey citizen and taxpayer of Rutherford and a parent of a pupil in a Rutherford public school. Each contends that the Gideon Bible is "a sectarian work of peculiar religious value and significance to members of the Protestant faith." Mr. Tudor claiming that "its distribution to children of the Jewish faith violates the teachings, tenets and principles of Judaism," while Mr. Lecoque states that "its distribution to children of Catholic faith violates the teachings, tenets and principles of Catholicism."

. . . .

. . . The charge here is sectarianism. The defendant board of education is accused of showing a preference by permitting the distribution of the King James version of the New Testament, which is unacceptable to those of the Jewish faith and, in fact, in conflict with their tenets. This violates the mandate of the First Amendment, as incorporated into the Fourteenth Amendment, prohibiting the making of any law "respecting an establishment of religion," and the requirement of Article I, paragraph 4 of the New Jersey Constitution that "there shall be no establishment of one religious sect, in preference to another." By its very terms the New Jersey constitutional provision prohibits any such religious preference, while the First Amendment to the Federal Constitution has been judicially interpreted as so providing. As stated by Mr. Justice Black in his opinion for the majority of the court in *Everson* v. *Board of Education:* . . .

The "establishment of religion" clause of the First Amendment means at least this: Neither a state nor the Federal Government can set up a church. Neither can pass laws which aid one religion, aid all religions, or prefer one religion over another. . . .

That amendment [First] requires the state to be a neutral in its relations with groups of religious believers and non-believers. . . .

In *Zorach* v. *Clauson,* 343 U.S. 306 . . . (1952), Mr. Justice Douglas in his opinion for the majority of the court stated: "The government must be neutral when it comes to competition between sects." . . .

We are well aware of the ever continuing debates that have been taking place in this country for many years as to the meaning which should be given to the First Amendment. There are those who contend that our forefathers never intended to erect a "wall of separation" between Church and State. On the other hand, there are those who insist upon this absolute separation between Church and State. The plaudits and the criticisms of the various majority, concurring and dissenting opinions rendered by the United States Supreme Court in *Everson* v. *Board of Education, People of State of Illinois* ex rel. *McCollum* v. *Board of Education,* and *Zorach* v. *Clauson* still continue.

But regardless of what our views on this fundamental question may be, our decision in this case must be based upon the undoubted doctrine of both the Federal Constitution and our New Jersey Constitution, that the state or any instrumentality thereof cannot under any circumstances show a preference for one religion over another. Such favoritism cannot be tolerated and must be disapproved as a clear violation of the Bill of Rights of our Constitution.

This brings us to the heart of our problem here—namely, whether the resolution of the board of education displays that favoritism that is repugnant to our Constitutions. By permitting the distribution of the Gideon Bible, has the board of education established one religious sect in preference to another? Although as to the Catholic plaintiff this action has become moot due to the withdrawal of his child from the public schools of Rutherford, some testimony was presented at the trial as to his claim of sectarianism so we will at times refer to such testimony in our opinion. Our decision, however, is based upon the claim of the Jewish plaintiff that the resolution of the Rutherford Board of Education constitutes a preference of one religion over the Hebrew faith.

A review of the testimony at the trial convinces us that the King James version or Gideon Bible is unacceptable to those of the Jewish faith. In this regard Rabbi Joachim Prinz testified:

The New Testament is in profound conflict with the basic principles of Judaism. It is not accepted by the Jewish people as a sacred book. The Bible of the Jewish people is the Old Testament. The New Testament is not recognized as part of the Bible. The teachings of the New Testament are in complete and profound conflict with what Judaism teaches. It pre-

supposes the concept of Jesus of Nazareth a divinity, a concept which we do not accept. . . .

. . . .

No, it is certainly not a nonsectarian book. It is a book that is—expresses the view of one denomination among the many religious denominations of the world.

Dr. Bernard J. Bamberger, rabbi of the West End Synagogue in New York City and former president of the Synagogue Council of America . . . concluded that the King James Version was "completely not a nonsectarian book." Rabbi Irving Schnipper, in answer to a question whether the teachings of the New Testament are in conflict with his teaching of children of the plaintiff Bernard Tudor, testified: "Definitely, the New Testament itself is in direct opposition to the teachings of Judaism." Nor is there any doubt that the King James version of the Bible is as unacceptable to Catholics as the Douay version is to Protestants. According to the testimony in this case the canon law of the Catholic Church provides that "Editions of the original text of the sacred scriptures published by non-Catholics are forbidden *ipso jure.*"

The defendant refers us to various statements by legal scholars and others to show that the Bible is not sectarian, but rather is the universal book of the Christian world, but in many of these statements the question of the New Testament was not discussed. In *Doremus* v. *Board of Education of Borough of Hawthorne*, 5 N.J. 345 (1950), . . . relied on by the defendant, the issue was whether R. S. 18:14–77 and 78, providing for compulsory reading in the public schools of five verses of the Old Testament and permissive reading of the Lord's Prayer violated the Federal Constitution. In upholding the constitutionality of the statutes we specifically stated . . . :

We consider that the Old Testament and the Lord's Prayer, pronounced without comment, are not sectarian, and that the short exercise provided by the statute does not constitute sectarian instruction or sectarian worship. . . .

We adhere to the *Doremus* case, but its holding does not apply here, where clearly the issue of sectarianism is present. Here the issue is the distribution of the New Testament. The uncontradicted evidence presented by the plaintiff reveals that as far as the Jewish faith is concerned, the Gideon Bible is a sectarian book, the teachings of which are in conflict with the doctrines of his religion as well as that of his child, who is a pupil in the Rutherford public school. The full force of the violation of both the State and Federal Constitutions is revealed when we perceive what might happen if a single school board were besieged by three separate applications for the distribution of Bibles—one from Protestants as here, another from Catholics for the distribution of the Douay Bible, and a third from Jews for the same privilege for their Bible.

We find from the evidence presented in this case that the Gideon Bible is a sectarian book, and that the resolution of the defendant board of education to permit its distribution through the public school system of the Borough of Rutherford was in violation of the First Amendment of the United States Constitution, as incorporated into the Fourteenth Amendment, and of Article I, paragraph 4, of the New Jersey Constitution. It therefore must be set aside.

The defendant contends that the dis-tribution of the Gideon Bible in no way injects any issue of the "free exercise" of religion, that "no one is forced to take a New Testament and no religious exercise or instrument is brought to the classrooms of the public schools." In other words, it asserts the arguments of *Zorach* v. *Clauson* . . . that the "accommodation" of religion is permissible. This argument, however, ignores the realities of life. . . .

. . . .

In *State* ex rel. *Weiss* v. *District Board*, 76 Wis. 177 (1890), it was stated:

When . . . a small minority of the pupils in the public school is excluded, for any cause, from a stated school exercise, particularly when such cause is apparent hostility to the Bible which a majority of the pupils have been taught to revere, from that moment the excluded pupil loses caste with his fellows, and is liable to be regarded with aversion, and subjected to reproach and insult. . . .

Professor Isidore Chein, Supervisor of Psychology and Acting Director of the Research Center for Mental Health at New York University, testified on behalf of the plaintiff:

. . . I would expect that a slip of this kind, distributed under the authority of the school, would create a subtle pressure on the child which would leave him with a sense that he is not quite as free as the statement on that slip says; in other words, that he will be something of an outcast and a pariah if he does not go along with this procedure.
. . . I think that they would be in a situation where they have to play along with this or else feel themselves to be putting themselves in a public position where they are different, where they are not the same as other people, and the whole pressure would exist on them to conform.

Dr. Dan Dodson, professor in the School of Education of New York University and director of curriculum and research in the Center for Human Relations Studies, when questioned as to the divisive effect of the distribution of the Gideon Bible stated:

I would say that any instance of this kind in which the . . . document that has the importance that this has to certain religious groups, including my own, would be distributed or used as a means of propaganda or indoctrination by official channels, such as the school system, would create tensions among the religious groups; there would be a controversial problem.

I would say that it would raise questions among the children as to who is and who isn't, in terms of receiving the Bible. It would also create problems as to why some accepted it and others didn't. That would be divisive.

. . . .

We cannot accept the argument that here, as in the Zorach case, the State is merely "accommodating" religion. It matters little whether the teachers themselves will distribute the Bibles or whether that will be done by members of the Gideons International. The same vice exists, that of preference of one religion over another. This is all the more obvious when we realize the motive of the Gideons. Its purpose is "to win men and women for the Lord Jesus Christ, through . . . (c) placing the Bible—God's Holy Word . . . or portions thereof in hotels, hospitals, schools, institutions, and also through distribution of same for personal use." The society is engaged in missionary work, accomplished in part by placing the King James version of the Bible in the hands of public school children throughout the United States. To achieve this end it employs the public

school system as the medium of distribution. It is at the school that the pupil receives the request slip to take to his parents for signature. It is at the school that the pupil actually receives his Gideon Bible. In other words, the public school machinery is used to bring about the distribution of these Bibles to the children of Rutherford. In the eyes of the pupils and their parents the board of education has placed its stamp of approval upon this distribution and, in fact, upon the Gideon Bible itself. . . .

. . . .

Dr. William Heard Kilpatrick stated:

The Protestants would feel that the school is getting behind this thing; the Catholics would feel that the school is getting behind a Protestant affair; the Jews would feel that the school is getting behind the Protestant religion as opposed to their religion; and the people who don't accept any religion would feel that the school is actually trying to teach the religion through this means.

This is more than mere "accommodation" of religion permitted in the Zorach case. The school's part in this distribution is an active one and cannot be sustained on the basis of a mere assistance to religion.

We are here concerned with a vital question involving the very foundation of our civilization. Centuries ago our forefathers fought and died for the principles now contained in the Bill of Rights of the Federal and New Jersey Constitutions. It is our solemn duty to preserve these rights and to prohibit any encroachment upon them. To permit the distribution of the King James version of the Bible in the public schools of this State would be to cast aside all the progress made in the United States and throughout New Jersey in the field of religious toleration and freedom. We would be renewing the ancient struggles among the various religious faiths to the detriment of all. This we must decline to do.

The judgment below is reversed and the resolution of the Board of Education of the Borough of Rutherford under review is stricken.

LATER CASES

A similar distribution of Gideon Bibles was voided likewise by a lower Florida court in *Brown* v. *Orange County Board of Public Instruction,* Fla., 128 So.2d 181 (1960). That decision was affirmed three years later by the Florida supreme court at Fla., 155 So.2d 371 (1963), upon the authority of *School District of Abington* v. *Schempp,* 83 S.Ct. 1560 (1963), and *Chamberlin* v. *Dade County,* 83 S.Ct. 1864 (1963), both of which are discussed below. Nonetheless, if news accounts are accurate, debates over the legality of permitting the distribution of Gideon Bibles in public schools in other parts of the nation continue. And there seems little likelihood of a solution to this problem until the United States Supreme Court rules definitively on the matter.

BIBLE READING IN THE UNITED STATES SUPREME COURT

Doremus v. *Board of Education,* 342 U.S. 429 (1952), was the first Bible-reading case heard by a federal court. A New Jersey statute provided for opening each public-school day by reading, without comment, five verses from the Old Testament. A declatory judgment was sought by the two appellants to determine whether the New Jersey Bible-reading act violated the establishment clause of the First Amendment. The New Jersey high court, 5 N.J. 435, 75 A.2d 880 (1950), upheld the statute on grounds that there was no contention by either of the plaintiffs or any religious sect that any religious beliefs, practices, or dictates had been violated. The action was sought by two parties, one as a taxpayer, and the other as a parent who had a daughter attending the school but who had since graduated. While the question was raised by respondents that the issue was moot, so far as the parent whose child had graduated was concerned, the New Jersey supreme court disposed of the appeal on its merits.

The United States Supreme Court dismissed the appeal for want of jurisdiction. It concluded from the facts involving the parent petitioner, that the case was moot because the child in question had graduated from the public school before the decision was appealed to the high court. The Court said that no decision could now protect the rights she had once had.

The Court treated the taxpayer's grievance in a similar fashion. "The facts stated by the appellants as taxpayers were not sufficient to constitute a justiciable case or controversy within the jurisdiction of this Court, because they do not show such direct and particular financial interest as is necessary to maintain a taxpayer's case or controversy." This dismissal, did not, of course, uphold the lower court's ruling, but merely left it standing. It should not, however, be construed as a direct or indirect indication of the Supreme Court's attitude concerning the constitutionality of Bible-reading exercises in public schools.

REACTIONS OF LEGAL PERIODICALS TO
DOREMUS v. *BOARD OF EDUCATION*

The reluctance of the Supreme Court of the United States to take on the thorny but long prevalent problem of Bible-reading programs in the public schools is revealed in the manner in which the Court side-stepped the merits in this case and disposed of the matter on jurisdictional grounds. The Court's decision that Bible-reading programs in the public school cannot be voided in a federal court when the controversy has become moot, and the complainants have no sufficient pocket book interest was of small solace to the education policy formulators who were increasingly being beset by objections to such exercises.

Law reviews generally were about as reluctant to take a stand as was the Supreme Court of the United States. The handful of reviews which ventured an opinion divided over the issue of whether precedent supported the Court's position on jurisdiction here. However, a finding that the Court's approach was legally correct was accompanied by statements of regret in the *Alabama Law Review* (4:284) and the *Harvard Law Review* (66:119) that such controversial litigation was not resolved.

A claim was made in the *Georgetown Law Journal* (40:619) that the Supreme Court had overlooked jurisdictional obstacles in the past when it felt that the issues warranted resolution. It suggested as an example, *Adler* v. *Board of Education*, 342 U.S. 485 (1952).

The reviews following the decision on the merits in the New Jersey supreme court seem more instructive. That 1951 ruling upholding Bible reading was hailed in the *Baylor Law Review* (3:456) and the *Rutgers Law Review* (5:553) for its recognition of our basic regard for religion. It was pointed out in the *Temple Law Quarterly* (25:89) that there is a favorable trend toward upholding Bible reading especially when no comment or interpretation is made by the teacher. The *Arkansas Law Review* (5:431) felt that an exposure to a "little religion" does not hurt anybody.

The denunciations of the decision although fewer were harsher. A prophetic position was taken in the *Harvard Law Review* (64:666) that such a statute, even though excusing objectors, may violate free exercise of religion by enforcing embarrassment of noncomformers, a situation of much concern to the four concurring justices in the McCollum case. That there could be no reconciliation of the decision with the Supreme Court dictates in either the McCollum or the Everson case was expressed in the *Marquette Law Review* (34:297). Meanwhile, the *Syracuse Law Review* (2:371) expressed doubts that the Bible was a sectarian book.

In the interim between the Doremus case and the Schempp case, discussed below, there were two more state cases. *Carden* v. *Bland*, 199 Tenn. 665, 288 S.W.2d 718 (1956), below, upheld a program of Bible reading in the public schools against contentions that the statute violated state and federal constitutional provisions. The state statute in question, required the teachers "to read, or cause to be read, at the opening of the school every day, a selection from the Bible."

Temporary solace for those supporting Bible-reading exercises was found in the declaration in the *Tennessee Law Review* (24:883) concerning the Carden case, that such a decision was favored generally by state court precedents. However, this journal also pointed out that the final resolution—the resolution of federal constitutional questions—involving such controversial areas as standing to sue, and the alleged sectarianism of the Bible, rested ultimately in the hands of the United States Supreme Court.

The Carden decision was criticized sharply in the *Nebraska Law Review* (36:357) for allowing the commingling of church and state within the school building itself. The *Georgia Bar Journal* (19:227) was critical of the Tennessee court for its neglect of minority rights in validating a process whereby the state forces a "sectarian" King James Version upon Jewish children. A similar opinion was expressed in the *Michigan Law Review* (55:715) where it was also felt that the state statute violated the First Amendment since it went far beyond the McCollum, Zorach, and Doremus decisions in its allowance of Bible-reading exercises directed in tax-supported classrooms by state-paid teachers with no provision for objectors to excuse themselves.

EVENTS FOLLOWING THE DOREMUS CASE

A similar conclusion that Bible reading was constitutional was reached by the Florida supreme court in *Chamberlin* v. *Dade County*, Fla., 143 So.2d 21 (1962), below. That case, which involved multiple issues of religious practices and considerable legal jockeying, is discussed further in the subsection, "The Schempp Case as a Controlling Precedent."

† † *CHAMBERLIN* v. *DADE COUNTY BOARD OF PUBLIC INSTRUCTION*

FLA., 143 SO.2D 21 (1962).

Justice CALDWELL delivered the opinion of the court, saying in part:

Harlow Chamberlin [and others] . . . brought separate actions against the Dade County Board of Public Instruction . . . to enjoin certain alleged religious practices in the Dade County public schools, praying that Section 231.09, F.S.A., be declared to be in violation of the First and Fourteenth Amendments to the United States Constitution and Sections 5 and 6 of the Declaration of Rights of the Florida Constitution, F.S.A. Neither suit alleged specific acts as being in violation of Section 5 of the Declaration of Rights of the Florida Constitution.

Both complaints seek relief by way of injunction and declaratory judgment and, as to the specific acts asserted to be in violation of the federal and state constitutions, they are identical.

. . . .

The plaintiff in the Chamberlin suit is an agnostic and the plaintiffs in the Resnick complaint are Jewish and Unitarian. The defendants in both suits are the Dade County Board of Public Instruction and its individual members.

. . . .

In substance, the complaints allege that, in the public schools, the defendant observes the following practices:

Regular reading of the Bible; comments on the Bible; distribution of sectarian literature to school children; after hours Bible instruction; regular recitation of the Lord's Prayer, grace and other sectarian prayers; singing of religious hymns; religious observance of the Christmas, Hanukka and Easter holidays, including instruction in the dogma of the Nativity and Resurrection; display of religious symbols, baccalaureate programs; conducting a religious census and the use of religious tests for employment and promotion of school employees.

After a prolonged trial and the taking of some 1400 pages of testimony, the chancellor enjoined: Sectarian comments on the Bible by public school teachers; the use of school premises after school hours for Bible instruction; the exhibition of films with religious content and the religious observance in the public schools of Christmas, Easter and Hanukka holidays.

The chancellor rejected the complaints alleging: The reading of the Bible; the distribution of sectarian literature to school children; the recitation of the Lord's Prayer, grace and other sectarian prayers; the singing of religious hymns; the display of religious symbols; baccalaureate programs; the conducting of a religious census and the use of religious tests for employment and promotion of school employees, all upon grounds hereinafter discussed.

. . . .

The plaintiffs contend that attendance upon or participation in the complained of religious practices is in violation of both the "establishment" and the "free exercise" clauses of the constitutional language above quoted, regardless of whether the alleged practices are sectarian or non-sectarian.

Also, notwithstanding the resolution of the Dade County Board of Public Instruction which required the school principal to excuse children from attendance upon request of their parents or guardians, the plaintiffs contend that the exclusion of expert testimony offered for the purpose of showing psychological compulsion and the effects thereof upon the school children was in error.

The plaintiffs lean heavily upon the Everson, McCollum, McGowan and Torcaso cases* for support and make much of the fact that in those cases, the court, defining the "establishment" clause, used this language:

Neither a state ʌor the Federal Government can set up a church. Neither can pass laws which aid one religion, aid all religions, or prefer one religion over another. Neither can force or influence a person to go to or remain away from church against his will or force him to profess a belief or disbelief in any religion. No person can be punished for entertaining or professing religious beliefs or disbeliefs, for church attendance or non-attendance. No tax in any amount, large or small, can be levied to support any religious activities or institutions, whatever they may be called or whatever form they may adopt to teach or practice religion. Neither a state nor the Federal Government can, openly or secretly, participate in the affairs of any religious organizations or groups and vice versa. In the words of Jefferson, the clause against establishment of religion by law was intended to erect 'a wall of separation between Church and State.'

We are not impressed with the language quoted as being definitive of the "establishment" clause. It goes far be-

yond the purpose and intent of the authors and beyond any reasonable application to the practical facts of everyday life in this country. We feel that the broad language quoted, must, in the course of time, be further receded from if weight is to be accorded the true purpose of the First Amendment. The quotation imputed to Jefferson, written by him ten years after the adoption of the First Amendment in a letter to the Danbury Baptists of Connecticut, has done little other than cause confusion.

The University of Virginia, wholly controlled by the State of Virginia, by regulation suggested by Mr. Jefferson and adopted by the Visitors of the University provided that the students would be expected to attend religious worship. As was pointed out by Mr. Justice Reed in the McCollum case:

Thus, the "wall of separation between church and State" that Mr. Jefferson built at the University which he founded did not exclude religious education from that school. The difference between the generality of his statements on the separation of church and state and the specificity of his conclusions on education are considerable. A rule of law should not be drawn from a figure of speech.

It is our view that Cooley [in *Principles of Constitutional Law*] more appropriately and accurately states the proposition as follows:

By establishment of religion is meant the setting up or recognition of a state church, or at least the conferring upon one church of special favors and advantages which are denied to others. It was never intended by the Constitution that the government

---

* [*Everson* v. *Board of Education*, 330 U.S. 1; *People* ex rel. *McCollum* v. *Board of Education*, 333 U.S. 203; *McGowan* v. *Maryland*, 336 U.S. 420; *Torcaso* v. *Watkins*, 367 U.S. 448.]

should be prohibited from recognizing religion . . . where it might be done without drawing any invidious distinctions between different religious beliefs, organizations or sects. The Christian religion was always recognized in the administration of the common law; and so far as that law continues to be the law of the land, the fundamental principles of that religion must continue to be recognized in the same extent as formerly.

. . . .

. . . In *Carden* v. *Bland* [199 Tenn. 665 (1956)] the Supreme Court of Tennessee refused to enjoin the reading of the Bible and the singing of religious hymns in the public schools and said:

In order to wipe out any and all right of the State to control their own system of public education great stress is laid upon the need of maintaining the doctrine of "Separation of Church and State." We concede that this is important. But it should not be tortured into a meaning that was never intended by the Founders of this Republic, with the result that the public school system of the several states is to be made a Godless institution as a matter of law.

. . . .

In *Engle* v. *Vitale* [10 N.Y. 2d. 174 (1961)] the court approved this language:

'We are a religious people whose institutions presuppose a Supreme Being.' . . . As Justic Bedlock of the Appellate Division wrote in this case: 'The contention that acknowledgments of and references to Almighty God are acceptable and desirable in all other phases of our public life but not *in our public schools* is, in my judgment, an attempt to stretch far beyond its breaking point the principle of separation of church and State and to obscure one's vision to the universally accepted tradition that ours is a Nation founded and nurtured upon belief in God.' . . .

. . . The concept of God has been and is so interwoven into every aspect of American institutions that to attack this concept is to threaten the very fiber of our existence as a nation. In *Wilkerson* v. *City of Rome,* [152 Ga. 762 (1922)] the Supreme Court of Georgia discussing the background of the doctrine of separation of Church and State in this country stated:

[U]nder the leadership of Roger Williams of Rhode Island, the movement for the separation of church and state proceeded with ever increasing volume and strength. It should be clearly understood, however, that this was not a movement for the separation of state from Christianity, but specifically a separation of church and state. Christianity entered into the whole warp and woof of our governmental fabric. Many of the statesmen of this country treated Christianity as a part of the law of the land.

By the Declaration of Independence, the Colonies asserted "certain unalienable rights" with which all men were "endowed by their Creator," and appealed "to the Supreme Judge of the world for the rectitude of our intentions." After the Revolution, the treaty exacted from Great Britain begins with these words: "In the name of the Most Holy and Undivided Trinity." In the light of these historic facts, can it be said that reference to the Scriptures or recognition of the Deity in our public schools is in violation of the constitutional rights of any person?

We think it significant that the federal government, in keeping with our traditional public recognition of religion and in harmony with Cooley's construction of the "establishment" clause has: Provided chaplains for both Houses of Congress who daily invoke Divine blessings upon the meetings;

commissioned chaplains for the Armed Forces who employ for religious purposes property belonging to the United States but dedicated to the cause of religions; approved the opening exercises of the public schools in the District of Columbia, a creature of the federal government, which exercises include a reading from the Bible and the Lord's Prayer; approved the requirement by the United States Naval and Military Academies of compulsory attendance of the Cadets at Sunday church services, presided over by chaplains paid by the United States Government and held in property owned by the government; authorized the flying of the church flag above or to the right of the national flag during church services conducted at sea by navy chaplains; required the President and Members of Congress, the Justices of the United States Supreme Court to subscribe to an oath in which the aid of Deity is invoked; inscribed the words "In God We Trust" upon the currency of the nation; designated a national anthem which proclaims the Deity; approved, along with the several states, the exemption of multiplied millions of dollars worth of church property from taxation.

In countless other instances the federal government accepts religion as an ever present fact without suggesting violation of the "establishment" and "free exercise" clauses which, we believe, have been tortured beyond the intent of the Authors.

It seems to us that Cooley, acclaimed as the foremost authority on the Constitution as it was in his time, by avoidance of gymnastic semanticisms and by the application of authentic definitions to simple words has fairly approximated the intended purposes of the constitutional safeguards.

. . . We, therefore, adopt for our guidance, Cooley's definition of the "establishment" clause as quoted above.
. . .

. . . The plaintiffs insist that each of the challenged practices violates not only the "establishment" but, also, the "free exercise" clause, and that, as to the facts before us, it is not necessary that "establishment" and "free exercise" guarantees be treated separately. If the offenses complained of conflicts with the safeguards provided by the Constitution, it must be because there is present compulsion requiring unwilling support of religion, in whatever its form.

. . . In this case the basic facts are that Florida Statute, §231.09, F.S.A. requires the daily reading of the Bible without sectarian comment. Moreover, the record shows that by appropriate regulation of the Dade County Board of Public Instruction it requires that pupils be excused from attendance upon request by the parents or guardians. Our problem is to determine whether the practices complained of violate the constitutional safeguards. If the facts constitute "establishment" of religion or restriction of the free exercise thereof it must be because there is compulsion. If the pupils are compelled to attend upon the practices cited, or if their free exercise of religion is otherwise circumscribed, then we must conclude that there is a violation of the "establishment" and "free exercise" safeguards.

We think it necessary that, unless otherwise clearly commanded by the plain language of the statutes of the Constitution, the courts refrain from purely philosophical invasions of the Constitution or long established and accepted customs of the vast majority of the American people. The recurrent whittling away of the bedrock foundations of our society can be nothing short of destructive of free government. . . .

. . . It is of interest here that the United States Supreme Court decision in the Zorach case makes it clear that the First Amendment does not say there must be in every and all respects a separation of church and state. Rather the First Amendment defines the manner and specific way in which there shall be no concert, or union, or dependency, one on the other. The court held that to be "the common sense of the matter" and that, otherwise, the state and religion would be aliens to each other—hostile, suspicious, and even unfriendly. . . .

In the light of this reasoning in the Zorach case the court held that the public schools of New York City, upon written request of the parents, were permitted to release, during the school day, those students who wished to attend religious exercises held outside the school building. The court found that it was proper that the school board assemble the students upon school property and, during the school day, excuse them from attendance upon classes of regular and secular instruction by teachers and in classrooms provided at public expense. . . .

In principle there is no substantial difference between the excusing of the Zorach students who wished to attend religious exercises elsewhere and the excusing of the Dade County students who do not wish to hear the Bible read in school. And, in substance, there is no difference in principle between the three and five minutes' use of Dade County public school facilities for the reading of the Bible to those who wish to hear it and the non-use, during school hours, of such facilities in Zorach while those who wish religious instruction elsewhere are excused from the premises. To beg the question between the facts in Zorach and the instant case is to engage in cynical trivialities.

It does not appear by the pleadings and testimony that there is any serious contention that the children of the plaintiffs have suffered or will suffer any measurable psychological trauma as a consequence of the reading of the Bible, either in or out of their presence. Rather, it seems that this is just another case in which the tender sensibilities of certain minorities are sought to be protected against the allegedly harsh laws and customs enacted and established by the more rugged pioneers of the Nation. In the instant case we are told that the primary objects of solicitude are the children of the plaintiffs, atheists, Unitarians and Jews, which children, although not required to be present at the time, will, so it is said, suffer some supposedly irreparable emotional stress if their classmates are permitted to hear the Bible read. It seems more likely that the children in question are the unwilling victims of a quasi-political contest.

The plaintiffs assume, inferentially at least, that minorities enjoy a peculiar susceptibility to psychological and emotional trauma and compulsions and are entitled to some peculiar and fatherly protection against the strange ways of the ordinary American citizen. But such is not the case. The minority is entitled to enjoy the same privileges and the same justice as are enjoyed by people generally as an inherent right. The minority and the majority are both denied the privilege of disrupting the lives of others because of some hyper-sensitivity or fractious temperament.

To say that the vast majority of students in the Dade County public school system are to be foreclosed of the privilege of living a few moments each day with the words of the Bible, the greatest of all literature, or of observing in the classroom, if such were possible, the magnificent painting of the Last Supper, or of listening to Caruso's recording of Adeste Fidelis, because a minority might suffer some imagined and nebulous confusion, is to approach the ridiculous.

We believe it necessary that public education give due recognition to the place of religion and the culture and convictions of our people but that in doing so the principle of separation of church and state must be safeguarded. The road is a difficult one but, certainly, we cannot agree that banishing the Bible and music and paintings of plaintiffs' children in any material religious connotation will benefit the way. We are of the opinion that erasing the influence of the best literature, music and art and gentler aspects of American life in general would be to create an anti-religious attitude in the schools and substantially injure the well being of the majority of the school children. And although it may be urged that to take such drastic action is to incur the good will of the nation's enemy we think the cost too great and the proposal illfounded in law.

We are sensible of the extent to which the sophistries of agnosticism have gained credence. And we acknowledge the trend toward the preference of minorities over the majority and toward the requiring of the majority, which seem never to suffer psychological trauma, to yield up its cherished customs and rights. Although we concede the duty to turn the other cheek to the enemy and to deal gently with the weak, we do not agree that it is our function to subvert the purpose and intent of the Constitution to those ends, nor do we feel impelled to indulge in flights of fanciful philosophy. When we

subscribed to our official oaths it was with "no mental reservations and with no purpose to construe the Constitution by any hypercritical rules."

For all practical purposes there are now in the world just two forms of government, loosely denominated Democracy and Communism. The vital difference between the two is that the Democracies accept religion and guarantee its free exercise, in one form or another, as part of the day to day lives of their people, whereas Communism has banished religion, except as it may be bootlegged in the dark and inhospitable corners. . . .

We feel it equally imperative that we preserve the safeguards of the Constitution against all violations of the "establishment" and "free exercise" clauses and, at the same time, preserve those clauses and the rights of the States and the people thereunder against weasel-worded constructions and distinctions designed to impute to them either more or less than was originally intended. But typical of the American custom of meeting the other side more than half way, is the paradox of the appellee school board insuring the free exercise of religion while, by mandatory statute, it must teach the history, doctrines, objectives and techniques of Communism. Thus the school board affords the atheists the freedom of hearing or not hearing the Bible read while it requires that all students, without choice, be taught the facts of Communism, the antithesis of the Bible.

. . . .

An examination of the Everson, Zorach and McCollum cases convinces us of the practical impossibility of drawing distinctions between nebulosities. The purpose of the First Amendment was to prevent the abuses prevalent prior to and at the time of its adoption. There is no occasion to strain at gnats in the cause under consideration. There is or there is not a violation of the substantial meaning of the "establishment" clause and the "free exercise" clause. We see no profit in a tweedle-dee, tweedle-dum uncertainty in which the complete and uncompromising separation of church from state is argued but the exception is allowed, nor the sort of indecisiveness thought by Justice Jackson to be best typified by Byron's Julia who "whispering 'I will ne'er consent,' —consented."

. . . .

[4] We have thus far limited our treatment of the merits of this cause to what we conceive to be the pivotal issue herein, the constitutionality of the statute requiring daily readings from the Holy Bible. The appellants have raised, and we have considered, a number of points relating to other religious practices allegedly being carried on in the public schools of Dade County, which the chancellor refused to enjoin.

It is our opinion that the legal issues raised in connection with these other points have been disposed of adequately by the foregoing consideration of the Bible readings. The principles governing the recitation of the Lord's Prayer, the singing of religious hymns and the holding of baccalaureate programs are much the same as those applicable to the reading of the Bible. It is our conclusion that such practices of the appellee school board are so con-

ducted as not to infringe the constitutional safeguards enjoyed by appellants.

[5] The appellants' prayer to enjoin the display of religious symbols in the schools was denied by the chancellor ". . . upon the ground that the religious displays were found by this court to be works of art created by the school children and were displayed on a temporary basis and not of a permanent nature." It is our opinion that this holding of the chancellor is well grounded both in fact and in law. This issue, moreover, serves to point up the delicate balance of rights involved in a case of this nature. Are school children to be forbidden from expressing their natural artistic talents through media including religious themes? Or, are the results of their efforts to be excluded from public display and recognition merely because they choose to adopt a religious, rather than a secular subject? The answer should be obvious. To impose such a restriction would more nearly approach a restraint upon the free exercise of religion than does the present practice of the school board in permitting such displays.

The chancellor found that there was no factual basis for the appellants' allegations regarding a religious census of school children and religious tests for teachers. His findings in this regard are adequately supported by the competent substantial evidence and therefore merit no further discussion here.

For the foregoing reasons the decree of the chancellor should be and it is hereby affirmed.

THE UNITED STATES SUPREME COURT AND BIBLE READING

Then in 1963, the United States Supreme Court came to grips for the first time with the substantive issue of Bible reading. In a joinder case of *School District of Abington* v. *Schempp* and *Murray* v. *Curlett*, 83 S.Ct. 1560, involving claims of direct injury to religious conscience of public school pupils the Supreme Court invalidated on federal constitutional grounds Bible reading and Lord's Prayer exercises.

† † *SCHOOL DISTRICT OF ABINGTON TOWNSHIP* v. *SCHEMPP*

374 U.S. 203, 83 S. CT. 1560, 10 L. ED.2D (1963).

Mr. Justice CLARK delivered the opinion of the Court, saying in part:

Once again we are called upon to consider the scope of the provision of the First Amendment to the United States Constitution which declares that "Congress shall make no law respecting an establishment of religion, or prohibiting the free exercise thereof. . . ." These companion cases present the issues in the context of state action requiring that schools begin each day with readings from the Bible. While raising the basic questions under slightly different factual situations, the cases permit of joint treatment. In light of the history of the First Amendment and of our cases interpreting and applying its requirements, we hold that the practices at issue and the laws requiring them are unconstitutional under the Establishment Clause, as applied to the States through the Fourteenth Amendment.

I.

The Facts in Each Case: No. 142. The Commonwealth of Pennsylvania by law . . . requires that "At least ten verses from the Holy Bible shall be read, without comment, at the opening of each public school on each school day. Any child shall be excused from such Bible reading, or attending such Bible reading, upon the written request of his parent or guardian." The Schempp family, husband and wife and two of their three children, brought suit to enjoin enforcement of the statute, contending that their rights under the Fourteenth Amendment to the Constitution of the United States are, have been, and will continue to be violated unless this statute be declared unconstitutional as violative of these provisions of the First Amendment. They sought to enjoin the appellant school district, wherein the Schempp children attend school, and its officers and the Superintendent of Public Instruction of the Commonwealth from continuing to conduct such readings and recitation of the Lord's Prayer in the public schools of the district pursuant to the statute. A three-judge statutory District Court for the Eastern District of Pennsylvania held that the statute is violative of the Establishment Clause of the First Amendment as applied to the States by the Due Process Clause of the Fourteenth Amendment and directed that appropriate injunctive relief issue. . . .

The appellees Edward Lewis Schempp, his wife Sidney, and their children, Roger and Donna, are of the Unitarian faith and are members of the Unitarian Church in Germantown, Philadelphia, Pennsylvania, where they as well as another son, Ellory, regularly attend religious services. The latter was originally a party but having graduated from the school system *pendente lite* was voluntarily dismissed from the action. The other children attend the Abington Senior High School, which is a public school operated by appellant district.

On each school day at the Abington Senior High School between 8:15 and 8:30 a.m., while the pupils are attending their home rooms or advisory sections, opening exercises are conducted pursuant to the statute. The exercises are broadcast into each room in the school building through an intercommunications system and are conducted under the supervision of a teacher by students attending the school's radio and television workshop. Selected students from this course gather each morning in the school's workshop studio for the exercises, which include readings by one of the students of 10 verses of the Holy Bible, broadcast to each room in the building. This is followed by the recitation of the Lord's Prayer, likewise over the intercommunications system, but also by the students in the various classrooms, who are asked to stand and join in repeating the prayer in unison. The exercises are closed with the flag salute and such pertinent announcements as are of interest to the students. Participation in the opening exercises, as directed by the statute, is voluntary. The student reading the verses from the Bible may select the passages and read from any version he chooses, although the only copies furnished by the school are the King James version, copies of which were circulated to each teacher by the school district. During the period in which the exercises have been conducted the King James, the Douay and the Revised Standard versions of the Bible have been used, as well as the Jewish Holy Scriptures. There are no prefatory statements, no questions asked or solicited, no comments or ex-

planations made and no interpretations given at or during the exercises. The students and parents are advised that the student may absent himself from the classroom or, should he elect to remain, not participate in the exercises.

It appears from the record that in schools not having an intercommunications system the Bible reading and the recitation of the Lord's Prayer were conducted by the home-room teacher, who chose the text of the verses and read them herself or had students read them in rotation or by volunteers. This was followed by a standing recitation of the Lord's Prayer, together with the Pledge of Allegiance to the Flag by the class in unison and a closing announcement of routine school items of interest.

At the first trial Edward Schempp and the children testified as to specific religious doctrines purveyed by a literal reading of the Bible "which were contrary to the religious beliefs which they held and to their familial teaching." . . . The children testified that all of the doctrines to which they referred were read to them at various times as part of the exercises. Edward Schempp testified at the second trial that he had considered having Roger and Donna excused from attendance at the exercises but decided against it for several reasons, including his belief that the children's relationships with their teachers and classmates would be adversely affected.

Expert testimony was introduced by both appellants and appellees at the first trial, which testimony was summarized by the trial court as follows:

Dr. Solomon Grayzel testified that there were marked differences between the Jewish Holy Scriptures and the Christian Holy Bible, the most obvious of which was the absence of the New Testament in the Jewish Holy Scriptures. Dr. Grayzel testified that portions of the New Testament were offensive to Jewish tradition and that, from the standpoint of the Jewish faith, the concept of Jesus Christ as the Son of God was 'practically blasphemous.' He cited instances in the New Testament which, assertedly, were not only sectarian in nature but tended to bring the Jews into ridicule or scorn. Dr. Grayzel gave as his expert opinion that such material from the New Testament could be explained to Jewish children in such a way as to do no harm to them. But if portions of the New Testament were read without explanation, they could be, and in his specific experience with children Dr. Grayzel observed, had been, psychologically harmful to the child and had caused a divisive force within the social media of the school.

Dr. Grayzel also testified that there was significant difference in attitude with regard to the respective Books of the Jewish and Christian Religions in that Judaism attaches no special significance to the reading of the Bible *per se* and that the Jewish Holy Scriptures are source materials to be studied. But Dr. Grayzel did state that many portions of the New, as well as of the Old, Testament contained passages of great literary and moral value.

Dr. Luther A. Weigle, an expert witness for the defense, testified in some detail as to the reasons for and the methods employed in developing the King James and the Revised Standard Versions of the Bible. On direct examination, Dr. Weigle stated that the Bible was non-sectarian. He later stated that the phrase 'non-sectarian' meant to him non-sectarian within the Christian faiths. Dr. Weigle stated that his definition of the Holy Bible would include the Jewish Holy Scriptures, but also stated that the 'Holy Bible' would not be complete without the New Testament. He stated that the New Testament 'conveyed the message of Christians.' In his opinion, reading of the Holy Scriptures to the exclusion of the New Testament would be a sectarian practice. Dr. Weigle stated that the Bible was of great moral, historical and literary value. This is conceded by all the parties and is also the view of this court.

The trial court, in striking down the practices and the statute requiring them, made specific findings of fact that the children's attendance at Abington Senior High School is compulsory and that the practice of reading 10 verses from the Bible is also compelled by law. It also found that:

The reading of the verses, even without comment, possesses a devotional and religious character and constitutes in effect a religious observance. The devotional and religious nature of the morning exercises is made all the more apparent by the fact that the Bible reading is followed immediately by a recital in unison by the pupils of the Lord's Prayer. The fact that some pupils, or theoretically all pupils, might be excused from attendance at the exercises does not mitigate the obligatory nature of the ceremony for . . . Section 1516 . . . unequivocally requires the exercises to be held every school day in every school in the Commonwealth. The exercises are held in the school buildings and perforce are conducted by and under the authority of the local school authorities and during school sessions. Since the statute requires the reading of the 'Holy Bible,' a Christian document, the practice . . . prefers the Christian religion. The record demonstrates that it was the intention of . . . the Commonwealth . . . to introduce a religious ceremony into the public schools of the Commonwealth.

No. 119. In 1905 the Board of School Commissioners of Baltimore City adopted a rule pursuant to Art. 77, §202 of the Annotated Code of Maryland. The rule provided for the holding of opening exercises in the schools of the city, consisting primarily of the "reading, without comment, of a chapter in the Holy Bible and/or the use of the Lord's Prayer." The petitioners, Mrs. Madalyn Murray and her son, William J. Murray III, are both professed atheists. Following unsuccessful attempts to have the respondent school board rescind the rule, this suit was filed for mandamus to compel its rescission and cancellation. It was alleged that William was a student in a public school of the city and Mrs. Murray, his mother, was a taxpayer therein; that it was the practice under the rule to have a reading on each school morning from the King James version of the Bible; that at petitioners' insistence the rule was amended to permit children to be excused from the exercise on request of the parent and that William had been excused pursuant thereto; that nevertheless the rule as amended was in violation of the petitioners' rights "to freedom of religion under the First and Fourteenth Amendments" and in violation of "the principle of separation between church and state, contained therein. . . ." The petition particularized the petitioners' atheistic beliefs and stated that the rule, as practiced, violated their rights

in that it threatens their religious liberty by placing a premium on belief as against non-belief and subjects their freedom of conscience to the rule of the majority; it pronounces belief in God as the source of all moral and spiritual values, equating these values with religious values, and thereby renders sinister, alien and suspect the beliefs and ideals of your Petitioners, promoting doubt and question of their morality, good citizenship and good faith.

The respondents demurred and the trial court, recognizing that the demurrer admitted all facts well pleaded, sustained it without leave to amend. The Maryland Court of Appeals affirmed, the majority of four justices holding the exercise not in violation of the First and Fourteenth Amendments, with three justices dissenting. . . .

II.

It is true that religion has been closely identified with our history and government. As we said in *Engel* v.

Vitale, 370 U.S. 421, 434 (1962), "The history of man is inseparable from the history of religion. And . . . since the beginning of that history many people have devoutly believed that 'More things are wrought by prayer than this world dreams of.'" In *Zorach* v. *Clauson,* 343 U.S. 306, 313 (1952), we gave specific recognition to the proposition that "[w]e are a religious people whose institutions presuppose a Supreme Being." The fact that the Founding Fathers believed devoutly that there was a God and that the unalienable rights of man were rooted in Him is clearly evidenced in their writings, from the Mayflower Compact to the Constitution itself. This background is evidenced today in our public life through the continuance in our oaths of office from the Presidency to the Alderman of the final supplication, "So help me God." Likewise each House of the Congress provides through its Chaplain an opening prayer, and the sessions of this Court are declared open by the crier in a short ceremony, the final phrase of which invokes the grace of God. Again, there are such manifestations in our military forces, where those of our citizens who are under the restrictions of military service wish to engage in voluntary worship. Indeed, only last year an official survey of the country indicated that 64% of our people have church membership, Bureau of the Census, U.S. Department of Commerce, Statistical Abstract of the United States (83d. ed. 1962), 48, while less than 3% profess no religion whatever. . . . It can be truly said, therefore, that today, as in the beginning, our national life reflects a religious people who, in the words of Madison, are "earnestly praying, as . . . in duty bound, that the Supreme Lawgiver of the Universe . . . guide them into every measure which may be worthy of his [blessing.]"

III.

. . . Almost a hundred years ago in *Minor* v. *Board of Education of Cincinnati,* Judge Alphonso Taft, father of the revered Chief Justice, in an unpublished opinion stated the ideal of our people as to religious freedom as one of absolute equality before the law, of all religious opinions and sects. . . . The government is neutral, and, while protecting all, it prefers none, and it *disparages none.*

Before examining this "neutral" position in which the Establishment and Free Exercise Clauses of the First Amendment place our Government it is well that we discuss the reach of the Amendment under the cases of this Court.

First, this Court has decisively settled that the First Amendment's mandate that "Congress shall make no law respecting an establishment of religion, or prohibiting the free exercise thereof" has been made wholly applicable to the States by the Fourteenth Amendment. Twenty-three years ago in *Cantwell* v. *Connecticut* 310 U.S. 296, 303 (1940), this Court, through Mr. Justice Roberts, said:

The fundamental concept of liberty embodied in that [Fourteenth] Amendment embraces the liberties guaranteed by the First Amendment. The First Amendment declares that Congress shall make no law respecting an establishment of religion or prohibiting the free exercise thereof. The Fourteenth Amendment has rendered the legislatures of the states as incompetent as Congress to enact such laws. . . .

In a series of cases since *Cantwell* the Court has repeatedly reaffirmed that doctrine, and we do so now. . . .

Second, this Court has rejected unequivocally the contention that the Establishment Clause forbids only governmental preference of one religion over another. Almost 20 years ago in *Everson,* the Court said that "[n]either a state nor the Federal Government can set up a church. Neither can pass laws which aid one religion, aid all religions, or prefer one religion over another." . . . The same conclusion has been firmly maintained ever since that time . . . and we reaffirm it now.

While none of the parties to either of these cases has questioned these basic conclusions of the Court, both of which have been long established, recognized and consistently reaffirmed, others continue to question their history, logic and efficacy. Such contentions, in the light of the consistent interpretation in cases of this Court, seem entirely untenable and of value only as academic exercises.

IV.

The interrelationship of the Establishment and the Free Exercise Clauses was first touched upon by Mr. Justice Roberts for the Court in *Cantwell* v. *Connecticut,* where it was said that their "inhibition of legislation" had a double aspect. On the one hand, it forestalls compulsion by law of the acceptance of any creed or the practice of any form of worship. Freedom of conscience and freedom to adhere to such religious organization or form of worship as the individual may choose cannot be restricted by law. On the other hand, it safeguards the free exercise of the chosen form of religion. Thus the Amendment embraces two concepts,—freedom to believe and freedom to act. The first is absolute but, in the nature of things, the second cannot be.

A half dozen years later in *Everson* v. *Board of Education,* this Court, through *Mr. Justice Black,* stated that the "scope of the First Amendment . . . was designed forever to suppress" the establishment of religion or the prohibition of the free exercise thereof. In short, the Court held that the Amendment

requires the state to be a neutral in its relations with groups of religious believers and non-believers; it does not require the state to be their adversary. State power is no more to be used so as to handicap religions than it is to favor them. . . . Our constitutional policy . . . does not deny that the state can undertake or sustain them in any form or degree. For this reason the sphere of religious activity, as distinguished from the secular intellectual liberties, has been given the twofold protection and, as the state cannot forbid, neither can it perform or aid in performing the religious function. The dual prohibition makes that function altogether private. . . .

Only one year later the Court was asked to reconsider and repudiate the doctrine of these cases in *McCollum* v. *Board of Education*. It was argued that "historically the First Amendment was intended to forbid only government preference of one religion over another. . . . In addition they ask that we distinguish or overrule our holding in the *Everson* case that the Fourteenth Amendment made the 'establishment of religion' clause of the First Amendment applicable as a prohibition against the States." . . . The Court, with Mr. Justice Reed alone dissenting, was unable to "accept either of these contentions." . . .

In 1952 in *Zorach* v. *Clauson, Mr. Justice Douglas* for the Court reiterated:

There cannot be the slightest doubt that the First Amendment reflects the philosophy that Church and State should be separated. An so far as interference with the 'free exercise' of religion and an 'establishment' of religion are concerned, the separation must be complete and unequivocal. The First Amendment within the scope of

its coverage permits no exception; the prohibition is absolute. The First Amendment, however, does not say that in every and all respects there shall be a separation of Church and State. Rather, it studiously defines the manner, the specific ways, in which there shall be no concert or union or dependency one on the other. That is the common sense of the matter. 343 U.S. at 312.

. . . Finally, in *Engel* v. *Vitale,* only last year, these principles were so universally recognized that the Court without the citation of a single case and over the sole dissent of *Mr. Justice Stewart,* reaffirmed them. The Court found the 22-word prayer used in "New York's program of daily classroom invocation of God's blessings as prescribed in the Regent's prayer . . . [to be] a religious activity." . . . It held that "it is no part of the business of government to compose official prayers for any group of the American people to recite as a part of a religious program carried on by government." . . . In discussing the reach of the Establishment and Free Exercise Clauses of the First Amendment the Court said

Although these two clauses may in certain instances overlap, they forbid two quite different kinds of governmental encroachment upon religious freedom. The Establishment Clause, unlike the Free Exercise Clause, does not depend upon any showing of direct governmental compulsion and is violated by the enactment of laws which establish an official religion whether those laws operate directly to coerce nonobserving individuals or not. This is not to say of course, that laws officially prescribing a particular form of religious worship do not involve coercion of such individuals. When the power, prestige and financial support of government is placed behind a particular religious belief, the indirect coercive pressure upon religious minorities to conform to the prevailing officially approved religion is plain.

And in further elaboration the Court found that the "first and most immediate purpose [of the Establishment Clause] rested on the belief that a union of government and religion tends to destroy government and to degrade religion." . . . When government, the Court said, allies itself with one particular form of religion, the inevitable result is that it incurs "the hatred, disrespect and even contempt of those who held contrary beliefs." . . .

V.

The wholesome "neutrality" of which this Court's cases speak thus stems from a recognition of the teachings of history that powerful sects or groups might bring about a fusion of governmental and religious functions or a concert or dependency of one upon the other to the end that official support of the State or Federal Government would be placed behind the tenets of one or of all orthodoxies. This the Establishment Clause prohibits. And a further reason for neutrality is found in the Free Exercise Clause, which recognizes the value of religious training, teaching and observance and, more particularly, the right of every person to freely choose his own course with reference thereto, free of any compulsion from the state. This the Free Exercise Clause guarantees. Thus, as we have seen, the two clauses may overlap. As we have indicated, the Establishment Clause has been directly considered by this Court eight times in the past score of years and, with only one Justice dissenting on the point, it has consistently held that the clause withdrew all legislative power respecting religious belief or the expression thereof. The test may be stated as follows: what are the purpose and the primary effect of the enactment? If either is the advancement or inhibition of re-

ligion then the enactment exceeds the scope of legislative power as circumscribed by the Constitution. That is to say that to withstand the strictures of the Establishment Clause there must be a secular legislative purpose and a primary effect that neither advances nor inhibits religion . . . The Free Exercise Clause, likewise considered many times here, withdraws from legislative power, state and federal, the exertion of any restraint on the free exercise of religion. Its purpose is to secure religious liberty in the individual by prohibiting any invasions thereof by civil authority. Hence it is necessary in a free exercise case for one to show the coercive effect of the enactment as it operates against him in the practice of his religion. The distinction between the two clauses is apparent—a violation of the Free Exercise Clause is predicted on coercion while the Establishment Clause violation need not be so attended.

Applying the Establishment Clause principles to the cases at bar we find that the States are requiring the selection and reading at the opening of the school day of verses from the Holy Bible and the recitation of the Lord's Prayer by the students in unison. These exercises are prescribed as part of the curricular activities of students who are required by law to attend school. They are held in the school buildings under the supervision and with the participation of teachers employed in those schools. None of these factors, other than compulsory school attendance, was present in the program upheld in *Zorach* v. *Clauson.* The trial court in No. 142 has found that such an opening exercise is a religious ceremony and was intended by the State to be so. We agree with the trial court's finding as to the religious character of the exercises. Given that finding, the exercises and the law requiring them are in violation of the Establishment Clause.

There is no such specific finding as to the religious character of the exercises in No. 119, and the State contends (as does the State in No. 142) that the program is an effort to extend its benefits to all public school children without regard to their religious beliefs. Included within its secular purposes, it says, are the promotion of moral values, the contradiction trends of our times, the perpetuation of our institutions and the teaching of literature. The case came up on demurrer, of course, to a petition which alleged that the uniform practice under the rule had been to read from the King James version of the Bible and that the exercise was sectarian. The short answer, therefore, is that the religious character of the exercise was admitted by the State. But even if its purpose is not strictly religious, it is sought to be accomplished through readings, without comment, from the Bible. Surely the place of the Bible as an instrument of religion cannot be gainsaid, and the State's recognition of the pervading religious character of the ceremony is evident from the rule's specific permission of the alternative use of the Catholic Douay version as well as the recent amendment permitting nonattendance at the exercises. None of these factors is consistent with the contention that the Bible is here used either as an instrument for nonreligious moral inspiration or as a reference for the teaching of secular subjects.

The conclusion follows that in both cases the laws require religious exercises and such exercises are being conducted in direct violation of the rights of the appellees and petitioners. Nor are these required exercises mitigated by the fact that individual students may absent themselves upon parental request, for that fact furnishes no defense to a claim of unconstitutionality under the Establishment Clause. . . . Further, it is no defense to urge that the religious practices here may be relatively minor encroachments on the First Amendment. The breach of neutrality that is today a trickling stream may all too soon become a raging torrent and, in the words of Madison, "it is proper to take alarm at the first experiment on our liberties." . . .

It is insisted that unless these religious exercises are permitted a "religion of secularism" is established in the schools. We agree of course that the State may not establish a "religion of secularism" in the sense of affirmatively opposing or showing hostility to religion, thus "preferring those who believe in no religion over those who do believe." . . . We do not agree, however, that this decision in any sense has that effect. In addition, it might well be said that one's education is not complete without a study of comparative religion or the history of religion and its relationship to the advancement of civilization. It certainly may be said that the Bible is worthy of study for its literary and historic qualities. Nothing we have said here indicates that such study of the Bible or of religion, when presented objectively as part of a secular program of education, may not be effected consistently with the First Amendment. But the exercises here do not fall into those categories. They are religious exercises, required by the States in violation of the command of the First Amendment that the Government maintain strict neutrality, neither aiding nor opposing religion.

Finally, we cannot accept that the concept of neutrality, which does not permit a State to require a religious exercise even with the consent of the majority of those affected, collides with the majority's right to free exercise of religion. While the Free Exercise

Clause clearly prohibits the use of state action to deny the rights of free exercise to *anyone,* it has never meant that a majority could use the machinery of the State to practice its beliefs. . . .

The place of religion in our society is an exalted one, achieved through a long tradition of reliance on the home, the church and the inviolable citadel of the individual heart and mind. We have come to recognize through bitter experience that it is not within the power of government to invade that citadel, whether its purpose or effect be to aid or oppose, to advance or retard. In the relationship between man and religion, the State is firmly committed to a position of neutrality. Though the application of that rule requires interpretation of a delicate sort, the rule itself is clearly and concisely stated in the words of the First Amendment. Applying that rule to the facts of these cases, we affirm the judgment in No. 142. In No. 110, the judgment is reversed and the cause remanded to the Maryland Court of Appeals for further proceedings consistent with this opinion.

It is so ordered.

Justices BRENNAN, GOLDBERG and HARLAN concurring, Justice STEWART dissenting.

REACTIONS OF LEGAL PERIODICALS TO *SCHOOL DISTRICT* v. *SCHEMPP*

The Supreme Court's ruling in the Schempp case that Bible-reading exercises, although voluntary and without comment, in the public schools violate the Establishment of Religion Clause, coupled with its earlier ruling in the Engel case caused a flurry of public reaction among lay groups, some congressmen, and certain special interest groups.

Surprisingly, however, the Schempp case stirred comparatively mild controversy among a small number of law journals discussing it. Perhaps the reviewers exhausted their energies in analyzing *Engel* v. *Vitale* the preceding year. It was a common statement in school-prayer reviews, whether they criticized or praised the Engel result, that the then pending Bible-reading case would undoubtedly be disposed of in similar fashion. On the other hand, the relative recentness of the case coupled with the normal delays inherent in the publishing process may account for the paucity of legal journal commentary.

Support for the Schempp decision centered on the fact that it continued in the tradition of the Everson and Engel decisions. The Court was also hailed in some circles for its recognition that a society must achieve good citizenship in a secular manner devoid of governmental involvements in religion.

Criticism was raised in several reviews on grounds that the Court dictated an inflexible policy which was unrealistic. A charge was made in the *Iowa Law Review* (49:560) that the Court's apparent approach of accepting jurisdiction under the free exercise clause and rendering the decision under the establishment clause implies that any taxpayer, with or without injury, could obtain standing to sue. The mere fact that the Court even adjudicated the Engel and Schempp cases was considered poor judg-

ment in the *Washington Law Review* (38:657). There it was declared
that the Court should not concern itself with controversial cases involving
such slight injuries, at a time when the Court badly needs popular approval
for controversial decisions involving significant issues.

The support for the Schempp philosophy was more pronounced following the federal District Court decision, 177 F.Supp. 398, of 1959. The question was raised in *George Washington Law Review* (28:579) that if such
readings are merely secular in nature, then why must there be no comment? That moral training is a task for the home and Church was found
to be a controlling logical point in the *Villanova Law Review* (5:486), while
a need to distinguish between objectives for educational purposes and for
devotional purposes was recognized in the *Virginia Law Review* (45:1376).
Both reviewers stressed the grounds of the unconstitutionality that were
to be found in the subtle but real compulsion involved in programs of
this nature. Meanwhile, a position was taken in the *Ohio State Law Journal*
(20:701) that Bible reading itself was allowable, but that the consolidation
of it with recitation of the Lord's Prayer made the program essentially
devotional.

In summary, those who criticized the decision did so on the grounds
that our American heritage is religious, and the government should officially recognize the importance of religion in the schools.

REACTIONS OF EDUCATION PERIODICALS TO
SCHOOL DISTRICT v. *SCHEMPP*

The reaction in education journals to the Schempp case was not as
violent as it was for the Engel decision, but was just as varied. Again,
some articles regarded the decision as further clarifying the place of
religion in public schools. Other writers approved of the Court's action
in ridding the schools of religious instruction and making them neutral,
thereby insuring freedom of religion. The opposite stand was taken in
other articles which maintained the decision actually allowed coercion by
the state, because of compulsory education, to the detriment of free
exercise of religion.

L. O. Garber in *Nation's Schools* (72:50, 51, 1963) felt that the decision might result in driving the Bible out of public schools, but also
might "make a place there for God and religion." An article in the
National Educational Association Journal (52:55, 1963) did not consider
the Schempp decision to have driven the Bible out of the schools. It argued
that the Bible could still be used to study about religion and for its historical and literary qualities. The American Jewish Committee in *Religious
Education* (50:232, 1955) agreed that the Bible could not be considered a
religious book if it were used to study literature, but Bible reading in
any other form would be religious in nature. R. U. Smith in *Religious*

Education (59:443, 1964) concluded that the Court specifically endorsed and encouraged teaching about religion and offering elective courses in religion. However, L. R. Ward in *Religious Education* (59:446, 1964) said that there are too many practical difficulties in teaching objectively *about* religion.

W. W. Brickman in an editorial in *School and Society* (91:272, 1963) thought that instead of securing free exercise of religion, free from compulsion from the state, the decision had just the opposite effect in its attempt to secularize public schools. Since attending school is compulsory, the state in essence coerces parents to send their children to school. If parents want a non-secular education for their children, they then must bear private school expenses in addition to public school taxes. This financial burden forces many parents to send their children to the less desired public school. Brickman argued that this is coercion by the state against individuals trying to follow their religious beliefs. O. C. D'Amour in *Religious Education* (59:455, 1964) agreed with this position. If our traditional forms of religion are withdrawn from the public schools, something has to take its place and that something is the religion of secularism, he concluded.

A series of articles in the November-December 1964 issue of *Religious Education* by religious and educational leaders supported Justice Clark's majority opinion that the public schools should objectively include religion as part of the curriculum.

Reaction by religious leaders to the Schempp decision seemed to indicate that the decision was generally supported by Protestant and Jewish leaders, while Roman Catholics tended to oppose it. The different stands were presented in an article in the *National Educational Association Journal* (52:56, 1963). In a 1963 policy statement, the National Council of Churches said that churches should not expect help from the state to fulfill its mission. Neither the churches nor the state should use public schools as a vehicle stressing a particular creed or practice. Rabbi J. Pring, President of the American Jewish Congress, agreed with and approved of the Court's decision as an aid to religious freedom. James Francis Cardinal McIntyre took just the opposite stand and said that the acceptance of secularism as evidenced by the Schempp decision was a denial of religious freedom and the American tradition.

In *Nation's Schools* (72:43, 1963) a poll similar to the one taken after the Engel decision, showed that 48 per cent of the school administrators personally disagreed with the Schempp decision and 52 per cent approved. Reactions to the question of supporting a constitutional amendment permitting Bible reading or recitation of prayers showed 57 per cent in favor of such an amendment and 43 per cent opposed. The poll was based on a 4 per cent proportional sampling of 16,000 administrators. Forty per cent of the administrators responded.

THE SCHEMPP DECISION AS CONTROLLING PRECEDENT

The uproar following the Bible-reading decision by the Supreme Court was revealed in subsequent litigation involving Bible-reading programs on both federal and state levels. Decisions were handed down by two United States district courts, two state supreme courts, and the Supreme Court itself. The Schempp ruling was considered controlling in each instance.

The first instance of acquiescence was in *Sills* v. *Board of Education,* 84 N.J. Super. 63, 200 A.2d 817 (1963). There the superior court of New Jersey was faced with New Jersey statutes "almost identical," in the court's opinion, to the Baltimore rule and Pennsylvania statute in the Murray and Schempp cases. One statute required the reading without comment, in each public school classroom, of at least five verses from the Old Testament. Another act forbade all religious services in the public schools except Bible-reading and Lord's Prayer exercises. Following a declaration by the New Jersey attorney general that both acts were within the strictures of the Schempp decision and therefore unconstitutional, the commissioner of education notified all county and local superintendents that such practices were unconstitutional and prohibited in the public schools.

Subsequently, a local board of education, in passing a resolution to continue Bible-reading exercises, declared that the United States Supreme Court decisions were not directly applicable to the pertinent New Jersey statutes. The court, after noting the similarity of the statutes, declared that it is a long-standing doctrine that one does not have to be a party to a case to be bound by its rulings, and that law and order must prevail. Furthermore, such a resolution would cause the school's teachers to violate their oath of allegiance to the United States Constitution and could subject them to federal criminal prosecution. An indication of possible future judicial thinking concerning church and state was injected: "A reading of the Abington and Murray cases leads the court to the conclusion that any law which requires religious exercises in the public schools is violative of the United States Constitution,"

Similarly, the high court of Massachusetts affirmed, without comment, in *Attorney General* v. *School Committee,* Mass., 199 N.E.2d 553 (1964), an order of a single justice enjoining a school committee from ordering continuation of Bible-reading and prayer exercises in the public schools of the municipality.

Comparable statutes in Delaware were attacked in *Johns* v. *Allen,* 231 F.Supp. 852 (1964). However, an attorney general's opinion there had upheld the statutes, and the state board of education had directed continuance of Bible reading and recitation of the Lord's Prayer. Against the defendant's contention that the prescribed exercises were of a cultural, educational and moral nature rather than religious, the court determined that the statutes violated the Establishment of Religion Clause of the First Amendment.

JUDICIAL MISGIVINGS OVER THE SCHEMPP DECISION

A three-judge federal district court voided in *Adams* v. *Engelking,* 232 F.Supp. 666 (1964), an Idaho statute requiring daily reading of the Bible in all public schools of the state. While declaring the act invalid and unenforceable because of its conflict with the Establishment of Religion Clause of the First Amendment, the court declared, "While members of the court may have personal reservations, we unanimously agree that the issue is settled by the United States Supreme Court ruling in . . . Schempp. . . ."

That the basic issue of church-state separation has not been settled is evidenced in *Chamberlin* v. *Dade County, Board of Public Instruction,* 84 S.Ct. 1272 (1964). Injunctions had been sought in the lower courts to enjoin regular reading of Bible verses in public school assemblies and classrooms, regular recitation of the Lord's Prayer and other religious sectarian prayers, conduct of religious and sectarian baccalaureate programs, conduct of religious census among children, and conduct of religious tests for qualification for employment of teachers.

Relief was denied by the Florida supreme court, at 143 So.2d 21 (1962), above, and an appeal was taken to the United States Supreme Court, 83 S.Ct. 1684 (1963). There, in a *per curiam* opinion, the lower judgment was vacated and the case remanded to the supreme court of Florida for further consideration in light of the Schempp ruling. On remand at 160 So.2d 97 (1964), the Florida court in apparent defiance of the United States Supreme Court again upheld the religious practices. It declared specifically that the statute relating to Bible reading was intended merely as a secular means of inculcating good moral training.

Upon appeal to the United States Supreme Court, the judgment with respect to prayer and devotional Bible reading was reversed. However, the appeal as to the other questions raised was dismissed "for want of properly presented federal questions."

Mr. Justice Douglas, joined by Mr. Justice Black, concurred in part:

> I join in reversing the Supreme Court of Florida on the main issue in the case.
> The "other questions raised" which the Court refuses to consider because not "properly presented" involve the constitutionality under the First and Fourteenth Amendments of baccalaureate services in the schools, a religious census among pupils, and a religious test for teachers. The Florida Supreme Court disposed of those issues on the authority of *Doremus* v. *Board of Education,* 342 U.S. 429, which held that a taxpayer lacks standing to challenge religious exercises in the public schools. Irrespective of *Doremus* v. *Board of*

Education, supra, I think it is arguable that appellant-taxpayers do have standing to challenge these practices.

I think, however, that two of those "other questions"—the baccalaureate services and the religious census—do not present substantial federal questions, and so I concur in the dismissal of the appeal as to them. As to the religious test for teachers, [Applicants for teaching positions are required to answer the question, "Do you believe in God?" Religious attitudes are also considered in making promotions.] I think a substantial question is presented. Cf. *Torcaso* v. *Watkins,* 367 U.S. 488. I would therefore put that question down for argument, postponing the question of jurisdiction to the merits.

SUMMARY

In 1963, when in its momentous decision in the Schempp case the Supreme Court struck down Bible-reading exercises in the public schools, it invalidated practices as old as the public school system itself and also one of the most widespread religiously oriented programs common to many public schools. There is no question that the Schempp decision profoundly affected state laws and educational programming in many states. There also is little doubt that the decision reflects a sophisticated awareness on the Court's part of the increasing pluralism of American society and the clear doctrinal differences among sects as to which is the "true" version of the Bible.

At the time of the Schempp ruling the constitutions and statutes of the states reflected an abiding desire to keep public funds from supporting sectarian institutions of any type. These enactments, however, were ambiguous as to what practices constituted sectarian instruction.

Thus, when the Court finally acted on the subject, thirty-seven states permitted Bible reading in their public schools. In only eleven states were Bible-reading exercises regarded as sectarian instruction prior to the Schempp decision. The high courts of eight states found such exercises to violate either the states' constitutions or statutes. On the other hand, the courts of fourteen states had upheld the constitutionality of Bible-reading exercises. The overwhelming number of state high courts which had upheld programs of this nature prior to 1963, however, insisted that the reading be done without comment, and attendance could not be made compulsory.

The state courts upholding Bible-reading exercises shared a number of underlying premises. The major one was that the Bible was not a sectarian book since they could see no significant differences between the King James Version of the Protestants and the Douay Version of the Roman Catholics. Since Christianity was so interwoven in the fabric of our government, these courts concluded, to prohibit such practices would violate our historic traditions. Moreover, the courts felt that Bible reading was important to an understanding of history and literature.

Prior to the Schempp decision, the state courts which struck down this practice as unconstitutional found the Bible clearly sectarian and concluded that such practices violated the religious sensibilities of non-Christians as well as nonbelievers. Programs of this nature violated the American tradition of church-state separation because in practice the King James Version of the Bible was the one normally used and it lacked the Apocryphal books of the Douay Version as well as containing references to the Christology of the New Testament which is objectionable to the Jews. Moreover, the democracy of the classroom was destroyed even though such exercises were voluntary since self-exclusion stigmatized the non-participating student in the eyes of his peers for he was leaving because of apparent hostility to a book which was revered by those students remaining.

The Schempp case ranks in prominence and controversial nature with the Court's decisions outlawing racial discrimination in the public schools and the decisions curtailing malapportionment in state legislatures and congressional districts. Furthermore, if possible, more public misunderstanding arose from the Schempp decision than in either of the other two areas. Perhaps for this reason, those opposed to the segregation decisions and those dealing with reapportionment may have joined forces to mount a most thorough attack designed to undercut the Supreme Court's authority through a constitutional amendment (known generally as the Becker Amendment).

In this connection, many well-intentioned laymen were convinced that the Court had completely banned the Bible from the schools. They did not understand that in both the Engel and Schempp cases the Court specifically pointed out that its decision did not prohibit the use of the Bible in the study of history or literature. The decision, in the Schempp case, of course, said merely that the Bible could not be used as a devotional tool.

Despite the public furor over the Schempp ruling, reactions in legal periodicals were scant and reflected little of the legal or public policy-making questions inherent in the case. Education journal reaction was equally subdued when contrasted to the stir caused by the Engel ruling. One public opinion poll showed that 52 per cent of school administrators favored the decision while 48 per cent opposed it.

Unlike some related areas the Supreme Court's ruling in the Schempp case seems to be accepted as a fact of law by courts of the land. Since its action on that case, two state high courts and two federal district courts have been faced with cases involving similar issues. In all instances, the courts have followed the Schempp doctrine and declared Bible-reading exercises in the public schools unconstitutional. Moreover, state courts have cast jaundiced eyes upon utilizing public school facilities to distribute Gideon Bibles.

Perhaps this is one area of church-state relations affecting public education that is relatively stabilized for the foreseeable future.

CHAPTER FIVE

State Distribution of Textbooks

† †

SCHOOL BOARDS generally are authorized by constitutional and statutory provisions to provide free textbooks to the public schools. However, similar distribution of textbooks to parochial schools has provoked much controversy, and sharply divided judicial opinions.

The decisions favoring an all-inclusive distribution of school books are based on the philosophy that such textbooks are given to the pupils, and thus do not constitute an aid to religion. The opposing position found in other cases holds that the textbooks are given directly to the (religious) schools, and thus constitute an unconstitutional aid to religion. Thus, this has been the controlling rationale in instances where the distribution was limited exclusively to public schools.

Until 1929, state legislatures, courts, and school boards followed a general policy of furnishing free textbooks only to public schools. State constitutional provisions prohibiting the appropriation of public funds for the support of any sectarian school were considered sufficient to deny equal distributions in private or parochial schools.

In this connection, an early case concerned the constitutional validity of an Ohio statute providing that pupils attending the public schools should be furnished school books free of charge. There, in *Mooney* v. *Bell*, 8 Ohio N.P. 658, 11 Ohio Dec. 786 (1901), a lower court could find neither a violation of the equal protection clause of the Fourteenth Amendment of the United States Constitution nor a violation of the provision of the Ohio constitution directing the general assembly to secure a thorough and efficient system of common schools throughout the state. The court, in denying the contention that the statute discriminated against those preferring to attend a nonpublic school, pointed out that the public schools were available to everyone of school age. The court further characterized the purpose of the statute as recognizing the preservation of the state.

The issue of the child-benefit theory began to materialize in *Smith* v. *Donahue*, 202 App. Div. 656, 195 N.Y.S. 715 (1922) below. There, the appellate division of the New York supreme court determined that the furnishing by the state of free textbooks to parochial schools constituted a grant directly to those schools rather than to their pupils. Consequently, the distribution violated the state constitutional prohibition against public financing of any denominational school. The court went on to say that even a statute clearly designed to furnish books to the pupils and not to the schools would still constitute at least an indirect aid to religious schools, in violation of the same constitutional provision.

† † *SMITH* v. *DONAHUE*
202 A.D. 656, 195 N.Y.S. 715 (1922).

Judge VANKIRK delivered the opinion of the court:

The principal question and in fact the only question urged seriously by the plaintiff is whether or not public funds may be used to furnish text-books and ordinary school supplies to pupils of private schools, or schools other than the public district schools, located in the city of Ogdensburg. . . . The article [in the Laws of 1917] provides for boards of education in the several cities of the state. In section 868, subd. 4, is the following:

To purchase and furnish such apparatus, maps, globes, books, furniture and other equipment and supplies as may be necessary for the proper and efficient management of the schools and other educational, social and recreational activities and interest under its management and control. To provide text-books or other supplies to all the children attending the schools of such cities in which free text-books or other supplies are lawfully provided prior to the time this act goes into effect.

This is one of the subdivisions of the section defining the powers and duties of boards of education in cities. Unless this subdivision authorizes the board of education of the city of Ogdensburg to furnish textbooks and supplies to schools other than the public schools in the district, or the pupils of

such, it is conceded that the judgment appealed from is erroneous.

To control and furnish education for the youth of the state is a governmental function, which was not delegated to the federal government, but reserved to the states; and the legislative department of each state has full control of its school and educational activities. In the exercise of this power the Legislature of this state has enacted the Education Law. Laws 1909, c. 21, as amended. In this law public schools were authorized in school districts, and, by the act of 1917, supra, in cities which are constituted school districts. These districts are civil divisions of the state, founded for the exercise of this governmental function. The boards of education have full control of the public schools and in the cities have the care, custody, and control of all school property or other property of the city used for educational, social, or recreational work, and not specifically placed by law under the control of some other body or officer and prescribe rules and regulations for the preservation of such property (section 868, subd. 3); also, in subdivision 5:

To establish and maintain such free elementary schools, high schools, training schools, vocational and industrial schools, kindergartens, technical schools, night schools, part-time or continuation schools, vacation schools, schools for adults, open air schools, schools for the mentally and physically defective children, or such other schools or classes as such board shall deem necessary to meet the needs and demands of the city—

also to direct and control the courses of study and the text-books to be used. Each board of education of a school district or city is a body corporate (section 300); and all their duties are confined to the public, educational, social, and recreational activities of the city, devoted to the welfare of the children; they have no authority or control over any other schools than public schools.

The first inquiry is whether or not the furnishing of "textbooks and ordinary school supplies" to parochial schools is in conflict with the Constitution. In the First Amendment to the federal Constitution is this:

Freedom of Religion, of Speech, of the Press and Right of Petition.—Congress shall make no law respecting an establishment of religion, or prohibiting the free exercise thereof.

In article 1 of the state Constitution is this:

Sec. 3. *Freedom of Worship—Religious Liberty.* The free exercise and enjoyment of religious profession and worship, without discrimination or preference, shall forever be allowed in this state to all mankind; and no person shall be rendered incompetent to be a witness on account of his opinions on matters of religious belief, but the liberty of conscience hereby secured shall not be so construed as to excuse acts of licentiousness, or justify practices inconsistent with the peace and safety of this state.

The direct provision of the Constitution which bears upon this case is in article 9, which refers to common schools and the university.

Section 1 is:

The legislature shall provide for the maintenance and support . . . of free common schools, wherein all the children of the state may be educated.

Section 4 is:

No Aid to Denominational Schools. Neither the state, nor any subdivision thereof, shall use its property or credit or any public money, or authorize or permit either to be used, directly or indirectly, in aid of maintenance, other than for examination or inspection, of any school or institution of learning wholly or in part under the control or direction of any religious denomination, or in which any denominational tenet or doctrine is taught.

At no time has it been the intent of government in our republic to permit the union of secular and religious education in any public school. The state has ever been jealous, since its organization, to protect against appearance of an encroachment upon the right of free worship of God as the conscience of the citizen may choose and direct. No law, has ever been permitted, or practice to that end condoned, respecting any establishment of religion or prohibiting the free exercise of religious belief without discrimination or preference or interference in any manner. . . .

. . . .

Under article 1, § 3, of the Constitution, and similar provisions in Constitutions of other states, which assure the free exercise and enjoyment of religious worship and belief without restraint, the reading of the Bible has been excluded from many of the public schools under protest that such practice was in conflict with the regulations and beliefs of a religious denomination, and, the public schools being furnished for all the children, the reading of the Bible was excluded in order that there could be no restraint upon their enjoyment of the public schools and without prejudicing their religious beliefs. The teaching of religious beliefs and principles to the youth of the state is recognized by all as of high importance to the welfare of the citizen, but still subordinate to freedom of conscience. The state may not join religious instruction with secular education, but a church may; and the parochial schools are furnished by the Roman Catholic Church, in order that, along with secular education, the youth of the church may receive instructions in its religious beliefs and rules. In accord with its principles in that respect, the state will not interfere, but it may not assist in aid of any distinct religious tenet. From these general observations, we turn more directly to the issues.

In practice in the city of Ogdensburg the principal and a teacher of a parochial school have made requisitions for the number of books of each kind required for the school, for readers, arithmetics, spellers, geographies, English, and history. These books have been procured by the board of education and delivered to the school; but the defendants say that books and supplies, while so procured and furnished, are furnished under the above section of the Education Law (section 868, subd. 4) to the children attending the schools, and not to the schools. Even though we accept the statute as meaning that the books and supplies are to be furnished to the pupils, and not to the school, we think the act plainly comes within the prohibition of the Constitution; if not directly in aid of the parochial schools, it certainly is in indirect aid. The scholars do not use text-books

and ordinary school supplies apart from their studies in the school. They want them for the sole purpose of their work there. There is no question but that the text-books and ordinary supplies are furnished direct to the public schools; there is no thought that they are furnished to the scholars as distinct from the schools; neither can there be such a thought in the case of the parochial schools.

It is claimed on the part of the defendants, and is found by the court, that the parochial schools of the city of Ogdensburg are recognized by law and by the education department of the state of New York as a part of the education system of the state. We think this is a mistaken view. The policy of this state is not only to furnish opportunities for education, but there are compulsory provisions of the Education Law, under article 23, entitled "Compulsory Education." . . . Every child between 7 and 16 must attend schools, except that, between 14 and 16 years of age, they need not attend, if engaged in a useful occupation. The state has not required that every child shall attend the public schools, but it has required that either they attend the public schools, or, if they attend elsewhere, they must be taught in the same subjects in English by a competent teacher.

It was the education of the youth that the state has required, and not this education necessarily in the public schools; but, if the education was to be had in a school other than the public schools, then it was necessary that those schools should be under the inspection of the state authorities. The state authorities have control of the education of the pupil and to require their attendance in school. In no sense does the state assume to employ teachers of schools other than the public schools; but it insists that in all schools other than the public schools, where children of compulsory school age are attending, the teachers must have the required qualifications, and there must be examinations to test the work done, and there must be attendance officers to insure attendance. . . . The only reference in the Education Law to the schools, other than the public schools, is in these provisions for compulsory education, and in no wise are any schools other than the public schools recognized as a part of the educational system of the state in the primary grades. This is in harmony with that expression in article 9, § 4 (supra), of the state Constitution, forbidding state aid "other than for examination or inspection."

We may turn now to a specific examination of the provisions of this subdivision 4 of section 868. The reading of the section with the other provisions of the Education Law shows that all its requirements, including the "powers and duties" of boards of education, refer to those schools and institutions which are under the control of the board of education and which are public institutions. The first sentence of this subdivision refers to several activities necessary for the proper and efficient management of schools, which are under the management and control of the board of education, and the last sentence provides for furnishing textbooks and other supplies "to all the children attending the schools of such cities in which free textbooks or other supplies are lawfully provided prior to the time this act goes into effect." The natural meaning of the wording of this section would apply to those schools only in such cities which are under the management and control of the board of education. There was no statute at the time containing general provisions

for the furnishing of text-books or supplies to the children of schools of cities. The only law under which the children attending the schools in Ogdensburg were supplied with their text-books was chapter 187, Laws of 1903. This act applied to the city of Ogdensburg alone; it is not a general law:

It provides (section 1), the electors of the city of Ogdensburg "are authorized to vote upon the question of furnishing at the expense of such city free text-books and ordinary school supplies for the use of the pupils of the school district of said city below the academic grade."

It is to be observed that these things were not to be furnished to the pupils, but were to be furnished, apparently to the schools "for the use of the pupils of the school district."

[Other sections provided that the moneys would be levied and collected in the school district of said city, and that the board of education would retain ownership of all books so furnished.]

The expression "pupils of the school district below the academic grade" naturally refers to the pupils of the public school where these grades are recognized. The moneys are to be raised as other moneys for school purposes are to be raised. They are to be used "for the use of the pupils of the several schools of the school district of the city and for no other purpose." The several schools there referred to, we think, considering all the provisions of the Education Law, are the public schools of the district under the control of the board of education. No other schools are "schools of the school district." There may be other schools in the district, but they are not the schools of the district; the parochial schools are schools of the parish, restricted to the parish, and there is nothing which implies that the books and supplies are to be furnished to the pupils as distinguished from the school. They are for the use of the pupils of the school district, to be furnished to the schools by the board of education, and they are the property of the board of education. A school district is a district of and for the public schools; it was organized as such and exists as such. The school is not the building and its equipment; it is the organization, the union of all the elements in the organization, to furnish education in some branch of learning—the arts or sciences or literature. It is the institution, and the teachers and scholars together, that make it up. The pupils are a part of the school.

Chapter 187, Laws of 1903, and chapter 786, Laws of 1917, are constitutional, but they do not bear the construction contended for by defendants. If the sections of these statutes complained of bore the construction contended for by defendants, our opinion is that they would be unconstitutional. We understand ordinary school supplies would mean pens, pencils, ink, paper, pads, slates—the ordinary things used by scholars in schools. These supplies are to be furnished in the same manner and to the same party as textbooks. It seems to us to be giving a strained and unusual meaning to words if we hold that the books and the ordinary school supplies, when furnished for the use of pupils, is a furnishing to the pupils, and not a furnishing in aid or maintenance of a school of learning. It seems very plain that such furnishing is at least indi-

rectly in aid of the institution, and that, if not in actual violation of the words, it is in violation of the true intent and meaning, of the Constitution, and in consequence equally unconstitutional. . . .

. . . .

The judgment dismissing the complaint, with costs, is reversed, and judgment is directed in accord with the foregoing opinion in favor of the plaintiff, restraining the defendants and all officers or agents acting in their behalf from purchasing or delivering text-books and ordinary school supplies for the use of pupils of schools in the city of Ogdensburg other than those public schools which are under the control and management of the board of education of the city of Ogdensburg.

. . . [W]e find that the parochial schools of the city of Ogdensburg are not a part of the education system of the state; that those schools are not "schools of the school district," but are "schools of the parish," and the pupils of those schools are not pupils of the school district, within the meaning of chapter 187 of Laws of 1903, or chapter 786 of Laws of 1917; that those schools are not schools of the city of Ogdensburg in which free text-books or other school supplies were lawfully provided for prior to the time chapter 786 of Laws of 1917 went into effect; that, under the Constitution of the state, text-books or school supplies cannot be furnished by defendants to the parochial schools, or the pupils of parochial schools, in the city of Ogdensburg.

THE SUPREME COURT RULES

The child-benefit argument triumphed in 1930, when the United States Supreme Court arrested the judicial trend of invalidating textbook distribution to nonpublic schools. In *Cochran* v. *Louisiana State Board of Education,* 281 U.S. 370 (1930), below, the Supreme Court affirmed the lower courts' refusals to grant an injunction to restrain the State Board of Education and certain other officials from expending tax funds for the purchase of free school books. No objection to such a policy could be found by the Court under the Fourteenth Amendment, since the books provided to private schools were granted to and for the use of the children and were the same as those furnished for public schools and were not religious or sectarian in character.

The Louisiana supreme court had followed a similar policy of allowing state distribution of free textbooks a year earlier in two companion cases, *Borden* v. *Louisiana State Board of Education,* 168 La. 1005, 123 So. 655 (1929), and *Bossier Parish School Board* v. *Louisiana State Board of Education,* 168 La. 1033, 123 So. 665 (1929). There, two statutes together authorized appropriations for school books, and directed the state board of education to provide free school books to school children, regardless of the type of school, public or private, they attended. For a thorough discussion of the judicial treatment of the above cases as well as the others involving free distribution of school books, consult *American Law Reports, Annotated,* 2d (93:985–91).

† † COCHRAN v. LOUISIANA STATE BOARD OF EDUCATION

281 U.S. 370, 50 S. CT. 335, 74 L. ED. 913 (1930).

Mr. Chief Justice HUGHES delivered the opinion of the Court, saying in part:

The appellants, as citizens and taxpayers of the State of Louisina, brought this suit to restrain the State Board of Educaion and other state officials from expending any part of the severance tax fund in purchasing school books and in supplying them free of cost to the school children of the State, under Acts No. 100 and No. 143 of 1928, upon the ground that the legislation violated specified provisions of the constitution of the State and also section 4 of Article IV and the Fourteenth Amendment of the Federal Constitution. The Supreme Court of the State affirmed the judgment of the trial court,

which refused to issue an injunction. . . .

Act No. 100 of 1928 provided that the severance tax fund of the State, after allowing funds and appropriations as required by the state constitution, should be devoted "first, to supplying school books to the school children of the State." The Board of Education was directed to provide "school books for school children free of cost to such children." Act No. 143 of 1928 made appropriations in accordance with the above provisions.

The Supreme Court of the State, following its decision in *Borden* v. *Louisiana State Board of Education,* 168

La. 1005, held that these acts were not repugnant to either the state or the Federal Constitution.

. . . The contention of the appellant under the Fourteenth Amendment is that taxation for the purchase of school books constituted a taking of private property for a private purpose. . . . The purpose is said to be to aid private, religious, sectarian, and other schools not embraced in the public educational system of the State by furnishing textbooks free to the children attending such private schools. The operation and effect of the legislation in question were described by the Supreme Court of the State as follows:

One may scan the acts in vain to ascertain where any money is appropriated for the purchase of school books for the use of any church, private, sectarian or even public school. The appropriations were made for the specific purpose of purchasing school books for the use of the school children of the state, free of cost to them. It was for their benefit and the resulting benefit to the state that the appropriations were made. True, these children attend some school, public or private, the latter, sectarian or non-sectarian, and that the books are to be furnished them for their use, free of cost, whichever they attend. The schools, however, are not the beneficiaries of these appropriations. They obtain nothing from them, nor are they relieved of a single obligation, because of them. The school children and the state alone are the beneficiaries. It is also true that the sectarian schools, which some of the children attend, instruct their pupils in religion, and books are used for that purpose, but one may search diligently the acts, through without result, in an effort to find anything to the effect that it is the purpose of the state to furnish religious books for the use of such children. . . . What the statutes contemplate is that the same books that are furnished children attending public schools shall be furnished children attending private schools. This is the only practical way of interpreting and executing the statutes, and this is what the state board of education is doing. Among these books, naturally none is to be expected, adapted to religious instruction.

The Court also stated, although the point is not of importance in relation to the Federal question, that it was "only the use of the books that is granted to the children, or, in other words, the books are lent to them."

Viewing the statute as having the effect thus attributed to it, we can not doubt that the taxing power of the State is exerted for a public purpose. The legislation does not segregate private schools, or their pupils, as its beneficiaries or attempt to interfere with any matters of exclusively private concern. Its interest is education, broadly; its method, comprehensive. Individual interests are aided only as the common interest is safeguarded.

Judgment affirmed.

REACTIONS OF LEGAL PERIODICALS TO *COCHRAN* v. *LOUISIANA STATE BOARD OF EDUCATION*

The Cochran decision received qualified support in *Law Notes* (34:233). There the reviewer, noting that private interests were not segregated for a special benefit, stated, "Individual interests are aided only as the common interest is safeguarded." He did, however, raise the question of how far the "child benefit" theory should or would go.

A similar question was raised in the *Illinois Law Review* (25:547) but in a more critical context. Expressing his concern over whether the agency which furnished the free textbooks would remain impartial in terms of the doctrines contained in said books, the reviewer conceded that the field of mathematics is a safe one. However, he quickly pointed out that the "histories of Galileo and Copernicus would lead us to believe that astronomy is a dangerous one." Considering all textbooks on biology, anthropology, history, and philosophy to be equally dangerous, he concluded that the whole policy of furnishing free textbooks "may be a questionable one."

REACTIONS OF OTHER PERIODICALS TO
COCHRAN v. *LOUISIANA STATE BOARD OF EDUCATION*

Reaction to the Cochran case was scattered and slight. Most periodicals took no notice of the decision.

An article in *Commonweal* (12:35, 1930) called the Cochran case a "decision of far-reaching importance." The author considered the possibility of some undesirable implications ensuing from the case. "May it not be deduced . . . that state educational authorities might justifiably claim other forms of control [besides textbooks] in the interest of education. . . ."

One article in *School and Society* (31:637, 1930) gave parts of the Supreme Court's rationale but did not discuss the merits of the case or its policy consequences. Several other articles were concerned with the general topic of textbooks, but the reviewers did not mention the case at hand. They dealt with legislative enactments and judicial decisions affecting the adoption, sale, and use of textbooks, and relations between state agencies and textbook publishers. But the question of providing textbooks for private schools was not mentioned.

AFTERMATH OF THE COCHRAN CASE

The Cochran rationale was followed by the Mississippi supreme court in *Chance* v. *Mississippi State Textbook Rating & Purchasing Board,* 190 Miss. 453, 200 So. 706 (1941). There, the court denied the appellant's allegation that a statute providing for free distribution of textbooks in the free public elementary schools and in all other elementary schools with equivalent standards violated state constitutional provisions denying religious sects to share in any of the educational funds of the states. Declaring that the pupils' needs should be emphasized rather than a strained construction of the statute, the court conceded that an incidental aid might accrue to the institution. It went on, however, to characterize the situation wherein a public-school student must give up his free textbooks if he chooses to attend a qualified parochial school as a "denial of equal privileges on sectarian grounds."

The Chance decision was characterized in the *Bill of Rights Review* (1:307) as allowing an invalid benefit to a sectarian school, in a situation where the public interests and the private interests were indivisible. The reviewer, noting that "courts have consistently invalidated such measures," argued that the instant appropriation should not stand even though it served a public purpose.

The focus of attention in *The Jurist* (2:370) was upon what its reviewer termed the "keen" rationale of the court in declaring that constitutional separation of church and state forbids only "the control of one over the other." The reviewer agreed that the state should not deny common benefits to any pupil because of his religious creed.

Shortly after the Chance case, however, the supreme court of South Dakota took a dim view of the point of view expressed in both the Cochran and Chance cases. While refusing to consider the constitutional question in *Haas* v. *Independent School District,* 69 S.D. 303, 9N.W.2d 707 (1943), the court ruled that the statute in question did not intend to empower or require public school corporations to aid any persons not enrolled in any part of the public school system of the state. The right of a sectarian school pupil to receive free textbooks from public funds of the state was thereby denied.

Two decades later, the supreme court of Oregon declared in *Dickman* v. *School District,* 232 Ore. 238, 366 P.2d 533 (1961), below, that a statute providing for the free and equal use of textbooks by all pupils could not be held constitutional if it permitted the district school board to supply free textbooks to church and parochial schools within its district. The court stated that the child-benefit theory must be qualified, because the pupil is benefitted to some extent by all educational aids. Otherwise, there would be no limit to the expenditure of public funds for educational purposes, the court asserted. After declaring that the expenditure of public funds to provide free textbooks was a function of the educational process, the court determined that the aid in question was extended to the pupil only as he was a member of the school he attended. The court reasoned, therefore, that such aid in reality specifically aided the schools themselves, the accompanying aid to the pupils notwithstanding.

The United States Supreme Court refused to grant certiorari in the Dickman case at 371 U.S. 823 (1962), thus causing speculation in some quarters as to whether the contemporary Supreme Court has reservations about the Cochran ruling of 1930.

† † DICKMAN v. SCHOOL DISTRICT NO. 62C

232 ore. 238, 366 p.2d 533 (1961).

Judge o'connell delivered the opinion of the court:

This is a suit in equity brought by plaintiff taxpayers against School District No. 62C, its board and clerk, to enjoin defendants from supplying textbooks without charge for the use of pupils enrolled in St. John's The Apostle School, a parochial school maintained and operated by the Catholic church. Plaintiffs also seek a judicial declaration that the socalled free textbook statute (ORS 337.150), under which distribution was made to the St. John's school and other parochial schools, does not authorize defendants to supply textbooks free of charge to church or parochial schools, or if the statute is so construed that it be declared unconstitutional.

. . . .

The statute in question, ORS 337.150, reads as follows:

337.150 (1) Each district school board shall, in the manner specified by ORS 328.520 and 328.525, provide textbooks, prescribed or authorized by law, for the free and equal use of all pupils residing in its district and enrolled in and actually attending standard elementary schools or grades seven or eight of standard secondary schools.

(2) For the purpose of ORS 328.520, 328.525 and 337.150 to 337.250 a school shall be standard when it meets the standards of the State Board of Education, except with respect to those standards applying to the ratio of pupils to the acre of school site, the square feet of classroom floor space per pupil and the ratio of pupils to teachers in classrooms, and when all teachers engaged in classroom instruction in said school hold a valid Oregon teaching certificate of the

proper teaching level. The holding of such a teacher's certificate shall be evidenced by annual registration with the county school superintendent of the county in which the school is situated.

Plaintiffs attack the constitutionality of the statute on four grounds; (1) it authorizes state aid to religion at public expense in violation of the First Amendment to the United States Constitution as made applicable to the states by the Fourteenth; (2) the furnishing of such textbooks constitutes a benefit to religious institutions contrary to the provisions of Article I, § 5 of the Oregon Constitution; (3) it, in effect, imposes a tax for a non-public purpose and thus deprives plaintiffs of property without due process of law; and (4) it authorizes the expenditure of money not exclusively for the support and maintenance of the common schools and is, therefore, in violation of Article VIII, § 2 of the Oregon Constitution.

Plaintiffs rely principally upon the first two grounds in attacking the constitutionality of the statute. The trial court held ORS 337.150 constitutional. Plaintiffs appeal.

For a period of several years the defendant district has furnished free textbooks for the use of the pupils of St. John's school. In a period of three school years these books have cost the district approximately $4,000. The books were purchased by the district from money in its General Fund, a part of which was derived from taxes levied upon real property in the district, including real property owned by plaintiffs. Books furnished by the district under ORS 337.150, whether to public or to parochial schools, are delivered to the persons in charge of the schools—not to the pupils individually. The district also furnishes teacher's editions of each text. The district retains title to the books, a matter of little practical significance however, because the books are not ordinarily retrieved by the district. Textbooks furnished for the use of parochial school students do not differ from those delivered to public schools. A school is not entitled to receive free textbooks unless it complies with standards established by the Oregon statutes as implemented by administrative regulation. The St. John's school met these standards.

The evidence establishes, and the trial judge found, that the purpose of the Catholic church in operating the St. John's school and other similar schools under its supervision is to permeate the entire educational process with the precepts of the Catholic religion. The study guides used by the teachers in St. John's school indicate that, to some extent at least, the use of the textbooks furnished by the district is inextricably connected with the teaching of religious concepts. These study guides were prepared by the superintendent of schools of the Archdiocese of Portland. There is no doubt that the teaching of the subject matter in this manner in a public school would be contrary to law.

Defendants first challenge plaintiffs' standing to raise any constitutional issue other than the violation of the due process clause of the Fourteenth Amendment. Plaintiffs have not shown, it is argued, a deprivation of any freedom guaranteed by the First Amendment since they do not appear as school children, parents of school children, or as persons whose own religious liberty is threatened. As will appear below, we have chosen to decide the issues presented in this case solely upon the basis of the Oregon Constitution. It is not necessary, therefore, to decide whether under federal law defendants' contention with respect to standing is sound.

. . . .

In the instant case the issue of plaintiffs' standing was not raised by defendants' pleadings. If standing were a jurisdictional matter, then, of course, defendants could raise the question at any stage in the proceedings. But we do not so regard it and we hold, therefore, that defendants' failure to raise the issue by a proper pleading constitutes a waiver of that issue.

The First Amendment, as interpreted in *Everson* v. *Board of Education,* 330 U.S. 1 (1946), and Article I, § 5 of the Oregon Constitution, prohibits the use of state funds for the benefit of religious institutions. The principal issue presented to us is whether the expenditure of public funds by the defendant school district for the purpose of furnishing textbooks free of charge to pupils of a parochial school is within these constitutional prohibitions.

We have concluded that the expenditure authorized by ORS 337.150 is within the proscription of Article I, § 5 of the Oregon Constitution. It is unnecessary, therefore, to consider plaintiffs' contention that the statute violates also the First or Fourteenth Amendments to the United States Constitution. Nor is it necessary to consider whether Article VIII, § 2 of the Oregon Constitution has been violated.

Article I, § 5 prohibiting the use of public moneys "for the benefit of any religeous (sic) or theological institution," was designed to keep separate the functions of state and church and to prevent the influence of one upon the other. In this respect our constitution follows the general pattern of other state constitutions and may be regarded as expressing, in more specific terms the policy of the First Amendment as it has been explained in the Everson case.

The historical setting in which constitutional provisions such as Article I, § 5 were written and the factors which prompted their adoption have been thoroughly explained elsewhere; it is not necessary, therefore, to restate those observations here. We need only say that we regard the separation of church and state no less important today than it was at the time Article I, § 5 and its counterpart in other constitutions were adopted.

The general policy is clear. Our problem is to determine whether that policy is violated by the distribution of free textbooks to parochial schools under ORS 337.150. A simple solution would be to declare that Article I, § 5 prohibits the legislature from conferring *any* benefit upon religious institutions including church supported schools, no matter how indirect it might be. But the principle of separation of church and state has not been applied in such strict form. A certain amount of interplay of influences exercised by state and church has been permitted. . . .

Moreover, the wall of separation has not been regarded as a barrier preventing all financial aid to religious institutions. In some instances the aid is direct and substantial. In others the financial aid flows indirectly and incidentally as a result of a tax exemption or other favored treatment, or through

an expenditure for a governmental purpose clearly within constitutional limits.

For the most part these cases afford us little assistance in the interpretation of our own constitution. This is so because in some of them the controlling constitutional provision differs from ours or is seen against a different historical background. In many instances it is obvious that constitutional principles have been sacrificed to serve urgent needs of the community and state; and in others there simply has not been any real analysis of the problem. Some of these cases are strongly relied upon by defendants. We do not propose to appraise each of the numerous cases which have attempted to draw the line of distinction between expenditures which are within and expenditures which are outside constitutional limits. The reasoning employed in these cases will be examined as we consider defendants' argument.

Defendants' principal argument in support of the statute is that the expenditure of public funds for the purpose of furnishing books to pupils of parochial and public schools benefits the pupils who receive these books and not the schools themselves. The leading case for this proposition is *Borden v. Louisiana State Board of Education*, 168 La. 1005, 123 So. 655, 67 A.L.R. 1183 (1929). In that case a statute similar to ORS 337.150 was attacked on constitutional grounds essentially the same as those asserted in the case at bar. The Louisiana court, with three Justices dissenting, sustained the statute on the ground, among others, that the expenditure was for the benefit of pupils and not in aid of schools.

This so-called "child benefit theory" has been applied in other cases in which the expenditure of public funds is made for the purpose of meeting the educational needs of pupils, including those attending parochial schools. The difficulty with this theory is, however, that unless it is qualified in some way it can be used to justify the expenditure of public funds for every educational purpose, because all educational aids are of benefit to the pupil. This criticism is made in *Gurney* v. *Ferguson,* 190 Okl. 254, 255, 122 P.2d 1002, 1003–1004 (1942). In passing upon expenditures for the transportation of children attending parochial schools the court said:

. . . It is true this use of public money and property aids the child, but it is no less true that practically every proper expenditure for school purpose aids the child. We are convinced that this expenditure, in its broad and true sense, and as commonly understood, is an expenditure in furtherance of the constitutional duty or function of maintaining schools as organizations or institutions. The state has no authority to maintain a sectarian school. Surely the expenditure of public funds for the erection of school buildings, the purchasing and equipping and the upkeep of same; the payment of teachers, and for other proper related purposes is expenditure made for schools as such. Yet the same argument is equally applicable to those expenditures as to the present one.

And, as observed by the same court, if the expenditure is not in aid of schools the use of school funds would be unauthorized and illegal.

The leading case rejecting the child benefit theory is *Judd* v. *Board of Education,* 278 N.Y. 200, 15 N.E.2d 576, 118 A.L.R. 789 (1938). In that case the validity of a statute authorizing the expenditure of public funds for the transportation of pupils to and from parochial and private schools was in question. The court said:

. . . Free transportation of pupils induces attendance at the school. The purpose of the transportation is to promote the interests of the private school or religious or sectarian institution that controls and directs it. 'It helps build up, strengthen and make successful the schools as organizations.' *State* ex rel. *Traub* v. *Brown,* 6 W. W. Hars. 36 Del. 181 [187], 172 A. 835, 837, writ of error dismissed Feb. 15, 1938, Del. Sup., 197 A. 478. Without pupils there could be no school. It is illogical to say that the furnishing of transportation is not an aid to the institution while the employment of teachers and furnishing of books, accommodations and other facilities are such an aid. *Id.* 278 N.Y. at 212, 15 N.E. 2d at 582.

The furnishing of textbooks even more clearly constitutes an educational aid. In the Everson case the expenditure for the transportation of parochial school pupils was upheld on the theory that the state could provide for the protection of all school children from traffic hazards irrespective of the religious or public character of schools which they attended. Assuming that the court's reasoning in Everson is sound, it is not applicable to the case at bar. The expenditure of public funds for textbooks supplied to pupils of parochial schools is clearly identified with the educational process, and does not warrant the assumption made in the Everson case that the expenditure is for the general welfare thus justifying the use of the state's police power.

The most recent appraisal of the child benefit theory which has been brought to our attention is *Matthews* v. *Quinton,* Alaska, 362 P.2d 932 (1961). In that case a statute authorizing the transportation of children attending non-public schools was held to be in violation of the Alaska constitutional provision prohibiting the appropriation of public money for the support or benefit of any sectarian, denominational or private school. After a careful examination of the cases in which the child benefit theory had been considered, the court rejected the theory, holding that the furnishing of transportation to pupils of non-public schools constituted a direct benefit to those schools. Mr. Justice Rutledge's dissent in the Everson case was relied upon to support this conclusion. There it was said:

Finally, transportation, where it is needed, is as essential to education as any other element. Its cost is as much a part of the total expense, except at times in amount, as the cost of textbooks, of school lunches, of athletic equipment, of writing and other materials; indeed of all other items composing the total burden. Now as always the core of the educational process is the teacher-pupil relationship. Without this the richest equipment and facilities would go for naught. See *Judd* v. *Board of Education*. . . . But the proverbial Mark Hopkins conception no longer suffices for the country's requirements. Without buildings, without equipment, without library, textbooks and other materials, and without transportation to bring teacher and pupil together in such an effective teaching environment, there can be not even the skelton of what our times require. Hardly can it be maintained that transportation is the least essential of these items, or that it does not in fact aid, encourage, sustain and support, just as they do, the very process which is its purpose to accomplish. No less essential is it, or the payment of its cost, than the very teaching in the classroom or payment of the teacher's sustenance. Many types of equipment, now considered essential, better could be done without. 330 U.S. 1, 47–48, 67 S.Ct. 504, 527.

We concur in the view that expenditures which aid a child as a pupil of a religious school cannot in that respect

be regarded as serving the public welfare as that term is used in defining the state's police power. The reason is stated by Mr. Justice Rutledge in his dissent in *Everson* v. *Board of Education:* the First Amendment "has removed this form of promoting the public welfare from legislative and judicial competence to make a public function. It is exclusively a private affair." The dissenting opinion in *Borden* v. *Louisiana State Board of Education* expresses the same idea: "Nor is there any room here for the application of the State's police power. That power is not absolute and cannot be invoked to sustain legislative acts which in their operation defeat the objects and purposes of the organic law." We are of the opinion that this analysis is correct.

It is argued that the aid to school children is for a public purpose because the compulsory school law compels all children to attend school and that the state may, therefore, make expenditures to further compliance. But this begs the basic question—the state may not compel compliance through the device of furnishing aid to religious schools if that aid is in violation of the constitution. Moreover, the state does not compel pupils to attend *parochial* schools; "their attendance upon the parochial school or private school is a matter of choice and the cost thereof not a matter of public concern." *Judd* v. *Board of Education,* supra.

The theory has been advanced in some cases that since the parochial schools are performing a task which the state itself must perform through the use of the public schools, the expenditures made are not "aid" but "remuneration" for services rendered and, therefore, not prohibited by the constitutional principle of separation of church and state. The distinction is specious and its application could be urged in the justification of the expenditure of public moneys for all educational needs of parochial schools.

In the instant case the evidence establishes that the defendant school district expended approximately $4,000 for textbooks used in the St. John's school. This constitutes a substantial benefit. The benefit is of such a character as to bring it within the proscription of Article I, § 5.

It seems obvious that as long as church and state continue to exist side by side there cannot be a complete isolation of each, with neither exerting influence upon the other. It is to be expected that in the operations of the state residual benefits will accrue to the various religious groups, not because they are religious organizations but because they are, like other organizations, a part of the community which the state will and must, serve indiscriminately. As Mr. Justice Black observed in the Everson case, the First Amendment (and its counterpart in state constitutions) "requires the state to be a neutral in its relations with groups of religious believers and non-believers; it does not require the state to be their adversary. State power is no more to be used so as to handicap religions, than it is to favor them."

Neither the federal nor the state constitutions prohibit the state from conferring benefits upon religious institutions where that benefit does not accrue to the institution as a religious organization. The proscription is against aid to religious *functions*. The benefits of police and fire protection, sewage disposal, and other community financed services accrue to churches, not as religious organizations but as owners of property in the community. And, the same principle applies when public expenditures benefit individuals who are engaged in carrying out a religious function. A government pension paid to a clergyman for his services in the Armed Forces may benefit religion but it is not constitutionally prohibited; in such case he receives the bounty not as a cleric but as any other citizen. On the other hand, the state obviously could not pay the clergyman's salary. The point is clearly seen by Cushman, Public Support of Religious Education in American Constitutional Law, 45 Ill. L. Rev. 333, 348 (1950):

The difference between providing police protection and providing teachers does not lie in the identity of the beneficiary but in the way in which the aid is extended. Aid is not normally extended to individuals or institutions by name, but rather to groups or classes of individuals or institutions. Any individual or institution falling under the restrictions of the law, or falling heir to its benefits, does so only as a member of such a group. An individual may be a pupil, a pedestrian, a property owner and a parent. A church is at once a corporation, a piece of property, a building, a meeting place, a religious institution and a non-profit institution. Furthermore, a church may receive police protection when classed as property, tax exemption when classed as a non-profit institution, sewage connections when classed as a building and yet be denied financial aid when classed as a religious institution, since such a class may not validly be given public aid. Since the aid goes to groups rather than the individual components of any one group, the eligibility of an institution to receive public aid would seem to depend on which group it is classed in, rather than on its individual characteristics.

The author then correctly concludes that where the aid is to pupils and schools the benefit is identified with the function of education and if the educational institution is religious, the benefit accrues to religious institutions in their function as religious institutions. And so it is the case at bar. Granting that pupils and not schools are intended to be the beneficiaries of the state's bounty, the aid is extended to the pupil only as a member of the school which he attends. Whoever else may share in its benefits such aid is an asset to the schools themselves. *State ex rel. Traub* v. *Brown.* The St. John's school shares in this benefit in a direct and vital way. We attach no significance to the fact that the books are loaned to the pupil or school rather than given outright; in either event a substantial benefit is conferred upon the recipient.

We recognize that whether an expenditure is an aid to a religious institution in its religious function or in some other capacity is a question of degree. But it seems clear that the line must be drawn to include within the constitutional proscription the furnishing of textbooks to pupils of parochial schools. This conclusion is compelled because such books are an integral part of the educational process. As we have already pointed out, the teaching of the precepts of Catholicism is an inseparable part of the educational process in the St. John's school. Considering the purpose of Article I, § 5, we are unable to see any substantial distinction between the furnishing of textbooks and the furnishing of blackboards, desks, laboratory instruments, or other equipment clearly necessary to the operation of the school. In comparing these various essential tools we agree with the dissenting opinion in *Everson* v. *Board of Education of Ewing Twp.* 133 N.J.L. 350, 359, 44 A.2d 333 (1945) that there is no way of "satisfactorily distinguishing one item of expense from another in the long process of child education."

It is argued that the strict notions of separation in vogue at the time of the adoption of our constitutional provisions no longer exist and that these provisions should be interpreted to reflect this change in attitude. Conceding that such change has occurred, there are still important considerations warranting the resolve that the wall of separation between church and state "must be kept high and impregnable." *Everson* v. *Board of Education,* supra, 330 U.S. at p. 18. Among other things, the extension of aid to religious educational institutions could, as observed in *Judd* v. *Board of Education,* supra 278 N.Y. at 209, 15 N.E.2d at 581, "open the door for a dangerous and vicious controversy among the different religious denominations as to who should get the largest share of school funds." More important, perhaps, is the danger that the acceptance of state aid might result in state control over religious instruction. Some religious leaders, including leaders in the Catholic church, have opposed the acceptance of public funds on this ground. These considerations convince us that the wall of separation in this state must also be kept "high and impregnable" to meet the demands of Article I, § 5.

We are not unmindful of the fact that parents who send their children to Catholic schools must bear the double burden of supporting not only their own parochial schools but the public schools as well. But the added burden is self-imposed; instruction in the public schools is available to all. Catholic schools operate only because Catholic parents feel that the precepts of their faith should be integrated into the teaching of secular subjects. Those who do not share in this faith need not share in the cost of nurturing it. Article I, § 5 so ordains.

Defendants argue that the denial of

the use of free textbooks to pupils solely because they attend parochial schools would constitute a violation of the equal protection clause of the Fourteenth Amendment. The argument is without merit. The classification which excludes such pupils from the state's bounty is not only reasonable, it is commanded by the constitution itself.

The principle announced in *Pierce v. Society of Sisters*, 268 U.S. 510, 45 S.Ct. 571, 69 L.Ed. 1070 (1925), relied upon by defendants, is not germane to the problem before us. That case simply recognizes the constitutional right of a parent to pursue freely his religious beliefs by sending his children to parochial schools. The court did not hold, nor was anything said in the case from which it could be implied, that the state must pay for the child's education if the parent elects to use the parochial schools.

. . . A decision of the Supreme Court of the United States holding that certain legislation is not in violation of the federal constitution is not an adjudication of the constitutionality of the legislation under a state constitution. In such a case it is not only within the power of the state courts, it is their duty to decide whether the state constitution has been violated. Our views on the policy or interpretation of a particular constitutional provision do not always coincide with those of the Supreme Court of the United States. As we have indicated, *Everson* v. *Board of Education*, supra, is distinguishable from the case at bar. Even if it were not, our conclusion would be the same.

The judgment is reversed. . . .

Judge ROSSMAN, dissenting:

I dissent.

Everson v. *Board of Education*, 330 U.S. 1, spent unusual effort upon a case which was governed by the same principle of law that governs the case at bar. It stated the principle with clarity and sustained the constitutionality of the challenged statute. We should apply the same principle of law in this case and recognize as valid the statute under attack. Certainty of law governing the relationship between the state and religious organizations, although difficult of expression, is peculiarly desirable. Confusion and controversy are certain to arise when the United States Supreme Court and this court interpret differently a constitutional principle that should have a single meaning. The Everson decision affords a good opportunity to achieve a high degree of certainty. It should

not be cast aside; it should be embraced.

. . . As I have indicated, the act in question clearly can be deemed an educational act. Its purpose was to bring to the avail of the pupils in denominational institutions textbooks which the legislature favored. The legislature was not concerned with any church, but with the youth of Oregon and believed that textbooks chosen by the State Board of Textbook Commissioners would afford superior education to those selected by the denominational schools.

I add that a parochial school is in no sense enriched through the operation of the statute under attack. If, prior to the enactment of ORS 337.150 the parochial school did not provide for its pupils free textbooks then obviously ORS 337.150 did not relieve it of any burden. But, if prior to the enactment of ORS 337.150 the parochial school provided free textbooks, then the act under question does not give to the parochial school any books whatever. ORS 337.200(2) renders it clear that the books are entrusted to the pupil and are not the property of the school. In fact, ORS 337.190 states:

All textbooks purchased under ORS 337.150 are, and shall remain, the property of the school district. Upon receipt thereof, each of said books shall be immediately and properly labeled as the property of the school district.

ORS 337.200 renders it the duty of the Superintendent of Public Instruction to see to it that all of the books thus rendered available to the pupils are returned to the school board. Without further analysis I express my conclusion that the act under review is constitutional and that this court should adhere to *Everson* v. *Board of Education*, supra.

REACTION TO *DICKMAN* v. *SCHOOL DISTRICT*

The Oregon court's approach was sharply attacked in the *University of Cincinnati Law Review* (31:335), where it was alleged that the court not only ignored the intent of the Oregon legislature, but it also rejected a child-benefit argument which had been upheld by courts in several other states. Pointing out that the parents and not the school had purchased the textbooks previous to the enactment of the statute in question, the reviewer further charged that the court had ignored the realities of the school's operation.

He continued: "If the court intends the term 'benefit' to include all indirect and incidental benefits, however remote, it imperils all state support of hospitals, child-care agencies, and other charitable institutions if maintained by a religious group."

That such a complete separation of church and state as envisaged by the court was not intended by the Oregon constitution seemed logical to the reviewer. He also could find no basis for refusing to grant benefits of general welfare legislation to a school child because of his religious belief.

SUMMARY

One of the most controversial areas in the field of church-state relations as it affects education, deals with the question of whether a public school district which undertakes to distribute free textbooks to public school students must also do so to parochial school pupils. As early as 1901 an Ohio court faced with this issue declared that the equal protection clause of the United States and Ohio constitutions was not violated if a school district provided free textbooks to public school students but not to those attending parochial schools.

Generally, it can be said that up to 1929 the practice of the states as enunciated by the state courts was to hold that providing free textbooks to parochial school students violated state constitutional or statutory provisions prohibiting the use of public funds for sectarian schools. For example, the New York court in 1922 seems to have been faced with the first systematized argument of what has come to be called the child-benefit theory. The court rejected it, however, and pointed out that free textbooks helped primarily the parochial school, not its students, and thus such a practice would violate the state constitutional prohibition against using public funds for denominational schools.

In 1930 the Supreme Court was faced with the issue in the Cochran case. In a relatively brief opinion that skirted the nuances of the two religion clauses of the First Amendment, the Court held that nothing in the United States Constitution prohibited a state from providing free texts to parochial school students so long as this was permissible under state constitutional or statutory provisions. The Court based its view on the conclusion that programs of this type aided the child and not religion. The upshot of the ruling, however, was that state courts were made the arena in which the battle was to continue to be waged.

An indication of the relatively unsophisticated attitude of the legal mind of that day to the complexities and ramifications of the two clauses on religion in the First Amendment is revealed by the paucity of commentary on the Cochran case in legal periodicals. The few reactions which did appear in print in these and other journals tended toward, at best, a lukewarm support of the Court.

State court opinions regarding the validity of providing textbooks to parochial schools from public funds, continued to be sharply divided. In two of the three cases to reach major state courts since the Cochran case, the practice was declared unconstitutional. In 1961, the Oregon supreme court rejected the child-benefit theory as controlling, by noting that pupils always benefit to some extent from all educational aid. But, the court concluded, the child received benefits from free textbooks only because he attended the parochial school, and thus state support of such programs was unconstitutional.

When this case was appealed to the Supreme Court, it refused to grant certiorari which meant that the decision of the Oregon court was left standing. This has led to speculation in some quarters that the Supreme Court may have serious reservations about the Cochran rule. The case of *Bowerman* v. *O'Connor* challenging the practice is presently pending in a Rhode Island trial court and raising federal questions. The Supreme Court may have another opportunity to reconsider the Cochran rule in the relatively near future.

Today, this area of controversy has been extensively magnified because of the enactment of the Elementary and Secondary Education Act of 1965. As Leo Pfeffer points out in his article in the *Saturday Review* of January

21, 1967, two suits were instituted in the federal and state courts of New York in December, 1966 challenging the constitutionality of the adminis-tration of some of the programs under the Act but not the Act itself. For example, Title I funds are used to provide remedial arithmetic programs in the New York parochial schools, but there are no such programs for the public schools. Remedial or special reading teachers are assigned to parochial schools at the ratio of one for every 157 eligible pupils, while in the public school the ratio is one for every 230. A public school must be located in an officially designated disadvantaged area to qualify for Title I funds while a parochial or private school need not be. The standard adopted by the New York authorities to qualify a disadvantaged private school for aid is the receipt of free lunches by 10 per cent of the children; however, substantially higher requirements are imposed for the public school, in some districts as much as 40 per cent.

The litigation in New York is merely a beginning one involving church-state problems inherent in the federal Elementary and Secondary Education Act. One need not be a prophet of doom to anticipate a deluge of similar actions.

CHAPTER SIX

Flag Salute

† †

THE MODERN FLAG-SALUTE CEREMONY originated in 1892. It resulted from the successful efforts by Francis Bellamy and James B. Upham, writers for the magazine *Youth's Companion,* to stimulate patriotism in the schools. Later in that same year, President Benjamin Harrison with Congressional authorization issued a proclamation declaring October 12, 1892, a national holiday to be suitably observed with mass tributes to the flag in the public schools in commemoration of Columbus' discovery of America.

The National Flag Conferences of 1923 and 1924 amended the original pledge of allegiance to read:

> I pledge allegiance to the Flag of the United States of America and to the Republic for which it stands; one nation, indivisible, with liberty and justice for all.

The original pledge referred to "my flag," rather than to "the Flag of the United States of America." For a definitive analysis of these and other developments, consult the comprehensive study which appeared in 1962 by David Manwaring, *Render Unto Caesar.*

New York passed the first flag salute statute in 1898, one day after the United States declared war on Spain. Several other states quickly followed her example. By 1940, "eighteen states had statutory provisions providing for some sort of teaching regarding the flag." Manwaring notes, moreover, that local use was being made of the ritual in at least thirty states, and in several of those states the local practices were common long before relevant supporting legislation was passed. Manwaring suggested that while none of the flag-salute statutes explicitly required individual recitations, the reality of classroom regimentation in practice made such a specific statement unnecessary.

The main support for the flag-salute ceremony came chiefly from such citizens' organizations aiming overtly at "Americanism" as the American Legion, the Veterans of Foreign Wars, the Ku Klux Klan, the Daughters of the American Revolution, the American Legion Auxiliary, and the Sons of the Revolution. Early opposition to flag-salute laws and parallel

139

statutory provisions, according to Manwaring, were generally weak and sporadic. The opposition centered within the teaching profession and with such religious groups as the Mennonites, the Jehovites, the Elijah Voice Society, and the Church of God.

The Jehovah's Witnesses spearheaded the drive against compulsory flag saluting in the public schools because of their profound conviction for basing all of their actions on their religious beliefs; they consider the act of saluting the flag as a form of idolatry and violative of the Biblical injunction, "Thou shalt not make unto thee any graven image," of the First Commandment.

EARLY FRUSTRATIONS

Early litigation in state courts resulted in complete defeat for the Jehovah's Witnesses. That group persisted in its efforts, though, and was finally granted a full hearing by the United States Supreme Court in 1940. That hearing in *Minersville School District* v. *Gobitis*, discussed below, coming after major litigation in seven states, however, proved temporarily disastrous for its cause.

The Witnesses reached the Supreme Court for the first time in *Leoles* v. *Landers*, 302 U.S. 656 (1937). However, the appeal was dismissed there *per curiam* for want of a substantial federal question. Consequently, the decision of the Georgia supreme court at 184 Ga. 580, 192 S.E. 218 (1937) was undisturbed. The latter court, while affirming the expulsion of a sixth-grader for refusing to salute the flag, expounded further on the "secular regulation" rule which had been formulated by the Massachusetts supreme court in *Nicholls* v. *Mayor*, 297 Mass. 65, 7 N.E.2d 577 (1937). According to that doctrine, the flag salute and pledge of allegiance observances were merely exercises in patriotism, and were not religious rites.

Three more rulings of state courts unfavorable to the Jehovah's Witnesses' position were appealed to the United States Supreme Court before 1940, all of them to no avail. The high Court let stand at 303 U.S. 624 (1938) the decision in *Hering* v. *Board of Education*, 117 N.J.L. 455, 189 A. 629 (1937), where the New Jersey supreme court had declared, "Those who do not desire to conform with the demands of the statute can seek their school elsewhere."

A slightly different situation was involved in *Gabrielli* v. *Knickerbocker*. California, lacking statutes regarding flag salutes and patriotic instruction, allowed local school boards to determine their own policies. A local board's actions in suspending and expelling pupils who refused to salute the American flag had been declared arbitrary and unwarranted by a district court of appeals at 74 P.2d 290 (1937). The California supreme court, however, reversed the lower decision at 12 Cal. 2d 85, 82 P.2d 391

(1938). In the process it invoked the secular regulation rule. The appeal to the United States Supreme Court was dismissed for want of jurisdiction at 306 U.S. 621 (1939).

The first case reaching the Supreme Court from a lower federal court also proved unsuccessful for the Jehovah's Witnesses. In *Johnson* v. *Deerfield,* 25 F.Supp. 918 (1939), a three-judge United States district court in Massachusetts refused to grant an injunction against continued enforcement of flag-salute requirements against Jehovah's Witnesses' children. That court considered the federal constitutional issues foreclosed by the Supreme Court's unfavorable dispositions of earlier appeals in flag-salute cases. It held further that *Nicholls* v. *Mayor,* discussed above, had settled the state constitutional arguments. The Supreme Court, at 306 U.S. 621 (1939), cited its earlier *per curiam* dispositions of flag-salute cases, as it summarily affirmed, *per curiam* the decision in the Johnson case.

The other actions in 1939 were settled in the state courts. The New York court of appeals while declaring, "The flag has nothing to do with religion," upheld a flag-salute requirement but reversed the convictions of parents who had failed to keep their daughter in some school. *People ex rel. Fish* v. *Sandstrom,* 279 N.Y. 523, 18 N.E.2d 840 (1939), thus ruled that the state may expel students who refuse to salute the flag, but it may not impose further penalties.

An application for mandamus to compel the board of education to re-admit a student who had upon religious grounds refused to salute the flag was denied in a scorching opinion by the supreme court of Florida in *State ex rel. Bleich* v. *Board of Public Instruction,* 139 Fla. 43, 190 So. 815 (1939). Declaring that such practices of refusal by conscientious objectors to salute the flag were "contrary to approved canons of morals [and] inimical to the public welfare," the court refused to permit such exemptions from the mandatory exercises even though the objections were raised in the name of religion. The court concluded: "To symbolize the flag as a graven image and ascribe to the act of saluting it a species of idolatry is too vague and far fetched to be even tinctured with the flavor of reason."

THE SUPREME COURT RULES ON THE FLAG-SALUTE ISSUE

The Supreme Court finally ruled on the merits of the constitutional issue in *Minersville School District* v. *Gobitis,* 310 U.S. 586 (1940). There, Justice Frankfurter, speaking for an eight-to-one majority, declared that freedom of religion of the First Amendment as made applicable to the states by the Due Process Clause of the Fourteenth Amendment was not violated by a statute requiring a flag salute and pledge of allegiance observance. A United States district court at 24 F.Supp 271 (1938) and circuit court of appeals at 108 F.2d 683 (1939) had held otherwise. Justice Stone dissented vigorously from the ruling by the United States Supreme Court.

Frankfurter, paying his usual respects to legislative deference, considered the matter to be solely an issue of education policy that was designed to foster national unity as the basis of national security. Manwaring characterized the decision as being a narrow holding which upheld the expulsion of nonsaluters but left unanswered the question of further punishment of the Jehovah's Witnesses students and their parents.

† † *MINERSVILLE SCHOOL DISTRICT* v. *GOBITIS*
310 U.S. 586, 60 S. CT. 1010, 84 L. ED. 1375 (1940).

Mr. Justice FRANKFURTER delivered the opinion of the Court, saying in part:

A grave responsibility confronts this Court whenever in course of litigation it must reconcile the conflicting claims of liberty and authority. But when the liberty invoked is liberty of conscience, and the authority is authority to safeguard the nation's fellowship, judicial conscience is put to its severest test. Of such a nature is the present controversy.

Lillian Gobitis, aged twelve, and her brother William, aged ten, were expelled from the public schools of Minersville, Pennsylvania, for refusing to salute the national flag as part of a daily school exercise. The local Board of Education required both teachers and pupils to participate in this ceremony. The ceremony is a familiar one. The right hand is placed on the breast and the following pledge recited in unison: "I pledge allegiance to my flag, and to the Republic for which it stands; one nation indivisible, with liberty and justice for all." While the words are spoken, teachers and pupils extend their right hands in salute to the flag. The Gobitis family are affili-

ated with "Jehovah's Witnesses," for whom the Bible as the Word of God is the supreme authority. The children had been brought up conscientiously to believe that such a gesture of respect for the flag was forbidden by command of Scripture.

The Gobitis children were of an age for which Pennsylvania makes school attendance compulsory. Thus they were denied a free education, and their parents had to put them into private schools. To be relieved of the financial burden thereby entailed, their father, on behalf of the children and in his own behalf, brought this suit. . . .

We must decide whether the requirement of participation in such a ceremony, exacted from a child who refuses upon sincere religious grounds, infringes without due process of law the liberty guaranteed by the Fourteenth Amendment.

Centuries of strife over the erection of particular dogmas as exclusive or all-comprehending faiths led to the inclusion of a guarantee for religious freedom in the Bill of Rights. The First

Amendment, and the Fourteenth through its absorption of the First, sought to guard against repetition of those bitter religious struggles by prohibiting the establishment of a state religion and by securing to every sect the free exercise of its faith. So pervasive is the acceptance of this precious right that its scope is brought into question, as here, only when the conscience of individuals collides with the felt necessities of society.

Certainly the affirmative pursuit of one's convictions about the ultimate mystery of the universe and man's relation to it is placed beyond the reach of law. Government may not interfere with organized or individual expression of belief or disbelief. Propagation of belief—or even of disbelief—in the supernatural is protected, whether in church or chapel, mosque or synagogue, tabernacle or meeting-house. Likewise the Constitution assures generous immunity to the individual from imposition of penalties for offending, in the course of his own religious activities, the religious views of others, be they a minority or those who are dominant in government. . . .

But the manifold character of man's relations may bring his conception of religious duty into conflict with the secular interests of his fellow-men. When does the constitutional guarantee compel exemption from doing what society thinks necessary for the promotion of some great common end, or from a penalty for conduct which appears dangerous to the general good? To state the problem is to recall the truth that no single principle can answer all of life's complexities. The right to freedom of religious belief, however dissident and however obnoxious to the cherished beliefs of others—even of a majority—is itself the denial of an absolute. But to affirm that the freedom to follow conscience has itself no limits in the life of a society would deny that very plurality of principles which, as a matter of history, underlies protection of religious toleration. . . . Our present task, then, as so often the case with courts, is to reconcile two rights in order to prevent either from destroying the other. But, because in safeguarding conscience we are dealing with interests so subtle and so dear, every possible leeway should be given to the claims of religious faith.

In the judicial enforcement of religious freedom we are concerned with a historic concept. . . . The religious liberty which the Constitution protects has never excluded legislation of general scope not directed against doctrinal loyalties of particular sects. Judicial nullification of legislation cannot be justified by attributing to the framers of the Bill of Rights views for which there is no historic warrant. Conscientious scruples have not, in the course of the long struggle for religious toleration, relieved the individual from obedience to a general law not aimed at the promotion or restriction of religious beliefs. The mere possession of religious convictions which contradict the relevant concerns of a political society does not relieve the citizen from the discharge of political responsibilities. The necessity for this adjustment has again and again been recognized. In a number of situations the exertion of political authority has been sustained, while basic considerations of religious freedom have been left inviolate. . . . In all [such] cases the general laws in question, upheld in their application to those who refused obedience from religious conviction, were manifestations of specific powers of government deemed by the legislature essential to secure and maintain that orderly, tranquil, and free society without which religious toleration itself is unattainable. Nor does the freedom of speech assured by Due Process move in a more absolute circle of immunity than that enjoyed by religious freedom. Even if it were assumed that freedom of speech goes beyond the historic concept of full opportunity to utter and to disseminate views, however heretical or offensive to dominate opinion, and includes freedom from conveying what may be deemed an implied but rejected affirmation, the question remains whether school children, like the Gobitis children, must be excused from conduct required of all the other children in the promotion of national cohesion. We are dealing with an interest inferior to none in the hierarchy of legal values. National unity is the basis of national security. To deny the legislature the right to select appropriate means for its attainment presents a totally different order of problem from that of the propriety of subordinating the possible ugliness of littered streets to the free expression of opinion through distribution of hand bills. . . .

Situations like the present are phases of the profoundest problem confronting a democracy—the problem which Lincoln cast in memorable dilemma: "Must a government of necessity be too *strong* for the liberties of its people, or too *weak* to maintain its own existence?" No mere textual reading or logical talisman can solve the dilemma. And when the issue demands judicial determination, it is not the personal notion of judges of what wise adjustment requires which must prevail.

Unlike the instances we have cited, the case before us is not concerned with an exertion of legislative power for the promotion of some specific need or interest of secular society—the protection of the family, the promotion of health, the common defense, the raising of public revenues to defray the cost of government. But all these specific activities of government presuppose the existence of an organized political society. The ultimate foundation of a free society is the binding tie of cohesive sentiment. Such a sentiment is fostered by all those agencies of the mind and spirit which may serve to gather up the traditions of a people, transmit them from generation to generation, and thereby create that continuity of a treasured common life which constitutes a civilization. "We live by symbols." The flag is the symbol of our national unity, transcending all internal differences, however large, within the framework of the Constitution. This Court has had occasion to say that ". . . the flag is the symbol of the Nation's power, the emblem of freedom in its truest, best sense. . . . It signifies government resting on the consent of the governed; liberty regulated by law; the protection of the weak against the strong; security against the exercise of arbitrary power; and absolute safety for free institutions against foreign aggression. . . ."

The case before us must be viewed as though the legislature of Pennsylvania had itself formally directed the flag-salute for the children of Minersville; had made no exemption for children whose parents were possessed of conscientious scruples like those of the Gobitis family; and had indicated its belief in the desirable ends to be secured by having its public school children share a common experience at those periods of development when their minds are supposedly receptive to its assimilation, by an exercise appropriate in time and place and setting, and one designed to evoke in them appreciation of the nation's hopes and dreams, its sufferings and sacrifices. The precise issue, then, for us to decide is whether the legislatures of the various states and the authorities in a thousand counties and school districts of this country are barred from determining the appropriateness of various means to evoke that unifying sentiment without which there can ultimately be no liberties, civil or religious. To stigmatize legislative judgment in providing for this universal gesture of respect for the symbol of our national life in the setting of the common school as a lawless inroad on that freedom of conscience which the Constitution protects, would amount to no less than the pronouncement of pedagogical and psychological dogma in a field where courts possess no marked and certainly no controlling competence. The influences which help toward a common feeling for the common country are manifold. Some may seem harsh and others no doubt are foolish. Surely, however, the end is legitimate. And the effective means for its attainment are still so uncertain and so unauthenticated by science as to preclude us from putting the widely prevalent belief in flag-saluting beyond the pale of legislative power. It mocks reason and denies our whole history to find in the allowance of a requirement to salute our flag on fitting occasions the seeds of sanction for obeisance to a leader.

The wisdom of training children in patriotic impulses by those compulsions which necessarily pervade so much of the educational process is not for our independent judgment. Even were we convinced of the folly of such a meas-

ure, such belief would be no proof of its unconstitutionality. For ourselves, we might be tempted to say that the deepest patriotism is best engendered by giving unfettered scope to the most crochety beliefs. Perhaps it is best, even from the standpoint of those interests which ordinances like the one under review seek to promote, to give to the least popular sect leave from conformities like those here in issue. But the courtroom is not the arena for debating issues of educational policy. It is not our province to choose among competing considerations in the subtle process of securing effective loyalty to the traditional ideals of democracy, while respecting at the same time individual idiosyncrasies among a people so diversified in racial origins and religious allegiances. So to hold would in effect make us the school board for the country. That authority has not been given to this Court, nor should we assume it.

We are dealing here with the formative period in the development of citizenship. Great diversity of psychological and ethical opinion exists among us concerning the best way to train children for their place in society. Because of these differences and because of reluctance to permit a single, iron-cast system of education to be imposed upon a nation compounded of so many strains, we have held that, even though public education is one of our most cherished democratic institutions, the Bill of Rights bars a state from compelling all children to attend the public schools. *Pierce* v. *Society of Sisters,* 268 U.S. 510. But it is a very different thing for this Court to exercise censorship over the conviction of legislatures that a particular program or exercise will best promote in the minds of children who attend the common schools an attachment to the institutions of their country.

What the school authorities are really asserting is the right to awaken the child's mind considerations as to the significance of the flag contrary to those implanted by the parent. In such an attempt the state is normally at a disadvantage in competing with the parent's authority, so long—and this is the vital aspect of religious toleration—as parents are unmolested in their right to counteract by their own persuasiveness the wisdom and rightness of those loyalties which the state's educational system is seeking to promote. Except where the transgression of constitutional liberty is too plain for argument, personal freedom is best maintained—so long as the remedial channels of the democratic process remain open and unobstructed—when it is ingrained in a people's habits and not enforced against popular policy by the coercion of adjudicated law. That the flag-salute is an allowable portion of a school program for those who do not invoke conscientious scruples is surely not debatable. But for us to insist that, though the ceremony may be required, exceptional immunity must be given to dissidents, is to maintain that there is no basis for a legislative judgment that such an exemption might introduce elements of difficulty into the school discipline, might cast doubts in the minds of the other children which would themselves weaken the effect of the exercise.

The preciousness of the family relation, the authority and independence which give dignity to parenthood, indeed the enjoyment of all freedom, presuppose the kind of ordered society which is summarized by our flag. A society which is dedicated to the preservation of these ultimate values of civilization may in self-protection utilize the educational process for inculcating those almost unconscious feelings which bind men together in a comprehending loyalty, whatever may be their lesser differences and difficulties. That is to say, the process may be utilized so long as men's right to believe as they please, to win others to their way of belief, and their right to assemble in their chosen places of worship for the devotional ceremonies of their faith, are all fully respected.

Judicial review, itself a limitation on popular government, is a fundamental part of our constitutional scheme. But to the legislature no less than to courts is committed the guardianship of deeply-cherished liberties. . . . Where all the effective means of inducing political changes are left free from interference, education in the abandonment of foolish legislation is itself a training in liberty. To fight out the wise use of legislative authority in the forum of public opinion and before legislative assemblies rather than to transfer such a contest to the judicial arena, serves to vindicate the self-confidence of a free people.

Reversed.

Mr. Justice STONE, dissenting:

I think the judgment below should be affirmed.

Two youths, now fifteen and sixteen years of age, are by the judgment of this Court held liable to expulsion from the public schools and to denial of all publicly supported educational privileges because of their refusal to yield to the compulsion of a law which commands their participation in a school ceremony contrary to their religious convictions. They and their father are citizens and have not exhibited by any action or statement of opinion, any disloyalty to the Government of the United States. They are ready and willing to obey all its laws which do not conflict with what they sincerely believe to be the higher commandments of God. It is not doubted that these convictions are religious, that they are genuine, or that the refusal to yield to the compulsion of the law is in good faith and with all sincerity. It would be a denial of their faith as well as the teachings of most religions to say that children of their age could not have religious convictions.

The law which is thus sustained is unique in the history of Anglo-American legislation. It does more than suppress freedom of speech and more than prohibit the free exercise of religion, which concededly are forbidden by the First Amendment and are violations of the liberty guaranteed by the Fourteenth. For by this law the state seeks to coerce these children to express a sentiment which, as they interpret it, they do not entertain, and which violates their deepest religious convictions. . . .

. . . This seems to me no less than the surrender of the constitutional protection of the liberty of small minorities to the popular will. We have previously pointed to the importance of a searching judicial inquiry into the legislative judgment in situations where prejudice against discrete and insular minorities may tend to curtail the operation of those political processes ordinarily to be relied on to protect minorities. . . . And until now we have not hesitated similarly to scrutinize legislation restricting the civil liberty of racial and religious minorities although no political process was affected. . . . Here we have such a small minority entertaining in good faith a religious belief, which is such a departure from the usual course of human conduct, that most persons are disposed to regard it with little toleration or concern. In such circumstances careful scrutiny of legislative efforts to secure conformity of belief and opinion by a compulsory affirmation of the desired belief, is especially needful if civil rights are to receive any protection. Tested by this standard, I am not prepared to say that the right of this small and helpless minority, including children having a strong religious conviction, whether they understand its nature or not, to refrain from an expression obnoxious to their religion, is to be overborne by the interest of the state in maintaining discipline in the schools.

The Constitution expresses more than the conviction of the people that democratic processes must be preserved at all costs. It is also an expression of faith and a command that freedom of mind and spirit must be preserved, which government must obey, if it is to adhere to that justice and moderation without which no free government can exist. For this reason it would seem that legislation which operates to repress the religious freedom of small minorities, which is admittedly within the scope of the protection of the Bill of Rights, must at least be subject to the same judicial scrutiny as legislation which we have recently held to infringe the constitutional liberty of religious and racial minorities.

With such scrutiny I cannot say that the inconveniences which may attend some sensible adjustment of school discipline in order that the religious convictions of these children may be spared, presents a problem so momentous or pressing as to outweigh the freedom from compulsory violation of religious faith which has been thought worthy of constitutional protection.

REACTIONS OF LEGAL PERIODICALS TO
MINERSVILLE SCHOOL DISTRICT v. *GOBITIS*

Over three-fourths of the law review articles condemned the Supreme Court's ruling in the Gobitis decision. Scattered support in some journals emphasized the importance of patriotism, the nonabsolute quality of religious freedom, the inherent desire of a democracy to maintain itself, and the wisdom of the legislative process. On the other hand, criticism centered upon the contentions that religious freedom was meant to be protected in just such situations as arose in the Gobitis case, that morality and loyalty cannot be legislated, that democracy was based on the very principles that were being violated, and that the policy of enforced loyalty was questionable both as to its effects and its effectiveness.

Attention was focused in the *St. John's Law Review* (15:95) on concern over the Court's emphasis upon school children's refusals to physically salute a flag where the child's loyalty is unquestionable (as the trial court found in the case of the Gobitis children). The Court, it was pointed out, should rather have been concerned over the greater danger of false professions of loyalty whereby the undetected enemy could physically salute a flag he "plans to destroy." A thoughtful alternative to enforced patriotism was set forth in the *University of Cincinnati Law Review* (14:570), where it was suggested that the schools should utilize history and civics courses to teach about the significance of our flag.

REACTIONS OF OTHER PERIODICALS TO
MINERSVILLE SCHOOL DISTRICT v. *GOBITIS*

There was a variety of comment in the education and general circulation periodicals concerning the Gobitis case. The great majority of the articles generally disapproved of the decision on the grounds that the Supreme Court had infringed upon individuals' constitutional rights. The remaining articles did not comment upon the merits of the case. Several articles mentioned the rash of anti-Jehovah's Witnesses acts that followed the Gobitis decision.

An article in *American Political Science Review* (36:1053, 1063, 1942) by V. W. Rotnem and F. G. Folsom, Jr., found the violence against Jehovah's Witnesses during the two years after the Gobitis decision "an eloquent argument in support of the minority contention of Mr. Justice Stone. . . . [P]ublic health, safety, and morals have not been fortified by the compulsory flag-salute laws. Indeed, the result has been quite contrary." An article in *Life* (9:20, 1940) also deplored the violence. "[P]ublic prejudice has short circuited due process of law and raised issues graver than the flag salute. From Maine to Wyoming, Witnesses have been jailed without charges, beaten, tarred and feathered, their property destroyed."

In another magazine, *New Republic* (102:843, 1940), an editorial also agreed with Stone's dissent. It stated: "[C]ivil rights are not absolute, . . . [the] government may infringe upon them to ensure its own survival and presumbaly to protect public morals, safety, health and order. But this right is not absolute; the question is one of adjustment between the power of government and the constitutional right of the individual." This article and another in the *New Republic* (103:173, 1940) likened the Gobitis decision to Hitler's philosophy of subordinating individual liberties to protect the state. Hodgdon in an article in *Clearing House* (20:430, 1946) was equally strong in denouncing the Supreme Court's decision. He felt that the Gobitis decision was a violation of free speech as guaranteed by the First Amendment.

Other articles took the same general stand that the decision was a restriction of individual liberties. See for example *Commonweal* (32:158, 1940), *Scholastic* (42:13, 1943), *American Political Science Review* (35:250, 271, 1941), *Harvard Educational Review* (76:81, 1941), and *Christian Century* (57:791, 1940).

Swisher in an article in *Political Science Quarterly* (55:321, 346, 1940) considered the Gobitis decision an indication that the Court was "in a frame of mind to support patriotic regimentation."

Time (35:21, 1940) and *Newsweek* (15:36, 1940) mentioned the Gobitis case briefly but made no comment upon its merits.

An editorial in *Clearing House* (15:554, 1941) indicated it thought "[t]he Supreme Court seems to have gone to bat on the [flag salute] problem and fanned out. . . . However it did suggest as a solution a method used in Rochester, Michigan, and approved by a probate judge whereby the dissenters gave their own pledge of allegiance without referring to the flag."

Reaction by newspapers to the Gobitis case generally opposed the decision. According to a survey made by D. R. Manwaring in *Render Unto Caesar* (1962, p. 161) "articulate newspaper response" was about two to one against the decision.

DISREGARD OF GOBITIS

The public reception of the Gobitis decision apparently was also hostile, as evidenced by the fact that following the 1940 decision three state courts directly repudiated the Gobitis precedent.

In this connection, a unanimous Kansas supreme court declared in *State* v. *Smith,* 155 Kan. 588, 127 P.2d 518 (1942), that the flag-salute statute in question did not authorize the expulsion of objectors professing sincere religious beliefs. The court went on to say, however, that a compulsory statute would violate the religious freedom guaranty of the state constitution.

Similarly, in *Brown* v. *Skustad,* an unreported decision in 1942 of the St. Louis County district court in Minnesota, an injunction was issued to restrain further enforcement of the flag-salute regulation. The opinion invoked religious freedom and Public Law 623, a joint resolution passed by Congress on June 22, 1942, in response to American Legion pressure for standard procedures of displaying respect to the flag.

See also *Bolling* v. *Superior Court,* 16 Wash.2d 373, 133 P.2d 803 (1943), where the Washington supreme court in rejecting the "secular regulation" rule suggested that the flag exercise could have great religious significance to conscientious persons such as Jehovah's Witnesses. The court held, therefore, that Washington's flag-salute law as applied to religious objectors such as the Jehovah's Witnesses violated religious freedom of the state's constitution.

Judicial defiance of the Gobitis decision was less pronounced in a number of other state cases. For instance, it was held in *Matter of Jones,* 175 Misc. 451, 24 N.Y.S.2d 10 (1940), that a child was not delinquent for refusing to pledge allegiance to and to salute the flag, where such refusal was based upon sincere religious beliefs. Declaring that its only course of action would be to take the child away from his parents, the court recognized that it could not compel: (1) the child to salute the flag, (2) the board of education to reinstate her as a pupil in the public schools, or (3) the parents to change their religion. The majority justices did add, however, that they could see no reason why any patriotic American would refuse to overtly display his loyalty. A similar conclusion was reached in *Matter of Reed,* 262 App. Div. 814, 28 N.Y.S.2d 92 (1941), where the rationale *Matter of Jones* was followed.

The opposite conclusion was reached in New Jersey, where it was ruled in *Matter of Latrecchia,* 128 N.J.L. 472, 26 A.2d 881 (1942), that compulsory flag-salute exercises in the public schools were allowable. The New Jersey supreme court went on to find, however, that the evidence there was not sufficient to convict parents of "disorderly conduct" who had refused to send their children to school because of religious convictions opposing saluting the flag.

A controversy had been pending in the Massachusetts supreme court at the time of the Gobitis ruling by the United States Supreme Court. It was settled in *Commonwealth* v. *Johnson,* 309 Mass. 476, 35 N.E.2d 801 (1941), where a divided court reversed the committal to a state training school of pupils who had been expelled twice for habitually refusing to salute the flag.

The court, noting that the legislature had provided no penalties for those refusing to participate in the mandatory exercises determined that a child refusing to salute the flag and recite the pledge of allegiance was not to be considered a "habitual school offender" within the provisions of a statute making such an offender subject to being committed to a training school. A similar result was reached in *State* v. *Lefebvre,* 91 N.H. 382, 20 A.2d 185 (1941).

Apparently only one major case clearly followed the dictates of the Gobitis decision. Required participation of public-school pupils in flag-saluting ceremonies was declared by the Arizona supreme court to be non-violative of the federal Constitution in *State* v. *Davis,* 58 Ariz. 444, 120 P.2d 808 (1942).

GOBITIS IS SPECIFICALLY OVERRULED

The Gobitis ruling was officially overruled by *West Virginia State Board of Education* v. *Barnette,* 319 U.S. 624 (1943). The latter decision, declaring that compulsory flag-salute exercises invade the sphere of intellect and spirit in violation of the First and Fourteenth Amendments, was handed down, ironically enough, on June 14, 1943—Flag Day.

Justice Jackson, speaking for a six-man majority, followed Justice Stone's dissenting rationale in the Gobitis decision, viz., that the state may require pupils to attend educational exercises utilizing studies of American history and civics to teach about patriotism. But ceremonies involving rituals such as a formal flag salute may not be compulsory.

Justice Frankfurter wrote a lengthy dissenting opinion in which he paid strong respects for legislative deference. Justices Reed and Roberts also dissented. All three had been part of the eight-man majority in the Gobitis decision. Three other Justices—Black, Douglas, and Murphy—had also been in favor of the requirement in the Gobitis case, but switched sides in the Barnette ruling. Their votes in the latter case came as no surprise, however, in the light of their declaration in *Jones* v. *Opelika,* 316 U.S. 584, 623–24 (1942) where they announced, "Since we joined in the opinion in the Gobitis Case, we think this is an appropriate occasion to state that we now believe that it was . . . wrongly decided." The two men who joined the Court after 1940—Justices Jackson and Rutledge—joined the new majority in the Barnette decision.

† † WEST VIRGINIA STATE BOARD OF EDUCATION v. BARNETTE

319 U.S. 624, 63 S. CT. 1178, 87 L. ED. 1628 (1943).

Mr. Justice JACKSON delivered the opinion of the Court saying, in part:

Following the decision by this Court on June 3, 1940, in *Minersville School District* v. *Gobitis*, 310 U.S. 586, the West Virginia legislature amended its statutes to require all schools therein to conduct courses of instruction in history, civics, and in the Constitutions of the United States and of the State "for the purpose of teaching, fostering and perpetuating the ideals, principles and spirit of Americanism, and increasing the knowledge of the organization and machinery of the government." Appellant Board of Education was directed, with advice of the State Superintendent of Schools, to "prescribe the courses of study covering these subjects" for public schools. The Act made it the duty of private, parochial and denominational schools to prescribe courses of study "similar to those required for the public schools."

The Board of Education on January 9, 1942, adopted a resolution containing recitals taken largely from the Court's *Gobitis* opinion and ordering that the salute to the flag become a "regular part of the program of activities in the public schools," that all teachers and pupils "shall be required to participate in the salute honoring the Nation represented by the Flag;

provided, however, that refusal to salute the Flag be regarded as an act of insubordination, and shall be dealt with accordingly."

The resolution originally required the "commonly accepted salute to the Flag" which it defined. Objections to the salute as "being too much like Hitler's" were raised by the Parent and Teachers Association, the Boy and Girl Scouts, the Red Cross, and the Federation of Women's Clubs. Some modification appears to have been made in deference to these objections, but no concession was made to Jehovah's Witnesses. What is now required is the "stiff-arm" salute, the saluter to keep the right hand raised with palm turned up while the following is repeated: "I pledge allegiance to the Flag of the United States of America and to the Republic for which it stands; one Nation, indivisible, with liberty and justice for all."

Failure to conform is "insubordination" dealt with by expulsion. Readmission is denied by statute until compliance. Meanwhile the expelled child is "unlawfully absent" and may be proceeded against as a delinquent. His parents or guardians are liable to prosecution, and if convicted are subject to fine not exceeding $50 and jail term not exceeding thirty days.

Appellees, citizens of the United States and of West Virginia, brought suit in the United States District Court for themselves and others similarly situated asking its injunction to restrain enforcement of these laws and regulations against Jehovah's Witnesses. The Witnesses are an unincorporated body teaching that the obligation imposed by law of God is superior to that of laws enacted by temporal government. Their religious beliefs include a literal version of Exodus, Chapter 20, verses 4 and 5, which says: "Thou shalt not make unto thee any graven image, or any likeness of anything that is in heaven above, or that is in the earth beneath, or that is in the water under the earth; thou shalt not bow down thyself to them nor serve them." They consider that the flag is an "image" within this command. For this reason they refuse to salute it.

Children of this faith have been expelled from school and are threatened with exclusion for no other cause. Officials threaten to send them to reformatories maintained for criminally inclined juveniles. Parents of such children have been prosecuted and are threatened with prosecutions for causing delinquency.

The Board of Education moved to dismiss the complaint setting forth these facts and alleging that the law and regulations are an unconstitutional denial of religious freedom, and of freedom of speech, and are invalid under the "due process" and "equal protection" clauses of the Fourteenth Amendment to the Federal Constitution. The cause was submitted on the pleadings to a District Court of three judges. It restrained enforcement as to the plain-tiffs and those of that class. The Board of Education brought the case here by direct appeal.

This case calls upon us to reconsider a precedent decision, as the Court throughout its history often has been required to do. Before turning to the *Gobitis* case, however, it is desirable to notice certain characteristics by which this controversy is distinguished.

The freedom asserted by these appellees does not bring them into collision with rights asserted by any other individual. It is such conflicts which most frequently require intervention of the State to determine where the rights of one end and those of another begin. But the refusal of these persons to participate in the ceremony does not interfere with or deny rights of others to do so. Nor is there any question in this case that their behavior is peaceable and orderly. The sole conflict is between authority and rights of the individual. The State asserts power to condition access to public education on making a prescribed sign and profession and at the same time to coerce attendance by punishing both parent and child. The latter stand on a right of self-determination in matters that touch individual opinion and personal attitude.

As the present CHIEF JUSTICE said in dissent in the *Gobitis* case, the State may "require teaching by instruction and study of all in our history and in the structure and organization of our government, including the guaranties of civil liberty, which tend to inspire patriotism and love of country. . . ." Here, however, we are dealing with a compulsion of students to declare a belief. They are not merely made acquainted with the flag salute so that they may be informed as to what it is or even what it means. The issue here is whether this slow and easily neglected route to aroused loyalties constitutionally may be short-cut by substituting a compulsory salute and slogan. This issue is not prejudiced by the Court's previous holding that where a State, without compelling attendance, extends college facilities to pupils who voluntarily enroll, it may prescribe military training as part of the course without offense to the Constitution. It was held that those who take advantage of its opportunities may not on ground of conscience refuse compliance with such conditions. *Hamilton* v. *Regents,* 293 U.S. 245. In the present case attendance is not optional. That case is also to be distinguished from the present one because, independently of college privileges or requirements, the State has power to raise militia and impose the duties of service therein upon its citizens.

There is no doubt that, in connection with the pledges, the flag salute is a form of utterance. Symbolism is a primitive but effective way of communicating ideas. The use of an emblem or flag to symbolize some system, idea, institution, or personality, is a short cut from mind to mind. Causes and nations, political parties, lodges and ecclesiastical groups seek to knit the loyalty of their followings to a flag or banner, a color or design. The State announces rank, function, and authority through crowns and maces, uniforms and black robes; the church speaks through the Cross, the Crucifix, the altar and shrine, and clerical raiment. Symbols of State often convey political ideas just as religious symbols come to convey theological ones. Associated with many of these symbols are appropriate gestures of acceptance or respect:

a salute, a bowed or bared head, a bended knee. A person gets from a symbol the meaning he puts into it, and what is one man's comfort and inspiration is another's jest and scorn.

Over a decade ago Chief Justice Hughes led this Court in holding that the display of a red flag as a symbol of opposition by peaceful and legal means to organized government was protected by the free speech guaranties of the Constitution. *Stromberg* v. *California,* 283 U.S. 359. Here it is the State that employs a flag as a symbol of adherence to government as presently organized. It requires the individual to communicate by work and sign his acceptance of the political ideas it thus bespeaks. Objection to this form of communication when coerced is an old one, well known to the framers of the Bill of Rights.

It is also to be noted that the compulsory flag salute and pledge requires affirmation of a belief and an attitude of mind. It is not clear whether the regulation contemplates that pupils forego any contrary convictions of their own and become unwilling converts to the prescribed ceremony or whether it will be acceptable if they simulate assent by words without belief and by a gesture barren of meaning. It is now a commonplace that censorship or suppression of expression of opinion is tolerated by our Constitution only when the expression presents a clear and present danger of action of a kind the State is empowered to prevent and punish. It would seem that involuntary affirmation could be commanded only on even more immediate and urgent grounds than silence. But here the power of compulsion is invoked without any allegation that remaining passive during a flag salute ritual creates a clear and present danger that would justify an effort even to muffle expression. To sustain the compulsory flag salute we are required to say that a Bill of Rights, which guards the individual's right to speak his own mind, left it open to public authorities to compel him to utter what is not in his mind.

Whether the First Amendment to the Constitution will permit officials to order observance of ritual of this nature does not depend upon whether as a voluntary exercise we would think it to be good, bad or merely innocuous. Any credo of nationalism is likely to include what some disapprove or to omit what others think essential, and to give off different overtones as it takes on different accents or interpretations. If official power exists to coerce acceptance of any patriotic creed, what it shall contain cannot be decided by courts, but must be largely discretionary with the ordaining authority, whose power to prescribe would no doubt include power to amend. Hence validity of the asserted power to force an American citizen publicly to profess any statement of belief or to engage in any ceremony of assent to one, presents questions of power that must be considered independently of any idea we may have as to the utility of the ceremony in question.

Nor does the issue as we see it turn on one's possession of particular religious views or the sincerity with which they are held. While religion supplies appellees' motive for enduring the discomforts of making the issue in this case, many citizens who do not share these religious views hold such a compulsory rite to infringe constitutional liberty of the individual. It is not necessary to inquire whether non-conformist beliefs will exempt from the duty to salute unless we first find power to make the salute a legal duty.

The *Gobitis* decision, however, *assumed,* as did argument in that case and in this, that power exists in the State to impose the flag salute discipline upon school children in general. The Court only examined and rejected a claim based on religious beliefs of immunity from an unquestioned general rule. The question which underlies the flag salute controversy is whether such a ceremony so touching matters of opinion and political attitude may be imposed upon the individual by official authority under powers committed to any political organization under our Constitution. We examine rather than assume existence of this power and, against this broader definition of issues in this case, reëxamine specific grounds assigned for the *Gobitis* decision.

1. It was said that the flag-salute controversy confronted the Court with "the problem which Lincoln cast in memorable dilemma: 'Must a government of necessity be too *strong* for the liberties of its people, or too *weak* to maintain its own existence?'" and that the answer must be in favor of strength. *Minersville School District* v. *Gobitis.* . . .

We think these issues may be examined free of pressure or restraint growing out of such considerations.

It may be doubted whether Mr. Lincoln would have thought that the strength of government to maintain itself would be impressively vindicated by our confirming power of the State to expel a handful of children from school. Such oversimplification, so handy in political debate, often lacks the precision necessary to postulates of judicial reasoning. If validly applied to this problem, the utterance cited would resolve every issue of power in favor of those in authority and would require us to override every liberty thought to weaken or delay execution of their policies.

Government of limited power need not be anemic government. Assurance that rights are secure tends to diminish fear and jealousy of strong government, and by making us feel safe to live under it makes for its better support. Without promise of a limiting Bill of Rights it is doubtful if our Constitution could have mustered enough strength to enable its ratification. To enforce those rights today is not to choose weak government over strong government. It is only to adhere as a means of strength to individual freedom of mind in preference to officially disciplined uniformity for which history indicates a disappointing and disastrous end.

The subject now before us exemplifies this principle. Free public education, if faithful to the ideal of secular instruction and political neutrality, will not be partisan or enemy of any class, creed, party, or faction. If it is to impose any ideological discipline, however, each party or denomination must seek to control, or failing that, to weaken the influence of the educational system. Observance of the limitations of the Constitution will not weaken government in the field appropriate for its exercise.

2. It was also considered in the *Gobitis* case that functions of educational officers in States, counties and school districts were such that to interfere with their authority "would in effect make us the school board for the country. . . ."

The Fourteenth Amendment, as now applied to the States, protects the citizen against the State itself and all of its creatures—Boards of Education not excepted. These have, of course, important, delicate, and highly discretionary functions, but none that they may not perform within the limits of the Bill of Rights. That they are educating the young for citizenship is reason for scrupulous protection of Constitutional freedoms of the individual, if we are not to strangle the free mind at its source and teach youth to discount important principles of our government as mere platitudes.

Such Boards are numerous and their territorial jurisdiction often small. But small and local authority may feel less sense of responsibility to the Constitution, and agencies of publicity may be less vigilant in calling it to account. The action of Congress in making flag observance voluntary and respecting the conscience of the objector in a matter so vital as raising the Army contrasts sharply with these local regulations in matters relatively trivial to the welfare of the nation. There are village tyrants as well as village Hampdens, but none who acts under color of law is beyond reach of the Constitution.

3. The *Gobitis* opinion reasoned that this is a field "where courts possess no marked and certainly no controlling competence," that it is committed to the legislatures as well as the courts to guard cherished liberties and that it is constitutionally appropriate to "fight out the wise use of legislative authority in the forum of public opinion and before legislative assemblies rather than to transfer such a contest to the judicial arena," since all the "effective means of inducing political changes are left free. . . ."

The very purpose of a Bill of Rights was to withdraw certain subjects from the vicissitudes of political controversy, to place them beyond the reach of majorities and officials and to establish them as legal principles to be applied by the courts. One's right to life, liberty, and property, to free speech, a free press, freedom of worship and assembly, and other fundamental rights may not be submitted to vote; they depend on the outcome of no elections.

In weighing arguments of the parties it is important to distinguish between the due process clause of the Fourteenth Amendment as an instrument for transmitting the principles of the First Amendment and those cases in which it is applied for its own sake. The test of legislation which collides with the Fourteenth Amendment, because it also collides with the principles of the First, is much more definite than the test when only the Fourteenth is involved. Much of the vagueness of the due process clause disappears when the specific prohibitions of the First become its standard. The right of a State to regulate, for example, a public utility may well include, so far as the due process test is concerned, power to impose all of the restrictions which a legislature may have a "rational basis" for adopting. But freedoms of speech and of press, of assembly, and of worship may not be infringed on such slender grounds. They are susceptible of restriction only to prevent grave and immediate danger to interests which the State may lawfully protect. It is important to note that while it is the Fourteenth Amendment which bears directly upon the State it is the more specific limiting principles of the First Amendment that finally govern this case.

Nor does our duty to apply the Bill of Rights to assertions of official authority depend upon our possession of marked competence in the field where the invasion of rights occurs. True, the task of translating the majestic generalities of the Bill of Rights, conceived as part of the pattern of liberal government in the eighteenth century, into concrete restraints on officials dealing with the problems of the twentieth century, is one to disturb self-confidence. These principles grew in soil which also produced a philosophy that the individual was the center of society, that his liberty was attainable through mere absence of governmental restraints, and that government should be entrusted with few controls and only the mildest supervision over men's affairs. We must transplant these rights to a soil in which the *laissez-faire* concept or principle of non-interference has withered at least as to economic affairs, and social advancements are increasingly sought through closer integration of society and through expanded and strengthened governmental controls. These changed conditions often deprive precedents of reliability and cast us more than we would choose upon our own judgment. But we act in these matters not by authority of our competence but by force of our commissions. We cannot, because of modest estimates of our competence in such specialties as public education, withhold the judgment that history authenticates as the function of this Court when liberty is infringed.

4. Lastly, and this is the very heart of the *Gobitis* opinion, it reasons that "National unity is the basis of national security," that the authorities have "the right to select appropriate means for its attainment," and hence reaches the conclusion that such compulsory measures toward "national unity" are

constitutional. Upon the verity of this assumption depends our answer in this case.

National unity as an end which officials may foster by persuasion and example is not in question. The problem is whether under our Constitution compulsion as here employed is a permissible means for its achievement.

Struggles to coerce uniformity of sentiment in support of some end thought essential to their time and country have been waged by many good as well as by evil men. Nationalism is a relatively recent phenomenon but at other times and places the ends have been racial or territorial security, support of a dynasty or regime, and particular plans for saving souls. As first and moderate methods to attain unity have failed, those bent on its accomplishment must resort to an ever-increasing severity. As governmental pressure toward unity becomes greater, so strife becomes more bitter as to whose unity it shall be. Probably no deeper division of our people could proceed from any provocation than from finding it necessary to choose what doctrine and whose program public educational officials shall compel youth to unite in embracing. Ultimate futility of such attempts to compel coherence is the lesson of every such effort from the Roman drive to stamp out Christianity as a disturber of its pagan unity, the Inquisition, as a means to religious and dynastic unity, the Siberian exiles as a means to Russian unity, down to the fast failing efforts of our present totalitarian enemies. Those who begin coercive elimination of dissent soon find themselves exterminating dissenters. Compulsory unification of opinion achieves only the unanimity of the graveyard.

It seems trite but necessary to say that the First Amendment to our Constitution was designed to avoid these ends by avoiding these beginnings. There is no mysticism in the American concept of the State or of the nature or origin of its authority. We set up government by consent of the governed, and the Bill of Rights denies those in power any legal opportunity to coerce that consent. Authority here is to be controlled by public opinion, not public opinion by authority.

The case is made difficult not because the principles of its decision are obscure but because the flag involved is our own. Nevertheless, we apply the limitations of the Constitution with no fear that freedom to be intellectually and spiritually diverse or even contrary will disintegrate the social organization. To believe that patriotism will not flourish if patriotic ceremonies are voluntary and spontaneous instead of a compulsory routine is to make an unflattering estimate of the appeal of our institutions of free minds. We can have intellectual individualism and the rich cultural diversities that we owe to exceptional minds only at the price of occasional eccentricity and abnormal attitudes. When they are so harmless to others or to the State as those we deal with here, the price is not too great. But freedom to differ is not limited to things that do not matter much. That would be a mere shadow of freedom. The test of its substance is the right to differ as to things that touch the heart of the existing order.

If there is any fixed star in our constitutional constellation, it is that no official, high or petty, can prescribe what shall be orthodox in politics, nationalism, religion, or other matters of opinion or force citizens to confess by word or act their faith therein. If there are any circumstances which permit an exception, they do not now occur to us.

We think the action of the local authorities in compelling the flag salute and pledge transcends constitutional limitations on their power and invades the sphere of intellect and spirit which it is the purpose of the First Amendment to our Constitution to reserve from all official control.

The decision of this Court in *Minersville School District* v. *Gobitis . . .* [is] overruled, and the judgment enjoining enforcement of the West Virginia Regulation is affirmed.

Mr. Justice BLACK and Mr. Justice DOUGLAS, concurring:

We are substantially in agreement with the opinion just read, but since we originally joined with the Court in *Gobitis* case, it is appropriate that we make a brief statement of reasons for our change of view.

Reluctance to make the Federal Constitution a rigid bar against state regulation of conduct thought inimical to the public welfare was the controlling influence which moved us to consent to the *Gobitis* decision. Long reflection convinced us that although the principle is sound, its application in the particular case was wrong. *Jones* v. *Opelika*, 316 U.S. 584, 623. We believe that the statute before us fails to accord full scope to the freedom of religion secured to the appellees by the First and Fourteenth Amendments.

The statute requires the appellees to participate in a ceremony aimed at inculcating respect for the flag and for this country. The Jehovah's Witnesses, without any desire to show disrespect for either the flag or the country, interpret the Bible as commanding, at the risk of God's displeasure, that they not go through the form of a pledge of allegiance to any flag. The devoutness of their belief is evidenced by their willingness to suffer persecution and punishment, rather than make the pledge.

No well-ordered society can leave to the individuals an absolute right to make final decisions, unassailable by the State, as to everything they will or will not do. The First Amendment does not go so far. Religious faiths, honestly held, do not free individuals from responsibility to conduct themselves obediently to laws which are either imperatively necessary to protect society as a whole from grave and pressingly imminent dangers or which, without any general prohibition, merely regulate time, place or manner of religious activity. Decision as to the constitutionality of particular laws which strike at the substance of religious tenets and practices must be made by this Court. The duty is a solemn one, and in meeting it we cannot say that a failure, because of religious scruples, to assume a particular physical position and to repeat the words of a patriotic formula creates a grave danger to the nation. Such a statutory exaction is a form of test oath, and the test oath has always been abhorrent in the United States.

Words uttered under coercion are proof of loyalty to nothing but self interest. Love of country must spring from willing hearts and free minds, inspired by a fair administration of wise laws enacted by the people's elected representatives within the bounds of express constitutional prohibitions. These laws must, to be consistent with the First Amendment, permit the widest toleration of conflicting viewpoints consistent with a society of free men.

Neither our domestic tranquility in peace nor our martial effort in war depends on compelling little children to participate in a ceremony which ends in nothing for them but a fear of spiritual condemnation. If, as we think, their fears are groundless, time and reason are the proper antidotes for their errors. The ceremonial, when enforced against conscientious objectors, more likely to defeat than to serve its high purpose, is a handy implement for disguised religious persecution. As such, it is inconsistent with our Constitution's plan and purpose.

Mr. Justice MURPHY, concurring:

. . . I am unable to agree that the benefits that may accrue to society from the compulsory flag salute are sufficiently definite and tangible to justify the invasion of freedom and privacy that is entailed or to compensate for a restraint on the freedom of the individual to be vocal or silent according to his conscience or personal inclination. The trenchant words in the preamble to the Virginia Statute for Religious Freedom remain unanswerable: ". . . all attempts to influence [the mind] by temporal punishments, or burdens, or by civil incapacitations, tend only to beget habits of hypocrisy and meanness. . . ." Any spark of love for country which may be generated in a child or his associates by forcing him to make what is to him an empty gesture and recite words wrung from him contrary to his religious beliefs is overshadowed by the desirability of preserving freedom of conscience to the full. It is in that freedom and the example of persuasion, not in force and compulsion, that the real unity of America lies.

Mr. Justice FRANKFURTER, dissenting:

. . . As a member of this Court I am not justified in writing my private notions of policy into the Constitution, no matter how deeply I may cherish them or how mischievous I may deem their disregard. The duty of a judge who must decide which of two claims before the Court shall prevail, that of a State to enact and enforce laws within its general competence or that of an individual to refuse obedience because of the demands of his conscience, is not that of the ordinary person. It can never be emphasized too much that one's own opinion about the wisdom or evil of a law should be excluded altogether when one is doing one's duty on the bench. The only opinion of our own even looking in that direction that is material is our opinion whether legislators could in reason have enacted such a law. In the light of all the circumstances, including the history of this Court, it would require more daring than I possess to deny that reasonable legislators could have taken the action which is before us for review. Most unwillingly, therefore, I must differ from my brethren with regard to legislation like this. I cannot bring my mind to believe that the "liberty" secured by the Due Process Clause gives this Court authority to deny to the State of West Virginia the attainment of that which we all recognize as a legitimate legislative end, namely, the promotion of good citizenship, by employment of the means here chosen.

. . . One's conception of the Constitution cannot be severed from one's conception of a judge's function in applying it. The Court has no reason for existence if it merely reflects the pressures of the day. Our system is built on the faith that men set apart for this special function, freed from the influences of immediacy and from the deflections of worldly ambition, will become able to take a view of longer range than the period of responsibility entrusted to Congress and legislatures. We are dealing with matters as to which legislators and voters have conflicting views. Are we as judges to impose our strong convictions on where wisdom lies? That which three years ago had seemed to five successive Courts to lie within permissible areas of legislation is now outlawed by the deciding shift of opinion of two Justices. What reason is there to believe that they or their successors may not have another view a few years hence? Is that which was deemed to be of so fundamental a nature as to be written into the Constitution to endure for all times to be the sport of shifting winds of doctrine? Of course, judicial opinions, even as to questions of constitutionality, are not immutable. As has been true in the past, the Court will from time to time reverse its position. But I believe that never before these Jehovah's Witnesses cases (except for minor deviations subsequently re-

traced) has this Court overruled decisions so as to restrict the powers of democratic government. Always heretofore, it has withdrawn narrow views of legislative authority so as to authorize what formerly it had denied.

In view of this history it must be plain that what thirteen Justices found to be within the constitutional authority of a state, legislators can not be deemed unreasonable in enacting. Therefore, in denying to the states what heretofore has received such impressive judicial sanction, some other tests of unconstitutionality must surely be guiding the Court than the absence of a rational justification for the legislation. But I know of no other test which this Court is authorized to apply in nullifying legislation.

. . . Of course patriotism can not be enforced by the flag salute. But neither can the liberal spirit be enforced by judicial invalidation of illiberal legislation. Our constant preoccupation with the constitutionality of legislation rather than with its wisdom tends to preoccupation of the American mind with a false value. The tendency of focussing attention on constitutionality is to make constitutionality synonymous with wisdom, to regard a law as all right if it is constitutional. Such an attitude is a great enemy of liberalism. Particularly in legislation affecting freedom of thought and freedom of speech much which should offend a free-spirited society is constitutional. Reliance for the most precious interests of civilization, therefore, must be found outside of their vindication in courts of law. Only a persistent positive translation of the faith of a free society into the convictions and habits and actions of a community is the ultimate reliance against unabated temptations to fetter the human spirit.

REACTIONS OF LEGAL PERIODICALS TO
WEST VIRGINIA STATE BOARD OF EDUCATION v. *BARNETTE*

The Barnett decision was received with as much enthusiasm as the Gobitis case was criticized three years earlier. Personal "freedom" was the theme that ranged throughout the law reviews which favored the Court's stands in the Barnette case as writers happily pointed to the broader sociological approach of the Barnette decision as an alternative to the "war hysteria" of the Gobitis ruling.

In this connection, the Constitution was considered in the *Temple University Law Quarterly* (17:465) to be "an expression of faith," and not a balancer of the competition between the state and the individual parents as to who should train the child. However, prophetic apprehension about the practical results of an otherwise realistic decision was expressed in the *George Washington Law Review* (12:70): "There is no knowing how far the freedom of religious beliefs may now be extended under the First Amendment as interpreted in the Barnette case."

The one review in plenary disagreement, the *Georgia Bar Journal* (6:249), followed Justice Frankfurter's dissent. The reviewer could find no arguments with the Justice's rationale that the purpose of the constitutional provision was to prohibit religious liabilities rather than to create civil immunity, but concluded, however, that it was the legislature's job to nullify undesirable legislation, and not the Court's.

REACTIONS OF OTHER PERIODICALS TO
WEST VIRGINIA STATE BOARD OF EDUCATION v. *BARNETTE*

The Barnette decision was greeted enthusiastically in education journals and general periodicals. As in the reactions to the Gobitis case, the decision was generally viewed in terms of individual's liberties.

Rodgdon in *Clearing House* (19:192, 1944) and an article in *American School Board Journal* (107:40, 1943) interpreted the Court's decision as meaning the Court would not sustain compulsory flag salutes at the expense of civil liberties in the Bill of Rights. Other articles such as in *Time* (41:16, 1943), also applauded the Court's decision as reaffirming "its faith in the Bill of Rights." In this same vein, an editorial in *The School Executive* (63:17, 1943) said "We hope the present position of the Court continues unchanged."

T. R. Powell in *New Republic* (109:16, 1943) considered the positions of the majority and minority to be essentially switched from the Gobitis case. In the Barnette decision, the majority took Stone's dissenting opinion and the dissent took Frankfurter's majority position.

An article in *Christian Century* (60:731, 1943) read more into the Barnette decision than others did. It stated: "By this flag salute decision the court has cleared up the whole range of cases involving freedom of conscience and freedom for the propagation of religious beliefs. . . ."

The press reactions to the Barnette decision followed the sentiments held toward the Gobitis decision. According to D. R. Manwaring in *Render Unto Caesar* (1962, p. 238), the majority of the papers commenting editorially on the Barnette ruling approved of the decision.

THE BARNETTE DECISION AS CONTROLLING PRECEDENT

At the time of the Barnette ruling, Witnesses claimed that more than two thousand Jehovah's Witnesses students had been expelled from the public schools, with expulsions taking place in all forty-eight states. In contrast, only fifteen states apparently had expelled pupils of the Jehovah's Witnesses faith for their refusal to salute the flag before the Gobitis decision of three years earlier.

That the Barnette ruling had apparently settled the flag-salute issue was evidenced by the willingness of several state courts to apply the full extent of its logic to questions concerning state constitutional provisions. See in this connection, *Commonwealth* v. *Conte,* 154 Pa. Super. 112, 35 A.2d 742 (1944), *Commonwealth* v. *Crowley,* 154 Pa. Super. 116, 35 A.2d 744 (1944), and *State* v. *Davis,* 69 S.D. 328, 10 N.W.2d 288 (1944). All of the above cases overturned convictions of Jehovah's Witnesses parents who had violated the compulsory education law of their respective states by refusing to send their children to schools requiring flag-saluting exercises.

A circular sent in November, 1943, by the Department of Justice to all United States attorneys, however, revealed that local school boards were disregarding the clear dictates of the Barnette decision. The circular ordered the attorneys to take the necessary legal actions against noncomplying officials upon receipt of complaints of interferences by state officials with religious liberty. Federal pressures appeared, therefore, as a guarantee that compulsory flag salutes would be eliminated everywhere.

One chapter remains to be told in the story of flag saluting. In 1954, Congress, at the urging of President Eisenhower, added a phrase to the standard pledge of allegiance. The pledge now reads at 36 U.S.C. §172, 36 U.S.C.A. §172:

> I pledge allegiance to the Flag of the United States of America and to the Republic for which it stands; one nation *under God,* indivisible, with liberty and justice for all. [Emphasis added.]

Action was brought in New York challenging the recommendation by the commissioner of education that the amended version of the allegiance pledge, as quoted above, be used in the public schools. A county court held in *Lewis* v. *Allen*, 5 Misc.2d 68, 159 N.Y.S.2d 807 (1957), that the regulation did not violate state or federal constitutional provisions. The court noted that the pledge was voluntary, and that no penalties were imposed for noncompliance.

That lower decision was affirmed by the appellate division of the New York supreme court at 11 App. Div.2d 447, 207 N.Y.S.2d 862 (1960), below. The court observed there, however, that any compulsion in the regulation would violate freedom of religion under the federal Constitution.

† † *LEWIS* v. *ALLEN*
11 APP. DIV. 2D 447, 207 N.Y.S.2d 862 (1960).

Judge BOOKSTEIN delivered the opinion of the court:

This is a proceeding by petitioners under Article 78 Sec. 1296, Par. 1, of the Civil Practice Act to compel respondent, the Commissioner of Education of the State of New York, to perform a duty which allegedly he has failed to perform. The duty which petitioners would compel him to perform is to revoke and rescind a certain regulation allegedly enforced in the public schools of the State of New York, "requiring the use of the phrase 'under God' in the Pledge of Allegiance to the Flag of the United States of America, and directing him to reestablish the use of said pledge, without that phrase."

The papers fail to indicate any demand or request for revocation or recision prior to the commencement of this proceeding.

No statutory duty has been shown which requires respondent to rescind or revoke the regulation. So it cannot be said that respondent has failed to perform a duty imposed upon him by statute.

But petitioners contend that such duty is imposed on respondent by the First and Fourteenth Amendments to the United States Constitution and by Article I, Sec. 3, and Article XI, Sec. 4, of the New York State Constitution.

Section 802 of the Education Law, as amended by Chapter 177 of the Laws of 1956, provides, in part:

1. It shall be the duty of the commissioner of education to prepare, for the use of the public schools of the state, a program providing for a salute to the flag and a *pledge of allegiance to the flag*, for instruction in its correct use and display and such other patriotic exercises as may be deemed by him to be expedient, under such regulations and instructions as may best meet the varied requirements of the different grades in such schools. (Emphasis supplied.)

Respondent had, prior to the 1956 amendment, promulgated Regulation 150, Par. 5, providing:

It is recommended that the schools use the following pledge to the flag:

'I pledge allegiance to the flag of the

United States of America and to the Republic for which it stands, one nation, indivisible, with liberty and justice for all.'

This recommended pledge is the precise pledge enacted by the Congress of the United States. U.S.C. Title 36, Chap. 10, Sec. 172, 36 U.S.C.A. § 172.

On June 14, 1954, the Congress amended Sec. 172 by inserting, between the words "nation" and "indivisible," the words "under God." The pledge of allegiance to the flag as amended by the Congress now reads:

I pledge allegiance to the flag of the United States of America and to the Republic for which it stands, one Nation under God, indivisible, with liberty and justice for all.

Thereafter respondent amended Regulation 150, Par. 5, recommending a pledge in the words enacted by the Congress.

Petitioners object to the use of the words, "under God" in the pledge of allegiance.

They have no objection to the former pledge but contend that respondent has the duty to revoke this revised regulation, deleting the words "under God" from the pledge recommended for use in the public schools and this duty petitioners say he has failed to perform.

It is clear that in making and amending Regulation 150 in accordance with the Education Law and with an act of Congress, respondent *was* performing his duties.

Respondent has made a regulation pursuant to express direction of a statute of this State and in conformance with a law of the United States. How then can he be charged with failing to perform his duty?

Petitioner's contention, in final analysis, is that the present pledge of allegiance to the flag of the United States violates the First Amendment to the United States Constitution (which by the Fourteenth Amendment binds this state), and, also violates the New York State Constitution. Therefore, petitioners contend respondent cannot and should not perform the duties which the Legislature of the State of New York has directed him to perform, since, by amending the regulation to include the words "under God," the regulation now contravenes the First Amendment.

To sustain that contention implies respondent has not only the right, but the duty, to determine the constitutionality of an act of the State Legislature or of the Congress and to refuse to perform, where in his judgment, such act is unconstitutional.

Clearly, this is in the exclusive domain of the judiciary. It is not a function of administrative officials.

As I read the petition, no claim is asserted that either the act of the Legislature or the act of Congress above referred to violates the Constitution of the United States or of the State of New York. The petition confines its charge to the regulation promulgated by the respondent and asserts the regulation contravenes those Constitutions.

The First Amendment to the United States Constitution, so far as pertinent, provides: "Congress shall make no law respecting an establishment of religion, or prohibiting the free exercise thereof . . . ." The Fourteenth Amendment makes the First Amendment applicable to and binding on the State of New York.

Article 1, Sec. 3 of the New York Constitution provides:

The free exercise and enjoyment of religious profession and worship, without discrimination or preference, shall forever be allowed in this state to all mankind; and no person shall be rendered incompetent to be a witness on account of his opinions on matters of religious belief; but the liberty of conscience hereby secured shall not be so construed as to excuse acts of licentiousness, or justify practices inconsistent with the peace or safety of this state.

Article 11, Sec. 4 of the New York Constitution provides:

Neither the state nor any subdivision thereof shall use its property or credit or any public money, or authorize or permit either to be used, directly or indirectly, in aid or maintenance, other than for examination or inspection, of any school or institution of learning wholly or in part under the control or direction of any religious denomination, or in which any denominational tenet or doctrine is taught, but the legislature may provide for the transportation of children to and from any school or institution of learning.

Petitioners claim that free thinkers, non-believers, atheists and agnostics cannot be compelled to recite the present pledge of allegiance because it includes the words "under God," and such compulsion violates the aforesaid constitutional provisions.

It is elementary that the First Amendment to the United States Constitution prohibits the establishment of religion and erects a wall of separation between church and State which may not and must not be breached.

In *People of State of Illinois* ex rel. *McCollum* v. *Board of Education*, 1948, 333 U.S. 203, 68 S. Ct. 461, 92 L. Ed. 648, the public schools were used for avowed religious instructions by members of the Protestant, Roman Catholic and Jewish faiths, although attendance at such instructions was only on request

of parents. The United States Supreme Court declared the system unconstitutional because public school buildings were there being used for dissemination of religious doctrines at the taxpayers' expense.

In *West Virginia State Board of Education* v. *Barnette*, 1943, 319 U.S. 624, at page 638, 633 S. Ct. 1178, at page 1185, 87 L.Ed. 1628, the United States Supreme Court indicated approval of the Congressional enactment of the pledge of allegiance but declared West Virginia flag salute law unconstitutional. In that instance, however, the salute to the flag was *compulsory*. The court pointed out, 319 U.S. at page 629, 63 S. Ct. at page 1181:

Failure to conform is 'insubordination' dealt with by expulsion. Readmission is denied by statute until compliance. Meanwhile the expelled child is 'unlawfully absent' and may be proceeded against as a delinquent. His parents or guardians are liable to prosecution, and if convicted are subject to fine not exceeding $50 and jail term not exceeding thirty days.

The regulation under attack here has no compulsory aspect. No penalties attach to a failure or refusal to recite the pledge. The pledge is made voluntarily and no penalties are imposed for non-compliance.

There are two general bases for attacking a statute or regulation on the grounds that it violates the First Amendment to the United State Constitution or the sections of the New York Constitution heretofore referred to:

First: Where a person is required to submit to some religious rite or instruction or is deprived or threatened with deprivation of his freedom for resisting that unconstitutional requirement; Second: Where a person is deprived of property for unconstitutional purposes (such as direct or indirect tax to support a religious establishment). See concurring opinion of Mr. Justice Jackson in the McCollum case, supra, 333 U.S. at pages 232–233, 68 S. Ct. at pages 475, 476.

Here, the second basis cannot be successfully urged. No tax or deprivation of property is involved whether or not the words "under God" are used in the pledge. We are, therefore, obliged to consider whether the first basis supports petitioners' contention.

If I properly apprehend the intent, design and purposes of the First Amendment, it was conceived to prevent and prohibit the establishment of a *State Religion;* it was not intended to prevent or prohibit the growth and development of a *Religious State.*

This concept finds judicial support in *Holy Trinity Church* v. *United States,* 1892, 143 U.S. 457, at page 470, 12 S. Ct. 511, at page 516, 36 L.Ed. 226, where the Court says "this is a religious nation."

In 1951, that Court said in *Zorach* v. *Clauson,* 343 U.S. 306, at page 313, 72 S. Ct. 679, at page 684, 96 L.Ed. 954, "We are a religious people whose institutions presuppose a Supreme Being."

The Declaration of Independence refers to "the Supreme Judge of the world," and "the protection of Divine Providence." Lincoln, at Gettysburg, spoke of "this nation, under God." Even the preamble to the New York Constitution expresses gratitude "to Almighty God for our Freedom." Indeed, the presidential oath of office concludes, "So Help Me, God." By Act of Congress, our coins are inscribed, "In God we trust."

If petitioners' contention be sound, it may be wondered whether the public school curriculum might properly include the Declaration of Independence and the Gettysburg address. Could "America" (". . . Protect us by thy might, Great God, our King!") be sung in a public school without offending the First Amendment? And might not the presidential oath of office have questionable constitutional status?

These questions find their answer in House Report No. 1693, note 2, supra. There, the Committee on Judiciary notes:

> The Supreme Court has clearly indicated that the references to the Almighty which run through our laws, our public rituals and our ceremonies in no way flout the provisions of the first amendment *(Zorach* v. *Clauson,* 343 U.S. 306, 312–313 [72 S.Ct. 679, 96 L.Ed. 954]). In so construing the first amendment, the Court pointed out that if this recognition of the Almighty was not so, then even a fastidious atheist or agnostic could object to the way in which the Court itself opens each of its sessions, namely, 'God save the United States and the Honorable Court' *(Id.,* [343 U.S.] 313 [72 S.Ct. 683])."

But evidently relying on Mr. Justice Frankfurter's concurring opinion in the McCollum case, supra, 333 U.S. at page 227, 68 S.Ct. at page 473, petitioners urge there is a compulsion which operates and, in substance, "requires" that a child recite the words "under God," when reciting the pledge of allegiance. In the circumstances of the McCollum case, Mr. Justice Frankfurter said, "That a child is offered an alternative may reduce the constraint; it does not eliminate the operation of influence by the school in matters sacred to conscience and outside the school's domain. The law of imitation operates, and non-conformity is not an outstanding characteristic of children. The result is an obvious pressure upon children. . . ."

Whatever the force of that argument in the circumstances of the McCollum case, here, the child of a non-believer may simply omit the words, "under God," in reciting the pledge. His "non-conformity," if such it be, will not, in the circumstances of this case, set him apart from his fellow students or bring "pressure" to bear in any real sense.

But assuming the contrary, Mr. Justice Jackson's concurring opinion in the McCollum case is nicely apposite. He there observed, 333 U.S. at pages 232–233, 68 S.Ct. at page 476:

The complaint is that when others join and he does not, it sets him apart as a dissenter, which is humiliating. Even admitting this to be true, it may be doubted whether the Constitution which, of course, protects the right to dissent, can be construed also to protect one from the embarrassment that always attends nonconformity, whether in religion, politics, behavior or dress. Since no legal compulsion is applied to complainant's son himself and no penalty is imposed or threatened from which we may relieve him, we can hardly base jurisdiction on this ground.

To grant this application "would be preferring those who believe in no religion over those who do believe." *Zorach* v. *Clauson*, supra, 343 U.S. at page 314, 72 S.Ct. at page 684. The First Amendment does not require this.

Petitioners' right to disbelieve is guaranteed by the First Amendment, and neither they nor their children can be compelled to recite the words "under God" in the pledge of allegiance. But the First Amendment affords them no preference over those who do believe in God and who, in pledging their allegiance, choose to express that belief.

Petition dismissed upon the merits, with costs.

SUMMARY

Throughout world history the religious beliefs of some minorities have conflicted with demonstrations which the majority of the public have regarded as manifestations of patriotism. The United States is no exception, despite two specific provisions in its Bill of Rights designed to protect the rights of religious minorities. One such patriotic demonstration which has placed a particular strain upon policy-formulation and certain religious sects in the United States has been the practice of holding compulsory flag-salute ceremonies.

The initiative for establishing an American flag-salute ceremony dates back to 1892, and New York passed the first "flag salute" statute in 1898. Support for ceremonies of this nature came generally from groups such as the American Legion, the Daughters of the American Revolution, and the Ku Klux Klan. Opposition to practices of this type came, on the other hand, from the teaching profession and some religious groups such as the Jehovah's Witnesses. In any event, by 1940, some ritual involving the flag was being used in the public schools of at least thirty states.

It was the Jehovah's Witnesses who generally sponsored the litigation attacking state laws authorizing programs of compulsory flag saluting in the public schools arguing they violated the Freedom of Religion Clause of the First Amendment. They objected that this practice violated a tenet of their religious belief in that it constituted a form of idolatry. Their efforts met with universal failure in the state courts prior to the time the Supreme Court took the subject under examination. The state courts usually adopted the "secular regulation" standard which has as its essence the notion that ceremonies in public schools involving saluting the flag and the pledge of allegiance are patriotic rather than religious exercises.

Indeed, the Supreme Court showed an early reluctance to enter the controversy. For example, the first case involving this issue reached the Court in 1937 but the Court dismissed it summarily in a *per curiam* opinion on the grounds that it did not pose a substantial federal question. In three later cases to come to the Supreme Court the Jehovah's Witnesses were equally unsuccessful since the Court either upheld the lower courts' decisions permitting such exercises or dismissed the appeals for want of a substantial federal question.

Not until 1940 did the Supreme Court rule on the merits of compulsory flag-salute programs in the public schools. In the Gobitis case, the Court by an eight to one vote upheld the constitutionality of such programs as non-violative of the Freedom of Religion Clause of the First Amendment. Concluding that "national unity is the basis of our security," and "that we live by symbols," the Court placed a higher priority on manifestations of patriotism than upon the injured religious sensibilities of a minority. In a blistering dissent, Justice Stone concluded that while voluntary expressions of loyalty might promote national unity it was quite another thing to compel certain children to violate their religious beliefs to participate in these programs and regard this as more important than the Freedom of Religion Clause of the Constitution.

The reaction of legal periodicals to the Gobitis decision was extremely hostile. Over three-fourths of those taking a stand on the case were critical of the Court. While comments on the subject in education journals and the popular media were limited, there was a general tendency to condemn the Court's action.

Of even more interest is the fact that state courts tended to reflect the public feeling of opposition. Whereas before the Gobitis decision state courts had regularly upheld flag-salute exercises, following it, three state courts directly repudiated the ruling, and four others ignored the principle of the case and ruled in favor of the religious scruples of the Jehovah's Witnesses. In only two states did the court follow the ruling of the Gobitis case and one of these cannot be considered a major case in point.

Two years after the Gobitis decision, in one of the most interesting examples of judicial behavior in recent history, several justices in a completely unrelated case undertook to state formally that they had changed their minds about their affirmative vote in the Gobitis case. Unsurprisingly enough, one year later in 1943, the Court reversed the Gobitis decision in the Barnette case. Speaking for the majority, Justice Jackson held that compulsory programs of flag saluting in the public schools invaded the spiritual and intellectual spheres of the individual in violation of the First Amendment.

The reaction of legal periodicals, education journals, general periodicals, and the newspapers all strongly supported the Barnette decision. Moreover, state courts accepted and followed the ruling as the three cases noted earlier indicate. Local school boards, however, were not so cooperative. Indeed, the situation reached the point where United States district attorneys were ordered to take action when they received complaints of noncompliance by state officials.

In a series of related cases, however, the New York supreme court upheld a regulation establishing voluntary programs involving the pledge of allegiance. It was argued that the words "under God" which had been added in 1954, violated First Amendment rights. The court based its conclusion on the fact that the program was voluntary and that a child did not really have to utter the words "under God" even if he participated in the ceremony.

CHAPTER SEVEN

School Buildings

† †

THERE ARE TWO GENERAL AREAS of litigation over church-state relations concerning the use of school buildings: the leasing of churches and sectarian buildings for public school use and, conversely, the renting of public school buildings for religious and other non-school purposes.

THE USE OF SECTARIAN BUILDINGS AS PUBLIC SCHOOLS

Several cases have involved holding public school classes in sectarian buildings of one sort or another. Many courts have ruled that such rentals do not violate state constitutional prohibitions of state aid to religion and of combining church and state functions. General approval has been given especially to emergency contracts and for other short-term arrangements.

In *Scripture* v. *Burns*, 59 Ia. 70, 12 N.W. 760 (1882), mandamus was held not to lie against the actions of school directors who rented a house owned by a bishop of the Roman Catholic church for use as a public schoolhouse. In doing so, the court noted that the arrangement was intended to be temporary and that there existed statutory authority for the directors to rent another building when it was not feasible to use the existing schoolhouse.

The high court of Illinois approved of an arrangement whereby a public school was maintained in the basement of a Roman Catholic church in *Millard* v. *Board of Education*, 121 Ill. 297, 10 N.E. 669 (1887). Declaring that the particular religious faith of the lessor was of "no importance whatever," the court noted that a school building was desperately needed in light of the defeat of a school-bond issue by the district taxpayers. Its ruling was further based on the conclusion that no religious doctrine during regular school hours was required by the board of education.

The rental and occupation for public school purposes of a building of a parochial character was allowed in *Swadley* v. *Haynes*, Tenn., 41 S.W. 1066 (1897). The Tennessee court nevertheless said that public money could not in normal circumstances be legally invested in any religious

171

property, but hastened to qualify the ban in the instant situation, where such a rental appeared to be necessary for the maintenance of the public school system in that district.

The mere fact that public school classes were held in churches was not considered in *Ford* v. *O'Shea,* 136 Misc. 921, 244 N.Y.S. 38 (1929), to be sufficient for finding a violation of the New York constitution, which prohibits the use of public money for support of any school controlled by a religious denomination. Although entertaining the taxpayer's suit, the supreme court of New York County found that the presiding teachers were public school teachers; that the curricula of studies was identical with those of other public schools; and that no religious paraphernalia was exhibited in the classroom.

A recent arrangement whereby the Roman Catholic church donated free of charge two buildings and leased another at a nominal charge to the public school board was upheld in *Rawlings* v. *Butler,* Ky., 290 S.W.2d 801 (1956). The Kentucky court could see no constitutional problem "so long as the church [did] not attempt to exercise any dominion or control over the school or classes taught therein." Constitutional difficulty was also precluded by the fact that the board maintained "full and complete control of the buildings throughout the school year," the opinion said.

The court noted further that there was no stipulation that there was any physical connection between the school buildings in question and the church or church schools. The record showed instead that the schools "were conducted in the same manner as other public schools in the respective counties."

On the other hand, in North Dakota, the leasing by the public school of a room in a Roman Catholic institution was invalidated in *Pronovost* v. *Brunette,* 36 N.D. 288, 162 N.W. 300 (1917). Although apparently not specifically deciding the question upon religious grounds, the court stated that under the circumstances the board lacked authority to rent a school room from anyone. It based that conclusion upon a finding that the public schoolhouse had sufficient room to accomplish its purposes.

The issue of who has authority over public school classes in sectarian buildings has also been a criteria for allowing sectarian buildings to be used. The high courts of several states have approved such practices when the board of education retained control. See for example, *New Haven* v. *Torrington,* 132 Conn. 194, 43 A.2d 455 (1945); *Millard V. Board of Education,* 121 Ill. 297, 10 N.E. 699 (1887); *State* ex rel. *Johnson* v. *Boyd,* 217 Ind. 348, 28 N.E.2d 256 (1940); *Crain* v. *Walker,* 222 Ky. 828, 2 S.W.2d 654 (1928); and *State* ex rel. *Conway* v. *District Board,* 162 Wis. 482, 156 N.W. 477 (1916).

A number of other cases presented the even stickier issue of the physical combining under one roof of a public school with a parochial school.

Grave doubts were then raised as to whether the public school maintained its public status and was, therefore, still entitled to its share of the common school fund.

It was held in *Dorner* v. *School District,* 137 Wis. 147, 118 N.W. 353 (1908), below, that a district could rent part of a parochial school building for holding common school classes when the district schoolhouse clearly was inadequate to handle the situation. Noting that the school district had "express power to vote a tax to hire a schoolhouse," the court could find "nothing either in the expression or policy of the statutes" to prevent the district from choosing a parochial school building.

† †   *DORNER* v. *SCHOOL DISTRICT No. 5*
137 WIS. 147, 118 N.W. 353 (1908).

The opinion of the court was delivered by Judge DODGE:

The defendant school district, for a period of about 20 years, rented from the defendant congregation of the Immaculate Conception, a Roman Catholic church corporation, certain rooms in its school building and expended the school moneys of the district in paying teachers to conduct schools therein, and also paid certain small amounts for fuel, cleaning, and the like. The building had been erected for the purposes of a parochial school by said church corporation, and the rest of the rooms therein not rented by the district were used to maintain the parochial school, and the public school conducted in the rooms rented by the school district was characterized by certain religious ceremonies, in that certain distinctive prayers of the Catholic Church were said at intervals throughout the school day, church hymns were sung, and the teachers were nuns specially designated to the service by the superior of a Catholic sisterhood to which they belonged.

In addition the scholars prior to school hours quite uniformly attended distinctively religious teaching in the adjoining church, and the school was suspended to enable their attendance upon weddings and funerals in the church. The pupils were all children of Catholic parents, members of the church congregation, with occasional exceptions of one or two at various times during said 20 years. The plaintiffs, members of the congregation, but also residents and taxpayers of the district, on behalf of themselves and others similarly situated, brought this action to enjoin the school board and district from persisting in maintaining the public school of the district in such manner and from paying out any moneys of the district for such purposes, and also to recover in behalf of the district all sums paid for maintenance of such school from the said church corporation and from the members of the school board who had joined in paying it out. The trial court found that the school so conducted had at all times been pervaded and characterized by sectarian instruction contrary to law, and granted injunction against continued maintenance thereof, but held that it was within the power of the school district and board to rent rooms as they deemed wise for the maintenance of a distinctively public school, and therefore refused to enjoin the maintenance thereof in the parochial school building. With regard to the moneys expended prior to the commencement of the suit, he held that the plaintiffs and all members of the school district had at all times had full knowledge, both before and immediately after the fact, of the manner in which the school was conducted, and of the expenditure of the school district moneys for the purposes aforesaid, and that, having made no objection, they were guilty of laches such as to warrant the court in denying the prayer for the repayment of moneys expended for services rendered in good faith and with the tacit approval and acquiescence of all interested parties. The plaintiffs appeal from those parts of the judgment which deny injunction against maintenance of a public school in the parochial school building, and deny recovery from the church corporation and from the members of the school board of the moneys paid out for teachers' salaries and other expenses of the school maintained heretofore.

But two questions arise upon this appeal, and they rather narrow ones. The very important questions as to what acts may constitute the giving or allowing sectarian instruction such as is prohibited in public schools by article 10, § 3, Const. Wis., and whether the acts done in the instant case are within

that inhibition, are treated in an able and exhaustive opinion by the trial court, but are not presented by the appeal. We are therefore to start with the fact that for nearly 20 years the school officers have annually paid school district moneys for support of a school where sectarian instruction was permitted. The question whether such payments were so unlawful that the school district, as a corporation, might maintain an action at law to recover them back from the recipients, or for damages against the district officers and their confederates for dissipating the school funds, was not decided, but affirmative answer was hypothetically assumed by the trial court, as also that the district will not bring any such action. The right of a member of a corporation to invoke the interference of a court of equity to practically coerce the reluctant corporation to enforce its legal rights against its officers and their confederates is abundantly established by our decisions. . . . [T]he circuit court . . . found as facts that plaintiffs and all other taxpayers had been cognizant of the manner of conducting the school, and that the electors of the district each year had been informed that the money had been spent for such purpose, and, without protest from any, at each meeting directed like expenditures for the ensuing year. Such finding is not antagonized by any clear preponderance of evidence. On the faith of such acquiescence, believing that all taxpayers approved, the defendant officers have parted with the money, and quite obviously, must lose it if compelled to reimburse the district. These plaintiffs at least cannot equitably ask that the defendants so suffer for acts induced and invited by plaintiff's own conduct.

We find no error in the trial court's refusal to enjoin the district and board from maintaining a common school in the parochial school building. Incidentally it may be noted that there is no prayer for such specific relief, but the court considered the question, and we will not rest upon that defect in the pleadings. Inferentially, at least, every school district is commanded to maintain a common school, for it shall be put out of existence if it does not. Section 423, St. 1808. True, this district owns a schoolhouse, 28 feet by 18, which is obviously wholly inadequate for a common school free to all the 200 or more scholars of the district. Non constat anything in the record or evidence, it may be wholly unable to construct a more commodious one. The school district has express power to vote a tax to hire a schoolhouse. Section 430, subd. 5, St. 1898. The school board are empowered, when directed by the electors, in the alternative to purchase or lease a site for a school-house, and to build, hire, or purchase a schoolhouse, and to sell and convey any site for schoolhouse the property of the district. Section 430, St. 1898. We find nothing either in the expression or policy of the statutes to prevent the school district in meeting assembled or the school board from hiring a building or part of a building in which to maintain the public school, not even though the district may already have a schoolhouse and the hiring may be by way of accommodation for overflow in excess of the accommodations of the schoolhouse so owned. Hence we think that the affirmative grant of powers above mentioned, fairly and reasonably construed, is sufficient to enable the district to maintain a common school in parochial school building and its discretion in that regard should not be controlled by the Court.

We are convinced that in the respects assailed by appeal the judgment is correct.

OTHER VIEWS

The physical combining of a public school with a parochial school within a Roman Catholic building, however, was declared in Iowa, to have caused the public school to take on a religious character in *Knowlton* v. *Baumhover,* 182 Ia. 691, 166 N.W. 202 (1918). The public school property had been sold, and the school's share of public funds continued to the new school.

The court noted that the newly-located "public" school was taught by garbed nuns who decorated the walls with religious pictures and their lectures with lessons in catechism; and that the nominal rent "was never demanded and never paid." Recognizing the right of maintaining a religious school on private property, the opinion was limited to ordering that the school no longer receive any public funds.

† † *KNOWLTON* v. *BAUMHOVER*
182 ia. 691, 166 n.w. 202 (1918).

Judge WEAVER delivered the opinion of the court, saying in part:

Maple River Township district is a school corporation of Carroll county. One of its subdistricts includes a small village bearing the name Maple River, and is spoken of in the record as "Maple River district" or "Maple district," and sometimes as "No. 4." For many years prior to March, 1905, a schoolhouse had been provided for the use of this subdistrict, and a public school regularly maintained therein. At the March, 1905, meeting of the board of directors, a resolution was adopted to the effect that, because of the "inadequacy" of the school building and for the "saving of expense," it was advisable to rent for school purposes "the north room of the second story of the building standing on lot 11, block 7, in the town of Maple River for a period of ten years at a yearly rental of $2.50, and that the president of the board be authorized to enter into such a lease with Joseph Kuemper." This was done, and the schoolhouse property was sold and disposed of. From that time forward the only public school, if any, in Maple district has been maintained in the place described in the lease above mentioned. In the year 1914 this suit was brought by the plaintiff, a resident taxpayer of the district, alleging that the school so maintained is not a public school within the meaning of the law, but is, in fact, a parochial or religious school, which was established, and has been and still is being conducted, by and in behalf of the religious organization known as the Roman Catholic Church, and that the board of directors and the treasurer of the district have paid out and expended, and, if not restrained from so doing, will continue to pay out and expend, the public funds of the district for the benefit and support of the said parochial school. Upon this showing an injunction was prayed forbidding all such use of the public funds and for other equitable relief. The answer of the defendants is a denial generally of the allegations of the petition.

The trial court, after hearing the evidence, found for the plaintiff, and entered a decree perpetually enjoining the defendants and their successors in office from using or appropriating the moneys of the district to such end, and commanding the board of directors to provide a school building for the use of the subdistrict, and meanwhile, until such building could be provided, that a suitable room be rented for that purpose elsewhere than in connection with the parochial school. From this decree the defendants have appealed.

While there is dispute at several points concerning certain matters of fact, very much of the testimony and enough to fairly determine the merits of the case is either undisputed or thoroughly well established by a clear preponderance of the evidence. It appears that the school township and subdistrict in question are peopled very largely by families of the Roman Catholic faith, and that parents of that communion prefer, whenever it is possible, that their children be trained or taught in parochial or religious schools of that faith until they have finished a course which is comparable to that which is covered by the first eight grades in public schools. A Roman Catholic house of worship known as the "St. Francis Church" had been erected in that vicinity, and there religious services were regularly conducted by priests to whom the pastoral charge of that parish was from time to time committed. By its side was also erected a building in which a parochial school was maintained. This building was of two stories, each having a schoolroom. The teachers in these rooms were Catholic Sisters, wearing the characteristic garb and regalia of their order, who gave daily instruction to their pupils not only in branches of secular learning, but also in the Catholic catechism and in elementary principles of Catholic faith. The building as a whole was to all intents and purposes a single schoolhouse, and the classes taught therein constituted a single school of two departments established and maintained for the express purpose of giving religious training to its pupils, and at the same time affording such pupils, as nearly as practicable, the equivalent of a common school education. Therefore, when we say that the property described in the resolution adopted by the board of directors as the "north room of the second story" of the building which we have described, and the nominal lessor, "Joseph Kuemper," was the priest in charge of St. Francis Church, which had the parochial school under its fostering care, the inevitable certainty of this controversy is plainly seen, and should have been visible to the parties to the transaction.

Let us now look briefly into the practical working of the arrangement thus made. Miss Martin, whose religious name is Sister Estella, and who was in charge of the upper room of the parochial school, was employed by the board of directors as teacher of the subdistrict school, and she took charge, or rather she remained in charge, of that room, while the lower room remained in charge of another Sister of the same order, who continued to conduct it as an avowedly church school. The pupils in both rooms were organized and graded after the manner of a single school of two departments, the younger children being taught in the lower room, and the older ones in the upper. From the beginning and for a period of more than nine years the study of the Catholic catechism and the giving of religious instruction were part of the daily program of instruction in both rooms. The walls were hung with pictures of the Holy Virgin, of Christ crowned with thorns, of the Crucifixion, and others all unmistakably appealing to Catholic sentiment, and the teachers were invariably arrayed in the striking robes of their order. Every influence of association and environment, and of precept and example, to say nothing of authority, were thus contrived to keep those of Catholic parentage loyal to their faith and to bias in the same direction those of non-Catholic parentage. In short, so far as its immediate management and control were concerned, the manner of imparting instruction, both secular and religious, and the influence and leadership exercised over the minds of the pupils, it was as thoroughly and completely a religious parochial school as it could well have been had it continued in name as well as in practice the school of the parish under the special charge and supervision of the church, its clergy and religious orders. The act of the board in thus surrendering its proper functions and duties is not to be explained as a mere change in the location of the public school or a mere exercise of the discretion which the law gives to the board to rent a schoolroom when circumstances render it necessary. It was a practical elimination of the public school as such and a transfer of its name and its revenues to the upper department of the parochial school. That the two departments, the so-called public school in the upper room and the church school in the lower room, were in practical operation considered and treated as a unit, a single school of two departments, is demonstrated by their organization and grading to which we have already referred. That Sister Estella was regarded as the head of this school as an entirety and the Sister in the lower room as her assistant is quite apparent. Indeed, on at least one occasion, when, in her alleged capacity as teacher of the public school, Sister Estella undertook to make her regular report of the pupils attending her school together with other statistics relating to the school and its work, she included therein the total number of pupils in both rooms, their average attendance, and other facts and figures relating thereto. It is true the secretary of the board, who came into office after this report was made and received it with other papers from his predecessor, to whom it had been delivered by the teacher, seems to have had an eye to the preservation of appearances, and wrote upon the document the words, "not accepted," but by what authority is not explained. It is further said by this secretary that he procured the teacher to make an amended report omitting therefrom all statistics except those pertaining to the school in the upper room. But if those schools were not in fact one and under the same control, if they were distinct and independent as is now claimed, it is quite

incredible that the Sister in charge being called upon for a report of her school could have been led into the blunder of including therein all the statistics of both. She was not produced as a witness, and no attempt is made to explain this inconsistency. It is much easier to believe that in the honest simplicity of her heart she made her report in accordance with what she understood to be the simple truth.

But it is argued in support of the appeal that, conceding the impropriety of teaching the catechism and the giving of religious instruction in the school, it was a mere irregularity which occurred without the knowledge or consent of the board of directors, and that when the practice became known to them they caused it to be abandoned. It is simply imposing too great a tax upon human credulity to believe that this school could have been conducted in the manner described for nine consecutive years and no notice or knowledge thereof come to the ears of these officers. All of them had for considerable periods been members of the board or held other official positions having to do with the public schools of the township. Some of them had children of their own attending this school. Several of them had served as directors of this subdistrict. The religious character and practices of the school do not appear to have been hidden from the directors under any veil of secrecy, and, assuming that these officers gave any attention whatever to their official trust, they must have known the facts as they existed, as indeed they must have been a matter of common knowledge throughout the district. The only explanation compatible with the entire candor of these denials is that, having surrendered the school to the care of the church, the officers cast off all thought of its further care or attention, except to go through the form from time to time of contracting with the teacher and providing for the support of the school from the public funds. That there is a large grain of truth in this theory is corroborated by the admission in testimony, that during all this period not one of the directors ever visited the school or gave to the Sister in charge any instruction, direction, or rule, with reference to her duties. The nominal rent reserved to St. Francis Church for the use of the schoolroom was never demanded and never paid. Nonresident pupils attended the school without paying tuition to the district. The statement that upon complaint being made the board ordered a discontinuance of the use of the catechism is not borne out by the record. There is no showing that the board or any officer or director of the district, even after complaint was made, took any action whatever to interfere with the practice or gave any order or instruction to the Sister in charge of the school to discontinue it. When complaint was made to the board, instead of taking up the investigation officially, it did no more than tell the complaining parties to investigate themselves and report again in the future. The county superintendent does say that when he "heard of the teaching of the catechism in this room" he at once "took measures to prevent it" and that such study was thereafter abandoned. The abandonment spoken of was in the form rather than in the substance of the practice to which the school was made a potent factor of religious propaganda. The change adopted was the omission of the catechism from the daily program of exercises, only to be taken up at once in the

church building near at hand, where the children were assembled each morning immediately before the school was open for the day, and there received instruction at the hands of the priest. Conceding for argument's sake that such attendance was voluntary in the sense that no requirement or command was laid upon non-Catholic pupils to attend to take part in such exercises yet, surrounded as they were by a multitude of circumstances all leading in that direction, impelled by the gregarious instincts of childhood to go with the crowd, and impressed with a sense of respect for their teachers, whose religious principles and church affiliation were unceasingly pressed upon their notice by their religious dress and strictly ordered lives, could a reasonable person expect the little handful of children from non-Catholic families to do otherwise than to enter the invitingly open door of the church and receive with their companions the instruction there given? That these conditions show any real or substantial removal of the objectionable features which differentiate this school from the public school provided for by law we cannot admit. When we speak of these matters as objectionable, it is not because of any danger of injury, morally or religiously, to children of another faith, but because they cannot be tolerated in public schools without infringing upon the common right of every citizen, whatever his faith, to rear his own children in his own way so long as he keeps within the law.

Again, it is argued that this school was approved by the acquiescence or consent of the people of the district, but this is setting up a standard which the law does not recognize. The board of directors had no authority to clothe a religious school with the character of a public school, and no estoppel could arise against the complaint of any patron or taxpayer simply because of delay in entering his protest.

Again, it is said that the public character of the school was guarded by providing that no child should be required to attend the school in the lower room, to receive all children of any grade applying for admission, and to give them instruction suited to their several needs. There is not a word of this kind in the records of the board or of the school which have been put in evidence. Some of the directors say, in substance, that such was their understanding, and the county superintendent testifies that in his talk with the board he "understood that, 'if any one refused to attend the parochial school,' he was at liberty to attend the other school and take work in the regular courses." This statement is a practical, though perhaps unconscious, admission that the general plan of the school was a grading of the pupils in both rooms in such manner as to send the lower grades into the lower room (an admittedly parochial department) and the higher grades into the upper room, except when such a plan was interrupted by the refusal of a young child to conform thereto, an exception which may well be dismissed as being a very negligible possibility. There is no evidence that any pupil below the sixth grade was ever taught in the upper room. The county superintendent himself says that when he visited this room he found Sister Estella teaching the sixth, seventh, and eighth grades, and, if it ever occurred to his supervisory discretion to inquire into the absence of the younger pupils who as a rule constitute the larger part of

every public school, he does not mention it.

It is also not without a bearing on this phase of the case that before the leasing of the parochial building of which we have spoken the attendance at the parochial school was so general as to materially deplete the attendance at the public school, but when the change was made the attendance was very largely increased, and soon thereafter the compensation paid to Sister Estella was increased from $56 to $70 per month. Two of the directors testify that this advance was made to enable this Sister to divide her salary in some proportion with the Sister who taught in the lower room. This is denied by others of the directors, while still others say they heard nothing of that kind. Neither of the teachers who could have settled the truth of this dispute was called as a witness. But, whatever the truth may be in this particular instance, it is an illuminating circumstance that when the public school had been metamorphosed or reorganized into the school in the second story of the parochial building under the auspices and organization which we have described, the objections which had led the supporters of the parochial school to found and maintain it at their private expense and to withdraw or withhold their patronage from the public school were somehow obviated, and the so-called public school became the recipient of the favor and confidence which it had before been denied. That these patrons had abandoned or renounced their religious scruples is scarcely to be believed, but if they accepted the school conducted by Sister Estella as affording their children all the advantages of religious training for which they formerly relied upon the parochial school, then their conduct is not only easily understood, but their conclusion in this respect was a reasonable deduction from the admitted and proved facts.

In short, it must be said that with the abandonment of the public schoolhouse and the transfer of the school into the parochial building and its organization and conduct as there perfected the school ceased to have a public character in the sense contemplated by our laws, and became, has since been, and now is a religious school, maintained and conducted with a special view to the promotion of the faith of the church under whose favor and guardianship it was founded.

Appellants misconceive the nature and purpose of this action when they undertake to treat it as a mere objection to the employment of a Sister of Charity as a teacher in a public school, or to the fact that such teacher arrays herself in the peculiar garb of her order, or to her practice of reading the Bible or repeating the Lord's Prayer in the presence of her school. The objection goes far deeper than that. The substance and effect of the complaint made by plaintiff is that a particular public school has been perverted into a sectarian or religious school contrary to the laws of our state, and that the defendants in their official capacity are unlawfully appropriating the public funds to its support. That charge being denied, the plaintiff properly put in evidence such facts as he was able to develop having any legitimate tendency to disclose the real nature and character of the school in question. Among these circumstances were not only the study of the Catholic catechism, but also the display of emblems of the Catholic faith, the giving of religious instruc-

tion, the use of the Catholic prayer book, the design and purpose of the parochial building for which the public schoolhouse was abandoned, the immediate proximity of the church where the children assembled to be taught by the priest, the religious dress in which the teachers were arrayed, together with other pertinent facts from which the court could determine whether this was in fact an ordinary public school from which all sectarian instruction and influence were strictly excluded or had been transformed into an efficient instrument of promoting and extending the work and influence of the church. That these are proper matters of evidence affording light upon the issues thus joined is not only manifest to every person of common observation and common sense, but also, as we shall show in another paragraph of this opinion, have been so treated by the courts over and over again. The law does not prescribe the fashion of dress of man or woman; it demands no religious test for admission into the teacher's profession; it leaves all men to worship God or to refrain from worship according to his own circumstance; it prefers no one church or creed to another. This principle of unfettered individual liberty of conscience necessarily implies, what is too often forgotten, that such liberty must be so exercised by him to whom it is given as not to infringe upon the equally sacred right of his neighbor to differ with him. To that end it is fundamental that the law itself shall be free from all taint of discrimination, and that the state shall be watchful to forbid the use or abuse of any of its functions, powers, or privileges in the interest of any church or creed. Nowhere is such abuse more likely to manifest itself than in our system of public schools, and it is not strange that the average parent is peculiarly sensitive concerning the influences there brought to bear upon his children. If there is any one thing which is well settled in the policies and purposes of the American people as a whole, it is the fixed and unalterable determination that there shall be an absolute and unequivocal separation of church and state and that our public school system, supported by the taxation of the property of all alike—Catholic, Protestant, Jew, Gentile, believer and infidel—shall not be used directly or indirectly for religious instruction, and above all that it shall not be made an instrumentality of proselyting influence in favor of any religious organization, sect, creed, or belief. So well is this understood, it would be a waste of time for us at this point to stop for specific reference to authorities or precedents or to the familiar pages of American history bearing thereon.

RELATED CASES

Similarly, the action of the school board of a Missouri public school district in taking a parochial school into the public school system was invalidated in *Harfst* v. *Hoegen,* 349 Mo. 808, 163 S.W.2d 609 (1942), below. In granting an injunction forbidding the school board to use any further public school funds for religious and sectarian purposes, the court noted that the compulsory religious exercises as continued in the Roman Catholic school constituted "a denial of constitutional guarantee of religious freedom."

† † *HARFST* v. *HOEGEN*
349 mo. 808, 163 s.w.2d 609 (1942).

Judge douglas delivered the opinion of the court:

This is a suit by parents of public school children, against members of a school board, seeking an injunction against the use of school funds for purposes alleged to be sectarian and religious. From a decree granting part of the relief sought, and refusing to grant more, plaintiffs have appealed. The suit involves the Missouri constitutional guaranties of religious liberty and presents questions which have never before been considered or decided by our appellate courts.

Some years ago in the town of Meta, in Osage County, the Catholic Parish of St. Cecelia established its usual parish or parochial school, which was conducted under the direction of the parish priest. The teachers were members of the Sisters of the Most Precious Blood, a Catholic teaching order, who came from St. Mary's Institute of O'Fallon at O'Fallon, Missouri, the motherhouse and novitiate for the training of teachers for parochial schools. The school building adjoined the parish church and had two school rooms on the first floor and a school room and a chapel on the second. After some time, and about ten years ago, this parish school was taken into the State public school system by the school board of the Meta school district as a public grade school. From then on it has been and is now supported by public funds. At that time the textbooks and the course of study prescribed by the State Superintendent of Schools were adopted, but otherwise the school seems to have been conducted as a parochial school in the same manner as before its inclusion in the public school system. It was continued under the same name, the St. Cecelia School, and in the same building, the three school rooms being rented from the parish priest by the school board. The same teachers or other Sisters of the same religious order were engaged and are paid by the school board and now constitute the teaching staff of the school. It is still referred to as the "Catholic school."

Harmony prevailed among the people of the school district about the conduct of this school until 1939 at which time there was a consolidation of another school district with the Meta district and the abandonment of the school in the other district. This action seems to have culminated in some bitterness between the peoples of the two districts and led to the filing of this suit. Almost all of the persons engaged in this controversy are of the same religion, Catholic. The questions involved do not arise from a strife between persons of opposing religious beliefs, but come from a dispute between those of the same faith.

We find the usual school day commencing with prayer in the morning. After prayer the pupils are marched, one room at a time, to the Catholic church next door for Holy Mass. After Mass the pupils are marched back to their school rooms where they receive religious instruction. In this they study the Catholic catechism and the child's Catholic Bible. On one or two days of each week the parish priest gives religious instruction to the pupils in the mid-morning, either at the church or in the schoolhouse chapel. On Friday afternoons the pupils are again marched to the church for confession. In the quarterly "Teacher's Report to the Parents" the subject "Religion" is included under "Branches Pursued" and a grade in this subject is given to each pupil.

Sister M. Berchmans, one of the present teachers, testified that the Sisters of the Most Precious Blood dedicate their lives to teaching the young which includes the teaching of the Catholic faith as well as the teaching of the usual secular educational subjects. She had been previously and was then teaching the Catholic faith to her pupils in the St. Cecelia public school. As accessories to the religious instruction, the school rooms have in them pictures and symbols of the Catholic faith, and there are holy water fonts for the benefit of the pupils at the doors of the school rooms. The one hundred or more pupils at this school are usually all of the Catholic faith, but in some years there have been one or two Protestant children enrolled there.

The school board maintains a second grade school in Meta which is attended entirely by Protestant children. The enrollment there is about one-half the number in the St. Cecelia school. The manner in which this school is conducted is not here in controversy, but the evidence shows that its facilities are not equal to those of the St. Cecelia school, and that Catholic children have been ordered by the school board to leave it and attend the St. Cecelia school.

Plaintiffs, who are parents of school children, taxpayers and residents of the school district, after stating the facts set out above allege that the members of the school board, the defendants, are maintaining a parochial school at public expense, contrary to our Constitution. They ask that the board be enjoined from using public funds in support of a parochial school; in employing as teachers persons garbed in the habiliments of a religious order; in employing sectarian teachers. The answer of the school board is a general denial.

The chancellor found that sectarian religion was being taught in the school by the Sisters and also by the parish priest with the knowledge of the board members. However, in his decree he fails to give the broad relief asked for but confines himself to enjoining what appellants contend are mere side issues. He enjoined the use of religious text books and accessories such as pictures and symbols and the holy water fonts, but he did not enjoin the teaching of sectarian religion. He did not enjoin the maintenance of a sectarian school by public officials at public expense. He did enjoin the parish priest from teaching within the school building, but he did not enjoin the payment of public funds to the teachers of religion. Under the decree as it now stands it is argued that defendants may continue

to ignore the constitutional provision insuring the freedom of worship.

. . . .

II

With the adoption of the federal Bill of Rights the whole power over the subject of religion, at that time, was left exclusively to the State governments.

Previously there had been controversies in the various colonies over the governmental support of the church, and the complete separation of the church from the state did not really come until the formation of our federal system of government, although the Virginia Bill of Rights had earlier guaranteed freedom of worship. At that time there was declared the principle which is of the warp and woof of democracy, namely, the people must enjoy religious freedom and religious equality. This principle has stood out as a guiding star in the growth and development of our form of government and has contributed to its solidarity. It is as vital to our people as the guaranty of civil liberty and political equality. Because of it, devotion to religious beliefs according to the dictates only of one's conscience without molestation or forcible direction became possible, thus permitting an unhampered growth of religious conviction of any sort and of every denomination. There could be no governmental discrimination in favor of or against any sect; each became entitled under the law to enjoy equal rights in a broad field. Yet, religion was in no way taken away from the individual. It has been recognized in the courts that generally we acknowledge with reverence the duty of obedience to the will of God. In the preamble to our Constitution the people of our

State acknowledge our "profound reverence for the Supreme Ruler of the Universe" and our gratitude for His goodness. But yet, beginning with our first Constitution, we have persistently declared "that all men have a natural and indefeasible right to worship Almighty God according to the dictates of their own consciences;" and, "that no human authority can control or interfere with the rights of conscience."

The fact that this is a case of first impression in this State is of itself an evidence that the policy separating religion from government can be maintained. It also demonstrates unusual restraint both on the part of church and state in view of the important roles played by the various pioneers of religion in the settlement of our State and in its transition from the frontier. A history starting with the first Jesuit Missionaries, followed in time by the frontiersman generally with a scorn of religion, and, finally, a period of Protestant revivals, has no doubt presented opportunities for vigorous controversy. But where such have occurred, settlement must have been made without resort to law. In other states numerous cases involving many phases of such controversies have reached the courts. There are decisions on public aid to a sectarian school, employment of a sectarian teacher, use of a church for school purposes, permitting the Bible in a school library, reading of the Bible with or without comment in a school, and so on. Each case necessarily turns on the particular constitutional provision of the state in which the case arises.

III–VII

Missouri follows generally the usual pattern of religious guaranties and safeguards in its Constitution. We have, as mentioned above, the provision for freedom of worship according to one's own conscience without control or interference of his rights of conscience. It is apparent therefore, that under our system of education the inclusion of the St. Cecelia school in the public school system and its maintenance as a part of and an adjunct to the parish church in its religious teaching, and where children of every faith may be compelled to attend and have attended, constitutes a denial of our guaranty of religious freedom. The fact that attendance at Mass is customarily before school hours or that religious instruction may be given during recess periods or that the participation of a non-Catholic child in these services may not be required does not make such conduct lawful in view of this provision. Particularly is this true under circumstances as in this case where the pupils must arrive and leave at the same time in the school buses. This court has already said that

it certainly could not have been the design of the legislature to take from the parent the control of his child while not at school and invest it in a board of directors or teacher of a school.

And we asked: "may they not prescribe a rule, which would forbid the parent from allowing the child to attend a particular church, or any church at all?"—assuming that the question answered itself and reduced the argument to absurdity. By the common law, control of children is parental and the father could "delegate part of his parental authority to the tutor or schoolmaster," said Blackstone, 1 Com. 452, 3. Now by statute the school board has been given certain powers, and it behooves the board to point to a statute, when its will and that of the parent conflict. This it has failed to do. And certainly the school board may not employ its power to enforce religious worship by children even in the faith of their parents. Furthermore, the segregation of the Catholic from the non-Catholic children and their mandatory attendance at one or the other of the two grade schools according to their religion, whether the schools be of equal or of unequal facilities, likewise constitutes a denial of complete religious freedom. The cases relied on by respondents may be distinguished on the facts; one involved only the garb of the teacher and two were about reading the Bible.

VIII

There is another constitutional inhibition which respondents do not observe. It forbids a school district to make payments from any public fund to sustain any private or public school controlled by any sectarian denomination. Respondents might argue that the St. Cecelia school is controlled by the school board and not by the church, but we find from the record that the nominal supervision by the school board is but an indirect means of accomplishing that which the Constitution forbids. The statement of the county superintendent of schools that "We put the St. Cecelia parochial school into the public school system" is fully borne out by the facts in evidence. It was not only put there but it was maintained there with public funds.

IX

But our Constitution goes even farther than those of some other states. In addition to the provisions already mentioned we have still another. Art. II, § 7 says:

That no money shall ever be taken from the public treasury, directly or indirectly, in aid of any church, sect or denomination of religion, or in aid of any priest, preacher, minister or teacher thereof, as such; and that no preference shall be given to nor any discrimination made against any church, sect or creed of religion, or any form of religious faith or worship.

Thus, we have an explicit interdiction of the use of public money for a teacher of religion as such which has been violated by the board. In the instant case it is true that the Sisters followed the course of secular instruction prescribed for public schools but in addition they also instructed in the faith of their religious belief as their obligation required them to do. The Sister Superior testified that the members of her order have dedicated their lives to teaching and to the Catholic faith; to both the religious training and education of children; to teach no other faith but that of their religion; to devote themselves to a religious life. She also testified that before coming to the St. Cecelia school she had taught in parochial schools and that the teaching was the same in them as in the St. Cecelia school, except that in the parochial schools there was even more time devoted to instruction in religion. "I couldn't teach any differently," she stated. She then told of the religious instruction she was giving to her pupils in the St. Cecelia public school using the Catholic catechism and the child's Catholic Bible as texts.

From her testimony we must conclude that the members of her religious order, their lives dedicated to the training of children both in religion and education, come within this constitutional interdiction as teachers of religion, and payment to them from public school funds is forbidden.

X

In reaching this conclusion we recognize that the members of these noble teaching orders are inspired only by the most unselfish and highest motives; that parochial education is an embodiment of one of the highest ideals that man may enjoy. The Supreme Court of the United States found that parochial education has been "long regarded as useful and meritorious." In the instant case it is admitted by all parties that the Sisters are fully qualified according to the standards set by the superintendent of instruction as teachers of a public school. We know of the great educational institutions conducted by the Jesuits and other Catholic Orders and of their high standards of excellence, St. Louis University being a leader among them. We recognize as well the great need of spiritual training not only in our own country, but throughout this troubled world. The right of freedom of worship, which at this time is being denied to the peoples of two foreign governments in particular must be restored before the world is again secure. Nevertheless, the question confronting us is one only of law; of upholding our Constitution as it is written which, as lawyers and judges, we have dedicated our professional life to do. The constitutional policy of our State has decreed the absolute separation of church and state, not only in governmental matters, but in educational ones as well. Public money, coming from taxpayers of every denomination, may not be used for the help of any religious sect in education or otherwise. If the management of this school were approved, we might next have some other church gaining control of a school board and have its pastor and teachers introduced to teach its sectarian religion. Our schools would soon become the centers of local political battles which would be dangerous to the peace of society where there must be equal religious rights to all and special religious privileges to none. The faithful observance of our constitutional provisions happily makes such a condition impossible.

XI–XIII

It is of no purpose to discuss or decide other questions raised except to point out that the long acquiescence of appellants in the management of the school cannot make such management proper. No one may waive the public interest; the constitutional provisions are mandatory and must be obeyed.

The members of the school board have unintentionally but unquestionably violated our constitutional provisions in the respects noted. We commend the candor of all parties and it has eased the labors of the court.

. . . .

This case must be remanded, with directions to the chancellor to supplement the decree for plaintiffs, giving them additional injunctive relief in conformity with the views expressed in this opinion.

It is so ordered.

All concur.

REACTIONS OF LEGAL PERIODICALS TO *HARFST* v. *HOEGEN*

Several aspects of the Missouri court's ruling were criticized in the law journal commentary. The sharpest attack, however, was made in couched language. Observing in the *Notre Dame Lawyer* (18:170) that the immediate ruling was not unexpected in the light of similar decisions involving religious liberty, the writer admitted that the "*legal* position of the Missouri supreme court is no doubt unassailable."

He went on to argue, however, that the decision overlooked "a Christian social policy." Noting that the early public attitude toward religion in the public schools "was not so adverse and repugnant," the writer queried in closing why the popular attitude should be changed now, especially in a situation such as the Harfst case presented.

On the other hand, a writer in the *Minnesota Law Review* (27:311) spoke in less critical tones as he argued that the approach of the litigation was incorrect. He suggested that state appropriations accruing to the benefit of sectarian schools should be attacked on the basis that they violate the principle of the separation of church and state, and not because "such expenditures constitute a diversion of public funds for private purposes."

The court's procedural approach was attacked in the *University of Detroit Law Journal* (6:174), also. The writer there argued that the relief sought in the Harfst case "was inconsistent with the facts presented." Because the parties in the case were of the same faith, he reasoned that the petitioners "would not desire to have a school of their own religion abolished."

He further submitted that a suit should not lie to recover public school funds paid to a sectarian school, when the taxpayers have given their consent to such an appropriation "for a long term of years." The author cited as support for his argument the propositions that the religious teachers in the school in question had been compensated for services rendered and that there is a lack of accord among authorities as to what particular forms of religious instruction are prohibited.

RELIGIOUS MEETINGS IN PUBLIC SCHOOLHOUSES —
VOTER AUTHORIZATION

Several courts were willing to permit a majority of the legal voters in a school district to be the ultimate policymakers concerning the question of after-hours use of public school buildings. In this connection, *Townsend* v. *Hagan*, 35 Ia. 194 (1872), and *Davis* v. *Boget*, 50 Ia. 11 (1878), upheld voters' authorizations for school buildings to be used for religious purposes. Both cases involved judicial interpretations of an Iowa Statute giving the voters the power to determine the uses to be made of public property.

The Connecticut court first held in *Sheldon* v. *Centre School District,* 25 Conn. 224 (1856), that a vote by a school district would not be void just because the proposed school building would also be used for religious purposes during the school year. However, the Connecticut rule was developed in *Scofield* v. *Eighth School District,* 27 Conn. 499 (1858), where the court reversed the Sheldon decision and held that a school board did not have the authority to allow religious meetings in school buildings even though the voters approved. A taxpayer could enjoin such practice even though use of the building resulted in minute wear and tear.

An instance of a court recognizing the right of district voters not to authorize the holding of religious meetings in public school buildings may be seen in *Echardt* v. *Darby,* 118 Mich. 199, 76 N.W. 761 (1898).

On the other hand, a single taxpayer was declared in *Scofield* v. *Eighth School District,* 27 Conn. 499 (1858), to have sufficient basis for negating majority approval by the district's voters for the use of the public school house for religious meetings and Sunday school classes. The court, in granting injunctive relief, recognized that the injury to a single taxpayer was very slight, but determined that he would have no other remedy under Connecticut law.

A taxpayer was able to convince the Kansas supreme court in *Spencer* v. *Joint School District,* 15 Kan. 259 (1875), that he could challenge the practice of leasing the public school building "for other than school purposes." Charging that religious and political meetings, social gatherings, and the like resulted in mutilation, misplacement, and destruction of his children's private property at the school, the appellant thus showed that he had a personal interest in the school fund to which he contributed.

The Kansas court in demanding that such extralegal activities stop, said that as the state may not levy taxes directly for the erection of a church it also may not countenance indirectly the practice of levying taxes to build a public schoolhouse which is then leased for church purposes. Such is the case even when a majority of the district's citizens and taxpayers, as here, favor the leasing arrangement, the court ruled.

The fact that the building was rented out only infrequently could not save the practice. The court said that "the use of a public schoolhouse for a single religious or political gathering, is, legally, as unauthorized as its constant use therefor."

The Indiana court in *Baggerly* v. *Lee,* 37 Ind. App. 139, 73 N.E. 921 (1905), interpreted an arrangement which had been approved by a majority of the district's legal voters in conjunction with statutory authorization, to mean that the public schoolhouse could be used for "other than school purposes" only in the time intervening between the school terms. The effect of the voters' approval was not to allow religious organizations to use the schoolhouse on Sundays and evenings during a school term, the court determined.

RELIGIOUS MEETINGS IN PUBLIC SCHOOLHOUSES —
STATUTORY DISCRETION BY LOCAL BOARDS OF EDUCATION

A variety of judicial attitudes may be seen in the handling of questions involving statutory discretionary powers of local boards of education in granting or denying the use of public school property for the holding of religious meetings.

A number of courts have refused to interfere with exercises by boards of education of their discretionary authority in allowing temporary and infrequent religious use of public school buildings.

In Illinois the temporary use of public schoolhouses, when not in use for school purposes, for religious meetings and Sunday school classes was sanctioned in *Nichols* v. *School Directors*, 93 Ill. 61 (1879). The opinion, declaring that the statutory authorization for such religious uses of school property did not conflict with the constitutional prohibition of public aid to any church, stated that religion is not meant to be banned absolutely from receiving any incidental benefit at all from the various public bodies.

Thirty years later in *Lagow* v. *Hill*, 238 Ill. 428, 87 N.E. 369 (1909), the Illinois supreme court determined that the state school law empowered the board of directors of a school district to permit any proper meetings in unoccupied rooms of the public school building. The court quoted as authority the provision of the state's educational code which authorized the board to "grant the temporary use of the school buildings" among other things for religious meetings.

The infrequent use of a public schoolhouse for Sunday school classes and religious meetings was not considered in *State* ex rel. *Gilbert* v. *Dilley,* 95 Neb. 527, 145 N.W. 999 (1914), to make the schoolhouse a "place of worship" within the Nebraska constitutional prohibition of preferring by law any religious society. All of the alleged meetings (held on four Sundays in each of the succeeding five years) did not interfere to any extent with the educational process.

The Nebraska court noted that the religious groups cleaned and repaired the facilities after each use. Therefore, a taxpayer had no grounds for challenging such use. The court stated nevertheless that the decision might have been different had there been proof that such practices did convert the school into a "place of worship," or that the taxpayers had been forced to contribute to upkeep chores created by the religious meetings.

The temporary use of a church for public school purposes was upheld in New York as an emergency measure in *Matter of Roche,* 26 N.Y. State Dept. Rep. 217 (1921). It was demanded, however, that the religious rights of the public school children in attendance there not be interfered with.

That a school board possessed limited discretion in authorizing the temporary use for religious purposes of public school facilities during off-school hours was recognized recently in *Southside Estates Baptist Church* v. *Board of Trustees, Fla.,* 115 So.2d 697 (1959). The Florida court noted that its decisions had consistently countenanced incidental benefits to religious groups from appropriate uses of public property. The opinion went on nevertheless to state definitively that neither the public school system nor its property can be permanently employed to promote any particular religious sect or denomination.

Other cases of this sort turned on technical grounds. An action by several Indiana taxpayers in *Hurd* v. *Walters,* 48 Ind. 148 (1874), to enjoin the school trustee from allowing the use of the public schoolhouse for purposes of religious worship when the school was unoccupied for common school purposes was allowed, but a legal technicality precluded the injunctive relief sought. Finding nothing in the record about whether, in conjunction with the Indiana common school law, "a majority of the legal voters of said district had expressed a desire that said schoolhouse might be used for religious worship," the court intimated that it had no bases for doubting that the trustee had acted within his legal authority. The opinion did state definitively, however that the court did have the necessary injunctive powers upon a showing that the trustee had exceeded his authority.

The decision in *South San Antonio Independent School District* v. *Martine,* Tex. Civ. App., 275 S.W. 265 (1925), turned upon the fact that the taxpaying appellee had failed to exhaust his legal remedies. Under Texas law he should have presented his grievances to the local school board first rather than directly to the courts.

As a result, there was no judicial decision on the merits of his charge that the school board had from time to time authorized various groups to use the school building for "sectarian, political, and religious purposes." Included among his allegations was the questioning of authorizing a Sunday school class to hold a "box supper" in the schoolhouse. While the proceeds went to the religious group the resultant increased cost of water, electricity, and upkeep of the building went to the district's taxpayers, the appellee charged.

On the other hand, several courts have taken the stand that the school buildings were built from public funds exclusively for state educational purposes, and that no religious groups shall be entitled to any type of use therein. That principle was adhered to in the following series of cases even though the boards of education had specifically authorized such uses.

In *Dorton* v. *Hearn,* 67 Mo. 301 (1878), the Missouri court overturned a resolution by a district school board which authorized the use of the school building "for teaching a Sunday school." While calling the purpose of the request "praiseworthy," the court refused to establish a precedent which it felt could "lead to great abuses and disagreeable altercations between different religious denominations."

A Pennsylvania county court stated categorically in *Bender* v. *Streabich,* 17 Pa. Co. Ct. 690 (1896), that school buildings are intended for use as common schools "and none other." In enjoining the school directors from permitting the use of school hours and school property for "church, Sunday-school or lyceum purposes," the court interpreted the state constitutional prohibition of public appropriations to sectarian schools to mean that public-financed school buildings cannot be used for any sectarian purposes.

An injunction was granted, however, in *Spring* v. *School Directors,* 31 Pittsb. L.J. 194 (1900), to restrain the school directors of a Pennsylvania school district from granting permission to outside parties to use the public schoolhouse for religious purposes.

There exist judicial precedents, of course, for the position that a school board may prohibit the use of public school facilities by religious and other groups.

The authority of a school board to prohibit religious worship in public schoolhouses was also recognized in Arkansas in *Boyd* v. *Mitchell,* 69 Ark. 202, 62 S.W. 61 (1901), even though the school in question was erected partly from private subscriptions upon the understanding that the school could be used for religious meetings when the buildings were not otherwise being used. The court nevertheless ruled that the schoolhouse from the beginning of the subscription drive was clearly intended to be under the control of the district directors.

Expanding upon that point, the Arkansas court determined that it was not only the board's province but its duty to maintain the buildings for "school purposes" only. To substantiate its holding, the court noted that books, seats, etc. had been damaged during such religious meetings held in the past.

An Illinois court in *School Directors* v. *Toll,* 149 Ill. App. 541 (1909), ruled that a church organization could not use a schoolhouse for religious meetings without the express permission of the school directors. The court went on to declare that the directors have a right to refuse permission at their discretion.

The statutory authority of a board of education to authorize the use of school property for any nonschool use carries the legal responsibility to ascertain the ulterior motives of the groups requesting such permission, said the Ohio supreme court in *State* ex rel. *Greisinger* v. *Board of Edu-*

cation, 88 Ohio App. 364, 100 N.E.2d 294 (1949). The board may arbitrarily deny such permission when the purposes do not "harmonize with the school's program of education, character building, and developing unprejudiced social attitudes," the court ruled. Such a selective process does not deny freedom of worship or any other federal or state constitutional right to those whose applications are denied, the court continued.

McKnight v. *Board of Public Education*, 365 Pa. 422, 76 A.2d 207 (1950), also involved a denial by a Pennsylvania school board to a religious organization requesting permission to use the high school auditorium on Sunday afternoons for religious purposes. Showing no particular interest in the scope of the contemplated religious activity, the court announced that petitioner's failure to show that the auditorium had previously been used in a similar fashion by other religious groups would result in his not being entitled to mandamus action to permit this activity.

The action in *Stanton* v. *Board of Education*, 190 Misc. 1012, 76 N.Y.S.2d 559 (1948), involved a slightly different situation. There the New York board refused to pass a resolution which would have denied the after-hours use of public buildings to organizations fostering religious or racial intolerance, in addition to Communist, Nazi, and Fascist groups.

OTHER ISSUES

In other cases involving tangential issues of determining the public character of schools, two courts ruled differently in factual situations concerned with whether particular circumstances converted the supposedly public school buildings into "houses of worship" within state constitutional bans on public financing.

People v. *McAdams*, 82 Ill. 356 (1876), involved the question of the power of the Illinois legislature to confer the taxing power upon a school controlled by a private corporation for maintenance of the school. The schoolhouse was erected by funds from a will and was to be "a building suitable for a school and for a place of public worship." The Illinois court ruled that the state legislature had no constitutional authority to invest the private school with taxing power.

However, the Michigan high court ruled in *Richter* v. *Cordes*, 100 Mich. 278, 58 N.W. 1110 (1894), that the school in question was a district school, even though the schoolhouse stood on land owned by the Roman Catholic church; the Roman Catholic faith was taught in the school; and the church contributed to the teachers' salaries. The court based its determination, in this forcible-entry case questioning the rightful title to the school's lease, upon a finding that the teachers were hired and primarily paid by the school board; that the school regularly received its share of the common school fund; and that the school's business was generally conducted in the usual fashion as that of other public schools in the district.

The New York court in *Lewis* v. *Board of Education,* 157 Misc. 520, 285 N.Y.S. 164 (1935), stated in no uncertain terms that the question of legality of public appropriations hinged upon "the use to which the school buildings are put, and not [upon] the identity of the users." It determined that the buildings in question were in fact being used as assembly places by sectarian religious groups but for the sole secular purpose of giving instruction in education, learning, and the arts.

The court declared that to "examine into the sectarianism of those seeking access to public school buildings would make a travesty of our glorified liberty of conscience." In fact, the groups in question are doing "a wholesome thing" when they use the school buildings for such purposes as here mentioned, the court added.

The court's decree that the mere use of New York public school buildings by student organizations with distinctive religious affiliations does not automatically constitute a constitutional violation was considered "unquestionably correct" in the *Michigan Law Review* (34:1237). The writer's approval of the decision was based upon the court's rationale that the controlling test is the purpose for which the building is used and not the religious ties of the user. He agreed with the court that the purpose in the instant situation was "primarily secular."

† † LEWIS v. *BOARD OF EDUCATION*
157 MISC. 520, 285 N.Y.S. 164 (1935).

Judge COLLINS delivered the opinion of the court, saying in part:

. . . The plaintiff, as a taxpayer, seeks to forbid the defendant, the Board of Education, from permitting school buildings to be used as assembly places for racial and religious groups, and to restrain reading from the Bible in public schools. The law which authorizes such readings is attacked as unconstitutional.

The amended complaint projects three causes of action. The first asserts that the board of education is illegally allowing the use of school buildings "to a large number of distinctively sec-

tarian religious denominations, societies and groups," among them "many Roman Catholic Newman Clubs, Protestant Young Men's and Young Women's Christian Associations and Hi-Y Clubs, and Hebrew Menorah and Junior Hadassah Clubs." Other Protestant, Jewish and Catholic organizations are enumerated as utilizing the school houses in disregard of law. . . .

The second cause attacks, as violative of the Federal and State Constitutions, the use of the Holy Scriptures in the public schools.

The third cause assails as unconstitutional that portion of section 1151 of the Greater New York Charter (Laws 1901, c. 466) which prohibits the board of education from excluding

the Holy Scriptures, without note or comment, or any selections therefrom, from any of the schools provided for by this chapter; but it shall not be competent for the said board of education to decide what version, if any, of the Holy Scriptures, without note or comment, shall be used in any of the schools; provided that nothing herein contained shall be so construed as to violate the rights of conscience, as secured by the constitution of this State and of the United States. . . .

Paragraph X of the answer alleges, as a defense to the first cause of action, that:

The so-called sectarian religious denominations, societies, and groups, mentioned and described in . . . the amended complaint . . . are not permitted by the defendant, Board of Education of the City of New York, to hold any religious denominational services in any of the public schools under the jurisdiction and control of the defendant and that the aforesaid denominations, societies and groups are only and solely permitted to have meetings in the aforesaid public schools for the purpose of conducting ethical, educational and cultural discourses and lectures for the moral uplift of the pupils in the public schools connected with the said so-called denominations, societies and groups; and the defendant alleges that at no time and for no purpose does it permit any pupil of the aforesaid public schools or the societies and groups to which they belong to use or occupy any public school in the City and City School District of New York for the inculcation of any of the tenents of any religious denomination or for any meeting or purpose, directly or indirectly, in which

any denominational tenet or doctrine is taught.

. . . .

Paragraph XII of the answer asserts a second defense to the second and third causes by averring

that the practice of singing hymns in the public school assemblies has never been universal and is declining rapidly, and that the reading of portions of the Bible or Bibles, mentioned in the amended complaint, without note or comment, at the opening exercises in the public schools of the City of New York is regular and lawful and not in violation of any provision of the Constitution of the State of New York or the Constitution of the United States or of any statute, but is duly permitted by and in accordance with the provisions of the said Constitutions and statute.

It is the validity of these defenses that this motion poses.

. . . .

Let it be emphasized that the concern here is with power, not policy. Within the boundaries of law what shall and shall not be done in the public schools is an educational function to be determined by those intrusted with the conduct and administration of the public schools. . . . The question here is not whether the Bible shall or shall not be read in the public schools; it is not whether permission to utilize the school buildings should be given or withheld from those of racial or religious affiliations. The board has resolved these questions of policy. The query here is whether the board in causing excerpts from the Bible to be read, and in allowing school buildings to be employed in the assailed fashion, is transgressing a constitutional guaranty, or is violating any other provision or concept of law.

Undisguised, the plaintiff's attack is on a belief and trust in God and in any system or policy or teaching which enhances or fosters or countenances or even recognizes that belief and trust. Such belief and trust, however, regardless of one's own belief, has received recognition in state and judicial documents from the earliest days of our republic.

Thus, the Declaration of Independence concludes with the riveting words: "And for the support of this declaration, with a firm reliance on the protection of Divine Providence, we mutually pledge to each other our lives, our fortunes, and our sacred honor."

"In God We Trust" has become an American aphorism, stamped on our coins.

And our State Constitution opens with the words, "We, The People of the State of New York, grateful to Almighty God for our Freedom, in order to secure its blessings, Do Establish this Constitution."

Nor have the courts ignored the existence of this declared policy.

In *People* ex rel. *Lewis* v. *Graves,* 219 App. Div. 233, 238, 219 N.Y.S. 189, 195, it was said: "A belief in religion is not foreign to our system of government."

Our highest court, in *Holy Trinity Church* v. *United States,* 143 U.S. 457, 465, said: "This is a religious people. This is historically true. From the discovery of this continent to the present hour, there is a single voice making this affirmation."

These quotations are not intended to convey the thought that state and church should be brought into closer harmony. Their separation is a funda-mental of immutable virility. Nor do the excerpts indicate the approval or proposal of a policy that religion be taught in the public schools. The principle that religion has no place in public temporal education is so inexorable that a reaffirmation of it would be supererogatory.

These concepts are not repugnant to the constitutional guaranty which safeguards freedom of conscience and of worship and the free entertainment and pursuit of religious beliefs. They are not hostile to section 3 of article 1 of the State Constitution, which declares that: "The free exercise and enjoyment of religious profession and worship, without discrimination or preference, shall forever be allowed in this State to all mankind."

With the foregoing as a setting, the adequacy of the defenses is examined.

1. As noted, the first defense answers the charge that the school buildings are being unlawfully used, and alleges that the assailed gatherings are in no sense sectarian or religious or denominational.

It seems to me that this defense pleads the law.

Section 455 of the Education Law, which covers the "Use of school-house and grounds out of school hours," provides:

. . . The Trustees or board of education of each district may, subject to regulations adopted as above provided, permit the use of the schoolhouse and rooms therein, and the grounds and other property of the district, when not in use for school purposes, for any of the following purposes:

1. By persons assembling therein for the purpose of giving and receiving instruction in any branch of education, learning or the arts. . . .

. . . .

3. For holding social, civic and recreational meetings and entertainments, and other uses pertaining to the welfare of the community; but such meetings, entertainment and uses shall be non-exclusive and shall be open to the general public.

4. For meetings, entertainments and occasions where admission fees are charged, when the proceeds thereof are to be expended for an educational or charitable purpose; but such use shall not be permitted if such meetings, entertainments and occasions are under the exclusive control and the said proceeds are to be applied for the benefit of a society, association or organization of a religious sect or denomination, or of a fraternal, secret or exclusive society or organization other than organizations of veterans of the military, naval and marine service of the United States and organizations of volunteer firemen.

We see, therefore, that, as education is, and must be, comprehensive, so the above language of subdivision 1 of section 455 is elastic.

The manifest vice of the plaintiff's position is that he has confused the racial and religious affiliations of the users of the school buildings with the purpose for which the buildings are used. The restrictions relate to the use. In this land where all races and creeds are equal before the law, regardless of color or religion, the doors of the schools should not be shut in the faces of those who by birth or otherwise belong to a particular race or adhere to a particular religion. Indeed, by opening the doors to all, the school authorities more honestly and faithfully cling to the enduring principles of our free institutions, and more sincerely and indiscriminately sustain the constitutional guaranties, than do those who would deny admission to certain persons because of creed or racial solidarity. The sanctified principle of freedom of religious belief does not distinguish between believers and nonbelievers. It embraces both, and accords one as much protection and freedom as the other. A sect or tenet which is intolerant of those of a different sect or tenet is the precise antithesis of religious liberty. Freedom is negated if it does not comprehend freedom for those who believe as well as those who disbelieve. The law is astute and zealous in seeing to it that all religious beliefs or disbeliefs be given unfettered expression. Authentic free thinking involves the indubitable right to believe in God, as well as the unfettered license not to believe or to disbelieve in a Deity.

To examine into the sectarianism of those seeking access to public school buildings would make a travesty of our glorified liberty of conscience. Liberty for nonbelievers in God, but denial to believers in a Deity, would be a mock liberty.

Rather than inimical to the educational policy of the state, or subversive of legitimate use, it is a wholesome thing to have the school buildings, which are maintained at large expense by the taxpayers, used for the purposes and by the groups whose exclusion is here sought.

It is the use to which the school buildings are put, and not the identity of the users, that is decisive of the lawfulness of the use.

Manifestly, therefore, the defense set forth in paragraph X of the answer, to the effect that the school buildings are being used for the purpose of giving and receiving instruction in education, learning, and the arts, is legally sufficient.

. . . .

Though it is not claimed that the board has not scrupulously adhered to the letter and spirit of section 1151, it is the plaintiff's thesis that any hymn singing or reading from the Scriptures, regardless of the hymn or version, is illegal.

To this notion of unconstitutionality of the challenged portion of section 1151 I cannot subscribe.

RELIGIOUS HOLIDAYS

On the other issues in the general area of use of schools and school sactioned events, the courts have entertained questions on religious holidays, baccalaureate, and religious displays.

In an early Vermont case, the constitutionality of requiring public school attendance of Roman Catholic children on days regarded by the faith as holy was questioned in *Ferriter* v. *Tyler,* 48 Vt. 444 (1876). Roman Catholic school children requested permission to be excused from the public school classes so that they could attend religious services on a holy day. The school committee refused to grant permission even after they received a note from the priest requesting the children be excused. The children who were absent that day were suspended from school until they agreed to follow the school's policy and rules concerning attendance.

The Vermont court determined that attendance at religious service on this particular holy day was neither required nor a matter of conscience. The court also found that some of the absent Roman Catholic children were seen playing in the streets, and that their parents had worked all day. This coupled with the fact that four years previously a similar request for authorized school absences on holy days had been denied, led the court to the conclusion that the school committee's actions in no way violated the state constitutional provision regarding freedom of worship. The committee did not dictate a mode of worship, nor did it "interfere with or control the rights of conscience in the free exercise of religious worship," the court concluded.

An action in *Cohn* v. *Townsend,* 48 Misc. 47, 94 N.Y.S. 817 (1905), to enjoin the practice in New York of holding examinations for prospective school teachers on Saturday was sought by the defendant whose Orthodox Jewish religion regarded Saturday as the Sabbath. She maintained that she could not take the examination on Saturday without violating the dictates of her faith and also maintained that holding the examinations on Saturday afternoon was contrary to the city ordinance making Saturday afternoon a public holiday. Therefore, the defendant alleged that she was being deprived "of the equal protection of the laws of the land and of the state," and was being discriminated against "on account of her race."

The New York court held that by statute the board of school examiners was not specifically restrained from holding examinations on Saturday, on the Sabbath of some religions, or granting those of that religion a special examination. Therefore, the court could not prevent the board at its discretion from holding examinations on Saturdays. The court concluded that a Jewish applicant was not deprived of the equal protection of the laws and discriminated against because of her race by being denied an examination on some day other than Saturday.

In an appeal from a summary conviction in a more recent action in Pennsylvania the defendant, a Moslem, alleged a violation of the Establishment and Free Exercise clauses of the First Amendment for requiring his children to attend school on Friday in *Commonwealth* ex rel. *Bey,* 92 Pittsb. Leg. J. 84 (1944). The court determined that the Koran did not forbid the defendant's children's attendance at school on Fridays and that the children were entitled to an education. Therefore, the court concluded that the school act requiring attendance did not violate the First Amendment.

† †   *COMMONWEALTH* ex rel. *BEY*

92 PITTSB. LEG. J. 84 (1944).

Judge GUNTHER delivered the opinion of the court:

This is an appeal from an alderman's decision based upon the alleged violation of the act of 1939, P. L. 786, which provides as follows:

. . . and such child or children shall attend school continuously through the entire term, during which the public elementary schools in their respective districts shall be in session. . . .

The act further provides:

Regular daily instruction in the English language for the time herein required, by a properly qualified private tutor, shall be considered as complying with the provisions of this section, if such instruction is satisfactory to the proper county or district superintendent of schools.

It is further provided that the compulsory attendance act shall not apply where failure to attend school results from:

. . . any mental, physical, or other urgent reasons . . . but the term 'urgent reasons' shall be strictly construed and shall not permit of irregular attendance. In every such case, such action by the board of school directors shall not be final until the approval of the department of public instruction has been obtained.

The defendant, Stevenson Bey, is of the Moslem faith, and is the father of Eleanor Bey, Stone Bey, Nathaniel Bey and Wallace Bey, who attend the public school of the city of Pittsburgh. The Moslem faith was embraced by him in

1927 when he assumed the surname of Bey. He refused to allow his children to attend the public school on Friday, and as a result thereof, he was charged with the violation of the above act. He was given a hearing before an alderman and fined. At a hearing before the court without a jury, there was testimony on the part of the defendant and his witnesses that the attendance of the defendant's children in the public schools on Friday would be in direct conflict with his religion.

The Koran was offered in evidence to establish the fact that Friday was a holy day or the sabbath day of the Moslem religion.

There was also some testimony offered by the defendant that his reason for embracing the Moslem religion was that his forefathers, although southern slaves, were not Negroes, but Moors; because the Moors professed the Moslem religion, he has adopted what he considered the religion of his forefathers.

The defendant contends that the alderman's decision is a violation of the constitutional amendment which protects the free establishment of religion and the exercise thereof. It is argued on behalf of the defendant that this question was settled by the supreme court of the United States in its recent decision in *West Virginia State Board of Education* v. *Barnett*, 319 U.S. 624, involving the refusal of Jehovah's Witnesses to salute the United States flag as required by the statutes of the state.

We are concerned in this appeal with the question whether children of the Moslem faith are required to attend school on Friday.

Turning first to the question whether Friday is the sabbath of the Moslem religion, we find in reading the Koran the following religious practices are obligatory: First: saying of the creed, second: saying of prayers five times each day, third: giving of alms, fourth: observing the feast of Ramadon, and fifth: a pilgrimage to Mecca.

The Koran does not forbid the Moslem from the carrying on of his ordinary business on Friday, and unlike the Jewish and Christian sabbath, it is not necessarily a day of rest. The idea underlying the sabbath is, no doubt, a cessation of the material and physical activities to give place to spiritual exercise and to holding communion with the Divine Being.

It is our judgment that sending Moslem children to school on Friday in no way violates the principles of the Moslem faith. But even granting that Friday is a holy day in Islam, and that defendant feels religious scruples about his children's attendance at school on Friday, it is also true that his children are entitled to an education.

The defendant as provided under the code has his choice of a public, parochial or private school, or any other adequate course of instruction approved by the school authority. But where the defendant chooses the public school system for his children, he cannot allow irregular attendance without violating the law.

The flag case cited by counsel for defendant does not involve the same question. There the court decided that an expression of belief cannot be compelled by law.

In our judgment, saluting the flag is a political belief and not a religious one, and is not a proper subject for the court's jurisdiction.

The constitution does not create any special religious privileges or immunities, but religious equality and freedom also carry along with them legal duties hat cannot be laid aside by religious iews or conscientious scruples. The tatute in this case does not undertake o educate the children of the defend-nt. It merely says that the children nust be educated.

We maintain that education under he statute, either private, parochial or public, depends upon the belief of the defendant, and we are forced to the conclusion that the school attendance act does not restrict the freedom of religion or violate the constitution.

This appeal is dismissed at the costs of the defendant, and the conviction stands.

UBSEQUENT DEVELOPMENTS

A similar situation arose six years later in *Commonwealth* v. *Bey,* 166 ᵃa. Super. 136, 70 A.2d 693 (1950), where the superior court ruled that arents electing to send their children to public schools must submit them o the full requirements of the school. Compulsory attendance require-nents could not be fulfilled if a child were excused on Fridays as part f his observance of religious holidays, the court ruled. The opinion uggested that other educational avenues existed, such as meeting school equirements in day schools or private and parochial schools.

REACTIONS OF LEGAL PERIODICALS TO *COMMONWEALTH* v. *BEY*

The court's action was characterized in the *Alabama Law Review* 2:320) and the *University of Pennsylvania Law Review* (98:923) as plac-ng an arbitrary hardship on religion. The criticism was more severe in he latter review, where the writer asserted that some alternative could e found to an otherwise arbitrary exercise of state power operating to leny the Moslem children the right of assembling with the congregation in worship. He could find little solace in the fact that the Moslem parents ould elect private education for their children. The financial burdens in-volved in that alternative could be prohibitive, the writer pointed out.

The position taken in the *Alabama Law Review* was that the test governing religious holidays should be "whether the asserted immunity is reasonable under the circumstances of the case." The analyst declared that "a state's police power is properly exercised somewhere between [the] two extremes of absolute refusal by the state to grant an occasional noliday" and the position that there is a "right to keep a child from school at all times if a religious belief so dictates." He went on to imply that an occasional absence, e.g. six times a year, would have little effect, but that planned absence on one day each week would defeat the whole educational process.

BACCALAUREATE PROGRAMS

The issue of baccalaureate has arisen in several cases with differen
opinions resulting in each.

In the earliest case a taxpayer's suit sought to enjoin the practice o
using churches and offering prayers for graduation exercises on th
grounds that it violated state constitutional guarantees of religious free
dom. The Wisconsin supreme court ruled in *State* ex rel. *Conway* v. *Dis
trict Board*, 162 Wis. 482, 156 N.W. 477 (1916), that the holding o
graduation services in churches and the use of nonsectarian prayer durin
these ceremonies did not violate state constitutional provisions. The cour
reasoned that attendance was not required at the exercises. The purpos
of the graduation exercise was not worship and the amount of time taken
by the nonsectarian prayer was incidental.

† † *STATE* ex rel. *CONWAY* v. *DISTRICT BOARD*
162 wis. 482, 156 n.w. 477 (1916).

Judge BARNES delivered the opinion of the court, saying in part:

The plaintiffs filed a petition in the circuit court, praying that a writ of mandamus issue from said court to the defendants, commanding that they discontinue the practice of holding graduating exercises in any of the churches of the city of Elroy or churches elsewhere, or permitting or suffering any minister or person to offer an invocation or prayer at the graduating exercises of such school district, and commanding the defendants to hold the graduating exercises in other places than in any of the churches of the city of Elroy, or churches elsewhere, and for further order or relief as might be proper. . . .

The petition then recites that for many years it has been the practice of the defendant board to hold graduating exercises for high school graduates and that the practice still prevails and is part of the district board's required ceremony before pupils are granted diplomas; that it has been the practice of the board to conduct a part of the graduating exercises in the different churches of the city of Elroy and a part of such exercises in the opera house and to invite and engage certain ministers and priests to officiate at such graduating exercises, their duty, while so officiating, being to give a so-called invocation, which consisted of a religious service, prayer, blessing, or religious exercise; that by reason of the practice followed by said board in engaging Protestant ministers and inviting Catholic priests to officiate at said graduating exercises, it has wounded the sensibilities of both Protestant and Catholic patrons of said schools alike, and subjected those patrons, and others similarly situated, to humiliation, and rced upon them "the offense of conscience" by reason of these religious xercises; and that by reason of such cts said board has allowed and enuraged sectarian instruction in the ublic school question.

The petition further recites that nce the establishment of the district ie practice complained of has been ursued against the ineffectual protests f taxpayers, parents, and patrons of he school, and that the board threatens continue such practice; that by reaon of the practice followed certain citens and taxpayers of Elroy belonging the Catholic Church and living in he school district refuse to allow their hildren, who are about to graduate, s well as other children of theirs, to ttend the graduating exercises, and lso refuse to attend themselves on account of the religious functions that are iade a part of such exercises; that although such practice has been followed or more than six years, the school oard has taken no steps to correct the buse, and such practice still continues, nd threatens to continue in the future; hat by reason of the school board reusing to omit the practice set forth, nd by reason of the believers in the Catholic faith refusing to allow their hildren to attend graduating exerises, such children did not receive their liplomas at such exercises, but were ranted them privately afterward by pecial request; that such a situation roduces a bad state of affairs, both to he parents, patrons, and graduates of he school, and causes young men and vomen who desire to participate in the ionors of graduation much chagrin and nortification at not being able to participate in the exercises with their fellow graduates; that because of conscientious scruples Catholic parents and itizens have refrained from taking

part in what they believe to be distinctly Protestant religious worship, and that the practice of having prayers offered by Protestant ministers is contrary to the right of conscience, and in violation of law; that petitioners have requested said board to discontinue the practice complained of to the extent of not holding the graduating exercises in churches and in not permitting prayers to be offered by denominational clergymen, and that said board has neglected and refused to comply with such request, and refused to interfere with the matter in any way; that such graduating exercises are an integral part of the curriculum of our public schools; that permitting religious service to take place in a public school, and permitting a minister to offer an invocation or prayer at such time, amounts to a sanction of the minister of one sect and an invitation to lend his personal influence and prestige to the particular sect in preference to all others, and that this action amounts to the teaching of certain religious doctrines of the particular sect so favored.

The petition further shows that permitting ministers of different denominations to offer prayers to the graduates and patrons assembled, irrespective of their religious creeds, and regardless of the wording of the prayer, amounts to giving sectarian instruction; that such prayers must necessarily be clothed with external form for delivery and reception and held with internal significance; that it is these various significances, which constitute the various sectarian churches, and that prayer in the Protestant service is delivered standing and received sitting, and in the Catholic service it is offered and received kneeling; that Protestants worship a Supreme Being by prayer alone, and hold that prayer is supreme worship; that Catho-

lics worship the Supreme Being by official sacrifice and prayer, and teach
that official sacrifice is supreme worship;
that prayer, therefore, as well in external form as doctrine, differs with the
different services and is sectarian, and
is therefore in violation of section 3,
art. 10, of the Constitution; that by permitting the acts complained of in a
public school, the board has permitted
and suffered the practice of religious
and sectarian instruction to become
part of the public school curriculum
which is conducted by those who are allied by profession to sectarianism and
who teach the same by suggestion; that
such practice interferes with religious
liberty and subjects the pupils to slight,
insult, and contempt because of their
religious faith.

The petition then recites that the petitioners enjoined the school board in
the year 1912 from carrying on any religious services in connection with the
graduating exercises, and that thereupon said board refused to hold any
graduating exercises at all; that such
action tends to engender strife and to
perpetuate in a public school curriculum religious and sectarian doctrines
and to impress upon the pupils that
they can expect no honors or favors at
the hands of the school board unless it
is permitted to hold graduating exercises in accordance with certain religious and sectarian forms.

. . . .

. . . Our Constitution makers wisely
sought to prevent, as far as they could,
the injection into the affairs of state of
anything that would tend to germinate
or foster religious rancor or bitterness.
It is wise and just that its provisions be
adhered to in spirit as well as in letter.
For reasons that will be stated later,
we conclude that the petitioners are not

entitled to relief on the facts stated
Nevertheless, we think it would be
wise exercise of official discretion to dis
continue such practices as are here com
plained of when objection thereto i
made by any substantial number o
school patrons. We do *not* underrat
the efficacy of prayer. Neither are w
prepared to say that the average high
school graduate may not need it. Bu
whenever it is likely to do more harm
than good, it might well be dispense
with. It is not at all times wise o
politic to do certain things although n
legal rights would be invaded by doin
them.

. . . .

III, IV

The plaintiffs' contentions are two
fold: (1) That the acts complained o
violate the constitutional rights guar
anteed to them by section 3, article 1
of our Constitution; and (2) that the
violate the rights guaranteed by section
18, of article 1 of that instrument. The
provision first referred to reads as fol
lows:

The Legislature shall provide by law fo
the establishment of district schools, which
shall be as nearly uniform as practicable
and such schools shall be free and without
charge for tuition, to all children between
the ages of four and twenty years; and no
sectarian instruction shall be allowed
therein.

Section 18 of article 1 provides:

The right of every man to worship Al
mighty God according to the dictates of
his own conscience shall never be infringed
nor shall any man be compelled to attend
erect, or support any place of worship, or
to maintain any ministry, against his con
sent; nor shall any control of, or interfer
ence with, the rights of conscience be
permitted, or any preference be given by

aw to any religious establishments, or modes of worship; nor shall any money be drawn from the treasury for the benefit of religious societies, or religious or theological seminaries.

The two things complained of are the use of a church building in which to hold graduation exercises and the delivery of an invocation or prayer thereat by a denominational clergyman. The holding of graduation exercises in a church is not in itself the giving of sectarian instruction, within the meaning of section 3 of article 10, above quoted. This is obvious, and presently eliminates from consideration the constitutional provision first quoted. Neither is it shown that the taxpayers were called upon to pay for the use of the churches in which the exercises were held, nor that the clergymen who gave the invocations were paid for doing so. Such being the case, no one has been called upon against his will to erect or support any place of worship or maintain any ministry, nor has any money been drawn from the treasury for the benefit of a religious society. A man may feel constrained to enter a house of worship belonging to a different sect from the one with which he affiliates, but if no sectarian services are carried on, he is not compelled to worship God contrary to the dictates of his conscience, and is not obliged to do so at all. The only clauses of section 18 of article 1 that are at all applicable to the question under discussion are those which provide that no person shall be compelled to attend any place of worship against his consent and which forbid interference with the rights of conscience. Obviously graduation exercises are a part of the school curriculum, and are under the direction and control of school boards. They may be dispensed with, but, so long as they are not,

school boards cannot escape responsibility for them. Parents and pupils of all denominations have a right to attend such exercises without their legal rights being invaded. It would be far-fetched, however, to say that by so doing they are compelled to attend a place of worship. True, the building is one ordinarily used for conducting religious services. Other buildings that are not churches are often used for like purposes. So are our public streets. Indeed, at the present day, churches are largely used for social gatherings of various kinds at which no religious services of any kind are carried on. The kind of a building is hardly the significant thing from the legal standpoint, but the fact that worship is carried on when there is actual or moral compulsion. Graduation exercises take place but once a year. Often in smaller places church auditoriums are more commodious and better calculated to take care of the overflow crowds that congregate at such times than any other building that is available. To say that a person attending such place once a year is compelled to attend a place of worship would be giving prominence to form rather than to substance. When the Constitution protects the individual from being compelled to attend a place of worship, it undoubtedly means that he shall not be required to attend a place where religious instruction is being given at the time he is required to be present. It protects a man from being obliged to attend the services of the Salvation Army in our public streets, or from being compelled to enter a hall or opera house while such services are being carried on just as much as it does against being forced to enter a church. It is what is done, not the name of the place where it is done, that is significant.

The fact that certain persons desire to attend graduation exercises with their children, and that they say that being compelled to enter a church of a different denomination from that to which they belong is violative of their assured rights of conscience, does not make it so. If it is clear that the thing complained of does not violate any right guaranteed by the Constitution, then the courts cannot interfere in their behalf, because the final decision on this question must necessarily rest with the courts and not with the individual. The individual must decide for himself whether his conscience tells him that he must not frequent a certain place. If it does, he should punctilliously regard its behests and stay away. But the court cannot turn casuist further than to determine whether a legal right has been invaded in any given case. Neither can it say that a thing offends against conscience when there is no substantial reason why it should. It is not sufficient for a person to say: "This thing is contrary to what my conscience tells me to be right, therefore, it must be stopped." The individual cannot foreclose inquiry into the reasonableness of his request by his bare assertion. Some consciences are very tender and very highly developed, so much so that the possessor regards as being wrong many things that the law regards as harmless. Some refrain from playing cards for amusement, some from dancing, some from attending places of amusement, and some from all these things, because they consider it wrong to participate in or countenance them. The law regards none of these things as being essentially wrong in itself. At the same time it recognizes the right of any one to stay away from them where the promptings of conscience indicate that it would be wrong to attend.

To the lay mind there is very little difference in principle between the case before us and *Dorner* v. *School District*, 137 Wis. 147, 118 N.W. 353, 19 L.R.A. (N.S.) 171. There a Catholic parochial school was built adjacent to a Catholic church, and some of the school rooms were rented and used for the purpose of a public school. The Catholic school children attended church services before school hours in the morning, and prayers were recited and hymns were sung during school hours in the portion of the school building used for parochial school purposes, and in rooms either adjoining or adjacent to those rented by the public school authorities. The parochial school was taught by Sisters clad in the conventional garb of the order to which they belonged. The lower court found that the public school conducted in the parochial school building had, at times, been pervaded and characterized by sectarian instruction, and very properly enjoined the continuance of such practices. It held, however, that the school board was acting within its legal rights in renting and using a part of the parochial school building for the purpose of a public school, and such decision was affirmed in this court. There are points of dissimilarity between the two cases, but it would be difficult to say that those who felt aggrieved in the Dorner Case did not have at least as strong a ground for complaint as did the plaintiffs in the present case. It is true that the public school was not conducted in the church building, and that certain rooms in the parochial school were exclusively devoted to the use of the public school. But it is also true that the school building was one in which sectarian instruction was given, and was within the shadow of a church which was attended daily by the children attending the parochial school; that the teachers in such school were clad in a religious garb, and that the public school attendants, or many of them, were within the hearing of prayers recited aloud in the parochial school rooms, as well as within the hearing of sectarian hymns sung in such rooms. We conclude that the holding of graduation exercises in a church building is not, in and of itself, contrary to either of the constitutional provisions relied on by the plaintiffs.

A somewhat different question is raised by the complaint about prayers being offered at graduation exercises by denominational clergymen. A prayer may be either sectarian or nonsectarian in character. The sessions of our national Congress, of our state Legislature, and of our great party conventions are customarily opened with prayer. These prayers are almost invariably nonsectarian in character, so much so that a person reading them or listening to them would be entirely at a loss to discover to what denomination the clergyman belonged. The enthusiast who places his desire to make proselytes to the faith he professes above his sense of propriety may occasionally "slop over," but it is only just to say that our clergy rarely offend in this regard. To be sure, offense may be very adroitly given if the clergyman is so minded, but there is no claim that any such thing has occurred in this case.

The court decided in the Edgerton Bible Case that the giving of a nonsectarian prayer was not sectarian instruction. We quote from the opinion:

The term 'sectarian instruction,' in the Constitution, manifestly refers exclusively to instruction in religious doctrines, and the prohibition is only aimed at such instruction as is sectarian; that is to say, instruction in religious doctrines which are believed by some religious sects and rejected by others. Hence, to teach the existence of a Supreme Being, of infinite wisdom, power, and goodness, and that it is the highest duty of all men to adore, obey, and love Him, is not sectarian, because all religious sects so believe and teach. The instruction becomes sectarian when it goes further, and inculcates doctrine or dogma concerning which the religious sects are in conflict. This we understand to be the meaning of the constitutional prohibition. *State* ex rel. *Weiss and Others* v. *District Board, etc.,* 76 Wis. 177, 192, 193, 44 N.W. 967, 973 [7 L.R.A. 330, 20 A. St. Rep. 41].

In the case before us it appears from the allegations of the petition that both Catholic priests and Protestant ministers had at different times been selected to deliver the invocation at graduation exercises. There is no claim that on any of these occasions any unseemly hint or suggestion was made by any of the reverend gentlemen who were so honored. In fact the contrary appears by inference at least. So it is clear that no showing was made that "sectarian instruction" was given, as that term is defined in the case last cited. Had it appeared that the invocations given were sectarian in character, and that the school board threatened to continue or permit such practices in the future, we do not wish to be understood as intimating that a court of equity would not enjoin the continuance of such practice.

We think it would be difficult to pick out any clause of section 18, art. 1, of the Constitution which by any fair or reasonable construction could be said to be violated by the delivery of a nonsectarian prayer at a graduation exercise. No man is compelled to worship, nor compelled to attend a place of worship, nor does he, as before stated, attend such a place, except in the most technical sense, when he attends graduation exercises. Pupils do not congregate on such an occasion for the purpose of worship, and the short nonsectarian invocation that is usually given is a mere incident, which occupies but a few moments of the two hours or more that is usually occupied with the program prepared for such occasions. If the prayer be nonsectarian, it does not interfere with any right of conscience that the law recognizes, and neither is the matter of permitting it the giving of any preference to any religious establishment or religious mode of worship in a constitutional sense. A very different question would arise if an attempt were made to introduce the practice of having prayer as part of the daily routine in our public schools. Considering what has been done here and the rare occasions on which it has been or can be done, the matter, complained of seems to be too inconsequential to furnish the subject of a lawsuit. It follows from what has been said that the judgment of the lower court was right.

Judgment affirmed.

LATER CASES

The New Mexico supreme court took a similar view over the question of holding baccalaureate and commencement exercises in churches in *Miller* v. *Cooper*, 56 N.M. 355, 244 P.2d 520 (1952). An attempt was made in a taxpayer's suit to enjoin the use of churches for commencement and baccalaureate services. The state court ruled that such practices did not violate the doctrine of separation of church and state and upheld the trial court's ruling that permitted such exercises to be held in Churches if there were no other suitable places available.

† †   *MILLER* v. *COOPER*
56 N.M. 355, 244 P.2D 520 (1952).

Mr. Justice MCGHEE delivered the opinion of the court:

The plaintiffs brought this action as taxpayers and members of the Board of Directors of the Lindrith School District in Rio Arelia County against the officers of the State Board of Education, the County Board of Education, the Director of the Certification Department of the State Board of Education, the principal of the school, three of its teachers, its janitor and the minister of the Baptist Church at Lindrith.

The object of the suit was to permanently bar the principal and teachers from again teaching in the public schools of New Mexico, because of their claimed teaching of religion in the public school at Lindrith, the dissemination of sectarian religious magazines among the pupils and other acts which were claimed to violate various provisions of the federal and our state constitutions relating to the separation of Church and State. The plaintiffs sought to invoke the penalty of Sec. 55–1102, N.M.S.A., 1941 Comp., which reads:

No teacher shall use any sectarian or denominational books in the schools or teach sectarian doctrine in the schools, and any teacher violating the provisions of this section shall be immediately discharged, his certificate to teach school revoked, and be forever barred from receiving any school moneys and employment in the public schools in the state. Provided, that this section shall not be construed to interfere with the use of school buildings for other purposes authorized by the county board after school hours.

The trial court entered judgment of dismissal as to all defendants except Cooper and Anson. Cooper was the principal and also taught in the school, while Anson was a teacher. The judgment enjoined Cooper and Anson from teaching religion in the school, but the plaintiffs were denied the other relief sought against them, and such denial is the sole basis of the appeal.

Only three acts of which the plaintiffs complain merit consideration here, and they are the holding of the Baccalaureate services in the Baptist Church, the holding of Commencement exercises in the Presbyterian Church, and the dissemination of religious pamphlets through the public schools.

The churches were the only buildings in the Lindrith community with sufficient seating capacity to accommodate the pupils and the people of the community who desired to attend these functions. The Legion Hall was large enough to accommodate those who desired to attend but it did not have sufficient seating capacity.

(1) These functions are of great interest to the pupils and their relatives, and like other communities throughout the state the churches are the only buildings which could comfortably accommodate those present. We are firmly committed to the doctrine of separation of Church and State, both by our constitutional provisions and statutes, as well as our decision in *Zellers* v. *Huff*, 55 N.M. 501, 236 P.2d 949; but we do not feel they require us to prohibit the holding of these time honored programs in a building where all who desire to attend may be accommodated. Neither are we fearful that those conducting the services or exercises will fail to observe the proprieties of the occasion and thus give offense to anyone attending.

The trial court correctly refused to enjoin the holding of such services or exercises in a church where there was no other suitable auditorium or place available.

(2) The charge the defendants were using the school as a medium for the dissemination of religious pamphlets published by the Presbyterian Church presents a different situation. It is true the teachers did not hand them to the pupils or instruct that they be taken or read. The pamphlets were, however, kept in plain sight in a school room and were available to the pupils and the supply was evidently replenished from time to time. We con-

demned such practice in *Zellers* v. *Huff,* supra, and condemn it here and hold the trial court was in error when it failed to enjoin such acts on the part of the defendants Anson and Cooper. The Pamphlets were kept in the room where Anson taught, but we assume such could only happen with the approval of the principal, Cooper. We will not, however, overturn the action of the trial court in refusing to bar the defendants Cooper and Anson from employment as teachers in the public schools. Instead, we follow the precedent set in the Zellers case where we accepted the judgment of the trial court that certain of the teachers should not be permanently barred from teaching in the public schools when the evidence disclosed far more flagrant violations than are present here.

The other practices of which the plaintiffs complain were only occasional and trivial; we pass them without notice as we did the same acts in the Zellers case.

This appeal was submitted ahead of the Zellers case and decision was delayed so both cases could be decided together. However, at the request of the plaintiffs in this case, we then withheld decision awaiting the determination by the United States Supreme Court of the case of *Doremus* v. *Board of Education from New Jersey,* 5 N.J. 435, 75 A.2d 880, in order to learn whether there would be a modification of the decision in *People of State of Illinois* ex rel. *McCollum* v. *Board of Education,* 333 U.S. 203, 68 S.Ct. 461, 92 L.Ed. 648, 649, where it was held there could be no religious instruction in the public schools. Unfortunately, the question in the Doremus case became moot by reason of the graduation of the pupil involved, and the appeal was dismissed without decision on its merits. 342 U.S. 429, 72 S.Ct. 394. We then learned of the case of *Zorach* v. *Clauson,* on appeal from a decision of the Court of Appeals of New York, 303 N.Y. 161, 100 N.E.2d 463, and postponed decision here awaiting the action of the United States Supreme Court in that case, 72 S.Ct. 679. That decision was announced April 28, 1952, but it does not aid us in the present determination.

The action of the trial court in refusing to enjoin the further employment of the defendants Cooper and Anson in the public school of Lindrith, or to bar them as teachers in the public schools of New Mexico will be affirmed, but its refusal to enjoin the dissemination of religious literature in the school was erroneous, and that part of the judgment is reversed and the cause remanded with instructions to enter a new judgment enjoining such practice.

RELATED CASES

For the first time the question of the actual constitutionality of baccalaureate services in public schools was raised in *Chamberlain* v. *Dade County,* 143 So.2d 21 (1962). The validity of a Florida statute which dealt with the allegedly religious practice was challenged as a violation of the Declaration of Rights of the Florida constitution and of the First and Fourteenth Amendments' religious freedoms.

The state court, rejecting the definition of the Establishment of Religion clause that the United States Supreme Court announced in *Everson*

v. *Board of Education*, 330 U.S. 1 (1948), said: "[That definition] goes far beyond the purpose and intent of the authors [of the Constitution] and beyond any reasonable application to the practical facts of every day life in this country." Rather, the lower court regarded establishment to mean the setting up of a state church or the preferment of one church over all others. Therefore, the Florida court found that the establishment clause was not violated. The court also held that the free exercise clause was not violated because there was no compulsion. By the same logic, the court determined that the Florida constitution had also not been violated.

Chamberlain v. *Dade County*, 374 U.S. 487, 83 S.Ct. 1864 (1963), reached the Supreme Court on appeal. Judgment was vacated and the case remanded to the Florida supreme court on the basis of *Murray* v. *Curlett*, 371 U.S. 809, 83 S. Ct. 21 (1963), and *School District Abington Township* v. *Schempp*, 374 U.S. 203, 83 S.Ct. 1560 (1963).

Upon remand, in *Chamberlain* v. *Dade County*, 160 So.2d 97 (1964), the Florida court held that the appellants had no standing to sue on the baccalaureate issue because none of the children were adversely affected since all the children but one junior high pupil were in elementary schools.

The case again came before the Supreme Court as *Chamberlain* v. *Dade County*, 377 U.S. 402, 84 S.Ct. 1272 (1964). Appeal on the issue of baccalaureate was dismissed by the Court in a *per curiam* opinion for lack of a properly presented federal question. (See Chapter 4 on Bible reading.)

NATIVITY SCENES AND RELIGIOUS DISPLAYS

The question of the constitutionality of religious displays was posed in *Baer* v. *Kolmorgen*, 181 N.Y.S.2d 230, 14 M.2d 1015 (1958) which involved an action to enjoin the building of a Nativity scene on public school property by a private group after the public school had been dismissed for Christmas vacation. The plaintiffs charged that the school board, which gave its permission for the erection of the creche, had violated the First and Fourteenth Amendments. The county court ruled that the erection of the Nativity scene was not unconstitutional since no public funds were used, no public employee was involved with its erection, and the public school was not in session.

† † BAER v. KOLMORGEN
181 N.Y.S.2D 230; 14 MISC.2D 1015 (1958).

Judge GALLAGHER delivered the opinion of the court:

In the year 1956 in the Village of Ossining a committee was formed, known and hereinafter designated as the Creche Committee. Its membership consisted of Catholics, Protestants and Jews. Its purpose was to solicit funds to enable the Committee to erect a Nativity Scene within the Village during the Christmas season.

An application was made by the Committee to the Board of Education of Ossining School District No. 1 for permission to construct the Scene on the lawn of the Ossining Junior-Senior High School. By resolution duly adopted the Board granted the Committee's request and the Creche was erected in December, 1956, a few days before school closed for Christmas vacation. It was dismantled before school reconvened. No suit was brought to restrain the Board or to obtain an adjudication as to the constitutionality of its resolution.

In 1957 the Creche Committee renewed its application but stipulated that the Creche would not be erected or maintained while school was in session. The Board of Education again passed a resolution authorizing the erection of the Creche on the lawn of the said school, after which this action was commenced for a permanent injunction and declaratory judgment. It is contended by the plaintiffs that the action of the School Board violates the First and Fourteenth Amendments to the United States Constitution and Article I, section 3 of the Constitution of the State of New York.

During the pendency of the action, the plaintiffs moved for an order restraining and enjoining, pendente lite, the defendant, Board of Education, from authorizing or permitting the erection of a Creche on any property subject to its jurisdiction and to rescind any permission previously granted in that regard. In denying the application Mr. Justice Coyne stated as follows:

Without prejudging the merits of the controversy, the following observation would appear germane. The constitutional prohibition relating to separation of church and state does not imply an impregnable wall or cleavage completely disassociating one from the other. While it is necessary that there be a separation of church and state, it is not necessary that the state should be stripped of all religious sentiment. It may be a tragic experience for this country and for its conception of life, liberty and the pursuit of happiness if our people lose their religious feeling and are left to live their lives without faith. . . .

The Court is of the opinion that of all the plaintiffs only one has alleged and proved sufficient interest in the controversy to entitle him to maintain this action.

The complaint alleges that all of the plaintiffs are residents and taxpayers of the school district. That allegation was put into issue by the defendants' answer. In most cases there was a failure by the plaintiffs to prove the fact alleged. In some cases the evidence establishes the contrary. Even were it admitted, however, that most if not all of the plaintiffs are taxpayers of the district, that fact alone would not give them a sufficient interest to maintain the suit. The erection of the Creche during the school holiday was not financed by any public appropriation, and there is no evidence that it has added any sum whatever to the cost of conducting the school or that any plaintiff is, will or possibly can be out of pocket because of it. *Doremus* v. *Board of Education*, 342 U.S. 429.

Moreover, the law in this State is long established that the interest which a taxpayer shares with all others in the community is not such a special, peculiar or personal interest as to entitle him to challenge in the courts the constitutionality of an act of a public official or body. . . .

The complaint must be dismissed as against those plaintiffs who have alleged no interest other than that they are residents and taxpayers. It must also be dismissed as against those whose claim to an interest is that they have children attending the grade schools within the district. Whether their children will ever even attend the Ossining Junior-Senior High School is entirely speculative and there is nothing in the record to indicate that the Board of Education has ever authorized or considered the erection of a Creche on other school property. In any event, those allegations were put in issue and with one possible exception there is no proof to sustain them.

. . . .

The remaining plaintiff, Stanley M. Estrow, is not entitled under the law to a permanent injunction. A basic requirement for such a decree is the danger of irreparable injury. . . . No such danger is shown in the case at bar.

Moreover, the act which plaintiff seeks to enjoin was terminated when the Creche was removed from the school grounds in January, 1958. It does not appear that any one has permission at the present time to erect or maintain a Creche on school property or that there is any pending application for such permission. Under the circumstances there is at present nothing to enjoin. . . .

However, plaintiff will not be deprived of his day in court. While the act which he seeks to enjoin terminated with the removal of the Creche in January, 1958, the controversy did not necessarily end at that time. The Creche was not removed because of any change in the policy of the Board, but because of the very nature of the display. A Creche is ordinarily exhibited only during the short Christmas season. The Creche which was erected on the school grounds in 1957 was up for only a few days during the vacation period. Because of this it would be extremely difficult for plaintiff to ever obtain a judicial determination of the constitutional question, even if the Creche were authorized year after year, unless the court were to view it as a continuing controversy. For that reason the complaint will be considered on the merits in so far as it seeks declaratory relief.

Proof was taken upon the trial as to the situation which existed in 1956 and the Court has considered such proof in determining that there is a continuing justiciable dispute. The constitutional question, however, must be decided on the facts which existed or were threatened at the time this action was commenced in December, 1957. The evidence establishes that the 1957 Creche was not erected or displayed while school was in session. The evidence further establishes that no public funds were expended, nor was the time of any public employee involved in its erection or display. Even the electricity used in the illumination of the Crib was paid for entirely by private contribution.

The testimony reveals that it has long been a tradition to receive and grant requests from various groups to erect signs or symbols on the school lawn. This privilege has been accorded to the Heart Fund, the Cancer Fund and the American Red Cross, among others. No similar privilege has been requested by any other religious group nor denied by the School Board.

The First Amendment, so far as pertinent, provides: "Congress shall make no law respecting an establishment of religion, or prohibiting the free exercise thereof. . . ."

The United States Supreme Court has held that by virtue of the Fourteenth Amendment to the Federal Constitution the prohibitions of the First Amendment are applicable to actions of the States and their subdivisions. *Cantwell* v. *State of Connecticut*, 310 U.S. 296.

Article I, Section 3 of the New York State Constitution reads, in part, as follows: "The free exercise and enjoyment of religious profession and worship, without discrimination or preference, shall forever be allowed in this State to all mankind. . . ."

Much has been written in recent years concerning Thomas Jefferson's reference in 1802 to "a wall of separation between church and State." It is upon that "wall" that plaintiffs seek to build their case. Jefferson's figure of speech has received so much attention that one would almost think at times that it is to be found somewhere in our Constitution. Courts and authors have devoted numerous pages to its interpretation. This Court has no intention of engaging in a dispute among historians as to the meaning of a metaphor. The only language which we are called upon to interpret and apply is the plain language quoted above from the Federal and State Constitutions.

Reason and precedent have given these provisions a somewhat broader meaning than a literal interpretation would indicate. Nevertheless, there appear to be two general bases for attacking a statute or resolution on the grounds that it violates the First Amendment to the United State Constitution or Article I, Section 3 of the State Constitution: First: Where a person is required to submit to some religious rite or instruction or is deprived or threatened with deprivation of his freedom for resisting that unconstitutional requirement; Second: Where a person is deprived of property for unconstitutional purposes (such as a direct or indirect tax to support a religious establishment). . . .

The second basis cannot be seriously or successfully urged in the case at bar. As previously mentioned, the erection and display of the Creche involved the use of no public funds nor the time of any school personnel. We consider then whether the first basis supports plaintiff's objection.

Plaintiff points out that Section 3212 of the Education Law requires him to send his minor children to school and that failure or refusal to do so renders him subject to punishment. He contends further that the Creche is a sectarian religious symbol. He concludes that "pupils compelled by law to attend public school classes for secular instruction, through such displays are subjected to sectarian religious influences and are obliged to attend and participate in the veneration of sectarian religious symbols of a religious faith to which some of them do not subscribe." Witnesses for the plaintiff testified that what is symbolized by the Creche is inconsistent with the religion of plaintiff and his children.

The fallacy in plaintiff's argument is apparent in view of the fact that school was not in session during the period when the Creche was displayed. Moreover, the Court is of the opinion that the influence, if any, of religious symbolism is inescapable during the Christmas season. It would be difficult to say that as a practical matter any greater influence exists by virtue of the fact that the symbol is permitted on public as well as private property.

Plaintiff has attempted to bring this

case within the decision of the United States Supreme Court in *People of State of Illinois* ex rel. *McCollum* v. *Board of Education,* 333 U.S. 203. That case involved the actual teaching of religion in the public schools, during school hours and by sectarian instructors. As expressed by Mr. Justice Frankfurter in his concurring opinion, 333 U.S. at page 227, religious instruction was "patently woven into the working scheme of the school." The program was held unconstitutional. The facts were in no way comparable to those in the case at bar.

Plaintiff claims that the presence of the Creche on school property constitutes "teaching" and, therefore, that the McCollum decision applies. Witnesses in the field of education testified that symbols are often employed as a means of education.

There can be no doubt that symbols are frequently and effectively employed in our schools as a teaching aid. Teaching, however, presupposes the presence of students and we must again repeat that school was not in session while the Creche was displayed in 1957. In any event the argument would be of little validity in the absence of evidence that instruction was given as to the meaning of the Creche or that it was in fact employed as a means of teaching.

Both of the bases for attacking a statute or resolution as being in violation of the First Amendment were present in the McCollum case. The use of public funds was involved, at least to the extent that the time of school personnel was utilized in the administration of the plan, and while religious instruction was offered on a voluntary basis the Court found inherent elements of compulsion. In the words of Mr. Justice Frankfurter there was "an obvious pressure upon children to attend." McCollum, supra, 333 U.S. at page 227. Neither element is present in the case at bar.

The Creche is undoubtedly a religious symbol. In viewing it, however, we are all free to interpret its meaning according to our own religious faith. If any public body were to limit that freedom or if any public institution were to give instruction as to its meaning there would, unquestionably, be a constitutional violation. That, however, is not this case. Here the School Board has done no more than to make a small portion of its property available for the display. To that extent they have accommodated a religious, though non-denominational, group. However, the accommodation of religious groups is not per se unconstitutional. *Zorach* v. *Clauson,* 343 U.S. 306. If such accommodation violates the doctrine of absolute separation between Church and State, then it is time that that doctrine be discarded once and for all. Absolute separation is not and never has been required by the Constitution. Mr. Justice Douglas, speaking for the United States Supreme Court in its most recent expression of opinion on the subject, stated, *Zorach* v. *Clauson,* supra, 343 U.S. at page 312:

The First Amendment, however, does not say that in every and all respects there shall be a separation of Church and State. Rather, it studiously defines the manner, the specific ways, in which there shall be no concert or union or dependency one on the other. That is the common sense of the matter. Otherwise the state and religion would be aliens to each other—hostile, suspicious, and even unfriendly.

By no process of legal reasoning could the permission granted to the Creche Committee be construed as an establishment of religion or a denial of the right to worship freely and without discrimination. The site was chosen by the Committee not because it was public school property, but because of its location and the amount of space available. The Board granted the Committee's application in the same spirit of cooperation which prompted it to accord a similar privilege to many other groups within the community. In this regard the facts are not unlike those in *Lewis* v. *Mandeville*, 201 Misc. 120, 107 N.Y.S.2d 865. There, the firehouse was made available for Catholic and Jewish services while their respective places of worship were being rected or repaired. Similar permission had been given from time to time to various local organizations, some with religious backgrounds and some without. The Court considered this a mere accommodation and held that there was no constitutional violation.

Privileges and benefits should not be denied to individuals or organizations merely because of their religious affiliations or because they may be engaged in some activity of a religious nature. . . . The test is the First Amendment. It has not been violated here. . . .

LATER CASES

Another New York county case questioned the constitutionality of the display of the Nativity scene on public school property in *Lawrence* v. *Buchmueller*, 40 Misc.2d 300, 243 N.Y.S.2d 87 (1963). The county court again held that the privately erected Nativity scene displayed during the Christmas recess did not violate the establishment clause of the First Amendment.

† † *LAWRENCE* v. *BUCHMUELLER*
40 MISC.2D 300, 243 N.Y.S.2D 87 (1963).

Judge COYLE delivered the opinion of the court:

This is an action by a number of parents whose children attend pubic schools maintained by the Board of Education of Union Free School District No. 7, at Hartsdale, New York, for a declaration that said Board has no legal or constitutional authority to permit the erection or display on school premises or property of any and all symbols of any deity or semi-deity belonging to any and all religions. The action was prompted by the Board of Education's authorization to a group of Hartsdale School District taxpayers, permitting them to erect a creche or Nativity scene on the Central Avenue school grounds during a portion of the 1962 Christmas recess, when school would not be in session and at no expense to the School District. The matter is now before the Court on plaintiffs' motion for summary judgment.

To grant the broad relief requested by the plaintiffs as above indicated would, in the opinion of the court, be tantamount to sanctioning judicially a policy of nonrecognition of God in the public schools resulting in a denial that religion has played any part in the formulation of the moral standards of the community. In such circumstances the State's declared purpose of fostering in the children of the State "moral and intellectual qualities," would be thwarted. The Legislature of the State of New York has mandated the Board of Regents to prescribe courses of instruction in patriotism and citizenship in all of the schools of the State "[i]n order to promote a spirit of patriotic and civic service and obligation and to *foster in the children of the state moral and intellectual qualities* which are essential in preparing to meet the obligations of citizenship in peace or in war." (Emphasis supplied) (Section 801, Education Law) To possess moral qualities one must be conformable to a standard of morality. "Accordingly to common understanding, the terms 'immoral' and 'morals' must be taken to refer to the moral standards of the community, the 'norm or standard of behavior which struggles to make itself articulate in law.' " . . .

There may be a difference of opinion with respect to the origin of the moral law, or the standards of morality which prevail in our modern society. The vast majority of men in the eras of recorded history have conceived the moral law as resting on a theistic foundation whether ascertained by the light of reason and thus rightly called natural law or promulgated by revelation and called divine law. The natural law is mentioned in the Declaration of In-

dependence as "the laws of nature and of Nature's God," and has been defined by sages. . . .

The basic foundation of such a philosophy of natural law is denied by some who advocate an adherence to moral principles because the experience of mankind has demonstrated that such conformity works, and has proved conducive, to a well-ordered and peaceful society. Theirs is pragmatic morality.

For school boards and school teachers to attempt a fostering of moral qualities in the children of the State without a recognition of the possibility, at least, that God is the fountainhead from which moral principles spring would have one of two consequences, either a stultification of their attempt to foster intellectual qualities in the children of the State or advocacy of a pragmatic morality in their attempt to foster moral qualities in the children of the State. This Court will not place school boards and school teachers upon the horns of such a dilemma, for as Mr. Justice Goldberg said in his concurring opinion in *Abington School District* v. *Schempp* and *Murray* v. *Curlett, Board of School Commissioners of Baltimore City,* 374 U.S. 203, 306:

Neither the state nor this Court can or should ignore the significance of the fact that a vast portion of our people believe in and worship God and that *many of our legal, political and personal values derive historically from religious teachings.* Government must inevitably take cognizance of the existence of religion and, indeed under certain circumstances the First Amendment may require that it do so. (Emphasis supplied)

While the plaintiffs' ultimate objective may be to remove from the public schools anything symbolic of God and religion, the Court must confine its decision to the matter at issue, namely, whether the Hartsdale School Board's resolution permitting a group of citizens to erect upon a small portion of spacious school grounds a creche or Nativity scene during a period of the Christmas Holidays, when school was not in session and without any involvement of the school personnel or school district's expense, constitutes a violation of the First Amendment. The First Amendment provides that Congress shall make no law respecting an establishment of religion, or prohibiting the free exercise thereof. Although the plaintiffs' complaint alleges that the action of the School Board interferes with the free enjoyment of their religious beliefs and constitutes an establishment of religion, for the purposes of this motion seeking summary judgment they have abandoned all claim that the free exercise of their religious beliefs has been interfered with. And indeed, they must take such position for the papers in support of their motion fail to disclose any such interference. Since school was in recess the compulsory attendance provisions of the Education Law pleaded in the complaint become irrelevant. There is no proof that plaintiffs or their children were compelled to look upon the creche and there is no statement or averment that any of the plaintiffs or any of their children even voluntarily, viewed the same. There is absolutely no indication in the moving papers as to what are the religious or nonreligious beliefs of the plaintiffs and their children. The only issue of law or fact then is whether the establishment clause of the First Amendment has been violated. This is made eminently clear by the statement in plaintiffs' brief:

Let there be no mistake, either, about the position of those plaintiffs who follow the Christian theology; objection is made therein, not on the basis of any religious antagonism with the creche as a symbol—but, rather, precisely because it *is* symbolic of a basic tenet of the Church and, as such, has no place in a secular atmosphere. . . . We contend most vigorously that one may follow the Christian religion and object most emphatically that his own constitutional rights and liberties are infringed by the display of a religious symbol upon public property.

It is the judgment of this Court that the resolution of the Hartsdale School Board permitting the erection of a creche under the circumstances here present does not constitute the establishment of religion. The plaintiffs' motion is therefore, denied. . . . Unlike *Engel* v. *Vitale*, 370 U.S. 421, 431 (Classroom recitation of so-called Regents' Prayer) or *Abington School District* v. *Schempp; Murray* v. *Curlett, Board of School Commissioners of Baltimore City*, 374 U.S. 203 (Classroom Bible reading and recitation of Lord's Prayer) which concerned active involvement by Government in religious exercises, the present case constitutes, at most, merely a passive accommodation of religion. . . .

REACTIONS OF LEGAL PERIODICALS TO LAWRENCE V. BUCHMUELLER

The New York court was criticized sharply in the *Brooklyn Law Review* (30:356) for not following the dictates and rationale of the United States Supreme Court in the latter's disposition of recent church and state questions. The reviewer argued that in line with the Supreme Court's action in the Everson, McCollum, Zorach, and Engel cases, the controlling test in matters of the instant nature is that there is a violation of the establishment clause of the First Amendment of the United States Constitution whenever there is a religious ceremony or activity upon public property.

He reasoned that the use of public property for religious exercises was the controlling factor in the McCollum decision (where released-time programs held in the public school buildings were declared unconstitutional) and the Zorach decision (where dismissed-time programs conducted off the school grounds were upheld). In a similar vein, the Everson ruling had decided that government may not aid any or all religions, and the Engel decision had ruled that an alleged violation of the Establishment of Religion Clause, unlike the Free Exercise of Religion Clause, requires no showing of official coercion of the students.

He argued in conclusion that the only constitutional justification for the erection of a creche on public property would be that the process was not a religious ceremony or activity. That conclusion would be difficult to achieve, he asserted.

In *Chamberlain* v. *Dade County,* 143 So.2d 21 (1962), discussed earlier, the Florida court took a similar view on the display of seasonal and Christmas drawings by the school children. The court ruled that the alleged religious displays, in reality compositions by the children, were not displayed on a permanent basis. Therefore, the court refused to enjoin the display of the pictures. This issue did not arise again in the subsequent appeals of the case.

SUMMARY

The use of school buildings and the possibilities of such use violating the religion clauses of the First Amendment is too complex and variegated to submit to meaningful generalizations. To be realistic, one must tend to view it on a case to case basis with careful attention paid to state statutory law as well as constitutions. This is especially true since the Supreme Court has remained aloof from the debate.

It may be said, however, that the litigation arising in state courts falls into two major categories. The first class of cases challenges the constitutionality of leasing churches or other sectarian buildings for public school use. The second class of cases, conversely, raises the issue of whether it is constitutional for public school authorities to rent public school buildings for religious or sectarian purposes either during or after the regular school day.

In Illinois, for example, the high court of that state upheld the constitutionality of maintaining a public school in the basement of the Roman Catholic church, inasmuch as the voters had rejected a public school bond issue and since no religious doctrine was taught during school hours. Two other state courts upheld the constitutionality of public school boards renting sectarian buildings for use as public schools, however, one state court emphatically prohibited such a proposal.

One of the stickiest questions in this area is how close may a public school be physically associated with a parochial school and still retain its public character by not violating prohibitions against the establishment of religion. In Wisconsin, the state supreme court permitted a public school board to rent rooms in a parochial school primarily because of the pragmatic reasons that public school rooms were desperately needed. In Iowa and Missouri, however, the courts prohibited such practices also on the pragmatic grounds that in point of fact the method of combining the public and parochial school caused the public school to take on a religious character.

In another area three state decisions held that public school buildings could be used by religious groups or for religious purposes when this was sanctioned by a majority of the school district's voters at a formal election. On the other hand, three other state courts concluded that such practices were unconstitutional. On the question of whether public school buildings could be used for religious meetings where formally sanctioned by a regulation of the public school board, state courts were again almost equally divided. Six courts upheld the validity of such practices, while five state courts invalidated them.

A related issue involved the problem of using public school buildings concurrently for religious purposes. When faced with this question, the New York court for one, held that the legality of public appropriation hinged upon "the use to which the school buildings are put not upon the identity of the user."

One of the most persistent controversies has involved the question of how far a public school must go in accommodating itself to account for the religious holidays of various sects which may conflict with the official school day. As early as 1876, the Vermont court ruled that the constitution or laws did not require a public school to dismiss Roman Catholic children from classes to observe a church holiday. In 1905, the New York court in somewhat the same vein concluded that to hold examinations for prospective public school teachers on Saturday afternoons did not violate a Jewish applicant's religious freedom. Similarly, the Pennsylvania court found no violation of the free exercise clause or the establishment clause of a public school's requirement that a Moslem child attend public schools on Friday. As late as 1950, this ruling was reaffirmed in *Commonwealth* v. *Bey* on the grounds that if parents elect to send their children to the public schools they must submit to the requirements of those schools.

The constitutionality of baccalaureate exercises is another issue that has bedeviled state public school administrators, especially when held in churches. The courts of Wisconsin, New Mexico, and Florida have upheld such programs with the New Mexico court emphasizing what seemed to be the controlling fact that this was only permissible "if there were no other suitable places available." The Florida decision of 1962 was appealed to the United States Supreme Court, but that Court refused jurisdiction on the ground that there was lack of a properly presented federal question. Nonetheless, from the wording of the dismissal there is reason to think that the Court might be willing to tackle the merits of these widely practiced programs.

In recent years the constitutionality of religious displays such as the nativity scene on public school property has been challenged. In 1958, a New York court upheld such a display since no public funds were involved, no public employees were utilized, and the public school was not in session. In 1963, another New York court again upheld the practice since the display was privately erected and it appeared only during the Christmas vacation. At this writing the case of *Lowe* v. *City of Eugene* is pending in Oregon involving an action seeking the removal of an illuminated 51-foot high neon re-enforced concrete cross erected in a public park.

It seems rather apparent that as the pluralism of American society increases, traditional manifestations of the Christian and frequently Protestant religious dogma in the public schools will come under increasing attack.

In 1963 the Maryland high court in *Horace Mann League* v. *Board of Public Works* declared three construction grants to three religiously affiliated colleges unconstitutional under the religion clauses of the First Amendment to the United States Constitution. Since then, that case was cited as potentially productive of judicial guidelines for Congress to follow in deciding the constitutionality of federal aid to religious institutions. Because of the refusal of the United States Supreme Court to review the case, on February 28, 1967, the Subcommittee on Constitutional Rights of the Senate Judiciary Committee unanimously approved Senate Bill 3. The Subcommittee indicated it had as its objective a desire to provide effective procedures for the enforcement of the establishment and free exercise clauses of the First Amendment, which was made imperative by the action of the Supreme Court.

CHAPTER EIGHT

Religious Garb in Public Schools

† †

THE QUESTION OF public school teachers wearing religious garb indicative of a particular religious order or society has been a source of considerable litigation and controversy. Such litigation, which has occurred only in state courts, goes back to 1894 and continues to the present day.

There does not seem to be any precise, single definition of religious garb. Several states have enacted legislation dealing with this problem and refer to the garb in a similar way. A 1919 Nebraska statute forbidding public school teachers from wearing religious garb while teaching, defined this apparel in terms of any dress or garb which showed the person belonged to or adhered to a particular religious sect, order, or denomination. A 1923 Oregon statute also outlawed the wearing of distinctive garb of a particular sect, denomination, or order while teaching. Robert G. Valentine, Commissioner of Indian Affairs, referred to religious garb as ecclesiastical robes and insignia in a hearing on April 8, 1912, before Secretary Fisher of the Department of the Interior over the wearing of religious garb while teaching in government Indian schools. See Johnson and Yost, *Separation of Church and State*, pp. 119–22 (1948).

In an early court action, *Hysong* v. *Gallitzin School District,* 164 Pa. St. 629, 30 A. 482 (1894), the supreme court of Pennsylvania determined that the wearing by nuns of the garb and insignia of the Sisterhood of St. Joseph (a religious society of the Roman Catholic church) while teaching in the public schools did not constitute sectarian teaching. To exclude such teachers from the public schools would violate the religious liberty guarantee of the Pennsylvania constitution, the court held. The court in ruling apparently was more impressed with the finding of a lack of religious instruction during the school day than it was with the evidence that Catholic children were required to study catechism at the school after the school hours.

That decision was overturned the following year by a legislative act prohibiting the wearing of such garb by public school teachers in performance of duty. In upholding that act fifteen years later in *Commonwealth* v. *Herr,* 229 Pa. 132, 78 A. 68 (1910), the Pennsylvania supreme court declared that time that the same religious liberty clause as above was not violated by a legislative prohibition against public school teachers wearing religious garb. Nor did the legislation violate the First and Fourteenth Amendments of the United States Constitution, the court determined. Characterizing the act as a reasonable means for regulating the state's public educational system in a manner so as to prevent sectarian control, the court observed that the legislation "is directed against acts, not beliefs, and only against acts of the teacher while engaged in the performance of his or her duties as such teacher."

† † *COMMONWEALTH* v. *HERR*
229 PA. 132, 78 A. 68 (1910).

Judge RICE delivered the opinion of the court:

. . . The remaining objections urged against the act [the title of the act of June 27, 1895, reads:

An act to prevent the wearing in the public schools of this commonwealth, by any of the teachers thereof, of any dress, insignia, marks or emblems indicating the fact that such teacher is an adherent or member of any religious order, sect or denomination, and imposing a fine upon the board of directors of any public school permitting the same.]

are that it violates sections 3 and 4 of article 1 of our Constitution, which so far as material here reads as follows:

Section 3.

All men have a natural and indefensible right to worship Almighty God according to the dictates of their own consciences; . . . no human authority can, in any case whatever, control or interfere with the rights of conscience, and no preferences shall ever be given by law to any religious establishments or modes of worship.

Section 4.

No person who acknowledges the being of a God and a future state of rewards and punishments shall, on account of his religious sentiments, be disqualified to hold any office or place of trust or profit under this commonwealth.

The inhibition of the act is thus expressed:

That no teacher in any public school of this commonwealth shall wear in said school or whilst engaged in the performance of his or her duty as such teacher any dress, mark, emblem or insignia indicating the fact that such teacher is a member or adherent of any religious order, sect or denomination.

A violation of the foregoing provision subjects the teacher to suspension from employment in the district for one year, and a second offense to permanent disqualification to teach in the district. If the question for our decision were whether the act prohibited by this legislation is contrary to the letter or the true intent and meaning of the sections of the Constitution above quoted, or of the constitutional prohibition against the appropriation or use of public school money for the support of any sectarian school, it would be sufficient for us to say that it has been authoritatively and conclusively answered in the negative by the Supreme Court in *Hysong* v. *Gallitzin Borough School Dist.* et al., 164 Pa. 629 [30 Atl. 482, 26 L.R.A. 203, 44 Am. St. Rep. 632]. . . .

. . . We cannot assent to the proposition that the intent or the effect of the legislation is to disqualify any person from employment as a teacher "on account of his religious sentiments." It is directed against acts of the teacher whilst engaged in the performance of his or her duties as such teacher. . . . Test oaths and religious disqualificacations belong to a period further back than the memory of the present generation can reach, and it is to be hoped they may never be restored. But broad as are these declarations of our Constitution, and sacred as are the religious freedom and the rights of conscience they secure, yet it must be apparent to any person upon reflection, and has been repeatedly declared by the highest judicial authority, that they do not mean unqualifiedly that it is beyond the power of the Legislature to enact any law which will restrain individuals from doing that which, if it were not for the law, their consciences would teach them to be their moral or religious duty. Indeed, it is impossible to see how civil government could exist, if the dictates of the individual conscience were in every instance where they come in conflict with the law of the land the paramount rule of action. Speaking of the act of Congress which forbids plural marriages in territories and places under the exclusive dominion of the United States, Chief Justice Waite . . . reviewed the history of the times in which the constitutional provision relating thereto was adopted, and in the course of his reasoning in support of

the conclusion that it was not intended to prohibit legislation forbidding polygamy, even by those adherents of a sect who believed it to be their religious duty to practice it, he used the following language, which is pertinent to the discussion of the question before us:

Laws are made for the government of actions, and, while they cannot interfere with mere religious belief and opinions, they may with practices. . . . So here, as a law of the organization of society under the exclusive dominion of the United States, it is provided that plural marriages shall not be allowed. Can a man excuse his practice to the contrary because of his religious belief? To permit this would be to make the professed doctrines of religious belief superior to the law of the land, and in effect to permit every citizen to become a law unto himself. Government could exist only in name under such circumstances.

Many other illustrations may be found in decided cases of the general principles that the religious freedom and the rights of conscience guaranteed by the Constitution do not necessarily and always stand in the way of the enforcement of laws commanding or prohibiting the commission of acts even by those who conscientiously believe it to be their religious or moral duty to do or refrain from doing them. For example, not to go outside of Pennsylvania, a Jew who refused to be sworn in the trial of a case on Saturday because it was his sabbath was fined. . . . The conscientious scruples of a Jew to appear in court and attend to the trial of his case on the same day were held to be no ground for the continuance of his cause. . . . The act prohibiting all worldly employment upon the first day of the week has been held not to be in contravention of the constitutional rights under consideration, even where applied to persons whose religious belief leads them to observe another day of the week as their Sabbath. . . . The same was held to be true as to persons who conscientiously believe it to be their religious duty to labor the first six days of the week and to keep the seventh day as the Sabbath. . . . The same was held to be organization who deem it their duty by divine command to go into the streets and there preach the gospel and who as a regular part of their service use the drum are not exempted by the Constitution from the operation of a city ordinance which prohibits the use of a drum or other musical instrument on the street without permit from the mayor. . . . The right of the individual to clothe himself in whatever garb his taste, his inclination, the tenets of his sect, or even his religious sentiments may dictate is no more absolute than his right to give utterance to his sentiments, religious or otherwise. In neither case can it be said that a statute cannot restrain him from exercising these rights whenever, wherever, and in whatever manner he conscientiously believes it to be his moral or religious duty to do so. That the right to wear a particular garb is not as absolute and as free from legislative control as that was expressly conceded by the Supreme Court in *Hysong* v. *Gallitzin Boro. School Dist.*, 164 Pa. 629 in the following terms:

The Legislature may by statute, enact that all teachers shall wear in the schoolroom a particular style of dress, and that none other shall be worn, and thereby secure the same uniformity of outward appearance as we now see in the city police, railroad trainmen, and nurses of some of our large hospitals.

It is urged that this part of the opinion is obiter dictum. It is true the precise question whether the Legislature could enact such a law was not before the court, and it may be conceded that for that reason the utterance is not a binding authority. Nevertheless it was pertinent in the discussion of the question then before the court, and was evidently made upon due deliberation. Besides that, the obiter, if so it may be regarded, comes from so high a source that it is entitled to great respect from us. Moreover, the proposition is so well supported by sound principle that we believe it to be unassailable. But any public school teacher who is restrained by the act of 1895 from doing that in the schoolroom which his conscience or his religious sentiments dictate would just as plainly and to the same extent be restrained by such a statute as is described in the case cited. Another case that may be appropriately referred to in this connection is *O'Connor* v. *Hendrick*, 184 N.Y. 421, 77 N.E. 612. It was there held in a well-considered opinion that a regulation established by the state superintendent of public instruction, who had implied authority under the statute to establish regulations as to the management of the public schools, prohibiting teachers in public schools from wearing a distinctively religious garb while engaged in the work of teaching therein was reasonable and valid exercise of the power vested in him. This is the only other decision that has been brought to our notice which deals with the precise question of the validity of a rule or statute of that nature.

The system of common school education in this commonwealth is the creature of the state, and its perpetuity and freedom from sectarian control are guaranteed by express constitutional provisions. Subject to these, the power to support and maintain an efficient system of public schools, wherein all the children of the commonwealth above the age of six years may be educated, is vested in the Legislature. This carries with it the qualifications of the teachers, but in prescribing them the Legislature may not make religious belief or church affiliation a test. Nevertheless, the power of the Legislature to make reasonable regulations for the government of their conduct whilst engaged in the performance of their du-

ties must be conceded. . . . As shown by the preamble of the act under consideration, the Legislature deemed it "important that all appearances of sectarianism should be avoided in the administration of public schools of the commonwealth." This was the ostensible object of the legislation, and we can discover no substantial ground for concluding that it was not the sole object which the Legislature had in contemplation. Nor are we able to conclude either that the object was beyond the scope of legislative power, or that the regulation adopted has no just and proper relation to that object.

The judgment is reversed.

RELATED CASES

A similar regulation of the superintendent of public instruction in New York was invalidated by the state's highest court in *O'Connor* v. *Hendrick*, 184 N.Y. 421, 77 N.E. 612 (1906), below. The court's ruling was based on its conclusions that "the influence of such apparel is distinctly sectarian," and that a regulation prohibiting the wearing of the religious garb was in accord with the state constitutional provision forbidding the use of property or credit of the state in the aid of sectarian influences.

The supreme court of Iowa ruled in the same vein in *Knowlton* v. *Baumhover*, 182 Ia. 691, 166 N.W. 202 (1918). It held that combining in one building of a public with a parochial school was unconstitutional. The court decided that the parish Roman Catholic school and the supposedly public school above it were for all intents and purposes one school under the same control. The record showed, among other things, that the teachers in both schools were Roman Catholic sisters adorned in the characteristic garb and regalia, and that they displayed several pictures, including the Holy Virgin, which unmistakably are appealing to Roman Catholic sentiment.

The court reasoned that the parent has the sacred right to guide his own children in the type of religious training, if any, that is desired, and that the state may not either use its official machinery to compel attendance at a sectarian school or exercise its taxing powers to support such a school. The opinion went on to say that those employed in public stations should not take advantage of their position to promote particular religious notions, when their employer—the state—cannot so do.

In *State* ex rel. *Public School District* v. *Taylor*, 122 Neb. 454, 240 N.W. 573 (1932), mandamus was later held not to lie against the Nebraska state superintendent of public instruction to require him to recognize a certain school district as a public school district eligible to share state educational trust funds. The school building in question was located on a tract of land belonging to the local Roman Catholic church, and the entrance to the building was adorned with a cross. Religious emblems were prominent throughout the building and its classrooms. Voluntary chapel services were conducted in the basement by the parish priest before commencement of the regular classes which were conducted by members of the Catholic sisterhood who were attired in distinctive garb including the rosary.

After finding evidence from the above record of an environment in the school that "reflects the spirit, example and belief of the Catholic religion," the court determined that "inculcation of that religion [as] part of the school work" was unconstitutional. The state superintendent's refusal to recognize that school as a public school was considered, therefore, by the court to be his duty rather than his neglect.

The wearing of religious garb, on the other hand, was upheld by three state supreme courts. A North Dakota case, *Gerhardt* v. *Heid*, 66 N.D. 444, 267 N.W. 127 (1936), involved four nuns who turned over the proceeds (above living expenses) from their salaries as public school teachers to the mother house of the Sisterhood of St. Benedict. The court, noting that there was no evidence that the nuns imparted any religious instruction even though they were attired in distinctive religious garb, determined that the above practices did not make the instant school a sectarian school within the meaning of the North Dakota constitution. The court went on to say that no public school teacher on duty had the right to proselytize for any religious purposes. The court considered the question of propriety of the dress of public school teachers to be nonjusticiable.

In *State* ex rel. *Johnson* v. *Boyd*, 217 Ind. 348, 28 N.E.2d 256 (1940), the Indiana high court determined that it was not sectarian teaching for a public school district to cause students to attend "voluntary" religious instruction at a nearby Roman Catholic church, and therefore the salaries of the teachers in question must be paid from the public treasury. The school, itself, was carried on in buildings contributed by the Catholic church. Catholic emblems and pictures remained on the walls, however, and the new school was left under the supervision of teachers—wearing distinctive garb—of Roman Catholic orders. The court, however, ruled that the schools in question were under public, and not sectarian, control. It based its conclusion on the fact that the teachers were duly licensed by the state, were in the employ of the city's board of trustees, and followed a course of study prescribed by the board of education.

† † *STATE* ex rel. *JOHNSON* v. *BOYD*
217 IND. 348, 28 N.E.2D 256 (1940).

Judge SWAIM delivered the opinion of the court, saying in part:

[Three separate actions were filed and consolidated for trial.]
. . . On July 28, 1933, a committee of priests of the Roman Catholic Parishes in the school city of Vincennes, advised the Board of School Trustees of said city that the Catholic Parochial Schools within the said school city would not be opened by the churches for the ensuing school year and asked said school trustees to provide necessary school facilities for the eight hundred school children who had theretofore attended the said parochial schools. . . . Thereupon the Board of Trustees of said school city passed a motion that they "assume the administrative and instructional obligation for the Catholic Parochial Schools included within the limits of said School City, in accordance with the constitutional and statutory laws of the state, the rules and regulations of the State Department of the Board of Education and the existing rules and regulations of the Board of School Trustees of the City of Vincennes with a definite understanding that the school city of Vincennes assumes no outstanding, existing or future financial obligations, either bonded temporary loans or other evidences of indebtedness, or the operation, maintenance and capital outlay costs for buildings and grounds belonging to the Catholic Parochial Schools";

and at the same time the board authorized the superintendent to proceed at once and work out the administrative details of the proposed plan of incorporation. On March 18, 1935, said board adopted a resolution, to be effective at the close of the school year 1934–35, rescinding said original motion. On August 25, 1935, said board of school trustees adopted a resolution reconsidering and amending the resolution of July 28, 1933, as follows:

Be it resolved by the Board of School Trustees of the School City of Vincennes, Indiana, that whereas the effects of the depression have brought about an economical condition in our city by reason of which an emergency exists regarding the operation and maintenance of the parochial schools of Vincennes and whereas the Board of School Trustees of said School City are of the opinion that the patrons of our parochial schools are entitled to public aid and assistance during these extraordinary times in which we are living; therefore, be it resolved by the Board of School Trustees of the School City of Vincennes that the School City of Vincennes assume the administrative and instructional obligation for the school children of the parochial schools included within the limits of said School City. . . .

The Superintendent of the Vincennes City Schools, acting under authority given him by said board of school trustees, procured recommendations for teachers for said schools from various Roman Catholic colleges. All teachers so recommended were Sisters and Brothers in various Catholic orders. The Board of School Trustees of said school city employed as teachers in said schools the teachers so recommended for the school year 1933–34 and for each subsequent year. Each teacher so employed was regularly licensed to teach school agreeable with the laws of the State of Indiana. The teachers taught in said schools the course of study prescribed by the State Board of Education. The school city of Vincennes at no time obtained a lease, rental contract or contract of any kind or character authorizing it to use the buildings of said parochial schools, but without any contract or other obligation to the school city of Vincennes to do so the Roman Catholic authorities have provided the several school buildings used by said schools together with all seats, desks, furniture and furnishings, heat, light, water, fuel, and janitor service for each building during the school years 1933–34 to and including the school years 1938–39, all without expense to or obligation upon the school city of Vincennes.

. . . .

In addition to other pictures the school rooms in each of said buildings had hanging on the walls, in view of said students, a picture of Jesus, The Holy Family, The Crucifixion, and George Washington. They also each have an American Flag and a Holy Water fount, in which is kept Holy Water for the use of the pupils. While teaching the teachers wore the characteristic robes of the orders to which they belonged and the sisters always wore a rosary and crucifix in view of the pupils.

On the grounds near each of said schools there is located a Roman Catholic Church, a rectory or Priests' Home and a Sisters' Home. Each morning immediately prior to the beginning of the school the pupils of each room were caused to attend at the nearby church where they were given religious instructions for thirty minutes by the parish priest. This particular service is said to be voluntary. So far as shown no pupil attending any of said schools has refused or failed to attend such morning services for religious instruction.

Prior to the school year 1933–34 the school city of Vincennes owned, maintained and operated nine public schools. Prior to the beginning of said school year the school authorities had divided said school city into school districts and assigned all the pupils below high school grades living in each district to a certain school, which they were required to attend unless transferred elsewhere. Beginning with the school year 1933–34 the children of the Roman Catholic families living within the school city of Vincennes were not required to attend the school assigned to the district in which they lived nor were they transferred elsewhere. They continued to attend the same schools that they had been attending theretofore, without regard to the boundaries of the school district in which they lived.

Since the beginning of the school year 1933–34 the schools in question have been visited, occasionally, by the superintendent of the Vincennes City Schools and, frequently, by the director of instruction in the elementary grades of the city schools. Throughout the period in question the school city of Vincennes "has paid the administrative and instructional obligations" of all of the schools mentioned from public school funds.

. . . .

. . . The principal question presented by this appeal is whether, under the facts in this case, the payments made by said school treasurers to said teachers are legal. The appellants contend that such payments were illegal and that the amount thereof should be returned to the school city because, according to the allegations of said complaint, the schools continued to be parochial schools, under the domination and control of the Roman Catholic Church, and the payments to said teachers were a mere subterfuge by which donations were actually made to said church.

Our state constitution expressly provides, "No money shall be drawn from the treasury, for the benefit of any religious or theological institution." Article I, § 6 and § 4 of said Article provides that, "No preference shall be given, by law, to any creed, religious society, or mode of worship; and no man shall be compelled to attend, erect, or support, any place of worship, or to maintain any ministry, against his consent." Neither of these provisions may be legally violated either directly or indirectly and any public official knowingly paying money from the public treasury in violation of these provisions would be required to reimburse said treasury for any amounts as paid. Have the appellants proved that the appellees, either directly or indirectly, violated either or both of these constitutional provisions?

. . . As the word is used in several places throughout the findings it was, undoubtedly, intended to mean or denote only a particular place for instruc-

tion. For instance, when the board of trustees of said school city in the first resolution passed spoke of assuming the administrative and instructional obligations for the Catholic Parochial schools included within the limits of said school city, and in the same resolution said that this was to be done in accordance with the constitution and statutory laws of the state, the rules and regulations of the State Department of the Board of Education and the existing laws and regulations of the Board of School Trustees of the City of Vincennes, the Board must have intended to say thereby that they were going to assume the instructional obligations or expense for schools to be conducted at the place where said parochial schools had been conducted. And again when the court in said special findings spoke of the treasurer as having "paid instructional obligations of said schools," naming them, it must have intended to designate only the names of the *places* where said schools were conducted, because the court also found that the teachers were employed by the board of trustees of the school city of Vincennes and it, therefore, necessarily follows that the obligation to pay said teachers under said contracts of employment was the obligation of said school city and not the obligation of the church society owning said school buildings and grounds.

It was the legal duty of the Board of School Trustees to provide necessary school facilities for all of the school children within said school city. A committee of priests of the Roman Catholic Parishes of said city informed the Board that the parochial schools, which had been theretofore conducted by the churches within said school city, would not be opened by the churches for the school year 1933–34, and said priests requested that said school trustees provide the necessary school facilities for the 800 or more school children of said school city who had theretofore been attending such parochial schools. The Board of School Trustees complied by employing teachers who were regularly licensed to teach school agreeable with the laws of the State of Indiana and with such teachers established schools in the school plants formerly occupied by said parochial schools. These teachers taught the course of study prescribed by the State Board of Education. No sectarian instruction was permitted in said schools during school hours. The schools were visited occasionally by the superintendent of the Vincennes City Schools and frequently by the Director of Instruction in the elementary grades of said city schools. The teachers were paid their salaries from public funds by the treasurer of the school city. In view of these findings it can not be said that the primary facts found by the court necessarily lead to the conclusion that the schools in question during this period were not public schools or that the salaries paid amounted to contributions made indirectly to parochial schools or to the church.

We must next determine whether any of the facts found, or any combination of them, made the payment of said teachers' salaries by said treasurers illegal.

The church authorities provided the several school buildings, in which said schools were conducted, together with the furniture, utilities and janitor services, during the school years 1933–34 to 1938–39, both inclusive. This was done without any lease or rental contract. Our statutes provide that the

school trustees shall take charge of the educational affairs of their respective townships, towns and cities. They shall employ teachers, establish and locate conveniently a sufficient number of schools for the education of children therein, and build, or otherwise provide, suitable houses, furniture, apparatus and other articles and educational appliances necessary for the thorough organization and efficient management of said schools.

§ 28–2410, Burns' 1933, § 5967, Baldwin's 1934. In this case we find the Board of Trustees faced with an emergency to provide school facilities for more than 800 additional school children. In the opinion of the trustees they could not be properly cared for in the buildings owned by the school city. There is no statutory provision in this state prohibiting school trustees under such circumstances from leasing for school purposes any buildings and equipment which are suitable for such purposes. Nor is there any statutory limitation as to the persons or societies from whom such buildings and equipment may be leased. We see no valid reason why the said school trustees should not have leased the buildings and equipment furnished by the church authorities.

Acting within their discretion, the Board of Trustees may well have assumed that the emergency was temporary and that they would not be justified in buying or building new buildings or in making additions to the buildings which the school city then owned, even if the finances of the school city had made it possible for them to do so. They may well have assumed that as soon as the churches became financially able to do so the parochial schools would be reestablished; and that the parents of the pupils in question would then desire their children to attend such parochial schools. In *Dorner* v. *School District,* No. 5, 1908, 137 Wis. 147, 118 N.W. 353, 19 L.R.A., N.S., 171, it was held that the lower court was not in error in refusing to enjoin the district and board from maintaining a common school in a parochial school building. It was held legal to maintain a public school in a church basement in the case of *Millard* v. *Board of Education,* 1887, 121 Ill. 297, 10 N.E. 669, 670. . . .

The fact that the church contributed the use of the buildings and equipment used for these schools does not make the schools conducted therein parochial schools. The acceptance of private donations to a public cause does not make the cause private. *Holt* v. *Town of Antrim,* 1887, 64 N.H. 284, 9 A. 389. Since the teachers in said schools were employed by the Board of School Trustees, teaching the course prescribed for the public schools, such teachers were the employees of the school city and their possession of said premises was the possession of the school city. *Richter* v. *Cordes,* 1894, 100 Mich. 278, 58 N.W. 1110. The fact that a church, a rectory or Priests' Home, and a Sisters' Home were located on the grounds near each of said schools does not affect the right of the school city to use said school buildings.

The appellants also stress the fact that in the school rooms in each of said buildings, in addition to other pictures in view of the pupils, there were the pictures of Jesus, The Holy Family, The Crucifixion and George Washington and that each room was also provided with an American Flag and with a Holy Water fount, in which Holy Water was kept for the use of the pupils. Such pictures and furnishings do not constitute sectarian teachings in the schools. No secret was made of the

fact that the equipment and buildings belonged to the Catholic Church and we see no valid reason why all evidence of that fact should have been concealed.

The appellant also complains of the fact that the teachers employed by the said school trustees were Catholic Sisters and Brothers, recommended for such positions by the authorities of various Catholic colleges and that such teachers, while teaching, wore the dress of their religious orders. The fact that these teachers were recommended by various Catholic normal schools can not be considered an important factor. The teachers were employed by the Board of School Trustees. They were chosen from persons regularly qualified and licensed to teach school agreeable to the laws of the State of Indiana. It is the duty of school trustees to investigate the character and fitness of teachers. The trustees may do this in any proper manner which they may choose, including the procurring of recommendations. Recommendations from any reliable normal college should be helpful. The choice of teachers is within the discretion of the school trustees and unless such discretion be abused the courts will not interfere. *State* ex rel. *Mitchell* v. *Gray,* 1884, 93 Ind. 303, 305.

Nor is there any law in Indiana which prevents school trustees from hiring persons of any religious faith or members of religious orders as school teachers.

Sections 2, 3, and 5 of Article I of the Constitution of Indiana provide as follows:

All men shall be secured in their natural right to worship Almighty God, according to the dictates of their own consciences.

No law shall, in any case whatever, control the free exercise and enjoyment of religious opinions, or interfere with the rights of conscience.

No religious test shall be required, as a qualification for any office of trust or profit.

No statute or rule prohibiting the employment of teachers belonging to a certain religious denomination or sect could be held valid. The employment of the teachers in this case certainly could not be held invalid because such teachers belonged to certain orders of the Catholic Church. The employment of teachers is within the discretion of the school trustees so long as such teachers meet the qualifications required by law. Membership in any particular church can neither legally qualify nor disqualify a teacher.

Nor does the fact that these teachers in question, while teaching, wore the robes of various orders to which they belonged constitute sectarian teaching or make it illegal for them to be paid their salaries as teachers. In *Hysong* v. *School District of Gallitzin Borough,* 1894, 164 Pa. 629, 30 A. 482, 484, 26 L.R.A. 203, 44 Am. St. Rep. 632, the court held that Catholic teachers appearing in the school room in the habits of their orders did not constitute sectarian teaching and in reference thereto said:

The religious belief of many teachers, all over the commonwealth, is indicated by their apparel. Quakers or Friends, Amish, Dunkards, and other sects, wear garments which at once disclose their membership in a religious sect. Ministers or preachers of many Protestant denominations wear distinctively clerical garbs. No one has yet thought of excluding them as teachers from the school room on the ground that the peculiarity of their dress would teach to pupils the distinctive doctrines of the sect

to which they belonged. The dress is but the announcement of a fact,—that the wearer holds a particular religious belief. The religious belief of teachers and all others is generally well known to the neighborhood and to pupils, even if not made noticeable in the dress, for that belief is not secret, but is publicly professed. Are the courts to decide that the cut of a man's coat or the color of a woman's gown is sectarian teaching, because they indicate sectarian belief: If so, then they can be called upon to go further. The religion of the teacher being known, a pure, unselfish life, exhibiting itself in tenderness to the young, and helpfulness for the suffering, necessarily tends to promote the religion of the man or woman who lives it. Insensibly, in both young and old, there is a disposition to reverence such a one, and at least to some extent, consider the life as the fruit of the particular religion. Therefore, irreproachable conduct, to that degree, is sectarian teaching.

To the same effect, see *Gerhardt* v. *Heid,* 1936, 66 N.D. 444, 267 N.W. 127.

The appellants also contend that it is significant that each morning, immediately prior to the beginning of school, the pupils were caused to attend at the nearby Roman Catholic Church where they were given religious instructions for thirty minutes by the Parish Priests. The findings do not disclose by whom the children were "caused" to attend. The finding does disclose that the service was said to be voluntary. Since the children in question were children of Catholic parents and the service was voluntary and not within the school hours we fail to see that this amounts to sectarian teaching within the schools or that it could be held to make the schools parochial schools rather than public schools.

Although it was alleged in the complaint that these schools were directed and controlled through the clerical government of the church exercised by and through the Bishop, there was no such finding by the court. Whether these schools, during the period in question, were parochial or public schools is determined by their control. They were in charge of teachers employed by the board of trustees of said school city. The teachers were regularly licensed under the laws of the State of Indiana. The teachers were regularly licensed by the Board of Education. The schools were visited and supervised by the Superintendent of City Schools and the Director of Instruction of the city schools. The teachers were paid from the public funds. The space occupied by the schools was in the possession of the school city through its employed teachers. It is our opinion that the board of school trustees of the said school city by their course of action did establish public schools in the buildings formerly occupied by the parochial schools and that the payment, by the various treasurers of the school city, to said teachers of salaries provided by their contracts of employment was valid.

. . . [T]he judgment in each of said three cases is affirmed.

REACTIONS OF LEGAL PERIODICALS TO *STATE* ex rel. *JOHNSON* v. *BOYD*

A writer in the *Notre Dame Lawyer* (16:148) was encouraged that the decision, in his words, rejected the religious bigotry that was flourishing in other lands. The constitutional test followed by the Indiana court, in making the determination of whether the Roman Catholic teachers imparted any sectarian instruction as the controlling element, seemed to that reviewer to be "the more logical and better reasoned rule."

The decision was considered in the *Yale Law Journal* (50:917) on the other hand as a judicial acceptance of a "program of religious subsidy" which "reawakens the slumbering forces of intolerance and hate." Declaring that the neighborhood common school is the best place overall for early education and that a *laissez-faire* policy traditionally has been "the key to a successful American solution of the church-state problem," the reviewer declared that this decision "is more sweeping in its approval of Catholic education at public expense than that of any other court to date."

He noted that two concessions for religion commonly were being made already—the option of meeting compulsory attendance requirements in parochial schools and the general release of public school pupils from their regular classes so they can attend denominational services either in the classrooms themselves (this was written before such practices were struck down by the U.S. Supreme Court in the McCollum case) or in nearby churches. Beyond that, he warned that a democratic society must not go.

To accept the Roman Catholic arguments in the instant case and in terms of the whole topic of church and state would, in his opinion, signa ublic support for the separate schools of "any legitimate religious, social, r even political group." That prospect was considered uninviting, coming t a time when our society already is "harassed by growing religious segre- ation and social and ideological stratification."

RELATED PROBLEMS

A parent in *New Haven* v. *Torrington,* 132 Conn. 194, 43 A.2d 455 1945), sought unsuccessfully to recover the costs of education of his hildren. The school was established by the public as a public school, pen to all children living in the neighborhood regardless of faith "to ring the school to the scholars rather than the scholars to the school . . . or reasons of convenience and economy." He claimed that the school in uestion was not a public school, and that he therefore owed none of the osts to the public treasury.

The court declared that a public school must be under the exclusive ontrol of the state agencies and must remain free from sectarian instruc- ion or influence. It, however, decided that a school within an all-Catholic rphanage may, consistent with the Constitution, be established under he control of the board of education, and its teachers may be nuns wear- ng the identifiable garb, *so long as* the school remained free from sec- arian influence.

† † *CITY OF NEW HAVEN* v. *TOWN OF TORRINGTON*
132 CONN. 194, 43 A.2D 455 (1945).

udge DICKENSON delivered the opinion of the court:

. . . .

The finding, on which no substantial ttack is made, is as follows: Prior to 880 there was, and ever since has been, n the city of New Haven a Roman Catholic charitable institution known s St. Francis Orphan Asylum dedi- ated to the care of orphans and ne- lected children. In 1879, the board of ducation of the city of New Haven ursuant to its duly passed vote, en-

tered into an arrangement with the or- phanage whereby it obtained the use of rooms in one of its institutional buildings for the purpose of establish- ing and maintaining a grammar school. The school was called the St. Francis Orphan Asylum School until 1934, when its name was changed by the board to "Highland Heights School." It has been maintained in the same building since 1879, which building is owned by the orphanage, a diocesan corporation having as its president the Roman Catholic bishop of the Hartford diocese. The building is not used exclusively for school purposes. There are eight rooms devoted to such purposes. Other rooms are used as a nun's waiting room, offices for two resident priests, a chapel for the celebration of religious exercises, and living quarters for nuns and priests. In another part of the building are dormitories where the inmates or pupils of the school live. Prayers are offered by them upon arising and before and after each meal; a retreat, lasting a week, is held for them once a year; and they attend mass on Sunday and on religious holidays. None of these religious exercises is held during the time allotted for school sessions. All of the inmates of the orphanage are of the Roman Catholic faith and all of them are required to attend the school except those who are too young or those who have completed their grammar school education and are attending local high schools, but the school has always been open to any child living in the neighborhood regardless of religious faith, and occasionally such children have been enrolled as pupils. The school day commences at 8:45 a.m. in conformity with the order of the board of education applying to all grammar schools in New Haven. An hour before, the pupils assemble in the classrooms and receive religious instruction from the nuns for one-half hour.

The teaching staff of the school consists of two lay women and eight nuns, and one of the latter is the principal. The nuns are attired in religious apparel while teaching and are employed as teachers because the practice conforms to the spirit of the orphanage. All of the teachers are appointed by the superintendent of schools of New Haven with the approval of the board of education and must be certified public school teachers. They are paid from the public treasury, their salaries being identical with those of similar classifications in the educational system of the city. They participate in the New Haven Teachers' Tenure and Retirement Acts. The board of education provides supplies for the school and the same textbooks which it uses in other grammar schools in the city, and the course of study are those prescribed by the board for all schools. Special studies such as shopwork, manual training, physical education, art, cooking, sewing and music are conducted at times at the school by special supervisors who teach these subjects throughout the school system. Medical, nursing and dental care are provided in conformity with the practice in other grammar schools. The equipment in the class rooms conforms to the requirements of state law and the teachers keep standard registers required by the state board of education. A uniform type of diploma given at graduation exercises of grammar schools in the city is used. The school complies in all respects to the requirements of state law. At no time during the school sessions is any form of religious exercise permitted or given.

. . . .

A main contention of the defendant is that the Highland Heights School is a parochial and not a public school, and that even if the plaintiff had authority to maintain it, which the defendant questions, the plaintiff had no recourse to the defendant for the expense of educating the children in such a school. The defendant claims that it is not a public school because it is conducted and maintained in a religious and sectarian atmosphere for children belonging to one, and only one, religious faith.

There are two essentials that must be present to constitute a school a public school. It must remain under the exclusive control of the state through the state's constituted agencies, and it must be free from sectarian instruction. The rationale of the rule is well stated in *State* ex rel. *Freeman* v. *Scheve*, 65 Neb. 853, 872, 91 N.W. 846, 847, 93 N.W. 169, 59 L.R.A. 927, where it is said that,

if the system of compulsory education is persevered in, and religious worship or sectarian instruction in the public schools is at the same time permitted, parents will be compelled to expose their children to what they deem spiritual contamination, or else, while bearing their share of the burden for the support of public education, provide the means from their own pockets for the training of their offspring elsewhere.

As might be expected where a religious question is involved, the authorities are not in agreement as to what constitutes interference with control and with secular teaching. . . . Many . . . decisions are based upon state constitutional provisions, but the principle is implicit in all public school systems that they must be under public control and secular in instruction.

In the maintenance and management of public schools the board of education of a town is the agent, not of the town, but of the state, and to that end is granted broad powers by the legislature. *Groton & Stonington Traction Co.* v. *Groton*, 115 Conn. 151, 155, 160 A. 902; *Board of Education of Stamford* v. *Board of Finance*, 127 Conn. 345, 349, 16 A.2d 601. That the plaintiff's board of education had authority to establish a school in the building of

the orphanage cannot be questioned, or that it had control of the school. *Millard* v. *Board of Education*, supra. It is not disputed that the courses of study in this school conformed to those required by the board of education of New Haven for all of its grammar schools, that its teachers are certified teachers appointed by the New Haven board of education, and that the school is conducted in conformity to the state laws.

The defendant, however, claims that it is not a public school because it is conducted and maintained in a religious and sectarian atmosphere for children of one sect. The fact that all of the children who attend the school are of the Catholic faith is not determinative of the question. General Statutes, § 1867, requires that when a child is committed to a custodial agency the court shall, as far as practicable, select one of the same faith as that of the child's parents. It was the apparent purpose of the New Haven board of education to bring the school to the scholars rather than the scholars to the school, as it did at the New Haven Orphan Asylum, for reasons of convenience and economy. It might do this if it maintained control over the school and kept it open to all children and free from sectarian instruction. It has been found by the trial court, and this finding is not attacked, that the school is not maintained exclusively for the inmates of the orphanage, but always has been open to any child living in the neighborhood regardless of religious faith.

There remain two circumstances concerning the operation of the school that might affect its nonsectarianism; several of its teaching staff are Roman Catholic nuns who wear their religious habits in the classrooms, and religious exercises are held in the schoolrooms before the sessions open. As to the holding of religious exercises in the schoolrooms, it does not appear that these immediately preceded the opening of the school sessions. They were held an hour before the opening of the session and lasted for one-half hour. Nor is it found that attendance at such exercises was compulsory to all pupils. The employment of teachers who dress in the habiliments of their religion as affecting the public character of a school has been the source of much controversy, as appears from the cases cited above. The decisions in these cases, however, are, as is to be expected, based upon a wide diversity of facts. The only definite conclusion that may be drawn from them is that whether sectarian influence connected with a school is such as to affect its public character is ordinarily a question of fact for the trial court. We cannot say upon the conceded facts in the case before us that the trial court's conclusion that this was a school such as is contemplated in the provision of the statute in question was so unreasonable as to be error as a matter of law.

. . . .

There is no error.

Judge BROWN, dissenting:

With the implication in the majority opinion that the plaintiff is not entitled to recover if the school in question is a sectarian rather than a public school, I agree. With the conclusion that upon the facts of this case the trial court was warranted in holding that this was a public and not a sectarian school, I disagree.

As the opinion suggests, a school to be a public school must (1) be under public control and (2) be free from sectarian instruction. It is primarily with regard to its interpretation of this second requisite that I differ from the majority. A child receives instruction by seeing, as well as by hearing. The impressions made upon him by being exposed day in and day out to the sectarian atmosphere implicit in the daily routine, the physical surroundings and the habit of their order worn by the teachers, set forth in the court's finding, may well prove as potent an influence in determining his religious development as would a regularly prescribed course of instruction in formulated precepts. . . .

. . . Although not a fact included in the finding, the undisputed evidence shows that during the four years in question this school was attended by an average of three hundred and seventy pupils, every one of whom was a Catholic and an inmate of the orphanage. Under the circumstances, to construe the court's finding that the school "always has been open to any child living in the neighborhood regardless of religious faith," as demonstrating the nonsectarian character of the school, is to substitute theory for reality. Whether this is a public school essentially depends upon the nature of the educational facilities which it affords the public, that is, non-Catholics as well as Catholics. Under our law, education is compulsory. This being so, the specific question is: Can a non-Catholic resident of the area served by this school, subject as he is to taxation to maintain it, lawfully be compelled to face the dilemma of either sending his children to it or paying for their education elsewhere? To my mind, to pose the question is but to emphasize that the answer must be no.

As the court well said in *Knowlton* v. *Baumhover*, 182 Iowa 691, 704, 166 N.W. 202, 206, 5 A.L.R. 841:

If there is any one thing which is well settled in the policies and purposes of the American people as a whole, it is the fixed and unalterable determination that there shall be an absolute and unequivocal separation of church and state and that our public school system, supported by the taxation of the property of all alike—Catholic, Protestant, Jew, Gentile, believer, and infidel—shall not be used, directly or indirectly, for religious instruction.

With this statement I am in full accord. Giving effect to the principle which it declared, it is my conclusion that the school here in question should not be held to be a public school.

OTHER VIEWS

The approach of the Connecticut supreme court was rejected, however, by the supreme court of New Mexico when it invalidated similar practices brought into question in *Zellers* v. *Huff*, 55 N.M. 501, 236 P.2d 949 (1951), below. The record there showed that the public school teachers —sisters and brothers of the Roman Catholic church—knowingly taught sectarian religion during regular school hours. The wearing of garb and insignia of religious significance by public school teachers was also specifically prohibited.

† †   ZELLERS v. HUFF
55 N.M. 501, 236 P.2D 949 (1951).

Judge MC GHEE delivered the opinion of the court, saying in part:

The general objects of the first cause of action were to have the teaching of sectarian religion in the public schools declared illegal, to bar permanently certain teachers from teaching in the public schools for having taught sectarian religion therein, to have all members of Roman Catholic Religious Orders declared ineligible to teach in the public schools of the state, and to have the expenditure of public funds in aid of Roman Catholic parochial schools declared illegal. In the second cause of action injunctions were asked to put into effect the declarations of law which might be made in the declaratory judgment.

Under our statutes the County, Town and independent Boards of Education named as defendants employed and had the supervision of the Sisters and Brothers (hereafter called the Religious) as teachers. Many additional facts regarding the Religious were pleaded, but it would unduly lengthen this opinion to detail them.

. . . .

Digest of Facts Found by the Trial Court.

. . . .

. . . The schools comprising the first group above are, in fact, Roman Catholic parochial schools being subsidized in part by funds raised through taxation by the State of New Mexico through the employment of teachers, furnishing of free bus transportation and free text-books; and funds so expended are used in furtherance of the dissemination of Roman Catholic religious doctrines to students attending these schools in compliance with the New Mexico compulsory attendance law. In all of the schools named in the first group, the following conditions exist, to-wit:

. . . .

(b) Religious are employed as teachers by the State of New Mexico and paid as such from funds raised through taxation in the State of New Mexico.

(c) Pupils attending these schools are given religious instruction in the principles of the Roman Catholic Church, commonly known as the catechism, during school hours by the Religious employed as teachers by the State of New Mexico.

(d) Students are taught and recite prayers during school hours which are peculiar to the Roman Catholic Church.

(e) Roman Catholic literature, pamphlets, leaflets and comic books are distributed to the students during school hours.

8. With respect to the schools enumerated in the second group, the court found:

. . . .

13. The Religious are employed as teachers and are paid salaries by the State of New Mexico out of funds produced by taxation in each of the schools involved, with the exception that in some schools the salaries are paid direct to the religious order to which the particular Religious belongs.

14. All of the Religious named as defendants were dressed in the distinctive garb of their Order at all times while school was in session and in a number of schools the Religious are employed to teach in said school by the Superior member of the Order to which they belong.

* * *

Summation of Facts

The record and trial court findings clearly establish that a part of the schools involved in this appeal (if not all except the Abiquiu school) were operated as Roman Catholic parochial schools where the Religious taught.

The Religious who taught in the public schools were selected and assigned to various schools by the heads of their respective Orders and were accepted by the school boards without question. . . .

In short, New Mexico had a Roman

Catholic school system supported by public funds within its public school system.

*   *   *

History of Present Controversy

A showdown finally came between irate school patrons, some of whom are plaintiffs in this case, and the school authorities over the teaching of religion in the Dixon schools, a rural community where the Roman Catholics and Protestants are about evenly divided. Public school had been held in that district for many years in Church property with Religious as teachers. The Protestants objected to the holding of public school in Roman Catholic owned buildings where Sisters taught the regular curriculum and in addition taught sectarian religion, but were advised by the County Board of education that funds were not available to erect a public school building. The Protestants then donated money and labor, erected a school building, gave it to the county and asked that it be opened and staffed with lay teachers. This request was denied and the new school was placed under a Sister as principal and the teaching of sectarian religion continued. Later a committee of Protestants appeared before the County Board of Education and demanded, among other things, that it stop the teaching of sectarian religion in the Dixon schools. The Board held it did not have jurisdiction and declined to act, referring the protestors to the State Board of Education.

They then appeared before the State Board and were told it was an appellate board and as it had no written appeal it could do nothing. The committee offered to make a tender of proof in of their protests but the offer was summarily denied following an objection by an attorney who later represented the Religious at the trial of this case. The meeting evidently waxed warm and for the first time the members of the State Board became exercised over the matter. After the protestors had been dismissed and the Board had been in practically closed session for a time the State Superintendent of Public Instruction, who was also a member ex-officio of the State Board, called on the Archbishop of the Diocese of Santa Fe, the Very Reverend Edwin V. Byrne, and solicited his help. Another meeting of the Board was held and finally the directive relative to the operation of the school at Dixon was adopted, the material portion of which is as follows:

1. That the new school recently completed at Dixon teach the first six grades, including the pre-first.

2. That this new school have all qualified lay teachers, with a lay principal.

3. That the public school, taught by Catholic Sisters, teach the 7–12 grades.

The Archbishop directed a letter to all religious teaching within the Archdiocese of Santa Fe, which, omitting formal parts, reads as follows:

In view of the present agitation against Sisters in Public Schools and to avert grave future difficulties that could prove disastrous to the continuation of Sisters in public schools in the State of New Mexico,

I request that no religious instructions be given in public school buildings by the teachers on school days. Catechism should be taught on Saturdays and Sundays.

* * *

The Archdiocesan Superintendent of Roman Catholic School in the Diocese of Sante Fe, Monsignor Bradley, accompanied two representatives of the Department of Education to Dixon to put the directives into effect. School was being held in the public school building and in the church property rented by the county. At that time the teachers in the church property were Sisters and those in the public school were lay teachers. Monsignor Bradley delivered the orders to the Sisters and then the representatives of the Department of Education gave the orders of the State Board to the lay teachers at the public school. The directives did not at that time effectively stop the teaching of sectarian religion. The State Board of Education did not give any orders to any other schools.

* * *

Question of Mootness of Appeal

The Religious appellees urge the questions raised by appellants in their brief (the teaching of religion, teaching by the Religious in public schools, teaching in religious garb and the fail-ure of the court to enjoin all Religious named as defendants who have taught in the public schools) are moot for the following reasons:

. . . .

2. The State Board of Education by resolution dated March 6, 1951, adopted a policy of prohibiting the wearing of religious garb by teachers in the public schools of New Mexico, declaring that church property shall not be used for public school purposes except in cases of emergency, the resolution, omitting recitals, reading as follows:

It is Hereby Resolved and Adopted as the policy of this board that all nuns, brothers, or priests of the Catholic Church, or members of any other sectarian religious group, wearing clothing of religious significance, should be removed from the public schools throughout the state as expeditiously as circumstances (of) each locality allows; and, it is further adopted as the policy of this board that insofar as possible no property owned by religious groups shall be leased or rented by the state from such religious or sectarian organization unless exceptional circumstances require such action.

3. Following the adoption of the foregoing resolution by the State Board of Education, the Archbishop of the Diocese of Santa Fe advised the State Board of Education that contracts by Religious would not be renewed at the close of the 1950–1951 school year, and that no Church property in this state was being used for public school purposes. . . .

We were advised at the argument in June that no Religious would be employed as teachers in the public schools of New Mexico for the 1951–1952 school year.

* * *

If the State Board of Education and the Archbishop continue the policies announced in the resolution and letter just quoted, then, indeed, the conditions of which plaintiffs so strongly complain would be entirely eliminated; but we must remember the membership of the Board changes somewhat with each administration and we have changes from time to time in the individual holding the high Church office of Archbishop. Lacking an authoritative declaration of law on the subjects the individuals holding such offices may change their policies when and as they might be advised. We decline to treat the questions as moot and will proceed to a decision of the matters raised by the appeal of the appellants and the cross appeal of the Religious.

* * *

Applicable Constitutional Provisions

Many of the assignments of error made by the plaintiffs relate to the right of the Religious to teach in the public schools, wear religious garb while teaching, draw public money for acting as such teachers, and further urge that payment of tax money to such members is, in fact, an aid to a religious order in aid of its particular religion (as the Re-

ligious all take vows of poverty and turn their earnings over to their respective orders) all in violation of the First Amendment to the United States Constitution, provisions of our Enabling Act and certain sections of our state Constitution. Therefore, we quote hereafter various constitutional and statutory provisions relative to the separation of church and state and to our schools.

* * *

*Effect of Relation Between the
Religious and Their Church*

It is argued by the plaintiffs that members of the Religious are bound by their oaths of obedience to obey their superiors in the church. They quote from Codex Juris Canonici, the official body of laws and regulations governing the Roman Catholic Church. . . .

. . . A number of the Religious testified they were bound to obey their superiors, the priest or the archbishop, in matters of religion, and that teaching of religion before or after classes was within the jurisdiction of their superiors. By virute of Sec. 9 of Art. 12 of our Constitution, supra, no religious tests can be prescribed for any teacher, or a member of any faith denied the right to teach because of his or her religious beliefs. But do the vow of obedience and the historic position of the Roman Catholic Church as to public schools and their own schools, the fact that all money received for teaching by members of the Religious is turned over to their Orders (which it is claimed is state aid to religion), and the wearing of religious garb disqualify them from teaching in the public schools?

* * *

Ruling Responsible Wearing of Religious Garb by Public School Teachers

The plaintiffs strongly urge that in any event the Religious should not be allowed to wear religious garb and insignia while discharging their duties as teachers, as this gives the Roman Catholic Church an advantage over all other churches and sects. In addition to the Everson and McCollum cases, supra, they rely on *O'Connor* v. *Hendrick,* supra, and *Knowlton* v. *Baumhover,* 182 Iowa 691, 166 N.W. 202, 5 A.L.R. 841.

In the O'Connor case the New York State Superintendent of Schools made a regulation prohibiting the wearing of religious garb by teachers in the public schools. One teacher, a member of a Roman Catholic Order, refused to comply with the regulation and brought suit for salary accruing after the effective date of the regulation. The constitution of that state provides substantially the same as ours, that public property, credit or money shall not be used directly or indirectly in the aid of any school under the control of any religious denomination. Applying this provision of the constitution to the facts as above noted, the court said:

. . . Here we have the plainest possible declaration of the public policy of the state as opposed to the prevalence of sectarian influences in the public schools. The regulation established by the state superintendent of public instruction through the agency of his order in the Bates appeal is in accord with the public policy thus evidenced by the fundamental law. There can be little doubt that the effect of the costume worn by these Sisters of St. Joseph at all times in the presence of their pupils would be to inspire respect, if not sympathy, for the religious denomination to which they so manifestly belong. To this extent the influence was sectarian, even if it did not amount to the teaching of denominational doctrine. [184 N.Y. 421, 77 N.E. 614.]

It is worthy of note the court approved the strong dissenting opinion of Mr. Justice Williams in *Hysong* v. *Gallitzin Borough School District,* 164 Pa. 629, 30 A. 482, 26 L.R.A. 203, 44 Am. St. Rep. 632, where a majority of the Pennsylvania court had refused to enjoin the wearing of religious garb in their public schools quoting from the dissent as follows:

. . . The teachers, said Mr. Justice Williams . . . , 'Come into the schools, not as common school teachers or as civilians, but as the representatives of a particular order in a particular church, whose lives have been dedicated to religious work under the direction of that church. *Now the point of the objection is, not that their religion disqualifies them. It does not. . . . It is not that holding an ecclesiastical office or position disqualifies, for it does not.* It is the introduction into the schools as teachers of persons who are by their striking and distinctive ecclesiastical robes necessarily and constantly asserting their membership in a particular church, and in a religious order within that church, and the subjection of their lives to the direction and control of its officers.' (Emphasis ours.)

The O'Connor case was based on a regulation, but the reasoning of the court is equally applicable here. In view of the fact we now have a like regulation made by our State Board of Education, we give specific approval to the holding of the New York court on that subject.

The O'Connor case and the dissenting opinion of Justice Williams in the Hysong case were likewise approved in *Knowlton* v. *Baumhover,* supra. The material facts in that case present a situation almost identical to the one we have in a number of schools in this case. A school building was closed and one room utilized as a public school was rented from the local priest of the Roman Catholic Church. A Religious was employed to teach in the public school room while another Religious taught in a room where a Roman Catholic parochial school was maintained. In the actual teaching, however, both rooms were operated the same, with the Religious teaching the catechism, having prayers and displaying Roman Catholic and religious pictures on the walls. When protest was made against the teaching of religion in the public classroom, it was discontinued, but the children of Catholic parents and others who wished to attend were marched to the adjoining church for religious instruction before school. The Iowa court in an exhaustive review of the authorities held the so-called public school was in fact a Roman Catholic school; that wearing of religious garb and the crucifix was an introduction of sectarian religion in the school, bound to make a strong impression on all children. Therefore, the court required the school directors to forthwith move out of the church property and enjoined the payment of public money to the Re-

ligious for teaching in her garb. While the opinion is lengthy, it is an able one and should interest those concerned with the subject.

The Religious rely strongly on the case of *Gerhardt* v. *Heid,* 66 N.D. 444, 267 N.W. 127, where the court refused to enjoin the Religious from teaching or the wearing of religious garb while teaching. However, it must be observed the court said there were no such conditions prevailing in the North Dakota school as had existed in the Iowa school. In the school before the court there was no teaching of religion or wearing of emblems, except for a few days at the opening of the school term, nor were there religious pictures on the walls. There is a strong intimation, as we read the opinion that if the conditions which obtained in the Iowa school had been present in North Dakota, a different result might have been reached.

So long as the resolution of March 6, 1951, by the State Board of Education barring the wearing of religious garb by teachers in our public schools is in effect and is enforced, there is, of course, no need for the issuance of an injunction preventing this practice. However, in view of the frequent changes in the personnel of the State Board of Education and the days of restoration of such practice, we feel compelled to announce our decision that the wearing of religious garb and religious insignia must be henceforth barred, during the time the Religious are on duty as public school teachers. We hold the trial court erred in denying an injunction on this feature of the case. Not only does the wearing of religious garb and insignia have a propagandizing effect for the church, but by its very nature it introduced sectarian religion into the school.

If the Religious are again employed as teachers in our public schools they must not dress in religious garb or wear religious emblems while in the discharge of their duties as such teachers. They must also refrain from the teaching of sectarian religion and doctrines and the dissemination of religious literature during such time. Furthermore, they must be under the actual control and supervision of the responsible school authorities. A church cannot be permitted to operate a school system within our public school system.

RECENT RULINGS

The latest declaration on the question of public school teachers attired in distinctive religious garb was made as a supplemental ruling in a case involving the key issues of the rental of public school buildings from churches and public-financed transportation to public schools. In *Rawlings v. Butler,* Ky., 290 S.W.2d 801 (1956), the Kentucky high court declared that the fact that members of a religious order who were engaged as public school teachers wore religious garb or emblems did not, of itself, constitute a violation of religious freedom, as guaranteed by the Constitution of the United States.

Pointing out that it is the woman within the garb who teaches, the court found instead that denying them the privilege of teaching in the public schools would in effect deny them equal protection of the law, as long as they neither imparted any religious instruction nor injected any dogma of the Roman Catholic church into the classroom activities. The Roman Catholic sisters could, therefore, constitutionally teach secular subjects in the public schools of Kentucky, and turn over the proceeds of such endeavors to a religious society if they so desired, the court determined.

REACTIONS OF LEGAL PERIODICALS TO *RAWLINGS* v. *BUTLER*

The Kentucky court was applauded in the *Wayne Law Review* (3:57) for its judicious use of a constitutional guideline to avoid invalidating the harmless practice of a public school employing as a teacher one who is attired in the distinctive garb of a particular religious order. In doing so, the writer agreed with the court's logic that "the wearing of sectarian attire alone" does not violate any provisions of the state or federal constitutions, as long as sectarian instruction is not imparted. Extending that logic further, he predicted that the outward wearing of religious symbols and ornaments by sisters teaching in other public schools would also stand a test of constitutionality.

He hesitated, however, about predicting what the results would have been if religious pictures and ornaments had been exhibited "in and about the school." He also expressed serious doubts about the constitutionality of maintaining a Roman Catholic church and a residence for the sisters near the public school where the sisters are employed. Neither of these two situations apparently was present in the Rawlings case, however.

On the other hand, a reviewer in the *Tulane Law Review* (31:676) expressed no direct opinion on the constitutionality of the garb question. He did note, however, that the Kentucky court was correct in finding insufficient evidence that the sisters were teaching religion in the public schools. In closing he suggested that the "proper way of preventing the influence of garb and emblem in public schools is by statute."

While the garb issue has provoked a flourish of state court opinions, question has never been raised in the United States Supreme Court. That the constitutionality of public school teachers attired in distinctive religious garb will be questioned before the nation's highest Court in the near future appears to be safe speculation.

State courts have been sharply divided over the constitutionality of such a practice, with at least five instances where the wearing of garb has been allowed and an equal number of times where the practice has been invalidated. The courts seemingly have looked at the peculiarities of each situation on a case-to-case basis, and have been unfavorable to only those programs where the nun clearly imparted sectarian instruction.

REACTIONS OF LAW REVIEWS IN GENERAL

The whole topic of religious garb received only limited attention in law review commentary. Because the few available articles were concerned more with the general topic than with the specific cases, the review is included as a unit here at the end of the chapter.

The general arguments for permitting the wearing of the distinctive garb were listed in 1955 in the *Chicago Law Review* (22:888), as primarily being that (1) the wearer's freedom of religion would be maintained; and (2) the garb, itself, has no sectarian effect on the public school pupils. The reviewer went on to say that the opposition to garb wearing has been "directed primarily at the Roman Catholic church, since typically clerics of other religions do not wear distinctive garb." He cited as evidence of the significance of the litigation to the Roman Catholic faith the fact that all nine garb cases to date had involved Roman Catholic teachers.

He then expressed his own opinion that "The wearer of religious garb has no greater right to wear garb which may effuse a sectarian influence than the right of the student to be free from such influence." Noting the difficulties that would be involved in attempting to draw the line between various degrees of sectarian influence in particular school systems, the writer concluded that any amout of that influence was sufficient to justify statutes prohibiting the wearing of distinctive garb by public school teachers on duty.

His conclusion apparently was based upon the argument that the garb constantly serves as an outward and conspicuous reminder of the wearer's religious affiliations. As a symbol of mystery to pupils of the Protestant faith, the distinctive garb is likely to provoke questions from the students concerning the significance and meaning of the garb and other accompanying regalia of the Roman Catholic faith. The writer felt that at that point the danger of sectarian teaching would become a potential hazard to the principle of secular public school education in the United States.

Two reviewers favored the constitutionality of teachers wearing distinctive religious attire. Charles Fahy, writing in 1949 in *Law and Contemporary Problems* (14:73), argued that the two religion clauses of the First Amendment to the United States Constitution could be properly harmonized only if the courts recognize that the wearing of such distinctive garments by a public school teacher—a public employee—does not constitute state aid to religion within the prohibitions of the Establishment of Religion Clause. He continued (at 90):

> [B]ut . . . to prohibit a teaching Sister from wearing the garb would infringe the free exercise of religion guaranteed by the second clause, and would establish an unconstitutional religious test as a qualification for public office.

In a somewhat similar vein, Virgil C. Blum, Jr., argued in 1955 in the *University of Chicago Law Review* (22:875) that:

> The right to the free exercise of religion is not an absolute right. But neither is the right of the legislature to enact laws restricting the religious liberty of the citizens.

He pointed out that traditionally there has existed liberty of the individual to choose his own attire, and that the question of religious dress is open to debate as to whether the particular garb is an insignia of belief, or merely a didactic device.

Blum, favoring the rationale in the Hysong and Gerhardt decisions, considered the whole question of whether a teaching nun may turn part of her salary, paid from public funds, over to religious societies to be purely "a personal matter."

He queried in conclusion in an interesting bit of logic whether a public school teacher who happens to be a nun should be dismissed merely because she prefers to publicly display evidence that she leads a virtuous life.

SUMMARY

The question of whether a public school teacher wearing distinctive religious garb may violate a state's constitution or statutes has been a recurrent one since the late nineteenth century. Originally the problem appears to have generally arisen in poor, religiously homogeneous communities whose financial resources were too limited to support both public and parochial schools. In the near future, however, the problem is likely to take on added dimension and complexity because of provisions in the federal Elementary and Secondary School Act which permits programs similar to shared time programs if they are authorized by a state's constitution and laws.

In the first case of this type to reach a state high court, the Pennsylvania court in 1894 could find nothing about the wearing of religious garb by teachers in the public school that violated the Pennsylvania constitution or laws. Shortly thereafter, the Pennsylvania legislature passed an enactment prohibiting such practices, and that law was subsequently upheld by the state high court.

The Pennsylvania precedent, notwithstanding, the courts of other states which have been faced with the question are almost evenly divided over its constitutionality. Four states—Iowa, Illinois, Nebraska, and New Mexico—have found the wearing of religious garb by public school teachers to violate the state constitutions. At least one additional state—Oregon—has a statute prohibiting this practice. On the other hand, its constitutionality has been upheld in five states—North and South Dakota, Indiana, Connecticut, and Kentucky.

An interesting sidelight on this subject is that this problem received very little attention in legal periodicals, and most of the articles that did appear tended to be strictly reportorial in nature. Of the remainder, one reviewer leaned slightly toward the position that practices of this type were unconstitutional while two others were at best lukewarm in their support of the constitutionality of this issue. It would be surprising if this noncommittal trend continues in light of the controversy brewing over this and related practices brought into the limelight by passage of the federal Elementary and Secondary Schools Act of 1965.

CHAPTER NINE

Curriculum

† †

THE CONSTITUTIONALITY of some of the subjects taught in schools has caused a large amount of litigation. Practically every conceivable area of teaching has been challenged.

SECTARIAN INSTRUCTION IN SCHOOLS

Several cases have dealt with the question of sectarian instruction in public schools. In an early case, *Scripture* v. *Burns*, 59 Iowa 70 (1882), a writ of mandamus was sought to compel school authorities to enforce the state constitutional provisions forbidding sectarian instruction in public schools. Plaintiff alleged that Roman Catholic catechism was being taught in a public school that was conducted in a building owned by a bishop of the Roman Catholic church.

The Iowa supreme court upheld the lower court's denial of the writ because the plaintiff had not shown "that he had demanded of the defendants that they perform their duty by prohibiting the acts complained of as illegal. This is required by the statute, to authorize a writ of *mandamus*."

Although finding "no evidence of any religious exercises of any character whatever during school hours," the Pennsylvania court in *Hysong* v. *School District*, 164 Pa. 629, 30 A. 482 (1894), did determine that Roman Catholic religious instruction was unconstitutionally imparted by the teachers in the school rooms after the regular day of classes was over.

The court enjoined that practice on the ground that "it was a use of the school property for sectarian purposes." The net effect of the decision was that Roman Catholic sisters attired in distinctive garb could not be barred from employment as public school teachers as long as they imparted no sectarian instruction either during or after the regular school hours.

As a side issue in a taxpayers' action in *Judd* v. *Board of Education*, 278 N.Y. 200, 15 N.E.2d 576 (1938), the court ruled that "education in state supported schools must be nonpartisan and nonsectarian, and such

250

requirement does not discriminate between individuals or classes and invades no religious rights."

The question of using University of Minnesota facilities and property to teach religious doctrine was raised in *State* ex rel. *Sholes* v. *University of Minnesota*, 236 Minn. 452, 54 N.W.2d 122 (1952). The state supreme court ruled that the university had no discretionary power to allow practices forbidden by its charter or the state constitution.

In a joinder opinion involving five cases, the Pennsylvania supreme court dealt with a taxpayer's suit which challenged the legality of appropriating money to an educational establishment which was alleged to be sectarian. The court held in *Collins* v. *Kephart*, 271 Pa. 428, 117 A. 440 (1921), that the maintenance of elective denominational courses and optional religious services made a college sectarian. The court further determined that a college whose name was selected in recognition of the relation between itself and a distinctly religious organization which furnished the college with most of its faculty and support was sectarian. Therefore, as a sectarian institution, the court concluded that the college could not receive state appropriations without violating the state constitutional provision prohibiting the appropriation of state funds to sectarian establishments.

In *Commonwealth* ex rel. *Wehrle* v. *School District*, 241 Pa. 224, 88 A. 481 (1913), involving the admittance of a private school pupil attempting to transfer into a public school, the Pennsylvania supreme court ruled that a pupil could not be refused entrance to public schools just because he had received prior schooling in other than public schools. Such admission into public school did not violate the state constitution by providing private or sectarian schools with public money intended for public school use, the court concluded.

The Washington supreme court in *State* ex rel. *Dearle* v. *Frazier*, 102 Wash. 369 (1918), ruled that a course studying the Bible for its literary, biographical, narrative, and historical contents was religious instruction within the meaning of the state constitutional provision which prohibited public funds or property from being used for religious instruction, worship, or exercises. The court reasoned that there was no single version of the Bible which was accepted by all religious groups. Any study of the Bible from a literary view, while not aiding particular sects, does serve the religious purposes of those intent upon aiding the growth of religion.

The Washington court further determined that no credit could be given toward graduation for such a course because the state constitution also said that schools receiving support from public funds had to be kept free of sectarian influence or control. Here again the court said that no one translation of the Bible was accepted by all religions. Credit would be given only to those answering questions in the way intended by the instructor. This would in essence mean giving credit for sectarian teaching, the very thing the state constitution prohibited.

† † *STATE* ex rel. *DEARLE* v. *FRAZIER*
102 WASH. 369, 173 P. 35 (1918).

Judge CHADWICK delivered the opinion of the court:

This cause is one brought by the petitioners below, respondents on this appeal, to compel appellants by writ of mandate to give petitioners an examination in the course of Bible study, and to compel appellants to give them high school credits for graduation for such Bible study.

. . . Two provisions of our state Constitutions to which the Attorney General has attended, and which have a bearing upon our present discussion are as follows:

All schools maintained or supported wholly or in part by the public funds shall be forever free from sectarian control or influence. Article 9, §4.

No public money or property shall be appropriated for, or applied to any religious worship, exercise or instruction or the support of any religious establishment. Article 1, §11.

The question calling for this opinion was:

Can a teacher employed in the common schools of this state, without violating any law of the state, or any provision of the state Constitution, conduct devotional or religious exercises at the opening of the school day, or during any part of the school day as prescribed by law, by the singing of hymns or other sacred music, or by reading passages from the Bible, without comment, or by repeating or causing to be repeated, without comment, what is usually known as the Lord's Prayer?

. . . .

Many people sincerely believe that a cultivation of religious sentiment, which we may admit is essential to the development of an enlightened citizenship, should be a part of the education and training of the children of our country, and they as firmly believe that the version of the Bible which is accepted and acknowledged by the great majority of the citizens of this country should be made the vehicle of that development. They believe that the Constitution can have no application, unless an attempt is made to advance the doctrine of a particular denomination, or to instill the dogma of sect in the mind of the pupil. Consequently it has been resolved by assemblies of teachers in this country and other countries that a course in Bible study should be a part of school work.

. . . .

Counsel for respondent bases his argument upon two propositions:

First. The resolution does not establish or maintain any school system which is under sectarian control or influence.

Second. There is no expenditure of public funds for any religious worship, exercise or instruction, or the aid or support of any religious establishment.

The first premise will be dismissed, not because it will not bear argument, for there is much argument and authority on either side, but because the case can be determined by reference to the second premise alone. The framers of the Constitution were not content to declare that our public schools should be kept free from sectarian control or influence; they went further and made it certain that their declaration should not be overcome by changing sentiments or opinions. They declared that "no public money or property shall ever be appropriated or applied to any religious worship, exercise or instruction," and in this respect our Constitution differs from any other that has been called to our attention.

. . . .

. . . Article 1, § 11, is all-significant. The words "no public money shall be appropriated for or applied to any religious worship, exercise, or instruction" are sweeping and comprehensive.

I

Our inquiry may be limited then to the one question whether an examination of pupils upon "the historical, biographical, narrative, and literary features" of the Bible is religious instruction within the meaning of the Constitution. To meet the premise of counsel for respondent, we would have to read the prohibition as if it were, "No public money shall be applied to any denominational or sectarian worship, exercise, or instruction," and reject the broader term "religious," for his argu-

ment proceeds as if the sole object of the Constitution was to keep the schools free of sectarian influences. While selections such as the Lord's Prayer, the Twenty-Third Psalm, and the Sermon on the Mount are regarded as masterpieces of literature, and inspiringly grateful to a thirsty soul, they are calculated to invite or excite the youthful mind to inquiry and the elder to resentment, for some, the Jew for instance, while accepting the Twenty-Third Psalm might reject the Lord's Prayer and the Sermon on the Mount as the work and words of one whom he regards as an impostor. Then too, the Twenty-Third Psalm as we understand it is not the Twenty-Third Psalm in the Douay Bible, but the Twenty-Second. Neither is the translation the same as in our own Bible. Nor is the Lord's Prayer translated in the same way. These objections to many of us would seem light and trivial, but history has been made over the controversies that have arisen out of such as these, and that such innocent uses of the Bible have led to civil strife and discussion is abundantly proved by the cases to which we have referred.

We have then not only "religious exercise" and "instruction" which are prohibited, but their natural consequence —religious discussion and controversy. The most ready and popular argument for the avoidance of these constitutional provisions has been that whereas the Bible inculcates a code of morality, which if understood and practiced will make for better citizenship, and whereas it is essential that the youth should be impressed with an understanding of the fundamental principles of right and wrong, and thus grow in moral stature, that Bible instruction by reading selected passages without comment can do no violence to the Constitution, no hurt to the principle of divorcement of church and state, and that it should be therefore not only tolerated, but encouraged. *Hackett* v. *Brooksville Graded School District.* . . .

It is upon these cases and those cited above that counsel relies, and as paradoxical as it may seem, our best authority for rejecting the doctrines announced is to be found in the cases themselves. Quickly put they distinguish religion in its broader sense from the dogmas, creeds, or opinions of sect, and hold that although the Bible may be the textbook of every sect, yet in its history, narrative, biography, and its moral persuasions, it serves no sect, but on the contrary is a spiritual stimulant in every individual whether he be a Jew or a Gentile, a Catholic or a Protestant, a Moslem or a Buddhist, a Christian or a Pagan, a believer or an atheist.

That the study of the Bible for its history, narrative, biography, or literary features serves the religious impulse and the ends of those who would aid the growth of religion as distinguished from mere sect is acknowledged.

. . . It will thus be seen that the cases cited were dealing only with the question whether the reading or study of the Bible might be a sectarian influence, and not with the question whether such reading or study was religious instruction. To prove that it is not sectarian instruction they affirm that it is no more than religious or moral instruction, and so affirming logically hold that if their Constitutions had been such as ours they would have held to the contrary.

II

But it is said that the teaching is to be upon the historical, biographical, narrative, and literary features of the Bible only, and in this the instruction will be neither sectarian, doctrinal, denominational, or religious. This might be true if all citizens were agreed that the King James' translation of the Bible is a true version of the Scriptures, and then only if the teaching were under the control of those who are selected through the means and methods provided by law. But the vice of the present plan is that school credit is to be given for instruction at the hands of sectarian agents. Then, too, all citizens are not agreed as to the narrative and historical worth of the Bible.

. . . That Bible history, narrative and biography cannot be taught without leading to opinion and ofttimes partisan opinion is understood and anticipated by the school board. They admit as plainly as language can admit that Bible teaching does lead to sectarian opinion and differences of opinion upon religious questions. They employ the word "religious" in a narrow and sectarian sense. They speak of "religious organizations," and provide that "interpretation" shall be given in the home, or by some "religious organization." Now we had thought that "history, biography and biblical narrative" would require no interpretation—certainly no interpretation calling for the doctrinal opinion of a religious organization. And who of authority in our schools is to say that a pupil shall or shall not have credit if he answers questions in a way that is different from the way intended by those who prepared the course of instruction. It may be said that the pupil is entitled to credit if he answers in a way that is consistent with the faith of his instructor. But there are two objections to this. The one is that the examiner may not know the faith and teachings of those of a different faith; the other and more conclusive objection is that to give a credit in the public school for such instruction is to give a credit for sectarian teaching and influence, which is the very thing outlawed by the Constitution.

. . . .

We shall not go far afield when we suggest that it is a matter within the common knowledge of those who followed the discussion attending the framing of our Constitution that it was the purpose of the men of that time to avoid all of the evils of religious controversies, the diversion of school funds to denominational schools and institutions, and the litigation that had occurred in other states. For it was known that religious opinion is a thing that men will fight for, and sometimes in most insidious ways. The question then was, and the people who adopted the Constitution were so advised, whether we should adopt a Constitution which provided in terms that no religious instruction should ever be a part, directly or indirectly, of the curriculum of our schools. To compromise opinion in these matters is to lead to confusion, which would make the courts the arbiter of what is and what is not religious worship, instruction, or influence, which would be as intolerable to the citizen as it would be to leave a decision to a school board. . . .

. . . .

. . . There is another reason for our holding which is not suggested in the briefs, but it nevertheless seems forceful to the writer. It is, that neither the board of education nor the school board has undertaken to define the meaning of the word "Bible." It may be said that they did not have the Jewish Bible in mind, for credit is provided for instruction and examination

in the New Testament, but we apprehend that this would not be binding on a Jewish school board. It would be free to prescribe the Talmud. A school board made up of Protestants would have in mind and provide for instruction and examination in the King James' version. A board made up of Catholics would no doubt insist upon the use of the Douay Bible, while a board made up of Lutherans would hold the pupil to the translations of Luther. . . .

. . . And it is not beyond the realm of imagination to believe that the framers of our Constitution foresaw the possibility of a school board divided in its religious beliefs.

. . . .

The resolution provides that the syllabus of course of study is to be made up by the school board. What guarantee has the citizen that the board having a contrary faith will not inject those passagers upon which their own sects rests its claims as the true church under the guise of "narrative or literary features," and if they did so, where would the remedy be found? Surely the courts could not control their discretion, for judges are made of the same stuff as other men, and what would appear to be heretical or doctrinal to one may stand out as a literary gem or as inoffensive narrative to another, and thus the evil at which the Constitution is aimed would break out with its ancient vigor. If the sentiment of the people has so far changed as to demand the things sought to be done, the remedy is by amendment to the Constitution.

Being controlled in our judgment by our conception of the Constitution, we are constrained to reverse the judgment of the court below, and to remand the case, with directions to deny the writ.

FOREIGN LANGUAGES

Teaching foreign languages in both public and private schools has been an area of controversy in the past. This litigation occurred around World War I and in all likelihood can be traced to the germanophobia of that era.

The conviction of a Nebraska teacher who had taught a parochial school pupil in the German language in violation of a state statute was overruled in *Meyer* v. *Nebraska*, 262 U.S. 390 (1923). The Supreme Court rejected the lower court's reasoning that by requiring all teaching of students before the eighth grade to be conducted in English, the students' health was fostered by limiting their mental activities. The lower court thereby accepted such legislation as within the authority of the police power of the state. The Supreme Court concluded, however, that by such action a state exceeded the state's power and violated liberties guaranteed by the Fourteenth Amendment.

† † *MEYER* v. *NEBRASKA*
262 u.s. 390, 43 s. ct. 625; 67 l. ed. 1042 (1923).

Mr. Justice MC REYNOLDS delivered the opinion of the Court, saying in part:

Plaintiff in error was tried and convicted in the District Court for Hamilton County, Nebraska, under an information which charged that on May 25, 1920, while an instructor in Zion Parochial School, he unlawfully taught the subject of reading in the German language to Raymond Parpart, a child of ten years, who had not attained and successfully passed the eight grade. The information is based upon "An act relating to the teaching of foreign languages in the State of Nebraska," approved April 9, 1919, which follows. . . .

Section 1. No person, individually or as a teacher, shall, in any private, denominational, parochial or public school, teach any subject to any person in any language other than the English language.

Sec. 2. Languages, other than the English language, may be taught as languages only after a pupil shall have attained and successfully passed the eighth grade as evidenced by a certificate of graduation issued by the county superintendent of the county in which the child resides.

Sec. 3. Any person who violates any of the provisions of this act shall be deemed guilty of a misdemeanor and upon conviction, shall be subject to a fine of not less than twenty-five dollars ($25), nor more than one hundred dollars ($100) or be confined in the county jail for any period not exceeding thirty days for each offense.

Sec. 4. Whereas, an emergency exists, this act shall be in force from and after its passage and approval.

The Supreme Court of the State affirmed the judgment of conviction. 107 Neb. 657. It declared the offense charged and established was "the direct and intentional teaching of the German language as a distinct subject to a child who had not passed the eighth grade," in the parochial school maintained by Zion Evangelical Lutheran Congregation, a collection of Biblical stories being used therefor. And it held that the statute forbidding this did not conflict with the Fourteenth Amendment, but was a valid exercise of the police power. . . .

. . . The problem for our determination is whether the statute as construed and applied unreasonably infringes the liberty guaranteed to the plaintiff in error by the Fourteenth Amendment. "No State shall . . . deprive any person of life, liberty, or property, without due process of law."

While this Court has not attempted to define with exactness the liberty thus guaranteed, the term has received much consideration and some of the included things have been definitely stated. Without doubt, it denotes not merely freedom from bodily restraint but also the right of the individual to contract, to engage in any of the common occupations of life, to acquire useful knowledge, to marry, establish a home and bring up children, to worship God according to the dictates of his own conscience, and generally to enjoy those privileges long recognized at common law as essential to the orderly pursuit of happiness by free men. . . . The established doctrine is that this liberty may not be interfered with, under the guise of protecting the public interest, by legislative action which is arbitrary or without reasonable relation to some purpose within the competency of the State to effect. Determination by the legislature of what constitutes proper exercise of police power is not final or conclusive but is subject to supervision by the courts. . . .

The American people have always regarded education and acquisition of knowledge as matters of supreme importance which should be diligently promoted. The Ordinance of 1787 declares, "Religion, morality, and knowledge being necessary to good government and the happiness of mankind, schools and the means of education shall forever be encouraged." Corresponding to the right of control, it is the natural duty of the parent to give his children education suitable to their station in life; and nearly all the States, including Nebraska, enforce this obligation by compulsory laws.

Practically, education of the young is only possible in schools conducted by especially qualified persons who devote themselves thereto. The calling always has been regarded as useful and honorable, essential, indeed, to the public welfare. Mere knowledge of the German language cannot reasonably be regarded as harmful. Heretofore it has been commonly looked upon as helpful and desirable. Plaintiff in error taught this language in school as part of his occupation. His right thus to teach and the right of parents to engage him so to instruct their children, we think, are within the liberty of the Amendment.

The challenged statute forbids the teaching in school of any subject except in English; also the teaching of any other language until the pupil has attained and successfully passed the eighth grade, which is not usually accomplished before the age of twelve. The Supreme Court of the State has held that "the so-called ancient or dead languages" are not "within the spirit or the purpose of the act." . . . Latin,

Greek, Hebrew are not proscribed; but German, French, Spanish, Italian and every other alien speech are within the ban. Evidently the legislature has attempted materially to interfere with the calling of modern language teachers, with the opportunities of pupils to acquire knowledge, and with the power of parents to control the education of their own.

It is said the purpose of the legislation was to promote civic development by inhibiting training and education of the immature in foreign tongues and ideals before they could learn English and acquire American ideals; and "that the English language should be and become the mother tongue of all children reared in this State." It is also affirmed that the foreign born population is very large, that certain communities commonly use foreign words, follow foreign leaders, move in a foreign atmosphere, and that the children are thereby hindered from becoming citizens of the most useful type and the public safety is imperiled.

That the State may do much, go very far, indeed, in order to improve the quality of its citizens, physically, mentally and morally, is clear; but the individual has certain fundamental rights which must be respected. The protection of the Constitution extends to all, to those who speak other languages as well as to those born with English on the tongue. Perhaps it would be highly advantageous if all had ready understanding of our ordinary speech, but this cannot be coerced by methods which conflict with the Constitution—a desirable end cannot be promoted by prohibited means.

For the welfare of his Ideal Commonwealth, Plato suggested a law which should provide:

That the wives of our guardians are to be common, and their children are to be common, and no parent is to know his own child, nor any child his parent. . . . The proper officers will take the offspring of the good parents to the pen or fold, and there they will deposit them with certain nurses who dwell in a separate quarter; but the offspring of the inferior, or of the better when they chance to be deformed, will be put away in some mysterious unknown place, as they should be.

In order to submerge the individual and develop ideal citizens, Sparta assembled the males at seven into barracks and intrusted their subsequent education and training to official guardians. Although such measures have been deliberately approved by men of great genius, their ideas touching the relation between individual and State were wholly different from those upon which our institutions rest; and it hardly will be affirmed that any legislature could impose such restrictions upon the people of a State without doing violence to both letter and spirit of the Constitution.

The desire of the legislature to foster a homogeneous people with American ideals prepared readily to understand current discussions of civic matters is easy to appreciate. Unfortunate experiences during the late war and aversion toward every characteristic of truculent adversaries were certainly enough to quicken that aspiration. But the means adopted, we think, exceed the limitations upon the power of the State and conflict with rights assured to plaintiff in error. The interference is plain enough and no adequate reason therefor in time of peace and domestic tranquility has been shown.

The power of the State to compel attendance at some school and to make reasonable regulations for all schools, including a requirement that they shall give instructions in English, is not questioned. Nor has challenge been made of the State's power to prescribe a curriculum for institutions which it supports. Those matters are not within the present controversy. Our concern is with the prohibition approved by the Supreme Court. . . . No emergency has arisen which renders knowledge by a child of some language other than English so clearly harmful as to justify its inhibition with the consequent infringement of rights long freely enjoyed. We are constrained to conclude that the statute as applied is arbitrary and without reasonable relation to any end within the competency of the State.

As the statute undertakes to interfere only with teaching which involves a modern language, leaving complete freedom as to other matters, there seems no adequate foundation for the suggestion that the purpose was to protect the child's health by limiting his mental activities. It is well known that proficiency in a foreign language seldom comes to one not instructed at an early age, and experience shows that this is not injurious to the health, morals or understanding of the ordinary child.

. . . Reversed.

RELATED CASES

A joinder of four cases concerned with teaching foreign languages in parochial schools was disposed of in summary fashion by the United States Supreme Court. *Bartels* v. *Iowa, Bohning* v. *Ohio*, and *Pohl* v. *Ohio*, 262 U.S. 404, 43 S.Ct. 628, 67 L.Ed. 1047 (1923), dealt with the conviction of a teacher for teaching German to parochial school students who had not attained the eighth grade. *Nebraska* v. *McKelvic*, 262 U.S. 404 (1923), pertained to the state supreme court's reversal of the trial court's ruling to issue an injunction to enjoin state officials from preventing modern foreign languages from being taught to young children. The above judgments were reversed upon the authority of *Meyer* v. *Nebraska*, 262 U.S. 390 (1923).

The United States Supreme Court in *Farrington* v. *Tokushige*, 273 U.S. 284 (1927), considered only the question of whether the trial court had abused its judicial discretion in issuing a temporary injunction to prevent the enforcement of an act aimed at foreign language schools. Finding that it had not, the Court determined that the Hawaiian statute apparently was intended to bring all foreign language schools under rigid territorial control.

In so doing, the Court extended the general Fourteenth Amendment protections for owners of private schools and parents of parochial school students against arbitrary state action as enunciated in *Meyer* v. *Nebraska*, 262 U.S. 390 (1923); *Bartels* v. *Iowa, id.* 404; and *Pierce* v. *Society of Sisters*, 268 U.S. 510 (1925), to include similar infringements by Congress and territorial legislatures under the Due Process Clause of the Fifth Amendment.

COMPULSORY R.O.T.C. AND CONSCIENTIOUS OBJECTORS

Conscientious objectors have sought release from military duties not only in the armed forces, but also in the compulsory Reserve Officer Training Corps (R.O.T.C.) programs required by many colleges and universities.

In the first of three cases involving conscientious objectors and compulsory R.O.T.C., the Maryland Court of Appeals in 1933 rendered a decision on the question of whether the University of Maryland could suspend students who refused to take prescribed courses in military science for reasons of conscientious religious convictions.

The Maryland Court, in *Pearson* v. *Coale,* 165 Md. 224, 167 A. 54 (1933), reversed the lower court which issued the writ of mandamus sought by Coale for reinstatement in the university without being required to takes the courses in military training. The court determined that the privilege of conscientious objection resulted from acts of Congress not from the Constitution. The Appellee had, in part, relied on the Fourteenth Amendment to support his claim. However, no federal or state laws existed which supported the appellee's stand. Nor was his position supported by the provisions of the charter of the university which forbade religious discrimination by the university authorities in pursuance of their duties, and which required the admittance of all students regardless of religion and without religious tests.

The court concluded that the appellee was not completely sincere in his request for exemption from compulsory R.O.T.C on grounds of conscientious religious conviction. Also, the court found that the university had recently embarked upon a policy of allowing no one to be excused except for physical disabilities. Therefore, the court concluded that the appellee's rights under the Fourteeth Amendment of the federal Constitution and the charter of the university had not been violated.

In *Hamilton* v. *Regents,* 293 U.S. 245 (1934), the appellants alleged that the provisions of the Morrill Land Grant Act, the state constitution, and regents' order which prescribed compulsory R.O.T.C., violated the Privileges and Immunities and the Due Process clauses of the Fourteenth Amendment and was repugnant to the Briand-Kellogg Peace Pact. The Court determined that the invoked privileges and immunities accrue only to citizens of the United States. Therefore, if the regents' denial of matriculation to the appellants for refusing to take military training did not violate the Due Process Clause of the Fourteenth Amendment, then it also did not violate the Privileges and Immunities Clause.

The Court concluded that requiring military training of all able-bodied males of junior classification did not violate any constitutional rights, and that the regents' order did not conflict with the Briand-Kellogg Peace Pact which renounced war as a solution for international problems.

† †   *HAMILTON* v. *REGENTS OF THE
UNIVERSITY OF CALIFORNIA*
293 U.S. 245, 55 S. CT. 197, 79 L. ED. 343 (1934).

Mr. Justice BUTLER delivered the opinion of the Court:

This is an appeal under § 237 (a), Judicial Code, 28 U. S. C., § 344 (a), from a judgment of the highest court of California sustaining a state law that requires students at its university to take a course in military science and tactics, the validity of which was by the appellants challenged as repugnant to the Constitution and laws of the United States.
. . . So far as they are material to the questions presented here, the allegations of the petition are:
In October, 1933, each of these minors registered, became a student in the university and fully conformed to all its requirements other than that compelling him to take the course in military science and tactics in the Reserve Officers Training Corps, which they assert to be an integral part of the military establishment of the United States and not connected in any way with the militia or military establishment of the State. The primary object of there establishing units of the training corps is to qualify students for appointment in the Officers Reserve Corps. The courses in military training are those prescribed by the War Department. The regents require enrollment and participation of the able-bodied male students who are citizens of the United

States. These courses include instruction in rifle marksmanship, scouting and patrolling, drill command, musketry, combat principles, books for use of students in such courses are furnished by the War Department of the United States Government.
These minors are members of the Methodist Episcopal Church and of the Epworth League and connected religious societies and organizations. For many years their fathers have been ordained ministers of that church.

. . . .

And in 1932 the General Conference of that Church adopted as a part of its tenets and discipline:

We hold that our country is benefited by having as citizens those who unswervingly follow the dictates of their consciences. . . . Furthermore, we believe it to be the duty of the churches to give moral support to those individuals who hold conscientious scruples against participation in military training or military service. We petition the government of the United States to grant to members of the Methodist Episcopal Church who may be conscientious objectors to war the same exemption from military service as has long been granted to members of the Society of Friends and other similar religious organizations. Similarly we petition all educational institutions which require military training to excuse from such training any student belonging to the Methodist Episcopal Church who has conscientious scruples against it. We earnestly petition the government of the United States to cease to support financially all military training in civil educational institutions.

. . . .

Appellants, as members of that church, accept and feel themselves morally, religiously and conscientiously bound by its tenets and discipline as expressed in the quoted conference resolutions; each is a follower of the teachings of Jesus Christ; each accepts as a guide His teachings and those of the Bible and holds as a part of his religious and conscientious belief that war, training for war, and military training are immoral, wrong and contrary to the letter and spirit of His teaching and the precepts of the Christian religion.

Therefore these students, at the beginning of the fall term in 1933, petitioned the university for exemption from military training and participation in the activities of the training corps, upon the ground of their religious and conscientious objection to war and to military training. Their petition was denied. Thereupon, through that church's bishop in California, they and their fathers petitioned the regents that military training be made optional in order that conscientious and religious objectors to war, training for war and military training might not be confronted with the necessity of violating and foreswearing their beliefs or being denied the right of education in the state university to which these minors are entitled under the constitution and laws of the State of California and of the United States.

The regents refused to make military training optional or to exempt these students. Then, because of their religious and conscientious objections, they declined to take the prescribed course, and solely upon that ground the regents by formal notification suspended them from the university, but with leave to apply for readmission at any time, conditioned upon their ability and willingness to comply with all applicable regulations of the university governing the matriculation and attendance of students. The university affords opportunity for education such as may not be had at any other institution in California, except at a greater cost which these minors are not able to pay. And they, as appellees at the time of their suspension well knew, are willing to take as a substitute for military training such other courses as may be prescribed by the university.

. . . .

The university is a land grant college. An act of Congress (Morrill Act approved July 2, 1862, 12 Stat. 503; 7 U.S.C., §§301–308) donated public lands to the several States in order that upon the conditions specified all moneys derived from the sale of such lands or from the sale of land script issued under the act should be invested and constitute a prepetual fund the interest of which should be inviolably appropriated by each State accepting the benefits of the act "to the endowment, support, and maintenance of at least one college where the leading object shall be, without excluding other scientific and classical studies, and including military tactics, to teach such branches of learning as are related to agriculture and the mechanic arts, in such manner as the legislatures of the States may respectively prescribe, in order to promote the liberal and practical education of the industrial classes in the several pursuits and professions in life."

March 23, 1868, the legislature of California passed an act creating the university "in order to devote to the largest purposes of education the benefaction made to the State" by the Morrill Act. Stats. 1867–8, p. 248. This law of the State, called the organic act, provides that "any resident of California, of the age of fourteen years or upwards, of approved moral character, shall have the right to enter himself in the University as a student at large, and receive tuition in any branch or branches of instruction at the time when the same are given in their regular course, on such terms as the Board of Regents may prescribe. . . ."

"[A]nd in order to fulfill the requirements of the said Act of Congress, all able-bodies male students of the University, whether pursuing full or partial courses in any college, or as students at large, shall receive instruction and discipline in military tactics in such manner and to such extent as the Regents shall prescribe, the requisite arms for which shall be furnished by the state."

. . .

[T]he state constitution as amended November 5, 1918, declares:

The University of California shall constitute a public trust, to be administered by the existing corporation known as 'The Regents of the University of California' with full powers of organization and government, subject only to such legislative control as may be necessary to insure compliance with the terms of the endowments of the university and the security of its funds . . . *provided*, that all moneys derived from the sale of public lands donated to this State by act of Congress approved July 2, 1862 (and the several acts amendatory thereof), shall be invested as provided

by said acts of Congress and the income from said moneys shall be inviolably appropriated to the endowment, support and maintenance of at least one college of agriculture, where the leading objects shall be (without excluding other scientific and classical studies, and including military tactics) to teach such branches of learning as are related to scientific and practical agriculture and mechanic arts, in accordance with the requirements and conditions of said acts of Congress.

September 15, 1931, pursuant to the provisions of the organic act and constitution, the regents promulgated the following order:

"Every able-bodied student of the University of California who, at the time of his matriculation at the University, is under the age of twenty-four years and a citizen of the United States and who has not attained full academic standing as a junior student in the University and has not completed the course in military science and tactics offered to freshmen and sophomore students at the University shall be and is hereby required as a condition to his attendance as a student to enroll in and complete a course of not less than one and one-half units of instruction in military science and tactics each semester of his attendance until such time as he shall have received a total of six units of such instruction or shall have attained full academic standing as a junior student."

In the court below appellants assailed the laws and order above referred to as repugnant to specified provisions of the California constitution, and political code. And they adequately challenged the validity of the state constitution, organic act and regents' order, in so far as they were by the regents construed to require these students to take the prescribed course in military science and tactics, as repugnant to the Constitution and laws of the United States.

The state court, without announcing an opinion, denied the petition for a writ of mandate. Appellants applied for a rehearing. The court, denying the application handed down an opinion in which it held that Art. IX, § 9, reposes in the regents full powers of organization and government of the university subject to legislative control in respect of its endowments and funds; that by § 6 of the organic act and Art. IX, § 9, military tactics is expressly required to be included among the subjects which shall be taught at the university and that it is the duty of the regents to prescribe the nature and extent of the courses to be given and to determine what students shall be required to pursue them, and that the suspension of the petitioning students because of their refusal to pursue the compulsory courses in military training involved no violation of their rights under the Constitution of the United States.

By their assignment of errors, appellants call upon this court to decide whether the challenged provisions of the state constitution, organic act and regents' order, in so far as they impose compulsory military training, are repugnant to the privileges and immunities clause of the Fourteenth Amendment, the due process clause of the amendment or the treaty that is generally called the Briand-Kellogg Peace Pact. . . .

. . . The allegations of the petition do not mean that California has divested itself of any part of its power solely to determine what military training shall be offered or required at the university. While, by acceptance of the benefits of the Morrill Act of 1862 and the creation of the university in order appropriately to comply with the terms of the grant, the State became bound to offer students in that university instruction in military tactics, it remains untrammeled by federal enactment and is entirely free to determine for itself the branches of military training to be provided, the content of the instruction to be given and the objectives to be attained. That State—as did each of the other States of the Union—for the proper discharge of its obligations as beneficiary of the grant made the course in military instruction compulsory upon students. Recently Wisconsin and Minnesota have made it elective. The question whether the State has bound itself to require students to take the training is not here involved. The validity of the challenged orders does not depend upon the terms of the land grant.

The petition is not to be understood as showing that students required by the regents' order to take the prescribed course thereby serve in the army or in any sense become a part of the military establishment of the United States. Nor is the allegation that the courses are prescribed by the War Department to be taken literally. We take judicial notice of the long-established voluntary cooperation between federal and state authorities in respect of the military instruction given in the land grant colleges. The War Department has not been empowered to determine or in any manner to prescribe the military instruction in these institutions. The furnishing of officers, men and equipment conditioned upon the giving of courses and the imposing of discipline deemed appropriate, recommended or approved by the Department does not support the suggestion that the training is not exclusively prescribed and given under the authority of the State. . . . And, when made possible by the national government, the State in order more effectively to teach and train its citizens for these and like purposes, may avail itself of the services of officers and equipment belonging to the military establishment of the United States. So long as its action is within retained powers and not inconsistent with any exertion of the authority of the national government, and transgresses no right safeguarded to the citizen by the Federal Constitution, the State is the sole judge of the means to be employed and the amount of training to be exacted for the effective accomplishment of these ends. . . .

The clauses of the Fourteenth Amendment invoked by appellants declare: "No State shall make or enforce any law which shall abridge the privileges or immunities of citizens of the United States; nor shall any State deprive any person of life, liberty or property, without due process of law." Appellants' contentions are that the enforcement of the order prescribing instruction in military science and tactics abridges some privilege or immunity covered by the first clause and deprives of liberty safeguarded by the second. The "privileges and immunities" protected are only those that belong to citizens of the United States as distinguished from citizens of the States— those that arise from the Constitution and laws of the United States as contrasted with those that spring from other sources. . . . The "privilege" of attending the university as a student comes not from federal sources but is given by the State. It is not within the asserted protection. The only "immunity" claimed by these students is

freedom from obligation to comply with the rule prescribing military training. But that "immunity" cannot be regarded as not within, or as distinguishable from, the "liberty" of which they claim to have been deprived by the enforcement of the regents' order. If the regents' order is not repugnant to the due process clause, then it does not violate the privileges and immunities clause. Therefore we need only decide whether by state action the "liberty" of these students has been infringed.

There need be no attempt to enumerate or comprehensively to define what is included in the "liberty" protected by the due process clause. Undoubtedly it does include the right to entertain the beliefs, to adhere to the principles and to teach the doctrines on which these students base their objections to the order prescribing military training. . . . The fact that they are able to pay their way in this university but not in any other institution in California is without significance upon any constitutional or other question here involved. California has not drafted or called them to attend the university. They are seeking education offered by the State and at the same time insisting that they be excluded from the prescribed course solely upon grounds of their religious beliefs and conscientious objections to war, preparation for war and military education. Taken on the basis of the facts alleged in the petition, appellants' contentions amount to no more than an assertion that the due process clause of the Fourteenth Amendment as a safeguard of "liberty" confers the right to be students in the state university free from obligation to take military training as one of the conditions of attendance.

Viewed in the light of our decisions

that proposition must at once be put aside as untenable.

Government, federal and state, each in its own sphere owes a duty to the people within its jurisdiction to preserve itself in adequate strength to maintain peace and order and to assure the just enforcement of law. And every citizen owes the reciprocal duty, according to his capacity, to support and defend government against all enemies. . . .

. . . .

Plainly there is no ground for the contention that the regents' order, requiring able-bodied male students under the age of twenty-four as a condition of their enrollment to take the prescribed instruction in military science and tactics, transgresses any constitutional right asserted by these appellants.

. . . Affirmed.

Mr. Justice CARDOZO, joined by Justices BRANDEIS and STONE, concurring:

I assume for present purposes that the religious liberty protected by the First Amendment against invasion by the nation is protected by the Fourteenth Amendment against invasion by the states.

Accepting that premise, I cannot find in the respondents' ordinance an obstruction by the state to "the free exercise" of religion as the phrase was understood by the founders of the nation, and by the generations that have followed. . . .

There is no occasion at this time to mark the limits of governmental power in the exaction of military service when the nation is at peace. The petitioners have not been required to bear arms for any hostile purpose, offensive or defensive, either now or in the future. They have not even been required in any absolute or peremptory way to join in courses of instruction that will fit them to bear arms. If they elect to resort to an institution for higher education maintained with the state's moneys, then and only then they are commanded to follow courses of instruction believed by the state to be vital to its welfare. This may be condemned by some as unwise or illiberal or unfair

when there is violence to conscientious scruples, either religious or merely ethical. More must be shown to set the ordinance at naught. In controversies of this order courts do not concern themselves with matters of legislative policy, unrelated to privileges or liberties secured by the organic law. The First Amendment, if it be read into the Fourteenth, makes invalid any state law "respecting an establishment of religion or prohibiting the free exercise thereof." Instruction in military science is not instruction in the practice or tenets of a religion. Neither directly nor indirectly is government establishing a state religion when it insists upon such training. Instruction in military science, unaccompanied here by any pledge of military service, is not an interference by the state with the free exercise of religion when the liberties of the constitution are read in the light of a century and a half of history during days of peace and war.

The meaning of those liberties has striking illustration in statutes that were enacted in colonial times and later. . . . From the beginnings of our history Quakers and other conscien-

ous objectors have been exempted as
a act of grace from military service,
ut the exemption, when granted, has
een coupled with a condition, at least
a many instances, that they supply the
rmy with a substitute or with the
oney necessary to hire one. . . . For
ne opposed to force, the affront to
onscience must be greater in furnish-
ıg men and money wherewith to wage
 pending contest than in studying
ıilitary science without the duty or the
ledge of service. Never in our history
as the notion been accepted, or even,
: is believed, advanced, that acts thus
ıdirectly related to service in the
amp or field are so tied to the prac-
ice of religion as to be exempt, in law
r in morals, from regulation by the
tate. On the contrary, the very law-
ıakers who were willing to give re-
ease from warlike acts had no thought

that they were doing anything inconsistent with the moral claims of an objector, still less with his constitutional
immunities, in coupling the exemption
with these collateral conditions.

Manifestly a different doctrine would
carry us to lengths that have never yet
been dreamed of. The conscientious
objector, if his liberties were to be thus
extended, might refuse to contribute
taxes in furtherance of a war, whether
for attack or for defense, or in furtherance of any other end condemned by
his conscience as irreligious or immoral. The right of private judgment
has never yet been so exalted above the
powers and the compulsion of the
agencies of government. One who is a
martyr to a principle—which may turn
out in the end to be a delusion or an
error—does not prove by his martyr-
dom that he has kept within the law.

REACTIONS OF LEGAL PERIODICALS TO
HAMILTON v. REGENTS

The Hamilton decision received mixed approval from slightly more
han half of the law review articles. The Court's position that a college edu-
ation is not required or is not a right but rather is a privilege attendant
ıpon meeting certain conditions and obligations was not disputed by the
eviewers. Dissenting reviews expressed the opinion, however, that such
onditions and obligations must not necessarily permit the violation of
eligious freedom and conscientious principles.

A proposal to make such collegiate military training optional was set
orth in the *University of Chicago Law Review* (2:331). The constitu-
ional vulnerability of the compulsory R.O.T.C. program was also men-
ioned in the *Indiana Law Journal* (10:361), although its reviewer found
he police power sufficient to uphold the decision here.

On the other hand, the emphasis in the *West Virginia Law Quarterly*
(41:281) seemed to be that the *Selective Draft Law Cases*, 245 U.S. 366
(1918), and other cases involving military exemptions had upheld "a wider
use of the war powers than is involved in a compulsory course in military
tactics with no obligation for further service."

Prior to this, the *Columbia Law Review* (33:1441) was the only review

that took a definite stand on *Pearson* v. *Coale,* 165 Md. 224, 167 A. ⁝
(1933), which had upheld the expulsion of a student who failed to comp〈
with the terms of a similar policy. The reviewer was highly critical 〈
what he called the head-on clash of compulsory military training with tl
"traditional policy of respecting religious scruples."

SUBSEQUENT CASES

More recently two cases turning on conscientious objection to con
pulsory R.O.T.C. were consolidated and appeared before the Marylan
court of appeals as *Hanauer* v. *Elkins,* 217 Md. 213, 141 A.2d 903 (1958
Two University of Maryland students petitioned for writs of mandamus 〈
allow them to continue their studies without complying with the universi〈
requirement of basic military training for all physically able male unde
graduates. The petitioners alleged violation of basic rights accorded b
the charter of the university which prohibited sectarian tests for admi
tance; the Maryland constitution which required equal protection of th
laws for a person's religious liberty and prohibited religious tests fc
holding public office; and the First and Fourteenth Amendments of th
United States Constitution. The court of appeals affirmed the lowe
court's denial of the writ. The decision, upon appeal to the United State
Supreme Court, was dismissed in *Hanauer* v. *Elkins,* 358 U.S. 643 (1961

The Maryland court of appeals cited *Pearson* v. *Coale,* 165 Md. 224
167 A. 54 (1933), when it rejected the contention that the compulsor
military course was the same as imposing a religious test which was fo〈
bidden by the university charter and the state constitution. The cour
also rejected the contention of violation of the First and Fourteent〈
Amendments. It based this ruling upon the Supreme Court's dismissal 〈
appeal for lack of substantial federal question in *Pearson* v. *Coale*
supra, and on *Hamilton* v. *Regents of the University of California,* 29〈
U.S. 245, 55 S.Ct. 197, 79 L.Ed. 343 (1934). In the latter decision, th
Supreme Court ruled that conscientious objectors could be legally ex
cluded from the state university for refusal to participate in the com
pulsory R.O.T.C. program. The Court concluded that even though th
appellants were sincere as conscientious objectors, the required course
in military science did not amount to an establishment of religion, a vic
lation of the Privileges and Immunities Clause, nor a denial of equa
protection of the laws of the Fourteenth Amendment.

The provision of the Selective Service Act of 1917 which exempte〈
ministers, theological students, and members of certain sects from strictl〈
military duty was challenged as violating the establishment and free exer
cise clauses of the First Amendment in the *Selective Draft Law Case〈*
245 U.S. 366 (1918). The lower court's ruling allowing theological exemp〈

tion for the draft was affirmed in this joinder of six cases. The Court touched only briefly upon the religious issues, saying: "And we pass without anything but statement the proposition that an establishment of a religion or an interference with free exercise thereof repugnant to the First Amendment resulted from the exemption clauses . . . because we think its unsoundness is too apparent to require us to do more."

A recent declaration by the United States Supreme Court on the question of conscientious objectors touched upon the question at hand. In *United States* v. *Seeger,* 85 S.Ct. 850 (1965), the Court reversed the conviction of a former college student who had refused induction into the armed services following a change in his draft classification from 2-S (student) to 1-A.

Justice Clark, speaking for a unanimous majority, reasoned that:

> We believe that under this construction the test of belief 'in a relation to a Supreme Being' is whether a given belief that is sincere and meaningful occupies a place in the life of its possessor parallel to that filled by the orthodox belief in God of one who clearly qualifies for the exemption.

REACTIONS OF LEGAL PERIODICALS TO
SELECTIVE DRAFT LAW CASES

Several law reviews gave overwhelming approval to the decision in 1918. The strong impetus for upholding the Draft Law Act seemed to stem from waves of highly emotionalized patriotism which characterized this era. Little concern was shown for the issue of religious freedom. Moreover, scant attention was paid to the rights or moral scruples of the conscientious objector.

As recent as 1964, however, the *Journal of Public Law* (13:16) strongly condemned what it termed the intellectual "sore spot" in modern constitutional interpretation that has developed from the decision. The article argued that sincerity must be the criteria for such conscientious objections. Otherwise, it was noted that there existed an unconstitutional establishment of religion whereby religious objectors *per se* are preferred over "sincere" pacifists solely because of an unresolved argument concerning the existence of a Supreme Being.

A similar opinion was expressed several months earlier in the *Virginia Law Review* (50:178), in its discussion of *United States* v. *Seeger,* 85 S.Ct. 850 (1965). The reviewer declared that continued upholding of draft exemptions for religious objectors was a violation of establishment of religion, because those professing theistic religion were preferred over those professing nontheistic religion. Furthermore, that reviewer argued that *Torcaso* v. *Watkins,* 37 U.S. 488 (1961), implies that incidental and unintentional preferences to religion are also forbidden.

THE SCHOOLS AND CONSCIENTIOUS OBJECTORS

The question of conscientious objectors arose in another fashion in *McDowell* v. *Board of Education,* 104 Misc. 564, 172 N.Y.S. 590 (1918), below. There the supreme court of New York County ruled that the local board of education had authority to dismiss a Quaker school teacher, who openly admitted that she was "opposed to all war, offensive and defensive."

Disregarding the teacher's contention that she should not be dismissed merely because of her belief, which she claimed was not "translated into action in the classroom," the court declared that the state must be able to expect its teachers to "inculcate . . . principles of justice and patriotism and a respect for our laws."

† † MC DOWELL v. BOARD OF EDUCATION
104 MISC. REP., 172 N.Y.S. 590 (1918).

Judge PHILBIN delivered the opinion of the court:

Application is made for a writ of mandamus, directing the reinstatement of the petitioner as an assistant teacher of Latin in one of the high schools under the control of the board of education, from which position she was dismissed on June 19, 1918. The dismissal occurred after a trial upon which petitioner was found guilty of the charges hereinafter mentioned. The statute under which the removal was made provides, in brief, that a teacher shall hold her position—

during good behavior and efficient and competent service, and shall not be removable except for cause after a hearing by the affirmative vote of a majority of the board.

Education Law, 872. . . .

On January 19, 1918, the petitioner was required to appear before the board of superintendents, and was then and there interrogated by them as to her views upon the present war and the attitude she would take and was taking with regard to her duties as a teacher in relation to the war. The petitioner is a Quakeress, and opposed to all war, offensive and defensive. Her answers to the questions propounded to her may be summarized as follows: She would not uphold this country in forcibly resisting invasion; she did not want to help the government of the United States in carrying on the present war; she would not urge her pupils to support the war; she would not urge them to perform Red Cross services, which better the condition of the soldiers in the field; she would not urge her pupils to buy thrift stamps; she does not believe a teacher is under a special obligation to train her pupils to support the government of the United States in its measures for carrying on the war; and she is opposed to the present war against the German government.

As a result of the foregoing expressions of belief and declarations of polcy and intention, the district superintendent assigned to high schools, on March 12, 1918, suspended the petitioner without pay from further service as a teacher, and at the same time notified her that he had preferred charges against her of conduct unbecoming a teacher. He also informed her that a copy of the charges would be served, with a notice to appear for trial. On April 24, 1918, the secretary of the board of education formally notified the petitioner that she was charged with conduct unbecoming a teacher, and a copy of the charges and specifications was annexed to the notice, which also informed the petitioner of the time and place of trial. The charges and specifications are expressly based on the answers given to the questions put by the members of the board of superintendents of January 10, 1918. A stenographic report of the meeting was taken, and a copy of the questions and answers is made part of the petition to this court, and there is no dispute as to what occurred. The charge, as above indicated, is of conduct unbecoming a teacher; the specifications set forth the making of the answers enumerated above.

It is claimed that the board of education was without jurisdiction to dismiss the petitioner, as no legal ground for removal was advanced. She calls attention to the fact that teachers hold their positions during good behavior and efficient and competent service, and that thereafter a teacher must be guilty of misbehavior, of inefficiency or of incompetency before she can be removed. The petitioner urges that she was not charged with either incompetency or inefficiency, and that if her dismissal can be sustained at all it must be sustained because of misbehavior—conduct unbecoming a teacher—which she says

was the specific ground on which she was tried. The petitioner asserts that she was not guilty of any misbehavior or misconduct within the meaning of the statute. She says that her offense, if any, was to disclose the state of her mind, her beliefs, and that there is no element of behavior or conduct in a mere belief. She claims the board of education should not have condemned her until her beliefs had been translated into action in the classroom.

This contention is unsound. While it is true that the offense of the petitioner was for the sake of brevity characterized in a certain manner—as conduct unbecoming a teacher—we must look to the specifications themselves in order to find the offense charged. The seven items of the specifications leave no doubt whatever that the petitioner was charged with entertaining certain beliefs and declaring certain intentions that may very well be regarded as clearly showing her to be both incompetent and inefficient as a teacher, within the meaning of section 872, supra. The substance of the finding of the board of education is that the petitioner is unfit to remain a teacher in our public schools, and this court will not, under the circumstances, undertake to say that the board is in error.

The contention that the petitioner, in spite of her views, may still be able to do her full duty as a teacher in the classroom cannot be upheld. The grounds of removal contemplated by the statute may in a given instance be wholly unrelated to the discharge of the scholastic duties, and a teacher may be both incompetent and inefficient, even though her class shows most gratifying results in the ordinary subjects of the curriculum. It is of the utmost importance to the state that the association of teacher and pupil should tend to inculcate in the latter principles of justice and patriotism and a respect for our laws. This end cannot be accomplished, if the pupil finds his teacher unwilling to submit to constituted authority.

It is further urged that in dismissing the petitioner upon the grounds assigned there was a violation of the federal and state Constitutions, in that she was discriminated against on account of her religion, and that there was an attempted restraint upon the observance of the Quaker faith. Such is not the case. The petitioner was not dismissed because she is a Quakeress. It has simply been found that certain views and beliefs, which she declares are based upon her religion, prevent her from properly discharging the duty she assumed. Where a person agrees with the state to perform a public duty, she will not be excused from performance according to law merely because her religion forbids her doing so. While the petitioner may be entitled to the greatest respect for her adherence to her faith, she cannot be permitted because of it to act in a manner inconsistent with the peace and safety of the state.

The board of education had jurisdiction to entertain the charges against the petitioner, and its decision was an exercise of the discretion vested in it. The only remedy, therefore, of the petitioner, was to appeal to the commissioner of education. . . . Any person conceiving himself aggrieved may appeal or petition to the commissioner of education, who is authorized and required to examine and decide the same. The commissioner may also institute such proceedings as are authorized under the Education Act, and his decision is final and conclusive, and not subject to question or review in any place or court whatever. . . .

. . . The state has always regarded the maintenance of an effective education system as of the highest importance to its well-being and has insisted upon exercising a supervision over the training of its children. The plan of having such appeals referred to the commissioner was advisedly and wisely adopted. By that means it was assured that all questions relating to the schools, of which the qualification of a teacher is not the least important, could be submitted to one whose experience is daily broadened in the administration of his duties as commissioner of education and whose power fully to investigate the circumstances is unrestricted. . . .

. . . [T]his court must hold that the board of education had jurisdiction to try the petitioner, and must therefore refuse to pass upon the merits of the petitioner's removal. Petition for writ denied.

RELIGIOUS EDUCATION STIPULATIONS IN DIVORCE DECREES

A tangential question in the controversy arising recently from the compulsory education requirements has been the matter of judicial enforcement of divorce decrees stipulating that children shall be both reared and educated in a particular faith. Courts generally have been most reluctant to enter into the controversy, however.

A popular reason given for not applying strict judicial enforcement to various types of custodial agreements has been that the choice of a religion is a private matter not to be influenced in any way by legislatures or by the courts. See for example, *Hackett* v. *Hackett*, 78 Abs. (Ohio) 485, 150 N.E.2d 431 (1958).

That decision was applauded in the *Harvard Law Review* (72:372) for not enforcing a decree that allegedly would furnish a more substantial aid to religion than did the furnishing of public bus transportation to parochial schools, a practice which was upheld in restrictive language in *Everson v. Board of Education,* 330 U.S. 1 (1947).

The reviewer's conclusion was based upon the fact that the state requires school attendance, and that those so desiring may choose a religious school to fulfill their obligations. But the child who forsakes the public schools *must* attend a private school of some sort.

Another key position has been that a court should grant such modifications of the decree which would be for the child's best interests and welfare. In this connection, see *Martin* v. *Martin,* 308 N.Y. 136, 123 N.E.2d 812 (1954).

Of a somewhat different nature, see *Lynch* v. *Uhlenhopp,* 248 Ia. 68, 78 N.W.2d 491 (1956). There an Iowa custody award in a divorce decree stating that the child "shall be reared in the Roman Catholic religion" was held unenforceable in contempt proceedings against the mother. The court noted that the decree did not specify which parent would rear the child or detail the exact duties expected of the parent.

An analyst, writing in the *North Carolina Law Review* (34:509) following the district court ruling in the Lynch case that the decree was enforceable, criticized Mrs. Lynch for openly violating the divorce decree. He suggested that the court may have permitted her to rear the child in the Protestant religion had she sought a modification of the decree on the ground that the mother "found it difficult to rear him in a religion different from her own," and that it would be in the "best interest and welfare of the child" for the change to be made.

He substantiated his assertion by citing as a precedent a case involving similar facts, where the court decided to grant the modification because of the best interests and welfare of the child concerned. See *Martin v. Martin,* above. He admitted that precedents for a holding to the contrary existed, however.

The reviewer went on to note that legal writers generally agree that the award of custody in divorce proceeding will settle questions concerning the religious education of children, and that the courts should not interfere except in exceptional cases involving the "children's interest and welfare to do so."

On the other hand, in *Ramon* v. *Ramon,* Dom. Rel. Ct., 34 N.Y.S.2d 100 (1942), the New York court upheld as binding an agreement whereby the child was placed in a Roman Catholic boarding school and the father assumed the cost of his care and education. This second agreement was made after the wife had commenced proceedings against the father, who had stopped supporting both the wife and child after the mother had withdrawn the child from a Roman Catholic church. An antenuptial agreement had been made that their children would be reared in the Roman Catholic faith, even though the mother was a Protestant.

COMPULSORY DANCING PROGRAMS

The major decision concerning dancing as a required part of the public school curriculum is *Hardwick* v. *Board of School Trustees*, 54 Cal. App. 696, 205 P. 49 (1921). The California supreme court determined that the school board regulation which required dancing as a form of exercise violated the plaintiff's religious freedom as guaranteed by both the United States Constitution and the California constitution. The school did not have the right to expel children from school for refusing to dance when so ordered by their parents, the court concluded.

The court went on to say that the religious provisions of these two constitutions were not restricted just to religious organizations, but that they also applied to persons having religious convictions since religion is primarily a personal matter. The question of requiring dancing also brought in the matter of parental control which cannot be eliminated, and must be considered by school authorities in matters of character building and welfare of the children. The court suggested that other forms of exercise be substituted in place of dancing for those children who object to dancing, or whose parents object to their dancing by reason of conscience.

† † *HARDWICK* v. *BOARD OF SCHOOL TRUSTEES*
54 CAL. APP. 696, 205 P. 49 (1921).

Judge HART delivered the opinion of the court, saying in part:

The appellant, C. C. Hardwick, is and was, at the time of the initiation of this proceeding, a resident and elector of Fruitridge school district, in Sacramento county, and was and is the father of Irma Hardwick, aged 13 years, and Douglas Hardwick, aged 9 years.

These children had been, at all time down to the happening of the circum stance leading to the controversy re sponsible for this action, attending sai school as students therein. Include within the curriculum of said school as the same was established by th school authorities (the defendants, trustees), are dancing exercises, inaugurated under the supposed authority vested in the school authorities of the state by section 1668 of the Political Code, authorizing the introduction into the public schools of a system of manual or physical training.

The remaining parts of the story may best be told in the language of the petition or complaint, as follows:

That in the teaching of such dancing the said children were and are taught, among other dances, the following: 'Ace of Diamonds,' 'Minuet,' 'Norwegian Mountain March,' and 'Children's Polka,' or what was formerly known as the 'Quadrille'; that in the formation of some of said dances, girls have boys as partners at times, and when boys are not available girls are designated to represent boys so as to form couples; that in such dancing the said children are taught the 'waltz' step, the 'polka' step, the 'two-step' and what is equal to the 'fox-trot'; that after such instructions are given for a period of time said children are prepared to participate on the regular dance floor, in up-to-date dancing.

That at the direction of plaintiff and his wife, Florence A. Hardwick, the said children of plaintiff, Irma and Douglas Hardwick, sought to be excused from joining in such dancing on the grounds that such exercise was offensive to the conscientious scruples and contrary to the religious beliefs and principles of the said children and of plaintiff and his said wife. . . .

That . . . because of the refusal of the said children to join in such dancing, the said trustees expelled the said Irma Hardwick and Douglas Hardwick from attendance upon said school.

That the said children are now without authority or right to attend any public school. . . .

. . . The whole theory of the argument of the respondents seems to be that the question presented here is one of religion, and that, to state a ground for relief in this proceeding, it was requisite for the appellant to have set forth in his complaint the fact, if it be a fact, that he is a member of a religious organization which is opposed to dancing. In other words, it seems to be conceded, or substantially so, that to require pupils who are the children of persons affiliated with a religious organization which is opposed to dancing to indulge in that exercise in the public schools, on pain of expulsion therefrom, would involve an abridgment of the constitutional rights of such parents and such pupils. Indeed, assuming that the question to be decided here is solely one of religion, in our opinion no other conclusion could justly be arrived at in the face of the mandate of the federal Constitution providing that "Congress shall make no law respecting an establishment of religion, or prohibiting the free exercise thereof" (Amendment No. 1) and the positive pronouncement of our own state Constitution (article 1, § 4), providing:

The free exercise and enjoyment of religious profession and worship, without discrimination or preference, shall forever be guaranteed in this state; and no person shall be rendered incompetent to be a witness or juror on account of his opinions on matters of religious belief; but the liberty of conscience hereby secured shall not be so construed as to excuse acts of licentiousness, or justify practices inconsistent with the peace or safety of this state.

These constitutional guaranties invest every citizen of this country with the right to worship Almighty God according to the dictates of his own conscience, free from molestation or interference by the Legislature or any other power in the government, so long as such worship is not offensive to the common sentiments of civilized mankind or is not against the public peace and good order. . . . In other words, there will not be permitted to exist in the state any power the execution of which would in any way impair or destroy the right of such organization to practice such doctrine or principle and teach it to the world as an essential of a proper worship of the Creator. . . .

But the principles above stated are not alone applicable or religious organizations or to persons actively affiliated with such organizations. They apply as well to any person having religious convictions irrespective of whether he is a member of any church or other religious society. . . . A man's religion is always "personal to himself," whether he be a member of a church or not. Whom could a man's religion concern but himself? . . .

The question involved in this controversy, however, is not necessarily one of religion or whether the dances mentioned in the complaint and to which the appellant is opposed are disapproved of by the religious organization to which he belongs, if, indeed, he is a member of any such organization. It is as much a question of morals, which may concern the consciences of those who are not affiliated with any particular religious sect as well as of those who are active members of religious organizations opposed to that form of amusement or exercise.

The writer of this opinion has no prejudice or holds no feeling of hostility against any form of dancing where the same is conducted with becoming propriety, and particularly has he none

against what is known as "folk dances" (the old style of dancing which has from time immemorial been common among the people generally, such as the "quadrille" or "cotillion," the "Virginia reel," etc.), and there are many others who see no wrong in dancing where the same is properly conducted under proper circumstances. But that such performances, particularly among the younger people—those of immature judgment—where the same are indiscriminately indulged in between males and females are regarded, as we know from common knowledge, by a considerable proportion of the people as tending in no small degree to develop in the young thoughts or propensities incompatible with that higher concept of morality which is a prime desideratum of life and which should be first among the teachings of all public or private institutions having more or less to do with the molding of human character, cannot for a moment be doubted. . . . Indeed, there may be persons (and undoubtedly there are many) who have absolutely no religious convictions whatever based upon the teachings of the Good Book—in fact, even atheists and agnostics—who are opposed to their children engaging in dancing in any form or under any circumstances upon the honest belief that such performances are not conducive to the moral uplift of the young. The proposition here may well be said to be something similar to that of the introduction of card playing in the public schools as a mental exercise, assuming that such a course should be pursued. . . . Games at cards are not in and of themselves harmful where they are not played for money or other stakes. They are common in the homes and are indulged in by people of the very highest character and of the most perfect ideals, yet nothing would appall the people more than to be told that such games had been introduced into the public schools as part of their system of mental training or for the purpose of developing the power for thinking in the pupils. Indeed, such an announcement would immediately bring forth widespread and emphatic remonstrances against such an innovation—not because the people regard such a practice as being harmful per se, but because of the evil results which might and which common experience has shown often do flow therefrom, and these remonstrances would be the outgrowth, as is true of plaintiff's opposition to dancing as practiced in the Fruitridge school, of the conscientious belief that such a practice might tend to the degradation of the moral standard of the pupils.

Thus it will be readily understood that, as before declared, the important proposition involved in this controversy is no more a question of religious liberty than it is a question of morals and the liberty of conscience upon a subject upon which people have the natural and the constitutional right to hold and put into practice divergent opinions. . . . It also involves the right of parents to control their own children—to require them to live up to the teachings and the principles which are inculcated in them at home under the parental authority and according to what the parents themselves may conceive will be the course of conduct in all matters which will the better and more surely subserve the present and future welfare of their children. Can it be true that a law which vests in others the authority to teach and compel children to engage in those acts which their parents, upon what they regard as a well-founded theory, have conceived that it is not conducive to their personal welfare to adopt and follow, have specially and strictly enjoined them not to engage in, is a valid enactment? Has the state the right to enact a law or confer upon any public authorities a power the effect of which would be to alienate in a measure the children from parental authority? May the parents thus be eliminated in any measure from consideration in the matter of the discipline and education of their children along lines looking to the building up of the personal character and the advancement of the personal welfare of the latter? These questions, of course, proceed upon the assumption the the views of parents affecting the education and disciplining of their children are reasonable, relate to matters in the rearing and education of their children as to which their voice and choice should first be heeded and not offensive to the moral well-being of the children or inconsistent with the best interests of society; and to answer said questions in the affirmative would be to give sanction to a power over home life that might result in denying to parents their natural as well as their constitutional right to govern or control, within the scope of just parental authority, their own progeny. Indeed, it would be distinctly revolutionary and possibly subversive of that home life so essential to the safety and security of society and the government which regulates it, the very opposite effect of what the public school system is designed to accomplish, to hold that any such overreaching power existed in the state or any of its agencies.

Addressing ourselves now particularly to the present case, it is first observed that the appellant does not voice any objection to the practicing of the dances described in the complaint in the school from which his children were expelled. . . . He merely objects to his children being coerced by the school authorities into taking part in those exercises contrary to the teachings they have received from their parents upon that subject; and the fact that he asks that his children be excused from participating in those dances is not unreasonable. We cannot perceive wherein the granting of his wishes in that particular can tend in any degree to interfere with the established discipline of the school. As there is not (and perhaps never will be) a general objection by parents or the public to that mode of physical education, the practice of dancing may be carried on, and those not hostile to it for religious or other sufficient reasons may avail themselves of that method of developing bodily vigor; and for those objecting to dancing for substantial, but not merely capricious reasons—indeed, such an objection as is bottomed by reason prompting the appellant's opposition to dancing—there are other physical exercises which may be adopted which will as effectually "develop organic vigor, provide neuro-muscular training, promote bodily and mental poise, and correct postural defects," etc., as will the kind of dancing that is, according to the complaint, included within the system of physical education which has been adopted and is habitually practiced in the school in question. There are the calisthenics and other athletics embracing a variety of physical exercises to which no reasonable opposition on moral or religious or other grounds can be urged. Then there is the military training which, if practiced, cannot but result, not only in developing bodily vigor and "bodily and mental poise" in those participating therein, but also in inculcating in some measure at least in the youths of the country sentiments of patriotism and thus educating them along lines which may be of great practical use and of infinite advantage to them and their country at some future time. These observations are suggested, not in a spirit of dictation to the school authorities as to what method or system of physical education shall be introduced in our public schools as a part of the system, but are offered only for the purpose of showing that the school authorities, in the management of the public schools, need not be seriously or at all embarrassed or the discipline of the school disturbed by the fact that there may be some pupils who, for reasons whose source is in the conscience, may not be permitted by their parents to take part in the dancing exercises as they are taught as a part of the physical education of the public schools.

. . . Accordingly, the judgment is reversed.

REACTIONS OF LEGAL PERIODICALS TO *HARDWICK* v. *BOARD OF TRUSTEES*

The court's action drew sharp rebuke in the *California Law Review* (10:249) for using a judicial theory of parental control to justify judicial protection of otherwise constitutionally unprotected moral scruples. Noting that the California constitution "protects freedom in religion only" and not "conscientious moral scruples of the pacifist," the reviewer suggested that a parent who elects public education for his children must either adhere to the prescribed course of study or else challenge the validity of the courses with an adequate statement of the grievances.

He went on to say, however, that a school should offer optional forms of physical education to avoid any constitutional conflict with the rights of religious liberty that could arise when any particular type of activity conflicts with the religious tenets of any students.

PHYSICAL EDUCATION PROGRAMS AND DRESS

A 1962 decision, *Mitchell* v. *McCall,* 273 Ala. 604, 143 So.2d 629 (1962), is the only case to date which has entertained the question of a similar nature concerning physical education and dress in reference to religion. A petition for writ of mandamus ordering readmittance to high school of petitioner's daughter was denied by a lower court. The daughter was expelled for refusing on religious grounds: to wear the prescribed physical education dress, to perform certain exercises, and to attend the physical education classes. However, the school authorities offered to exempt her from wearing the required uniform and performing the certain exercises. These concessions were incorporated by the lower court, which then ordered the readmittance of the girl and required her attendance at the physical education classes subject to the above conditions.

The Alabama state supreme court, in *Mitchell* v. *McCall,* affirmed the lower court's denial of the writ. In doing so, the court held that the state law, requiring public and private schools to have physical education courses following the format prescribed by the department of education was reasonable, and that its scope was within the authority of the state's responsibilities.

While admitting that compulsory attendance at such classes could offend some religious beliefs, the court determined that such action did not violate the appellant's rights under the First and Fourteenth Amendments. The court concluded that the daughter was required to attend the physical education course with the concessions made by the school authorities and incorporated by the lower court, as basic grounds for its decision that she not be required to wear the repugnant apparel nor be required to participate in those exercises regarded by her or her parents as immodest when performed in ordinary clothing.

† † *MITCHELL* v. *MC CALL*

273 ALA. 604, 143 SO.2D 629 (1962).

Mr. Chief Justice LIVINGSTON delivered the opinion of the court:

. . . .

Appellant's daughter, Eulene, was suspended from Vigor High School, a public school in Mobile County, for refusing to participate in the physical education program lawfully prescribed for that school. This refusal was originally based upon the three objections which follow:

A. A refusal to wear the costume prescribed for the students while participating in the course on the ground that said costume is immodest and sinful according to the religious beliefs of the appellant.

B. A refusal to perform certain physical exercises on the same grounds as listed above.

C. A further refusal to attend the physical education course because such attendance would require appellant's daughter to be in the presence of the other girls and the instructress who wore the prescribed costume and performed all the exercises.

The school authorities offered to allow appellant's daughter to wear clothing which appellant would consider modest and suitable, and further agreed that she would not have to perform any exercises that seemed to her or her parents immodest for a girl to perform when clad in ordinary feminine clothing.

The court below incorporated these concessions in its decree and ordered the school authorities to readmit the girl on the further condition that she would attend the physical education course and participate therein subject to the concessions. Since these concessions were made by the school board and adopted by the lower court, and since no complaint is made of them here, this Court is not concerned with the concessions and expresses no opinion on their legality or illegality.

Appellant appeals from the decree of the lower court on the theory that the requirement that his daughter attend and participate in the course in the presence of the other girls and the instructress violates her freedom of religious belief secured to her by Art. 1, Sec. 3 of the Constitution of Alabama 1901, and the First and Fourteenth Amendments of the Constitution of the United States.

Appellant vigorously argues what he describes as his constitutional right to have his children educated in the public schools of the state. In this connection, it should be observed that the State of Alabama is under no constitutional obligation to provide public schools. . . .

Clearly, appellant's daughter does have a right to make use of such facilities if they are in fact provided by the state. However, appellant's daughter is free to refrain from attending the public schools since Alabama does not require public school attendance. . . . Her attendance in a public school is therefore voluntary. . . .

Sec. 555 of Title 52, Code of Alabama 1940, provides as follows:

Every public school and private or parochial school shall carry out a system of physical education, the character of which shall conform to the program or course outlined by the department of education.

. . . .

In *Desribes* v. *Wilmer*, 69 Ala. 25, page 26, Justice Stone stated the following:

. . . All religions, save such as shock the public morals, *or offend our statutes,* are alike tolerated and protected by the broad philanthropy of our republican policy. . . . We disturb no man's faith, unless it is manifest in acts which violate municipal regulation. We deal with the physical and secular, and not with the mere moral which is not uttered in voice or act, *offensive to our legislative policy.* (Emphasis supplied.)

The legislation involved in the case at bar is unquestionably reasonable, and it touches only matters which are the legitimate concern and responsibility of the state and its agencies.

This is not the first instance of exacting obedience to general laws that have offended deep religious scruples. Compulsory vaccination, see *Jacobson* v. *Massachusetts,* 197 U.S. 11, 25 S.Ct. 358, 49 L.Ed. 643, 3 Ann. Cas. 756; food inspection regulations, see *Shapiro* v. *Lyle* (D.C.) 30 F. 2d 971; the obligation to bear arms, see *Hamilton* v. *Regents of University of California,* 293 U.S. 245, 267, 55 S.Ct. 197, 79 L.Ed. 343, 355; testimonial duties, see *Stansbury* v. *Marks,* 2 Dall. 213, 1 L.Ed. 353; compulsory medical treatment, see *People* v. *Vogelgesang,* 221 N.Y. 290, 116 N.E. 977—these are but illustrations of conduct that has often been compelled in the enforcement of legislation of general applicability even though the religious consciences of particular individuals rebelled at the exaction.

Every precaution has been taken to insure that the course is conducted in a manner consistent with modesty and good taste. The classes which Eulene Mitchell, appellant's daughter, is required to attend are composed entirely of girls and the teacher is also a female. When the class is conducted in the gymnasium, the girls are completely excluded from male eyes, and when conducted outdoors, there is a school building between the girls and the boys. In spite of these facts, reasonable concession has been made to appellant's religious beliefs, and this Court therefore holds that the legislative policy overrides appellant's objections, and Art. 1, Sec. 3 of the Constitution of Alabama 1901 has not been violated.

It is the opinion of this court that appellant's rights under the First and Fourteenth Amendments of the United States Constitution have not been infringed. In *Hamilton* v. *Regents of University of California,* supra, the Supreme Court of the United States unanimously held that a student attending a state-maintained university cannot refuse to attend required courses in military training on the ground that such courses offend his religious beliefs. Later, the Supreme Court of the United States held that the First and Fourteenth Amendments were violated by a West Virginia Statute which required all public school pupils to salute the flag of the United States and recite a pledge of allegiance. This requirement was held to violate the freedom of pupils who considered such conduct to be contrary to their religious beliefs. *West Virginia State Board of Education* v. *Barnette,* 319 U.S. 624, 63 S.Ct. 1178, 87 L.Ed. 1628. However, the Hamilton case, supra, was specifically distinguished on the basis that attendance at the state institution in question in that case was voluntary, and therefore a pupil could not refuse to comply with the reasonable conditions lawfully required and still demand admission.

The Hamilton decision is therefore authority for the proposition that the State of Alabama can place reasonable, nondiscriminatory conditions on the privilege of attending public schools since such attendance is voluntary.

Moreover, even if this is not the case, *West Virginia State Bd. of Education* v. *Barnette,* supra, is clearly distinguishable on its facts. The statute involved in that case, as construed by the court, was invalid because it called for a compulsory statement of belief. There is nothing analogous to that in the case at bar. Indeed, the Barnette case, supra, would only be analogous if the complaining pupils in that case had further alleged that it was unconstitutional to require them to be present when other students professed their allegiance. The Alabama Constitution and the United States Constitution do not require such a result. Indeed, a decision supporting such an allegation would place an intolerable burden on the state and federal governments in the discharge of their responsibilities to the people of the state and the nation. Such a decision would give every citizen the power to nullify all state and federal legislation by simply asserting in a court of law that the behavior required is contrary to his religious beliefs. A power of nullification of such extreme scope would undermine the very foundation of our "democratic" institutions and undercut the very concept of ordered liberty protected by our state and federal constitutions.

Every reasonable concession has been made to the appellant in this case.

This Court cannot go further and hold that appellant's religious belief that his daughter should not be placed in the presence of others whose dress and behavior is contrary to his scruples imposes upon the school the legal obligation to conduct a separate class in conformity with appellant's belief.

Appellant further complains that unless the school is required to conduct a separate class composed of those who share his and his daughter's belief that she will be made to appear a "speckled bird," and will be subject to the contumely of her fellow students.

All citizens in so far as they hold views different from the majority of their fellows are subject to such inconveniences. And this is especially true of those who hold religious or moral beliefs which are looked upon with disdain by the majority. It is precisely every citizen's right to be a "speckled bird" that our constitutions, state and federal, seek to insure. And solace for the embarrassment that is attendant upon holding such beliefs must be found by the individual citizen in his own moral courage and strength of conviction, and not in a court of law.

Our conclusion is, that in the posture of this case, the appellant's daughter is not required to participate in the exercises which would be immodest in ordinary apparel, nor is she required to wear the prescribed outfit. However, subject to these concessions previously made she is obligated to attend the course in physical education. . . .

The decision of the lower court is affirmed.

TEACHING THEORIES OF EVOLUTION

The celebrated Scopes trial of 1927 created a national furor; not so much over the constitutional issue of governmental aid to religion, but rather over the validity of the Darwinian theory of evolution. In *Scopes v. State*, 154 Tenn. 105, 289 S.W. 363 (1927), the Tennessee supreme court determined that the state law forbidding the teaching of evolution in public schools did not violate the state constitutional provision prohibiting giving preference to any religious establishment or mode of worship, and did not violate the Due Process Clause of the Fourteenth Amendment of the federal Constitution.

The court reasoned that as far as it could determine, no religious body either affirmed or denied the theory of evolution as a part of its creed or confession of faith. Therefore, belief or disbelief in this theory could not be considered characteristic to any particular religion. Also, while the theory could not be taught by law, nothing contrary to that theory was required to be taught. The court then concluded that no preference was given to any religion or mode of worship.

However, the court reversed the lower court's decision because of the trial judge's error in imposing the minimum $100 fine that the jury failed to assess. By state statute, only a jury could levy fines exceeding $50, the Tennessee high court concluded.

† † *SCOPES* v. *STATE*
154 T.N. 105, 289 S.W. 363 (1927).

Judge GREEN delivered the opinion of the court, saying in part:

Scopes was convicted of a violation of chapter 27 of the Acts of 1925, for that he did teach in the public schools of Rhea county a certain theory that denied the story of the divine creation of man, as taught in the Bible, and did teach instead thereof that man had descended from a lower order of animals. After a verdict of guilty by the jury, the trial judge imposed a fine of $100, and Scopes brought the case to this court by an appeal in the nature of a writ of error.

. . .While the act [known as the Tennessee Anti-Evolution Act] was not drafted with as much care as could have been desired, nevertheless there seems to be no great difficulty in determining its meaning. It is entitled:

An act prohibiting the teaching of the evolution theory in all the Universities, normals and all other public schools in Tennessee, which are supported in whole or in part by the public school funds of the state, and to provide penalties for the violations thereof.

Evolution, like prohibition, is a broad term. In recent bickering, however, evolution has been understood to mean the theory which holds that man has developed from some preexisting lower type. This is the popular significance of evolution, just as the popular significance of prohibition is prohibition of the traffic in intoxicating liquors. It was in that sense that evolution was used in this act. It is in this sense that the word will be used in this opinion, unless the context otherwise indicates. It is only to the theory of the evolution of man from a lower type that the act before us was intended to apply, and much of the discussion we have heard is beside this case. . . .

Thus defining evolution, this act's title clearly indicates the purpose of the statute to be the prohibition of teaching in the schools of the state that man has developed or descended from some lower type or order of animals.

. . . Supplying the ellipsis in section 1 of the act, [the act] reads that it shall be unlawful for any teacher, etc.—

to teach any theory that denies the story of the divine creation of man as taught in the Bible, and to teach instead [of the story on the divine creation of man as taught in the Bible] that man has descended from a lower order of animals.

. . . The undertaking of the statute was to prevent teaching of the evolution theory. It was considered this purpose could be effected by forbidding the teaching of any theory that denied the Bible story, but to make the purpose clear it was also forbidden to teach that man descended from a lower order of animals.

. . . It thus seems plain that the Legislature in this enactment only intended to forbid teaching that men descended from a lower order of animals. The denunciation of any theory denying the Bible story of creation is restricted by the caption and by the final clause of section 1.

So interpreted, the statute does not seem to be uncertain in its meaning nor incapable of enforcement for such a reason notwithstanding the argument to the contrary. . . .

It is contended that the statute violates section 8 of article 1 of the Tennessee Constitution, and section 1 of the Fourteenth Amendment of the Constitution of the United States—the law of the land clause of the federal Constitution, which are practically equivalent in meaning.

We think there is little merit in this contention. The plaintiff in error was a teacher in the public schools of Rhea county. He was an employee of the state of Tennessee or of a municipal agency of the state. He was under contract with the state to work in an institution of the state. He had no right or privilege to serve the state except upon such terms as the state prescribed. His liberty, his privilege, his immunity to teach and proclaim the theory of evolution, elsewhere than in the service of the state, was in no wise touched by this law.

The statute before us is not an exercise of the police power of the state undertaking to regulate the conduct and contracts of individuals in their dealings with each other. On the other hand, it is an act of the state as a corporation, a proprietor, an employer. . . . In dealing with its own employees engaged upon its own work, the state is not hampered by the limitations of section 8 of article 1 of the Tennessee Constitution, nor of the Fourteenth Amendment to the Constitution of the United States.

. . . Since the state may prescribe the character and the hours of labor of the employees on its works, just as freely may it say what kind of work shall be performed in its service, what shall be taught in its schools, so far at least as section 8 of article 1 of the Tennessee Constitution, and the Fourteenth Amendment to the Constitution of the United States, are concerned.

But it is urged that chapter 27 of the Acts of 1925 conflicts with section 12 of article 11, the educational clause, and section 8 of article 1, the religious clause of the Tennessee Constitution. It is to be doubted if the plaintiff in error, before us only as the state's employee, is sufficiently protected by these constitutional provisions to justify him in raising such questions. Nevertheless, as the state appears to concede that these objections are properly here made, the court will consider them.

The relevant portion of section 12 of article 11 of the Constitution is in these words:

". . . It shall be the duty of the General Assembly in all future periods of this government, to cherish literature and science."

The argument is that the theory of the descent of man from a lower order of animals is now established by the preponderance of scientific thought and that the prohibition of the teaching of such theory is a violation of the legislative duty to cherish science.

While this clause of the Constitution has been mentioned in several of our cases, these references have been casual, and no act of the Legislature has ever been held inoperative by reason of such provision. . . .

. . . If the Legislature thinks that, by reason of popular prejudice, the cause of education and the study of science generally will be promoted by forbidding the teaching of evolution in the schools of the state, we can conceive of no ground to justify the court's interference. The courts cannot sit in judgement on such acts of the Legislature or its agents and determine whether or not the omission or addition of a particular course of study tends "to cherish science."

The last serious criticism made of the act is that it contravenes the provision of section 3 of article 1 of the Constitution, "that no preference shall ever be given, by law, to any religious establishment or mode of worship."

The language quoted is a part of our Bill of Rights, was contained in the first Constitution of the state adopted in 1796, and has been brought down into the present Constitution.

. . . We are not able to see how the prohibition of teaching the theory that man has descended from a lower order of animals gives preference to any religious establishment or mode of worship. So far as we know, there is no religious establishment or organized body that has in its creed or confession of faith any article denying or affirming such a theory. So far as we know, the denial or affirmation of such a theory does not enter into any recognized mode of worship. Since this cause has been pending in this court, we have been favored, in addition to briefs of counsel and various amici curiae, with a multitude of resolutions, addresses, and communications from scientific bodies, religious factions, and individuals giving us the benefit of their views upon the theory of evolution. Examination of these contributions indicates that Protestants, Catholics, and Jews are divided among themselves in their beliefs, and that there is no unanimity among the members of any religious establishment as to this subject. Belief or unbelief in the theory of evolution is no more a characteristic of any religious establishment or mode of worship than is belief or unbelief in the wisdom of the prohibition laws.

It would appear that members of the same churches quite generally disagree as to these things.

Furthermore, chapter 277 of the Acts of 1925 *requires* the teaching of nothing. It only *forbids* the teaching of the evolution of man from a lower order of animals. Chapter 102 of the Acts of 1915 requires that ten verses from the Bible be read each day at the opening of every public school, without comment, and provided the teacher does not read the same verses more than twice during any session. It is also provided in this act that pupils may be excused from the Bible readings upon the written request of their parents.

As the law thus stands, while the theory of evolution of man may not be taught in the schools of the state, nothing contrary to that theory is required to be taught. It could scarcely be said that the statutory scriptural reading just mentioned would amount to teaching of a contrary theory.

Our school authorities are therefore quite free to determine how they shall act in this state of the law. . . . If they believe that the teaching of the science of biology has been hampered by chapter 27 of the Acts of 1925 as to render such an effort no longer desirable, this course of study may be entirely omitted from the curriculum of our schools. If this be regarded as a misfortune, it must be charged to the Legislature. It should be repeated that the Act of 1925 deals with nothing but the evolution of man from a lower order of animals.

It is not necessary now to determine the exact scope of the religious preference clause of the Constitution and other language of that section. The situation does not call for such an attempt. Section 3 of article 1 is binding alike on the Legislature and the school authorities. So far we are clear that the Legislature has not crossed these constitutional limitations. If hereafter the school authorities should go beyond such limits, a case can then be brought to the courts. . . .

THE NATIONAL ANTHEM AND RELIGIOUS FREEDOM

The plaintiffs in *Sheldon* v. *Fannin*, 221 F. Supp. 766 (1963), were suspended from school for refusing to stand for the singing of the national anthem. They claimed that as Jehovah's Witnesses, their religion would not let them participate in the singing even by standing. Therefore, by being suspended, they were deprived of their First Amendment rights.

The United States district court determined that the singing of the national anthem was a patriotic, not a religious ceremony. Therefore, the anthem could be sung in public schools and prescribed participation in the singing did not violate the establishment clause of the First Amendment. However, the court further stated that the First Amendment guaranteed a religious sect the right to base their objections to standing in public schools during the singing of the national anthem upon religious belief. The sincerity or reasonableness of such a claim could not be examined by a court to determine if First Amendment rights have been violated.

The court concluded, however, that the suspension of the students for refusing to stand during the singing of the national anthem, in accordance with their religious beliefs as Jehovah's Witnesses, violated the First Amendment rights of the students.

† † *SHELDON* v. *FANNIN*
221 F. SUPP. 766 (1963).

Judge MATHES delivered the opinion of the court:

This is a suit for injunctive relief, brought pursuant to the Civil Rights Act of 1871. . . .

. . . .

The defendants are the Arizona State Board of Education, the individual members thereof, the Superintendent of Public Instruction of the State of Arizona, the Board of Trustees of Pinetop Elementary School, a public grade school of Pinetop, Arizona, and the individual members thereof.

The facts are without controversy, and may be briefly stated. On September 29, 1961, the plaintiffs were suspended from Pinetop Elementary School for insubordination, because of their refusal to stand for the singing of the National Anthem. This refusal to participate, even to the extent of standing, without singing, is said to have been dictated by their religious beliefs as Jehovah's Witnesses, requiring their literal acceptance of the Bible as the Word of Almighty God Jehovah. Both precedent and authority for their refusal to stand is claimed to be found in the refusal of the three Hebrew children Shadrach, Meshach and Abed-nego, to bow down at the sound of musical instruments playing patriotic-religious music throughout the land at the order of King Nebuchadnezzar of ancient Babylon. [Daniel 3:13–28.] For a similar reason, members of the Jehovah's Witnesses sect refuse to recite the Pledge of Allegiance to the Flag of the United States, viewing this patriotic ceremony to be the worship of a graven image. [Exodus 20:4–5.] However, by some process of reasoning we need not tarry to explore, they are willing to stand during the Pledge of Allegiance, out of respect for the Flag as a symbol of the religious freedom they enjoy. . . .

The plaintiffs were expelled from Pinetop Elementary School solely because of their refusal to stand for the National Anthem. They were not accused of any other misconduct of any kind, and were in no scholastic difficulty. They have since continued their education at home, and are therefore subject to a charge of truancy and delinquency under Arizona law for failing to attend school until they have passed the compulsory education age.

Their parents too face possible prosecution for a violation of Arizona's school laws. . . .

. . . .

The plaintiffs also allege that their conduct does not present any clear or present danger to the orderly operation of the school, which the State has the Constitutional power to prevent, and they deny that their refusal to stand while other pupils sing the Star Spangled Banner is conduct which is in anywise contrary to morals, health, safety or welfare of the public, the State, or the Nation.

. . . .

Turning now to the merits, I like to recall that the founding fathers inscribed upon the Great Seal of the United States the Latin phrase *novus ordo seclorum*—"a new order of the ages." This proud boast proclaimed their pride and their faith in the new nation they had founded here—a nation where everyone from the highest official to the most humble citizen must act under and in accordance with the law.

The keystone of this "new order" has always been freedom of expression —the widest practicable individual freedom to believe, to speak, to act.

Our forbears realized that ideas for preservation and improvement of a free society must come, not from the government, but from the people, and must compete for acceptance by the people, just as goods and services compete for acceptance in our free-enterprise economy. They realized too that in order to compete for acceptance, these ideas must be freely expressed by act and deed; that only in this way can the truth prevail; that only in this

way can an idea despised today win the acceptance of reason tomorrow, or be thoroughly discredited; and that only by protecting the freedom of the smallest minority to express unpopular ideas by word or deed can the majority insure freedom to believe and express its own ideas, and to dispute and criticize those of others. . . .

This principle of freedom of belief and expression was so esteemed by the founding fathers that it was embodied in the First Amendment to the Constitution of the United States with the unqualified declaration that:

Congress shall make no law respecting an establishment of religion, or prohibiting the free exercise thereof; or abridging the freedom of speech, or of the press; or the right of the people peaceably to assemble, and petition the Government for a redress of grievances.

And these freedoms have since been held protected against State action by the Fourteenth Amendment. . . .

However, the unqualified declaration of the First Amendment has never been literally enforced. . . . The right to believe, to speak, to act, in the exercise of freedom of expression, like all legal rights under our common-law system of justice, presupposes the correlative legal duty always to do whatever is reasonable, and to refrain from doing whatever is unreasonable, under the circumstances; and hence these fundamental rights are ever subject to such abridgements or restraints as are dictated by reason. . . .

But we so prize freedom of expression—deem it so essential to the maintenance of "a government of laws and not of men"—that the bounds of restraint upon First Amendment rights which will be tolerated as reasonable are narrow in the extreme.

If there is any fixed star in our constitutional constellation, it is that no official, high or petty, can prescribe what shall be orthodox in politics, nationalism, religion, or other matters of opinion or force citizens to confess by word or act their faith therein.

[*West Virginia State Board of Education* v. *Barnette*, 319 U.S. 624, 642 (1943).]

It was in *Schenck* v. *United States* [249 U.S. 47, 52 (1919)]—a prosecution under the Espionage Act of 1917 . . . —that the criteria of permissible restraint upon freedom of expression were stated by Mr. Justice Holmes:

The question in every case is whether the words used are used in such circumstances and are of such a nature as to create a clear and present danger that they will bring about the substantive evils that Congress has a right to prevent. It is a question of proximity and degree.

"This is a rule of reason," Mr. Justice Brandeis later wrote, adding:

Correctly applied, it will preserve the right of free speech both from suppression by tyrannous, well-meaning majorities and from abuse by irresponsible, fanatical minorities. . . . [I]t can be applied correctly only by the exercise of good judgment; and to the exercise of good judgment, calmness is, in times of deep feeling and on subjects which excite passion, as essential as fearlessness and honesty.

The standard of permissible restraint upon freedom of speech applies as well to freedom of religion. Thus, although the State may not establish a religion, it may curtail religious expressions by word or deed which create a clear and present danger of impairing the public health or safety, or of offending widely accepted moral codes, or of resulting in a more-than-negligible breach of the peace. . . .

Notwithstanding offense to certain religious beliefs, the State may declare a uniform day of rest for its citizens . . . regulate the practice of polygamy . . . regulate child labor . . . and require military training upon attendance at non-compulsory schools. . . .

Where, however, a particular application of a general law not protective of some fundamental State concern materially abridges free expression or practice of religious belief, than the law must give way to the exercise of religion. . . .

Clearly, then, if the refusal to participate in the ceremony attendant upon the singing or playing of the National Anthem had not occurred in a public-school classroom, but in some other public or private place, there would be not the slightest doubt that the plaintiffs were free to participate or not as they chose. Every citizen is free to stand or sit, sing or remain silent, when the Star Spangled Banner is played.

But the case at bar involves refusal to participate in a public-school classroom ceremony. Relying upon the recent "school-prayer" decisions [*School District of Abington* v. *Schempp*, 374, U.S. 203 (1963); *Engel* v. *Vitale*, 370 U.S. 421 (1962)], the plaintiffs first argue that the National Anthem contains words of prayer, adoration and reverence for the Deity, and that a State's prescription of participation therein amounts to a prohibited "establishment of religion." This contention must be rejected. The singing of the National Anthem is not a religious but a patriotic ceremony, intended to inspire devotion to and love of country. Any religious references therein are incidental and expressive only of the faith which as a matter of historical fact has inspired the growth of the nation. [Cf., *Engel* v. *Vitale,* 370 U.S. 421, at 435, n. 21. . . .] The Star Spangled Banner may be freely sung in the public schools, without fear of having the ceremony charcterized as an "establishment of religion" which violates the First Amendment.

The plaintiffs next urge that coercing their participation, even to the extent of requiring them on pain of expulsion merely to stand while the other pupils sing the Star Spangled Banner, unreasonably abridges their rights to the free exercise of religion under the First Amendment. In considering this contention, it should be observed that lack of violation of the "establishment clause" does not *ipso facto* preclude violation of the "free-exercise clause." For the former looks to the majority's concept of the term religion, the latter the minority's.

In view of the plaintiffs' avowed willingness to stand for the Pledge of Allegiance to the Flag, it may strain credulity that their claim of religious objection to standing as well for the National Anthem is bona fide or sincere. But all who live under the protection of our Flag are free to believe whatever they may choose to believe and to express that belief, within the limits of free expression, no matter how unfounded or even ludicrous the professed belief may seem to others. While implicitly demanding that all freedom of expression be exercised reasonably under the circumstances, the Constitution fortunately does not require that the beliefs or thoughts expressed be reasonable, or wise, or even sensible. The

First Amendment thus guarantees to the plaintiffs the right to claim that their objection to standing is based upon religious belief, and the sincerity or reasonableness of this claim may not be examined by this or any other Court. . . .

Accepting, then, the plaintiffs' characterization of their conduct as religiously inspired, this case is ruled by *West Virginia State Board of Education* v. *Barnette,* where the Supreme Court held unconstitutional the expulsion of Jehovah's Witnesses from a public school for refusal to recite the Pledge of Allegiance to the Flag. The decision there rested not merely upon the "free-exercise clause," but also upon the principle inherent in the entire First Amendment: that governmental authority may not directly coerce the unwilling expression of any belief, even in the name of "national unity" in time of war.

Manifestly, the State's interest was much stronger in Barnette than in the case at bar. The sole justification offered by the defendants here is the opinion of the school authorities that to tolerate refusal of these plaintiffs to stand for the National Anthem would create a disciplinary problem. Evidence as to this is speculative at best and pales altogether when balanced against the "preferred position" of First Amendment rights. . . . Indeed, there is much to be said for the view that, rather than creating a disciplinary problem, acceptance of the refusal of a few pupils to stand while the remainder stand and sing of their devotion to flag and country might well be turned into a fine lesson in American Government for the entire class.

. . . .

Since it appears that the conduct of

the pupils involved here was not disorderly and did not materially disrupt the conduct and discipline of the school, and since there is a lack of substantial evidence that it will do so in the future, a writ of injunction will issue permanently restraining the Board of Trustees of Pinetop Elementary School from excluding the plaintiffs from attendance at the school solely because they silently refuse to rise and stand for the playing or singing of the National Anthem. The injunction will run against the defendant members of the Board of Trustees only since, as the three-judge panel found, it is their action alone which brought about the expulsion. . . .

LITERARY CLASSICS AND RELIGION

Rosenberg et al. v. *Board of Education*, 92 N.Y.S.2d 344 (1949), dealt with the question of allowing certain books in public and secondary school libraries of New York City. The petitioners applied for an order to review pursuant to the Civil Practice Act, the choice of *Oliver Twist* by Charles Dickens and *The Merchant of Venice* by Shakespeare for use in study and in school libraries. They contended that offensive characters in the books fostered a hatred for Jews.

The New York court denied the motion for review and dismissed the petition. The court held that the respondents in no way abused their discretion in permitting the two particular books to be used in the schools even though they portrayed certain characters in a derogatory fashion. The apparent aim of the respective authors did not seem to be that of promoting racial or religious bigotry. Any suppression must be based upon a clear malevolent intent by the author's portrayal, not just because some unduly sensitive people feel that the literature is offensive to a racial or religious group.

The court concluded that the discretion of administrative officials of public schools must not be interfered with by a court in absence of proof of actual malevolent intent.

† † ROSENBERG v. BOARD OF EDUCATION
196 MISC. 542, 92, N.Y.S.2D 344 (1949).

Judge DI GIOVANNA delivered the opinion of the court:

This is an application pursuant to Article 78 of the Civil Practice Act for review of a determination permitting and allowing the use of "Oliver Twist" by Charles Dickens and "The Merchant of Venice" by William Shakespeare, in the secondary schools of the City of New York as approved reading and study material.

In exercising its duty under Section 2516, subd. 3, of the Education Law, the respondents select text books regarded as preferable for instruction of pupils in English and English literature. These two books were selected together with many others.

Petitioner charges that the two books are objectionable because they tend to engender hatred of the Jew as a person and as a race.

It is not contended herein that the respondents, collectively or individually, approved the books because of anti-religious or anti-racial inclinations. As a matter of fact, because of public discussion concerning books of this nature, respondents have expressly required teachers to explain to pupils that the characters described therein are not typical of any nation or race, including persons of the Jewish faith, and are not intended and are not to be regarded as reflecting discredit on any race or national group.

Except where a book has been maliciously written for the apparent purpose of promoting and fomenting a bigoted and intolerant hatred against a particular racial or religion group, public interest in a free and democratic society does not warrant or encourage the suppression of any book at the whim of any unduly sensitive person or group of persons, merely because a character described in such book as belonging to a particular race or religion is portrayed in a derogatory or offensive manner. The necessity for the suppression of such a book must clearly depend upon the intent and motive which has actuated the author in making such a portrayal.

Literary value of a work of fiction does not depend upon the religious or national origin of the characters portrayed therein. If evaluation of any literary work is permitted to be based upon a requirement that each book be free from derogatory reference to any religion, race, country, nation or personality, endless litigation respecting many books would probably ensue, dependent upon sensibilities and views of the person suing.

Public education and instruction in the home will remove religious and racial intolerance more effectively than censorship and suppression of literary works which have been accepted as works of art and which are not per se propaganda against or for any race, religion or group. Removal from schools of these books will contribute nothing toward the diminution of anti-religious feeling; as a matter of fact, removal may lead to misguided reading and unwarranted inferences by the unguided pupil.

Educational institutions are concerned with the development of free inquiry and learning. The administrative officers must be free to guide teachers and pupils toward that goal. Their discretion must not be interfered with in the absence of proof of actual malevolent intent. Interference by the court will result in suppression of the intended purpose of aiding those seeking education.

The Court therefore finds that respondents, in exercising their judgment, did not abuse their discretion; that they acted in good faith without malice or prejudice and in the best interests of the school system entrusted to their care and control, and, therefore, that no substantial reason exists which compels the suppression of the two books under consideration. Motion for review is denied and the petition is dismissed.

THE BIBLE IN PUBLIC SCHOOL LIBRARIES

In *Evans* v. *Selma Union High School District*, 193 Cal. 54, 222 P. 801 (1924), the California supreme court was faced with the question of whether the King James Version of the Bible was of sectarian character and as such not allowed in public school libraries under the state constitutional provision which prohibited using public funds for sectarian purposes and excluded sectarian books from the libraries. The court ruled that the King James Version of the Bible was not sectarian even though it was accepted by certain religions and rejected by others. "The mere act of purchasing a book to be added to the school library does not carry with it any implication of the adoption of the theory or dogma contained therein, or any approval of the book itself, except as a work of literature fit to be included in a reference library."

† † *EVANS* v. *SELMA UNION HIGH SCHOOL DISTRICT*
193 CAL. 54, 222 P. 801 (1924).

The opinion of the court was given per curiam:

Plaintiff brought this action to enjoin the trustees of the Selma Union high school district of Fresno county from carrying into effect a resolution for the purchase of 12 copies of the Bible in the King James version for the library of the high school. . . . Both complaints rest on the contention that the King James version of the Bible is a book of a sectarian character, and that its purchase for the library of a public school is therefore contrary to constitutional and statutory provisions in this state.

The trial court held that the Bible in the King James version was not a publication of sectarian, partisan, or denominational character, and accordingly gave judgment for the defendants. This appeal is from that judgment.

The Constitution of this state provides (Article 1, § 4) that—

The free exercise and enjoyment of religious profession and worship, without discrimination or preference, shall forever be guaranteed in this state.

It prohibits (Article 4, § 30) appropriations, grants, or payments of public moneys in aid of any "religious sect, church, creed, or sectarian purpose," or to support or sustain any school or other institution "controlled by any religious creed, church, or sectarian denomination whatever." In section 8 of article 9 it provides that—

No public money shall ever be appropriated for the support of any sectarian or denominational school, or any school not under the exclusive control of the officers of the public schools; nor shall any sectarian or denominational doctrine be taught, or instruction thereon be permitted, directly or indirectly, in any of the common schools of this state.

Political Code, § 1607 . . . makes it the duty of boards of education and school trustees—

to exclude from school and school libraries all books, publications, or papers of a sectarian, partisan, or denominational character.

Section 1672 of the same Code provides that—

No publication of a sectarian, partisan, or denominational character must be used or distributed in any school, or be made a part of any school library; nor must any sectarian or denominational doctrine be taught therein.

The question before us is different from those dealt with in the reported cases which consider the question of Bible instruction in the public schools. We have examined with care all decisions cited by counsel and all that our independent research has discovered, and not one of them deals with the precise question now under consideration, namely, the placing of the Bible in a public school library. These decisions all deal with questions growing out of the use of the Bible in devotional exercises or for religious instruction or as a text-book in the public schools; for that reason we do not discuss these decisions in detail in arriving at our conclusion, although some of these decisions consider and decide whether or not the Bible is sectarian. In our opinion, for the reasons hereafter stated, it is clear that for reference and library purposes in the public schools, it is not a book of the class prohibited by our statute.

It will be seen from the provisions of our statutes above quoted that they do not in terms exclude from these schools "religious" books as such. Indeed, there is nothing in our statutes aimed at religious works. To be legally objectionable they must be "sectarian, partisan, or denominational in character." It is under our Code provisions that this question immediately arises, and their terms must be construed with their intent and purpose in view and the mischief at which they were aimed. The terms used are "sectarian" and "denominational." "Sect," strictly defined, means "a body of persons distinguished by peculiarities of faith and practice from other bodies adhering to the same general system" (Standard Dict.), and "denominational" is given much the same definition. But the term "sect" has frequently a broader signification, the activities of the followers of one faith being regarded as sectarian as related to those of the adherents of another. Since the object of these Code provisions was to exclude controversial matters of any kind from the school libraries; in so far as that object could be attained by the exclusion of printed matter of partisan tendency, we have no doubt that the term "sectarian" was used in its broad signification. The purpose was to bar from school libraries books and other publications of factional religion—those whose character is "sectarian, partisan, or denominational." As a book on almost any subject may adopt a partisan tone, so a book on religion, instead of confining itself to broad principles and simple fundamentals, may emphasize particular points—those upon which differences of opinion have arisen. In a word, a book on any subject may be strongly partisan in tone and treatment. A religious book treating its subject in this manner would be sectarian. But not all books of religion would be thus excluded. The fact that it was not approved by all sects of a particular religion, nor by the followers of all religions, would not class it as sectarian for library purposes. There is no religion that has found universal acceptance, and therefore no book of religion that has.

· · · · · · · · · · · · ·

Turning to the character of the King James version, it appears that the original manuscripts of the Bible have been lost for centuries. Those available for translation are themselves "versions," and either copies or translations or still older texts. There have been numerous English translations, but those most generally in use today are the King James version, and its subsequent English and American revisions, and the Douai version.

The Douai version consists of a translation of the New Testament made in the English College at Rheims, published there in 1582, and of the Old Testament published at Douai in 1609.

The King James version is a translation made at the direction of James I of England, and published at London in 1611. The work was done by a commission of forty-seven scholars drawn largely from the universities of Oxford and Cambridge. The work of its revision by English and American committees was begun in 1870, and the revised New Testament published in 1881, and the revised Old Testament in 1884.

The Douai version is based upon the text of the Latin Vulgate, the King James version on the Hebrew and Greek texts. There are variances in the rendering of certain phrases and passages. The Douai version incorporates the Apocrypha, which are omitted from the texts of the Testaments in the King James version, though in many editions they have been printed between the two Testaments. The Douai version

was the work of Catholics, and is the translation used by the Roman Catholic Church in English-speaking countries. The King James version and its revisions are the work of Protestants, and are used in Protestant churches.

The contention that the Bible in the King James translation is a book of a sectarian character rests on the fact that there are differences between it and, among others, the Douai version; that it is of Protestant authorship; that it is used in Protestant churches; and that it is not approved by the Catholic Church. According to such a test the Bible in any known version or test is sectarian. In fact, until all sects can agree upon the manuscript texts that should be used, no English version of the Bible not "sectarian" in this view can be produced.

The statute, however, deals with publications of a sectarian character. It makes the character of the book the test of whether it is "sectarian," not the authorship or the extent of its approval by different sects or by all. That the authors of religious books belong to a sect or church does not necessarily make their books of a sectarian character. Nor does the fact that the King James version is commonly used by Protestant churches and not by Catholics make its character sectarian. Its character is what it is, a widely accepted translation of the Bible. What we have said of the King James translation is equally applicable to the Douai version. Both are scholarly translations of the Bible, and neither is a book "of a sectarian character" within the meaning of the statute relating to school libraries for reference purposes. Each version has claims. Regarded merely as literature, the King James version is a recognized classic. For centuries it has been the version most generally used in Protestant churches in England and America. The Douai version has merits of its own. It is the text approved by one of the world's greatest churches. Many children base their religious education upon its text. We do not assume to decide the comparative merits of the two versions. We do, however, hold that either or both may be purchased for and placed in a public school library without violation of the law of this state.

If it were a fact that the King James version of the Bible was sought to be placed in the public school library to the exclusion of all other versions of the Bible, or if it appeared to be a fact that this particular version or any other version of the Bible was to be used as a text-book for a prescribed course of study or to be used in reading therefrom to the pupils as a part of school exercises, it might then be well argued that such circumstances amounted to an implied declaration that this version was the only true version of the Scrip-

tures, and that all others were false in so far as not in accord therewith. So used and under such circumstances it might be justly claimed to be used as a basis for sectarian instruction. Such are not the facts in the case at bar. The mere act of purchasing a book to be added to the school library does not carry with it any implication of the adoption of the theory or dogma contained therein, or any approval of the book itself, except as a work of literature fit to be included in a reference library. For aught that appears in the instant case the library in question may already contain copies of the Douai version of the Bible as well as copies of the Talmud, Koran, and teachings of Confucius. If the Douai version and these other books are not already in the library, we have no right to assume that they will not be added thereto in the future. That such action would be legal and appropriate we have no doubt.

. . . .

The judgment is affirmed.

OTHER ISSUES

A number of other areas of litigation pertaining to schools have been brought before the courts.

A devotional program in which Roman Catholic students and teachers in a public school maintained in the basement of a Roman Catholic church were required to assemble in the school before the start of regular classes for mass and catechism exercises was upheld in *Millard* v. *Board of Education*, 121 Ill. 297, 10 N.E. 669 (1887). The Illinois court refused to grant injunctive relief on the ground that the bill of complaint did not disclose who, if anybody, required the exercises and attendance at them.

A few years later in *North* v. *Board of Trustees of University of Illinois*, 137 Ill. 296, 27 N.E. 54 (1891), the question of compulsory attendance at nonsectarian religious exercises in a university chapel was raised. North petitioned for a peremptory writ of mandamus against the institution's board of trustees to reinstate him after having been expelled five years previously for refusing to attend chapel. The petitioner alleged that his

state constitutional rights were violated in having been required to attend
a place of worship against his consent.

In original proceeding, the Illinois supreme court determined that
mandamus does not lie when a private citizen merely wishes to settle a
doubtful question. Rather, such a writ will be granted only upon proof
that a legal right has been denied on other than discretionary action by
officials.

The court further found that the petitioner had not notified the university's faculty that he intended to refuse to attend chapel, nor had requested to be excused in accordance with the university rules which
allowed students to be excused for good cause from attending chapel.
Therefore, his expulsion resulted from his own wrong.

The court then concluded that the required attendance at chapel
under such circumstances did not violate the state constitutional provision
forbidding the requiring of persons to attend a place of worship against
his consent.

† † *NORTH* v. *BOARD OF TRUSTEES OF UNIVERSITY OF ILLINOIS*
137 ILL. 296, 27 N.E. 54 (1891).

Judge WILKIN delivered the opinion of the court, saying in part:

[In original proceedings, petitioner
sought a peremptory writ of mandamus
against the board of trustees of the University of Illinois to compel the board
to reinstate said petitioner as a student.
North had been expelled therefrom for
his refusal to comply with a rule of the
trustees of the state university requiring
students to attend nonsectarian religious exercises in the university chapel.
The court, declared that mandamus
will not lie on the petition of a private
citizen merely to settle some doubtful
question, but rather shall be granted
only upon proof of a legal right being
denied.]
. . . The petitioner here seeks to
compel the defendants to readmit him
to the University of Illinois without requiring him to obey one of its rules,
and without requiring him to ask to
be excused from obedience thereto.
First, does he show by his petition that
his purpose in so doing is to vindicate
a personal right, or protect an individual interest? He states no facts in
his petition from which it can be seen
that he will be injured in any way if
the writ is denied. He simply shows
that, after nearly five years' acquiescence in the action of the faculty and
board of trustees suspending him, he
"applied for admission to classes in
said university, and was refused because
of said suspension." What classes he
made application to enter, what his
purpose was in making such application, whether to pursue his course of

studies therein, or merely for the purposes of this suit, he does not say. After these years of unexplained delay he cannot even claim that it should be inferred that he made such application with the desire and intention of in good faith resuming his course of study in said university. But if he could as we have seen, his right and interest is not to be left to inference, but must be clearly averred when this extraordinary writ is invoked. More than this, when his allegation of application for readmission is considered in connection with the other averments of the petition, it is clear that the application was made, not for the purpose of securing an individual right but for the sole purpose of questioning the right of the board of trustees to adopt the rule, which he condemns as an infringement upon the constitutional rights of students generally in the institution. By his own showing, from the inception of his disobedience, his purpose has been, not to protect a personal interest, but to compel respondents to abrogate one of the long-established regulations of the university. This motive was clearly disclosed in his communication to Dr. Peabody, dated April 23, 1885. He there says to ask to be excused would be asking a favor for himself not accorded to others, which he will never do. He also says, the first thing to be settled is whether or not the faculty has the legal authority to adopt the rule which he had violated; thus clearly showing that he had resolved to disregard the rule, not because it interfered with his personal or individual interests, but because he sought an opportunity to test the legality of a regulation of the university, as applied to all students attending the same. His theory throughout has been that, even though he could receive absolute immunity for himself from the requirement by asking it, yet, the rule existing, he was within the meaning of the constitution required to attend a place of worship against his consent. It needs no citation of authorities or argument to show that if respondents have exceeded their authority in adopting rules for the government of students, and any one desires to question such rules on behalf of the public, they must do so in the name of the people of the state of Illinois.

But independently of this question we think the petition wholly fails to show that the defendants have acted unlawfully, or been guilty of any wrong. Their answer avers that they had the lawful right to adopt all reasonable rules and regulations for the government of the university, and in pursuance of that right did adopt the rule in question. This averment the demurrer to the answer admits. Moreover, the act of the legislature establishing the institution clearly confers upon them such power. It follows that in enacting such rules they exercise an official discretion, *McCormick* v. *Burt*, 95 Ill. 263, and with that discretion courts will not interfere by *mandamus*. "The rule is that in all matters requiring the exercise of official judgment, or resting in the sound discretion of the person to whom a duty is confided by law, *mandamus* will not lie, either to control the exercise of that discretion, or to determine upon the decision which shall be finally given." High, Extr. Rem. § 42. It certainly will not be insisted that the rule requiring students to attend chapel exercises is unreasonable or unlawful as applied to those who are willing to obey it. The legality of the rule is questioned on the sole ground that it violates that clause of section 3, art. 2, of the constitution f this state which says: "No person shall be required to attend or support any ministry or place of worship against his consent." It is not pretended by the petitioner that the exercises at chapel meetings were sectarian, and therefore objectionable; but the only objection to those exercises was and is that they were in part religious worship within the meaning of the above-quoted language of the constitution. In the view we take of the case, that fact may be conceded. The real question on this branch of the case is, was it a violation of that constitutional provision for repondents to adopt the rule, and require obedience thereto by those attending the university unless excused therefrom? There is certainly nothing in this section of our constitution prohibiting this and like institutions of learning from adopting reasonable rules requiring their students to attend chapel exercises of a religious nature, and to use all at least moral suasion and all argumentative influences to induce obedience thereto.

. . . Shall a court say such a requirement is, in and of itself, a violation of said constitutional provision, merely because some one or more students attending the university may object to obeying it? More especially should this be done when, as is here shown by the answer, the rules expressly provide that for good cause students may be excused from obedience to such regulation? We have said in construing this section of the constitution: "Religion and religious worship are not so far placed under the ban of the constitution that they may not be allowed to become the recipient of any incidental benefit whatever from the public bodies or authorities of the state." ¶*Welch* v. *Sherer*, 93 Ill. 64. It may be said with greater reason that there is nothing in that instrument so far discountenancing religious worship that colleges and other public institutions of learning may not lawfully adopt all reasonable regulations for the inculcation of moral and religious principles in those attending them. We are clearly of the opinion that the rule is not unlawful. At most it could only be fairly contended that under said clause of the constitution one so desiring it should for reasonable cause be excused from its observance. The whole of said section 3 being considered, it is clear that it is designed to protect the citizen in the free exercise of his religious opinions, and it should be liberally construed to that end. It is doubtless true that one owing obedience to no one else cannot be required to explain or give an excuse why he does not attend places of religious worship; but a moment's reflection will convince any one that the reasons for so holding cannot be applied to those who voluntarily place themselves under the government of others, or who are by parents and guardians placed in institutions of learning, where a code of rules must be adopted for the general government of all students attending them. In the one case the citizen has the right to use his time as he pleases, and, so long as he does not interfere with the rights of others, he may go where he will, and conduct himself as he sees proper. This he may do independently of all questions of conscience. In the other case, however, the will of the student is necessarily subservient to that of those who are for the time being his masters. By voluntarily entering the university, or being placed there by those having the right to control him, he necessarily surrenders very many of his individual rights. How his time shall be occupied, what his habits shall be, his general deportment, that he shall not visit certain places, his hours of study and recreation—in all these matters, and many others, he must yield obedience to those who for the time being are his masters; and yet, were it not for the fact that he is under the government of the university, he could find ample provision in the constitution to protect him against the enforcement of all rules thus abridging his personal liberty. In this case petitioner could not say the faculty had not the right to require him to spend his time in attending chapel, because they, and not himself, had the right to say how he should spend his time. He admits that the rule requiring him to attend chapel was obligatory upon him, and that he was bound to obey it as to all exercises held there except those of a religious character. What personal right, then, has he been deprived of that the faculty did not have complete legal authority to take away from him, unless it be a right of conscience? But this right he expressly stated to the faculty was not in any way interfered with. The answer expressly avers (and this the demurrer admits) that he arbitrarily and in defiance of the authority of said "board of trustees and faculty refused to attend chapel meetings, and also refused to ask to be excused therefrom, and denied the right or authority of said trustees to ask such attendance." We think the conclusion is irresistible that in his controversy with the faculty he was not attempting to protect himself in the exercise of a constitutional privilege, but was only using that clause of the constitution as a shield for insubordination himself, and endeavoring to furnish others an excuse for disobedience. In placing an estimate upon his conduct towards the authorities of the institution it is to be noted that the rule in question was in force from the time he became a student therein to the time he began to disobey it, and that he not only gave his consent to obey it, but for more than five years without objection, did obey it. Will it be contended that during the period he was compelled to attend a place of worship against his consent? Was the rule unconstitutional as to him during that time? According to his own showing, when he made up his mind to no longer observe the rule he did not so much as inform the faculty of that determination, much less make a request to be allowed to withdraw his former consent to obey it. As we have seen, he was requested to base his application to be excused from attending chapel exercises on the only reasonable ground that it could be based. He not only refused to do that, but, according to the allegations of the answer, which he admits, refused to ask to be excused on any ground. His expulsion was the result of his own wrong. Neither the respondents nor the faculty have been guilty of a violation of law, or the doing of any wrong. The authorities cited by counsel for petitioner do not militate against this conclusion. . . . None of the questions there decided are necessarily involved here. We are clearly of the opinion that there is no sufficient grounds here shown to authorize the ordering of the peremptory writ of *mandamus,* and it is therefore denied.

SUMMARY

It is impossible to adequately summarize an area as diverse as that covered in this chapter. What is clear is that almost every conceivable area of the public school curriculum has been challenged at one time or another someplace in the United States. Thus what follows is intended to be merely illustrative of some of the controversies covered in the chapter.

The use of the Bible in public schools other than in Bible-reading exercises (covered in Chapter 4) has continued to be a source of contention. For example, the high court of Washington state held that it would be unconstitutional there to study the Bible for its literary, biographical, narrative, or historical content. On the other hand, in 1924, the California supreme court held that the King James Version of the Bible was not sectarian and thus it might be placed in public school libraries without violating the state constitution. Biblical and religious overtones are, of course, prominent in the famous Scopes case where the Tennessee court upheld a state law forbidding the teaching of evolution in the public schools.

The contents of public school libraries, always a prime target for various interest groups, was the subject of litigation in a somewhat related case. In 1949, the New York supreme court ruled that placing copies of *Oliver Twist* and the *Merchant of Venice* in public school libraries was not a violation of the religion clauses of the United States or the New York constitutions. The court held that the apparent aim of the authors did not appear to be that of promoting racial or religious bigotry. Furthermore, it concluded that suppression of a work must be based on this intent of the author not on some unduly sensitive person's feelings.

A United States district court held in 1963 that singing of the national anthem in public schools did not in and of itself violate the religion clauses of the First Amendment. The court went on to note, however, that suspending pupils who were Jehovah's Witnesses for not standing during such singing violated the First Amendment rights. In a somewhat related area the New Jersey supreme court in 1966, in *Holden* v. *Board of Education* held that a New Jersey law that required public school students to pledge allegiance to the flag only if they had no "conscientious scruples against such pledge" prevented a public school principal from suspending Black Muslim children for refusing to salute the flag.

Conscientious objectors and their attitudes toward military service and war have posed critical questions concerning public school and university practices in a number of states. In 1934, the Supreme Court held in the Hamilton case, that for a state board of regents of a public university to require military training of all college juniors did not violate either the Due Process Clause or the Equal Protection Clause of the Fourteenth Amendment. The Court went on to say that conscientious objectors could legally be excluded from a state university for their failure to participate in compulsory R.O.T.C. programs. Following the same logic, the Maryland high court in 1961 ruled that students could not continue their studies without complying with the university requirement of basic military training. In probably the most extreme case of this nature the New York supreme court ruled that a local school board could dismiss an otherwise qualified Quaker teacher merely because she admitted that she was "opposed to all war."

In another type of case involving a state university, the Illinois supreme court in 1891 again authorized wide discretionary power to the university. There it held that the University of Illinois' requirement making chapel services compulsory to all students did not violate the state constitutional provision prohibiting action requiring a person to attend a place of worship against his consent.

Even the area of physical education in the public schools has been involved in disputes over church-state relations. The California supreme court in 1921 ruled that a public school could not expel a student who because of religious convictions refused to participate in a compulsory physical education course which involved dancing. And in a rather unique case in 1962, the Alabama court held that a state could not compel an individual to wear prescribed physical education attire or to take part in exercises regarded by the parents to be immodest on religious grounds, even when performed in ordinary clothes.

A final case grew out of the anti-German sentiment of World War I. When it ultimately reached the Nebraska supreme court, that body ruled that teaching of a parochial school pupil in the German language was not a violation of the state constitution or laws.

CHAPTER TEN

Compulsory Education

† †

EVERY STATE in the union requires in some form or other that its children regularly attend some school, whether it be public, parochial, or private. The United States Supreme Court gave its approval to the movement when Justice McReynolds stated in the modern foreign language case of *Meyer v. Nebraska*, 262 U.S. 390 (1923):

> The power of the state to compel attendance at some school and to make reasonable regulations for all schools, including a requirement that they shall give instructions in English, is not questioned.

The choice of the particular type of school is left entirely to the child and his parents. The state generally will interfere only when the child is not considered to be receiving an adequate education which is comparable to that being received by other children of the same age. Consequently, a parent who does not wish for his children to take advantage of free education at the public schools may choose private or parochial schooling for them, even though they must continue to pay taxes in support of the public schools. Nevertheless, those choosing to meet their state educational requirements in private or parochial schools may not have their education furnished at public expense. For a ruling of this nature, see *Judd* v. *Board of Education*, 278 N.Y. 200, 15 N.E.2d 576 (1938).

Massachusetts was the first state to pass a compulsory education law. That 1852 statute has acted as a guiding format for succeeding compulsory education statutes of other states. Compulsory education requirements generally prescribe only limited discretion in such matters at various types of schools as the specific studies in the secular curricula, the qualifications of the teachers, attendance records, and similar matters.

The above requirements among others were held as early as the 1890's to apply to parochial or private schools. In *Quigley* v. *State*, 5 Ohio Cir. Ct. Rep. 638 (1891), the court determined that the term "private schools," as used in the compulsory attendance statute, was intended to cover the religious schools as well.

303

The first state education laws were originally tied to religious motives. The basic reason for schooling in Colonial times was to enable systematic reading of the Bible and catechism. As a colony, Massachusetts passed the first school law in 1642. That law and another passed in 1647 dealt with providing children with enough schooling so that they could read the Bible.

Religious questions have continued to present some of the most interesting problems for educators to cope with in their drive to educate a pluralistic society. In fact, the whole question of the legal right of private or parochial schools to exist has been raised in a few instances.

The right of a parent to have his child meet the requirements of compulsory education in a qualified non-public school was settled by the United States Supreme Court in *Pierce* v. *Society of Sisters,* 268 U.S. 510 (1925), below. Oregon had passed a statute in 1922 requiring the attendance at public schools only of children between eight and sixteen. A unanimous Court, Mr. Justice McReynolds speaking, declared that "the child is not the mere creature of the state," and that the state may not standardize its children by demanding that only public school teachers instruct them.

† † *PIERCE* v. *SOCIETY OF SISTERS*
268 U.S. 510, 45 S. CT. 571, 69 L. ED. 1070 (1925).

Mr. Justice MC REYNOLDS delivered the opinion of the Court, saying in part:

The challenged Act effective September 1, 1926, requires every parent, guardian or other person having control or charge or custody of a child between eight and sixteen years to send him "to a public school for the period of time a public school shall be held during the current year" in the district where the child resides; and failure so to do is declared a misdemeanor. There are exemptions—not specially important here—for children who are not normal, or who have completed the eighth grade, or who reside at considerable distances from any public school, or whose parents or guardians hold special permits from the County Superintendent. The manifest purpose is to compel general attendance at public schools by normal children, between eight and sixteen, who have not completed the eighth grade. And without doubt enforcement of the statute would seriously impair, perhaps destroy, the profitable features of appellees' business and greatly diminish the value of their property.

Appellee, the Society of Sisters, is an Oregon corporation, organized in 1880, with power to care for orphans, educate and instruct the youth, establish and maintain academies or schools, and acquire necessary real and personal property. It has long devoted its property and effort to the secular and religious education and care of children, and has acquired the valuable good will of many parents and guardians. It conducts interdependent primary and high schools and junior colleges, and maintains orphanages for the custody and control of children between eight and sixteen. In its primary schools many children between those ages are taught the subjects usually pursued in Oregon public schools during the first eight years. Systematic religious instruction and moral training according to the tenets of the Roman Catholic Church are also regularly provided. All courses of study, both temporal and deligious, contemplate continuity of training under appellee's charge; the primary schools are essential to the system and the most profitable. It owns valuable buildings, especially constructed and equipped for school purposes. The business is remunerative—the annual income from primary schools exceeds thirty thousand dollars—and the successful conduct of this requires long time contracts with teachers and parents. The Compulsory Education Act of 1922 has already caused the withdrawal from its schools of children who would otherwise continue, and their income has steadily declined. The appellants, public officers, have proclaimed their purpose strictly to enforce the statute.

After setting out the above facts the Society's bill alleges that the enactment conflicts with the right of parents to choose schools where their children will receive appropriate mental and religious training, the right of the child to influence the parents' choice of a school, the right of schools and teachers therein to engage in a useful business or profession, and is accordingly repugnant to the Constitution and void. And, further, that unless enforcement of the measure is enjoined the corporation's business and property will suffer irreparable injury.

Appellee, Hill Military Academy, is a private corporation organized in 1908 under the laws of Oregon, engaged in owning, operating and conducting for profit an elementary, college preparatory and military training school for boys between the ages of five and twenty-one years. The average attendance is one hundred, and the annual fees received for each student amount to some eight hundred dollars. The elementary department is divided into eight grades, as in the public schools; the college preparatory department has four grades, similar to those of the public high schools; the courses of study conform to the requirements of the State Board of Education. Military instruction and training are also given, under the supervision of an Army officer. It owns considerable real and personal property, some useful only for school purposes. The business and incident good will are very valuable. In order to conduct its affairs long time contracts must be made for supplies, equipment, teachers and pupils. Appellants, law officers of the State and County, have publicly announced that the Act of November 7, 1922, is valid and have declared their intention to enforce it. By reason of the statute and threat of enforcement appellee's business is being destroyed and its property depreciated; parents and guardians are refusing to make contracts for the future instruction of their sons, and some are being withdrawn.

. . . The court ruled that the Fourteenth Amendment guaranteed appellees against the deprivation of their property without due process of law consequent upon the unlawful interference by appellants with the free choice of patrons, present and prospective. It declared the right to conduct schools was property and that parents and guardians, as a part of their liberty, might direct the education of children by selecting reputable teachers and places. Also, that these schools were not unfit or harmful to the public, and that enforcement of the challenged statute would unlawfully deprive them of patronage and thereby destroy their owners' business and property. Finally, that the threats to enforce the Act would continue to cause irreparable injury; and the suits were not premature.

No question is raised concerning the power of the State reasonably to regulate all schools, to inspect, supervise and examine them, their teachers and pupils; to require that all children of proper age attend some school, that teachers shall be of good moral character and patriotic disposition, that certain studies plainly essential to good citizenship must be taught, and that nothing be taught which is manifestly inimical to the public welfare.

The inevitable practical result of enforcing the Act under consideration would be destruction of appellees' primary schools, and perhaps all other private primary schools for normal children within the State of Oregon. These parties are engaged in a kind of undertaking not inherently harmful, but long regarded as useful and meritorious. Certainly there is nothing in the present records to indicate that they have failed to discharge their obligations to patrons, students or the State. And there are no peculiar circumstances or present emergencies which demand extraordinary measures relative to primary education.

Under the doctrine of *Meyer* v. *Nebraska,* 262 U.S. 390, we think it entirely plain that the Act of 1922 unreasonably interferes with the liberty of parents and guardians to direct the upbringing and education of children under their control. As often heretofore pointed out, rights guaranteed by the Constitution may not be abridged by legislation which has no reasonable relation to some purpose within the competency of the State. The fundamental theory of liberty upon which all governments in this Union repose excludes any general power of the State to standardize its children by forcing them to accept instruction from public teachers only. The child is not the mere creature of the State; those who nurture him and direct his destiny have the right, coupled with the high duty, to recognize and prepare him for additional obligations.

. . . Generally it is entirely true, as urged by counsel, that no person in any business has such an interest in possible customers as to enable him to restrain exercise of proper power of the State upon the ground that he will be deprived of patronage. But the injunctions here sought are not against the exercise of any *proper* power. Plaintiffs asked protection against arbitrary, unreasonable and unlawful interference with their patrons and the consequent destruction of their business and property. Their interest is clear and immediate, within the rule[s] approved in . . . many . . . cases where injunctions have issued to protect business enterprises against interference with the freedom of patrons or customers. . . .

. . . .

The decrees below are affirmed.

REACTIONS OF LEGAL PERIODICALS TO
PIERCE v. *SOCIETY OF SISTERS*

Of those law review articles and notes analyzing the Pierce case, twice as many approved the Supreme Court's stand as those that objected to the ruling. A major argument of the reviews supporting the decision was based on the grounds that it struck down governmental action threatening the very existence of the private and parochial school system. Another main theme of the Pierce decision supporters was that the ruling formalized important guarantees against the arbitrary denial of property rights by government.

The arbitrary nature of the law as revealed by the fact that there was no charge levied against private schools of bad influence or downgrading of the educational process was mentioned in the *California Law Review* (12:509). That philosophy was enlarged upon in the *Virginia Law Review* (12:146), which pointed out that parochial schools are "oftentimes much better equipped and fitted for the educational process than (are) public schools."

Meanwhile, the policy of judicially balancing the interests of the majority as evidenced by legislation against the rights of the individual to freedom of religion was considered in the *Texas Law Review* (4:93). There it was concluded that judicial interference was not a good alternative to that of allowing the states to be sole determinors of their own new legislative policy. A similar state's right approach was suggested in the *Illinois Law Review* (20:378) along with more detailed constitutional arguments. There, it was argued that the Fourteenth Amendment was adopted solely for the protection of the Negro and thus could not be utilized in cases of this nature. Moreover, the author insisted that the Oregon statute was constitutional since it did not establish any religion, promote any sectarian purpose, or prohibit the enjoyment of any religion. In no uncertain terms, it was concluded that children should be forced to attend that great old American "melting pot"—the *public* school.

THE AMISH PROBLEM

The Pierce ruling was reiterated forty-six years later in *State* ex rel. *Chalfin* v. *Glick*, 172 Ohio St. 249, 175 N.E.2d 68 (1961). An administrative proceeding was brought by the attendance officer and county board of education of the Ohio public school system to enjoin the operation of certain Amish private schools, and to force the Amish children to attend the public schools in the district.

The Amish, who have presented a number of interesting problems for various courts, are generally willing to educate their children during the first eight grades in the public schools or preferably in Amish schools, but hold as a tenet of their faith that their children should not receive any secular education after they are fourteen years old and have completed the eighth grade. The children then are considered fully equipped to cope with any problems which might arise in an agricultural culture.

In refusing to order the closing of the Amish school, the court in the Glick case recognized that the instruction there adequately met state educational requirements. It, therefore, could see no justification for ruling the Amish schools out of existence. The Pierce case was not mentioned, however, and the Ohio court added little to systematic theory on the whole topic.

The court recognized in *State* v. *Hershberger,* 103 Ohio App. 188, 144 N.E.2d 693 (1955), that it is well settled that the Amish may establish and maintain their own private schools. But that the educational program in the Amish schools must be equivalent to the free instruction offered in the public schools was also deemed essential by the court. The school involved in this litigation, however, was not considered by the court to be adequate to meet state educational requirements. The school in question crowded all eight grades into one room, and the sole teacher lacked an eighth-grade education plus teaching experience.

No question of religious freedom was involved in the case, according to the court. The basis for that conclusion was the position that merely requiring proper education of children does not infringe the rights of worship, nor does it interfere with the parent's "right to instruct his children in the tenet of his chosen faith." The sole question is whether such education "is equivalent to that given in the public schools of the district," the court added.

Objections by state educational officers to practices whereby Amish parents have denied advanced formalized education to their children have been successful the most part. The court in *Commonwealth* v. *Beiler,* 168 Pa. S. 462, 79 A.2d 134 (1951), below, ruled that parents do not have a constitutional right (state or federal) to deprive their children of education even though their religion apparently commands that formal education be limited. And the parent's religious liberty is not violated when the state demands that Amish children become intelligent members of society, the court concluded.

† † COMMONWEALTH v. BEILER
168 PA. SUPER. 462, 79 A.2D 135 (1951).

Judge RENO delivered the opinion of the court:

Samuel and Levi Beiler were convicted in summary proceedings before a justice of the peace and on appeal in the court below of violating the compulsory attendance provisions of the Public School Code of 1949. . . . They are members of the Old Order Amish Church, and their separate appeals invoke the protection of religious freedom guaranteed by the State and Federal Constitutions.

Samuel is the father of Naomi Beiler; Levi is the father of Jacob Beiler. Both children are 14 years of age, have completed and passed the eighth grade in the public schools, and are eligible for instruction in the high school grades. Appellants refused to send their children for further instruction in the schools to which they had been assigned, and this constitutes the alleged violations of the Code. Nor have they attended private or denominational schools or received instruction from qualified tutors. Their parents hold, in conformity with the tenets of their religion, that children should not receive secular education after they have attained the age of fourteen and have completed the eighth grade of the public schools.

The Code . . . requires:

Every parent . . . of any child or children of compulsory school age [between the ages of eight and seventeen] . . . to send such child or children to a day school in which subjects and activities prescribed by the State Council of Education are taught in the English language.

A "day school" includes a public school but does not exclude other methods of education, and parents may send their children to private or parochial schools or have them instructed by qualified tutors. A subsequent section of the Code . . . provides various exemptions, but appellants did not apply for or secure permits which might have exempted their children from attending school.

The Amish are our "plain people," a quiet, pious, industrious, thrifty people, whose vitalizing contributions to the welfare, and especially to the development of the agricultural resources, of the Commonwealth have always been gratefully recognized. Their ancestors came to Pennsylvania in response to William Penn's personal invitation and his promise of religious liberty. They adhere, devoutly and unchangingly, to the strict and literal interpretation of the Dortricht Creed, a confession of faith adopted at Dort, Holland, in 1632, by the followers of Menno Simmons, the founder of the Mennonite Church, from which sprang the Amish under the leadership of Jacob Amman. Upon it, they have patterned their lives and followed it, consistently, conscientiously and faithfully.

The specific doctrinal pronouncement of the Dortricht confession here relevant is:

And since it is a known fact that a lack of faithful ministers, and the erring of the sheep because of the lack of good doctrine, arise principally from the unworthiness of the people; therefore, the people of God, needing this, should not turn to such as have been educated in universities, according to the wisdom of man, that they may talk and dispute, and seek to sell their purchased gift for temporal gain; and who according to the custom of the world do not truly follow Christ in the humility of regeneration.

With that credal declaration as the doctrinal basis, and fortifying it with the citation of Biblical proof-texts, a group of ruling bishops wrote, and during the pendency of these prosecutions, revised a "Statement of Position of Old Order Amish Church Regarding Attendance in Public Schools" from which we extract the pertinent articles:

2. We believe that our children should be properly trained and educated for manhood

and womanhood. We believe that they need to be trained in those elements of learning which are given in the elementary schools. Specifically, we believe that our children should be trained to read, to write, and to cipher. 3. We believe that our children have attained sufficient schooling when they have passed the eighth grade of the elementary school. This attainment is ordinarily made at age fourteen. 4. We believe that when our children have passed the eighth grade that in our circumstances, way of life and religious belief, we are safeguarding their home and church training in secular and religious belief and faith by keeping them at home under the influence of their parents.

I. Seeing that the Dortricht Creed refers to men who "have been educated in universities" while the bishops' statement relates to post-eighth grade schools, the Commonwealth argues that the inconsistency indicates that the true Amish faith "does not prohibit or restrict children of their faith from going to high school."

Where property rights of members of a church are not involved, courts will not investigate or determine its faith or doctrine. The courts accept as true definitions of faith the expressions and interpretations of ecclesiastical officers, governing councils and judicatories which the church has authorized to speak for it. "Any other than those [ecclesiastical] courts must be incompetent judges of matters of faith, discipline and doctrine": *German Reformed Church* v. *Com.* ex rel. *Seibert*, 3 Pa. 282, 291. . . . So, even though the bishops' statement should be in conflict with the Dortricht confession, we nevertheless accept it as the authorized exposition of the Amish faith in regard to the public schools.

II. Thus, we are squarely faced with competing demands of the Common-

wealth, evidenced by its compulsory school law, and of religious liberty, guaranteed by the Constitution. Or to state the problem in other terms: In the realm of secular education, which is paramount? The State, functioning according to democratic processes and depending for its virility upon enlightened citizens; or parents, whose deep and sincere religious convictions reject advanced education as an encroachment upon their way of life? The responsibility of the Court is to find a solution which will reasonably accommodate both demands in a manner that will preserve the essentials of each.

We analyzed this question in *Com.* ex rel. *School District of Pittsburgh* v. *Bey,* 166 Pa. Super. 136, 140. . . .

. . . .

. . . Its major premise is that there is no interference with religious liberty where the State reasonably restricts parental control, or compels parents to perform their natural and civic obligations to educate their children. They may be educated in the public schools, in private or denominational schools, or by approved tutors; but educated they must be within the age limits and in the subjects prescribed by law. The life of the Commonwealth—its safety, its integrity, its independence, its progress, and the preservation and enhancement of the democratic way of life, depend upon the enlightened intelligence of its citizens. . . . These fundamental objectives are paramount, and they do not collide with the principles of religious or civil liberty. Unless democracy lives religious liberty cannot survive.

Religious liberty includes absolute right to believe but only a limited right to act. A Mormon believed that plural marriages were divinely ordained but when he acted upon his belief he was convicted of polygamy. *Reynolds* v. *U.S.,* 98 U.S. 145. A Jew held his Sabbath a holy day but when he refused to be judicially sworn on Saturday he was fined. *Stansbury* v. *Marks,* 2 Dall. 213. A Seventh Day Baptist believed he should rest from his labors on Saturday and follow the divine command, "six days shalt thou labor," but when he worked on Sunday he was convicted under the Act of 1794. *Specht* v. *Com.,* 8 Pa. 312. . . .

III. Appellants' able counsel argues that Bey and similar authorities do not rule this appeal and pins his faith on the flag salute cases, *West Virginia State Board of Education* v. *Barnette,* 319 U.S. 624, *Com.* v. *Conte,* 154 Pa. Super. 112, 35 A.2d 742; and *Com.* v. *Crowley,* 154 Pa. Super. 116, 35 A.2d 744. He contends that since a public school pupil cannot be compelled to salute the flag, he cannot be compelled to attend school and his parents cannot be punished for refusing to send him.

The Barnette opinion announces no such doctrine and nothing in it supports the corollary which counsel seeks to draw from it. It decides only that the compulsory salute to the flag and the accompanying pledge constitute denial of the freedoms of speech and worship, because they require "students to declare a belief." (Access to Pennsylvania's common schools is not conditioned upon participation in a flag salute ceremony.) The opinion does not declare that states may not enforce compulsory school laws against religious dissidents. To the contrary, it approvingly quoted, 319 U.S. at page 631, an extract from Chief Justice Stone's dissent in overruled *Minersville School Dist.* v. *Gobitis,* 310 U.S. 586, 604. There the Chief Justice said:

Without recourse to such compulsion [flag salute] *the state is free to compel attendance at school* and require teaching by instruction and study of all in our history and in the structure and organization of our government, including the guaranties of civil liberty which tend to inspire patriotism and love of country.
(Emphasis added.)

Furthermore, Barnette did not expressly or otherwise overrule *Pierce* v. *Society of the Sisters of the Holy Names,* 268 U.S. 510, which recognized "the power of the state . . . to require that all children of proper age attend some school." And *after* Barnette was decided, the United States Supreme Court held that "the state as parens patriae may restrict the parent's control by requiring school attendance," and that, "Its authority is not nullified merely because the parent grounds his claim to control the child's course of conduct on religion or conscience": *Prince* v. *Com. of Massachusetts,* supra. This is the latest interpretation and application of the First and Fourteenth Amendments of the Federal Constitution by the highest court of the land. That judgment binds this Court, appellants, and their brethren.

OTHER AMISH PROBLEMS

The action in *Commonwealth* v. *Smoker,* 177 Pa. Super. 435, 110 A.2d 740 (1955), involved an application by an Amish boy for a work permit, which apparently was required in order for him to waive compulsory education requirements. The boy was over fourteen and had completed the eighth grade.

In upholding the refusal by the superintendent of public instruction to grant the permit, the court declared that the question of religious freedom in such matter had already been settled in *Commonwealth* v. *Beiler,* above. Noting that the statutory exemption of school age children from compulsory attendance requirements was intended primarily for those children whose families were in dire financial circumstances, the court denied the relief on the additional ground that there was an older brother who was available to accomplish the contemplated family tasks.

In a similar case, *Gingerich* v. *State,* 226 Ind. 678, 83 N.E.2d 47 (1948), the conviction of an Amish father who had caused his son not to attend high school was upheld. The religious issue was not considered by the court, however, because the question was not raised properly in the lower court.

However, a father, who took his son from the public schools a month or so before their closing for the term and enrolled him in a two-month private course of instruction, was held to be not subject to the penalties of the truancy law, in *State* v. *Will,* 99 Kan. 167, 160 P. 1025 (1916). The curriculum at the private school consisted primarily of German exercises in reading, grammar, spelling, and writing; plus lessons in Bible history and but a small amount of arithmetic.

The Kansas court declared that it was not within its prerogative to fill the gaps left by the legislature, which did not prescribe the curricula in private, denominational, or parochial schools. The acts had merely demanded that they employ competent instructors.

RELATED CASES

The court in *People* v. *Donner,* 302 N.Y. 883, 100 N.E.2d 57 (1951), nevertheless made it clear that any formal school must meet certain qualifications in order for children in attendance there to satisfy state educational requirements. Their parents had contended that their religious beliefs "forbad systematic secular education," and that, therefore, the Education Law must give way to religious law which was protected by the First Amendment of the United States Constitution.

Their children were in the meantime attending a small religious school where there was no instruction in the customary eleven subjects and the teachers lacked the minimum qualifications as prescribed by the board of education. In addition, the instruction was not given in English, and attendance records were not kept. Without expounding further, the court held that the compulsory education statute "did not violate any of [their] rights [as] guaranteed by the Constitution of the United States."

In *People* ex rel. *Shapiro* v. *Dorin*, Dom. Rel. Ct., 99 N.Y.S.2d 830 (1950), children attended a small religious school which functioned "as an entirely independent organization." The school was not recognized by the Jewish Education Committee of New York, which "supervises secular instruction in Hebrew Parochial schools." The school, furthermore, offered instruction only in "the Bible, the Talmud and elementary Jewish law," and was taught by a noncertified teacher.

The New York court, in upholding the conviction of the parents for not complying with proper schooling requirements, said that the federal constitutional protection of religious freedom obliges the states to maintain separation of church and state. That means that the state cannot accept sectarian education as a substitute for the secular education which is prescribed by state law, the court determined.

The effect of that decision was that a court had once again taken the position that secular law takes precedence over a conflicting religious law when the interests of society are at stake.

HOME INSTRUCTION

Another court added to the weight of judicial precedents demanding that any child, not attending public schools, must be instructed nevertheless by the qualified teacher. In *Meyerkorth* v. *State*, 173 Neb. 889, 115 N.W.2d 585 (1962), the Nebraska court quoted with favor the state's insistence "upon a qualified teacher under reasonable statutes providing for such qualifications to teach school."

Meyerkorth, a member of the Emmanuel Association, had hired a tutor to educate his children spiritually and intellectually in a religious atmosphere. Although the teacher obviously was qualified to handle such sectarian instruction, the court agreed with the state that the standards of teachers' qualifications must be based upon a program of secular learning.

The religious beliefs of parents was held by the Virginia high court, in *Rice* v. *Commonwealth*, 188 Va. 224, 49 S.E.2d 342 (1948), not a sufficient basis to allow a child to remain illiterate. The deeply religious parents interpreted the Bible as "commanding, at the risk of God's displeasure, that parents teach and train their children in the ways of life." The court, however, stated that any home instructor must be a qualified teacher who prescribes a course of study that will prepare the students to meet general academic standards. Claims based upon religious freedom cannot negate a reasonable civil requirement, the opinion suggested.

On the other hand, the fact that a child was receiving private instruction at home was not considered in *Commonwealth* v. *Renfrew*, 332 Mass. 492, 126 N.E.2d 109 (1955), below, to be justification for the parents to remove the child from the public schools without gaining prior approval from the superintendent of the school committee. The fact that the children objected to daily exercises in the public schools consisting of reading of the Bible and recital of the Lord's Prayer did not justify their arbitrary actions in leaving before the superintendent could ascertain whether the contemplated home instruction would be adequate under state standards, the court added.

† † *COMMONWEALTH* v. *RENFREW*
332 MASS. 492, 126 N.E.2D 109 (1955).

Judge RONAN delivered the opinion of the court, saying in part:

The defendants, husband and wife, were charged jointly in two complaints, each complaint alleging a different period of time in neglecting to cause their minor child to attend school as required by [statute in 1939] the said minor having failed during each of the said periods to attend school for seven day sessions or fourteen half day sessions within a period of six months as set forth in . . . 1947. Both complaints were tried together and each defendant was found guilty on each complaint.

The first witness for the Commonwealth testified that the defendants resided in Boston; that their minor child was eight or nine years of age; that the said child, during the periods alleged in the complaints, did not attend the public schools which were then in session or a private school approved by the superintendent or the school committee nor pursue a course of study which had been approved in advance by the superintendent or the committee; and that the child was under the control of both defendants. The defendants subject to their exceptions

were not permitted to show through this witness the subjects which were taught in public schools for the purpose of showing that the child had been otherwise instructed in the branches of learning required in the public day schools and in order to meet the allegations contained in each complaint, to wit, "and the said child not having been otherwise instructed in the branches of learning required to be taught in the public day schools." The judge ruled that these words were surplusage, and also ruled that the issue before him was whether the child during the times alleged attended a public day school or a private day school approved by the superintendent or the committee or was otherwise being instructed in a manner approved in advance by the superintendent or the committee, and that, if he was not being educated in one of these three methods, the defendants were guilty. The defendants saved exceptions to these rulings. The parties then agreed on the facts, and a statement of agreed facts was submitted to the judge who ruled that under the first eight paragraphs no issue of fact was left open and, subject to the exceptions of the defendants, ordered the jury to return verdicts of guilty.

. . . .

None of the various other enumerated admitted facts constituted any defense to these complaints. Home education of their child by the defendants without the prior approval of the superintendent or the committee did not show a compliance with the statute and bar the prosecution of the complaints. . . . The right to religious freedom is not absolute. . . . The defendants and their child were Buddhists. One of the grievances of the defendants was that the mental health of the child was being affected because he was not being educated according to his capacity to learn. This is ambiguous as it might mean that he was attending a grade either above or below his capacity to learn. If his difficulty consisted merely of being in the wrong grade, it undoubtedly would have been remedied if such had been known to the teacher or the school authorities, but there is nothing in the record that shows that any such particular complaint was ever brought to their attention or any definite request made to change his grade. Another grievance of the defendants is that some things that he was taught were causing conflict with the principles of Buddhism although they conceded that these principles were in no way in conflict with the law. There is no specification whatever as to what were "some of the things" just mentioned. They may well have been the secular subjects ordinarily taught in the public schools. The defendants state that their child has been taught the Twenty-Third Psalm and the Lord's Prayer. The mere reading of the Bible and the recital of the Lord's Prayer in the public schools do not justify the failure of the defendants to have him attend school. For more than a century our statute has provided that a portion of the Bible shall be read daily in the public schools without written note or comment and that no pupil shall be required to take any personal part in the reading if his parent or guardian informs the teacher in writing that he has conscientious scruples against the pupil participating in such reading. . . . The purpose and validity of such a statute were explained and upheld, as was a regulation of a school committee that the schools should be opened each morning with a reading from the Bible and the offering of prayer, in *Spiller* v. *Inhabitants of Woburn*, 12 Allen 127. We think the case cited is in accord with the weight of authority. . . .

. . . .

Exceptions overruled.

RELATED PROBLEMS

Of a similar nature, *State* ex rel. *Shoreline School District* v. *Superior Court*, 55 Wash.2d 177, 346 P.2d 999 (1960), below, ruled that parents were guilty of violating the compulsory school attendance law when the child was withdrawn from the public school so that she could be taught at home by her mother. The mother, who lacked a teacher's certificate allegedly was giving the child instruction in the regular school subjects, however.

Finding no record that the mother attempted to qualify her alleged school as a private school within the statutory confines, the court went on to deny relief for her claim that certain practices at the school were repugnant to the family's religion (Seventh Elect Church In Spiritual Israel).

† † *STATE* ex rel. *SHORELINE SCHOOL DISTRICT* v. *SUPERIOR COURT*
55 WASH.2D 177, 346 P.2D 999 (1960).

Judge OTT delivered the opinion of the court, saying in part:

William and Maude Wold are husband and wife, and have been residents of the state of Washington since August, 1952. Alta Lee Wold, their daughter, was born June 6, 1945. Prior to March 14, 1955, she was regularly enrolled as a grade school student at the Ronald public school in Shoreline school district No. 412 in King county. On that date, her parents withdrew her from the fourth grade. After several demands were made upon the parents by the truant officer of the school district that Alta Lee attend a public or private school, as required by Laws of 1909 . . . a petition was filed in the juvenile court for King county which alleged that Alta Lee Wold was a delinquent child, because of her violation of the compulsory school attendance law of this state, and that William and Maude Wold, her parents, were contributing to her delinquency.

At the hearing upon the petition, the parents admitted that Alta Lee had not been attending public school, and that she had not been excused from attendance by any school authority. Their

defense was that Alta Lee's mother had graduated from a Colorado high school in 1937; that Alta Lee was being taught the regular public grade school subjects by her mother in their home, and that this constituted a private school. A further defense was that they were members of the Seventh Elect Church In Spiritual Israel; that eating meat, fish or fowl, listening to music, and dancing were forbidden by the tenets of their church, and that, to be present where meat, fish or fowl was served or music played violated their religious belief.

After considering the evidence, the juvenile court found that the "school" Alta Lee was attending did not constitute a private school as contemplated by law; that, although their church tenets were violated by public school attendance, this was not a defense to violation of the compulsory school attendance law; that Alta Lee was a dependent and delinquent child and that the parents, William and Maude Wold, were contributing to her dependency and delinquency.

. . . .

The trial court further found that the mother's teaching methods had improved in the two and one-half years she had been maintaining the home school; that the legislature had not provided standards for private schools, and that, since Alta Lee was receiving a book learning comparable to that of the public schools, she was attending a private school as contemplated by law. . . .

The principal assignment of error relates the court's finding that the Wolds' home school constituted a qualified private school contemplated by law.

We agree with relator's contention that the court's findings are inconsistent. It found that Alta Lee Wold was not attending a public or private school, provided by law, and was therefore a dependent child. After so finding, it then found that the home school which she was attending and which caused her to be adjudicated a dependent child, was a qualified private school. In other words, the juvenile court obtained jurisdiction of Alta Lee Wold and made her a ward of the court because the court found that she was not attending a qualified private school, as contemplated by law. After obtaining jurisdiction of Alta Lee on this basis, the court then found that the welfare of its ward would best be served by her attending the same unqualified school because its method of education was "in conformity with the laws of this state."

The juvenile court's decision is inconsistent with *State* v. *Counort*, 1912, 69 Wash. 361, 124 P. 910, (to which decision we adhere), wherein this court held that a father teaching his children at home was doing so in violation of the compulsory school attendance law. In the cited case, this court said:

. . . We do not think that the giving of instruction by a parent to a child, conceding the competency of the parent to fully instruct the child in all that is taught in the public schools, is within the meaning of the law 'to attend a private school.' Such a requirement means more than home instruction. It means the same character of school as the public school, a regular, organized and existing institution, making a business of instructing children of school age in the required studies and for the full time required by the laws of this state. . . . This provision of the law is not to be determined by the place where the school is maintained, nor the individuality or number of the pupils who attend it. It is to be determined by the purpose, intent and character of the endeavor.

Article IX, § 1, of our state constitution, provides that "It is the paramount duty of the state to make ample provision for the education of all children residing within its borders. . . ." The legislature, in compliance with this constitutional mandate, provided for compulsory school attendance for all children between the ages eight and sixteen years (unless excused from attendance for reasons not here material) at either a public or private school. Laws of 1909. . . .

. . . .

Although the trial court found that there are no legislative standards governing private schools in this state, such a conclusion is not supported by law. A school is an institution consisting of a teacher and pupils, irrespective of age, gathered together for instruction in any branch of learning. . . . The three essential elements of a school are (1) the teacher, (2) the pupil or pupils, and (3) the place or institution. If the alleged school has no teacher, then it does not qualify as a school. There is one standard which the legislature made applicable to all schools, both public and private, and that standard is that the teacher must be qualified to teach and hold a teaching certificate. . . .

No person shall be accounted as a qualified teacher within the meaning of the school law, who is not the holder of a valid teacher's certificate or diploma issued by lawful authority of this state.

The Wolds had the place and the pupil, but not a teacher qualified to teach in the state of Washington. Their alleged private school did not legally qualify as such.

. . . .

Although the legislature did not expressly provide that *all* of the legislative standards for a public common school must be maintained by a private school in order to qualify as such, it is reasonable to assume that the legislature intended that the one to whom it had delegated the power and authority to determine whether a child was attending a *qualified* private school would be guided in that decision by the minimum standards required by the legislature for a public common school. . . .

. . . Under the compulsory school attendance law, the legislature delegated to the district or county superintendent the authority to determine the mini-mum standards for a private school, in order that, in the exercise of his discretion, attendance at a qualified private school may be approved.

In the instant case, the Wolds' alleged private school did not have a qualified teacher. The Wolds did not report that their daughter was attending a private school, nor did they attempt in any manner to qualify their alleged school as a private school with the person whose duty it was to exercise his discretion in granting the waiver to students of public school attendance.

We find no merit in the contention of the Wolds that they are excused from the penalties of the compulsory school attendance law because school attendance is repugnant to their religion. . . .

Although the freedom to believe remains absolute, religious beliefs, whatever they may be, are not a legal justification for violation of positive law. See *State* ex rel. *Holcomb* v. *Armstrong*, 1952, 39 Wash.2d 860, 239 P.2d 545.

The judgment of the trial court is affirmed in the following particulars: Alta Lee Wold is a dependent child because she is in violation of the compulsory school attendance act, and will remain a ward of the court until such time as she is purged of dependency by attendance at either a public or qualified private school.

The judgment is reversed. . . .

REACTIONS OF LEGAL PERIODICALS TO *STATE* ex rel. *SHORELINE SCHOOL DISTRICT* v. *SUPERIOR COURT*

The Washington court's holding was supported in the *Washington Law Review* (35:151), where the opinion was expressed that the child's position was not so extreme that a reasonable alternative could not be worked out. The writer suggested that a stronger case could be made in attacking the validity of the compulsory education requirement if the particular religious beliefs "would bar association with large groups."

That principle was not involved in the case at hand, however. Had it been, though, the analyst argued that the state might have been required to allow the private tutoring. He went on nevertheless to say that a certified teacher would be required in that situation.

QUALITY OF PRIVATE INSTRUCTION

The quality of the instruction in private schools was considered adequate under state compulsory educational requirements in a number of cases. In this connection, *State v. Peterman*, 32 Ind. App. 665, 70 N.E. 550 (1904), ruled that a child could satisfy his state educational requirements in a private school which was conducted by an accredited teacher who had formerly taught in the public schools. The opinion noted that the teacher maintained a regular schedule of classes, but made no mention of religion or of the child's specific objections to formalized education.

The latter situation was present also in *People v. Turner*, 121 Cal. App.2d Supp. 861, 263 P.2d 685 (1953). There the children were taught in their home, but the court ruled that such teachers must possess valid state credentials. This was so even though teachers in certain other types of private schools were exempted from the certification requirements.

Members of the Seventh-Day Adventist faith were successful in a number of cases in convincing the respective courts that they could better undertake and manage the education of their children at home. For example, a parent was not held in contempt of court in *Wright v. State*, 21 Okl. Crim. 430, 209 P. 179 (1922), when it was shown that as a qualified teacher he had conducted a private school for his child in a fitting and proficient manner.

The child was shown furthermore to be proficient in all of the branches of general study as taught in the district's public school. The parent apparently had desired his children to become a missionary or a minister, and felt that the training in the public schools was "not favorable to that end."

Seventh-Day Adventist parents claimed in *People v. Levisen*, 404 Ill. 574, 90 N.E.2d 213 (1950), that competitive educational processes cause a "pugnacious character" in children, and that a child should receive his early years of education (until he is about eight or ten years old) in the field or garden with nature the best lesson book and the mother the best teacher. Consequently, a seven-year old girl, receiving her instruction at home from her mother was considered to be attending a "private" school within the allowable limits of the Illinois compulsory education statute.

The Illinois court, noting that the mother had had two years of college with additional training in pedagogy and educational psychology and that the child showed average proficiency for her age, declared that the object of the compulsory education law if that "All children shall be educated, not that they shall be educated in any particular manner or place."

The opinion in the Levisen case was sharple criticized in a number of reviews. One writer charged in the *University of Chicago Law Review* (18:105) that the court not only ignored the legislative history of compulsory education statutes but also constructed the statute at hand in a fashion unsupported by ordinary connotations of the term "private school." Personally stressing the values of social conduct and educational association, he concluded that our school laws are designed to guard our children against the dangers of developing incompetent citizenship.

The same flavor of disgust with the decision and reverence for the purpose of formalized education en masse was apparent in the *Virginia Law Review* (36:682). In rejecting both the majority opinion, which was premised upon the theory that a "quantum of book learning" comprises the entire educational process, and the dissenting view, which expressed concern over the practicalities of enforcement of the attendance statute, the reviewer stressed the importance of the "melting pot" idea in the common classroom as a training ground for good citizenship.

Several other cases illustrate reluctance on the part of many courts to find that the particular "school" or type of instruction adequately met the state educational standards. For example, in *Knox* v. *O'Brien*, 7 N.J. Super. 608, 72 A.2d 389 (1950), a child in New Jersey attending a private school in his home was considered not to be receiving an education equivalent to that received in the public schools. The conclusion was based upon a finding that the teacher, although certified, had not taught within the last twenty years.

That the requirements of compulsory education have reached a stage where the instruction must be given in a particular way was the central theme in the *George Washington Law Review* (19:361). Pointing out that educators and social workers applauded the decision in the Knox case, the reviewer added that a child needs the educational association which is inherent in a large and diverse student body. Learning to live and associate with others at an early age before various prejudices are developed will produce better citizens, he argued.

The supervisory factor was prevalent in several decisions. In *State* v. *Counort*, 69 Wash. 361, 124 P. 910 (1912), the court rejected the idea that place is the determining factor in education. It emphasized instead that the quality of an adequate education should be measured by the "purpose, intent, and character of the endeavor." In the process, an educational program lacking a regular schedule of classwork similar to that in the public schools was declared not to be a "private school," even thought the parent-teacher was personally competent and qualified.

In a similar vein, *State* v. *Hoyt,* 84 N.H. 38, 146 A. 170 (1929), ruled that a mere exhibition of competency in the educational areas comparable to the public school children was no enough to offset the fact that the child in question was unsupervised in her instruction. The court thus suggested that the education of children involves something more than mere "book-learning."

HEALTH REGULATIONS

It is one thing for the state to require attendance in its schools, public or private, and to provide for bus transportation to get them there. It is another to ensure the health and welfare of the children while there. Pupils must not be forced from their homes to a gathering place of disease.

The school system took an early lead in establishing regular innoculation programs to ensure the health of the young people in this country. But not all of the parents appreciated the fact that their children were receiving vaccinations at the schools.

Compulsory vaccination received federal judicial sanction in *Jacobson* v. *Massachusetts,* 197 U.S. 11 (1904). There, the Supreme Court held that the public health justified a state statute requiring compulsory vaccination. Although that case involved a municipal regulation aimed at all residents, it clearly pointed up the continuing trend toward justification on police power grounds of various violations of bodily privacy.

School vaccination programs first were attacked as being violative of due process. Some petitioners alleged that vaccination would in fact endanger their children's health; while others claimed that vaccine was just a worthless expense.

Objections to vaccination regulations were based upon health considerations in a number of cases. In *Zucht* v. *King,* Tex. Civ. App., 225 S.W. 267 (1920), petitioner's claim that vaccination would endanger her health was disregarded by the Texas court. The decision turned on the issue of equal protection of the laws, however.

The fact that parents believed only in divine healing through the miracle of faith was considered in *Anderson* v. *State,* 84 Ga. App. 259, 65 S.E.2d 848 (1951), not to overcome their obligation to have their children vaccinated before admission to the Georgia public schools. Noting that their pastor refused to sign a certificate declaring official opposition by that religious sect to the use of medicine, the court went on to rule that "A person's right to exercise religious freedom ceases where it overlaps and transgresses the rights of others."

Individual opinions of parents failing to send their unvaccinated children to school were held in *State* v. *Drew*, 89 N.H. 54, 192 A. 629 (1937), to be irrelevant and immaterial in New Hampshire when no question of religious liberty was involved. In denying the petition which was based partly upon religion and partly upon a hostility to having "that poison injected into his child," the court reasoned that anarchy would replace law if all men could claim that their individual opinion had the weight of natural rights.

The religious issue was nevertheless the paramount question in the comparatively recent case of *Board of Education* v. *Maas*, 56 N.J. Super. 245, 152 A.2d 394 (1959). There a foster mother of three Grecian exchange students, who were temporarily in the United States, refused to have the children vaccinated before admitting them to the public school system. A Christian Scientist, she claimed immunity for the children from the New Jersey statutory requirement upon the ground that she came under the act's provision authorizing local school boards to admit unvaccinated pupils whose parents stated that immunization conflicted with free exercise of religious principles.

The New Jersey court, in refusing admission to the children until they were vaccinated, stated categorically that the objection to the immunization was made solely by the foster mother. The children, adherents of the Greek Orthodox faith, had been innoculated, without raising religious objections, against smallpox before they came to America. Stating that a statute may be attacked only by the one whose personal rights are adversely affected, the court ruled that the defendant could not "use the children to champion her own rights and beliefs."

Meanwhile, a father's conviction for failing to send his child to any school was upheld in *People* v. *Ekerold*, 211 N.Y. 386, 105 N.E. 670 (1914). The father had submitted his child for admission to a public school, which refused the child because of his refusal to be vaccinated. The father apparently then used that situation as an excuse for not schooling his child.

Calling the fatherly actions "arbitrary and capricious," the New York court pointed out that it was his duty to either have his child comply with the vaccination requirements at the public schools or send him to a private school (where the vaccination requirement did not apply). Any additional expense for private schooling would be the price the father would have to pay for his refusal to conform with society in general, the court determined.

A contention that appellants' faith, religion, and conscience forbade them to submit their children to vaccination was to no avail in *Staffel* v. *Board of Education*, Tex. Civ. App., 201 S.W. 413 (1918). The Texas civil appeals court held that the law gives control of the schools to the board of education, rather than to individual parents. The above situation is so regardless of the parents' particular consciences, convictions, faiths, or religious beliefs, the court decided.

Other statutory vaccination requirements as prerequisites to admission and attendance at public schools were upheld against claims of violations of religious freedom in *Commonwealth* v. *Green,* 268 Mass. 585, 168 N.E. 101 (1929); In re *Whitmore,* N.Y. Dom. Rel. Ct., 47 N.Y.S.2d 143 (1944); and *State* ex rel. *Dunham* v. *Board of Education,* 154 Ohio St. 469, 96 N.E.2d 413 (1951.

In the face of the danger of a smallpox epidemic, the supreme court of Indiana ruled in *Vonnegut* v. *Baun,* 206 Ind. 172, 188 N.E. 677 (1934), that a resolution by the city board of health excluding unvaccinated children from school did not violate rights of conscience as protected by the First Amendment of the United States Constitution and the bill of rights of the Indiana constitution.

Noting that there was no mention in the record of how those constitutional rights were infringed, the court reasoned that the resolution merely involved an emergency action to prevent the spread of a deadly disease. Dismissing the complaint against the enforcement by appellant school board of the health resolution, the court declared that in the instant situation the "right of the state to require vaccination is not involved."

Other actions of a similar nature included *Auten* v. *School Board,* 83 Ark. 431, 104 S.W. 130 (1907), and *McSween* v. *School Trustees,* 60 Tex. Civ. App. 270, 129 S.W. 206 (1910). Certificates of vaccination were required for school attendance in both instances, but an objector in the latter case was authorized to be excluded by the terms of the statute from school only during the smallpox epidemic, which was raging at the time. The respective states upheld the expulsion of nonconforming students in both cases.

On the other hand, a city ordinance in Texas requiring all children to be vaccinated before they were admitted to either public or private schools was upheld in *New Braunfels* v. *Waldschmidt,* 109 Tex. 302, 207 S.W. 303 (1918). While conceding that there was only one case of smallpox in the town at the time, the court nevertheless considered the regulation to be a reasonable exercise of police power which under the circumstances did not infringe upon the rights of conscience as guaranteed by the Texas constitution.

In the latest judicial declaration on the subject, the highest court of Arkansas ruled in *Cude* v. *State,* Ark., 377 S.W.2d 816 (1964), below, that a probate court has jurisdiction to vest the control of unvaccinated children in the custody of the child welfare division of the state welfare department. The fact that the father had been fined on three occasions for his failure to have his children vaccinated against smallpox was considered by the court to be an insignificant consideration. In upholding the order of the probate court in transferring the custody of the children to the child welfare division guardian, the court stressed that its objective was to make it possible for the children "to obtain a reasonable education." Punishing a noncomplying father was not a sufficient means for obtaining the educational goal, the court determined.

† † *CUDE* v. *STATE*
ARK., 377 s.w.2d 816 (1964).

Judge ROBINSON delivered the opinion of the court, saying in part:

The issue is the authority of the courts to appoint a guardian for children between the ages of 7 and 15, inclusive, who are not attending school, and to give the guardian custody of the children with directions to have them vaccinated to facilitate school attendance.

Appellants . . . are the parents of eight children, three of whom are between the ages of 7 and 15, inclusive. . . . Wayne [age 12] went only to the second grade; the other two [ages 10 and 8] have not attended school at all. The children are not in school for the reason that the school authorities will not permit them to attend school because they have not been vaccinated against smallpox. The Cudes will not permit such vaccinations; they contend that it is contrary to their religion.

. . . . . † . . † . . . . . .

For the purposes of the appeal, we will assume that the Cudes, in good faith because of their religious beliefs, will not permit the children to be vaccinated. Then the question is whether they have the legal right to prevent vaccination. The answer is that they do not have such right.

. . . . . † . . † . . . . . .

It is clear that the law requires that the children attend school, and a valid regulation requires that they be vaccinated. The next question is: Are appellants, because of their religion, exempt from the law and the regulation requiring that the children be vaccinated so that they can go to school? It will be remembered that appellants do not object to the children going to school; it is the vaccination that is objectionable to them. But, according to a valid regulation, the children are not permitted to go to school without having been vaccinated.

Article 2, Sec. 24 of the Constitution of Arkansas provides:

All men have a natural and indefeasible right to worship Almighty God according to the dictates of their own consciences; no man can, of right, be compelled to attend, erect or support any place of worship; or to maintain any ministry against his consent. No human authority can, in any case or manner whatsoever, control or interfere with the right of conscience; and no preference shall ever be given, by law, to any religious establishment, denomination or mode of worship above any other.

The foregoing provision of the Constitution means that anyone has the right to worship God in the manner of his own choice, but it does not mean that he can engage in religious practices inconsistent with the peace, safety and health of the inhabitants of the State, and it does not mean that parents, on religious grounds, have the right to deny their children an education.

The U.S. Supreme Court said in *Prince* v. *Commonwealth of Massachusetts,* 321 U.S. 158:

The right to practice religion freely, does not include liberty to expose the community or the child to communicable disease or the latter to ill health or death. . . . Parents may be free to become martyrs themselves. But it does no follow they are free, in identical circumstances, to make martyrs of their children before they have reached the age of full and legal discretion when they can make that choice for themselves.

It is a matter of common knowledge that prior to the development of protection against smallpox by vaccination, the disease, on occasion, ran rampant and caused great suffering and sickness throughout the world. According to the great weight of authority, it is within the police power of the State to require that school children be vaccinated against smallpox, and that such requirement does not violate the constitutional rights of anyone, on religious grounds or otherwise. In fact, this principle is so firmly settled that no extensive discussion is required.

. . . .

. . . Affirmed.

RELATED CASES

A novel situation arose in *Williams* v. *Wheeler,* 23 Cal. App. 619, 138 P. 937 (1913). The board of regents of the state passed a regulation which provided for the vaccination of *all* students at the University of California. The state legislature passed a law requiring children in all public and private schools to be vaccinated, *except* those children whose parents were "conscientiously opposed to vaccination." The court held that the state statute "is not a health regulation so as to be within the general police power, and hence would not nullify a regulation of the boards of regents of the state university requiring all students to be vaccinated." Effectively, then, the court held that all students entering the university had to be vaccinated, while pupils in public and private schools could be exempted if they objected on religious grounds.

The fact that a resolution of a local board of education, corresponding to a statute requiring vaccination as a prerequisite for admission to public schools, did not also require children in private schools to be vaccinated was not considered by the New Jersey supreme court in *Sadlock* v. *Board of Education,* 137 N.J.L. 85, 58 A.2d 218 (1948), to negate its application to public schools. The court, characterizing the act as a measure for the general welfare, declared furthermore that the statute did not violate personal or religious liberties.

State health regulations involve more than mere immunization against various diseases. The several cases discussed below illustrate that courts have been just as willing to uphold other regulatory matters, which have generally been based upon the states' police powers.

The right of a school board to require from all children seeking admission to the school a "Physical Record Card" based upon an examination by a physician was upheld in *Streich* v. *Board of Education*, 34 S.D. 169, 147 N.W. 779 1914). In doing so, the court determined that the school board had authority through its police powers to so act as to protect the school premises and school children from the spread of infectious and contagious diseases, even though the board of health is usually responsible for such matters.

The South Dakota court could find no question of religious liberty involved under the circumstances. It noted that counsel repeatedly said in oral argument that a religious question was not involved, even though appellant's brief suggested that the requirement of the physical examination was violative of his freedom of mental determination which "may be a part of his worship of Deity." In its agreement with counsel's oral arguments, the court declared that school boards should not base rules for public schools "upon the tenets of any particular religious sect or sects."

A tangential element regarding health issues arose in *Application of President and Directors of Georgetown College*, 331 F.2d 1000 (1964), where a federal court entered an order authorizing the university hospital on a sectarian campus to administer blood transfusions to a dying patient, whose husband refused upon religious grounds to authorize them. In doing so, the court noted among other things that the patient wanted to live; that the transfusions were necessary to maintain her life; and that the hospital would run the risk of civil and criminal liability if it failed to administer such treatment.

In *State* ex rel. *Holcomb* v. *Armstrong*, 39 Wash. 2d 860, 239 P.2d 545 (1952), below, an objection was made by a member of the Christian Science faith that submission to a required X-ray examination of her chest as a prerequisite to her enrollment at the University of Washington for her senior year would be contrary to the doctrine of her church and "to her personal religious convictions." Deciding that the primary concern of the regulation was to merely detect incidences of infectious tuberculosis and thus prevent the spread of that dreaded disesae to others in the student body, the court noted that the regulation did not require any infected person to "take any prescribed treatment," but merely denied him admission to the university.

Tuberculosis constituted a "clear and present danger" that could be safeguarded against by the board of regents as an essential means for maintaining effective operation of the state university, the court determined.

† † *STATE* ex rel. *HOLCOMB* v. *ARMSTRONG*
39 wash.2d 860, 239 p.2d 545 (1952).

Judge OLSON delivered the opinion of the court, saying in part:

Since 1941, the respondent board has required all entering freshmen to have this [X-ray] examination as a condition precedent to registration. The appellant entered the university in 1947 as a freshman and, after voicing her objections, submitted to the examination.

In 1950, upon the advice of the health officer of the university, the respondent board extended this requirement to all students desiring to register. When she applied for registration for her senior year, appellant would not comply with this rule. She is a member of the Christian Science church and adheres to its doctrine. She requested exemption from the examination because of her belief that submission to it is contrary to that doctrine and to her personal religious convictions.

The health officer of the university testified to certain facts regarding the nature of tuberculosis, its incidence on the university campus, and the reasons for making the requirement in question. His testimony was uncontroverted and, in summary, was that tuberculosis is an insidious, slow, and progressive disease and is infectious; that a person may be infected with it and show no symptoms of the disease nor be aware of his infection; that its early discovery is difficult, except by an X-ray of the chest; that this method of exploration is generally considered best adapted to mass screening by the medical profession; that a tubercular lesion in the lungs will show as a shadow upon an X-ray film; and that further tests will then permit a positive diagnosis.

. . . .

He stated it to be his conclusion that, in order to protect the health of the student body, it is imperative that every effort be made to discover the presence of the disease on the campus, and that for this purpose the requirement of an X-ray examination of all registering students is necessary.

Whether compliance with the questioned regulation is contrary to the doctrine to which appellant adheres is not in controversy, nor is her sincerity.

It is not the proposal of the respondents that any person found to be infected take any prescribed treatment. The regulation is purely for the purpose of discovery. It does not say to this appellant, you must be treated if you are ill; it only says, if you are so unfortunate as to be ill and not know it, you cannot spread your infection to others at the university. Its primary concern is not for the possibly infected student, but is for those jeopardized by contact with such an individual. It is a preventive measure. Noncompliance with it for any reason by one or more of the group tends to make such a measure ineffective.

Appellant's assignments of error raise two questions: the constitutionality of the regulation, and the power of the respondent board to make it.

The material portion of the first

amendment to the constitution of the United States is "Congress shall make no law respecting an establishment of religion, or prohibiting the free exercise thereof. . . ."

This right is protected against infringement by state action. *Cantwell* v. *State of Connecticut,* 1940, 310 U.S. 296. . . . Here the action of the regents is the action of the state.

There is no presumption in favor of the constitutionality of any regulation involving civil rights. *Schneider* v. *State of New Jersey,* 1939, 308 U.S. 147.

Amendment 4 to the constitution of the state of Washington provides, in part:

Absolute freedom of conscience in all matters of religious sentiment, belief and worship, shall be, guaranteed to every individual, and no one shall be molested or be disturbed in person or property on account of religion; but the liberty of conscience hereby secured shall not be so construed as to excuse acts of licentiousness or justify practices inconsistent with the peace and safety of the state. . . .

Religious freedom embraces two concepts:

. . . freedom to believe and freedom to act. The first is absolute but, in the nature of things, the second cannot be. Conduct remains subject to regulation for the protection of society. . . .

Cantwell v. *State of Connecticut,* supra.

This freedom can be restricted "only to prevent grave and immediate danger to interests which the state may lawfully protect." *West Virginia State Board of Education* v. *Barnette,* 1943,

319 U.S. 624, 639. . . . Other restatements of the "clear and present danger" test have been made in numerous cases since Justice Holmes gave it life in 1919 in *Schenck* v. *United States,* 249 U.S. 47. Their citation or review would not be helpful. The test must be applied to the facts of each case because, as its author said, "It is a question of proximity and degree."

With these principles in mind, we cannot say the questioned regulation violates any constitutional inhibition. Here the public interest threatened is the health of all of the students and employees of the university. It may lawfully be protected. In this case, it is of more importance than the right of appellant which is infringed. The danger to this interest is clear and present, grave and immediate. Infringement of appellant's rights is a necessary consequence of a practical attempt to avoid the danger. The questioned requirement utilizes the generally approved method of combating the danger, and no practical method which might not possibly infringe a constitutional right is shown. It is a regulation pertaining to the second aspect of the constitutional inhibition, mentioned in the Cantwell case, supra, in which aspect the conduct of appellant is subject to regulation for the protection of others. Her "freedom to believe" remains absolute.

. . . .

. . . We therefore conclude that the board of regents had the power to make and enforce the regulation in question, and that the disallowance of the exemption claimed by appellant was proper.

REACTIONS OF LEGAL PERIODICALS TO *STATE* ex rel. *HOLCOMB* v. *ARMSTRONG*

The court's approach in applying the clear and present danger doctrine to the situation at hand drew sharp criticism in a number of law journals.

In that connection, the writer in the *Rocky Mountain Law Review* (24:388) argued that the test was designed to give judicial protection to the expression of innocent ideas. The test, however, was not intended to be used to settle arguments over preventive medicine, the reviewer asserted.

Developing a similar argument in the *Washington Law Review* (27:228), the writer there declared that the sole question to be determined by the courts is whether the requiring of an X-ray examination is reasonably within the general powers of the regents. That such an inquiry would not involve questions of the free exercise of religion or of clear and present danger seemed clear to the analyst. In closing, he reasoned that a blanket requirement of examination is a reasonable means for the regents to discover infected persons on the campus.

TEACHERS

A number of courts, as is evidenced above, have gone on record in opposition to instruction imparted by inadequately qualified teachers regardless of the type of school. Other courts have been divided over the constitutional question of whether a public school teacher may wear distinctive religious garb in the classroom. (In this connection, see the chapter on religious garb in public schools.)

A sample of some of the other church-state problems involving teachers follows. Only one area of controversy in this field has been decided by the nation's highest court.

An absolute exclusion of any type of religious instruction under an interpretation of a ban against ecclesiastics, missionaries, and ministers of any kind from ever serving in or visiting in a college established by one Girard's will was challenged in *Vidal* v. *Girard's Executor,* 2 How. (U.S.) 127 (1844), below. There the United States Supreme Court, Mr. Justice Story speaking, determined that the effect of the above provision was not to exclude either Christianity or the Bible from the school. The Court reasoned therefore, that there could be no restrictions on the religious opinions of the instructors and officers of the college.

† † *VIDAL* v. *GIRARD'S EXECUTORS*
2 HOWARD 127 (1844).

Mr. Justice STORY delivered the opinion of the Court, saying in part:

. . . The late Stephen Girard, by his will dated the 25th day of December, A.D. 1830, after making sundry bequests to his relatives and friends, to the city of New Orleans, and to certain specified charities, proceeded in the 20th clause of that will to make the following bequest, on which the present controversy mainly hinges.

And, whereas, I have been for a long time impressed with the importance of educating the poor, and of placing them, by the early cultivation of their minds and the developments of their moral principles, above the many temptations to which, through poverty and ignorance, they are exposed; and I am particularly desirous to provide for such a number of poor male white orphan children, as can be trained in one institution, a better education, as well as a more comfortable maintenance, than they usually receive from the application of the public funds [etc]. . . .

. . . And so far as regards the residue of my personal estate, in trust, as to two millions of dollars, part thereof, to apply and expend so much of that sum as may be necessary, in erecting, as soon as practicably may be, a permanent college, with suitable out-buildings, sufficiently spacious for the residence and accommodation of at least three hundred scholars, and the requisite teachers and other persons necessary in such an institution. . . .

. . . .

The testator then, after suggesting that in relation to the organization of the college and its appendages, he leaves necessarily many details to the mayor, aldermen, and citizens of Philadelphia, and their successors, proceeded to say:

there are, however, some restrictions which I consider it my duty to prescribe, and to be, amongst others, conditions on which my bequest for said college is made and to be enjoyed, namely . . . I enjoin and require that no ecclesiastic, missionary, or minister of any sect whatsoever, shall ever hold or exercise any station or duty whatever in the said college; nor shall any such person ever be admitted for any purpose, or as a

visitor, within the premises appropriated to the purposes of the said college.

In making this restriction, I do not mean to cast any reflection upon any sect or person whatsoever; but, as there is such a multitude of sects, and such a diversity of opinion amongst them, I desire to keep the tender minds of the orphans, who are to derive advantage from this bequest, free from the excitement which clashing doctrines and sectarian controversy are so apt to produce; my desire is, that all the instructors and teachers in the college shall take pains to instil into the minds of the scholars the purest principles of morality, so that, on their entrance into active life, they may, from inclination and habit, evince benevolence towards their fellow-creatures, and a love of truth, sobriety, and industry, adopting at the same time such religious tenets as their matured reason may enable them to prefer.

. . . The present bill is brought by the heirs at law of the testator, to have the devise of the residue and remainder of the real estate to the mayor, aldermen, and citizens of Philadelphia in trust as aforesaid to be declared void. . . .

. . . That if otherwise capable of taking effect, the trust would be void, because the plan of education proposed is anti-christian, and therefore repugnant to the law of Pennsylvania, and is also opposed to the provision of Art. IX. sect. iii. of the Constitution of Pennsylvania, that "no human authority can in any case whatever control or interfere with the rights of conscience."

. . . .

This objection if that the foundation of the college upon the principles and exclusions prescribed by the testator, is derogatory and hostile to the Christian religion, and so is void, as being against the common law and public policy o

Pennsylvania; and this for two reasons: First, because of the exclusion of all ecclesiastical missionaries, and ministers of any sect from holding or exercising any station or duty in the college, or even visiting the same; and Secondly, because it limits the instruction to be given to the scholars to pure morality, and general benevolence, and a love of truth, sobriety, and industry, thereby excluding, by implication, all instruction in the Christian religion.

In considering this objection, the court are not at liberty to travel out of the record in order to ascertain what were the private religious opinions of the testator, (of which indeed we can know nothing,) nor to consider whether the scheme of education by him prescribed, is such as we ourselves should approve, or as is best adapted to accomplish the great aims and ends of education. Nor are we at liberty to look at general considerations of the supposed public interests and policy of Pennsylvania upon this subject, beyond what its constitution and laws and judicial decisions make known to us. The question, what is the public policy of a state, and what is contrary to it, if inquired into beyond these limits, will be found to be one of great vagueness and uncertainty, and to involve discussions which scarcely come within the range of judicial duty and functions, and upon which men may and will complexionally differ; above all, when that topic is connected with religious polity, in a country composed of such a variety of religious sects as our country, it is impossible not to feel that it would be attended with almost insuperable difficulties, and involve differences of opinion almost endless in their variety. We disclaim any right to enter upon such examinations, beyond what the state constitutions, and laws, and decisions necessarily bring before us.

It is also said, and truly, that the Christian religion is a part of the common law of Pennsylvania. But this proposition is to be received with its appropriate qualifications, and in connection with the bill of rights of that state, as found in its constitution of government. The constitution of 1790, (and the like provision will, in substance, be found in the constitution of 1776, and in the existing constitution of 1838,) expressly declares.

That all men have a natural and indefeasible right to worship Almighty God according to the dictates of their own consciences; no man can of right be compelled to attend, erect, or support any place of worship, or to maintain any ministry against his consent; no human authority can, in any case whatever, control or interfere with the rights of conscience; and no preference shall ever be given by law to any religious establishments or modes of worship.

Language more comprehensive for the complete protection of every variety of religious opinion could scarcely be used; and it must have been intended to extend equally to all sects, whether they believed in Christianity or not, and whether they were Jews or infidels. So that we are compelled to admit although Christianity be a part of the common law of the state, yet it is so in this qualified sense, that its divine origin and truth are admitted, and therefore it is not to be maliciously and openly reviled and blasphemed against, to the annoyance of believers or the injury of the public. Such was the doctrine of the Supreme Court of Pennsylvania in *Updegraff* v. *The Commonwealth*, 11 Serg. and Rawle, 394.

It is unecessary for us, however, to

consider what would be the legal effect of a devise in Pennsylvania for the establishment of a school or college, for the propagation of Judaism, or Deism, or any other form of infidelity. Such a case is not to be presumed to exist in a Christian country; and therefore it must be made out by clear and indisputable proof. Remote inferences, or possible results, or speculative tendencies, are not to be drawn or adopted for such purposes. There must be plain, positive, and express provisions, demonstrating not only that Christianity is not to be taught; but that it is to be impugned or repudiated.

Now, in the present case, there is no pretence to say that any such positive or express provisions exist, or are even shadowed forth in the will. The testator does not say that Christianity shall not be taught in the college. But only that no ecclesistic of any sect shall hold or exercise any station or duty in the college. Suppose, instead of this, he had said that no person but a layman shall be an instructor or officer or visitor in the college, what legal objection could have been made to such a restriction? And yet the actual prohibition is in effect the same in substance. But it is asked; why are ecclesiastics excluded, if it is not because they are the stated and appropriate preachers of Christianity? The answer may be given in the very words of the testator. "In making this restriction," says he,

I do not mean to cast any reflection upon any sect or person whatsoever. But as there is such a multitude of sects and such a diversity of opinion amongst them, I desire to keep the tender minds of the orphans, who are to derive advantage from this bequest, free from the excitement which clashing doctrines and sectarian controversy are so apt to produce.

Here, then, we have the reason given and the question is not, whether it is satisfactory to us or not; nor whether the history of religion does or does not justify such a sweeping statement; but the question is, whether the exclusion be not such as the testator had a right consistently with the laws of Pennsylvania, to maintain, upon his own notions of religious instruction. Suppose the testator had excluded all religious instructors but Catholics, or Quakers or Swedenborgians; or, to put a stronger case, he had excluded all religious instructors but Jews, would the bequest have been void on that account? Suppose he had excluded all lawyers, or all physicians, or all merchants from being instructors or visitors, would the prohibition have been fatal to the bequest? The truth is, that in cases of this sort, it is extremely difficult to draw any just and satisfactory line of distinction in a free country as to the qualifications or disqualifications which may be insisted upon by the donor of a charity as to those who shall administer or partake of his bounty.

But the objection itself assumes the proposition that Christianity is not to be taught, because ecclesiastics are not to be instructors or officers. But this is by no means a necessary or legitimate inference from the premises. Why may not laymen instruct in the general principles of Christianity as well as ecclesiastics. There is no restriction as to the religious opinions of the instructors and officers. They may be, and doubtless under the auspices of the city government, they will always be, men, not only distinguished for learning and talent, but for piety and elevated virtue and holy lives and characters. And we cannot overlook the blessings, which such men by their conduct, as well as their instructions, may, nay must im part to their youthful pupils. Why may not the Bible, and especially the New Testament, without note or comment, be read and taught as a divine revelation in the college—its general precepts expounded, its evidences explained, and its glorious principles of morality inculcated? What is there to prevent a work, not sectarian, upon the general evidences of Christianity, from being read and taught in the college by lay-teachers? Certainly there is nothing in the will, that proscribes such studies. Above all, the testator positively enjoins,

that all the instructors and teachers in the college shall take pains to instil into the minds of the scholars the purest principles of morality, so that on their entrance into active life they may from inclination and habit evince benevolence towards their fellow-creatures and a love of truth, sobriety, and industry, adopting at the same time such religious tenents as their matured reason may enable them to prefer.

Now, it may well be asked, what is there in all this, which is positively enjoined, inconsistent with the spirit or truths of Christianity? Are not these truths all taught by Christianity, although it teaches much more? Where can the purest principles of morality be learned so clearly or so perfectly as from the New Testament? Where are benevolence, the love of truth, sobriety, and industry, so powerfully and irresistibly inculcated as in the sacred volume? The testator has not said how these great principles are to be taught, or by whom, except it be by laymen, nor what books are to be used to explain or enforce them. All that we can gather from his language is, that he desired to exclude sectarianism from the college, leaving the instructors and officers free to teach the purest morality, the love of truth, sobriety, and industry, by all appropriate means; and of course including the best, the surest, and the most impressive. The objection, then, in this view, goes to this,—either that the testator has totally omitted to provide for religious instruction in his scheme of education, (which, from what has been already said, is an inadmissible interpretation,) or that it includes but partial and imperfect instruction in those truths. In either view can it be truly said that it contravenes the known law of Pennsylvania upon the subject of charities, or is not allowable under the article of the bill of rights already cited? Is an omission to provide for instruction in Christianity in any scheme of school or college education a fatal defect, which avoids it according to the law of Pennsylvania? If the instruction provided for is incomplete and imperfect, is it equally fatal? These questions are propounded, because we are not aware that anything exists in the constitution or laws of Pennsylvania, or the judicial decisions of its tribunals, which would justify us in pronouncing that such defects would be so fatal. Let us take the case of a charitable donation to teach poor orphans reading, writing, arithmetic, geography, and navigation, and excluding all other studies and instruction; would the donation be void, as a charity in Pennsylvania, as being deemed derogatory to Christianity? Hitherto it has been supposed, that a charity for the instruction of the poor might be good and valid in England even if it did not go beyond the establishment of a grammar-school. And in America, it has been thought, in the absence of any express legal prohibitions, that the donor might select the studies, as well as the classes of persons, who were to receive his bounty without being compellable to make religious instruction a necessary part of those studies. It has hitherto been thought sufficient, if he does not require any thing to be taught inconsistent with Christianity.

Looking to the objection therefore in a mere juridical view, which is the only one in which we are at liberty to consider it, we are satisfied that there is nothing in the devise establishing the college, or in the regulations and restrictions contained therein, which are inconsistent with the Christian religion, or are opposed to any known policy of the state of Pennsylvania.

. . . .

Upon the whole, it is the unanimous opinion of the court, that the decree of the Circuit Court of Pennsylvania dismissing the bill, ought to be affirmed . . .

PUBLIC FUNDS FOR PAROCHIAL SCHOOL TEACHERS

The question of paying from public funds the salaries of parochial teachers arose in several cases. A taxpayer's suit to enjoin the payment from public school funds of a public school teacher, who in maintaining a sectarian school violated the terms of her contract calling for the teaching of "a public free school," was rejected in *Nance* v. *Johnson*, 84 Tex. 401, 19 S.W. 559 (1892). The court ruled that such a suit could not be maintained until the taxpayers had exhausted the administrative remedies as provided by law which included a preliminary appeal to the superintendent of public instruction.

A taxpayer sought an injunction in *Millard* v. *Board of Education*, 121 Ill. 297, 10 N.E. 669 (1887), to stop the operation after ten years of a public school which was conducted in the basement of a Roman Catholic church by Roman Catholic teachers only. The court, noting that the Illinois school law did not prescribe "any religious belief as qualification of a teacher in a public school," determined that the school authorities could select their teachers "as they may think best."

† † *MILLARD* v. *BOARD OF EDUCATION*
121 ILL. 297, 10 N.E. 669 (1887).

Mr. Justice CRAIG delivered the opinion of the court:

. . . It is alleged that complainant is a taxpayer in a certain school district in St. Clair county; that the schools are under the control of a board of education instead of school directors; that for the last 10 years the school authorities of said district have maintained one of the schools in the base-nent of a church which is under the control of a congregation of Roman Catholics; that such congregation is sectarian; that during the last year the board of education appointed as teachers for such school persons who alone were members of such church; that the board paid the church, as rent for the use of the basement, for the school year of 10 months, $600; that the children of Catholic parents and the teachers were required to assemble at the church on all school days by 8 o'clock A.M., and have mass said to them by the priest of the congregation until half past 8 o'clock; that the teachers and pupils were then required to repair to the school-room, in the basement, and engage in religious instruction by teaching and learning catechism until 9 A.M.; that the common-school exercises were then commenced, and continued until 12 o'clock, when the *angelus* prayer was said by pupils and teachers. It is also alleged that the basement of said church was never established or located as a school-site by a vote of the people of the district, or petition of the voters, as required by statute; that the board of education threatens to and will appoint only members of said church as teachers for the ensuing year, and will pay for the use of the basement same rent as heretofore, and will conduct the school therein at public expense, with the religious exercises above set forth, in the same manner as during the last year. It is also alleged that on the first day of February, 1885, a school-site other than that named in the bill was located in pursuance of a petition of a majority of the voters of the district, and on the tenth of March, 1885, the board submitted a proposal to issue $30,000 of the bonds of the district to the voters with which to pay for the site, which was voted down by a

majority of 18. The bill concludes with a prayer as follows:

Wherefore complainant prays that said board of education may be summoned to answer this bill; that, upon a hearing hereof, said board may be perpetually enjoined from in any manner maintaining, supporting, or conducting a public school in such church basement, or expending any of the school funds of said district for that purpose; and that in the meantime a temporary injunction issue to restrain the defendant from so doing; and that complainant may have such other relief as to equity appertains.

As to the first allegation, that the schools have been maintained in the basement of a Catholic church, no importance whatever can be attached to a fact of that character. If the district where the school was maintained had no school-house, and it became necessary for the board of education to procure a building to be used for school purposes, they had the right to rent of any person who had property suitable for school purposes; and whether the owner of the property was a Methodist, a Presbyterian, a Roman Catholic, or any other denomination, was a matter of no moment, nor was it material that the building selected had been used as a church.

The next allegation is that the board employed Catholic teachers in the school. The statute has not prescribed any religious belief as a qualification of a teacher in a public school. The school authorities may select a teacher who belongs to any church, or no church, as they may think best.

The next allegation is that children of Catholic parents, and the teachers, are required to attend at the church at a certain hour on school-days, and hear mass said by the priest. Who requires this attendance is not disclosed by the bill. Whether it is the priest or church authorities, or somebody else, is left to mere conjecture. There is no intimation that the board of education requires anything of this character, and, so long as they are not connected with the matter, the allegation forms no ground of relief in favor of complainant. Besides, attending mass at the church has nothing to do with the school or its management, and upon what ground complainant can complain, because others in no manner connected with him may be required to attend mass at the church, we cannot comprehend.

Another part of this allegation is that the teachers and pupils are required to meet at the school-room each morning, for a half hour before 9 o'clock, and engage in religious instruction, by reading and learning catechism. What the nature of this religious instruction may be is not disclosed by the bill, nor is it claimed that it is directed, ordered, or required by the board of education, or that they have anything to do with it, nor is it claimed that complainant's children are required, against his will or desire, to attend any religious or sectarian instruction in the school. Under such circumstances, we see no ground for relief under this part of the bill.

The next allegation found in the bill is that, when school closes at noon each day, the *angelus* prayer was said by pupils and teachers. It is not claimed in the bill that this prayer is required by any regulation of the board, or any rule of the school. So far as it appears, it is a mere voluntary matter among teachers and scholars, which in no manner injures complainant. Had the board of education required any religious doctrine to be taught in the pub-

lic schools, or established any religious exercises sectarian in character, and complainant's children were required to receive such religious instruction in the school, and conform to the sectarian exercises established, he might have good ground of complaint, as our public schools are established for the purpose of education. The free schools are institutions provided where all children of the state may receive a good common-school education. The schools have not been established to aid any sectarian denomination, or assist in disseminating any sectarian doctrine, and no board of education or school directors have any authority to use the public funds for such a purpose.

The next and only remaining allegation of the bill to be considered questions the authority of the board to lease the basement of the church for school purposes. It appears from the bill that on the first day of February, 1885, the voters of the district located a school-house site in pursuance of the statute, and that the board of education submitted the question of issuing bonds, in amount $30,000, to erect a school-house on the site selected, to a vote of the people, and that on the tenth day of March, 1885, the proposition was defeated by a vote of the people. Section 80, c. 122, Rev. St., made it the duty of the board of education to establish and support free schools, not less than six, nor more than ten, months in each year. What course should the board pursue? Money to build could not be raised, because the voters had defeated the proposition. The school was required to be kept in operation. Under such circumstances no remedy was at hand except to lease, which may be done under the section of the statute last named. What building the board hould lease for school purposes is a matter for that body to determine, and not for the courts to decide. After the building is procured, of course the school will have to be conducted in the same manner that other free schools of the state are conducted, regardless of any opinion that may be entertained by the owner of the building in regard to the propriety of any school exercises.

As no ground for equitable relief is shown in the bill, the judgment of the appellate court was right, and it will be affirmed.

ASSOCIATED PROBLEMS

For a discussion of the court's disposition of the issue involving the holding of public school in a church, see the chapter on buildings.

A peculiar situation developed in *McDonald* v. *Parker*, 130 Ky. 501, 110 S.W. 810 (1908), where several faculty members of a sectarian college were "loaned" to a nearby graded school district. A fire had destroyed the college's administration building, and thereby resulted in limited operations for the ensuing school year. Three professors were then allowed to resign so they could conduct the graded school. The teaching services of two ladies, who lacked teaching certificates necessary for employment in public schools, were donated by the college to the graded school.

In an action brought by the treasurer of the graded common school district to obtain a mandamus requiring the county superintendent of common schools to pay over to him the district's pro rata share of the common school fund, the court ruled that the salaries of the three male teachers from the college must be paid from the public funds. Emphasizing that the money would go to individuals for services rendered, the court discounted the argument that such a payment would be an unconstitutional allocation of public funds to aid "any church, sectarian or denominational school."

Conceding that the ladies could not be employed by the public schools, the court nevertheless pointed out that they "were eminently qualified to teach young children." Noting that the statute establishing teacher requirements was intended to prevent the squandering of public money on incompetent teachers, the court said that the law was not meant to "prevent charitable persons from donating their services," especially at a time when philanthropy was "not so prevalent in [the] state."

A side issue in the controversy over public funds to religious teachers in a constitutional scheme of separation of church and state arose in *Gubler* v. *Utah State Teachers' Retirement Board*, 113 Utah 188, 192 P.2d 580 (1948). There the court ruled that statutory expansion in 1945 of the Teachers' Retirement Act of 1938 to give retirement credits to public school teachers whose duties prior to 1937 were in parochial schools did not violate either the constitutional provision concerning religious liberty or the one forbidding public aid to church schools.

The legislative intent in enacting the Amendment of 1945 was interpreted by the court as a design for improving the quality of the state's public school system and secular education in general by extending state retirement benefits to parochial teachers who were willing to switch their employment to the public school system. The court answered the constitutional questions by pointing out that:

> Under the present plan, no money is being appropriated or used to maintain any school operated or controlled by a church and no funds are used to assist in maintaining any essential element of such a school.

The court continued:

> Likewise, no public money or property has been appropriated or is being applied to any religious worship, exercise, or instruction.

It said, in closing, that the amendment did not operate retroactively "so as to pay these teachers for being instructors in church schools." Rather "the amendment pays for services in future," the court pointed out.

SUMMARY

This chapter like the last one does not submit easily to a meaningful summary because of the variety of nuances involved in the question of compulsory education. Except for a few general categories, most of the points to be suggested here are merely illustrative of some of the many facets rather than a comprehensive summation of all the points included in this chapter.

At the outset it should be stressed that the United States Supreme Court made clear in 1923 that there was no question about the constitutional power of a state to compel attendance at some school. The decision also upheld the constitutionality of a state's authority to establish reasonable regulations for all schools both public and private. On the other hand, just two years later the Supreme Court in the Pierce case was to make equally clear that children are not creatures of the state and the state of Oregon could not standardize them by a law which required that children attend only public schools.

There has been considerable litigation over the question of what are "reasonable regulations" insofar as they affect religious freedom. There has been significant litigation in this respect regarding the Amish. The

Pennsylvania supreme court, for example, held in 1951 that Amish parents do not have a constitutional right to deprive their children of an education even though their religion demands that the child's education be more limited than that required by state law. Although there has been no litigation at this writing, the state of Iowa for four years has been anguishing over finding a solution to the problem created by fifteen families of Old Order Amish. The problem is, of course, how to maximize the religious freedom of the Amish within the framework of the state's compulsory school law and its requirement of certified teachers. A temporary solution was arrived at in 1966 when the Danforth Foundation provided the necessary funds to hire certified teachers for the Amish schools for several years.

Other states, such as Nebraska, in 1962, have held that among "reasonable regulations" a state may require the use of certified teachers in all scools, public and private, in the state.

A number of cases concerning qualifications of teachers have had religious overtones. The Massachusetts supreme court in 1955 held that simply because a child is receiving instruction at home does not justify his parents in removing him from a regular school. The key to the problem, the court pointed out, was the determination of the competency of the home instruction. In a similar vein, the Washington high court in 1960, ruled that a child could not for religious reasons be taken from a school to receive home instruction from a parent who is not a certified teacher. The New Jersey supreme court went even further in following this trend when in 1950 it held that a child was not receiving a legally acceptable education in his home even though the parent was a certified teacher. The problem, as the court saw it, was that the parent had not been an active school teacher for the past twenty years.

These rulings must be considered as constituting the mainstream of judicial thought on the subject. Apart from a few early decisions reflecting a more casual attitude toward qualifications and certification where the religious issue was involved, such as one state court which concluded that education consists of more than "book-learning," only one modern state case stands against the general trend mentioned above. In 1950, the Illinois supreme court in a case in which religious beliefs were at issue held that the object of compulsory education meant that a child "shall be educated" not necessarily that he "shall be educated in any particular manner or place." Legal periodical articles were sharply critical of the decision.

Various health regulations incident to one's attendance in a public school have resulted in a host of cases in which the issue of church-state relations was central. Compulsory vaccination requirements adopted by public schools or municipalities have been responsible for most of the litigation in this area. Seventeen state courts, on various grounds, have held that neither the Due Process Clause of the Fourteenth Amendment nor the religion clauses of the First Amendment were violated by compulsory vaccination requirements. The Supreme Court of the United States as early as 1904 had upheld the constitutionality of such practices if they were authorized by a state's constitution or laws. In general the courts adopted the police power doctrine, that is, that a government has reasonable power to protect its citizens' health, welfare and morals and promote their education, as overriding the religious issues.

The issue is far from dead, however. In 1965, for example, the supreme court of Arkansas was faced with the question and concluded that state health regulations which required all students to be vaccinated against smallpox was a reasonable regulation and did not violate the constitutional right of the free exercise of religion. In the same year, the supreme court of North Carolina was confronted with a similar case, but remanded it for a retrial because of the trial court's improper instructions to the jury.

In a related case, the Washington state supreme court devised an interesting rationale. Holding that requiring a student to have a chest X-ray to detect infectious tuberculosis was not contrary to petitioner's religious beliefs that healing must come from heaven, the court concluded that the X-ray was a detection device, not a treatment. Somewhat more to the point, the court also noted that tuberculosis was a clear and present danger to society.

CHAPTER ELEVEN

Incidental and Public Benefits for Religious Purposes

† †

CHURCHES, PAROCHIAL SCHOOLS, and other religious institutions are aided in many ways by the state. The "wall of separation" between church and state has been a difficult structure for the courts to maintain for the rulings of the many courts are not always consistent. Moreover, practices once begun are difficult to terminate after years of being part of the warp and woof of the community pattern. They, like eggs, are difficult to unscramble.

SPECIAL EDUCATION

Several state courts have allowed public funds to be used by sectarian institutions for special education purposes. Violations of both state and federal constitutional provisions have been alleged in challenging this use of state money.

The supreme court of Mississippi ruled in *Craig v. Mercy Hospital Street Memorial,* 209 Miss. 427, 47 So.2d 867 (1950), that a state grant for construction to a sectarian hospital did not violate state constitutional provisions prohibiting the use of state funds for the support of any sectarian schools.

In *Shade v. Allegheny County Institution District,* 386 Pa. 507, 126 A.2d 911 (1956), a taxpayer's suit sought to enjoin the institution district administrators from paying public funds to sectarian children's homes for children placed in them by the juvenile court.

Such payments were charged with violating the establishment clause of the First and Fourteenth Amendments and with violating the state constitutional provisions which prohibited appropriations from public funds for charitable, educational, or benevolent purposes to sectarian institutions. The Pennsylvania supreme court held that "payments made by the Institution District for the support and maintenance of neglected or dependent children, who are under the jurisdiction and control of the Juvenile Court, are not appropriations within the meaning of that term." The maintenance of such children is, rather, a governmental duty. The court cited *Everson v. Board of Education* and concluded that the payment did not tend toward governmental establishment of religion.

341

A statute authorizing public appropriations to private institutions for the education of "exceptional children" was construed in *Butler* v. *United Cerebral Palsy,* Ky., 352 S.W.2d 203 (1961), not to extend to the allocation of public funds to sectarian or denominational schools. The Kentucky court reasoned that statute was a welfare rather than an educational measure, but ruled that in the challenged situation there was no attempt to spend money "for education" or from "the public school fund."

PUBLIC FUNDS FOR SECTARIAN SCHOOLS

Challenging the use of state money for sectarian schools has caused a number of cases to be brought before the courts, the bulk of which are state cases. For this reason, and also because some of the judgments date back to the 1800's the decisions rendered are frequently inconsistent.

The use of public funds for the construction "of a house to be used as a schoolhouse and for religious services" was allowed in *Swadley* v. *Haynes,* Tn., 41 S.W. 1066 (1897). The Tennessee court ruled that the appropriation was "just a part of the construction cost and was in the nature of a loan made out of public funds in consideration of getting the use of the building for a public school and [was] under an arrangement by which it was to be returned by five annual contributions of $20 each. . . ."

Schools on Indian reservations were held by the United States Supreme Court in *Quick Bear* v. *Leupp,* 210 U.S. 50 (1908), not to fall under the general ban on appropriations of public funds to sectarian schools. The Supreme Court declared that the provisions in the five Indian Appropriation Acts between 1895 and 1899 were intended to forbid educational contracts in sectarian schools only in those instances where the appropriations of public moneys were raised by general taxation from all persons.

The Court refused to extend that ban to Indian treaty and trust funds which belong to the Indians themselves. The net effect of the decision was that governmental officials could not be enjoined from contracting with the Indians to the *pro rata* extent that the Indians wished to go with tying their trust funds to sectarian schools.

† † *QUICK BEAR* v. *LEUPP*
210 U.S. 50, 28 S. CT. 690, 52 L. ED. 954 (1908).

Mr. Chief Justice FULLER delivered the opinion of the Court:

The appellants filed their bill in equity in the Supreme Court of the District of Columbia, alleging that:

1. The plaintiffs are citizens of the United States, and members of the Sioux tribe of Indians of the Rosebud Agency, in the

State of South Dakota. . . .

2. The defendants . . . are sued in this action as the Commissioner of Indian Affairs, the Secretary of the Interior, the Secretary of the Treasury, the Treasurer of the United States, and the Comptroller of the Treasury respectively.

3. That by article VII of the Sioux treaty of April 29, 1868 (15 Stat. 635, 637) . . . the United States agreed that for every thirty children of the said Sioux tribe who can be induced or compelled to attend school, a house shall be provided, and a teacher competent to teach the elementary branches of an English education, shall be furnished, who will reside among said Indians and faithfully discharge his or her duties as a teacher.

4. That for the purpose of carrying out the above provision of the said treaty during the fiscal year ending June 30, 1906, the following appropriation was made . . .
'For support and maintenance of day and industrial schools, including erection and repairs of school buildings. . . .'
The fund so appropriated is generally known as the Sioux treaty fund.

5. That section 17 of the said act of March 2, 1889, further provides as follows:
'And in addition thereto there shall be set apart out of any money in the Treasury not otherwise appropriated, the sum of three million dollars, which said sum shall . . . be so expended for the promotion of industrial and other suitable education among said Indians, and the other half thereof in such manner and for such purposes, including reasonable case payments *per capita* as, in the judgment of said Secretary, shall, from time to time, most contribute to the advancement of said Indians in civilization and self-support.'
This fund of three million dollars is generally known as the Sioux trust fund.

. . . .

7. That the act of June 7, 1897, c. 3, § 1, 30 Stat. 62, 79, contains the following provision:
'And it is hereby declared to be the

settled policy of the Government to hereafter make no appropriation whatever for education in any sectarian school.'

8. That, in violation of the said provision of the act of June 7, 1897, the said Francis E. Leupp, Commissioner of Indian Affairs as aforesaid, has made or intends to make, for and on behalf of the United States, a contract with the Bureau of Catholic Indian Missions of Washington, D.C., a sectarian organization, for the care, education, and maintenance, during the fiscal year ending June 30, 1906, of a number of Indian pupils of the Sioux tribe, at a sectarian school on the said Rosebud Reservation, known at the St. Francis Mission Boarding School, and in the said contract has agreed to pay or intends to agree to pay to the said Bureau of Catholic Indian Missions of Washington, D.C., a certain rate per quarter as compensation for every pupil in attendance at the said school. . . .

9. That all payments made to the said Bureau of Catholic Indian Missions of Washington, D.C., under the said contract, either out of the said Sioux treaty fund or out of the interest of the said Sioux trust fund, will be payments for education in a sectarian school, and will be unlawful diversions of funds appropriated by Congress, and in violation of the above-recited provision of the act of June 7, 1897. . . .

10. That the plaintiffs have never requested nor authorized the payment of any part of the said Sioux treaty fund, or the interest of the said Sioux trust fund, to the said Bureau of Catholic Indian Missions of Washington, D.C., or any other person or organization whatever, for the education of Indian pupils of the said Sioux tribe in the said St. Francis Mission Boarding School, or any other sectarian school whatever, but have on the contrary protested against any use of either of the said funds, or the interest of the same, for the purpose of such education.

11. That the plaintiffs have no remedy at law. Wherefore the plaintiffs ask relief, as follows:
I. That a permanent injunction issue

against the said Francis E. Leupp, Commissioner of Indian Affairs, to restrain him from executing any contract with the said Bureau of Catholic Indian Missions of Washington, D.C., or any other sectarian organization whatever, for the support, education or maintenance of any Indian pupils of the said Sioux tribe at the said St. Francis Mission Boarding School, or any other sectarian school on the said Rosebud Reservation or elsewhere. . . .

II. And for a permanent injunction against the drawing, countersigning and paying

any warrants in favor of the said Bureau of Catholic Indian Missions of Washington, D.C., or any other sectarian organization whatever, for the support, education, and maintenance of any Indian pupils of the said Sioux tribe. . . .

III. And for the general relief.
The defendants answered . . .

. . . .

2. Admitting

. . . These defendants, as officers of the Government of the United States, have no interest in the controversy raised by the bill, except to perform their duties under the law, and they, therefore, as such officers, respectfully submit the validity of the contract hereinafter referred to, and the payments thereunder, to the judgment of this honorable court. The real defendant in interest is the 'Bureau of Catholic Indian Missions,' a corporation duly incorporated by chapter 363 of the Acts of Assembly of Maryland for the year 1894, for the object, *inter alia,* of educating the American Indians directly and also indirectly by training their teachers and others, especially to train their youth to become self-sustaining men and women, using such methods of instruction in the principles of religion and of human knowledge as may be best adapted to these purposes.

. . . .

The case was submitted on record and briefs, and the court affirmed the decree below in respect of the income of the "Trust Fund," and reversed the injunction against the payment from the "Treaty Fund," and remanded the case with directions to dismiss the bill at the cost of the complainants, whereupon the case was brought to this court on appeal.

We concur in the decree of the Court of Appeals of the District and the reasoning by which its conclusion is supported. . . .

The validity of the contract for $27,-000 is attacked on the ground that all contracts for sectarian education among the Indians are forbidden by certain provisos contained in the Indian Appropriation Acts of 1895, 1896, 1897, 1898 and 1899. But if those provisos relate only to the appropriations made by the Government out of the public moneys of the United States raised by taxation from persons of all creeds and faiths, or none at all, and appropriated gratuitously for the purpose of education among the Indians, and not to "Tribal Funds," which belong to the Indians themselves, then the contract must be sustained. The difference between one class of appropriations and the other has long been recognized in the annual appropriation acts. The gratuitous appropriation of public moneys for the purpose of Indian education has always been made under the heading "Support of Schools," whilst the appropriation of the "Treaty Fund" has always been under the heading "Fulfilling Treaty Stipulations and Support of Indian Tribes," and that from the "Trust Fund" is not in the Indian Appropriation Acts at all. One class of appropriations relates to public moneys belonging to the Government;

the other to moneys which belong to the Indians and is administered for them by the Government.

From the history of appropriations of public moneys for education of Indians, set forth in the brief of counsel for appellees and again at length in the answer, it appears that before 1895 the Government for a number of years had made contracts for sectarian schools for the education of the Indians, and the money due on these contracts was paid, in the discretion of the Commissioner of Indian Affairs, from the "Tribal Funds" and from the gratuitous public appropriations. But in 1894 opposition developed against appropriating public moneys for sectarian education. Accordingly, in the Indian Appropriation Act of 1894, under the heading of "Support of Schools," the Secretary of the Interior was directed to investigate the propriety of discontinuing contract schools and to make such recommendations as he might deem proper. The Secretary suggested a gradual reduction in the public appropriations on account of the money which had been invested in these schools, with the approbation of the Government. He said: "It would be scarcely just to abolish them entirely—to abandon instantly a policy so long recognized," and suggested that they should be decreased at the rate of not less than twenty per cent a year. Thus in a few years they would cease to exist, and during this time the bureau would be gradually prepared to do without them, while they might gather strength to continue without Government aid.

Accordingly Congress introduced in the Appropriation Act of 1895 a limitation on the use of public moneys in sectarian schools. This act appropriated under the heading "Support of Schools"

for the support of Indian and industrial schools and for other purposes . . . $1,164,-350 . . . provided, that the Secretary of the Interior shall make contracts, but only with the present contract schools for the education of Indian pupils during the fiscal year ending June 30, 1896, to an extent not exceeding eighty per cent of the amount so used in the fiscal year 1895, and the Government shall as early as practicable make provision for the education of the Indians in Government schools.

This limitation of eighty per cent was to be expended for contract schools, which were those that up to that time had educated Indians through the use of public moneys, and had no relation and did not refer to "Tribal Funds."

. . . .

Since 1899 public moneys are appropriated under the heading "Support of Schools" "for the support of Indian and industrial schools and for other educational purposes," without saying anything about sectarian schools. This was not needed, as the effect of the legislation was to make subsequent appropriations for education mean that sectarian schools were excluded in sharing in them, unless otherwise provided.

As has been shown, in 1868 the United States made a treaty with the Sioux Indians, under which the Indians made large cessions of land and other rights. In consideration of this the United States agreed that for every thirty children a house should be provided and a teacher competent to teach the elementary branches of our English education should be furnished for twenty years. In 1877, in consideration of further land cessions, the United States agreed to furnish all necessary aid to assist the Indians in the work of civilization and furnish them schools and instruction in mechanical and agricultural arts, as provided by the Treaty of 1868. In 1889 Congress extended the obligation of the treaty for twenty years, subject to such modifications as Congress should deem most effective, to secure the Indians equivalent benefits of such education. Thereafter, in every annual Indian appropriation act, there was an appropriation to carry out the terms of this treaty, under the heading "Fulfilling Treaty Stipulations with and Support of Indian Tribes."

These appropriations rested on different grounds from the gratuitous appropriations of public moneys under the heading "Support of Schools." The two subjects were separately treated in each act, and, naturally, as they are essentially different in character. One is the gratuitous appropriation of public moneys for the purpose of Indian education, but the "Treaty Fund" is not public money in this sense. It is the Indians' money, or at least is dealt with by the Government as if it belonged to them, as morally it does. It differs from the "Trust Fund" in this: The "Trust Fund" has been set aside for the Indians and the income expended for their benefit, which expenditure required no annual appropriation. The whole amount due the Indians for certain land cessions was appropriated in one lump sum by the act of 1889, 25 Stat. 888, chap. 405. This "Trust Fund" is held for the Indians and not distributed *per capita,* being held as property in common. The money is distributed in accordance with the discretion of the Secretary of the Interior, but really belongs to the Indians. The President declared it to be the moral right of the Indians to have this "Trust Fund" applied to the education of the Indians in the schools of their choice, and the same view was entertained by the Supreme Court of the District of

Columbia and the Court of Appeals of the District. But the "Treaty Fund" has exactly the same characteristics. They are moneys belonging really to the Indians. They are the price of land ceded by the Indians to the Government. The only difference is that in the "Treaty Fund" the debt to the Indians created and secured by the treaty is paid by annual appropriations. They are not gratuitous appropriations of public moneys, but the payment, as we repeat, of a treaty debt in installments. We perceive no justification for applying the proviso or declaration of policy to the payment of treaty obligations, the two things being distinct and different in nature and having no relation to each other, except that both are technically appropriations.

Some reference is made to the Constitution, in respect to this contract with the Bureau of Catholic Indian Missions. It is not contended that it is unconstitutional, and it could not be. . . . But it is contended that the spirit of the Constitution requires that the declaration of policy that the Government "shall make no appropriation whatever for education in any sectarian schools" should be treated as applicable, on the ground that the actions of the United States were to always be undenominational, and that, therefore, the Government can never act in a sectarian capacity, either in the use of its own funds or in that of the funds of others, in respect of which it is a trustee; hence that even the Sioux trust fund cannot be applied for education in Catholic schools, even though the owners of the fund so desire it. But we cannot concede the proposition that Indians cannot be allowed to use their own money to educate their children in the schools of their own choice because the Government is necessarily undenominational, as it cannot make any law respecting an establishment of religion or prohibiting the free exercise thereof.

The Court of Appeals well said:

The 'Treaty' and 'Trust' moneys are the only moneys that the Indians can lay claim to as matters of right; the only sums on which they are entitled to rely as theirs for education; and while these moneys are not delivered to them in hand, yet the money must not only be provided, but be expended, for their benefit and in part for their education; it seems inconceivable that Congress should have intended to prohibit them from receiving religious education at their own cost if they so desired it; such an intent would be one 'to prohibit the free exercise of religion' amongst the Indians, and such would be the effect of the construction for which the complainants contend.

The *cestuis que trust* cannot be deprived of their rights by the trustee in the exercise of power implied.

Decree affirmed.

AID TO PAROCHIAL JUVENILE HOME

In *St. Hedwig's Industrial School* v. *Cook County*, 289 Ill. 432, 124 N.E. 629 (1919), a Roman Catholic industrial school for girls sued the county to recover "charges for the unpaid tuition, maintenance, and care of dependent children" who were committed there by the juvenile branch of the circuit court. A similar action in the joinder was pursued by the Polish Manual Training School for Boys. See also, *Trost* v. *Ketteler Manual Training School*, 282 Ill. 504, 118 N.E. 743 (1918).

The court determined that the remittance by the county of the full costs of the education of dependent children in Roman Catholic industrial schools was necessary. In denying the county's motion to recover all of the appropriations already channeled to the industrial schools in question on the ground that the state constitution prohibited any appropriation in aid of any church or sectarian purpose, the court reiterated its position in the Dunn and Trost cases that "one who pays less for benefits or services than the actual cost of the same is not making a donation by such a payment."

REACTIONS OF LEGAL PERIODICALS TO
ST. HEDWIGS SCHOOL v. *COOK COUNTY AND*
TROST v. *KETTELER MANUAL TRAINING SCHOOL*

The Illinois court's logic in both cases came under sharp attack in the *University of Detroit Law Journal* (6:174) and the *Minnesota Law Review* (27:311). Both reviewers characterized as erroneous the court's rationale that the appropriations for sectarian education were valid because the amount of such grants would be, in the words of the writer in the latter review, "less than was founded by a charitable bequest which dictated that the school be under the control of a board of trustees who were to be of a particular religious denomination." The court ruled that "[t]he fact that [the school] is not under the control of the town authorities is its objectionable feature, and constitutes the reason why moneys raised by taxation or appropriated by the Commonwealth for the support of common schools cannot be applied to its support."

PUBLIC FUNDS FOR PAROCHIAL SCHOOLS

In *Otken* v. *Lamkin,* 56 Miss. 758 (1879), the Mississippi state high court determined that an act which allowed private school children the same share of a public fund as public school children was unconstitutional. The act violated the state constitutional provision which stipulated that school funds could be used only for those schools which were under state and local supervision, open to all, and free of sectarian control, the court concluded.

A Texas public school board was held, in *Ussery* v. *City of Laredo,* 65 Tex. 406 (1886), not to be empowered to apply public school funds to the payment of the salary of a district teacher who clearly maintained a private school. In addition, the court ruled that the State Superintendent of Public Instruction lacked authority to order the local board to make such a payment.

The supreme court of South Dakota ruled in *Synod of Dakota* v. *State,* 2 S.D. 366, 50 N.W. 632, 14 LRA 418 (1891), that the state constitutional provision forbidding the use of lands, money, or credit for sectarian schools prohibited the appropriation of state funds for such schools as donations or as payment for services rendered to the state. The state constitutional provision prohibiting sectarian instruction in public schools was also quoted when the court held unconstitutional the payment of tuition by the state for students studying in the sectarian university to become public school teachers.

In an advisory opinion rendered to the Senate and House of Representatives of Massachusetts, *Opinion of the Justices,* 214 Mass. Supp. 595, 102 N.E. 464 (1913), the court ruled that the state constitutional provision prohibiting the use of public school funds for schools maintained in whole or in part by sectarian groups required that the funds be used only for public schools. However, the court went on to say that higher educational institutions under sectarian control were not prohibited by the state constitution.

A taxpayer's action was sustained in *Wright* v. *School District,* 151 Kan.

485, 99 P.2d 737 (1940), where the district's extra tax funds were being siphoned by the school board to a second school even though it appeared that the existing public school building was adequate. That second school clearly was controlled by a religious sect, and sectarian religious doctrines were taught within it, the Kansas supreme court held.

In another case, an Ohio court determined in *Findley* v. *City of Conneaut*, 121 Ohio Supp. 161 (1943), that a school set up by funds from a will as a private Protestant technical school was necessarily sectarian, and, therefore, could not be supported by public funds without violating the state constitution.

In the light of the school in question being characterized as controlled by and managed and administered for the interests of the adjacent Roman Catholic church, the Missouri high court ruled in *Berghorn* v. *Reorganized School District*, 364 Mo. 121, 260 S.W.2d 573 (1953), that tax money could not be used to maintain the school where sectarian religion was taught by Roman Catholic teachers attired in distinctive garb. To allow the practice of a public school district, which lacked a school system of its own, of paying tuition charged of its residents for their schooling at the sectarian school would countenance a violation of the Missouri and United States constitutions, the court determined.

The question of reimbursing the tuitions of high school students attending nonpublic schools was raised in *Donoghue* v. *Smith*, 126 A.2d 93, 119 Vt. 259 (1956). Under state statute, state aid could be obtained for students attending public school districts in other towns. The Vermont court ruled that restricting state aid to the repayment of tuitions of only those students attending public schools did not violate the statute which authorized towns not having a high school to pay the tuition of the students attending a high school in another town. The court concluded saying that "the courts in construing the statute, may not take into consideration the injustice which may be caused thereby."

In *Swart* v. *South Burlington Town School District*, 122 Vt. 177, 167 A.2d 514 (1961), below, a taxpayer challenged the expenditure of public funds for meeting tuition charges to religious denominational schools. Several religious schools within the school district had been declared by the state board of education to possess adequate "scholastic standards and educational facilities" to qualify them for tuition benefits within the provisions of the restrictive state statute governing the matter. The court determined that tuition payments from public funds to a nonpublic school, which was operated as an integral part of a religious society, fell within a literal interpretation of the statute but nevertheless violated the Establishment of Religion Clause of the First Amendment of the United States Constitution.

† † SWART v. SOUTH BURLINGTON TOWN SCHOOL DISTRICT

122 vt. 177, 167 a.2d 514 (1961).

Judge HOLDEN delivered the opinion of the court:

The immediate concern of this appeal is the expenditure of public funds to meet the charges of tuition for the attendance of students at high schools operated by the Roman Catholic Diocese of Burlington, Vermont. The cause has been well argued and thoughtfully presented, in keeping with the sensitive and solemn issues that confront the Court.

. . . .

The South Burlington Town School District does not maintain a public high school. It has transferred the task of furnishing plant, faculty and curricula for the higher education of the youth of the town to schools beyond its control that have been selected by the parents and approved by the state department of education.

The aspects of this enactment of which the plaintiff complains provide:

(a) Each town district shall maintain a high school or furnish secondary instruction, as hereinafter provided, for its advanced pupils at a high school or academy, to be selected by the parents or guardian of the pupil, within or without the state. The board of school directors may both maintain a high school and furnish secondary instruction elsewhere as herein provided as in the judgment of the board may best serve the interest of the pupils.
(b) Each town school district shall pay tuition per pupil per school year as billed, but not in execess of $325.00 unless authorized by a vote of the town school district, but in no case shall the tuition exceed the cost per pupil per year for the maintenance of such school for the previous year.

Acting according to the terms and formula specified in the statute the defendant school district and its officers, during the years from 1952 to 1958 authorized and made payments in varying amounts to the Cathedral High School of Burlington. This institution ceased operations at the close of the first semester of the 1958–59 school year. Its land, buildings and equipment are owned by the Roman Catholic Diocese of Burlington. During the time of operation as an educational establishment, it was conducted as a religious denominational high school of the Roman Catholic Faith.

The Rice Memorial High School, located at South Burlington, opened its courses of instruction at the time of the closing of Cathedral High School on January 30, 1959. Like Cathedral, this school is owned by the Diocese of Burlington. In the 1958–59 school year, the defendants caused the sum of $19,687.50 to be expended and paid directly to the Rice Memorial High School, for the attendance of South Burlington students at this high school.

Mount Saint Mary's Academy is located in the city of Burlington. The land, buildings and equipment are owned by The Sisters of Mercy of the Diocese of Burlington. The defendants have paid tuition to this school, in varying amounts since 1952. The payment for the 1958–59 school year was $2,025.

The chancellor made detailed findings concerning the specific payments to each of these schools and the corresponding tax payments made by the plaintiff over the same period. It is made to appear that the taxes collected from the plaintiff became a part of the public school funds of the South Burlington Town School District which were disbursed by the defendant officials to the institutions named. The chancellor specifically found that these disbursements were in payment of tuition and not for scholarships nor as awards of merit.

Mount Saint Mary's Academy and Rice Memorial High School were determined by the chancellor to be religious denominational high schools of the Roman Catholic Faith, controlled and principally supported by the Roman Catholic Church. Instruction in the religion of that denomination is included in the curricula of both institutions, and is a required subject for students of that faith. There is no requirement that students of other denominations attend the instruction in religion although some students in this category have elected to do so.

Each of the schools concerned has furnished the Department of Education for the State of Vermont the information relating to the cost per pupil in compliance with the statute. The state department of education has established no policy or regulation to specify whether tuition payments under the statute are to be made to the parents of the students receiving instruction or to the school which furnishes the courses of study.

The provisions of 16 V.S.A. § 799 forbid a town school district to pay tuition of a student receiving advanced instruction except to a high school or academy approved by the state board of education. Cathedral High School, Mount Saint Mary's Academy and Rice Memorial High School have received approval from the state board of education as to scholastic standards and educational facilities.

. . . .

The facts reported by the chancellor are not challenged by any of the appellants. The appeal centers on the declaration of the decree that

payment of tuition by the South Burlington Town School District to sectarian high schools in prohibited by the First and Fourteenth Amendments to the United States Constitution and Article 3, Chapter 1 of the Vermont Constitution.

. . . The record certified to this Court includes the written opinion of the chancellor which states his analysis of the issues relating to religious liberty and separation of Church and State as defined in these provisions of the state and federal constitutions. In this memorandum the court observed that all parties had seemingly agreed, and the chancellor adopted the theory that the constitutional provisions of the paramount law of Vermont and of the United States establish a common protection, with the effect that a violation of one infringes upon the other. Noting that the issue presented in relation to the Vermont Constitution has not been previously reported in the decisions of this Court, the court below resorted exclusively to the First Amendment and the decisions of the United States Supreme Court. . . .

. . . The correctness of the analogy adopted by the chancellor as to the state and federal guaranties is not essential to our decision. In order for the statute to prevail, it must not exceed the limitations of either. In the domain of religious liberty, the resolute history of the First Amendment seems the more demanding. Following the pattern established below, we search the question from the federal aspect.

The basic concept of religious liberty and the separation of Church and State was made applicable to the states with the ratification of the Fourteenth Amendment. . . . On questions arising under these amendments the decisions of the Supreme Court of the United States are controlling upon the Court. . . .

. . . " 'Despite the delicate and highly important functions entrusted to local school boards, they must perform within the limits of the Bill of Rights. . . .' " But the First Amendment must be cautiously applied to the end that the agency of the state is not inadvertently forbidden from extending a public benefit to all its citizens without regard to religious beliefs. . . . The mere fact that public funds are expended to an institution operated by a religious enterprise does not establish the fact that the proceeds are used to support the religion professed by the recipient. . . .

. . . The doctrine of these cases [*Cochran* v. *Louisiana State Board of Education,* 281 U.S. 370 (1930); *Everson* v. *Board of Education,* 330 U.S. 1 (1947); *McCollum* v. *Board of Education,* 333 U.S. 203 (1948); *Zorach* v. *Clauson,* 343 U.S. 306 (1952)] narrows our problem to this: Does the payment of tuition to a religious denominational school by a public entity finance religious instruction, to work a fusion of secular and sectarian education?

16 V.S.A. § 793 is the instrument which the Legislature has provided to the local school districts for furnishing the educational training required by the Vermont Constitution, Ch. II, § 64. The enactment entrusts to the school board the decision of whether secondary education will be provided in schools maintained by the district, or elsewhere. If it is to be furnished outside the facilities of the district, the institution to be selected is the choice of the parents or guardian. . . . Whatever the decision, attendance at least until the age of sixteen at the institution provided is compulsory. . . .

In this instance the defendant school board has elected to discharge its duty by furnishing secondary education outside the public facilities of the district. For a substantial number of its advanced students at least, the legal and public duty of the district is undertaken in religious denominational high schools that are an integral part of the Roman Catholic Church. The Church is the source of their control and the principal source of their support.

This combination of factors renders the service of the Church and its ministry inseparate from its educational function. That this is a high and dedicated undertaking is not to be questioned, and deserves the respect of all creeds. Yet however worthy the object, the First Amendment commands the State shall not participate.

The Bill of Rights secures to those of the Catholic Faith that the State shall not intrude in the affairs of their Church or its institutions. It assures to those of different persuasion that it will not lend assistance to them or those of differing faith in the pursuit of their religious beliefs. Our government is so constituted to the end that the schisms of the churches shall not be visited upon the political establishment.

Neither shall the conflicts of the political establishment attend the churches.

Considerations of equity and fairness have exerted a strong appeal to temper the severity of this mandate. The price it demands frequently imposes heavy burdens on the faithful parent. He shares the expense of maintaining the public school system, yet in loyalty to his child and his belief seeks religious training for the child elsewhere. But the same fundamental law which protects the liberty of a parent to reject the public system in the interests of his child's spiritual welfare, enjoins the state from participating in the religious education he has selected. . . .

Equitable considerations, however compelling, cannot override existing constitutional barriers. Legislatures and courts alike cannot deviate from the fundamental law.

We conclude that the defendants, while acting within the literal provisions of the statute, have exceeded the limits of the United States Constitution. . . .

REACTIONS OF LEGAL PERIODICALS TO *SWART* v. *SCHOOL DISTRICT*

The limited reaction to the Swart decision was favorable. Any type of grant involving state funds for parochial schools and colleges was considered in the *Michigan Law Review* (59:1254) to aid the teaching of religion. In that connection, the writer argued that "the ultimate recipient [of the aid] will be the school or college in which the parent enrolls his child."

The tenor of the educational process in the program in question provided the avenue for criticism in the *Louisiana Law Review* (22:266). Declaring that neutrality could not be expected when education was administered by a religious order, the writer argued that *any* governmental aid, both of direct and indirect forms, freed school funds for diversion by the parent religious organization "to other religious purposes."

He added, however, that the wrong approach to the question of church and state was generally being taken by the courts, including the Supreme Court of the United States. In placing primary concern on a determination of whether the religious schools are being aided and, if so, then quibbling over whether the aid is "direct" or "indirect" the courts were skirting the real crux of the problem, the writer argued. His suggested criterion in judging "aid" projects would be to determine " to what extent the program aids secular education which is objectionably colored by sectarian philosophy."

PUBLIC FUNDS FOR PAROCHIAL HIGHER EDUCATION

The issue of using public funds for sectarian schools is not limited to primary and secondary schools. The following cases involve using these funds for sectarian colleges.

A corporate taxpayer's suit in *Atchison, T. & S.F.R. Co.* v. *City of Atchison*, 47 Kan. 712, 28 P. 1000 (1892), successfully recovered the portion of the city taxes which was levied on a railroad's property for the public maintenance therein of two private and sectarian colleges. The Kansas court noted at the start of its opinion that the parties did not dispute the facts that the legislature lacked authority to grant public benefits for sectarian purposes and that the schools in question were sectarian institutions. It then qualified the city's argument that a public benefit inures with an increase in the number of schools and wider spread of learning and knowledge with the controlling observation that institutions receiving public benefits necessarily must be under public control.

In another case several college professors were released from their contracts with a sectarian college to teach in a public school after the college suffered heavy damage in a fire. Two other instructors, who did not have the required teaching certificates were loaned to the public school. Action was brought in *McDonald* v. *Parker*, 130 Ky. 501, 110 S.W. 810 (1908), to compel payment of these teachers' salaries. The Kentucky court ruled that no school funds were paid to the college. Therefore, the state constitutional provision prohibiting public funds for sectarian schools was not violated.

An arrangement of "sharing" expenses, whereby public funds ultimately were allocated to a sectarian educational institution, was declared in *Williams* v. *Board of Trustees*, 173 Ky. 708, 191, S.W. 507 (1917), to be violative of the Kentucky constitution. The contract in question called for free religious training in the nearby sectarian college for common school pupils in exchange for public funds to keep the buildings of the sectarian institution in repair. A declared purpose of the Presbyterian college was to teach "the tenets of its creed, mode of worship, and ecclesiastical polity."

It was determined in *State* ex rel. *Atwood* v. *Johnson*, 170 Wis. 251, 176 N.W. 224 (1920), below, that the state G.I. Bill benefits for Wisconsin citizens who had served in the United States military and naval service during the First World War could be extended to education at religious schools.

Declaring that "Mere reimbursement is not aid," the court based its ruling upon a finding that the benefits were given to the religious schools merely to reimburse them for the increased costs of operation caused by the influx of veterans into their classrooms.

The Wisconsin decision was viewed with favor in a limited number of review articles. Regarding the veterans' benefits "in the light of a payment for past services done for and in the behalf of the state," the reviewer in the *Michigan Law Review* (18:535) argued that the public interest involved in the program was apparent and compelling. In less definitive terms, the opinion was expressed in the *Yale Law Journal* (29:690) that the decision seemed to be in "accord with the authorities."

The precedents were interpreted in the *Harvard Law Review* (33:846) on the other hand as providing "no sound ground upon which a bonus statute can be supported." Failing to see in the statute either a direct or an indirect public benefit, the reviewer suggested that a medal would be more effective and permanent "as a means of encouraging patriotism."

A taxpayer's suit challenging an allocation by the Emergency Joint Housing Board to a Roman Catholic college on the ground that such an appropriation would be "a gift by the state to a religious institution" in violation of the New York and United States constitutions was dismissed in *Bull* v. *Stichman,* 298 N.Y. 516, 80 N.E.2d 661 (1948). In denying plaintiff's contention that his standing "stems from common law," the court, without elucidation, quoted the lower court's rationale that the plaintiff had "no special or peculiar interest in the matter other than that common to all taxpayers and citizens."

The commentary in law journals following the Bull decision was more instructive in terms of analyzing the New York court's approach to taxpayer's suits than it was for commenting on the particular decision at hand. The fact that the New York court did not rule on the merits of the case was considered in a number of reviews to be in good taste, even though a number of precedents existed in other states for the maintenance of a taxpayer's suit.

In that connection, the writer in the *Fordham Law Review* (17:107) declared that the practice is judicially settled in New York against allowing such suits against the state. Any changes in that situation would have to be made through legislation, he argued.

The writer then discussed some of the key arguments that could be made for and against taxpayer's actions against state officials or state instrumentalities. Considering sheer expedience as "the soundest view" for allowing the suits, he pointed out that allegedly unconstitutional expenditure of state funds conceivably would go unchallenged if the taxpayer's action is disallowed. He reasoned that the beneficiary of the appropriation would not, even if he legally could, "challenge the constitutionality of the grant he is to enjoy," and that the state agency making the grant undoubtedly would not either.

Citing state judicial precedents in each instance, he continued in the same vein pointing out that the majority of the state decisions have allowed a citizen or taxpayer to challenge unconstitutional expenditures of public funds. That author believed that some of the favorable points in the court's rationale included: (1) there is no real distinction between a taxpayer's suit against a state or similar litigation against a municipality; (2) actions against state officials are personal suits and are not suits against the state because the state official who violates his oath of office by performing unconstitutional acts is "not acting for or in the interest of the state"; and (3) the state constitutional right of action for any citizen of any town, county, or city to protect himself from "any illegal exaction" includes remedies against "state wide exactions alleged to be illegal."

On the opposite side of the ledger, he listed these arguments against taxpayer's suits: (1) allowing one or a few taxpayers to challenge some appropriations could signal a right for every taxpayer in the United States to challenge any and every appropriation; (2) one person cannot assume the role of community guardian; (3) the statutory permission for taxpayer's actions against municipalities does not extend by analogy to state actions; (4) and courts have consistently refused to decide "questions of academic abstractions."

In a similar fashion, a writer in the *Virginia Law Review* (34:335) noted that other theories upon which taxpayer's actions have been allowed include: "A taxpayer has a direct interest in state funds procured by taxation . . . and that a taxpayer is the equitable owner of public funds." He also pointed out that in at least one jurisdiction "the action is allowed by statute."

On the other hand, he listed several bases for not allowing taxpayers to bring suit. With judicial precedents cited in each instance, these included:

> (1) an injunction should not issue against a state officer unless the complainant can show some special and direct interest . . . (2) the state is a sovereignty whose programs should not be disorganized by such suits . . . (3) the action is in effect a suit against the state . . . and (4) the assumption of jurisdiction would be interference by one department of the government with another department.

ORPHANS AND DELINQUENTS IN SECTARIAN INSTITUTIONS

The use of public funds for the education of orphans, delinquents, and neglected children in the schools of sectarian orphanages, some of whom had been placed there by the state, has been another source of considerable litigation. Generally this use of public money has been challenged as violating state constitutional provisions prohibiting public aid for sectarian purposes. However, in a majority of the opinions, the courts declared that some public funds could be used for the education of orphanage children attending the schools set up by the sectarian orphanages.

A New York state court held in *People* ex rel. *Roman Catholic Orphan Asylum Society* v. *Board of Education*, 13 Barb. 400 (1851), that the state's common school funds could not be constitutionally distributed to the number of students cared for in the institutions and the number educated in common schools.

St. Patrick's Orphan Asylum v. *Board of Education*, 34 How. Prac.

(N.Y.) 229 (1867), found another New York court allowing distribution of city and district school funds to the schools of the Orphan Asylum Societies, except for those in New York City. The funds were to be apportioned to these schools in accordance with the proportion between the number of students therein and the number of students in the common schools. However, the court ruled that under the state constitution, state funds intended for common schools could not be used to support the asylums or their corresponding schools because these schools did not come within the constitutional definition of common schools.

In a later case, *Sargent* v. *Board of Education*, 69 N.E. 722, 177 N.Y. 317 (1904), a New York court again allowed the distribution of city funds, but not common school funds, to a school run by a sectarian orphanage. The court reasoned that the orphanage could not be considered a school or institution under the constitutional provision prohibiting aid to sectarian schools.

A particular arrangement whereby per capita pro rata payments from the state school fund for the education in the graded common school district of inmates of a Baptist orphan's home was countenanced in Kentucky in *Crain* v. *Walker,* 222 Ky. 828, 2 S.W.2d 654 (1928), below.

Distinguishing its ruling in *Williams* v. *Board of Trustees*, 173 Ky. 708, 191 S.W. 507 (1917), the court noted that the present facts showed that no sectarian instruction was required; that inmates of the home were not required to be of Baptist parentage; that the home had no influence on the employment of any of the graded school district teachers; and that the teachers need not be of the Baptist faith.

CRAIN v. *WALKER*
222 KY. 828, 2 S.W.2D. 654 (1928).

Judge THOMAS delivered the opinion of the court, saying in part:

There is a duly organized graded school district in Hardin County, known as the Glendale graded common school district, which, when this action was filed, was under the management of appellees and some of the defendants below . . . and within the confines of its boundary there is located and maintained by the Kentucky Baptist Children's Home, a charitable corporation organized under the provisions of section 879 of our present Statutes, a children's home, in which there has been gathered, exclusively from various points within the commonwealth, a number of children to be reared, provided for, and educated by the charitable corporation, and at the time of the institution of this action there was in the home 221 of such inmates within the public school age. Practically all of them were qualified for entrance into only the primary grades of our public school system. The home was established in 1915, and began by acquiring the property theretofore owned and operated by an institution known as Lynnland College, and which has since been converted into the present home for orphan children, and the facilities for its maintenance have been considerably enlarged.

In 1919 its then manager, who was a man of considerable experience in the management of such institutions, and who is known in this record as "Daddy" Moore, entered into a verbal arrangement with the trustees of the school district whereby the latter agreed to furnish and pay the salaries of three teachers in the primary grades, and they taught the school for such grades in three rooms that the home agreed to, and did, furnish and equip with heat, light, seats, and all other equipment for the teaching of such a school, the home being located some mile or more away from the site of the graded school building of the Glendale graded common school district; but it was a part of that agreement that any other child in the district who was entitled to receive instruction in such grades would be permitted to attend the schools being taught at the place and in the manner indicated. It was also agreed that the transportation of any pupils from the home who took any course of instruction furnished at the high school building would be transported by the home free of charge—in consideration for all of which the district was permitted to receive the state per capita for all of the students in the home, and an additional donation of $675, which

for the scholastic year of 1926–27 was increased to $775. . . .

This equity action was filed by appellants and plaintiffs below, F. L. Crain, and two other citizens and taxpayers residing in the school district, against its trustees and the charitable corporation that maintained the home, in which it was sought to perpetually enjoin defendants from carrying out the above arrangement, upon the grounds: (1) That the inmates of the home were not entitled to attend the schools of the district, because they were not residents therein; (2) that the corporate defendant had no right to continue to bring into the district the orphaned inmates of the institution and to demand or require for them the privilege of attending the public schools of the district; and (3) that the arrangement was in direct violation of the provisions of section 189 of the Constitution, saying:

No portion of any fund or tax now existing, or that may hereafter be raised or levied for educational purposes, shall be appropriated to, or used by, or in aid of, any church, sectarian or denominational school.

. . . 2. What we have said in disposing of ground 1. in a large measure disposes of ground 2. Grave apprehension is manifested in briefs for plaintiffs that in the course of time there will be gathered in the school district by the Baptist Orphans' Home such a great number of inmates as to greatly and unnecessarily burden the taxpayers of the district, and to disastrously operate upon the maintenance of its schools; but that apprehension is rendered less alarming by the payment to the district of each pupil's pro rata of the state public school funds, as is demonstrated by the proven facts in this case. The expenses of the district in carrying out the arrangement sought to be enjoined is shown to be in the neighborhood of $1,900, when the increased income to the district thereby, as we have seen, is about $3,400, thereby creating a surplus to be expended by the school trustees for the benefit of the schools. It would, perhaps, not be proper, however, to give that fact legal weight in arriving at our conclusion, but it does demonstrate that plaintiffs and those whom they represent are not detrimentally affected by the arrangement. Whatever may be the eventual result of such apprehension, if it should finally occur, it would present a situation to be then dealt with, and which, no doubt, would be solved so as to do justice to all concerned. It is sufficient for our present purposes to say that no such situation is presented.

3. In support of this ground, chief reliance is had upon the domestic case of *Williams* v. *Board of Trustees of Stanton Graded School District*, 173 Ky. 708, 191 S. W. 507, L. R. A. 1917D, 453. In that case a denominational school, operated under the auspices of the Presbyterian church, was located within the school district. The school "was organized for the purpose of teaching and spreading the ecclesiastical polity of the Presbyterian church," and the church employed the teachers in the school. The curriculum included not only the common school branches and others necessary for the acquisition of a liberal education, but also "religious tenets and dogmas of the Presbyterian church." The trustees of the graded school district entered into a contract with the authorities of the Presbyterian school whereby the latter leased to the former the grounds and

school buildings of the denominational school for the purpose of conducting therein the graded school for the district. The trustees of the public school employed two of the former teachers employed in the church school, while the church board employed the four other teachers therein, and practically the management of the district school was turned over exclusively to the church authorities, and the money arising from taxation for the purpose of maintaining the district school was thereby unlawfully diverted by being practically turned over to the church authorities maintaining the denominational school. That arrangement was sought to be enjoined as violative of the provisions of section 189 supra, of our Constitution. This court so held in its opinion in that case and in which it is stated, inter alia:

The evidence further conduces to show that the teachers and pupils of the graded school conducted in the college building are really as much under the control of Mr. Hanley [the head of the denominational school] as the teachers and pupils of Stanton College; that the graded common school trustees have virtually surrendered to Mr. Hanley all control over the conduct and management of the graded school; that the two graded school teachers, although nominally contracted with by the graded school trustees and paid out of the common school fund, were really selected by Mr. Hanley. . . . And if the arrangement between Stanton College and the graded school should be subjected to the scrutiny of this not too comprehensive or rigid test, the evidence makes it plain that it was of such a nature as to reasonably create the belief that the graded school trustees had abdicated all control and authority over the graded school and delivered its conduct entirely to Mr. Hanley, the head of the sectarian institution.

If the facts herein measured up to those contained in the excerpt from that opinion, the only course would be to sustain this ground, and grant the relief praved for in the petition. But we have no such facts in this case, nor any approaching thereto. The Baptist Orphans' Home has no voice in the employment of any of the teachers of the graded school district, nor are any of them required to be members of the Baptist religious denomination or any other church. No control of any character is exercised over them by the officers, superintendents, or managers of the home. As a matter of fact, only one of the three teachers of the primary grades taught in the rooms furnished by the home is a member of the Baptist Church, the other two being members of the Christian Church. No requirement is made that any inmate of the home shall receive sectarian instruction or be taught any creed of any religious denomination; nor are the inmates required to be children of Baptist par-entage—all of which widens the gulf separating the facts of the Williams Case from those in this one.

Because of such difference of facts, the conclusions therein reached find no application here, since prior announced legal principles are only valuable as precedents when similar states of fact are involved. It was never intended by the section of the Constitution, supra, to withhold the right to teach public schools in buildings rented, or their use otherwise acquired, from others, if the circumstances justified it, although the building may be owned by a particular religious denomination. The vice sought to be prevented by the constitutional provision was the teaching of religious sectarianism in schools maintained by public funds, and which it is indisputably shown was not true in this case, but which was true in the relied on Williams Case. We therefore conclude that this ground is also without merit. . . .

While the children in *State* ex rel. *Johnson* v. *Cotton*, 67 S.D. 63, 289 N.W. 71 (1939), did not attend a school set up by the sectarian orphanage, the resulting benefits to the sectarian institution amounted to the same as granting public funds to a similar institution's school, the South Dakota supreme court held.

The right of residents of a charitable institution for homeless children maintained by the Norwegian Lutheran Church of America to attend public schools without paying tuition was recognized in *State* ex rel. *Johnson* v. *Cotton*. Noting that the children in the institution in question had no other home or legal guardians, the court declared the contention, that the ruling would impose an unjust burden upon the public school district, was "a matter to be dealt with by the legislature rather than the court."

A parent in *New Haven* v. *Torrington*, 132 Conn. 194, 43 A.2d 455 (1945), sought unsuccessfully to recover the costs of education of his children. He claimed that the school was not a public school, and that he therefore owed none of the costs to the public treasury. The court declared that a public school must remain free from sectarian instruction or influence. It, however, decided that a school within an all-Roman Catholic orphanage may, consistent with the Constitution, be established under the control of the board of education *as long as* the school remained free from sectarian influence.

The state of Oklahoma contracted with a Baptist orphans' home to care for dependent children. This arrangement raised the question of whether such a contract violated the state constitutional provision prohibiting the state from adopting sectarian principles or supporting religious sects.

The Oklahoma supreme court ruled in *Murrow Indian Orphans Home v. Childers,* 197 Okl. 249, 171 P.2d 600 (1946), that the arrangement was valid because either the state legislature or the people had the authority to provide for needy children by contracting with sectarian eleemosynary stitutions. The court concluded that such a contract with an eleemosynary institution was legal when it involved a substantial return to the state in the discharge of a state duty and when the appropriation was not a donation.

However, two state courts did rule in opposition to the majority of the other courts.

In *State* ex rel. *Nevada Orphan Asylum* v. *Hallock,* 16 Nev. 373 (1882), the Nevada supreme court ruled that the appropriation of public funds to a sectarian orphan asylum was unconstitutional under the provision forbidding the use of tax money for sectarian purposes. The court found it impossible to separate the money that was spent legally and that spent for sectarian purposes.

The use of public funds under a Virginia statute to pay the tuitions of orphans of service men was declared unconstitutional in *Almond* v. *Day,* 197 Va. 419, 89 S.E.2d 851 (1955). The Virginia high court found that the tuition was available to sectarian secondary schools and colleges and thereby violated the state constitution forbidding aid for sectarian purposes and to schools not under public control. The establishment clause of the First Amendment was also violated by the state statute, the court concluded, by raising public funds for religious purposes, by aiding sectarian purposes with the state compulsory school machinery, and by compelling taxpayers to contribute their money for sectarian purposes.

† † *ALMOND* v. *DAY*
197 VA. 419, 89 S.E.2D 851 (1955).

Judge EGGLESTON delivered the opinion of the court, saying in part:

This is a petition for a writ of mandamus filed by the Attorney General of Virginia to determine the validity of Item 210 of the Appropriation Act of 1954 . . . which appropriates funds for the "education of orphans of soldiers, sailors and marines" who were citizens of Virginia and were "killed in action or died, or who are totally and permanently disabled as a result of service during the World War."

In September, 1955, the Superintendent of Public Instruction contemplated presenting to the Hon. Sidney C. Day, Jr., State Comptroller, approved vouchers authorizing the payment of certain funds appropriated by Item 210 of the Appropriation Act to the parents, guardians, or other persons having custody of children attending public and private institutions and eligible for benefits under the Act. The State Comptroller forwarded to the Attorney General, in writing, an expression of his doubt of the validity of such payments, in view of Section 141 of the State Constitution, and notifying him that he would decline to make them until there was a final adjudication of their validity by this court.

Pursuant to the provisions of Code, § 8-714, the Attorney General filed in this court a petition for a writ of mandamus directing the State Comptroller to issue warrants upon the State Treasurer for the payment of such amounts. . . .

The respondent State Comptroller filed an answer . . . expressing the view that he should not make such payments until it had been adjudicated whether the appropriation contravened Section 141 of the State Constitution, and also Sections 16, 58 and 67 of that Constitution, and the Fourteenth Amendment to the Federal Constitution.

. . . .

It thus appears that the provision in Item 210 of the 1954 Appropriation Act for the payment of tuition, institutional fees, etc., of eligible children "at any educational or training institution of collegiate or secondary grade in the State of Virginia, approved in writing by the Superintendent of Public Instruction," is by force of its broad language made available for use while such children are attending either sectarian or nonsectarian private schools.

Section 141 of the Constitution of Virginia, as amended in 1952, reads thus:

State appropriations prohibited to schools or institutions of learning not owned or exclusively controlled by the State or some subdivision thereof; exceptions to rule.— No appropriation of public funds shall be made to any school or institution of learning not owned or exclusively controlled by the State or some political subdivision thereof; provided, first, that the General Assembly may appropriate funds to an agency, or to a school or institution of learning owned or controlled by an agency, created and established by two or more states under a joint agreement to which this State is a party for the purpose of providing educational facilities for the citizens of the several states joining in such agreement; second, that counties, cities, towns and districts may make appropriations to nonsectarian schools of manual, industrial, or technical training, and also to any school or institution of learning owned or exclusively controlled by such county, city, town, or school district.

The first question presented is whether the provisions of this section of the Constitution prohibit the payments authorized by Item 210 of the Appropriation Act for tuition, institutional fees and other designated expenses of eligible children attending private schools.

The argument of the petitioner Attorney General runs thus: Section 141, being a restraint on the plenary power of the General Assembly, must be strictly construed; the express language of the section merely prohibits a *direct* "appropriation of public funds" *to* "any school or institution of learning not owned or exclusively controlled by the State or some political subdivision thereof;" Item 210 is not an appropriation *directly to* the institutions which the eligible children may attend, but is an appropriation to the parents or guardians of such children, is primarily for the benefit of such children, and only incidentally for the benefit of the selected private schools. Hence, it is said, the appropriation is "not antagonistic either to the letter or spirit of Section 141."

The position of the respondent State Comptroller is that the constitutionality of a statute is to be tested by its normal effect and the practical consequences to which it leads; that the provision for the payment of tuition, institutional fees and other designated expenses at a private school, to be attended by children eligible under the Act, is a direct and substantial aid to such institution, and falls within the inhibition of Section 141 which was designed to prohibit such diversion of public funds from the public school system to the aid or benefit of private schools.

Section 141 is found in Article IX of our Constitution embracing the provisions for "Education and Public Instruction." Section 129, the first of these provisions, provides that "The General Assembly shall establish and maintain an efficient system of public free schools throughout the State." The other sections in Article IX make provision for the establishment and maintenance of such system. Among these is Section 141 which insures that public funds raised by taxation will be under the exclusive control of public authorities, used for the benefit of the public schools, and that no part thereof will be diverted from that purpose to private schools.

It will be observed that the prohibition in Section 141 is in broad and inclusive language. It says, "*No appropriation* of public funds shall be made to *any school or institution of learning* not owned or exclusively controlled by the State or some political subdivision thereof" (italics supplied), with two provisos or exceptions then spelled out. The effect is thus to prohibit all appropriations of public funds to institutions of learning other than those expressly permitted. The prohibition is against any or all aid to the excluded institutions.

The Record of the Debates of the Constitutional Convention of 1901–02 during the framing and adoption of Section 141 shows that its dominant purpose was to aid and maintain the public free school system and to guard against any diversion of public school funds from that purpose.

The first sentence of the section as originally reported by the Committee on Education and Public Instruction prohibited appropriations of public funds to any school or institution of learning "not owned and exclusively controlled" by the State or some political subdivision thereof. (Debates, Constitutional Convention, Vol. 1, p. 1019.) During the debates the phrase "not owned *and* exclusively controlled" (italics supplied) was broadened to read, "not owned *or* exclusively controlled" (italics supplied) to conform to the wording in what is now Section 67 of the Constitution, limiting appropriations to charitable and other institutions. (Debates, Constitutional Convention, Vol. 1, p. 1239.) There is no suggestion in the debates that the opening sentence of Section 141 was intended, as the petitioner argues, merely to prohibit *direct* aid *to* such institutions, and, by implication, to permit *indirect* aid to them.

. . . Giving the words their commonly accepted meaning, "to appropriate to" means "to appropriate for the benefit of" a specific purpose, and none other. Hence, the prohibition in Section 141 against an appropriation "to" any school not under public control means that no money can be lawfully appropriated "for the benefit of" that school.

A glance at the 1954 Appropriation Act will show that appropriations are not usually made directly "to" the various beneficiaries, whether they be State educational institutions or State departments. They are stated to be "for" a specific purpose; for example, "For maintenance and operation of" the particular educational institution, or "for" some specific purpose at the institution, or "For expenses of administration" of a department of the State. But no one would question that these appropriations are in effect "to" these institutions and departments in the sense that they are "set apart" for their use.

Similarly the appropriation in Item 210, now before us, for the purpose of "providing for tuition, institutional fees," etc., at private schools to be approved by the Superintendent of Public Instruction, is an appropriation for the benefit of such schools. The fact that in the administration of the Act the funds may be paid to the parents or guardians of the children and not directly to the institutions does not alter their underlying purpose and effect. As a matter of fact the record shows that from July, 1950, through June, 1954, payments of these appropriations have usually been made directly to the institutions.

It is urged that we should apply the reasoning of certain recent cases which have validated appropriations for transportation of children to private schools, and the furnishing of textbooks for the use of children at such schools, upon the theory that such aid is primarily for the benefit of the children and only incidentally for the benefit of the institutions involved. Typical of these is *Everson* v. *Board of Education,* 330 U.S. 1, in which the Supreme Court in a 5 to 4 decision held that a New Jersey statute . . . authorizing school district boards to provide for the transportation of pupils to and from parochial schools was not violative of the "establishment of religion" clause of the Federal Constitution, Amendment 1.

Upon the same theory *Borden* v. *Louisiana State Board of Education,* 168 La. 1005, 123 So. 655, relied upon by the petitioner, validated the expenditure of public funds to provide free school books to pupils at private schools against a constitutional provision similar to Section 141 in the Virginia Constitution. The crux of that case, as stated in the court's opinion, is that "The schools, however, are not the beneficiaries of these appropriations. They *obtain nothing from them,* nor are they relieved of a single obligation, because of them. The school children and the state alone are the beneficiaries." (Italics supplied.) . . .

Clearly such reasoning does not apply to the appropriation here under consideration. Assuming, but not deciding, the soundness of the view that the private institutions involved receive no direct benefit from the transportation of pupils or the furnishing of textbooks to them, the same cannot be said of provisions for the payment of tuition and institutional fees at such schools. Tuition and institutional fees go directly to the institution and are its very life blood. Such items are the main support of private schools which are not sufficiently endowed to insure their maintenance. Surely a payment by the State of the tuition and fees of the pupils of a private school begun on the strength of a contract by the State to do so would be an appropriation to that school.

Furthermore, the argument that the appropriation in Item 210 is not for the benefit of private schools is entirely inconsistent with the concession in petitioner's reply brief that, "tuition paid for the benefit of a child attending a *sectarian* school would undoubtedly violate the 1st Amendment of the Constitution of the United States as incorporated into the 14th Amendment. The trend of recent U.S. Supreme Court decisions and decisions in other foreign jurisdictions strongly indicates this. Those decisions further indicate the strong possibility that the provisions of the Virginia Constitution dealing with separation of Church and State would also be construed as prohibiting the type of appropriation here under consideration."

The basis of this concession is that the payment of such tuition would directly benefit and support a *sectarian* school contrary to the purpose and spirit of these constitutional provisions. The same principle would, of course, apply to the payment of tuition at a private *nonsectarian* school. In both cases the parent or guardian to whom the tuition fees are paid is merely the conduit or channel through whom the aid from the State to the school is transmitted. Such natural and reasonable effect of the appropriation is proof of its invalidity.

"The general rule is that in whatever language a statute may be framed, its purpose and its constitutional validity must be determined by its natural and reasonable effect. . . ." . . .

When we consider, the natural, reasonable and realistic effect of the provision in Item 210 for the payment of tuition, institutional fees and other designated expenses of eligible children who attend private schools approved by the Superintendent of Public Instruction, we are forced to the conclusion that it constitutes a direct and substantial aid to such institutions and falls within the prohibition of Section 141 of our Constitution.

We further agree with the position of counsel for the respondent State Comptroller that in so far as Item 210 purports to authorize payments for tuition, institutional fees and other designated expenses of eligible children who attend *sectarian* schools, it falls within the prohibitions of Sections 16, 58 and 67 of the Constitution of Virginia and the First and Fourteenth Amendments to the Federal Constitution. Section 16 provides:

Religious freedom.—That religion or the duty which we owe to our Creator, and the manner of discharging it, can be directed only by reason and conviction, not by force or violence and, therefore, all men are equally entitled to the free exercise of religion, according to the dictates of conscience and that it is the mutual duty of all to practice Christian forbearance, love and charity towards each other.

Section 58, so far as here pertinent, reads as follows:

Prohibitions on General Assembly as to suspension of writ of habeas corpus, and enactment of laws referring to religion and other laws.— . . . No man shall be compelled to frequent or support any religious worship, place, or ministry, whatsoever. . . . And the General Assembly shall not . . . pass any law requiring or authorizing any religious society, or the people of any district within this State, to levy on themselves, or others any tax for the erection or repair of any house of public worship, or for the support of any church or ministry; but it shall be left free to every person to select his religious instructor, and to make for his support such private contract as he shall please.

Section 67 provides:

Limitations on appropriations by General Assembly to charitable and other institutions; exceptions. — The General Assembly shall not make any appropriation of public funds, or personal property, or of any real estate, to any church, or sectarian society, association, or institution of any kind whatever, which is entirely or partly, directly or indirectly, controlled by any church or sectarian society; nor shall the General Assembly make any like appropriation to any charitable institution which is not owned or controlled by the State; except that it may, in its discretion, make appropriations to nonsectarian institutions for the reform of youthful criminals; but nothing herein contained shall prohibit the General Assembly from authorizing counties, cities, or towns to make such appropriations to any charitable institution or association.

These provisions in our basic law guarantee freedom of religion and complete separation of Church and State in civil affairs.

The First Amendment to the Federal Constitution provides that, "Congress shall make no law respecting an establishment of religion. . . ."

It has been settled by the decisions of the Supreme Court that the Due Process Clause of the Fourteenth Amendment "has rendered the legislatures of the states as incompetent as Congress to enact such laws." *Cantwell* v. *State of Connecticut*, 310 U.S. 296. See also, *Everson* v. *Board of Education*, supra, 330 U.S. at page 15.

The payment of such items to sectarian schools as directed or authorized by the terms of Item 210 is unconstitutional because, (1) It utilizes public funds to support religious institutions contrary to the principles laid down in *Everson* v. *Board of Education*, supra, 330 U.S. at page 16, (2) It "affords sectarian groups an invaluable aid in that it helps to provide pupils for their religious classes through use of the state's compulsory public school machinery," condemned in *People of State of Illinois* ex rel. *McCollum* v. *Board of Education*, 333 U.S. 203, 212, (3) It compels taxpayers to contribute money for the propagation of religious opinions which they may not believe. . . .

. . . .

Since, in our opinion, Item 210 is unconstitutional and void . . . the writ prayed for is denied.

REACTIONS OF LEGAL PERIODICALS TO
ALMOND v. *DAY*

The Almond ruling was sharply criticized in the *Virginia Law Review* (42:437). That reviewer argued that tuition payments should be considered in the light of the child benefit theory, as are textbooks, meals, and transportation. Admitting that tuition could be considered the lifeline of a private school, he reasoned that the child would be benefited to a greater degree by state payment of the tuition because of the fact that many children cannot afford to pay the high tuition rates at private schools. Continuing in that vein, he argued that tuition payments made by the state without religious discrimination were not intended by our Founding Fathers, nor should be considered by contemporary courts, to constitute a violation of the Establishment of Religion Clause.

Closing in patriotic tones he declared that the Almond rationale would necessitate the invalidation of the federal "G.I. Bill" as it applies to "attendance of veterans at hundreds of sectarian colleges and universities over the nation."

RELIGIOUS INSTRUCTION IN PAROCHIAL SCHOOLS

The question of allowing religious instruction in both private and public schools has arisen in a number of cases. (See also the chapters on Bible reading, flag, prayer, released and dismissed time, and sectarian instruction in chapter on curriculum.)

The use of public premises for religious preaching when the buildings were not needed for school purposes was allowed in *Harmon* v. *Driggers,* 116 S.C. 238, 107 S.E. 923 (1921). The controlling principle, however, was the court's construction concerning a condition in a deed which conveyed the school property to the school trustees.

The South Carolina court ruled that the provision calling for the land in question to be used "for the purpose of erecting and maintaining a public school for white children only," meant that only white children were to be admitted to the school and not that the use of the building was confined to school purposes only.

That a private school does not possess absolute authority to regulate its own curricula affairs became apparent in *Miami Military Institute* v. *Leff,* 129 Misc. 481, 220 N.Y.S. 799 (1926), below. There a city court in New York ruled that a Jewish cadet could not be required to attend Christian chapel services, and that he could therefore recover the balance of his tuition for the period following his expulsion from a private military academy in Ohio. The court did say, nevertheless, that the regulation was reasonable, except as it applied to Jewish students, and did not violate religious liberty as guaranteed by the Ohio constitution.

† † *MIAMI MILITARY INSTITUTE* v. *LEFF*
129 MISC. 481, 220 N.Y.S. 799 (1926).

Judge HARTZELL delivered the opinion of the court, saying in part:

This action was brought by the plaintiff to recover of the defendant the balance of $325 due for tuition of his son in the Miami Military Institute of Germantown, Ohio. . . .

The answer to this is a general denial, and sets up as an affirmative defense that on or about the 25th day of September, 1924, and within two weeks after the defendant's son entered the institute, he was expelled without just cause. . . .

The case was called for trial, and the defendant, through his attorney, moved to amend his answer to set up as a valid and separate defense, the following:

For a third and separate defense, the defendant admits the allegations contained in paragraphs 1 and 2 of the plaintiff's complaint, and alleges that on or about the 24th day of September, 1925, the plaintiff wrongfully and unlawfully broke the contract, if any there was, by expelling the defendant from the academy, upon the grounds he did not attend church, as directed by the persons in charge; that any such provision or regulation of the plaintiff, requiring the defendant to attend church, which was contrary to his religious belief, is void, under the provisions of section 7 of article 1 of the Bill of Rights of the Constitution of the state of Ohio; that the defendant's son was of Jewish religion, and it was contrary to his religious instructions to attend the church directed to be attended by the plaintiff and its agents and unjustly interfered with his religious rights and is and was null and void under such provisions of the state Constitution.

Article 1, § 7, of the Bill of Rights, referred to in said amendment reads as follows:

All men have a natural and indefeasible right to worship Almighty God according to the decision of their own conscience. No person shall be compelled to attend, erect, or support any place of worship, or maintain any form of worship, against his consent; and no preference shall be given, by law, to any religious society; nor shall any interference with rights of conscience be permitted. No religious test shall be required, as a qualification for office, nor shall any person be incompetent to be a witness on account of his religious belief; but nothing herein shall be construed to dispense with oaths and affirmations. Religion, morality, and knowledge, however, being essential to good government, it shall be the duty of the General Assembly to pass suitable laws to protect every religious denomination in the peaceable enjoyment of its own mode of public worship, and to encourage schools, and the means of instruction.

. . . The youth had been at the school for a period of about 10 days when he was expelled by the plaintiff for the reason he refused to attend the Presbyterian Church in the village at the Sunday services, upon the grounds that it was contrary to his religious instruction and faith, in which conduct he was sustained by the defendant. It appears that the defendant and his son are both of the Hebrew faith.

By the boy's refusal to attend the

church on Sunday as above mentioned, correspondence passed between the plaintiff and the defendant in reference to the matter, wherein the plaintiff stated that the boy would be expelled unless he complied with the requirements of the school in this respect. The defendant begged the plaintiff to make an exception in his son's case in view of the fact that, being of the Jewish faith, attendance at the Presbyterian Church would be contrary to his religious belief and in violation of his conscience. The youth offered to attend a synagogue of his own faith in the village, but, there being none available, it appears that permission was given to him to attend a synagogue in a town 14 miles distant at his own expense, which the defendant declined to accept.

During the 10 days of the boy's presence at the institute he attended regularly to the duties of the school, which included attendance at the daily chapel where religious exercises were held by the school without objection on his part. His conduct in this respect during his entire stay at the institute was in strict compliance with the rules of the school, and met with the satisfaction of the president and faculty of the institute.

The facts in this case present an interesting and important question, and which has received careful consideration on the part of the court.

The two main questions that arise are: First. Does a contract between the parties grant the right to the plaintiff to recover from the defendant the full amount of the year's tuition, together with the incidental expenses as claimed by the plaintiff under the facts in this case? Second. If such contract existed, is such a violation of the defendant's constitutional rights, as expressed in the Ohio state Constitution, as above quoted?

We will first examine the question of the contract. The contract consists of the signed application, together with the catalogue of the institution and the correspondence that had passed between the parties at the time thereof. It will therefore be necessary to examine the contract in all its detail to determine whether or not there is anything in the said contract that constitutes an obligation upon the defendant's son to attend the services at the Presbyterian Church on Sunday, as claimed by the plaintiff. It is apparent that the correspondence between the parties is silent upon that proposition. The matter of religious attendance was not in the minds of the parties so far as the correspondence is concerned, neither does the application suggest it in any way.

The learned counsel for the plaintiff calls the court's attention to pages 41 and 42 of the catalogue, which he claims is a regulation in reference to the subject binding upon the defendant.

. . . .

It is upon these statements of the catalogue that the foundation of the plaintiff's claim must rest, and the question is, Are these statements a part of the contract between the parties, and binding upon the defendant?

The learned counsel for the defendant suggests that the first above mentioned at the foot of page 42, in reference to the cadet corps attending Sunday morning services in one of the several churches in the village, is but a mere part of the advertisement, set forth in the catalogue to attract attention and arouse the interest of patrons. Counsel for the plaintiff on the other hand, claims it is a regulation which he adopts by signing the application for his son and agrees to comply therewith. If the latter interpretation is true, there can be no doubt but that a contract is established between the plaintiff and the defendant.

The learned counsel for the plaintiff in his able brief, lays down the rule that it is a well-recognized principle of law that colleges and schools possess a discretionary power to regulate discipline as long as such rules do not violate either the divine or human law, and, in case of the refusal of the pupil to obey such reasonable regulations, he may be expelled as a matter of right. The counsel cites various cases sustaining this proposition, which the court has examined with care, although it is hardly necessary to examine at any great length authorities upon the proposition that seems to be so well established. He also advances the proposition that, where a student has entered for a scholastic year and violates some regulation of the institute that he is attending, he becomes liable, upon expulsion, to the payment of the full amount for the entire school year, called for by the contract. Authorities are cited in support of this proposition, which as I understand it, seems to be well established.

I

The important question in this case is whether or not the defendant and the plaintiff entered into a contract, wherein their minds met upon the proposition in question. It will be noted, in an examination of the catalogue, that on pages 45, 46, 47, and 48, are laid down certain matters in great detail, which are headed "Miscellane-

ous Regulations," among those, for example several may hereafter be mentioned merely as an illustration.

The paragraph in reference to religious attendance at church on Sunday does not come under the heading of "Regulations" in the catalogue; but under another heading, entitled "M.M.I. School Home" (Miami Military Institute School Home). Under the heading there are various things of interest and importance spoken of, and the learned counsel advertisement. Under this heading there are subdivisions, as follows: Devotions, Health, Music, Military Band. Under this heading "Devotions," the small paragraph in question, is found at the bottom of the page

Under the said heading of "Devotions" there is more than a page of attractive and beautiful description of the aims of the school, in reference to not only the physical, social, and mental, but also the spiritual development of the student.

There is a statement that new emphasis has been added to this work by the substitution of a special religious department at the institute, for the old method of permitting the Sunday schools of the village churches to take care of the more specific spiritual education of the boy. And, although the greatest stress has been laid upon the study of the Christian religion, the greatest truths of other religions have been considered, not in a condemnatory, but in a sympathetically critical, spirit. Above all has been impressed the broadminded acceptance of the reasonableness of religion. The second ideal sought has been accomplished by the study of men's lives, beginning with the leaders of the Old Testament times, progressing with leaders of New Testament times; a special course being devoted to the life of Jesus Christ, and ending with the study of a modern man's life at its best. . . .

. . . It seems to me that if the attendance of a pupil was to be mandatory at some church service on each Sunday in the village of Germantown, Ohio, to be selected by the president or the faculty of the school, that such provision would have been set forth in the catalogue under the heading of "Miscellaneous Regulations," and would have taken its place among the carefully prepared and numerous announcements of this kind set forth on pages 45, 46, 47, and 48, of the said catalogue. There are 41 regulations of this kind, set forth in the catalogue on these pages, that become part of the contract upon the signing of the application by the patron, and which are binding upon him to the fullest extent. I am quite confident that the small paragraph, that has been quoted in reference to this matter, set out at the bottom of page 42 in the general description and discussion preceding it, concerning the advantages of a religious life and the methods employed to instill it in the minds of the pupil, has not the force of a binding character, for the last sentence of that paragraph, after describing what may be called a custom for Sunday morning service, says no creed is preferred, but genuine religious character is sought by daily devotions in the School chapel. This inference is made prominent by the president stating in plain words, in a preceding paragraph, at the top of page 42, that a special religious department at the institute has been substituted for the old method of permitting the Sunday schools of the village churches to take care of the more spiritual education of the boy.

Under these circumstances a patron might well feel that daily devotions at the chapel of this school, upon which so much emphasis has been laid by the catalogue, and as a substitute for the old method of attendance at the Sunday schools of the village churches on Sunday, was the one requirement in reference to religious attendance desired, and which he could conscientiously attend without any conflict in his faith or his conscience, whatever the same might be, and to which his son might faithfully and fairly subscribe. It is apparent to me that it was with this fact in mind that the defendant's son entered the institute and complied with all the regulations and requirements in reference to the daily exercises at the school chapel.

II

If my reasoning is not correct, and if the paragraph in question, notwithstanding its position in the catalogue, should be considered as one of the regulations of the school, then I am of the opinion that the same is not binding on the defendant, for the reason that its general language fails to convey the idea that attendance upon the student at other churches in the village on Sunday is mandatory. . . .

As I view it, the language used is but a pleasant description of—to many—an interesting event in the life of the school. It has the lure of an advertisement of one of the attractive features of the institution. It says:

The cadet corps attend the Sunday morning services of one of the several churches in the village, visiting each in turn.

At best the language used implies an occasional visit, parceled impartially among the several churches of the village. It might indeed be assumed, also, by one reading the paragraph, that a Jewish or a Catholic place of worship would be among the churches so visited.

If it had been the intention of the plaintiff to make this a condition of membership in the school and have the force of a regulation which the student was to obey, surely it would have used some language to convey that meaning. It would have been an easy matter to use specific language setting forth in plain words such requirement. . . .

. . . Turning to the heading "regulations" where this paragraph belongs, if it is to have any force, we find no lack of specific language, in the various regulations that are binding on the student. . . .

. . . My views harmonize with those of the learned counsel for the defendant, in that there was no contract between the parties to the effect that the defendant's son would attend any church other than that consistent with his own religion. The expulsion of the defendant's son from the school was therefore without just cause, and by such act the plaintiff committed a breach of the contract actually made, and was therefore not entitled to receive any compensation whatsoever called for by the contract, and thereby forfeited all rights to the same.

I also adopt the theory of the learned counsel for the defendant upon the question of waiver. I determine that there has been no waiver of the constitutional rights vouchsafed the defendant's son by the said section, quoted above, of the Bill of Rights of the Constitution of the state of Ohio. I find in the whole case no element of evidence in relation either to the contract between the parties, or any action on the part of the defendant or his son, upon which such a waiver could be predicated. . . .

The contract must fail for lack of mutual understanding. There is nothing to charge the defendant with notice of any requirement concerning Sunday attendance at Christian churches for his son. It is not necessary to refer to the correspondence to establish the fact that the defendant would not have sent his son to the school had he known of this requirement.

Furthermore, I am of the opinion that if the said paragraph in reference to compulsory attendance upon Sunday services of the churches in the village could be construed as being within the purview of the parties and part of the contract between them, it cannot be sustained as valid and binding upon the plaintiff, for the reason that it is an unreasonable rule or regulation under the circumstances of this case.

III

The authorities all hold that a school has full power to enforce its rules and regulations and to carry into effect its disciplinary methods among its students, and that any disobedience of the student may be punished, not only by suspension or other penalty, but even by expulsion from the institution, and that he still remains liable to pay the full amount of the tuition and charges for the entire year, stipulated in the contract.

But there is one important provision upon which the entire law rests in such a case, and that is that the rule or regulation must be reasonable.

IV

The regulation that the student shall attend religious exercises at the school chapel is held to be reasonable, and a refusal of a student to this requirement entails such penalty as the institution may prescribe.

V

But that is not the case at bar. There is no complaint that the defendant's son refused to attend the chapel services of the school. In fact it appears that he did attend such services and made no complaint thereof. The only thing that he did complain of was the requirement to attend other and different religious services, outside of the institution itself, and at churches of different denominations conducted in the village in which the school is located.

This was an unusual, and unreasonable requirement, which he was justified in refusing to obey. The courts do not go so far as to sanction such a requirement. The regulations of a school in this respect that are sustained by the courts are only those requiring attendance upon the exercises or religious services conduced by the school itself, as being a part of the curriculum and instruction of the institution. Certainly the proposition to compel a student to march from one church to another of various denominations and of conflicting faiths, independent of the school itself, and located outside its boundaries and beyond its authority and control, cannot by any wild stretch of the imagination come within the principle laid down by the courts in sanctioning compulsory attendance by the student upon the religious services conducted by the school itself.

VI

Secondly, I find the contract to be void as violating the constitutional rights of the defendant's son in compelling him to attend and support a place of worship against his consent. . . .

. . . In considering the facts of this case, I cannot escape the thought that there is involved here a great principle that has always been regarded by the American people as the very heart beat of its national life.

This republic was founded by our forefathers, not to escape the injustice of political aggressions, but to seek freedom in a region where every man could worship God according to his own conscience. It was for this that they braved the perils of an unknown sea and the dangers of a savage wilderness.

. . . It is plain to me that the strenuous effort of the plaintiff to compel the defendant's son, a boy of Jewish faith, to attend the church services of various Christian churches in the village of Germantown, against his will, and in opposition to his religious faith and convictions, is clearly a violation of his constitutional rights. This, to my mind, is so, unless the language of the Bill of Rights of the state Constitution of Ohio is composed of empty words, and the ideas and ideals of the American people as to freedom of conscience through all these years has been but a pleasant dream. . . .

. . . In view of the foreging, judgment is found in favor of the defendant and against the plaintiff of no cause of action, dismissing plaintiff's complaint upon the merits, and judgment for defendant for his counterclaim in the amount of $475 and interest from September 25, 1924, together with costs and disbursements herein, amounting in the aggregate to the sum of $580.84.

REACTIONS OF LEGAL PERIODICALS TO *MIAMI MILITARY INSTITUTE* v. *LEFF*

The New York court's ruling drew limited reaction in law journals. The importance of the case was the underlying principle of religious freedom, a writer in the *Alabama Law Journal* (2:270) concluded.

He went on to characterize religious freedom as "a primal aim of the American people." In that connection, he cited the court's quotation, to wit: "A man's right to his own religious convictions . . . are as sacred in the eye of the law as his rights of person or property."

Although he said nothing in the review article in addition to what is mentioned here, a logical argument could be made that he was implying that the Christian student should not be compelled to attend the Christian chapel services either. One wonders whether that writer might have foreseen the then emerging problems of church and state in a perspective similar to the pattern of development during the past four decades.

The United States Supreme Court finally settled the issue in 1962, when it ruled in *Engel* v. *Vitale,* among other things, that religious liberty is violated when state coercion is present in sectarian matters.

INCIDENTAL BENEFITS TO RELIGION

In addition to the indirect benefits given to parochial schools; sectarian institutions, churches, and other religious groups have also received indirect aid. Some of this aid has been struck down by courts and some has been allowed.

The New York court in *St. Patrick's Church Society* v. *Heermans*, 68 Misc. 487, 124 N.Y.S. 705 (1910), ruled that providing free water to parochial schools did not violate state constitutional provisions regarding using state property, credit, or money for schools maintained by sectarian institutions. It was held that since the waterworks were leased to a private concern the lessee under the lease could give away the water to sectarian schools.

An advisory opinion by the New Hampshire supreme court, *Opinion of Justices,* 99 N.H. 519, 113 A.2d 114 (1955), ruled that state grants to all hospitals in the state offering nurses training were not unconstitutional as using tax money for religious purposes. The court reasoned that the proposed grants were not meant to aid any or all religious sects but rather were meant to aid the teaching of nursing.

The question of granting aid to or subsidizing a sectarian corporation was raised in *64th St. Residence* v. *New York City*, 4 N.Y.2d 268, 150 N.E.2d 396 (1958). An area condemned for urban renewal was acquired by the city for $16 per foot. A sectarian university purchased part of the land for $7 per square foot with the agreement to raze buildings, relocate the accupants of the buildings, and to use the cleared land only for the campus and buildings.

The $7 per square foot price was determined by several appraisers to be at least equal to the re-use value of the land. Therefore, the New York court ruled that while the university was benefiting by acquiring desirable land at a price lower than it could have been negotiated for with the private owners, the university was not "getting a gift grant or subsidy of public property."

The side issue of using college registration fees to support the Y.M.C.A. and Y.W.C.A. was raised in *Connell* v. *Gray*, 33 Okl. 591, 127 P. 417 (1912). The payment of $5 from each student's registration fee for the Agriculture and Mechanical College in Oklahoma was invalidated by the Oklahoma supreme court. The high court ruled that "[a]s to Young Men's and Young Women's Christian Associations, it is not permissible for [the] . . . board to make it compulsory upon any student of said institution to contribute to the maintenance of same."

TAX EXEMPTIONS FOR PAROCHIAL EDUCATION

Tax exemption has been one of the main ways in which religious groups have received indirect state aid.

A New Hampshire court ruled in *Warde* v. *Manchester*, 56 N.H. 509 (1876), that property in the state owned by the Roman Catholic church and used exclusively for academies and seminaries, wherein the faith and practices of that church were taught, was exempted from taxes. The court determined that the land was used solely for learning and the schools, while teaching moral and religious principles, were doing their duty in education.

An Iowa court ruled in *Trustees of Griswold College* v. *State of Iowa*, 46 Ia. 275 (1877), that the state constitution only prohibited the state from levying tithes, taxes, or other rates for use by churches. Therefore, the indirect benefit of tax exemption is not prohibited if the legislature thinks the exemption proper.

Property belonging to the Roman Catholic church and used exclusively for parochial schools in Minnesota was declared tax exempt by the state supreme court in *In re Grace*, 27 Minn. 503, 8 N.W. 761 (1881). The court determined that the parochial schools were free, run on a nonprofit basis, and were open to all children regardless of religion. Therefore, the court concluded that the schools were "in the legal sense, not only Charit-

[ies], but . . . wholly and entirely of a public nature, and therefore [are] purely public [schools]." However, the parsonage was not included in the tax exemption.

The supreme court of Illinois held in *Garrett Biblical Institute* v. *Elmhurst State Bank*, 331 Ill. 308, 163 N.E. 1 (1928), that the school for Bible study, set up and controlled by the Methodist church, was exempted from taxation. The court further determined that the tax exemption did not violate the state constitution, or the First Amendment provisions regarding religious freedom.

A Kentucky court determined in *Rawlings* v. *Butler Ky.*, 290 S.W.2d 801 (1956), that religious teachers who had taken vows of poverty and were employed in public schools could turn over their salaries to their religious orders. Such action, the court concluded, did not violate the constitutional prohibition concerning using public funds for religious purposes as long as the religious teachers were not "conduits" through which public funds were channeled into the church.

In a recent case, the supreme court of Wisconsin allowed tax exemption for parochial school property as a side issue. The court held in *State* ex rel. *Reynolds* v. *Nusbaum*, 17 Wis.2d 148, 115 N.W. 761 (1962), that "this tax exemption [did] not transcend the religious classification prohibition" regarding the use of public money for the benefit of religious societies.

A resident taxpayer challenged the legality of a tax exemption to religious property "used exclusively for school purposes" in a nonprofit manner in *Lundberg* v. *County of Alameda*, 46 Cal.2d 644, 298 P. 1 (1956), below. The court determined that the term "charitable" as used in the California constitutional provision providing exemptions for "religious, hospital or charitable" purposes should be interpreted broadly to include an exemption for a religious school. Thus construed, the Revenue and Taxation Code's specific exemption of religious school property was not an establishment of religion, the court ruled.

† † LUNDBERG v. COUNTY OF ALAMEDA
46 CAL.2D 644, 298 P. 1 (1956).

Judge GIBSON delivered the opinion of the court, saying in part:

Plaintiff, a citizen resident of defendant county and a taxpayer therein, brought this suit to challenge the legality of a tax exemption. Such actions are authorized by section 526a of the Code of Civil Procedure. . . .

The suit involves the constitutionality of that portion of section 214 of the

Revenue and Taxation Code which grants a tax exemption to property

used exclusively for school purposes of less than collegiate grade and owned and operated by colleges, hospital or charitable funds, foundations, or corporations,

provided that the property is used for nonprofit purposes and owned by nonprofit organizations. The exemption in question was added to section 214 in 1951 and was approved by the people on referendum at the general election of 1952. This appeal was taken from a judgment declaring the exemption invalid.

In California all property must be taxed unless an exemption is authorized by the state Constitution or granted by the laws of the United States. Section 1c of article XIII of the Constitution declares,

In addition to such exemptions as are now provided in this Constitution, the Legislature may exempt from taxation all or any portion of property used exclusively for religious, hospital or charitable purposes and owned by community chests, funds, foundations or corporations organized and operated for religious, hospital or charitable purposes, not conducted for profit and no part of the net earnings of which inures to the benefit of any private shareholder or individual.

The validity of the statutory exemption depends, first, upon whether an educational purpose may be regarded as a charitable purpose within the meaning of section 1c of article XIII. The term charity has been defined in a number of California cases as

'a gift, to be applied consistently with existing laws, for the benefit of an indefinite number of persons, either by bringing their hearts under the influence of education or religion, by relieving their bodies from disease, suffering or constraint, by assisting them to establish themselves in life, or by erecting or maintaining public buildings or works or otherwise lessening the burdens of government.' . . .

It thus appears that the word charitable has been given a broad construction in tax exemption cases as well as others, and it would seem clear that nonprofit schools owned by nonprofit organizations and operated for the benefit of the public come within the term charitable as defined by our decisions. Moreover, both the Legislature and the people have construed the term charitable in section 1c of article XIII as authorizing exemption of such schools. . . .

It is next argued that the exemption, as applied to schools owned or operated by religious organizations, is contrary to section 30 of article IV of the California Constitution which provides that the Legislature shall not

grant anything to or in aid of any religious sect, church, creed, or sectarian purpose, or help to support or sustain any school, college, university, hospital, or other institution controlled by any religious creed, church, or sectarian denomination whatever. . . .

This section does not expressly mention tax exemptions, but, even if we assume that it prohibited them, it was superseded by the subsequent adoption of section 1½ of article XIII, which exempts property used exclusively for religious worship, and of section 1c, which, as we have seen, authorizes exemption of nonprofit schools and specifically refers to property owned and operated by religious organizations.

The validity of the exemption is also

challenged on the theory that it contravenes that portion of the First Amendment of the federal Constitution which forbids the enactment of laws respecting the establishment of religion. This argument is, of course, pertinent only insofar as the exemption would be available to nonprofit schools operated by religious groups. There are two answers to the contention.

In the first place, it is apparent that the exemption was enacted to promote the general welfare through encouraging the education of the young and not to favor religion, since it is not limited to schools maintained by religious groups but applies also to those operated by other charitable organizations. Under the circumstances, any benefit received by religious denominations is merely incidental to the achievement of a public purpose. An analogous situation was presented in *Everson* v. *Board of Education,* 330 U.S. 1, where it was held that a statute authorizing the use of public funds to transport pupils could constitutionally be applied to include the furnishing of transportation to parochial schools. The court reasoned that the statute was designed to promote the general welfare, that a parochial school would benefit upon the same terms as would other schools and that the First Amendment does not require that government be hostile to religion in enacting public welfare legislation. . . .

Secondly, even if we regard the ex-

emption as benefiting religious organizations, it does not follow that it violates the First Amendment. The practice of granting tax exemptions benefiting religious sects began in the colonial period. . . . Today, at least some tax exemption for religious groups is authorized by statutory or constitutional provisions in every state and the District of Columbia, as well as by federal law. . . . No case has been found holding that the granting of such exemptions is contrary to state or federal constitutional provisions prohibiting the support or establishment of religion, and, where the matter has been raised, the exemptions have been upheld. . . . The United States Supreme Court, in discussing the prohibition of laws respecting the establishment of religion, recently stated that the standard of constitutionality is the separation of church and state, and that the problem, like many others in constitutional law, is one of degree. *Zorach* v. *Clauson,* 343 U.S. 306. The principle of separation of church and state is not impaired by granting tax exemptions to religious groups generally, and it seems clear that the First Amendment was not intended to prohibit such exemptions. Accordingly, an exemption of property used for educational purposes may validly be applied to school property owned and operated by religious organizations.

The judgment is reversed. . . .

REACTIONS OF LEGAL PERIODICALS TO
LUNDBERG v. *COUNTY OF ALAMEDA*

The decision was sharply criticized in a number of reviews. An argument was made in the *U.C.L.A. Law Review* (4:280) that the decision disregarded both legislative history and fiscal necessity.

In that connection, the writer argued that the legislative intent had been to "grant tax exemptions to 'charitable' organizations in the narrow sense of the term, and not to include educational institutions." He asserted further that the decision would have the effect of considerably narrowing the tax base in California at a time when the state government was in vital need of tax revenues.

A somewhat different approach in reasoning emerged in the *Stanford Law Review* (9:366). The writer there focused his attack upon the United States Supreme Court's dismissal of the appeal of this case "for want of a substantial federal question." In failing to hear the case on its merits the United States Supreme Court rejected the language which had been controlling in earlier decisions by the nation's highest tribunal, the analyst charged.

Continuing in that vein, he declared that the effect of leaving the California decision undisturbed was that the Supreme Court has "conclusively rejected the argument that the establishment clause prohibits all aid to religion and that it prohibits no more than the establishment of a state church." The result of all that has been, in his estimation, the absence of judicial guidelines in determining the "validity of other aids to religion."

Indicting the California court for not inquiring further into the matter of whether the tax exemptions were in the form of an indirect aid as well as an incidental one, the writer pointed out that the Everson case language seems to bar all governmental action which benefits religion. In that connection, he added that the amount of financial benefit to religion and cost to the taxpayers "may have been tacitly recognized as negligible" in the Everson decision, but that the amount in the Lundberg case was "over $900,000 annually."

That the tax exemption could not be justified on grounds of public welfare considerations either was plain to him, in light of the McCollum case. He also argued that there was more coercion sanctioned in the Lundberg case (where taxpayer support of religious instruction was guaranteed by the state itself) than was invalidated in the McCollum case (where social pressures were the primary forms of coercion).

SUMMARY

Because of the conglomerate nature and miscellaneous character of the issues covered in this chapter no cogent summary is possible. There are, however, a number of general themes that seem worthy of noting, again recognizing that they in no fashion exhaust the problems alluded to in the chapter. Moreover, it should be recognized that many of these decisions are of nineteenth-century vintage and do not necessarily reflect the sophistication of thought concerning the complexities inherent in church-state relations of today.

Eight state supreme court decisions ranging in time from 1879 to 1961 reflect a unanimous view that allowing public funds for schools which are clearly parochial in nature violates the state's constitution. Still another state high court held unconstitutional a practice whereby public funds were used to pay a teacher in a private school. Payment from public funds for tuition in a parochial school was voided by the South Dakota court. The Ohio court held that a school which was established from a will as a private, Protestant, technical school was sectarian and thus could not receive state funds.

While the general judicial attitude of opposition to use of public funds for parochial schools is present when dealing with sectarian-supported colleges and universities, the decisions lack the degree of consistency that is present when parochial elementary and secondary schools are involved. For example, in Wisconsin the supreme court of that state held that the state funds from the state's World War I G.I. Bill of Rights could be used by veterans attending sectarian colleges without violating the state's constitutional prohibition against aid to sectarian institutions. The basic theory of the court was that the benefits accrued to the veterans and not to the sectarian colleges and universities. In New York, a taxpayer's suit challenging an allocation of state funds to a Roman Catholic college because such an appropriation would be "a gift by the state to a religious institution" was dismissed on jurisdictional grounds. The major premise of the court was that an individual's tax contributions to the state treasury was so small that he could not have a good-faith, pocketbook interest in the case sufficient to justify a taxpayer's suit.

In a somewhat related case, however, a New York court held that a Jewish cadet at a private military academy in Ohio could not be required to attend Christian church services. The New York court held that while the regulation, in general, was reasonable, it could not be applied to Jewish students. The practical question is, however, what jurisdiction does a New York court really have to interpret the constitution and laws of Ohio?

The majority of state courts have a much more permissive attitude toward the use of state funds for special schools of one sort or another which are of a sectarian nature. It appears that most state courts have adopted a double standard when applying the religion clauses of the state or national constitutions to orphans' homes, and schools for delinquent and neglected children, on the one hand, and general parochial elementary or secondary schools, on the other. There are two notable exceptions to this generalization. The Nevada high court struck down an appropriation of public funds to a sectarian orphan asylum and the Virginia supreme court prohibited the use of public funds to pay for the tuition of servicemen's orphans to parochial schools, because the state law authorized such payments for veterans' orphans in any school.

The courts of three states have ruled that providing free water to parochial schools does not violate the religious provisions of the state constitutions. Another state court has permitted the use of public funds to support nurses' training programs in hospitals even though they are under the control of a religious sect. Still, another court upheld an authorization permitting a church to purchase future college buildings at a reduced price. On the other hand, however, the Oklahoma court prohibited the use of part of all students' tuition fees to help support the Y.M.C.A. and the Y.W.C.A.

Finally, those courts who have faced the issue, have been unanimous in ruling that property tax exemption for churches or sectarian schools, when authorized by state action, was not prohibited by constitutional provisions forbidding the use of public funds for sectarian purposes. In a related area, the Kentucky court held that religious teachers who had taken a vow of poverty and were employed in public schools could turn over their earnings to their religious orders without violating the Kentucky constitution.

On the subject of tax exemption, given the opposition of some important religious denominations in recent years to exempting property owned by sects from real property taxes coupled with the more detailed analysis by the United States Supreme Court of the establishment clause of the First Amendment recently, it might be expected that the litigation potential in this area may increase.

APPENDIX

---

† † *RHOADES* v. *SCHOOL DISTRICT OF ABINGTON TOWNSHIP*
226 A.2D 53 (1967).

Mr. Justice MUSMANNO delivered the opinion of the court, saying in part:

The Act of June 15, 1965, amending Article XIII, Section 1361 of the Public School Code of 1949, provides, inter alia:

"When provision is made by a board of school directors for the transportation of resident pupils to and from the public schools, the board of school directors shall also make provision for the free transportation of pupils who regularly attend non-public elementary and high schools not operated for profit."

On August 30, 1965, Brenard G. Rhoades and five others filed a suit in equity in Montgomery County, averring that the Act of June 15, 1965 . . . was unconstitutional, unlawful and invalid, and asking that the Court enjoin the defendant School District of Abington Township from entering into any contract under the indicated legislation.

. . . Betty J. Worrell filed a similar suit in Delaware County against the School Directors and Officers of Rose Tree Union School District. . . .

The issue is one on which adversaries feel deeply, although in reality the opposing points of view do not bristle with as much contention as might at first appearance seem likely. The plaintiffs and those who support their position see in Act 91 an infringement on the First Amendment to the Federal Constitution and to Article I, Sec. 3; Article III, Sections 17 and 18; and Article X, Sections 1 and 2 of the Pennsylvania Constitution, P.S.

The purpose of Act 91, as announced in its title, is to provide for the "health, welfare and safety of the children of the Commonwealth." The phrase "health, welfare and safety" is not to be treated lightly or as a superfluity. "The Legislature cannot be deemed to intend that its language be superfluous and without import." (*Daly* v. *Hemphill*, 411 Pa. 263, 191 A.2d 835.)

The larger number of schools in Pennsylvania are located so far away

382

from the homes of the pupils who attend them that the pupils are required either to walk long distances or to make use of vehicular transportation. In recent years the foot traveler, because of the volume of motor traffic which more and more is approaching the grim appearance of a foreign invasion, is in constant jeopardy of death or physical disablement, as he proceeds, warily or carefreedly over the highways of the nation. . . .

Testimony before a United States Senate Committee advanced the dire prediction that:

"It seems probable that over the next 5 years we will kill on the highways of this country as many people as we lost to enemy action in all four years in World War II. In the next decade, we can expect to kill more than 500,000 people and injure about 40 million." (89th Cong. 2d Sess. 112 Cong. Rec. 6576.)

In view of the peril hovering over our streets and roads like a miasmatic fog, those charged with concern for the safety of children are duty bound to devise methods and means for saving the little travelers from harm on their way to and from school. Obviously the manner in which to provide these youthful wayfarers with a fair measure of protection against highway mishap is to keep them pedally off the roads and to transport them in vehicles so formidably constructed that they may ward off and parry, to the maximum extent possible, aggression from other vehicles. The school bus with its large heavy wheels and steel fabricated body seems to be the answer to the worrisome problem. Pennsylvania Secretary of Public Welfare, in testifying on House Bill 381 (later to become Act 91) before the Senate Education Committee, said:

". . . school bus transportation clearly involves the safety and health of our children. The busing of school children is for their protection against hazards of the roadways and of traffic, against dangers occasioned by exposure to weather, against evils of child molestation."

He stated further that "with respect to injuries," a person is five times as safe in a school bus as in a car. With respect to death, a person is ten times as safe in a school bus as in a car. . . .

. . . The opponents of Act 91 do not contest the desirability, indeed even the imperativeness, of transporting children to school by means of school buses, but argue that they may not be used to ferry children attending non-public schools which, of course, include parochial schools. They point to the First Amendment to the Constitution of the United States which declares, inter alia, "Congress shall make no law respecting an establishment of religion," and argue that Act 91 offends against it.

Despite the wondrous flexibility of the English language it is still difficult to see how one can conclude that placing children on a school bus establishes a religion. And even if the children are transported to a school which, in addition to teaching state-approved subjects, offers guidance in the world of faith, this still does not establish a religion. Our whole body of school law is predicated on the proposition that once children are served educationally according to State criteria, their extracurricular activities cannot adversely affect the State, constitutionally. . . .

. . . .

Pennsylvania State laws compel all children up to 18 years of age to attend school—not public school, but *any* school so long as it teaches an approved curriculum and meets other State requirements. The State awards to nonpublic school students the same scholastic credits as those which are earned by public school students. It would be grossly illogical, therefore, to say that the State which does not differentiate between public and nonpublic pupils, so far as grades, promotion, and graduation are concerned, cleaves a line of distinction between them according to whether they arrive at the school on buses, in private motor cars or on foot.

Not only do law and reason refute any such differentiation, but economics in good government dispels the concept. . . . [A]ny procedure which may lighten that [heavy tax] burden, consistent with maintaining the highest State educational standards, is warmly welcomed by the taxpayers. Thus, for every nonpublic school pupil picked up on the road by a public school bus, that much weight is lifted from the back of the taxpayer because the maintenance of nonpublic schools, of course, does not depend upon public funds.

. . . Indeed, if nonpublic schools were to be abolished, the increase in tax burden to the citizens of the Commonwealth would be noteworthy and the Commonwealth would be hard put to provide the buildings, teachers and equipment for the flood of additional children released into their care and responsibility.

Where children are involved, the laws of the Commonwealth and the decisions of our Court make no distinction between public school and nonpublic school pupils. In 1911 the Pennsylvania Legislature enacted a law providing for the establishment of manual training schools for all children, public and nonpublic. . . .

. . . .

The Public School Code provides for children, without distinguishing between public and nonpublic schools, many facilities, as, for instance, medical, dental and nurse services . . .; driver safety . . .; food and milk supply . . .; board and lodging . . .; tuition and maintenance of blind, deaf and cerebral palsied children. . . . The School Code provides that school district funds may be used for traffic safety purposes. . . .

On the basis of logic and sustained reasoning it would be absurd to allow nonpublic school children into all these public services but deny them a ride on a bus to attend a school conforming to the requirements of the State educational program.

But the plaintiffs in the Montgomery County case argue that Act 91 is unconstitutional because five of the schools that educate children riding the school buses are owned and operated by the Roman Catholic Church and that, therefore, the plaintiffs contend,

"a primary and direct effect of the expenditures necessary or reasonably attendant upon such maintenance and operation is to advance the Roman Catholic Church. . . . "

This same argument was pressed in the case of *Everson* v. *Board of Education,* 330 U.S. 1, . . . where the constitutionality of a New Jersey statute was attacked because it authorized reimbursement to parents for fares paid for transporting by public carrier children attending public and Catholic schools. The Supreme Court of the United States ruled that the statute did not offend against the Federal Constitution. . . .

The United States Supreme Court found that the parochial schools there under consideration met New Jersey's school requirements. The State contributed no money to these schools; it did not support them. The legislation which provided for the busing of the parochial children did "no more than provide a general program to help parents get their children, regardless of their religion, safely and expeditiously to and from accredited schools." Therefore, the law was not at odds with the First Amendment. The same is true of Pennsylvania's Act 91. . . .

. . . .

The Supreme Court also pointed out that the First Amendment, in addition to abjuring the establishment of religion, also declared that there must be no prohibition in the "free exercise" of religion. Thus, while government may not use a legislative tool to build a church, neither may it employ a parliamentary bulldozer to demolish a church already constructed. "State power is no more to be used so as to handicap religions than it is to favor them." (*Everson*, supra, p. 18 . . . .)

Religion is part of the American way of life. . . .

. . . .

The constitutional prohibition against the establishment of religion was never intended to deny the free exercise of religion. . . .

Any interpretation of legislation, therefore, which would deny the fullest voluntary freedom in religious worship would not only be contrary to these American historical expressions of faith, but would also offend against the First Amendment with its bell-clanging proclamation of religious freedom. It was because the Founding Fathers foresaw the possibility of forces and influences working to destroy the faith of man in a Supreme Being that they made the free exercise of religion part of the same swing of the pendulum which prohibits the establishment of a State religion.

. . . .

Act 91 is public welfare legislation and, from the reservoir of public welfare, all races and religions may drink unimpededly in the quenching of normal thirsts. Indeed one of the fundamental reasons for the State in a civilized society is to provide for the public welfare.

The *Everson* case is the law of the land and rules squarely against the contentions of the plaintiffs in the Courts below in so far as the Federal Constitution is concerned. Our own Court upheld the *Everson* case by name in 1956 in *Schade* v. *Allegheny County Institution District*, 386 Pa. 507, 126 A.2d 911. . . .

We here hold that Act 91 does not offend against the First or Fourteenth Amendment to the Constitution of the United States. Does it transgress any provision or provisions of the Constitution of Pennsylvania? We have already touched on certain phases of the State Constitution in connection with a discussion of alleged trespassing on the domains of the United States. We will now examine specifically the argument that Act 91 cannot survive under prohibitory provisions of our own State organic law.

The plaintiffs contend that Act 91 violates Art. 1, Sec. 3 of the State Constitution:

"All men have a natural and indefeasible right to worship Almighty God according to the dictates of their own consciences; no man can of right be compelled to attend, erect or support any place of worship, or to maintain any ministry against his consent; no human authority can, in any case whatever, control or interfere with the rights of conscience, and no preference shall ever be given by law to any religious establishments or modes of worship."

The Abington Township brief asserts precisely that Act 91—

"compels all the real property owners of the Township to support places of worship and to maintain a particular religious ministry against their consent; and (2) it gives preference by law to certain religious establishments and modes of worship."

These assertions are so feeble of merit that they must fall in the slightest breeze of analysis. When the Constitution of 1874 was being debated in convention, no reference was made to the subject of pupil transportation. Supporting a place of worship meant providing funds for the maintenance of a church. The phrase certainly could not have referred to motor transportation. The concept of a horseless buggy was as unimaginable in 1873, as walking on air 150 miles above the earth was inconceivable in 1946. . . . Thus, it can be stated with historic conclusiveness that the framers of the 1874 Constitution could not have had in mind a prohibition against motor transportation for children when they declared that no citizen of the State should be required to support a place of worship.

Even in quixotic imagination, a school bus cannot be regarded a place of worship. . . . Nor can transporting a child to a church-connected school be regarded as supporting a place of worship. The purpose of the school bus is to take children to a structure where they will receive a secular education. Thus the bus serves a secular, public purpose, and as stated in *Everson*, "it is much too late to argue that legislation intended to facilitate the opportunity of children to get a secular education serves no public purpose."

. . . .

The plaintiffs' assertion that Act 91 "gives preference by law to certain religious establishments and modes of worship" is self-defeating on its face because there is nothing in the Act which speaks of preference for nonpublic schools. Indeed the Act states that the buses on which the nonpublic school pupil may ride "shall be over established public school bus routes." Thus, while nonpublic students eventually reach the nonpublic school, there is no provision that the bus is to take them to the doorstep of that school, or that the bus will pick them up at their homes. So far as nonpublic school children are concerned, they must, in a universal Mohammed sense, go to the buses rather than that the buses come to them.

It is also to be noted particularly that Act 91 makes no special provision for parochial schools. It applies all-sweepingly to children attending nonpublic schools, whether those schools have an association with a church or not. In addition, it is significant that the nonpublic schools will not be the donee of funds or busing facilities, nor will they have any control over them.

The plaintiffs do not charge that nonpublic schools would, under Act 91, be the recipient of financial benefits. But even if this were to be an indirect result of the legislation, this fact in itself would not unconstitutionalize the law. In order to come within the constitutional ban, financial benefits accruing to a nonpublic school would have to be direct and not merely incidental, supplemental or peripheral. . . .

The plaintiffs find in Act 91 a violation of Article 3, Section 18 of the Pennsylvania Constitution, which reads, inter alia:

"No appropriations shall be made for charitable, educational or benevolent purposes to any person or community nor to any denominational and sectarian institution, corporation or association."

. . . Educating the children of the state is a governmental duty, and, if excessive distance builds a wall around the place of education, government must level that wall.

Moreover, Act 91 does not require any appropriation from the Commonwealth.

. . . The school buses under Act 91 are operated for the benefit of the children who ride them and not for the benefit of the church which may be associated with the school in which the children receive a State-supervised education.

. . . "'The Constitution does not prohibit the State or any of its agencies from doing business with denominational or sectarian institutions, nor from paying just debts to them when incurred at its direction or with its approval. Numerous cases can be readily visualized where such situations have occurred: i.e. payment of the bill of an injured employee to a sectarian hospital.'" *(Schade* v. *Allegheny County Dist.,* supra, 386 Pa. p. 512, 126 A.2d p. 914).

. . . .

Section 2 of Article 10 states that:

"No money raised for the support of the public schools of the Commonwealth shall be appropriated to or used for the support of any sectarian school."

Abington sees in this section another bulldozer crushing out the life of Act 91, but Abington itself throws the bulldozer off its track with its own statement, namely.

"One section of the Public School Code, viz., sec. 1401, relating to school health services, does extend to children in private schools and results in public expenditures for the benefit of all children of school age, whether they attend public or private schools. Of course, the health of all children residing within the Commonwealth is a matter of legitimate concern of the General Assembly. . . . Programs such as health and dental examinations for all children of certain ages are unrelated to the 'support of any sectarian school'."

Indeed, under existing law, children in sectarian schools receive tax-supported health services. . . .

If the health of *all* children in the Commonwealth is a matter of legitimate concern of the General Assembly, why would not their safety also be a matter of legitimate concern of the General Assembly?

. . . .

In all the briefs which have been filed in opposition to Act 91, there is not one statement or word remotely suggesting that the transportation of nonpublic school children will in the slightest be deleterious to the public, the individuals involved, or the educational program of the State. On the contrary, we have seen how this school busing will be protective of the health and the safety of the children. . . .

[Plaintiff] . . . argues that three is no analogy between bus transportation and the provision for lunches and medical care for nonpublic school children, specifying: "Lunch and medical care are things which a child must have, irrespective of whether or not he attends school." In our society it is accepted that food for the mind in the form of education is no less necessary than food for the stomach. With regard to medical care, the supplying of bus transportation may be the means of protecting children from illness-producing exposure which would lessen the need for medical care.

It was also argued before us that Act 91 will "accelerate the fragmentation of our society and increase religious conflicts." The exact reverse is true. The closer different religions get to one another, the less will be the reason for dissension. . . .

. . . .

Justices JONES and ROBERTS wrote separate concurring opinions.
Chief Justice BELL dissented.
Mr. Justice COHEN dissented, saying in part:

The act in question violates, in my opinion, both the Pennsylvania Constitution and the Federal Constitution, and is further void for vagueness and incompleteness. Moreover, it is premised upon the subterfuge of the "child benefit" theory, and the present case comes before us with a record insufficient to substantiate the arguments made in support of the statute.

. . . .

. . . The act was passed as an aid to education and that is all. Since it grants tax supported benefits to sectarian educational institutions it is unconstitutional. That is all there is to it.

I dissent.

BIBLIOGRAPHY

BOOKS

American Association of School Administrators. *Religion in the Public Schools.* Washington: National Education Association, 1964.

American Association of School Administrators, Commission on Religion in the Public Schools. *Religion in the Public Schools.* New York: Harper, N.D.

Bannerjee, D. N. *Our Fundamental Rights: Their Nature and Extent (As Judicially Determined).* Cleveland: World Press, 1960.

Barker, E. *Church, State and Education.* Ann Arbor: University of Michigan Press, 1957.

——. *Church, State and Study: Essays.* Ann Arbor: University of Michigan Press, 1957.

Barrett, P. *Religious Liberty and the American Presidency: A Study in Church-State Relations.* St. Louis: Herder & Herder, 1963.

Berns, W. *Freedom, Virtue, and the First Amendment.* Baton Rouge: Louisiana State University Press, 1957.

Beth, L. P. *The American Theory of Church and State.* Gainesville: University of Florida Press, 1958.

Blanshard, P. *American Freedom and Catholic Power.* Boston: Beacon Press, 1958.

——. *Religion, and the Schools.* Boston: Beacon Press, 1963.

Blum, V. *Freedom in Education; Federal Aid for All Children.* Garden City: Doubleday, 1965.

Boles, D. E. *The Bible, Religion, and the Public Schools.* Ames: Iowa State University Press, 1965.

Boone, A. *Our Hypocritical New National Motto: In Good We Trust.* New York: Exposition Press, 1963.

Brady, J. *Confusion Twice Confounded; The First Amendment and the Supreme Court, an Historical Study.* South Orange: Seton Hall University Press, 1955.

Brickman, W. W. and S. Lehrer (eds.). *Religion, Government, and Education.* New York: Society for the Advancement of Education, 1961.

Brown, N. C. (ed.). *The Study of Religion in the Public Schools: An Appraisal.* Washington: American Council on Education, 1958.

Brown, W. A. *Church and State in Contemporary America.* New York: Scribner's Sons, 1936.

Burstein, A. *Law Concerning Religion.* Dobbs Ferry: Oceana, 1950.

Butts, R. F. *American Tradition in Religion and Education.* Boston: Beacon Press, 1950.

Cobb, S. H. *The Rise of Religious Liberty in America.* New York: Macmillan Co., 1902.

Conference on Religion and Public Education. *Religion and Public Education.* Washington: American Council on Education, 1945.

Conference on Religion in State Universities. *Religion in the State University.* Minneapolis: Burgess Publishing Co., 1950.

Coughlin, B. J. *Church and State in Social Welfare.* New York: Columbia University Press, 1965.

389

Cousins, N. (ed.). *'In God We Trust.'* New York: Harper, 1958.

Curry, J. E. *Public Regulation of the Religious Use of Land.* Charlottesville: The Michie Company, 1964.

Dawson, J. *Separate Church and State Now.* New York: Richard R. Smith, 1948.

Dierenfield, R. B. *Religion in American Public Schools.* Washington: Public Affairs Press, 1962.

Douglas, W. O. *The Bible and the Schools.* Boston: Little, Brown & Co., 1966.

Drinan, R. F. *Religion, the Courts and Public Policy.* New York: McGraw-Hill, 1963.

Drouin, E. *The School Question.* Washington: Catholic University of America Press, 1963.

Ehler, S. Z. *Church and State Through the Centuries.* Westminster: Newman Press, 1954.

Ellul, J. *Theological Foundation of Law.* New York: Doubleday, 1960.
Buffalo: Dennis & Co., 1958.

Emerson, T. I. and D. Haber. *Political and Civil Rights in the United States.* Vol. II.

Fellman, D. *Religion in American Public Law.* Boston: Boston University Press, 1965.

—— (ed.). *The Supreme Court and Education.* New York: Teachers Press, Columbia University, 1960.

Foote, H. W. *Thomas Jefferson: Champion of Religious Freedom; Advocate of Christian Morals.* Boston: Beacon Press, 1947.

Freund, P. A. and R. Ulrich. *Religion and the Public Schools.* Cambridge: Harvard University Press, 1965.

Friedrich, C. J. *Transcendent Justice: the Religious Dimension of Constitutionalism.* Durham: Duke University Press, 1964.

Frommer, A. B. (ed.). *The Bible and the Public Schools.* New York: Liberal Arts Press, 1963.

Gabel, R. J. *Public Funds for Church and Private Schools.* Washington: Catholic University of America Press, 1937.

Gausted, E. S. *Historical Atlas of Religion in America.* New York: Harper, 1962.

Goslin, R. C. *Church and State.* New York: The Foreign Policy Association, 1937.

Greene, E. B. *Religion and the State.* Ann Arbor: University of Michigan Press, 1958.

Healey, R. M. *Jefferson on Religion in Public Education.* New Haven: Yale University Press, 1962.

Herberg, W. *Protestant, Catholic, Jew: An Essay in American Religious Society.* Magnolia, Massachusetts: Peter Smith Publisher, 1960.

Howe, M.deW. *Cases on Church and State in the United States.* Cambridge: Harvard University Press, 1952.

——. *The Garden and the Wilderness: Religion and Government in American Constitutional History.* Chicago: University of Chicago Press, 1965.

Huegli, A. *Church and State Under God.* St. Louis: Concordia, 1964.

Hyneman, C. *The Supreme Court on Trial.* Englewood Cliffs: Prentice-Hall, 1963.

Institute of Church and State, Villanova University School of Law, D. A. Gianella, ed. *Religion and the Public Order.* Chicago: University of Chicago Press, 1963.

James, J. B. *The Framing of the Fourteenth Amendment.* Urbana: University of Illinois Press, 1965.

Johnson, A. W. *Legal Status of Church and State Relationships in the United States.* Minneapolis: University of Minnesota Press, 1934.

—— and F. H. Yost. *Separation of Church and State.* Minneapolis: University of Minnesota Press, 1948.

Johnson, F. E. (ed.). *American Education and Religion: The Problems of Religion in the Schools.* New York: Harper, 1952.

Jones, H. W. (ed.). *The Courts, The Public and the Law Explosion.* Englewood Cliffs: Prentice-Hall, 1965.

Katz, W. G. *Religion and American Constitutions.* Evanston: Northwestern University Press, 1959.

Kauper, P. G. *Religion and the Constitution.* Baton Rouge: Louisiana State University Press, 1964.

Kerwin, J. G. *The Catholic Viewpoint on Church and State.* New York: Doubleday, 1960.

Kurland, P. *Religion and the Law of Church and State and the Supreme Court.* Chicago: Aldine, 1962.

Landis, B. Y. *Religion in the United States.* New York: Barnes and Noble, 1965.

Levy, L. W. *Jefferson and Civil Liberties.* Cambridge: Harvard University Press, 1963.

Lindstrom, D. E. *American Foundations of Religious Liberty.* Champaign: Garrard Press, 1950.

Littel, F. H. *From State Church to Pluralism.* Chicago: Aldine, 1962.

Loder, J. E. *Religion and the Public Schools.* New York: Association Press, 1965.

McCollum, V. *One Woman's Fight.* Boston: Beacon Press, 1961.

McGill, R. *A Church, A School.* Nashville: Abington, 1959.

McGrath, J. J. *Church and State in American Law.* Milwaukee: Bruce Publishing Co., 1962.

McLean, M. D. and H. H. Kimber. *The Teaching of Religion in State Universities.* Ann Arbor: University of Michigan Press, 1960.

Madden, W. *Religious Values in Education.* New York: Harper, 1951.

Manwaring, D. R. *Render Unto Caesar: The Flag-Salute Controversy.* Chicago: University of Chicago Press, 1962.

Marnell, W. H. *The First Amendment: The History of Religious Freedom in America.* Garden City: Doubleday, 1964.

Mason, A. *The Supreme Court: Palladium of Freedom.* Ann Arbor: University of Michigan Press, 1962.

Miller, W. L., *et al. Religion and the Free Society.* New York: Fund for the Republic, 1958.

Moehlman, C. H. *School and Church.* New York: Harper, 1944.

——. *The Wall of Separation Between Church and State.* Boston: Beacon Press, 1951.

Moody, J. N. *Church and Society.* New York: Arts, Inc., 1953.

Munger, F. J. and R. Fenno. *National Politics in Federal Aid to Education.* Syracuse: Syracuse University Press, 1962.

Murray, J. C. *Problem of Religious Freedom.* Westminster: Newman Press, 1965.

——. *We Hold These Truths: Catholic Reflections on the American Proposition.* New York: Sheed & Ward, Inc., 1960.

Nichols, R. F. *Religion and American Democracy.* Baton Rouge: Louisiana State University Press, 1959.

——. *Religion and Education.* Cambridge: Harvard University Press, 1945.

O'Brien, F. *Justice Reed and the First Amendment.* Washington: Georgetown University Press, 1958.

O'Neill, J. M. *Religion and Education Under the Constitution.* New York: Harper, 1949.

Oaks, D. H. *The Wall Between Church and State.* Chicago: The University of Chicago Press, 1963.

Olmstead, C. E. *History of Religion in the United States.* Englewood Cliffs: Prentice-Hall, 1960.

Olson, B. E. *Faith and Prejudice: Intergroup Problems in Protestant Curricula.* New Haven: Yale University Press, 1963.

Parsons, W. P. *The First Freedom: Considerations on Church and State in the United States.* New York: McMullen, 1948.

Patterson, C. P. *Constitutional Principles of Thomas Jefferson.* Austin: University of Texas, 1953.

Perry, R. L. (ed.). *Sources of Our Liberties: Documentary Origins of Individual Liberties in the U.S. Constitution and Bill of Rights.* Chicago: American Bar Foundation, 1959.

Pfeffer, L. *Church, State and Freedom.* Boston: Beacon Press, 1953.

———. *Creeds in Competition.* New York: Harper, 1960.

———. *The Liberties of An American: The Supreme Court Speaks.* Boston: Beacon Press, 1956.

Politella, J. *Religion in Education: An Annotated Bibliography.* Oneonta: American Association of Colleges for Teacher Education, 1956.

Powell, T. *The School Bus Law: A Case Study in Education, Religion and Politics.* Middletown: Wesleyan University Press, 1961.

Regan, R. J. *American Pluralism and the Catholic Conscience.* New York: Macmillan Co., 1963.

Rice, C. E. *The Supreme Court and Public Prayer, the Need for Restraint.* New York: Fordham University Press, 1964.

Ryan, M. P. *Are Parochial Schools the Answer.* New York: Holt, Rinehart and Winston, Inc., 1964.

Sanders, T. G. *Protestant Conceptions of Church and State.* New York: Holt, Rinehart and Winston, Inc., 1964.

Schaff, P. *The Progress of Religious Freedom as Shown in the History of Toleration Acts.* New York: Scribner's Sons, 1889.

Schubert, G. *The Judicial Mind: The Attitudes and Ideologies of Supreme Court Justices, 1946–1963,* Evanston: Northwestern University Press, 1965.

Schultz, H. E. *Religious Education and the Public Schools.* Los Angeles: UCLA, 1955.

Shaver, E. L. *The Weekday Church School.* Philadelphia: Pilgrim, 1956.

Smith, J. W. and A. L. Jamison (eds.). *The Shaping of American Religion.* Princeton: Princeton University Press, 1961.

Snavely, G. *The Church and the Four-Year College: An Appraisal of their Relation.* New York: Harper, 1955.

Spicer, G. W. *The Supreme Court and Fundamental Freedoms.* New York: Appleton-Century-Crofts, 1959.

Spurlock, C. *Education and the Supreme Court.* Urbana: University of Illinois Press, 1955.

Stedman, M. S., Jr. *Religion and Politics in America.* New York: Harcourt, Brace & World, 1966.

Stokes, A. P. and L. Pfeffer. *Church and State in the United States.* New York: Harper, 1964.

Strickland, R. C. *Religion and the State in Georgia in the Eighteenth Century.* New York: Columbia University Press, 1939.

Sturzo, L. *Church and State.* New York: Longmans, Green and Co., 1939.

Sweet, W. W. *Religion in the Development of American Culture 1765–1840.* New York: Scribner's Sons, 1952.

Torpey, W. G. *Judicial Doctrines of Religious Rights in America.* Oxford: University of North Carolina Press, 1948.

Tussman, J. (ed.). *Supreme Court on Church and State.* New York: Oxford University Press, 1962.

Umbreit, K. P. *Our Eleven Chief Justices; A History of the Supreme Court in Terms of Their Personalities.* New York: Harper, 1938.

Walter, E. A. (ed.). *Religion and the State University.* Ann Arbor: University of Michigan Press, 1958.

Ward, L. R. *Federal Aid to Private Schools.* Westminster: Newman Press, 1964.

———. *Religion in All the Schools.* Notre Dame: Fides Publishing, Inc., 1960.

Wilson, J. F. (ed.). *Church and State in American History.* Boston: Heath, 1965.

Zabel, O. H. *God and Caesar in Nebraska: A Study of the Legal Relationship Between Church and State, 1854–1954.* Lincoln: University of Nebraska Press, 1955.

Zollman, C. F. *Church and School in the American Law.* St. Louis: Concordia, 1918.

PERIODICALS

EDUCATION AND GENERAL PERIODICALS

"After June 25, 1962," *America,* 107:483 (1962).

Allison, C. W. "What Spiritual Values Should Be Included in the Secondary-School Program?" *National Association of Secondary-School Principals Bulletin,* 33:83 (1949).

American Jewish Committee. "Religion in Public Education," *Religious Education,* 50:232 (1955).

"And Now School Buses: Transportation to Parochial Schools," *Commonweal,* 65:651 (1957).

Ball, W. B. "The Forbidden Prayer," *Commonweal,* 76:419 (1962).

——. "Religion in Education: A Basis for Consensus," *America,* 108:528 (1963).

Baumeister, E. "Religion and the Public Schools, Reply," *School and Society,* 67:473 (1948).

"Bible and Stuff; McCollum Case: Should Religion Be Taught in Public Schools?" *Time,* 46:66 (1945).

"Bible Reading Decision Splits Administrators into Two Camps; School Administrators, Opinion Poll," *Nation's Schools,* 72:43 (1963).

"Black Monday Decision," *America,* 107:456 (1962).

"Blot Removed," *Time,* 41:16 (1943).

Brickman, W. W. "Bible Reading, Prayers, and Public Schools," *School and Society,* 91:272 (1963).

——. "Educational Literature Review: Religion and Education," *School and Society,* 67:245 (1948).

Canavan, F. "New Pluralism or Old Monism," *America,* 109:556 (1963).

"Celebrating Holidays," *Nation's Schools,* 59:92 (1957).

"Champaign Case," *Christian Century,* 65:308 (1948).

"Champaign Case: Religious Instruction in Public School," *Christian Century,* 65:449 (1948).

Cocking, W. D. "Public Schools and the Teaching of Religion," *School Executive,* 67:5 (1948).

Coffey, W. L. "Judicial Status of Textbooks," *American School Board Journal,* 84:66 (1932).

Commager, H. S. "Civil Liberties and Democracy," *Scholastic,* 42:13 (1943).

"Comments by Lay and Religious Leaders," *National Education Association Journal,* 52:56 (1963).

"The Court Abdicates," *Christian Century,* 57:845 (1940).

"The Court Decides Wisely," *Christian Century,* 80:851 (1963).

"The Court on Prayer," *Commonweal,* 76:387 (1962).

"Court Upholds Freedom of Conscience," *Christian Century,* 60:732 (1943).

Cushman, R. E. "Constitutional Law in 1930–1940," *American Political Science Review,* 35:250 (1941).

Dano, E. H. "Mounting Church-State Issues: Time for a Showdown," *Education,* 69:124 (1948).

Dawson, J. M. "Public Schools Catholic Model," *Christian Century*, 65:627 (1948).

Driuan, R. F. "The Supreme Court and Religion," *Commonweal*, 56:554 (1952).

Dukir, S. "Supreme Court Ruling on School Prayer," *Educational Forum*, 27:71 (1962).

"The Editorial Stand," *American School Board Journal*, 146:38 (1963).

Elbin, P. N. "Religion in State School," *Christian Century*, 69:106 (1952).

"The Flag Salute," *National Education Association Journal*, 32:265 (1943).

"The Flag Salute Case," *Christian Century*, 57:791 (1940).

"Flag Salute Issue Finally Settled," *American School Board Journal*, 107:40 (1943).

"Flag-Salute Ruling Reversed," *The School Executive*, 63:17 (1943).

Fosdick, H. E. "Shall American School Children Be Religiously Illiterate?" *School and Society*, 66:401 (1949).

"Frankfurter vs. Stone," *New Republic*, 102:843 (1940).

Franklin, S. P. "The Language of the Problem," *Religious Education*, 43:193 (1948).

"Free Textbooks Constitutional," *Commonweal*, 12:35 (1930).

Fuller, E. "Public Schools and Separation of Church and State," *The Education Digest*, 14:3 (1949).

Garber, L. O. "Confusing Decisions on Released Time," *Nation's Schools*, 50:67 (1952).

———. "Court Bars Bible Reading, but Finds Place for Religion in Schools," *Nation's Schools*, 72:50 (1963).

———. "Four Big Educational Issues Dominate Court Cases," *Nation's Schools*, 73:76 (1964).

———. "Four Church-State Controversies: How They Affect Education," *Nation's Schools*, 69:66 (1962).

———. "How the Courts Are Changing the Education Scene," *Nation's Schools*, 69:92 (1962).

———. "Prayer Barred: What It Means," *Nation's Schools*, 70:54 (1962).

———. "What the New Jersey Courts Say About Bible Reading in the Public Schools," *Nation's Schools*, 50:61 (1952).

Gauss, C. "Should Religion Be Taught In Our Schools?" *Ladies Home Journal*, 65:40 (1948).

Hamilton, W. and G. Braden. "The Supreme Court Today," *New Republic*, 103:178 (1940).

Heffron, E. J. "Supreme Court Oversight," *Commonweal*, 46:9 (1947).

Hess, M. W. "Devil Newly Invented! Released Time Cases; Reply to A. E. Meyer," *Catholic World*, 168:295 (1949).

"High Court Finale," *Newsweek*, 15:36 (1940).

"High Court Rules as Anticipated," *Christian Century*, 80:820 (1963).

Hodgdon, D. R. "Excusing Public—Public Pupils for Religious Instruction," *Clearing House*, 23:374 (1949).

———. "Religious Instruction in a School Building," *Clearing House*, 23:436 (1949).

———. "School Law Review: Flag Salute Issue Settled," *Clearing House*, 19:192 (1944).

———. "School Law Review: Patriotism and Compulsion," *Clearing House*, 20:430 (1946).

Holmes, J. H. "The Case of Jehovah's Witnesses," *Christian Century*, 57:896 (1940).

Howlett, W. M. "The Case for Released Time," *Education*, 71:370 (1951).

Hunt, C. L. "Religious Instruction versus Secularization: German Experience," *Journal of Educational Sociology*, 22:304 (1948).

Jarman, B. H. "Religious Education and the Public Schools," *School and Society*, 67:44 (1948).

"Jehovah's Witnesses, Who Refuse to Salute the U.S. Flag, Hold Their National Convention," *Life*, 9:20 (1940).

Johnson, F. E. "Church, State and School," *Education*, 71:353 (1951).

———. "Religion and Public Education," *National Association of Secondary- School Principals Bulletin,* 31:95 (1947).

———. "Religion and the Schools—What Can We Hope For," *Religious Education,* 43:201 (1948).

Kandel, I. L. "Religion and Public Education: Review of American Council on Education Report," *School and Society,* 66:53 (1947).

Kuenzli, L. R. "Federal Aid for Transportation to Public and Non-Public Schools," *American Teacher,* 32:2 (1948).

Larson, J. "Released Time for Religious Education?" *National Education Association Journal,* 47:572 (1958).

"Legal Status of Religious Teaching in Various States, 1949–1950," *Nation's Schools,* 48:651 (1951).

Little, L. C. "Syllabus on a Religion and Public Education," *Religious Education,* 44:163 (1949).

Lookstein, J. "Strategies for Making Adequate Provision of Religious Education for All Our Young," *Religious Education,* 49:95 (1954).

"Majority Decision in Engel v. Vitale," *Overview,* 3:60 (1962).

Miller, E. O. "True Piety and the Regent's Prayer," *Christian Century,* 79:934 (1962).

Morrison, C. C. "What Did the Supreme Court Say? McCollum Case Concerning Released Time," *Christian Century,* 66:707 (1949).

O'Gara, J. "Religion and the Court," *Commonweal,* 78:391 (1963).

O'Neill, N. M. "Supreme Court on Separation of Church and State: Released Time for Religious Education," *Commonweal,* 49:466 (1949).

Oxnam, G. B. "Church, State and Schools," *Nation,* 168:67 (1949).

Pfeffer, L. "State-Sponsored Prayer," *Commonweal,* 76:417 (1962).

Powell, T. R. "The Flag Salute Case," *New Republic,* 109:16 (1943).

———. "Public Rides To Private Schools," *The Harvard Educational Review,* 17:73 (1947).

"Prayer and the Schools," *America,* 108:898 (1963).

"Prayer Still Legal in Public Schools," *Christian Century,* 79:832 (1962).

"Protestants: Come Clean!" *Christian Century,* 65:591 (1948).

"Protestants Take Catholic Line," *Christian Century,* 65:643 (1948).

"Public Schools Can Teach Religion," *Christian Century,* 65:374 (1948).

Punke, H. H. "Recent Court Ruling on Pupil Transportation," *National Association of Secondary-School Principals Bulletin,* 45:49 (1961).

"Radicals: Fifth Column," *Time,* 35:21 (1940).

"Reaction to Supreme Court Prayer Rule," *Nation's Schools,* 70:80 (1962).

"Recent Supreme Court Decisions: Separation of Church and State," *Social Education,* 26:439 (1962).

"Released Time Decision," *National Education Association Journal,* 37:209 (1948).

"Releasing the Time: Religious Teaching in Champaign," *Commonweal,* 47:581 (1948).

"Religion in Public Education," *Religious Education,* 50:232 (1955).

"Religious Teaching in School Buildings or on School Time," *American City,* 63:7 (1948).

Remmlein, M. K. "The Legal Situation Resulting From the Recent Supreme Court Decision," *Religious Education,* 43:211 (1948).

Rosenfield, H. N. "Nobody Has to Salute U. S. Flag," *Nation's Schools,* 32:45 (1943).

Rotnem, N. W. and F. G. Folsom. "Recent Restrictions Upon Religious Liberty," *American Political Science Review,* 36:1053 (1942).

"Roundup on Prayer Case," *America,* 107:541 (1962).

"School News Digest," *Clearing House,* 15:554 (1941).

Seyfert, W. C. "Religious Education and The Schools; Analysis of Recent Supreme Court Decision," *School Review*, 56:249 (1948).

Shaver, E. L. "Weekday Religious Education Secures its Charter and Faces a Challenge," *Religious Education*, 48:38 (1953).

Shaw, A. B. "Symposium: Religion in the Public Schools," *Religious Education*, 59:451 (1964).

"Should Schools Teach 'About Religion,'" *Nation's Schools*, 66:74 (1960).

Southworth, H. R. "Jehovah's 50,000 Witnesses," *Nation*, 151:110 (1940).

Starr, I. "Recent Supreme Court Decisions: Separation of Church and State," *Social Education*, 16:361 (1952).

————. "Recent Supreme Court Decisions: Separation of Church and State," *Social Education*, 26:439 (1962).

"State Rulings on Religious Observances in Public Schools," *School Life*, 44:89 (1962).

"State and Sectarian Education," *National Education Association Research Bulletin*, 24:1 (1946).

"The State and Sectarian Education," *National Education Association Research Bulletin*, 34:169 (1956).

"Supreme Court Bans Released Time," *Christian Century*, 65:294 (1948).

"Supreme Court Bans Released-Time Classes," *The Education Digest*, 13:4 (1948).

"Supreme Court Decision on Bible Reading and Prayer Recitation," *National Education Association Journal*, 52:55 (1963).

"Supreme Court on Free School Books," *School and Society*, 31:637 (1930).

"Supreme Court Prayer Decision," *National Education Association Journal*, 51:38 (1962).

Sutherland, A. E. "The Supreme Court and the Public School," *The Harvard Educational Review*, 24:71 (1954).

Swisher, C. B. "Civil Liberties in War Time," *Political Science Quarterly*, 55:321 (1940).

Taft, C. P. "Religion and the Public School," *Christian Century*, 69:944 (1952).

"Taking it Out on the Aliens," *Commonweal*, 32:158 (1940).

Tapp, R. B. "Released Time For Religious Education?" *National Education Association Journal*, 47:573 (1958).

"Ten Commandments," *Nation's Schools*, 60:45 (1957).

Tey, H. E. "They Stand for Free Schools!" *Christian Century*, 64:824 (1947).

Toner, J. L. "Does A.F.T. Support 'Zeal for Democracy' Program?" *The American Teacher*, 32:2 (1948).

"Unser Gott and Jehovah's Witnesses," *New Republic*, 103:173 (1940).

Ward, L. R. "Things to be Done," *Religious Education*, 51:250 (1956).

Weigle, L. A. "Crisis of Religion in Education," *Religious Education*, 49:73 (1954).

"We Must Permit Prayer in the Schools: School Administrators Poll Findings," *Nation's Schools*, 70:101 (1962).

Wetzel, W. A. "Religious Education, A Layman's Analysis," *National Association of Secondary-School Principals Bulletin*, 33:66 (1949).

Whelan, C. M. "Textbook and the Constitution," *America*, 107:399 (1962).

LEGAL PERIODICALS

Baker, R. C. "The Supreme Court and the Freedom of Religion Melange," 49 *American Bar Association Journal* 439 (1955).

Blum, V. C. "Religious Liberty and the Religious Garb," 22 *University of Chicago Law Review* 875 (1955).

Casad, R. C. "On Teaching Religion at the State University," 12 *University of Kansas Law Review* 405 (1964).

"Cases and Studies—Free Textbooks in Mississippi," 2 *The Jurist* 370 (1942).

"Case Law—Released Time for Religious Instruction During School Day—Constitutional Aspects of School Participation in Religious Program," 35 *Washington Law Review* 143 (1960).

"Case Notes—Expulsion From School For Refusal to Salute the Flag," 14 *Southern California Law Review* 73 (1940).

—— Right to Keep Children Out of Public Schools on Religious Holidays," 2 *Alabama Law Review* 320 (1950).

—— Use of Legislative History," 4 *U.C.L.A. Law Review* 280 (1957).

"Cases Notes—Bible Reading in Public Schools," 24 *Tennessee Law Review* 883 (1957).

—— Requirement of Interest in Appeal to United States Supreme Court," 4 *Alabama Law Review* 284 (1952).

"Cases of Interest—State Law Requiring Public School Pupils to Salute the Flag Held Unconstitutional," 6 *Georgia Bar Journal* 249 (1944).

—— Statute Providing For Free School Books Held Unconstitutional," 34 *Law Notes* 233 (1931).

"Comment—Appropriations of Public Funds Beneficial to Sectarian Schools," 6 *University of Detroit Law Journal* 174 (1943).

"Comment of Cases—Prescribed Courses of Study in Public Schools and the Constitutional Guaranty of Religious Liberty," 10 *California Law Review* 249 (1922).

—— Personal Liberty: Includes the Right to Teach Foreign Languages in Private Schools," 12 *California Law Review* 136 (1924).

"Comments—, Application of the First Amendment to State Action Through the Fourteenth Amendment," 22 *Southern California Law Review* 423 (1949).

—— Church and State in American Education," 43 *Illinois Law Review* 374 (1948).

—— Compulsory Military Training," 8 *Southern California Law Review* 302 (1935).

—— Distribution of Gideon Bibles in Public Schools," 34 *Boston University Law Review* 375 (1954).

—— The New York Released Time Program," 50 *Michigan Law Review* 1359 (1952).

—— Private Tutoring and Compulsory Education," 18 *University of Chicago Law Review* 105 (1950).

—— Public Aid to Parochial Schools," 45 *Michigan Law Review* 1001 (1947).

—— Released Time," 26 *Southern California Law Review* 186 (1953).

—— Religious Garb in the Public Schools, A Study in Conflicting Liberties," 22 *University of Chicago Law Review* 888 (1955).

—— Result of the 'Everson Amendment'—The McCollum Case," 32 *Marquette Law Review* 138 (1948).

—— State Tax Exemptions and the Establishment Clause," 9 *Stanford Law Review* 366 (1957).

—— Taxpayer's Action Against State Officials to Prevent Alleged Unconstitutional Use of State Funds," 17 *Fordham Law Review* 107 (1948).

"Comments on Recent Cases—Statute Authorizing Use of School District Funds to Provide Transportation for Parochial School Children," 32 *Iowa Law Review* 769 (1947).

—— Personal, Civil and Political Rights—Compulsory Flag Salute," 23 *Iowa Law Review* 424 (1938).

—— Power of State to Compel Students at a State University to Pursue a Course in Military Training," 23 *Illinois Bar Journal* 270 (1935).

—— Separation of Church and State—'Released Time' Religious Education Program," 37 *Iowa Law Review* 286 (1952).

—— Teaching of English Language in Schools," 18 *Illinois Law Review* 394 (1924).

"Constitutionality of the New York Released Time Program," 49 *Columbia Law Review* 826 (1949).

"Contributed Matter—Interpreting the Constitution," 33 *Law Notes* 121 (1929).

Corwin, E. S. "The Supreme Court as a National School Board," 14 *Law and Contemporary Problems* 1 (1949).

"Current Decisions—'Released Time' Held Valid if School Buildings Not Used," 25 *Rocky Mountain Law Review* 104 (1952).

"Decisions—Compulsory Military Study in State Universities," 33 *Columbia Law Review* 1441 (1933).

——— Distribution of 'Gideon' Bibles Through the Public School System," 29 *New York University Law Review* 1290 (1954).

——— State Appropriations for Education of War Orphans Held Unconstitutional Insofar as It Could Be Used to Finance Attendance at Private or Sectarian Schools," 42 *Virginia Law Review* 437 (1955).

——— Statute Providing for Free Transportation of Children to Nonpublic Schools Violated a State Constitutional Provision Prohibiting Appropriation of Public Money for Support of Nonpublic Schools," 8 *New York Law Forum* 424 (1962).

——— Use of School Property for the Temporary Erection of a Privately Financed Religious Symbol," 30 *Brooklyn Law Review* 356 (1963).

——— Validity of Released Time Program for Religious Instruction," 19 *Brooklyn Law Review* 134 (1952).

Donnici, P. J. "Governmental Encouragement of Religious Ideology: A Study of the Current Conscientious Objector Exemption from Military Service," 13 *Journal of Public Law* 16 (1964).

"Editorial Notes—Constitutional Implications of Compulsory Flag Salute Statutes," 12 *George Washington Law Review* 70 (1943).

——— Permissible Limits of 'Released Time' In Public Schools," 17 *George Washington Law Review* 516 (1949).

Emerson, T. I. and D. Haber. "The Scopes Case in Modern Dress," 27 *University of Chicago Law Review* 522 (1959).

Fahy, C. "Religion, Education, and the Supreme Court," 14 *Law and Contemporary Problems* 73 (1949).

Fellman, D. "Religion in American Public Law," 44 *Boston University Law Review* 287 (1964).

Fielden, A. E. "Constitutional Law; Constitutionality of Transporting Nonpublic School Children on Public School Buses," 17 *Oklahoma Law Review* 174 (1964).

"The Flag Salute Cases," 1 *Bill of Rights Review* 9 (1940).

Hannan, J. D. "Not One Cent for Religion," 7 *The Jurist* 45 (1947).

Hartogensis, B. H. "Denial of Equal Rights to Religious Minorities and Nonbelievers in the United States: (Bible Reading in the Schools)," 39 *Yale Law Journal* 678 (1929).

Kalvern, H., Jr. "A Commemorative Case Note—Scope v. State," 27 *University of Chicago Law Review* 505 (1959).

Lee, B. "Anti-Evolution Laws Unconstitutional," 11 *American Bar Association Journal* 417 (1925).

"The McCollum Decision and the Public School," 37 *Kentucky Law Journal* 402 (1949).

McKenna, W. J. "The Transportation of Private and Parochial School Chlidren at Public Expense," 35 *Temple Law Quarterly* 259 (1962).

Manion, C. E. "The Church, the State and Mrs. McCollum," 23 *Notre Dame Lawyer,* 456 (1948).

Meiklejohn, A. "Educational Cooperation Between Church and State," 14 *Law and Contemporary Problems* 61 (1949).

Murray, J. C. "Law or Prepossessions?" 14 *Law and Contemporary Problems* 23 (1949.)

"Notes—Are Bonuses to Soldiers and Sailors Given for A Public Purpose?" 33 *Harvard Law Review* 846 (1920).

—— Catholic Schools and Public Money," 50 *Yale Law Journal* 917 (1940).

—— Church-State: A Legal Survey 1963–64," 39 *Notre Dame Lawyer* 427 (1963–64).

—— Compulsory Flag Salutes and Religious Freedom," 51 *Harvard Law Review* 1418 (1938).

—— The First Amendment and Distribution of Religious Literature in the Public Schools," 41 *Virginia Law Review* 789 (1955).

—— The Furnishing of Free Textbooks to Private Schools," 25 *Illinois Law Review* 547 (1931).

—— *Illinois v. Board of Education,*" 9 *Detroit Law Review* 119 (1948).

—— Members of Religious Orders as Teachers in Public Schools," 31 *Tulane Law Review* 676 (1957).

—— The Place of Religion in the Schools of the State of Iowa," 49 *Iowa Law Review* 771 (1964).

—— Public Funds for Sectarian Schools," 60 *Harvard Law Review* 793 (1947.)

—— Religious Instruction in Public Schools," 9 *Louisiana Law Review* 409 (1949).

—— Separation of Church and State and the Application of the First Amendment to State Powers," 36 *Nebraska Law Review* 357 (1957).

—— Tuition Payments by State to Sectarian Schools," 22 *Louisiana Law Review* 266 (1961).

—— The Unconstitutionality of the Foreign Language Law," 72 *Pennsylvania Law Review* 46 (1923).

—— Validity of the Tennessee Anti-Evolution Law," 5 *Tennessee Law Review* 242 (1947).

"Note and Comment—Constitutionality of Soldiers' Bonus Law," 18 *Michigan Law Review* 535 (1920).

—— The United States Supreme Court and Everson v. Board of Education of Ewing Township," 27 *Oregon Law Review* 150 (1948).

—— Validity of Foreign Language Statutes," 22 *Michigan Law Review* 248 (1924).

"Notes and Comments—Aid to Parochial School Students," 27 *Boston University Law Review* 281 (1947).

—— The Compulsory Flag Salute in Schools," 9 *Journal of Kansas State Bar Association* 276 (1941).

—— Compulsory Flag Salute; Interference with Religious Freedom," 26 *Cornell Law Quarterly* 127 (1940).

—— Compulsory Military Training," 15 *Boston University Law Review* 332 (1935).

—— Court's Jurisdiction over the Religious Upbringing of Children," 34 *North Carolina Law Review* 509 (1956).

—— Refusal to Salute Flags Because of Religious Beliefs," 20 *Boston University Law Review* 356 (1940).

—— Right of Japanese in Hawaii to Direct Education of Child; Government Power of Control," 11 *Marquette Law Review* 158 (1927).

—— Schools and School Districts," 2 *Alabama Law Journal* 270 (1927).

O'Brien, K. R. and D. E. O'Brien. "Separation of Church and State in Restatement of Inter-Church-and-State Common Law," 7 *The Jurist* 259 (1947).

Pfeffer, L. "Religion, Education and the Constitution," 8 *Lawyers Guild Review* 387 (1948).

"Recent Case Comments—Compulsory Military Training in Land Grant Colleges," 41 *West Virginia Law Quarterly* 281 (1935).

"Recent Case Notes—Compulsory Military Training in Land Grant Colleges," 10 *Indiana Law Journal* 361 (1935).

—— Soldier's Bonus Laws," 29 *Yale Law Journal* 690 (1920).

"Recent Cases—Agreement Concerning Child's Religious Education Incorporated in Divorce Decree Held Unenforceable," 72 *Harvard Law Review* 372 (1958).

—— Chest X-Ray as a Condition of Admission to State University," 27 *Washington Law Review* 228 (1955).

—— Compulsory Education Laws—Equivalent Education," 19 *George Washington Law Review* 361 (1950).

—— Compulsory Flag Salute," 6 *Missouri Law Review* 106 (1941).

—— Compulsory Flag Salute by School Children," 14 *Temple University Law Quarterly* 545 (1940).

—— Compulsory Flag Salute by School Children," 17 *Temple University Law Quarterly* 465 (1943).

—— Compulsory Military Training," 2 *University of Chicago Law Review* 331 (1935).

—— Constitutionality of Statute Providing Free Transportation for Private and Parochial School Children," 51 *Harvard Law Review* 935 (1938).

—— Distribution of Bibles in Public Schools," 3 *St. Louis Law Journal* 269 (1955).

—— Distribution of Bibles Through Public Schools," 38 *Minnesota Law Review* 663 (1954).

—— Laws Affecting the Establishment of Religion," 15 *George Washington University Law Review* 361 (1947).

—— Oregon Textbook Statute Unconstitutional as a Benefit to a Religious Institution," 31 *University of Cincinnati Law Review* 335 (1962).

—— Power of a State to Compel Mohammedan Children to Attend School on Friday," 98 *University of Pennsylvania Law Review* 923 (1950.)

—— Power of School Board to Compel Pupils to Salute Flag," 92 *University of Pennsylvania Law Review* 103 (1943).

—— Public Schools," 27 *Temple Law Quarterly* 339 (1954).

—— Released Time Program for Religious Instruction of School Children," 28 *North Dakota Law Review* 222 (1952).

—— Released Time Religious Education—Laws Respecting An Establishment of Religion," 27 *Texas Law Review* 256 (1948).

—— Religious Freedom and Compulsory Saluting of the Flag," 14 *University of Cincinnati Law Review* 444 (1940).

—— Religious Freedom and Compulsory Saluting of the Flag," 14 *University of Cincinnati Law Review* 570 (1940).

—— Religious Instruction in the Public Schools," 31 *Texas Law Review* 327 (1953).

—— Requiring Public School Pupils to Salute Flag," 15 *Washington Law Review* 265 (1940).

—— Right of Land Grant College to Expel Conscientious Objectors for Refusal to Take Course in Military Training as Required by State Statute—The Morrill Act," 83 *University of Pennsylvania Law Review* 529 (1934).

—— Statute Requiring Reading of Old Testament by Teacher in Public Schools Not an Establishment of Religion," 64 *Harvard Law Review* 666 (1950).

—— Statutes Prohibiting Teaching of Foreign Languages," 37 *Harvard Law Review* 151 (1924).

—— Teaching Foreign Languages," 6 *Illinois Law Quarterly* 86 (1923).

—— Transportation of Parochial School Pupils," 3 *St. Louis University Law Journal* 273 (1955).

—— Use of Public Funds for Transportation of Parochial School Students," 51 *Dickinson Law Review* 276 (1947).

—— Use of Public School Facilities for Sectarian Instruction Held Unconstitutional Under the First Amendment," 61 *Harvard Law Review* 1248 (1947).

—— Use of School Time," 21 *University of Cincinnati Law Review* 481 (1952).

——— Validity of Appropriations of Public Funds that Inure to the Benefit of Sectarian Schools," 29 *Minnesota Law Review* 311 (1942).

——— Validity of Released Time Programs," 28 *Washington Law Review* 156 (1953).

——— Voluntary Religious Instruction in Public Schools, Violation Under First and Fourteenth Amendments," 16 *George Washington Law Review* 556 (1948).

"Recent Cases of Interest—Public Funds for Transportation to Parochial Schools," 9 *Georgia Bar Journal* 471 (1947).

——— Validity of Released Time Program," 15 *Georgia Bar Journal* 363 (1953).

——— Validity of Statute Requiring Bible Reading in Public Schools," 19 *Georgia Bar Journal* 227 (1956).

"Recent Decisions—Bible Reading in the Public Schools," 55 *Michigan Law Review* 715 (1957).

——— Compulsory Flag Salute," 39 *Michigan Law Review* 149 (1940).

——— Compulsory Flag Salute and Religious Liberty," 4 *University of Detroit Law Journal* 38 (1940).

——— Compulsory Salute and Pledge of Allegiance to Flag by School Children," 36 *Michigan Law Review* 485 (1938).

——— Compulsory School Attendance Statute Construed to Permit Instruction at Home by Parent," 36 *Virginia Law Review* 682 (1950).

——— Distribution of Bible in Public Schools Declared Unconstitutional," 25 *Mississippi Law Journal* 271 (1954).

——— Distribution of Gideon Bible in Public School," 52 *Michigan Law Review* 1057 (1954).

——— Distribution of Gideon Bible through Use of Public School Machinery Held Unconstitutional as Violating 'Establishment of Religion' Clause," 40 *Virginia Law Review* 487 (1954).

——— The Distribution of the King James Version of the Bible, Accomplished through the School System, is Violative of Both the Federal Constitution and that of the State," 42 *Georgetown Law Journal* 455 (1954).

——— The Establishment Clause of the First Amendment," 29 *Notre Dame Lawyer* 478 (1954).

——— Federal Statute Limiting Draft Exemption to Those Religious Objectors Professing Belief in Supreme Being Does Not Violate Establishment Clause," 50 *Virginia Law Review* 178 (1964).

——— Flag Salute in Public Schools," 15 *St. John's Law Review* 95 (1940).

——— New York Released Time Program Held Constitutional," 4 *Syracuse Law Review* 157 (1952).

——— Private Parochial Schools—Transportation of Pupils—Use of Public Funds," 37 *Michigan Law Review* 335 (1938).

——— Prohibition of Teaching of German Language not Valid Exercise of Police Power," 9 *St. Louis Law Review* 68 (1923).

——— 'Released Time' Religious Instruction of Public School Students," 10 *University of Pittsburgh Law Review* 409 (1949).

——— Religion in the Public Schools," 34 *Michigan Law Review* 1237 (1936).

——— Religious Education in Publicly Supported Schools," 1 *Baylor Law Review* 79 (1948).

——— Resolution of State Board of Education Compelling Salute to Flag Held Unconstitutional," 32 *Georgetown Law Journal* 93 (1943).

——— Saluting Flag," 29 *Georgetown Law Journal* 112 (1940).

——— State Taxpayer Denied Standing as Party in Interest in Bible Reading Case," 50 *Michigan Law Review* 1100 (1952).

——— Taxpayer's Standing in Court to Question Expenditures of State Funds," 34 *Virginia Law Review* 335 (1948).

—— Transportation of School Children," 9 *University of Pittsburgh Law Review* 56 (1947).

—— Validity of 'Released Time' Program," 35 *Marquette Law Review* 385 (1952).

—— Validity of Salary Payments to Teachers Wearing Religious Garb While Teaching," 16 *Notre Dame Lawyer* 148 (1941).

—— Validity of State Law Requiring School Children to Salute Flag," 42 *Michigan Law Review* 186 (1943).

—— Voluntary Religious Classes Held in Public School Building During School Hours," 46 *Michigan Law Review* 828 (1948).

"Recent Decisions and Statutes—Compulsory Flag Salute Sustained," 18 *New York University Law Quarterly Review* 124 (1924).

"Recent Important Decisions—Foreign Language Schools—Due Process Under the Fifth," 25 *Michigan Law Review* 906 (1927).

—— Support of Parochial Schools," 16 *Michigan Law Review* 559 (1918).

Reed, G. E. "Church and the Zorach Case," 27 *Notre Dame Lawyer* 529 (1952).

Reeves, H. C. "Higher Education and State Tax Policy," 15 *National Tax Journal* 291 (1962).

Schmidt, G. P. "Religious Liberty and the Supreme Court of the U.S.," 17 *Fordham Law Review* 173 (1948).

Setzler, E. A. and O. Linford. "A Constitutional Analysis of the Wisconsin School Bus Law," 1962 *Wisconsin Law Review* 500 (1962).

Stout, W. D. "The Establishment of Religion Under the Constitution," 37 *Kentucky Law Journal* 220 (1949).

"The Supreme Court, 1951 Term—Case or Controversy," 66 *Harvard Law Review* 119 (1952).

"The Supreme Court, 1951 Term—Establishment of Religion," 66 *Harvard Law Review* 118 (1952).

Sutherland, A. E., Jr. "Establishment According to Engel," 76 *Harvard Law Review* 25 (1962).

Swancara, F. "The Colorado Bible Case," 21 *Lawyer and Banker* 164 (1928).

Tochman, G. "The Constitutionality of Furnishing Publicly Financed Transportation to Private and Parochial School Students in Missouri," 1963 *Washington University Law Quarterly* 455 (1963).

"Washington Case Law—1959—Compulsory School Attendance Law," 35 *Washington Law Review* 151 (1960).

Wirin, A. L. "Supreme Court and Freedom," 10 *California State Bar Journal* 38 (1935).

Zollman, C. "Parental Rights and the Fourteenth Amendment," 8 *Marquette Law Review* 53 (1923).

INDEX